3-

Supreme Court Jurisprudence in Times of National Crisis, Terrorism, and War

Supreme Court Jurisprudence in Times of National Crisis, Terrorism, and War

A Historical Perspective

Arthur H. Garrison

LEXINGTON BOOKS
A division of

ROWMAN & LITTLEFIELD PUBLISHERS, INC.
Lanham • Boulder • New York • Toronto • Plymouth, UK

Published by Lexington Books
A division of Rowman & Littlefield Publishers, Inc.
A wholly owned subsidiary of The Rowman & Littlefield Publishing Group, Inc.
4501 Forbes Boulevard, Suite 200, Lanham, Maryland 20706
http://www.lexingtonbooks.com

Estover Road, Plymouth PL6 7PY, United Kingdom

British Library Cataloguing in Publication Information Available

Library of Congress Cataloging-in-Publication Data

Garrison, Arthur H., 1966-
  Supreme court jurisprudence in times of national crisis, terrorism, and war : a historical perspective / Arthur Garrison.
     p. cm.
  Includes bibliographical references and index.
  ISBN 978-0-7391-5102-0 (cloth : alk. paper) — ISBN 978-0-7391-5104-4 (electronic)
  1. United States. Supreme Court—History. 2. Executive power—United States.
  3. War and emergency powers—United States. 4. Separation of powers—United States. I. Title.
  KF8742.G378 2011
  342.73'0412—dc22   2010053775

∞™ The paper used in this publication meets the minimum requirements of American National Standard for Information Sciences—Permanence of Paper for Printed Library Materials, ANSI/NISO Z39.48-1992. Printed in the United States of America

To *Him* who helped me in all parts of this book

Deuteronomy 8:18, Proverbs 3:13

To my two God sons, Nicholas and Alexander Fleming

Micah 6:8

Contents

Introduction

> I know that some people question if America is really in a war at all. They view terrorism more as a crime, a problem to be solved mainly with law enforcement and indictments. After the World Trade Center was first attacked in 1993, some of the guilty were indicted and tried and convicted, and sent to prison. But the matter was not settled. The terrorists were still training and plotting in other nations, and drawing up more ambitious plans. After the chaos and carnage of September the 11th, it is not enough to serve our enemies with legal papers. The terrorists and their supporters declared war on the United States, and war is what they got.—President George W. Bush (2004)[1]

On one level the whole debate over the actions of President Bush post-9/11 can be understood by this simple question—were the events of September 11 a criminal act or an act of war? Less than two weeks after the attacks, with fires still burning and bodies both alive and dead yet to be recovered from the destruction of the World Trade Center, the Bush Administration, before a joint session of Congress, defined the attacks in both moral and military terms. The President informed Congress:

> Tonight we are a country awakened to danger and called to defend freedom. Our grief has turned to anger, and anger to resolution. Whether we bring our enemies to justice, or bring justice to our enemies, justice will be done. . . .
> On September the eleventh, enemies of freedom committed an act of war against our country. Americans have known wars but for the past 136 years, they have been wars on foreign soil, except for one Sunday in 1941. Americans have

known the casualties of war but not at the center of a great city on a peaceful morning. Americans have known surprise attacks but never before on thousands of civilians. All of this was brought upon us in a single day and night fell on a different world, a world where freedom itself is under attack. . . .

Our war on terror begins with al-Qaida, but it does not end there. It will not end until every terrorist group of global reach has been found, stopped, and defeated. . . .

Our response involves far more than instant retaliation and isolated strikes. Americans should not expect one battle, but a lengthy campaign, unlike any other we have seen. It may include dramatic strikes, visible on television, and covert operations, secret even in success. We will starve terrorists of funding, turn them one against another, drive them from place to place, until there is no refuge or rest. And we will pursue nations that provide aid or safe haven to terrorism. Every nation, in every region, now has a decision to make. Either you are with us, or you are with the terrorists. From this day forward, any nation that continues to harbor or support terrorism will be regarded by the United States as a hostile regime. . . .

Our Nation has been put on notice: We are not immune from attack. We will take defensive measures against terrorism to protect Americans. . . .

These measures are essential. But the only way to defeat terrorism as a threat to our way of life is to stop it, eliminate it, and destroy it where it grows. . . .

Great harm has been done to us. We have suffered great loss. And in our grief and anger we have found our mission and our moment. Freedom and fear are at war. The advance of human freedom—the great achievement of our time, and the great hope of every time—now depends on us. Our nation—this generation—will lift a dark threat of violence from our people and our future. We will rally the world to this cause, by our efforts and by our courage. We will not tire, we will not falter, and we will not fail.

It was to be the policy of the Bush administration that Al Qaeda declared war and war is what they got; and the dictates of war, not the criminal justice system, will be used to answer the soldiers of Osama Bin Laden, period.

Others acknowledged that 9/11 was an international criminal act not seen in recent history and its impact on the United States was rivaled only by Pearl Harbor, but it was a criminal act nonetheless. But even if the acts of 9/11 were analogous to war it was not uniformly agreed that it authorized the President to use his power as Commander-in-Chief without constraint. As Attorney General Reno asserted to the Supreme Court,

The government thus had the authority to arrest, detain, interrogate, and prosecute . . . . The difference between invocation of the criminal process and the power claimed by the President here, however, is one of accountability. The criminal justice system requires that defendants and witnesses be afforded access to counsel, imposes judicial supervision over government action, and places congressionally imposed limits on incarceration. The government . . .

claims the authority to imprison citizens without counsel, with at most extremely limited access to the courts, for an indefinite term.[2]

But there is more at stake than the question of whether 9/11 was an act of war or an act of international criminality. Assuming the truth of President Bush's view that 9/11 was an act of war, it does not follow that the rule of law and Constitutional structures and limitations on Executive power are made subservient to the need for military victory and national security. As Attorney General Reno asserted to the Supreme Court,

> The broad and largely unsupervised authority claimed by the Executive Branch is also inconsistent with the fundamental principles of our Constitution. Arbitrary arrest and imprisonment by the King was one of the principal evils that the Constitution and the Bill of Rights were meant to address. See *Duncan v. Kahanamoku*, 327 U.S. 304, 322 (1946). These principles have been adhered to even when national security is implicated. . . .
>
> Amici recognize that these limitations might impede the investigation of a terrorist offense in some circumstances. It is conceivable that, in some hypothetical situation, despite the array of powers described above, the government might be unable to detain a dangerous terrorist or to interrogate him or her effectively. But this is an inherent consequence of the limitation of Executive power. . . . [O]ur Nation has always been prepared to accept some risk as the price of guaranteeing that the Executive does not have arbitrary power to imprison citizens. . . . This Court has never countenanced the untrammeled authority the Executive Branch seeks in this case; it should not do so now.[3]

Concurring with this sentiment Justice Kennedy observed, "Liberty and Security can be reconciled"[4] but this reconciliation is found in the law and the traditions and principles of limited government, not in the need for security.

After the terrorist attacks on America on September 11, 2001, the question of the legitimate role of the judiciary during times of war or national crisis has become more than an academic discussion appearing in law reviews and journal articles. Within two months of the attacks of 9/11 Congress passed the Authorization to Use Military Force (AUMF) authorizing President Bush to use military force against Al Qaeda and its host country Afghanistan as well as against those individuals the President determined were involved in the attacks and those who would plan future attacks. In the resulting "War on Terrorism" with Afghanistan and Al Qaeda and later in Iraq President Bush asserted that, under his powers as Commander-in-Chief and through the AUMF, he had the authority to capture and detain various individuals as "enemy combatants." President Bush maintained four propositions in regard to his powers as Commander-in-Chief during the current national security crisis, known as the War on Terror. First, as President he is authorized to detain enemy combatants at the U.S. Naval Base at Guantanamo, Cuba without judicial review; second, the citizenship status of a captured enemy combatant has no bearing on his detention and classification as an enemy combatant; third, the Geneva Conventions do not apply to those the President designates enemy combatants; and fourth, he has the power to submit such individuals to military commissions without judicial interference. President Bush concluded that in time of war, the "war on terrorism" in this instance, the President acting as Commander-in-Chief has exclusive powers and responsibilities in protecting the nation, and Congress with the Court to an even lesser degree are tertiary players in conducting the war. In March 2002 the Defense Department published Military Order No. 1, which created the procedures for military commissions which would be used to put enemy combatants and members of Al Qaeda on trial for acts of terrorism. Military Order No. 1 was issued in response to an executive order issued by President Bush in November 2001 which declared that captured enemy combatants and members of Al Qaeda would not be subject to trial by civilian or military courts. In July 2004 President Bush authorized the creation of a formal system of classification and review of individuals suspected of being enemy combatants and members of Al Qaeda through the Combatant Status Review Tribunal (CSRT).

Beginning in 2002 President Bush argued in various federal courts that under the Constitution he should be accorded wide discretion in the use of his Constitutional powers as Commander-in-Chief in times of war and that the judiciary has little, if any, voice in the review of that discretion. Eventually, the Supreme Court rejected the Bush Administration's broad definition of the Commander-in-Chief's power. Three years after the events of 9/11 the Supreme Court in *Hamdi v. Rumsfeld* (2004), *Rumsfeld v. Padilla* (2004), and *Rasul v. United States* (2004) collectively held that the President did not exercise exclusive powers over Congress and the Courts in how the war on terrorism would be conducted. Two years later in *Hamdan v. Rumsfeld* (2006) and four years later in *Boumediene v. Bush* (2008) the Supreme Court would continue to assert that the principles of separation of powers and limited powers in the Constitution, even in times of war, will prevail over the assertion of necessity by the President. It is how the Supreme Court has interpreted and applied various Constitutional and statutory laws to Presidential authority during the current and in past national security threats and wars that is the subject of this book. The thesis of this book is that in times of war and national crisis the judiciary maintains the Constitutional boundaries on Presidential power. The Constitution grants to the judiciary the responsibility to establish the outer boundaries of policy options, not to make its own policy determinations within those boundaries.

This book provides a historical review of the growth of Presidential power and judicial power in times of military and national crisis. In times of crisis various Presidents, both with and without Congressional authorization, have sought to use the Commander-in-Chief's power to secure needed materials, silence detractors, and protect the nation from both internal and external threats. These historic examples include President Lincoln and his suspension of habeas corpus, President Wilson and Sedition Acts placing limits on political speech during World War I, the infamous raids by Attorney General Palmer and the deportation of suspected anarchists, President Roosevelt and the internment camps of World War II, and President Truman's attempted seizure of the American steel industry during the Korean War. All of these actions have been posited as evidence that in times of war or national crisis, Presidential power is used to restrict, if not abridge, civil liberties. It is almost a maxim in the academic circles of law, history, and political science that in times of war the law is silent and the judiciary provides little protection of civil liberties and opposition to executive power exercised during a national security crisis. Chief Justice Rehnquist and Justice Brennan, for example, have both publicly asserted this view of American and Constitutional history as established fact. The goal of this book is to provide the reader with a walk through history and to use this history as background for reviewing the decisions and policies of the Bush Administration and the post-9/11 cases decided by the Rehnquist Court. This book challenges the maxim that the judiciary will retreat from protecting civil liberties in times of national crisis. The primary audience for this book includes criminal justice, legal studies and political science scholars and professors looking for primary or secondary reading materials for courses on Constitutional law, selected topics in Constitutional history, selected topics in political science, legal history, terrorism, Supreme Court history as well as specific courses on civil liberties, first amendment history, topical studies in American government and judicial decision making.

This book is divided into two main parts and provides a historical chronological review of how the judiciary developed a jurisprudence of judicial deference in times of war and national security crisis as well as how the Supreme Court articulated the parameters of acceptable executive and legislative action within the Constitutional principles of separation of powers and limited powers in times of crisis and war. The first two chapters of part I will review the historical development of the President as Commander-in-Chief and how the Supreme Court participated in making the President the sole organ of American foreign policy. Chapters 3 and 4 will focus on the rise of the two Red Scares of World War I and World War II. Chapters 3 and 4 will also review how the Court handled freedom of speech and assembly in times of national crisis and how the national fear of communism infiltrated the American society. Chapters 3 and 4 will focus on the Espionage Act of 1917 and the Sedition Act of 1918 and the power of Congress to criminalize antiwar and communist speech during World War I and the rise of modern free speech jurisprudence. Chapters 5 and 6 will use the internment camp policy of President Roosevelt during World War II and the seizure of the steel industry by President Truman during the Korean War as case studies on how the Supreme Court both defined and defended the boundaries of Presidential power and how both cases establish the limits on executive power. Although the Supreme Court case *Korematsu v. United States* (1944) is the poster case for the internment policy and has been universally condemned as the Dred Scott case of the twentieth century, the Supreme Court support for the internment policy originated in *Hirabayashi v. United States* (1943) and the true error in both cases was not that the Court affirmed the internment policy but that it applied the wrong legal standard to the justifications made by the Roosevelt Administration. The failure of the Court to reign in the power of the President as Commander-in-Chief during World War II was not repeated during the Korean War. In *Youngstown Sheet & Tube v. Sawyer* (1952) the Court rejected the arguments made by President Truman that Presidential power included the power to seize the American Steel industry to prevent a strike from interfering with the production of steel to support the war effort. More importantly the concurring opinion by Justice Jackson has become the gold standard regarding categorizing and evaluating the boundaries of Presidential Commander-in-Chief powers in general and especially when those powers are used in domestic policymaking.

Part II of the book focuses on the key terrorism cases after 9/11. Chapter 7 reviews the Constitutional and political arguments that the Bush Administration submitted during the first two years after 9/11 to the federal judiciary in context with past assertions of power made by former Presidents and legal opinions issued by former attorneys general and the Office of Legal Counsel. Chapter 8 reviews the first round of post-9/11 terrorism cases, specifically focusing on the Bush Administration's assertion that the judiciary has a very limited role in the "War on Terrorism" and that the President is due very broad deference from the judiciary in his determination of how the war is to be fought. In *Hamdi v. Rumsfeld* (2004) the Court agreed that the President had the power to declare American citizens who are captured on the field of battle (outside of the United states) as enemy combatants but held that his designation was not without appeal and that he had to submit to some level of review by a neutral decision making body. The Supreme Court ruled that the President had certain powers to address national security threats during times of war that could not be used in times of peace but that these powers were not without limit.

Chapter 9 continues to review the post-9/11 policies of the Bush Administration, specifically the assertion that it had the power to detain enemy combatants at the U.S. Naval Base at Guantanamo Bay, Cuba without any fear of judicial interference through habeas corpus. In *Rasul v. Bush* (2004) the President suffered a more clear defeat when the Court held that the right of statutory habeas corpus was fully applicable to the detainees and that they could not be separated from the courts by Presidential fiat. The Court also addressed the procedures established by President Bush by executive order to place various terrorists and enemy combatants on trial through military commissions. The Court held in *Hamdan v. Rumsfeld* (2006) that although the President had the power to establish military commissions he could not do so in violation of statutory law governing such commissions and could not violate standing treaties ratified by the Senate which, in part, defined the laws of war. In *Boumediene v. Bush* (2008) the Court addressed if the right to habeas corpus, as a Constitutional matter, was applicable to the detainees at Guantanamo. The Court held that the President could not establish a "constitutional free zone" in which he could act to detain individuals without any judicial review of the detention. The Court held for the first time that the Constitution fully applies to Guantanamo because the United States exercises full de facto control over the area and as such is governed by the Constitution and is subject to judicial enforcement of individual Constitutional rights. Chapter 9 reviews the *Rasul, Hamdan,* and *Boumediene* decisions, specifically regarding the values and purposes of separation of powers and limited powers embodied in the Constitution and the Court protection of those principles under the rule of law.

Chapter 10 concludes with an essay on the rule of law in times of crisis. Much ink has been spilled over the question of "how" and to "what" extent the Judiciary should exercise deference to the political branches in times of war and national security crisis. Chapter 10 addresses the question from a different perspective: Under the Madisonian model, why does the judiciary have a role in national security policy in the first place? Hamilton described the Judicial Department as the least dangerous branch because it neither controls the sword or the purse. Madison designed a Constitutional system in which the Constitution would be the Supreme Law of the Land. With the Constitution as the pantheon of all laws and actions under our system of government, the Supreme Court has developed into the final arbiter of "what" the Supreme Law of the Land allows the three branches of government to do both in peace and war. Concurrent with Madison's and Hamilton's design, history has placed its own requirements on the three branches and has made its own determinations on the power of the judiciary.

⁂

From the earliest days of the republic it has been debated what role the President, outside of Congressional sanction, has in developing and implementing foreign policy, including the power to use the armed forces of the United States to implement that policy. For the first half of the nineteenth century the judiciary did not enter the debate, but beginning with the war of rebellion by the southern slave states, the Supreme Court began to develop a jurisprudence to place boundaries on the power of the President in times of war. The power of the President to create commissions and to try American citizens not involved in active rebellion was rejected but the power of the President to respond to acts of war without Congressional recognition of war was affirmed. The first three decades of the twentieth century saw the Court develop limits on the protection of the First Amendment in times of national crisis and world war, but by the end of middle of the century the Court had asserted that times of crisis do not elevate the President to Commander-in-Chief of the nation. The Court has consistently defended the power of the government to act, but has developed and enforced the outer boundaries of Constitutional power. Even in war, there are limits to governmental power and those limits belong to the Court to defend and for the Constitution to impose.

The rule of law in times of crisis is not easily defended; for those who suffer under the lack of protection are easily sacrificed for the greater good as perceived by those who guard the good. But it is asked who will guard the guardians? The history of the Supreme Court in times of crisis is far from simple or without controversy. The goal of this book is to review how the federal judiciary and the Supreme Court developed the jurisprudence that the power of government is not without limits and by the middle of the twentieth century had developed a jurisprudence to control the power of the President in what the Court itself held was an area in which the President was the "sole organ" to implement: foreign policy. It will be asserted throughout this book that the Court has adopted a historical jurisprudence that although acknowledges that the weighing of choices within the scales of politics is not for the Court to review, but the boundaries of the choices that can be put in those scales are governed by the scales of justice. And the Constitution requires that the principles of limited powers and separation of powers require that the rule of law govern Presidential action in both peace and war. The Court has historically agreed that in times of war the elected branches can approach the outer limits of Constitutional power but as the muse of the Constitution, the Court has historically said to the proud waves of national protection and security: You may come so far and here your proud waves must stop.

From the earliest days of western history even before Rome, kings have been above men. But there was also the law and before Greece became one nation and the cradle of democracy, it was said of the principles of the law in the face of kings that no one, subject or citizen, man or woman, slave or king, is above the law.[5]

NOTES

1. President Bush, State of the Union Address, January 20, 2004.
2. Brief of Amicus Curiae Janet Reno et al. in *Rumsfeld v. Padilla* 524 U.S. 426 (2004), 2–3.
3. Ibid., 27, 29–30.
4. *Boumediene v. Bush* and *Al Odah v. United States* 553 U.S. 723, 128 S. Ct. 2229, 171 L. Ed 2d 41, 96–97(2008).
5. Legendary Pictures, *300*, DVD (Burbank, CA: Warner Home Video, 2007).

I

National Security, the Rise of Presidential Power, the Rule of Law, and the Development of Constitutional Boundaries on Political Necessity and the War Power

1

The Rise of Presidential Authority in Times of National Crisis

One of the most significant and longstanding Constitutional debates in American history is whether it belongs to the President or the Congress to *initiate war*. Notice, not declare war, but to initiate war; to sanction the initiation of hostilities and the use of military force. The Constitution is clear in Article I, Section 8, Clause 11 that Congress shall have the power to declare war. The war powers of Congress, in Article I, Section 8, are clearly spelled out to include the power to "provide for the common defense," to "grant letters of Marque and Reprisal" and to make "rules concerning Captures on Land and Water." Article I, Section 8 also grants to Congress the power to "raise and support Armies" to "provide and maintain a Navy" as well as to "make rules for the Government and Regulation of the land and naval Forces" including the power to "provide for calling forth the Militia to execute the laws of the Union, suppress Insurrections and repel invasions." The list continues by granting Congress the power to provide for "organizing, arming, and disciplining, the Militia, and for governing such part of them as may be employed in the service of the United States." The Constitution provides control of the Militia to the states "according to the discipline prescribed by Congress." Thus Congress is tasked by the Constitution to raise, fund, support, discipline and regulate the armed forces of the United States. Further the Constitution grants Congress the power to declare war.

According to Article II, Section 1 of the Constitution, "the executive power shall be vested in a President of the United States of America." Unlike Article I, Article II does not provide a specific list of powers and responsibilities granted to the President. The powers of the President are described in Section 1 to include the statement that the "President shall be the Commander-in-Chief of the Army and Navy of the United States, and of the Militia of the several states, when called into actual Service of the United States." Later, Section 2 grants the President the "power, by and with the Advice and Consent of the Senate, to make treaties . . . and he shall nominate, and by and with the Advice and Consent of the Senate, shall appoint Ambassadors, other public ministers and Consuls."

Thus on first reading one could conclude that the Constitution grants to Congress the preeminent role in foreign affairs because it is the branch that holds the power to raise an army and the power to use one of the major tools of foreign policy, the decision to use military force, to achieve foreign policy objectives. Congress is given the power to raise, discipline and regulate the military and is given the power to determine how the military will be trained and maintained. But Congress is not granted the power to "command" the armed forces of the United States. The entity that commands the armed forces is the President. As Commander-in-Chief the President dictates the action of the military. Congress establishes the rules of behavior and laws governing the military and the President commands military actions.

But what does the interplay of the Congressional power to declare war, to raise and maintain the military and the Presidential power as Commander-in-Chief mean in application? Is the power of Commander-in-Chief a power granted to the President only to ensure that the will of Congress is fulfilled and to be a conduit for Congressional action in times it declares war? Is the power of Congress to declare war synonymous with the power to initiate war or hostilities? Or is the power to initiate war vested with the President under his powers as Commander-in-Chief and as the holder of the executive powers of the United States? These questions are not new to American history. Two of the greatest founders and theorists of our Constitutional system, Alexander Hamilton and James Madison, allies in the drafting and ratification of the Constitution, developed diametrically opposing views of the Article I, Section 8 powers of Congress and the Article II, Section 1 powers of the President in the area of foreign affairs just within a few years after the drafting and ratification of the Constitution. Their debate on which branch of government, the Congress or the President, is preeminent in setting and implementing foreign affairs policy for the United States set the stage for the debates on those powers from then till today. Even in the minds of the founders, it was not settled which branch of government was preeminent in foreign affairs.

When the founding generation had to implement both the words and the theories of the Constitution in real world circumstances, they had as much debate and disagreement about the meaning of the words as we have today. Madison, Hamilton, Adams and the men of the Constitutional Convention did not perceive the Constitution they were drafting and themselves as analogous to Moses coming down from the mountain with immutable truth on tablets written by the finger of God Himself. As history shows, the men of the founding generation of our Madisonian Constitutional system were not a monolithic group with a single, clear and unambiguous view of the document they drafted to be referred to by later generations as one would refer to the Seventh Commandment—thou shall not steal. Debates over the words of the Constitution, we should remember, started with the debates over ratification itself. The meaning of the Constitution was never beyond debate. Its meaning has always been the result of debate, real world politics, history and the development of law. This does not mean that the Constitution is a "living" document in which political desires can or should be elevated to Constitutional principles and be placed beyond the politics of majority rule. Although the Constitution is not as immutable as the tablets of the Ten Commandments, it is the Supreme Law of the Land not a text written on a laptop, subject to the edit features of a word processor. The implementation of the Constitution and its principles have changed and adapted as the nation changed from being a rural, agricultural, small-town-based nation to an international nation with worldwide interests. One of the first adaptations and applications of the Constitution to the changing world was the interpretation and application of Presidential powers versus Congressional powers in the realm of foreign policy.

The first debate on the power of the President versus the Congress in dealing with foreign policy and national security was engaged in by Hamilton and Madison in the summer of 1793. Out of this debate on the meaning of the Constitution came the formation of the political party system, party acrimony, the politicalization of foreign policy, and the beginning of the spilling of immeasurable amounts of ink on theories of Constitutional interpretation.

ALEXANDER HAMILTON AND JAMES MADISON: PACIFICUS-HELVIDIUS: LET THE DEBATE BEGIN

In 1793 the two major world powers, Great Britain and France, were at war as a result of the French Revolution in 1789. President Washington sought to keep the United States neutral and issued a statement of neutrality on April 22, 1793, which touched off the earliest debates of the power of the President to take action in foreign affairs and which branch of government, Congress or the President, has the "final" authority to determine the state of peace or war. Although Congress passed the Neutrality Acts of 1794 which outlawed any American citizen from serving on a vessel engaging in hostilities with a nation not at war with the United States, thus sustaining Washington's actions, it was the decision of President Washington to act in the first place and the belief that his act was a hostile act against France in the second that touched off a political firestorm in Philadelphia. The decision to remain neutral rather than honor treaties of friendship and alliance with France split the nation and placed Hamilton and Washington on one side and further pushed Jefferson and his supporters, including Madison, on the other side.

On the political level, one side was supportive of neutrality in an effort to protect business and trade with Britain (Hamilton being the key leader of this interest) and those wanting to honor agreements with America's Revolutionary War ally (Jefferson being the leader for this interest) on the other. Jefferson saw the French Revolution as the next step in the destruction of monarchies and the ascendancy of the liberation of man from kings and priests. The Federalists, led by Hamilton, saw the Reign of Terror and the Jacobins of the guillotine during the fall of 1793 through the early summer of 1794 as the rise of the mob, the destruction of law, justice and order. To Hamilton and the Federalists, those who supported the ideals and actions of the French Revolution were a practical and political threat to the stability and viability of the young republic. These diametrically opposed views, with others, later led to the drafting of the internal security acts of 1798, political trials and convictions of outspoken Republicans, the rise of Jeffersonian democracy and the fall of the Federalist Party.

On the debate over Congressional and Presidential power in foreign affairs on the level of Constitutional theory, Jefferson and Madison believed that it was not within the power of the President to declare a state of peace or war between the United States and other nations. That power belonged to the Congress. Hamilton and Washington believed that it was within the power of the President as the head of the department responsible for making sure that the laws are faithfully executed to make such assessments. The President has the power as the Chief Executive and as Commander-in-Chief to determine if a state of war or peace exists and to take measures to secure peace until Congress acts otherwise.

In response to the criticism of Washington's neutrality declaration, an article in the *Gazette of the United States*, a Philadelphia newspaper, was published on June 29, 1793, which was signed Pacificus.[1] The article, written by Alexander Hamilton, defended the power of the President to issue the declaration of neutrality. Hamilton got straight to the point and summarized his argument as follows:

> The Legislative Department is not the organ of intercourse between the United States and foreign Nations. It is charged neither with making nor interpreting Treaties. It is therefore not naturally that Organ of the Government which is to pronounce the existing condition of the Nation, with regard to foreign Powers, or to admonish the Citizens of their obligations and duties as

founded upon that condition of things. Still less is it charged with enforcing the execution and observance of these obligations and those duties.

Hamilton wrote that since it was "equally obvious that the act in question is foreign to the Judicial Department of the Government. . . . It must then of necessity belong to the Executive Department to exercise the function in question." Now taking it as a given that it is not for the Judiciary to make declarations on the state of foreign affairs, Hamilton moved to why it was not an area for the Legislative branch.

Hamilton asserts that the organ of government that handles the "intercourse between the Nation and foreign Nations" and is "the interpreter of the National Treaties" is the same organ that is "charged with the Execution of the Laws, of which treaties form a part" and "is charged with the command and application of the Public Force." Thus according to Hamilton the branch that has the power to enforce the laws and execute treaties also has the power to interpret those treaties in part by its power to deal with other nations in international relations. That branch, or course, is the Executive, not the Legislative. It is this view of presidential Constitutional power that the "vesting theory" and "sole organ" theory of Presidential authority in the area of foreign affairs originates. The *vesting theory* is based on Article II, Section 1, which states that the "executive power shall be *vested* in a President of the United States." The *sole organ theory* supports the proposition that it is an inherent power of the executive to be the sole voice of a nation in the realm of foreign affairs out of the need, in part, to have one voice in the international arena of nations.[2]

After noting that the Constitution empowers the President to be the Commander-in-Chief, to make treaties with the advice and consent of the Senate, to receive ambassadors and to take care that the laws are faithfully executed, Hamilton introduces what has come to be called the *theory of inherent powers* of the President. He asserts the following:

> It would not consist with the rules of sound construction to consider this enumeration of particular authorities as derogating from the more comprehensive grant contained in the general clause, further than as it may be coupled with express restrictions or qualifications; as in regard to the cooperation of the Senate . . . which are qualifications of the general executive powers of appointing officers and making treaties: Because the difficulty of a complete and perfect specification of all the cases of Executive authority would naturally dictate the use of general terms—and would render it improbable that a specification of certain particulars was design[e]d as a substitute for those terms, when antecedently used.

According to Hamilton, the Constitutional limitations on the general executive power of the President to make treaties and appoint ambassadors, does not otherwise limit the general power of the President to exercise executive power in other areas of activity. "The different mode of expression employed in the Constitution in regard to the two powers, the Legislative and the Executive, serves to confirm this inference." He notes that Article I reads, "*All Legislative powers herein granted* shall be vested in a Congress of the United States" while Article II reads, "The *Executive power shall be vested in a President* of the United States of America," the difference being the legislative powers that are granted to Congress are specifically enumerated and those enumerated give Congress the power to exercise legislative power. But all executive powers are granted to the President, some of which are subject to exceptions and qualifications. Thus executive power is defined by a "general grant" of power with limitations and qualifications within certain executive action, while Congress is granted legislative power defined by specific limiting expressions of legislative power and governmental jurisdiction.

In regard to the issuance of the neutrality proclamation, Hamilton asserted that the issuing of such a proclamation is the exercise of general executive power not qualified by the Constitution.

> The issuing of a proclamation of neutrality is merely an Executive Act; since also the general Executive Power of the Union is vested in the President, the conclusion is, that the step, which has been taken by him, is liable to no just exception on the score of authority.

Hamilton concludes the foreign policy power is a general power of the executive. In the American Constitutional system the foreign policy power is generally granted to the President with certain specific qualifications, but Congressional concurrent power on the issuance of a proclamation on the state of peace and war is not one of those specific qualifications. To the proposition that the Constitution places the power to declare war with Congress alone, and with it, the inherent power to judge whether the nation is obligated to make war, Hamilton answered,

> That however true it may be, that the right of the Legislature to declare war includes the right of judging whether the Nation be under obligations to make War or not—it will not follow that the Executive is in any case excluded from a similar right of Judgment, in the execution of its own functions.
>
> If the Legislature have a right to make war on the one hand—it is on the other the duty of the Executive to preserve Peace till war is declared; and in fulfilling that duty, it must necessarily possess a right of judging what is the nature of the obligations which the treaties of the Country impose on the Government; and when in pursuance of this right it has concluded that there is nothing in them inconsistent with a *state* of neutrality, it becomes both its province and its duty to enforce the laws incident to that state of the Nation.

If Congress and the President share a concurrent power to set policy in the area of recognition of war or peace, "it will not follow" says Hamilton, "that the Executive is in any case excluded from a similar right of Judgment, in the execution of its own functions." Here Hamilton asserts, *aguendo*, that Congress may have the power to determine that a treaty requires the United States to support France, but as the branch responsible for the execution of the laws of the United States, treaties being part of those laws, the President has independent authority to interpret those treaties apart from Congress and the President is not obligated to the judgment of Congress. On this point Hamilton explained:

> The Executive is charged with the execution of all laws, the laws of Nations as well as the Municipal law, which recognizes and adopts those laws. It is consequently bound, by faithfully executing the laws of neutrality, when that is the state of the Nation, to avoid giving a cause of war to foreign Powers.

Hamilton further argued that the executive power of the President is limited by the Congress in his power to declare war, but unless Congress changes the state of peace with foreign nations, the decision of the President to maintain the peace is his alone.

Hamilton continued his defense of the President's authority to make determinations on the application and enforcement of treaties and executive authority to make determinations of neutrality even if it affects Legislative areas of authority. He explains:

> The right of the Executive to receive ambassadors and other public Ministers may serve to illustrate the relative duties of the Executive and Legislative Departments. This right includes that of judging, in the case of a Revolution of Government in a foreign Country, whether the new rulers are competent organs of the National Will and ought to be recognized or not: And where a treaty antecedently exists between the United States and such nation, that right involves the power of giving operation or not to such treaty. For until the new Government is *acknowledged,* the treaties between the nations, as far at least as regards *public* rights, are of course suspended. . . .
>
> This serves as an example of the right of the Executive, in certain cases, to determine the condition of the Nation, though it may consequentially affect the proper or improper exercise of the Power of the Legislature to declare war. . . . The Legislature is free to perform its own duties according to its own sense of them—though the Executive in the exercise of its Constitutional powers, may establish an antecedent state of things which ought to weigh in the legislative decisions. From the division of the executive power there results, in reference to it, a *concurrent* authority, in the distributed cases.
>
> Hence in the case stated, though treaties can only be made by the President and Senate, their activity may be continued or suspended by the President alone.

Thus Hamilton concludes that though the President shares some foreign policy powers flowing from his general grant of executive powers, his general powers allow him to make decisions that can dictate the manner in which those determinations, made together with the Congress, will be implemented. One example of this has come to be known as Presidential signing statements.[3] Hamilton, in his conclusion, puts it bluntly:

> It deserves to be remarked, that as the participation of the senate in the making of Treaties and the power of the Legislature to declare war are exceptions out of the general "Executive Power" vested in the President, they are to be construed strictly—and ought to be extended no further than is essential to their execution. . . .
>
> It is the province and duty of the Executive to preserve to the Nation the blessings of peace. The Legislature alone can interrupt those blessings, by placing the Nation in a state of War.
>
> But though it has been thought advisable to vindicate the authority of the Executive on this broad and comprehensive ground—it was not absolutely necessary to do so. That clause of the Constitution which makes it his duty to "take care that the laws be faithfully executed" might alone have been relied upon, and this simple process of argument pursued.
>
> The President is the Constitutional Executor of the laws. Our Treaties and the laws of Nations form a part of the law of the land. He who is to execute the laws must first judge for himself of their meaning. In order to the observance of that conduct, which the laws of nations combined with our treaties prescribed to this country, in reference to the present War in Europe, it was necessary for the President to judge for himself whether there was any thing in our treaties incompatible with an adherence to neutrality. Having judged that there was not, he had a right, and if in his opinion the interests of the Nation required it, it was his duty, as Executor of the laws, to proclaim the neutrality of the Nation, to exhort all persons to observe it, and to warn them of the penalties which would attend its non observance.

As discussed in more detail in chapters 2 and 5, Hamilton's views on plenary and inherent executive power have prevailed as the dominant view of the Presidency held by both subsequent Presidents and the Supreme Court from the late nineteenth century to the present.

Jefferson, after reading Hamilton's article, was incensed. The declaration of neutrality interfered with his goal of maintaining a relationship with France as well as addressing British violations of American shipping and commerce.[4] If it had only involved the complaints of the Secretary of State and his radical Francophile forces, Secretary of the Treasury Hamilton might not have written Pacificus. But it was the "public outcry against the Washington Administration's evident tenderness toward England [that] alarmed Hamilton" as well as the efforts of the French Ambassador to the United States to stir up war feelings in favor of France and against Britain that drove Hamilton to act.[5] Hamilton's defense of the neutrality policy was so successful that Jefferson wrote to Madison on July 7, 1793, imploring him, "For God's sake, my dear Sir, take up your pen, select the most striking heresies and cut him to pieces in the face of the public."[6] Madison came to the aid of his friend and published four articles in the *Gazette of the United States*, between August 24 and September 18, 1793, which he signed Helvidius.[7]

Jefferson asked for heresies and that is what he got from the very first paragraph of Madison's first article. In Helvidius 1, Madison opened with the following:

> Several pieces with the signature of Pacificus were lately published, which have been read with singular pleasure and applause, by the foreigners and degenerate citizens among us, who hate our republican government, and the French revolution.

"Degenerate citizens among us, *who hate our republican government!"* Such a description by one of the writers of the Federalist Papers about the other key writer of those same papers goes to evidence how divisive and hardened positions had become on the war in Europe, which nation was the just side in that war (the French or the British), how a Constitutional republic functions, and what was America's future and destiny.

The harshness of Madison's beginning notwithstanding, his four articles were written as if given by a professor of political philosophy to his students. While Hamilton asserted his arguments based on the construction of the Constitution, Madison's articles were drafted on the level of political theory dissertation reflecting on what the Constitution was, how it established a republican government, the threat to that government Hamilton's theory of the Presidency presented, the nature of executive power, and the threat of corruption of any one person holding the office of the Presidency. The first two articles focused on Hamilton's theories on the nature of executive authority and the nature of treaties as laws to be executed. The third article focused on the specific meaning of the power of the President to receive ambassadors.

In the fourth article, Madison turned to a different tone of argument regarding presidential power. Madison focused on the threat of corrupting influences on the President and the possibility of Presidential action being influenced by vice over virtue. In Madison's view, the proposition that the power to make peace or war was exclusively or significantly placed in the hands of one person should be avoided because a single person while President could be bribed by foreign powers to enter or refrain from war against the interests of the country. Madison wrote, citing Hamilton's Federalist 75:

> An hereditary monarch, though often the oppressor of his people, has personally too much at stake in the government to be in any material danger of being corrupted by foreign powers: but that a man raised from the station of

a private citizen to the rank of chief magistrate, possessed of but a moderate or slender fortune, and looking forward to a period not very remote, when he may probably be obliged to return to the station from which he was taken, might sometimes be under temptations to sacrifice his duty to his interest. . . . An avaricious man might be tempted to betray the interests of the state to the acquisition of wealth. An ambitious man might make his own aggrandizement, by the aid of a foreign power, the price of his treachery to his constituents.

Madison, again citing Hamilton's Federalist 75, concluded,

The history of human conduct does not warrant that exalted opinion of human virtue, which would make it wise in a nation to commit interests of so delicate and momentous a kind, as *those which concern its intercourse* with the rest of the world, to the *sole* disposal of a magistrate created and circumstanced as would be a president of the United States.

Madison's fear of a single executive, with the power of war and peace placed in his hands, rather than being spread among the hands of a collective body of elected officials, is at the heart of the fourth article's assault on the Hamiltonian theories of Presidential power. The Constitution, Madison asserts, reflects this fear of placing the power of implementing war in the hands of one person and divides the power to determine the presence of war and peace between the two branches of Congress and not in the hands of the President alone. "In no part of the Constitution is more wisdom to be found, than in the clause which confides the question of war or peace to the legislature, and not to the executive department. . . . War is in fact the true nurse of executive aggrandizement." But what is it that Madison saw in war that was so alluring to a single executive and dangerous to freedom and liberty?

War is in fact the true nurse of executive aggrandizement. In war, a physical force is to be created; and it is the executive will, which is to direct it. In war, the public treasures are to be unlocked; and it is the executive hand which is to dispense them. In war, the honours and emoluments of office are to be multiplied; and it is the executive patronage under which they are to be enjoyed. It is in war, finally, that laurels are to be gathered; and it is the executive brow they are to encircle. The strongest passions and most dangerous weaknesses of the human breast; ambition, avarice, vanity, the honourable or venial love of fame, are all in conspiracy against the desire and duty of peace.

Hence it has grown into an axiom that the executive is the department of power most distinguished by its propensity to war: hence it is the practice of all states, in proportion as they are free, to disarm this propensity of its influence. . . .

The Constitution has manifested a similar prudence in refusing to the executive the *sole* power of making peace. The trust in this instance also, would be too great for the wisdom, and the temptations too strong for the virtue, of a single citizen.

If one is prone to dismiss, out of hand, Madison's fears of the power of war and its allure, especially in regard to opening of the "public treasuries," one should remember the warnings of President Eisenhower in his farewell speech on January 17, 1961, on the growth of a permanent military-industry complex in American life: "Three and a half million men and women are directly engaged in the defense establishment. *We annually spend on military security more than the net income of all United States corporations. . . .* The total influence [of the military establishment and the arms industry]—economic, political, even spiritual—is felt in every city, every Statehouse, every office of the Federal government." Eisenhower concluded with this warning:

> Only an alert and knowledgeable citizenry can compel the proper meshing of the huge industrial and military machinery of defense with our peaceful methods and goals, so that security and liberty may prosper together.

Madison would agree that the meshing of security and liberty so both can live together is a process envisioned in the Constitution but the balance is to be established by Congress, not placed in the sole hands of the Executive; we are reminded "in no part of the Constitution is more wisdom to be found, than in the clause which confides the question of war or peace to the legislature, and not to the executive department."

Madison's Helvidius no. 1 starts with the proposition that the "natural province of the executive magistrate is to execute laws . . . [a]ll his acts, therefore, properly executive, must presuppose the existence of the laws to be executed." Thus Madison starts his lesson with the proposition that executive power does not include inherent powers, but rather "the executive power" vested in the President is exclusively dependent on Congressional actions: "To see the laws faithfully executed constitutes the essence of the executive authority." He cites Hamilton's Federalist 75 for the agreed proposition that the "essence of the legislative authority, is to enact laws . . . while the execution of the laws and the employment of the common strength, either for this purpose, or for the common defense, seems to comprise all the functions of the executive magistrate. The power of making treaties . . . relates neither to the execution of the subsisting laws, nor the inaction of new ones, [for they] are contracts with foreign nations, which have the force of law."

With that said, treaties, Madison explains, are laws "to be carried into execution, like all other laws, by the executive magistrate." Treaties, being laws, are established and given meaning by that branch that has the power to make laws and not to the department that executes laws. "To say then that the power of making treaties [or interpreting them], which are confessedly laws, belong naturally to the department which is to execute laws, is to say, that the executive department naturally includes a legislative power. In theory this is an absurdity—in practice a tyranny." This is no small point to Madison, because the Constitutional system developed at the Constitutional convention assumed that to protect liberty the powers of government and the types of powers in government must be separated so that freedom can be maintained. To Madison, there is little difference between the power to make laws and the power to interpret them. If the President can enforce the laws and interpret them to his own liking, there is no check on the power of one man holding the power of one-third of the government. To Madison, such a system was the foundation of tyranny. In the mind of Madison, the power of the purse and the sword were separated for a specific reason. Hamilton's theory, at least on paper, threatened the republican system.

Madison rejected the proposition that the determination of war or peace is in any way an executive function. "A declaration that there shall be war . . . is, on the contrary, one of the most deliberative acts that can be performed; and when performed, has the effect of repealing all laws operating in a state of peace [and in] like manner, a conclusion of peace annuls all the laws peculiar to a state of war, and revives the general laws incident to a state of peace." Clearly, according to Madison, the act of making war and peace is legislative because it involves the changing of laws. Madison did agree that the President has a role in foreign affairs apart from naming Ambassadors, with advice and consent of the Senate, and receiving ministers, but that role was subservient to Congress:

> The executive may be a convenient organ of preliminary communications with foreign governments, on the subjects of treaty or war; and the proper agent for carrying into execution the final determinations of the competent authority; yet it can have no pretensions, from the nature of the powers in question compared with the nature of the executive trust, to that essential agency which gives validity to such determinations.

Hamilton's proposition that the power of the President to receive and accept the credentials of ambassadors and other public ministers evidenced the power of the President to make independent assessments in foreign policy was of little weight to Madison. In Helvidius no. 3 he described this responsibility of the chief magistrate amounts to

> little, if anything, more . . . than to provide for a particular mode of communication, *almost* grown into a right among modern nations; by pointing out the department of the government, most proper for the ceremony of admitting public ministers, of examining their credentials, and of authenticating their title to the privileges annexed to their character by the law of nations.

Citing Hamilton's Federalist 69, Madison asserted that the power to

> receive ambassadors and other public ministers . . . [this] is more a matter of dignity than authority. It is a circumstance, that will be without consequence in

the administration of the government, and it is far more convenient that it should be arranged in this manner, than that there should be a necessity for convening the legislature or one of its branches upon every arrival of a foreign minister.

Concluding on this point, Madison asserted that in regard to the function of receiving ambassadors and other public ministers

> two questions immediately arise: Are his credentials from the existing and acting government of his country? Are they properly authenticated? These questions belong of necessity to the executive; but they involve no cognizance of the question, whether those exercising the government have the right along with the possession. . . . The questions before the executive are merely questions of fact; and the executive would have precisely the same right, or rather be under the same necessity of deciding them, if its function was simply to receive *without any discretion to reject* public ministers. It is evident, therefore, that if the executive has a right to reject a public minister, it must be founded on some other consideration than a change in the government, or the newness of the government; and consequently a right to refuse to acknowledge a new government cannot be implied by the right to refuse a public minister . . . the authority of the executive does not extend to a question, whether an *existing* government ought to be recognized or not.

To Hamilton's proposition that the President is the organ of government that handles the "intercourse between the Nation and foreign Nations" and as such is "the interpreter of the National Treaties" because the President is the head of the Constitutional branch "charged with the Execution of the Laws, of which treaties form a part," Madison responds:

> In the general distribution of powers, we find that of declaring war expressly vested in the Congress, where every other legislative power is declared to be vested; and without any other qualification than what is common to every other legislative act. The Constitutional idea of this power would seem then clearly to be, that it is of a legislative and not an executive nature.

Hamilton asserted that the power of treaties, meaning their interpretation and the judgment of whether war or peace was to be pursued, was concurrently provided to both the executive and the legislative branches. To this Madison wrote,

> Whatever difficulties may arise in defining the executive authority in particular cases, there can be none in deciding on an authority clearly placed by the Constitution in another department. In this case, the Constitution has decided what shall not be deemed an executive authority; though it may not have clearly decided in every case what shall be so deemed. The declaring of war is expressly made a legislative function. The judging of the obligations to make war, is admitted to be included as a legislative function. Whenever, then, a

question occurs, whether war shall be declared, or whether public stipulations require it, the question necessarily belongs to the department to which those functions belong—and no other department can be *in the execution of its proper functions,* if it should undertake to decide such a question.

As to the power of the President as Commander-in-Chief, Madison rejected the proposition that the title endued the Presidency with war-making power.

> There can be no relation worth examining between this power and the general power of making treaties. And instead of being analogous to the power of declaring war, it affords a striking illustration of the incompatibility of the two powers in the same hands. Those who are to *conduct a war* cannot in the nature of things, be proper or safe judges, whether *a war ought* to be *commenced, continued,* or *concluded.* They are barred from the latter functions by a great principle in free government, analogous to that which separates the sword from the purse, or the power of executing from the power of enacting laws.

Madison concluded with the question of where does this theory originate that the power of making, interpreting and enforcing treaties belongs with the executive power, if it is not found within the Constitution. His answer is tied to his opening paragraph—"The power of making treaties and the power of declaring war, are royal prerogatives in the British government, and accordingly treated as executive prerogatives by British commentators." In 1793 to imply a person supports a British-style government or advocates the President has powers similar in nature and scope to the British king was to propose that such a person was bordering on treason against the American form of government. Hamilton, in his own time, much less judged by certain historians, was seen as an anglophile who wanted to institute as much of an oligarchy as possible into the culture of the new nation. He supported close economic ties with Britain and opposed Jeffersonian efforts to side with France and risk war with Britain. The linking of Hamilton's views on executive power with the executive prerogatives of the British government was intended to imply Hamilton would impose upon the American system a President one step away from being a king, which at the time was the very definition of tyranny.

In Helvidius no. 2, Madison focused on the proposition that the President has the right to interpret a treaty independently of Congressional interpretation. Madison begins with Hamilton's general concession that the power to declare war includes the power to determine if there is an obligation to go to war. Madison proposed that Hamilton's concession to this point defeats the assertion that the President shares the power of interpretation.

> He had before admitted, that the right to declare war is vested in the legislature. He here admits, that the right to declare war includes the right to judge,

whether the United States be obliged to declare war or not. Can the inference be avoided, that the executive, instead of having a similar right to judge, is as much excluded from the right to judge as from the right to declare?

If the right to declare war be an exception out of the general grant to the executive power, every thing included in the right must be included in the exception; and, being included in the exception, is excluded from the grant.

He cannot disentangle himself by considering the right of the executive to judge as *concurrent* with that of the legislature: for if the executive have a concurrent right to judge, and the right to judge be included in (it is in fact the very essence of) the right to declare, he must go on and say, that the executive has a concurrent right also to declare. And then, what will he do with his other admission, that the power to declare is an exception out of the executive power?

Madison concludes that if the Congress has the admitted exclusive power to declare war and decide if war should occur, the President can't claim to share the same power that is strictly granted to another branch. More specifically, the power to judge whether war should occur cannot be a concurrent power. Either it is a power provided to Congress or the President; and the shared power of appointing ambassadors or making treaties does not equate to concurrent powers of determining war. "The power to judge of the causes of war, as involved in the power to declare war, is expressly vested, where all other legislative powers are vested, that is, in the Congress of the United States. It is consequently determined by the Constitution to be a legislative power. Now . . . in what respects a compound power may be partly legislative, and partly executive, . . . or jointly in both . . . the same power cannot belong, in the whole to both . . . or be properly so vested as to operate separately in each. Still more evident is it, that the same specific function or act, cannot possibly belong to the two departments, and be separately exercised by each."

To Hamilton's supplemental argument that two branches of government, each acting within its authority to expound the meaning of the Constitution, can interpret the Constitution and lay claim to the same power, Madison accepted that such an event can happen under the Constitution:

But this *species* of concurrence is obviously and radically different from that in question. The former supposes the Constitution to have given the power to one department only; and the doubt to be, to which it has been given. The latter [Hamilton's view] supposes it to belong to both; and that it may be exercised by either or both, according to the course of exigencies.

A concurrent authority in two independent departments, to perform the same function with respect to the same thing, would be as awkward in practice, as it is unnatural in theory.

Madison concluded that since the power of declaring war and the power to determine if war is required belongs to Congress alone, the assertion that each branch can interpret the Constitution is irrelevant because there is no interpretation debate on which branch has the power to declare war—Article I, Section 8 settles that question on its face.

ALEXANDER HAMILTON AND JAMES MADISON: SOME OBSERVATIONS ON THE FIRST DEBATE

On a Constitutional level, Madison was a firm believer that Congress was to be the main policy making body in the area of foreign affairs and decisions of war. The Congress, in Madison's view, was to be the first branch of government and the President as Commander-in-Chief was to be the governmental organ that carries out policies of war, not the branch that makes those policies. To Hamilton's proposition that the power to declare war belonged to Congress but it was up to the President to protect the peace until Congress declared war, Madison asserted that the move from war to peace and from peace to war are Congressional prerogatives because to move in either direction positive law is required. The President is the chief magistrate and as such implements the law and he has a subservient role in the development of law or the policies that foster the creation of law. Although both men used the description of the President, "Chief Magistrate," each had completely different meanings for the term. To Hamilton, the Chief Magistrate is the leader of the nation in regard to foreign policy and responsible for maintaining relations with other nations and protecting the interests of the nation, almost exclusively. To Madison, the President is simply the arm of execution of Congressional policy. Congress, not the President, is responsible for the protection of the interest of the nation in the area of foreign affairs.

Hamilton understood that in the area of war a single department under the leadership of a single individual was needed to deal with the necessities of diplomacy and war; Madison simply did not accept this concept as true. One of the differences between these two men was that Hamilton understood the necessities of war that Madison did not. Hamilton was with Washington during the Revolutionary War and saw the limitations of war policy making and providing for a nation at war by a deliberative body of divergent interests. Hamilton saw men starve barefoot in the snow due to the inability of the Continental Congress to act. Hamilton also saw an army, which on paper should have been defeated in a few months if not in a few weeks, defeat the reigning super power of the day due to the strong leadership of one Commander-in-Chief. Madison was not at Valley Forge and was not with Washington. With the exception of perhaps James Wilson, Madison was without rival as the greatest theorist of governmental theory and construction among the Founding Fathers, but Hamilton was schooled in both the theory and the practicalities of governmental construction. It was this difference that allowed Hamilton to see the need for a strong President and that a strong President was not a synonym for tyranny. Madison did not have this perspective. An example of Madison's limited practical perspective is evidenced in Helvidius 3 and 4.

In the last two Helvidius articles, the reader is struck by Madison's twin fears of a general distrust of executive power and his distrust in the virtues of those who would become the chief magistrate. In Helvidius 4 he made clear that he feared the outright successful bribery of the chief executive and in Helvidius 3 he demonstrated a disregard for executive functions. The latter fear was reflected in part from his inability to separate the executive power of the President from the executive power of the King. His distain for any hint of a British-type executive in the American Presidency colored his ability to perceive that a strong American President was not synonymous with tyranny. As it did with Jefferson, eight years as President (1809–1817) and the events of the war of 1812 changed Madison's mind on the power of the Presidency and the virtues of those who hold the office.

Hamilton's view of the Presidency has prevailed as the foundation for the development of a strong independent Presidency with inherent powers to act decisively. The theories of the "unitary executive" President; or the President being the "sole organ" of foreign policy; or the view that the President is the "steward" of the nation whose powers are limited only by the specific limitations of the Constitution; or the proposition that it is the "prerogative" of the President to preserve the nation in times of crisis even if doing so would violate the law; are all reflective of Hamilton's proposition that the President exercises inherent powers as well as specific powers under the Constitution. The President is "vested" with all the executive power of the United States and is the Commander-in-Chief of the armed forces of the nation.

Although Madison may have been correct that at the birth of the republic, and as understood in eighteenth-century governmental theory, that executive power was a term of art to mean the power to execute the laws and policies decided by Congress—thus not empowering the President to make his own policies that he himself would implement—the growth of the nation in the nineteenth century fostered both the need and the inevitability of a strong President that could provide leadership in times of war and national crisis, as well as the protection and projection of American interests on the stage of world affairs. Madison was correct that the Constitution intended that Congress was to be the first among equal branches of government in both the determination of war and peace and domestic policy; but two hundred years of history has placed its own gloss over the republic and has changed the relationship of the Congress and the President by empowering the Presidency to be the first and primary branch of government it is today. Madison did not agree that, in a time when the question of if war should be entered,

Congress would not act. He did not accept the proposition that Congress, being a deliberative body, could not act with deliberate speed or with deliberate conviction. To the assertion that in times when foreign policy may require war in dealing with foreign nations, the Constitution requires the President to act, Madison provided this observation in Helvidius 2:

> It is certain that a faithful execution of the laws . . . may tend as much in some cases, to incur war . . . as in others to avoid war. . . . The executive must nevertheless execute the laws . . . and leave it to the legislature to decide, whether they ought to be altered or not. *The executive has no other discretion than to convene and give information to the legislature* on occasions that may demand it; *and whilst this discretion is duly exercised, the trust of the executive is satisfied, and that department is not responsible for the consequences.* It could not be made responsible for them without vesting it with the legislative as well as with executive trust.

In the Madisonian model, Congress is a deliberative body, with various interests represented, thus serving as a reflection of the nation as a whole. These different interests can create inaction or delay in action. Each of these interests, or what Madison called factions, have their own voice and leaders and each proposing to claim to be representing the voice of the people. This is how it should be. Madison was correct that with all interests reflected in Congress, no one voice can dominate Congress and threaten the liberty of those in the minority. Madison also put great stock in the fact that through the legislative process, the advent of war would be slow and the pride of executive power would not be able to inflict war upon the people. The deliberative process would make war more difficult, and that was a positive, not a negative.

But the avoidance of war is not the highest value or even the purpose of foreign policy. The avoidance of war is but one aspect of international relations. Madison believed, despite the nature of a legislature, Congress could develop a long-term coherent foreign policy for the Executive to implement. Hamilton believed that though Congress had a role in the formulation of foreign policy, the President was equally, if not primarily, vested with a role of determining how the interests of the nation were to be implemented and protected on the international stage. To Madison the "aggrandizement" of the fruits of war provided a "temptation . . . to great for any one man" and the "sole power of making peace . . . would be too great for the wisdom, and the temptations too strong for the virtue, of a single citizen" to handle. To Hamilton, the President was given the responsibility by the Constitution "to preserve to the Nation the blessing of peace" and it was Congress, not the President, that was the source and organ of government that "can interrupt those blessings, by placing the Nation in a state of War." As we will discuss, history has provided Hamilton with the victory in this argument.

The Presidency has grown into the primary instrument of foreign policy. Although the President is acknowledged the primary organ of American foreign policy, history has also taught that the "laws of politics"[8] and "party politics"[9] and cycles of presidential elections[10] have tempered the power of the President and at times empowered Congress to temper, if not dictate, the policy initiatives of the President.

ALEXANDER HAMILTON AND JAMES MADISON: THE ADVENT OF A HAMILTONIAN PRESIDENCY

Although the debate between Hamilton and Madison is significant in understanding the beginning of our republic and the dispute over which branch of government controls the power of war, the debate between these two men has developed over the last two hundred years. Although Madison's views have their adherents, the history and practice of American Constitutionalism has made its own determinations. Madison's theory, that "the executive power . . . vested in a President of the United States of America" only provides the chief magistrate with the power to execute the laws as passed by Congress and that Congress is the first and primary organ to deliberate and decide on matters of war, has lost to Hamilton's theory that the President has independent power to determine if the nation is to initiate or respond to war with or without prior Congressional approval.

Although some scholars have dated the post–World War II era and the advent of the Cold War as the date of the rise of the Presidency as the de facto branch that decides questions of war and peace and the reduction of Congress to a secondary role,[11] the advent of the President as the controlling branch of government was well established by the middle of the nineteenth century if not earlier.[12] Every President from Washington to the present has developed and implemented a foreign policy designed to meet the times they were in. President Adams in 1798–1800 pursued a dual foreign policy of war preparation over the objections of the Republicans in early 1798 and peace treaty negotiations with France over the objections of his own Federalist party in Winter 1799; both resulted in avoidance of full-scale war with France and a peace treaty confirmed by the Senate in February 1801.[13]

President Jefferson, a disciple of the Madisonian version of the Presidency, as one historian observed,

> Took office . . . with a number of cherished principles . . . among them not only opposition to entangling alliances, a large army and navy, and war but support of the strict construction of the Constitutional powers of the president. . . . It was ironic that before he left the White House in 1809, he had to sacrifice almost every one of these principles. Yet it was vastly to his credit that he

surrendered those ideas when they conflicted with what he considered to be the national interest.[14]

Jefferson's foreign policy began with the war against the Barbary pirates of Tripoli in May 1801. Although Jefferson complied with his views on the limitation of his powers as Commander-in-Chief by ordering the navy to take a defensive posture against the Tripolitan Navy and requesting from Congress authorization to take an aggressive posture against the Tripolitan Navy,[15] it was Jefferson's foreign-policy decision not to pay the tribute demanded by Tripoli that precipitated hostilities in the first place. His next significant foreign-policy initiative included the famous Louisiana Purchase. On April 30, 1803, Jefferson's agents in France signed the Louisiana Purchase treaty.[16] Jefferson submitted the treaty to the Senate which was received with serious challenges to the legality of the treaty as well as to the Constitutionality of the President signing such a treaty without gaining prior "advice" of the Senate.

As a Madisonian theorist of the Presidency, Jefferson had acted outside of the Constitution because Congress did not authorize the negotiation, much less the purchase and signing of a treaty to gain possession of the Louisiana Territory. Jefferson's answer was to lay claim to *ex post facto* Congressional Indemnity. Under this theory, the executive officer admits that the action taken was not within the law but was committed under circumstances that required the action to prevent harm to the nation and the failure to act would constitute dereliction in the fulfillment of the duties of his office.[17] The theory has been described as follows:

> The Constitutional doctrine which lies under [this theory] is simply this: Imperious circumstances may sometimes require the high officers of government to act outside the law; but when such action is taken, the causes of it ought to be truly imperious, and ought to be stated immediately to Congress, who is the only judge of the propriety of the measure, and not the man who has usurped its decision. If . . . the officer has acted honestly, under the pressure of such urgent necessity . . . then it becomes the duty of Congress to sanction his illegal act . . . to indemnify him.[18]

Jefferson, in his famous 1810 letter to John B. Colvin, a State department official, who inquired about the power of the Executive to act when the law did not authorize the action but the action was beneficial to the security of the country, expounded on both the justification of executive power, Presidential responsibility, and the justification of extra-legal action by the executive under the theory of *ex post facto* Congressional Indemnity. In his letter to Colvin, Jefferson used as an example Washington's destruction of private property during the Revolutionary War so as to protect his army and a hypothetical naval ship starving for supplies attacking another ship with extra supplies that refuses to provide assistance. Jefferson concludes that, "[i]n all these cases, the unwritten laws of necessity, of self-preservation, and of the public safety, control . . .," such circumstances "constituted a law of necessity and self-preservation, and rendered the *salus populi* supreme over the written law."[19]

But Jefferson does not limit the use of this indemnification for military emergencies. In defending his actions in the Louisiana Purchase, Jefferson posits that political necessity is equally applicable to military necessities. He writes,

> Suppose it had been made known to the Executive of the Union in the au-
> tumn of 1805, that we might have the Floridas for a reasonable sum, that that
> sum had not indeed been so appropriated by law, but that Congress were to
> meet within three weeks, and might appropriate it on the first or second day of
> their session. Ought he, for so great an advantage to his country, to have risked
> himself by transcending the law and making the purchase? . . . But suppose it
> foreseen that a John Randolph would find means to protract the proceeding
> on it by Congress, until the ensuing spring, by which time new circumstances
> would change the mind of the other party. Ought the Executive, in that case,
> and with that foreknowledge, to have secured the good to his country, and to
> have trusted to their justice for the transgression of the law? I think he ought,
> and that the act would have been approved.[20]

Thus Jefferson, the famed advocate of limited powers for the national govern-
ment and a Madisonian who feared Presidential power, advocated that the President is duty bound to protect the national interest from both threats to national security and political obstruction, even when that obstruction originates in Congress. Hamilton wrote that the President has the right "to determine the condition of the Nation, though it may consequently affect the proper or improper exercise of the power of the Legislature," and though the "Legislature is free to perform its own duties according to its own sense of them . . . the Executive in the exercise of its Constitutional powers, may establish an antecedent state of things which ought to weigh in the legislative decisions." More than a decade later, Jefferson proposes that the President, knowing that delay in action would prevent the purchase of land that is in the interest of the nation to possess and knowing that Congress would be "pro-tracted" in approval due to political opposition, is obligated to act because of his specific executive knowledge of matters in foreign and domestic policy, and has a duty to protect the interests of the nation *salus populi suprema lex esto*. Hamilton would have viewed his victory with some amusement, being vindicated through the pen of Jefferson! No wonder Jefferson concluded his letter to Colvin with a request that his letter be for Colvin's eyes only.

But Jefferson, now writing with the actual experience of being President for two terms as supposed to his antifederalists Francophile experience of the 1790s, made an interesting and valid observation in regard to how the actions of the President should be judged when he takes action to preserve the nation, especially when such actions are not specifically authorized by the law. Jefferson wrote,

> The officer who is called to act on this superior ground, does indeed risk himself on the justice of the controlling powers of the Constitution, and his station makes it his duty to incur that risk. But those controlling powers, and his fellow citizens generally, are bound to judge according to the circumstances under which he acted. They are not to transfer the information of this place or moment to the time and place of his action; but to put themselves into his situation.[21]

In times of war and national security crisis, presidential actions have been taken that have been either explained or condemned as overreactions at best or intentionally unlawful at worst but during the actual time of the events appeared reasonable and necessary. Jefferson correctly proposes that a President should be judged by the facts as he knew them at the time and not those understood in the calmness of historical hindsight. We will return to Jefferson's theory of judging Presidential actions in later chapters.

Accepting that the President is liable for his actions to the Congress, the "controlling powers of the Constitution," and "his fellow citizens generally," Jefferson defends the Madisonian model of checks and balances but through the lens of the duty of the President to use inherent executive power for the defense of the interests of the nation—the Hamiltonian model. Implementing the Hamiltonian view, Jefferson posits his famous statement on the balance between the obedience to the law and the laws of necessity.

> A strict observance of the written law is doubtless *one* of the highest duties of a good citizen, but it is not *the* highest. The laws of necessity, of self-preservation, of saving our country when in danger, are of higher obligation. To lose our country by a scrupulous adherence to written law, would be to lose the law itself, with life, liberty, property and all those who are enjoying them with us; thus absurdly sacrificing the end to the means. . . .
>
> It is incumbent on those only who accept of great charges, to risk themselves on great occasions, when the safety of the nation, or some of its very high interests are at stake. An officer is bound to obey orders; yet he would be a bad one who should do it in cases for which they were not intended, and which involved the most important consequences. The line of discrimination between cases may be difficult; but the good officer is bound to draw it at his own peril, and throw himself on the justice of his country and the rectitude of his motives.[22]

Twoscore and eleven years later, Lincoln would be in total agreement.

The theory of *ex post facto* Congressional Indemnity, theoretically, validates the Madisonian theory of Presidential power because it acknowledges that the action in question required Congressional authorization, that the executive action was taken outside of the law or the Constitutional system, and that the executive does not make claims that the action was within Presidential powers, all the while protecting and justifying the action taken. Of course, the theory has no utility if one supports the Hamiltonian "inherent" and "vested" executive powers theory of the Presidency because the assertion is made that the act in question was within the Constitutional powers of the President and thus not outside the law and indemnification is not required. With the prevailing of the Hamiltonian view of presidential power, the theory of *ex post facto* Congressional Indemnity has not been used by any President since Jefferson or discussed by presidential scholars.

Of course, Jefferson was indemnified in that the Senate ratified the treaty in October 1803 due to the need to protect the economic growth and viability of the nation by having possession of the Port of New Orleans and Florida. In May 1803 England and France entered the second and final war resulting from the French revolution of 1789. Napoleon was emperor and after settling with America with the Louisiana Purchase, he was ready to address England. By 1806 both England and France had imposed worldwide economic embargoes to starve the other into submission. These intersecting embargoes involved the seizure of ships belonging to neutral nations found in violation of the embargo order. America suffered the most, being the world's biggest neutral nation and needing European trade for the majority of its economic growth. Of course, England, having the superior navy to France, was the chief violator of American commerce on the seas. To make things worse, British naval ships seized and searched American ships for British deserters and many American sailors were impressed into service of the British navy either by mistaken identity as British sailors or by need for men. The French proved to be little better in respecting American naval commerce and its standing orders to its navy included the provision that any neutral person found on a British ship was to be considered a pirate regardless of impressment. The total of American sailors impressed was six thousand between 1808 and 1811 and Americans were incensed and ready for war, but Jefferson was not.[23] Jefferson with a Republican Congress passed the Embargo Act of 1807 to force England to end her policy of seizure and searching American ships for deserters. Jefferson had violated his last prized Constitutional value—that the national government had no power to interfere with property rights, in this case, commerce. In March 1809 the Embargo was repealed under pressure from Federalists in New England and Western farmers. Three months later President James Madison took office.

Fifteen years after writing in Helvidius that the President of the United States was simply the organ of action for the Congress and accusing Hamilton of being a monarchist for supporting a more independent Presidency, Madison was now President himself. Madison, backed by the "War Hawks" of the Twelfth Congress, submitted a war message to Congress on June 1, 1812, after two unsuccessful diplomatic initiatives to avoid war. Madison implemented his Presidency without violation to his core principles of the Constitution. He provided Congress with reports on the actions of England and France and recommended a year before his war message that Congress implement measures to put the United States in a state of preparedness for war. Although he continued the tradition of active diplomacy by the President, he did not use military force against England until Congress approved through a declaration of war. But, although he did not claim powers beyond his views of the Presidency, he did not leave the development of policy completely in the hands of Congress and then enter the process after a declaration of war was made. The active diplomacy of Madison alone conceded to Hamilton's view that the President is the organ of foreign policy for the nation. Madison simply did not take Hamilton's theory as far as Hamilton advocated. *Hamilton prevailed nonetheless.*

James Madison was the last of the "Founding Fathers" to hold the Presidency. Subsequent presidents continued the development of a strong independent Presidency. President Monroe issued his famous doctrine declaring that the American continent was to be free from future European colonization and that any attempt to impose European governance in the Americas would be considered a threat to the peace and security of the United States. President Monroe acted in order to maintain American interests. After Texas won independence from Mexico in 1829, Texas sought recognition and annexation by the United States. President Jackson, fearing war with Mexico and disruption of the Democratic Party (split between pro and antislavery factions) in annexing Texas as a slave state, refused to recognize the independence or to support the annexation of Texas. Jackson later relented and provided official recognition of Texas independence on March 3, 1837, as the acceptance of the lesser of two evils.

By 1844 President Tyler for political reasons supported annexation[24] and upon signing a treaty of annexation made assurances to Texas that he, under his powers as President of the United States would employ all of the means at his disposal as President to protect Texas from any invasion by foreign powers.[25] The presumption that the President had independent power to pledge United States military intervention and protection without prior consent of the Senate caused protest by some members of Congress. As one Congressman protested, President Tyler's pledge "makes an act of defeasance from the Senate necessary to undo a treaty . . . instead of requiring our assent to give it validity. . . . This, indeed, is not merely reading, but spelling the Constitution backwards! It is reversing the functions of the Senate and making it a nullifying, instead of a ratifying body."[26] The treaty failed in the

Senate, in part, because of Senator Calhoun's vigorous defense of slavery in general and specifically supporting the institution of slavery in Texas.[27]

The issue of Mexican and additional territorial expansion by the United States as well as the blossoming of Presidential power to shape foreign policy occurred with the ascendancy of President Polk. President Polk, not to mention Congress, full well knowing that it meant war with Mexico, annexed Texas on December 29, 1845. President Polk, determining that it was in the interests of the United States to have California as well as needing to finalize the territorial boundaries of Texas, developed the dual strategy of diplomatic overtures to Mexico and sending the military (under General Zachary Taylor) into the disputed territory of the Nueces River in July 1845. President Polk also sent Thomas Larkin to foment revolt in California. With the diplomatic overture to buy California rebuffed by Mexico in January 1846, President Polk ordered Taylor to move across the Rio Grande. In April 1846 Mexican forces attacked General Taylor and war was declared by Congress on May 13, 1846.

There was little doubt that Polk had orchestrated the war but he did so with the full support of Congress. Congress supported the declaration with both enthusiasm and little reservation two days after President Polk asked for it on May 11, 1846 (House vote 174 to 14 and Senate vote 40 to 2). What would Madison have said of an American President actively through diplomatic and military policy seeking to create a war? Polk's actions would have confirmed his assertion that the "aggrandizement of war" was too much for one person to resist. But, and this is important, Congress was aware of Polk's diplomacy and supported it. As President Polk sent his message to Congress asking for a declaration of war against Mexico in 1846, few in Congress had political, much less, Constitutional complaints in regard to Polk's actions. The observation of one Congressman was that the "Constitution gives Congress the sole power to declare war. Perhaps some gentlemen may suppose that that clause in the Constitution simply means that when the President gets us into war, it is the business of Congress to make it known—to declare it—or recognize the fact"[28] fell on deaf ears.

Polk acted and Congress supported. The Congress did not lead in the policy of wanting war. It merely affirmed the President in actions he initiated. This is something Madison never contemplated in his debate with Hamilton. That Congress would accede to Presidential action when that action was acceptable to them and that the Constitutional principle that the President is not to act but to implement policy would give way to political approval of a Presidential policy implementation independent of prior direction from Congress. The actions of the nineteenth-century Presidents post-Madison established that they could act independent of Congress. The lack of Congressional resistance solidified this power so that in the future when Congress did not approve of Presidential action, it was and has been proposed that historically the President has the power to act in the areas of foreign policy independently of Congressional approval. When disagreements on Presidential action now arise, those who support Presidential action assert that it is a historical and Constitutional fact that the President has inherent powers in foreign policy and is the sole organ of that policy.

President Pierce sent Commodore Perry to secure a trade treaty with Japan and with a naval force of several ships pointing their guns at Yeddo Bay he secured the treaty in 1854. The prominence and significance of executive power greatly increased and were institutionalized with President Lincoln and the necessities of the Civil War. President Lincoln suspended habeas corpus, blockaded southern ports and seized ships under a blanket assertion that as Commander-in-Chief he had the power and the responsibility to save the union. He made clear that he would do so regardless of technical Constitutional violations. On July 4, 1861, President Lincoln in a special session of Congress explained the use of executive power in the face of a national domestic threat:

> And this issue embraces more than the fate of these United States. It presents to the whole family of man, the question, whether a Constitutional republic, or a democracy—a government of the people, by the same people—can, or cannot, maintain its territorial integrity, against its own domestic foes. It presents the question, whether discontented individuals, too few in numbers to control administration, according to organic law, in any case, can always, upon the pretences made in this case, or on any other pretences, or arbitrarily, without any pretence, break up their Government, and thus practically put an end to free government upon the earth. It forces us to ask: "Is there, in all republics, this inherent, and fatal weakness?" "Must a government, of necessity, be too strong for the liberties of its own people, or too weak to maintain its own existence?"[29]. . . .
>
> Soon after the first call for militia, it was considered a duty to authorize the Commanding General, in proper cases, according to his discretion, to suspend the privilege of the writ of habeas corpus . . . the legality and propriety of what has been done . . . are questioned; and the attention of the country has been called to the proposition that one who is sworn to "take care that the laws be faithfully executed," should not himself violate them. Of course some consideration was given to the questions of power, and propriety, before this matter was acted upon. The whole of the laws which were required to be faithfully executed, were being resisted, and failing of execution, in nearly one-third of the States. . . . To state the question more directly, are all the laws, but one, to go unexecuted, and the government itself go to pieces, lest that one be violated? Even in such a case, would not the official oath be broken, if the government should be overthrown, when it was believed that disregarding the single law, would tend to preserve it?[30]

In justifying his actions, Lincoln explained that the southern rebellion was a direct threat to the principles of elective government and the rule of law. Lincoln believed that the Civil War was a test as to whether a Republic can survive a challenge to its processes of choosing its government through elections only. He stated that

> our popular government has often been called an experiment. Two points in it, our people have already settled—the successful establishing, and the successful administering of it. One still remains—its successful maintenance against a formidable internal attempt to overthrow it. It is now for them to demonstrate to the world, that those who can fairly carry an election, can also suppress a rebellion—that ballots are the rightful, and peaceful, successors of bullets; and that when ballots have fairly, and Constitutionally, decided, there can be no successful appeal, back to bullets; that there can be no successful appeal, except to ballots themselves, at succeeding elections. Such will be a great lesson of peace; teaching men that what they cannot take by an election, neither can they take it by a war—teaching all, the folly of being the beginners of a war."[31]

He concluded his speech with this observation: "No popular government can long survive a marked precedent that those who carry an election can only save the government from immediate destruction by giving up the main point upon which the people gave the election."[32]

Reminiscent of Jefferson and the theory of *ex post facto* Congressional Indemnity, Lincoln posits that although the President is charged with the faithful execution of the laws, the higher law of taking actions to preserve the nation and its interest can present the President with the choice of acting within the law and endangering the union or acting outside of the law to protect it. The choice of which, for both Jefferson and Lincoln, is to act outside the law. But Jefferson would assert if the President must act outside of the law to preserve the union he must present the action to Congress with full admission that the act was outside the law and seek Congressional indemnity, thus protecting the Madisonian view that if an action is needed and the law does not allow it, Congress must be so informed and invited to make the change to the law. But Lincoln, in presenting his act of suspending habeas corpus, did not propose that his action was outside the law but was at best within his power and at the very least was not prohibited by the law. Lincoln explained his actions to Congress as follows:

> But it was not believed that this question was presented. It was not believed that any law was violated. The provision of the Constitution that "The privilege of the writ of habeas corpus, shall not be suspended unless when, in cases of rebellion or invasion, the public safety may require it," is equivalent to a provision—is a provision—that such privilege may be suspended when, in cases of rebellion, or invasion, the public safety does require it. It was decided that we have a case of rebellion, and that the public safety does require the qualified suspension of the privilege of the writ which was authorized to

be made. Now it is insisted that Congress, and not the Executive, is vested with this power. But the Constitution itself, is silent as to which, or who, is to exercise the power; and as the provision was plainly made for a dangerous emergency, it cannot be believed the framers of the instrument intended, that in every case, the danger should run its course, until Congress could be called together; the very assembling of which might be prevented, as was intended in this case, by the rebellion.[33]

Close to the end of his speech, Lincoln makes an observation on the legitimacy of the ends to support the legality of the means.

> The Constitution provides, and all the States have accepted the provision, that "The United States shall guarantee to every State in this Union a republican form of government." But, if a State may lawfully go out of the Union, having done so, it may also discard the republican form of government; so that to prevent its going out, is an indispensable *means*, to the *end*, of maintaining the guaranty mentioned; and when an end is lawful and obligatory, the indispensable means to it, are also lawful, and obligatory.[34]

Leaving aside Lincoln's first premise, with which I have no argument, his second premise is interesting when looking at the growth of Presidential power in times of crisis and foreign policy or war. Is it true that "when an end is lawful and obligatory, the indispensable means to it, are also lawful, and obligatory"? If this is true, what are its limits? What can't a President do in the agreed legitimacy of the end? Is there a line that can't be crossed? If so, who draws that line? As we have reviewed and will continue to see, the power of the President to act, in his estimation, to preserve and protect the interests of the United States has evolved the office of the President far beyond what the Founders, even what Hamilton, may have imagined. But as history has progressed, the limits on what Lincoln stated and implied have been political, historical, and legal, but not necessarily Constitutional.

With the end of the civil war, the nation quickly healed its wounds and turned to continuing to secure foreign territories. The rise of "Social Darwinism" and full blossoming of the theory of "Manifest Destiny" increased America's view of its national interests and its belief that those interests were almost divine in origin and equally divine in necessity of completion. These two world views were supplemented by the publication of *The Influence of Sea Power Upon History, 1600–1783* by Alfred Thayer Mahan in 1890 which asserted that great nations were born and maintained through international commerce backed by a strong naval presence in the world. By the late 1800s the Office of the President had become the predominant political branch for the formation and implementation of the national vision of the nation.

During the late nineteenth and early twentieth centuries of American history (1865–1917) the United States asserted itself in the Pacific and in Latin

America. Reminiscent of President Tyler in 1844 in Texas, President Grant sent forces to Santo Domingo to protect American interests and prevent foreign intervention while the Senate debated a treaty annexation. Even after the failure of the treaty in the Senate, Grant continued to keep forces in Santo Domingo. In a letter to Rear Admiral Lee, Secretary of the Navy Robeson wrote that "the President of the United States has by the Constitution the right to make treaties, subject to the ratification of the Senate. . . . In pursuance of this Constitutional right he did negotiate such treaties . . . but by such treaties and pending such final action, the United States acquired an interest in the thing negotiated for, which could not be rightfully disturbed by any other power; and it was the plain duty of the Executive to protect, if need be, the integrity of this Constitutionally acquired interest."[35] As with President Tyler's use of military force to protect interests created by a negotiated treaty, President Grant's assertion of American military power without Congressional authorization raised Constitutional protest. Senator Sumner proposed a resolution asserting that the President could not send forces to foreign lands without Congressional approval.[36] The resolution was defeated.

President Cleveland sent warships to face down German warships over the Samoan Islands. President Harrison nearly went to war with Chile in 1892 over diplomatic insults and minor military harassment by the Chilean navy. In February 1893, President Harrison's minister to Hawaii, with the help of 150 Marines and sailors, raised the American flag over the government house of the Queen and declared Hawaii an American protectorate. This was done, in part, because of the Queen's actions in drafting a new Constitution that was seen as an economic and political threat to the white business settlers. The Queen was deposed. President Cleveland, unable to convince the new President of Hawaii to return power to the Queen, offered recognition of the new government but refused requests for annexation and formally withdrew a treaty of annexation left over by the Harrison administration. In 1895 America faced down Great Britain over the territorial boundaries of Venezuela.

The Spanish American war was the capstone on the nineteenth-century emergence of America as a world power. Cleveland, followed by President McKinley, had eyes on securing Cuba from Spain. Both Presidents initially tried to purchase Cuba from Spain but failed. After Cuba declared independence, President Cleveland established a policy of neutrality over the rebellion, ignoring a Senate resolution (41–14) to recognize the Cuban rebellion.[37] McKinley sent the USS *Maine* and other naval ships into the Cuban harbor, a war zone, under his powers as Commander-in-Chief to protect U.S. interests. The explosion of the USS *Maine* on February 15, 1898, was almost uniformly blamed on Spain even though official investigations did not hold Spain responsible. McKinley subsequently presented his war message to Congress on April 11, 1898, and Congress passed a resolution authorizing the President to eject Spain from Cuba and saying that the United States had no interest in annexing Cuba on April 19, 1898. By August 1898 the war was over. The United States entered the twentieth century possessing Puerto Rico, Guam, and the Philippines—Hawaii was annexed in July 1898.[38] In 1900 McKinley sent an expeditionary force of five thousand troops as part of an international force to put down the Boxer Rebellion in China. In 1903 Theodore Roosevelt sent the U.S. Navy to Panama to prevent the Colombian navy from landing troops to put down a Panamanian uprising, which he was in no small part responsible for starting. In 1913 President Taft sent two thousand marines to occupy Nicaragua in order to maintain a friendly government, an occupation that was sustained until 1933. In 1914 and in 1916 President Wilson sent American forces into Mexico to protect American political and economic interests. After the abdication of Czar Nicolas II in February 1917 and the fall of the Provisional government of October 1917 at the hands of the Bolshevik government, the Russian Civil War (1918–1920) ensued and by July 1918 a multinational force invaded the Siberian area of Russia. Wilson sent a thirteen thousand strong expeditionary force to aid the allies in supporting the White Army against the communists in both Siberia and Northern Russia in July and August 1918 to prevent German capture of munitions stationed there. FDR, before Pearl Harbor, occupied Greenland and Iceland, and issued a "sink on sight" order to the U.S. Navy if they found any German or Japanese submarines in U.S. defensive waters. Wilson's actions could be viewed as necessary under the state of war with the axis powers, but FDR had no such justification. He issued orders that placed U.S. forces in hostile situations that could lead to military engagement without prior approval by Congress.

Needless to say, this summary of history is not exhaustive. But our review provides a foundation for understanding how the Office of the President has become the primary branch of government in the area of foreign affairs. From Washington through Wilson, each President established a foreign policy based on the times in which they lived. The early Presidents sought to avoid war with the major world powers because of the weakness of the nation both militarily and economically. As the strength of the nation grew, later Presidents protected economic interests on the American continent and later in Latin America. Foreign powers were bought off or militarily pushed out of North America so the United States could meet its "manifest destiny" to have a nation from sea to shining sea with preeminence in the Western Hemisphere. The issue of slavery was finally recognized as an issue that only war could solve. President Lincoln used powers to maintain the union and established the President as the single political leader responsible for protecting the nation. The later Presidents of the nineteenth century brought the country to first-rate status in the eyes of the world and governed the country through a world view of nationalism and imperialism. The twentieth century was called the American Century and by its end the President was universally acknowledged as the Chief Diplomat of the nation and the sole organ of foreign policy. Congress receded to the role of providing political support or opposition to Presidential policy. Congress, by the early twentieth century, was no longer considered the originator of American foreign and national security policy, assuming that it ever was.

Woodrow Wilson's book *Constitutional Government in the United States* (1908) is instructive on how the Presidency was viewed at the dawn of the American Century. In chapter 3 he discusses how the Presidency and the Hamiltonian view of the Presidency again prevailed over Madison. Wilson wrote that the "makers of the Constitution constructed the federal government upon a theory of checks and balances which was meant to limit the operation of each part and allow to no single part or organ of it a dominating force; but no government can be successfully conducted upon so mechanical a theory. Leadership and control must be lodged somewhere . . . bringing the several parts of government into effective cooperation."[39] The President, Wilson wrote, is that leadership. Wilson, in the time when Social Darwinian thinking was the predominant social and political theory in the leading circles of academia, government and business, wrote that government is not a machine of parts but is a living thing that grows and adapts to its environment and such growth cannot occur if its parts are in opposition to each other in the operation of the organism. The parts are the politicians and institutions that govern and lead the nation.

In describing the Office of the President, Wilson accepts that the founders intended to create a President in Madison's image, a President "only [being a] legal executive, the presiding and guiding authority in the application of law and the execution of policy. . . . He was empowered to prevent bad laws, but he was not to be given an opportunity to make good ones. As a matter of fact he has become very much more. He has become the leader of his party and the guide of the nation in political purpose."[40] The President, Wilson explained, had become more than an executor of Congressional will and policy. History had made the President a national leader, and the only leader, selected by the people through a national election—thus granting him the position to be the single voice of the people. Wilson writes,

> What the country will demand of the candidate will be, not that he be an astute politician, skilled and practiced in affairs, but that he be a man such as it can trust, in character, in intention, in knowledge of its needs, in perception of the best means by which those needs may be met, in capacity to prevail by reason of his own weight and integrity. . . .
>
> There is no national party choice except that of President. No one else represents the people as a whole, exercising a national choice. . . .
>
> The nation as a whole has chosen him, and is conscious that it has no other political spokesman. His is the only national voice in affairs. Let him once

win the admiration and confidence of the country, no other single force can withstand him.[41]

In regard to Congress, Wilson observed that the "President is at liberty, both in law and conscience, to be as big a man as he can. His capacity will set the limit; and if Congress be overborne by him, it will be no fault of the makers of the Constitution—it will be from no lack of Constitutional powers on its part, but only because the President has the nation behind him, and Congress has not."[42]

"One of the greatest of the President's powers," Wilson wrote, is "his control, which is very absolute, of the foreign relations of the nation."[43] Although the President must submit a treaty to the Senate for confirmation, "he may guide every step of diplomacy, and to guide diplomacy is to determine what treaties must be made."[44] Hamilton could not have said it better himself. The power of foreign affairs

> has been decisively influential in determining the character and influence of the office . . . first, when the government was young [second,] . . . in our day when the results of the Spanish War . . . [made] it necessary that we should turn our best talents to the task of dealing firmly, wisely, and justly with political and commercial rivals. The President can never again be the mere domestic figure. . . . The nation has risen to the first rank in power and resources. . . . Our President must always, henceforth, be one of the great powers of the world.[45]

Wilson's view of the rise of the President as the sole organ of foreign policy and the expansion of his powers were not unique. Hamilton, Jefferson, Lincoln and Theodore Roosevelt all wrote of a Presidency that, when necessary, was not only able but duty bound to act in the best interests of the nation. They were to be held accountable for those actions, but none the less were expected to act, not simply implement policy. Lincoln wrote,

> I did understand however, that my oath to preserve the Constitution to the best of my ability, imposed upon me the duty of preserving, by every indispensable means, that government—that nation—of which that Constitution was the organic law. Was it possible to lose the nation, and yet preserve the Constitution? By general law life *and* limb must be protected; yet often a limb must be amputated to save a life; but a life is never wisely given to save a limb. I felt that measures, otherwise unconstitutional, might become lawful, by becoming indispensable to the preservation of the Constitution, through the preservation of the nation. Right or wrong, I assumed this ground, and now avow it. I could not feel that, to the best of my ability, I had even tried to preserve the Constitution, if, to save slavery, or any minor matter, I should permit the wreck of government, country, and Constitution all together.[46]

Theodore Roosevelt similarly wrote of the growth and significance of the Presidency in his autobiography in 1913.

The most important factor in getting the right spirit in my Administration, next to the insistence upon courage, honesty, and a genuine democracy of desire to serve the plain people, was *my insistence upon the theory that the executive power was limited only by specific restrictions and prohibitions appearing in the Constitution or imposed by the Congress under its Constitutional powers. My view was that every executive officer,* and above all every executive officer in high position, *was a steward of the people bound* actively and affirmatively *to do all he could for the people,* and not to content himself with the negative merit of keeping his talents undamaged in a napkin. *I declined to adopt the view that what was imperatively necessary for the Nation could not be done by the President unless he could find some specific authorization to do it.* My belief was that it was not only his right but his duty to do anything that the needs of the Nation demanded unless such action was forbidden by the Constitution or by the laws. Under this interpretation of executive power I did and caused to be done many things not previously done by the President and the heads of the departments. *I did not usurp power, but I did greatly broaden the use of executive power.* In other words, I acted for the public welfare, I acted for the common well-being of all our people, whenever and in whatever manner was necessary, unless prevented by direct Constitutional or legislative prohibition. . . .[47] There have long been two schools of political thought, upheld with equal sincerity. The division has not normally been along political, but temperamental, lines. The course I followed, of regarding the executive as subject only to the people, and, under the Constitution, bound to serve the people affirmatively in cases where the Constitution does not explicitly forbid him to render the service, was substantially the course followed by both Andrew Jackson and Abraham Lincoln. Other honorable and well-meaning Presidents, such as James Buchanan, took the opposite and, as it seems to me, narrowly legalistic view that the President is the servant of Congress rather than of the people, and can do nothing, no matter how necessary it be to act, unless the Constitution explicitly commands the action. . . . My successor in office took this, the Buchanan, view of the President's powers and duties.[48]

President Roosevelt was also astute in observing that the debate on the powers of the Presidency and those who supported what he called the Buchanan-Taft view of the Presidency did so "because it enables them to attack and to try to hamper, for partisan or personal reasons, an executive whom they dislike."

History, political necessities, wars, national ambition, civil war, the end of slavery, and the rise of international economic and political interests have all conspired to increase the power and prestige of the President. The power of the President as Commander-in-Chief to use the armed forces of the United States to protect the nation against internal and external threats grew into the power to use those forces to project and protect American interests, first in the Western United States, then in Latin America and later the Pacific and the Atlantic oceans around the world. By the close of the twentieth century the United States military was present on or had access to every continent of the globe. Even scholars who assert that Congress is the only branch with the authority to initiate hostilities admit that Presidents over the past two centuries "in probably more than two hundred instances, have used military force without first receiving Congressional authority."[49] Although such scholars, like Louis Fisher, qualify this fact by noting that these military "actions generally fall under the category of 'protecting life or property,' . . . [and none] of these actions come close to anything approaching [initiating] a major war,"[50] the qualification misses the point. Congressional acquiescence or complicity with Presidential use of military force and deployment without Congressional approval has established a history that has placed in the power of the President as Commander-in-Chief the ability to use military force as he determines the need with or without the strict need to gain Congressional approval. The difference between the power to initiate small military deployments and large deployments is a matter of degree and not substance. Even if the "Founding Fathers" had intended otherwise (and as we have discussed, they were not of one mind on the powers of the President) history and practice has made its own determination and that is the determination that has prevailed.

But another factor which has not yet been reviewed also played a significant role in the growth of the Presidency in the nineteenth century. That factor was the rise of the Supreme Court as a coequal branch of government and its interpretation of the Constitutional power to declare war and the role of the President as Commander-in-Chief to initiate war and protect the nation in times of rebellion and national crisis. The Court had its own views on how these two clauses and powers operated and the Hamilton view of the Presidency, again, prevailed. It is to how the Supreme Court undergirded the rise of Presidential power in times of war and national crisis in the nineteenth century that we now turn our attention.

NOTES

1. The following citations for Pacificus are taken from the University of Chicago *The Founders' Constitution* research page, http://press-pubs.uchicago.edu/founders/documents/a2_2_2-3s14.html, reprinting of Harold C. Syrett et al., eds., *The Papers of Alexander Hamilton*, 26 vols. (New York: Columbia University Press, 1961–1979).

2. See *United States v. Curtis-Wright Exports* 299 U.S. 304 (1936).

3. The Presidential signing statement is one of the major tools used by Presidents to enforce their policy prerogatives and initiatives when applying acts of Congress. First developed during the Monroe administration to defend his appointment powers, the Presidential "signing statement, because of the aggressiveness to which the Reagan administration pushed it as an important tool to advance presidential power, became standard fare for all administrations that followed. In fact, both the Bush I administration and the Clinton administration made sure to not only

aggressively use the signing statement to protect presidential prerogative but also as a policy tool." Christopher S. Kelly, "Rethinking Presidential Power—The Unitary Executive and the George W. Bush Presidency" (paper presented at the 63rd Annual Midwest Political Science Association Conference, April 7–10, 2005); Phillip J. Cooper, "George W. Bush, Edger Allen Poe, and the Use and Abuse of Presidential Signing Statements," *Presidential Studies Quarterly* 35, no. 3 (2005): 515–32.

4. Albert H. Bowman, "Realism versus Moralism in Foreign Policy: Jefferson, Hamilton, and the Franco-British War," in *The President's War Powers: From the Federalists to Reagan,* ed. Demetrios Caraley (New York: Academy of Political Science, 1984).

5. Ibid.

6. Thomas Jefferson letter to James Madison, July 7, 1793. Thomas A. Mason, Robert A. Rutland, and Jeanne K. Sisson, eds., *The Papers of James Madison,* vol. 15 (Charlottesville: University Press of Virginia, 1985), 43.

7. The following citations for Helvidius are taken from the University of Chicago *The Founders' Constitution* research page, http://press-pubs.uchicago.edu/founders/documents/a2_2_2-3s15.html, reprinting of Gaillard Hunt, ed., *The Writings of James Madison,* 9 vols. (New York: Putnam, 1900–1910).

8. "Laws of politics" refers to the politically acceptable options a President can consider and still maintain popular support, or in the converse, options that will create large and/or vocal opposition in the public. A President is not a king who can act without support of the people. Maintaining support of the people provides the President with the political capital to act or not act. It is the art of gaining and maintaining political support and avoiding political rejection that more times than not provides the President with the power to act or not act.

9. "Party politics" was a fact that Madison accepted from the Federalist papers. He assumed, expected, and depended on the clash of interests as the best way to protect liberty and freedom. His theory was that with all interests forced into a collective body and only a majority of the body able to take action, no one interest could gain power and impose tyranny on the rights of others. History focused the divergent interests into political parties from the very beginning of the Republic. The Federalist split into the Federalists and Republicans based on differences of Constitutional interpretation, domestic policy, foreign policy, and the view of what the republic was to become. As parties became the focal machine for the selection and election of Presidents, the power of the President to act became governed by the majority of his party in Congress. Over time, Congress changed from an institution of policy and struggle with the President to an institution in which the party not holding the Presidency would oppose the party holding the Presidency. Party control of Congress has become a major force in giving a President a free or obstructed hand in foreign and domestic policy determination.

10. Between Washington and Franklin Roosevelt, Presidents served two terms. FDR changed the generally accepted reign of a President and the Twenty-Second Amendment to the Constitution has established that the President can only serve two terms. As such, the laws of politics and party fight for control of the Presidency, which reduces the President's power within two years of his second term. With politicians of both parties gearing up for a fight for the soon-to-be-vacant chair of the President, the power of the sitting President to reward loyalty or punish adverse behavior is lost because he no longer can aid in the election or threaten public con-

demnation of those seeking office. He is a "lame duck" to both parties and to those from each who seek his job. Those who seek his chair gain political support with the electorate by opposing him or supporting him. Of course this truth can provide some power to the President if he is significantly popular during his last two years. The laws of politics and party politics interplay at much higher levels during the election session of a "lame duck" President.

11. See generally the work of Louis Fisher. For example, see *Presidential War Power* (Lawrence: University Press of Kansas, 1995) and *Military Tribunals & Presidential Power* (Lawrence: University Press of Kansas, 2005).

12. Abbot Smith, "Who Decides War? Madison in 1812," in Caraley, ed., *The President's War Powers.*

13. Armin Rappaport, *A History of American Diplomacy* (New York: Macmillan, 1975).

14. Ibid., 51.

15. Thomas Jefferson, First Annual Address to Congress (December 8, 1801).

16. Rapaport, *A History of American Diplomacy*, 54.

17. Lucius Wilmerding, Jr., "Seizure of Industry under War Powers: Truman and the Steel Mills," in Caraley, ed., *The President's War Powers.*

18. Ibid., 116.

19. Andrew A. Lipscomb and Albert Ellery Bergh, eds., *The Writings of Thomas Jefferson*, vol. 12 (Washington, DC: The Thomas Jefferson Memorial Association of the United States, 1903), 419, 421.

20. Ibid., 419–20.

21. Ibid., 420.

22. Ibid., 418, 421–22.

23. Rappaport, *A History of American Diplomacy*, 60.

24. Ibid., 100.

25. Charles C. Tansill, "The President and the Initiation of Hostilities: The Precedents of the Mexican and Spanish-American Wars," in Caraley, ed., *The President's War Powers.*

26. Ibid., 78.

27. Rappaport, *A History of American Diplomacy*, 101.

28. Smith, "Who Decides War? Madison in 1812," in Caraley, ed., *The President's War Powers*, 29.

29. Joseph R. Fornieri, *The Language of Liberty: The Political Speeches and Writings of Abraham Lincoln* (Washington, DC: Regnery, 2003), 578–79.

30. Ibid., 581.

31. Ibid., 587.

32. Ibid., 587–88.

33. Ibid., 581.

34. Ibid., 587.

35. Tansill, "The President and the Initiation of Hostilities," in Caraley, ed., *The President's War Powers*, 80.

36. Congressional Globe (March 24, 1871), 42nd Congress, 1st Session, p. 294.

37. Rappaport, *A History of American Diplomacy*, 192.

38. Ibid., 198.

39. Woodrow Wilson, *Constitutional Government in the United States* (New York: Columbia University Press, 1908), 54.

40. Ibid., 60.

41. Ibid., 66, 68.

42. Ibid., 70.

43. Ibid., 77.

44. Ibid.

45. Ibid., 78.

46. Letter to A. G. Hodges, April 4, 1864. Fornieri, *The Language of Liberty*, 788.

47. Theodore Roosevelt, *An Autobiography* (New York: Macmillan, 1913), 388–89 (emphasis added).

48. Ibid., 394–95. After providing an example of the difference between "what may be called the Lincoln-Jackson and the Buchanan-Taft schools, in their views of the power and duties of the President," President Roosevelt concluded:

> There are many worthy people who reprobate the Buchanan method as a matter of history, but who in actual life reprobate still more strongly the Jackson-Lincoln method when it is put into practice. These persons conscientiously believe that the President should solve every doubt in favor of inaction as against action, that he should construe strictly and narrowly the Constitutional grant of powers both to the National Government, and to the President within the National Government. In addition, however, to the men who conscientiously believe in this course from high, although as I hold misguided, motives, there are many men who affect to believe in it merely because it enables them to attack and to try to hamper, for partisan or personal reasons, an executive whom they dislike. There are other men in whom, especially when they are themselves in office, practical adherence to the Buchanan principle represents not well-thought-out devotion to an unwise course, but simple weakness of character and desire to avoid trouble and responsibility. Unfortunately, in practice it makes little difference which class of ideas actuates the President, who by his action sets a cramping precedent. Whether he is high-minded and wrongheaded or merely infirm of purpose, whether he means well feebly or is bound by a mischievous misconception of the powers and duties of the National Government and of the President, the effect of his actions is the same. The President's duty is to act so that he himself and his subordinates shall be able to do efficient work for the people, and this efficient work he and they cannot do if Congress is permitted to undertake the task of making up his mind for him as to how he shall perform what is clearly his sole duty.

Ibid., 397–99.

49. Louis Fisher, "Exercising Congress's Constitutional Power to End War" (testimony before the Senate Committee on the Judiciary, January 30, 2007), www.loc.gov/law/help/usconlaw/pdf/Feingold2007rev.pdf.

50. Ibid.

2

The Supreme Court and Presidential Authority in Times of National Crisis

The war that engulfed Great Britain and France and the rest of the world had, as we have discussed, a significant impact on the development of the power of the President to deal with national security. President Washington, defended by Hamilton, made independent assessments of treaties and on the obligations those treaties imposed and did not impose on the United States. The Supreme Court, although the most silent of the three branches of government on the development of national power and the power of the Presidency in the area of foreign affairs, lent its interpretation of Presidential power and that interpretation added, rather than detracted, from the growth of Presidential power.

In the advent of the War of 1812 President Madison called for the service of the militia to serve in its capacity as part of the armed forces of the United States. Subsequent to that general call, Governor of New York Daniel D. Tompkins called out the New York militia to serve in accordance with the President's general call. Jacob E. Mott, a private in the New York militia, refused to report for service and was subsequently court-martialed, convicted and fined due to his failure to report for service. He sued, challenging his conviction and fine. The case of *Martin v. Mott*[1] was the first case in which the Supreme Court specifically described and defined the power of the President as Commander-in-Chief.

Justice Story wrote that Congress, under the Constitution, has the power to raise the armed forces of the United States and to provide for those forces in times of war, insurrection and invasion. "In pursuance of this authority, [Congress enacted] the act of 1795 [which] provided, 'that whenever the

41

United States shall be invaded, or be in imminent danger of invasion from any foreign nation or Indian tribe, it shall be lawful for the President of the United States to call forth such number of the militia of the State or States most convenient to the place of danger, or scene of action, as he may judge necessary to repel such invasion, and to issue his order for that purpose to such officer or officers of the militia as he shall think proper.'"[2] Justice Story pointed out that it

> has not been denied here, that the act of 1795 is within the Constitutional authority of Congress, or that Congress may not lawfully provide for cases of imminent danger of invasion, as well as for cases where an invasion has actually taken place. In our opinion there is no ground for a doubt on this point, even if it had been relied on, for the power to provide for repelling invasions includes the power to provide against the attempt and danger of invasion, as the necessary and proper means to effectuate the object. One of the best means to repel invasion is to provide the requisite force for action before the invader himself has reached the soil.[3]

The Court ruled that Congress can and did delegate the power to call out the military to the President from the earliest years of the republic. The Court held that the power to call out the militia is a limited power based on the circumstances, but the question that presents itself is "by whom is the exigency to be judged of and decided? Is the President the sole and exclusive judge whether the exigency has arisen, or is it to be considered as an open question?"[4] To which the Court answered, "*We are all of opinion, that the authority to decide whether the exigency has arisen, belongs exclusively to the President, and that his decision is conclusive upon all other persons. We think that this construction necessarily results from the nature of the power itself*, and from the manifest object contemplated by the act of Congress."[5]

The Court ruled the exclusive power of the President to determine if an exigency has arisen is an inherent power flowing out of the general grant of power to call out the militia as Commander-in-Chief.

The Court wrote broadly that the "nature of the power itself" of the President, as Commander-in-Chief, to call out the militia and the armed forces of the United States "is to be exercised upon sudden emergencies, upon great occasions of state, and under circumstances which may be vital to the existence of the Union."[6] The Court, as early as 1827, recognized that the nature of Presidential decision making may require both exigency and secrecy and such decisions may not be subjected to technical proof by the public, Congress or the Judiciary.[7] The Constitution, the Court reasoned, invests the President, as Commander-in-Chief and as the branch of government responsible to ensure that the laws are faithfully executed, with the exclusive power to determine when the forces of the United States are to be activated due to the President's determination that circumstances justify that action. The Court ruled that Congress, by its Act of 1795, similarly recognized the inherent Constitutional powers of the President as Commander-in-Chief to use the militia in times of exigent circumstances of rebellion, insurrection or invasion in order to carry out his responsibilities to ensure the effective execution of the laws.

> If we look at the language of the act of 1795, every conclusion drawn from the nature of the power itself, is strongly fortified. The words are, "whenever the United States shall be invaded, or be in imminent danger of invasion, &c. it shall be lawful for the President, &c. to call forth such number of the militia, &c. as he may judge necessary to repel such invasion." The power itself is confided to the Executive of the Union, to him who is, by the Constitution, "the commander in chief of the militia, when called into the actual service of the United States," whose duty it is to "take care that the laws be faithfully executed," and whose responsibility for an honest discharge of his official obligations is secured by the highest sanctions. *He is necessarily constituted the judge of the existence of the exigency in the first instance, and is bound to act according to his belief of the facts.*[8]

The Court concluded that, aside from the President's inherent powers as Commander-in-Chief, Congress has supplemented the power of the President to call out the military under circumstances that the President deems appropriate. The Court held that such Congressional action has vested in the President exclusive and sole discretion in making determinations of emergencies and situations justifying the activation of the military.

> *Whenever a statute gives a discretionary power to any person, to be exercised by him upon his own opinion of certain facts, it is a sound rule of construction, that the statute constitutes him the sole and exclusive judge of the existence of those facts.* And, in the present case, we are all of opinion that such is the true construction of the act of 1795. It is no answer that such a power may be abused, for there is no power which is not susceptible of abuse. The remedy for this, as well as for all other official misconduct, if it should occur, is to be found in the Constitution itself. In a free government, the danger must be remote, since in addition to the high qualities which the Executive must be presumed to possess, of public virtue, and honest devotion to the public interests, the frequency of elections, and the watchfulness of the representatives of the nation, carry with them all the checks which can be useful to guard against usurpation or wanton tyranny.[9]

The Court addressed the assertion that even if the President has exclusive authority to determine exigencies that justified the use of the military, that "power confided to the President is a limited power, and can be exercised only in the cases pointed out in the statute, and therefore it is necessary to aver the facts which bring the exercise within the purview of the statute."[10] The Court rejected the assertion that the President must prove, in fact, the exigency that justified his use of his powers as Commander-in-Chief. The Court wrote, "It is the opinion of the Court, that this objection cannot be maintained. When the President exercises an authority confided to him by law, the presumption is, that it is exercised in pursuance of law."[11]

In *Luther v. Borden*[12] the Court addressed the power of the President to act in the case of armed insurrection within a state of the United States. Rhode Island, after the colonies gained their independence from Great Britain and formed the United States, retained the governmental structure that Charles the Second created in 1663. Minor changes were made to the structure by the legislature to allow for Rhode Island entrance to the Union. In May 1841 a Constitutional convention was created and it passed a new Constitution, which was claimed to have been approved by the people of Rhode Island, later resulting in the election of a Governor and other officials on May 3, 1842, to take power and govern the new Constitutional state. The convention and its resulting elected officers were not recognized by the charter government. On January 25, 1842, while the unauthorized Constitutional government was being organized, the charter government passed a resolution placing the state under martial law and called out the militia to protect the charter government from military insurrection and ordered arrests of those who planed to take up arms against it in support of the opposition-formed government. The charter government also took steps to call for a Constitutional convention to revise the charter. A new government was formed as a result of the new Constitution and elections pursuant to it. In May 1843, the charter government surrendered power and the new government began to govern under the new Constitution.

It was during the period between the installation of martial law by the charter government and the formation of the recognized Constitutional government of 1843 that military forces protecting the charter government broke into the home of Martin Luther for the purposes of search and arrest for his activities supporting the May 1841 government. Luther claimed that the charter government was not lawful at the time its agents broke into his home and committed criminal trespass on his property. During this period the Governor of the charter government was recognized by President John Tyler as the legitimate executive power of Rhode Island and the President publicly declared that he was prepared to call out the militia to protect the charter government. His public declaration of support, the Court explained, of the charter government "put an end to the armed opposition to the charter government, and prevented any further efforts to establish by force the proposed Constitution."[13] The Court, in supporting the President's power to act, affirmed *Martin v. Mott* and further discussed the power of the President as Commander-in-Chief.

The Court wrote that under Article IV of the Constitution, "it rests with Congress to decide what government is the established one in a State. For as the United States guarantees to each State a republican government, Congress must necessarily decide what government is established in the State before it can determine whether it is republican or not. . . . And its decision is binding on every other department of the government, and could not be questioned in a judicial tribunal."[14] Furthermore, the Court explained, Congress implemented this responsibility by the passage of

> the act of February 28, 1795, [which] provided, that, in case of an insurrection in any State against the government thereof, it shall be lawful for the President of the United States, on application of the legislature of such State or of the executive (when the legislature cannot be convened), to call forth such number of the militia of any other State or States, as may be applied for, as he may judge sufficient to suppress such insurrection.
>
> By this act, the power of deciding whether the exigency had arisen upon which the government of the United States is bound to interfere, is given to the President. He is to act upon the application of the legislature or of the executive, and consequently he must determine what body of men constitute the legislature, and who is the governor, before he can act.[15]

The Court, again, recognized implied powers necessary to implement specific powers and responsibilities. The Court held that if the President is authorized to call out the militia to support a state government and put down insurrection or rebellion upon a request from that state, he has the implied power to determine if the request from such a state has been made by the legitimate government officials. The Court held that when the President is empowered to take action, military if necessary, that power includes the ability to make an independent assessment of the facts that may require the use of military force.

Interestingly, the Court in explaining the sole and exclusive power of the President to act by calling on the militia in cases of insurrection in a state, limited only by the requirement of a formal request for assistance by the governor or the legislature of the state, analogized the power of the President to exercise sole authority to recognize foreign nations. The Court held that "the President must, of necessity, decide which is the government, and which party is unlawfully arrayed against it"[16] just as in "the case of foreign nations, the government acknowledged by the President is always recognized in the courts of justice. And this principle has been applied by the act of Congress to the sovereign States of the Union."[17]

In both the *Luther* and *Mott* cases the Court made clear that the President, both under his powers as Commander-in-Chief and under the 1795 Act of Congress, has the power to act to repel invasion and to act in the event of armed insurrection in any of the States and protect the right of each State to have a republican government. This power includes "sole authority" to make determinations of fact in the implementation of these responsibilities. It is at the sole discretion of the President to determine if a threat of invasion or actual invasion exists and to determine the lawfulness of a State government in the event of rebellion in that State. The Court determined, in *Mott*, that the President's discretion is conclusive on the government and in *Luther*, the Court held that his determination of the lawful State government in times of insurrection and rebellion resulting in calling on the militia is equally conclusive, limited only by formal request by the State and by Article IV which gives Congress the power of recognition when disputes involve delegates sent to Congress. The Court concluded, in *Luther*, that once Congress provided the President with the power to act in his discretion, his power to act was exclusive and binding. The Court in *Luther* also recognized that the "sole authority" of the President to recognize the legitimacy of a State government is the same as his power to recognize the legitimacy of foreign governments. His decision on that recognition is also obligatory on the other branches of government.

This is not to imply that the Supreme Court supported an unfettered President, with power without any Constitutional limits. In *Fleming v. Page*, the Court held that his powers as Commander-in-Chief even during times of war have limits.

> The United States, it is true, may extend its boundaries by conquest or treaty, and may demand the cession of territory as the condition of peace, in order to indemnify its citizens for the injuries they have suffered, or to reimburse the government for the expenses of the war. But this can be done only by the treaty-making power or the legislative authority, and is not a part of the power conferred upon the President by the declaration of war. *His duty and his power are purely military. As Commander-in-Chief, he is authorized to direct the movements of the naval and military forces placed by law at his command, and to employ them in the manner he may deem most effectual to harass and conquer and subdue the enemy.* He may invade the hostile country, and subject it to the sovereignty and authority of the United States. *But his conquests do not enlarge the boundaries of this Union, nor extend the operation of our institutions and laws beyond the limits before assigned to them by the legislative power.*[18]

Supreme Court Justice William Paterson, in *U.S. v. Smith*,[19] on circuit, addressed various assertions made by William S. Smith, who was indicted for violation of a 1794 Act of Congress making it illegal to engage in military activities against a nation that is at peace with the United States. Smith argued, among other things, that the actions of President Jefferson gave him license to participate in a military operation against Spain. Justice Paterson first rejected the proposition that the Constitutional requirement that the President "shall from time to time give to the Congress information of the Union" in Article II gives the President the power to determine whether the United States is or is not in a state of war. Justice Paterson wrote that "'the

Congress shall have power to declare war.' Here this power is given in a most explicit manner."[20] In explaining the Constitutional power to make war, the framers of the Constitution put

> in the Congress . . . solely and exclusively, . . . the power of making war. As it is the people who are to endure the fatigues and calamities, and sustain the waste of blood and treasure inseparable from war, they have confided the power of making it to their immediate representatives. They have, therefore, declared that "the Congress shall have power to declare war . . . ." But if the proposition contended for by the defendant's counsel be correct . . . the President [through his power] to "give to the Congress information on the state of the union," by necessary implication give[s] to him also the power of declaring that the United States are in a state of war, or, in other words, of declaring war.[21]

Justice Paterson rejected the proposition that the President reporting to Congress that Spanish troops entered the United States in a hostile manner and committed acts of aggression on citizens of the United States is tantamount to recognition of war, thus excusing Smith from obedience to the 1794 Act of Congress.[22]

Justice Paterson also rejected the defense that the President and his subordinates knew of the military expedition of Smith and that knowledge exempted him from the prohibition by Congress. Smith asserted in an affidavit that Secretary of State James Madison, Secretary of the Navy Robert Smith and two officers within the State Department knew and approved of his actions and requested the court admit evidence supporting his assertions. Justice Paterson held that "the first question is, whether the facts stated [by] the defendant . . . be material."[23] Justice Paterson reasoned:

> If, then, the President knew and approved of the military expedition . . . it would not justify the defendant in a court of law, nor discharge him from the binding force of the act of Congress; because the President does not possess a dispensing power. Does he possess the power of making war? That power is exclusively vested in Congress . . . .
>
> [T]herefore, the organ instructed with the power to declare war, should first decide whether it is expedient to go to war, or to continue in peace; and until such a decision be made, no individual ought to assume an hostile attitude; and to pronounce, contrary to the Constitutional will, that the nation is at war.[24]

Upon charging the jury, District Judge Tallmadge instructed the jury that

> it is also the opinion of the court . . . that the previous knowledge or approbation of the President to the illegal acts of a citizen can afford him no justification for the breach of a Constitutional law—The President's duty is faithfully to execute the laws, and he has no such dispensing power. . . . The United States cannot be Constitutionally at war, but when war is authorized by Congress, or is rendered an act of necessity by the invasion of a foreign enemy.[25]

In *Little v. Berreme*, the Court held that an officer implementing an order from the President based on an incorrect interpretation of a statute by the President is not indemnified from liability because the action was taken in obedience to the President.[26] The Court held that the President and his officers are bound to the actual meaning of the law and subject to sanctions for failure to conform to it regardless of a good faith misinterpretation of it. Thus the Court in *Berreme* and Justice Paterson in *Smith*, ruled that the President, even acting within his authority as Commander-in-Chief, is bound by specific acts of Congress. Authorization to act contrary to a specific act of Congress cannot be granted by Presidential indifference or disobedience and neither is it a defense to act contrary to an act of Congress based on Presidential misinterpretation of the law. The Court made clear that the President is bound to faithfully execute the law and his powers as Commander-in-Chief are limited by specific laws when enacted. More than a century and half later, the Court will remind President Truman of these boundaries of Presidential power in *Youngstown Sheet and Tube v. Sawyer in* 1952.

The Court continued to support broad Presidential powers in the area of foreign affairs. In *Durand v. Hollins* Supreme Court Justice Samuel Nelson, on circuit, wrote expansively on the power of the President to protect life and property of American citizens in foreign nations. A year before the advent of the Civil War, Justice Nelson upheld the action of Lt. Hollins who bombarded Greytown, Nicaragua after a mob attacked the U.S. Counsel Office. Hollins was sued by Durand for damages to his property due to the attack. Justice Nelson broadly defined the power of the President in foreign affairs:

> The Executive power, under the Constitution, is vested in the President of the United States. He is commander-in-chief of the army and navy and has imposed upon him the duty to "take care that the laws are faithfully executed". . . .
>
> As the Executive head of the nation, the President is made the only legitimate organ of the General Government, to open and carry on correspondence or negotiations with foreign nations, in matters concerning the interests of the country or of its citizens. It is to him, also, the citizens abroad must look for protection of person and of property, and for the faithful execution of the laws existing and intended for their protection. For this purpose, the whole Executive power of the country is placed in his hands, under the Constitution, and the laws passed in pursuance thereof; and different Departments of government have been organized, through which this power may be most conveniently executed, whether by negotiation or by force—a Department of State and a Department of the Navy.
>
> Now, as it respects the interposition of the executive abroad, for the protection of the lives or property of the citizen, the duty must, of necessity, rest in the discretion of the President. Acts of lawless violence, or of threatened violence to the citizen or his property, cannot be anticipated and provided for; and the protection, to be effectual or of any avail, may, not unfrequently, require the most prompt and decided action.

... The interposition of the President abroad, for the protection of the citizen, must necessarily rest in his discretion. ... The question whether it was the duty of the President to interpose for the protection of the citizens at Greytown against an irresponsible and marauding community that had established itself there, was a public political question, in which the government, as well as the citizens whose interests were involved, was concerned, and which belonged to the executive to determine; and his decision is final and conclusive, and justified the defendant in the execution of his orders given through the secretary of the navy.

The Justice concluded that

under our system of Government, the citizen abroad is as much entitled to protection as the citizen at home. The great object and duty of Government is the protection of the lives, liberty, and property of the people composing it, whether abroad or at home; and any Government failing in the accomplishment of the object, or the performance of the duty, is not worth preserving.[27]

"The great object and duty of Government is the protection of the lives, liberty, and property of the people composing it . . . any Government failing in the accomplishment of the object, or the performance of the duty, is not worth preserving." Lincoln could not have said it better himself. With the advent of the Civil War, the powers of the President in times of insurrection and rebellion were fully implemented but the Court made clear that even in times of Civil War those powers had limits.

On March 4, 1861, Abraham Lincoln took office as President of the United States and seven states had already seceded from the union.[28] Four additional states[29] seceded two months after Lincoln took office. On April 12, 1861, Confederate troops, under orders from Jefferson Davis and his Secretary of War, attacked Fort Sumter and forced its surrender two days later. President Lincoln called for enlistments for the army and called into service the militia of the several states to put down the rebellion. At the same time, Lincoln feared the presence of spies, saboteurs, and sympathizers of the confederate cause. To prevent their activities from having a detrimental affect on the subduing of the insurrection of the southern states, Lincoln issued to General Winfield Scott, then Commander-in-Chief of the Army, the following orders on April 27, 1861:

You are engaged in repressing an insurrection against the laws of the United States. If at any point on or in the vicinity of the military line which is now used between the city of Philadelphia via Perryville, Annapolis City and Annapolis Junction you find resistance which renders it necessary to suspend the writ of habeas corpus for the public safety, you personally or through the officer in command at the point where resistance occurs are authorized to suspend that writ.

On December 2, 1861, Lincoln issued similar orders suspending the writ in the entire state of Missouri. Although Lincoln had issued various military orders and proclamations suspending the writ in specific jurisdictions, on September 24, 1862, a year and half after his first suspension order, Lincoln issued a formal proclamation suspending the writ of habeas corpus applicable to "all persons arrested . . . by any military authority."

PROCLAMATION SUSPENDING THE WRIT OF HABEAS CORPUS

By the President of the United States of America: A Proclamation

Whereas, it has become necessary to call into service not only volunteers but also portions of the militia of the States by draft in order to suppress the insurrection existing in the United States, and disloyal persons are not adequately restrained by the ordinary processes of law from hindering this measure and from giving aid and comfort in various ways to the insurrection;

Now, therefore, be it ordered, first, that during the existing insurrection and as a necessary measure for suppressing the same, all Rebels and Insurgents, their aiders and abettors within the United States, and all persons discouraging volunteer enlistments, resisting militia drafts, or guilty of any disloyal practice, affording aid and comfort to Rebels against the authority of United States, shall be subject to martial law and liable to trial and punishment by Courts Martial or Military Commission:

Second. That the Writ of Habeas Corpus is suspended in respect to all persons arrested, or who are now, or hereafter during the rebellion shall be, imprisoned in any fort, camp, arsenal, military prison, or other place of confinement by any military authority or by the sentence of any Court Martial or Military Commission.

In witness whereof, I have hereunto set my hand, and caused the seal of the United States to be affixed.

Done at the City of Washington this twenty fourth day of September, in the year of our Lord one thousand eight hundred and sixty-two, and of the Independence of the United States the 87th.

Abraham Lincoln

By the President:

William H. Seward, Secretary of State.

Finally, Congress acted on March 3, 1863, by passing the Habeas Corpus Suspension Act which authorized the President to suspend habeas corpus during the duration of the rebellion.[30] Although Congress indemnified the actions of the President and subordinate officers acting under his orders, it remains true that Congress did not act until the war was almost half over—thus Lincoln suspended the writ of habeas corpus one month short of two years under his own authority.

Prior to Lincoln's suspension of the Writ, the Supreme Court had occasion to review the writ. In *Ex parte Bollman and Swartwout*[31] the Court was challenged with the question of whether the federal courts had the authority to issue a Writ of Habeas Corpus. Chief Justice Marshall held that section 14 of the Judiciary Act of 1789 gave the Court such powers. After discussing at length the authorization of the judiciary to make effective the right to the writ through appeal to the federal judiciary, in the last paragraph of his opinion, arguably *dicta*, the Court wrote the following observation on the power to suspend the great writ.

> The decision that the individual shall be imprisoned must always precede the application for a writ of habeas corpus, and this writ must always be for the purpose of revising that decision, and therefore appellate in its nature.
>
> But this point also is decided in Hamilton's case and in Burford's case. *If at any time the public safety should require the suspension of the powers vested by this act in the courts of the United States, it is for the legislature to say so.*
>
> *That question depends on political considerations, on which the legislature is to decide.* Until the legislative will be expressed, this court can only see its duty, and must obey the laws.[32]

Chief Justice Marshall also commented on what the drafters of the Judiciary Act were trying to accomplish in implementing the protections and procedures of the Constitutional right to the writ.

> It may be worthy of remark, that this act was passed by the first Congress of the United States, sitting under a Constitution which had declared "that the privilege of the writ of habeas corpus should not be suspended, unless when, in cases of rebellion or invasion, the public safety might require it."
>
> Acting under the immediate influence of this injunction, *they must have felt, with peculiar force, the obligation of providing efficient means by which this great Constitutional privilege should receive life and activity; for if the means be not in existence, the privilege itself would be lost,* although no law for its suspension should be enacted. *Under the impression of this obligation, they give, to all the courts, the power of awarding writs of habeas corpus.*[33]

The Supreme Court did not address President Lincoln's suspension of the writ, but Chief Justice Taney had an opportunity to do so when he issued a writ for John Merryman and it was refused by General George Cadwalader. On May 25, 1861, John Merryman was arrested under orders of General William Keim, Commander of the District of Pennsylvania and placed in the custody of General Cadwalader, the commander of Fort Henry which housed the military headquarters for the army responsible for Maryland. On May 26, 1861, Chief Justice Taney ordered the clerk of the court to issue a writ of habeas corpus and have the U.S. Marshall for Maryland serve the writ to General Cadwalader. The serving of the writ was not completed because the U.S. Marshall was not granted access to the fort. Upon failure to enter the fort and serve the court order, the Marshall returned the writ and reported the failure to Chief Justice Taney. Unable to enforce the issuance and service of the order, Chief Justice Taney issued his opinion in *Ex parte Merryman.*[34]

The Chief Justice asserted from the beginning of his opinion that the "President has exercised a power which he does not possess under the Constitution"[35] because "the privilege of the writ [can] not be suspended, except by act of Congress."[36] Chief Justice Taney proclaimed simply that the power of suspension of the writ is mentioned in the Constitution within Article I, Section 9, which is listed within the powers of the Congress under the Constitution. Furthermore, the list of powers of the executive, Taney asserted, did not include the suspension of the writ. Taney concluded, "If the high power over the liberty of the citizen now claimed, was intended to be conferred on the President, it would undoubtedly be found in plain words in this article; but there is not a word in it that can furnish the slightest ground to justify the exercise of the power."[37] Furthermore, the power to suspend the writ is specific and limited. The framers placed limits on the power to suspend the writ both by placing the power to suspend it in the branch of government that is directly responsible to and representative of the people—namely Congress—and limited the ability of Congress to suspend it only in times of insurrection, rebellion or invasion.

Defending judicial authority in the area of adjudication of criminal activity, Taney stated that it is a judicial function, not executive, to make determinations of arrest and guilt. The Chief Justice explained that the President

> is not empowered to arrest any one charged with an offence against the United States, and whom he may, from the evidence before him, believe to be guilty; nor can he authorize any officer, civil or military, to exercise this power, for the fifth article of the amendments to the Constitution expressly provides that no person "shall be deprived of life, liberty or property, without due process of law," that is, judicial process.
>
> Even if the privilege of the writ of habeas corpus were suspended by act of Congress, and a party not subject to the rules and articles of war were afterwards arrested and imprisoned by regular judicial process, he could not be detained in prison, or brought to trial before a military tribunal, for the article in the amendments to the Constitution immediately following the one above referred to (that is, the sixth article) provides, that "in all criminal prosecutions, the accused shall enjoy the right to a speedy and public trial by an impartial jury of the state and district wherein the crime shall have been committed, which district shall have been previously ascertained by law; and to be informed of the nature and cause of the accusation; to be confronted with the witnesses against him; to have compulsory process for obtaining witnesses in his favor; and to have the assistance of counsel for his defense."[38]

Furthermore, the judiciary, asserted Taney, can handle cases involving acts of treason or other unlawful acts during war. The principle that would be argued one hundred and forty years later before the Supreme Court that the civilian courts are not to be supplanted by the military was first asserted by Chief Justice Taney:

> For, at the time these proceedings were had against John Merryman, the district judge of Maryland, the commissioner appointed under the act of Congress, the district attorney and the marshal, all resided in the city of Baltimore, a few miles only from the home of the prisoner. *Up to that time, there had never been the slightest resistance or obstruction to the process of any court or judicial officer of the United States,* in Maryland, except by the military authority. And if a military officer, or any other person, had reason to believe that the prisoner had committed any offence against the laws of the United States, it was his duty to give information of the fact and the evidence to support it, to the district attorney; it would then have become the duty of that officer to bring the matter before the district judge or commissioner, and if there was sufficient legal evidence to justify his arrest, the judge or commissioner would have issued his warrant to the marshal to arrest him; and upon the hearing of the case, would have held him to bail, or committed him for trial, according to the character of the offence, as it appeared in the testimony, or would have discharged him immediately, if there was not sufficient evidence to support the accusation. *There was no danger of any obstruction or resistance to the action of the civil authorities, and therefore no reason whatever for the interposition of the military.*[39]

The President's authority, under the Constitution, asserted Taney,

> Where the "life, liberty or property" of a private citizen is concerned, is the power and duty prescribed in the third section of the second article, which requires "that he shall take care that the laws shall be faithfully executed." He is not authorized to execute them himself, or through agents or officers, civil or military, appointed by himself, but he is to take care that they be faithfully carried into execution, as they are expounded and adjudged by the coordinate branch of the government to which that duty is assigned by the Constitution. It is thus made his duty to come in aid of the judicial authority . . . but in exercising this power he acts in subordination to judicial authority, assisting it to execute its process and enforce its judgments.[40]

The President has the power to faithfully execute the laws, but he "certainly does not faithfully execute the laws, if he takes upon himself legislative power, by suspending the writ of habeas corpus, and the judicial power also, by arresting and imprisoning a person without due process of law."[41] Echoing the thoughts of Madison, Taney asserted that the United States government is one of delegated and limited powers of which each of the branches of government can only exercise powers specifically granted. Taney rejected the proposition that the President had any inherent powers or could have been contemplated to have the power to suspend the writ on his own authority.

If the President of the United States may suspend the writ, then the Constitution of the United States has conferred upon him more regal and absolute power over the liberty of the citizen, than the people of England have thought it safe to entrust to the crown; a power which the queen of England cannot exercise at this day, and which could not have been lawfully exercised by the sovereign even in the reign of Charles the First.[42]

And no one can believe that, in framing a government intended to guard still more efficiently the rights and liberties of the citizen, against executive encroachment and oppression, they would have conferred on the President a power which the history of England had proved to be dangerous and oppressive in the hands of the crown; and which the people of England had compelled it to surrender, after a long and obstinate struggle on the part of the English executive to usurp and retain it.[43]

The Chief Justice posited that the threat to civil liberty and executive tyranny, that the founders sought to prevent, was realized with the actions of President Lincoln's suspension of the writ.

T]he military authority . . . has, by force of arms, thrust aside the judicial authorities and officers to whom the Constitution has confided the power and duty of interpreting and administering the laws, and substituted a military government in its place, to be administered and executed by military officers. . . . Yet, under these circumstances, a military officer . . . assumes to himself the judicial power in the district of Maryland; undertakes to decide what constitutes the crime of treason or rebellion; what evidence (if indeed he required any) is sufficient to support the accusation and justify the commitment; and commits the party, without a hearing, even before himself, to close custody, in a strongly garrisoned fort, to be there held, it would seem, during the pleasure of those who committed him.

The Constitution provides, as I have before said, that "no person shall be deprived of life, liberty or property, without due process of law." It declares that "the right of the people to be secure in their persons, houses, papers and effects, against unreasonable searches and seizures, shall not be violated; and no warrant shall issue, but upon probable cause, supported by oath or affirmation, and particularly describing the place to be searched, and the persons or things to be seized." It provides that the party accused shall be entitled to a speedy trial in a court of justice.

These great and fundamental laws, which Congress itself could not suspend, have been disregarded and suspended, like the writ of habeas corpus, by a military order, supported by force of arms. Such is the case now before me, and *I can only say that if the authority which the Constitution has confided to the judiciary department and judicial officers, may thus, upon any pretext or under any circumstances, be usurped by the military power, at its discretion, the people of the United States are no longer living under a government of laws, but every citizen holds life, liberty and property at the will and pleasure of the army officer in whose military district he may happen to be found.*[44]

The Chief Justice concluded that he would provide the President with a copy his opinion so as to give the President time to provide an answer and "determine what measures he will take to cause the civil process of [the Court] to be respected and enforced."[45] The Chief Justice did not wait long for his answer. As discussed in chapter 1, on July 4, 1861, President Lincoln before a special joint session of Congress rhetorically asked "are all the laws, but one, to go unexecuted, and the government itself go to pieces, lest that one be violated? Even in such a case, would not the official oath be broken, if the government should be overthrown, when it was believed that disregarding the single law, would tend to preserve it?" To Lincoln, the issue was quite simple. Assuming that he did not have the power to suspend the writ in times of rebellion, it would be ridiculous to comply with such limitations with the result being the destruction of the union. If he had not the power, Lincoln would act so as to preserve the union regardless of legal niceties. This Constitutional principle, the preservation of the union, he implied, was higher than the legal strict reading of one section of the Constitution. To follow one line to the detriment of the whole document and the government formed upon it, Lincoln thought, would sacrifice the ultimate end to a specific mean.

Lincoln's actions introduced the maxim *Salus Populi, Suprema Lex* into the continuing growth of Presidential power and American political thought. The maxim that "the safety of the people is the supreme law"[46] and that the President is duty bound by the "law of saving our country when in danger" has been adopted by every President since. It was strenuously advocated by President Bush. This maxim of protecting the "safety of the American people" being the highest law coupled with the "law of necessity" was the centerpiece of President Bush's actions after the attacks of September 11, 2001. After the attacks of 9/11 the American people were in congruence with this view. It was to the President that the nation turned for action and protection after 9/11, not the Congress. Members of Congress who demanded that Congress take the lead in the redrafting of laws dealing with antiterrorism strategy and those who asserted that the legislation proposed by the President threatened civil liberties were assailed as providing assistance to the terrorists.[47] Within the body of a strong democracy are the seeds of its destruction; because a democracy can elect itself out of all of its freedoms and rights if the fear of destruction overrides considerations of liberty for a long enough period of time. The founding generation understood this. The Federalist's theory of government, developed by Madison and others, asserted that the protection against this possibility was limited and divided government. The Anti-Federalists, although losing the fight to keep the Articles of Confederation, won the promise to amend the Constitution with specific amendments spelling out the rights that government could not disregard regardless of the system of checks and balances.

Madison taught us in Federalist 51 that

> if men were angels, no government would be necessary. If angels were to
> govern men, neither external nor internal controls on government would be
> necessary. In framing a government which is to be administered by men over
> men, the great difficulty lies in this: you must first enable the government to
> control the governed; and in the next place oblige it to control itself. *A depen-*
> *dence on the people is, no doubt, the primary control on the government; but experi-*
> *ence has taught mankind the necessity of auxiliary precautions.*

One of the reasons for the need for auxiliary precautions is due to the tendency of society to give up liberty for security. Benjamin Franklin warned
against believing in the utility of safety bought at the price of liberty. He
warned that a society that "would give up essential liberty to purchase a little
temporary safety, deserves neither liberty nor safety."[48] The founding generation understood that in a democracy security and order are not secured when
the people no longer hold dear the virtues of liberty and freedom. Madison
observed, "To suppose that any form of government will secure liberty or
happiness without any virtue in the people, is a chimerical idea."[49] Benjamin
Franklin said as much when he observed, "Only a virtuous people are capable of freedom. As nations become corrupt and vicious, they have more need
of masters."[50] Only a virtuous nation can know how to balance the need for
security with the protection of liberty. It is only the virtue of liberty, freedom,
and the rule of law in a nation that sets the outer boundaries of the range
of options to secure internal security. To the powerful and mighty waves of
necessity for safety and security, liberty says this far you may come but no
farther and here your proud waves must stop. But we digress.

On July 5, 1861, Attorney General Edward Bates answered the Chief
Justice with his opinion on the questions of whether the President has the
power to arrest and hold suspected insurgents and others who are suspected
of criminal support of those in rebellion and whether the President has
the power to refuse to obey a writ of habeas corpus issued from a federal
court.[51] The publication of the opinion by General Bates was the only legal
response of the Lincoln administration on the Constitutional issues regarding the suspension of the writ by President Lincoln.

Is the arrest of spies, saboteurs, sympathizers, and men engaged in supporting those who are in armed rebellion against the United States a political or
judicial matter? Is it a question of war or crime? General Bates in his opinion
on the power of the President to suspend the writ of habeas corpus answered
that the suspension was a political and military matter, not a judicial matter
and as such it was not for the courts to interfere in political/military determinations of the President in times of military rebellion.[52] General Bates wrote,

> Besides, the whole subject-matter is political and not judicial. The insurrec-
> tion itself is purely political. Its object is to destroy the political government of

this nation and to establish another political government upon its ruins. And the President, as the chief civil magistrate of the nation, and the most active department of the Government, is eminently and exclusively political, in all his principal functions. As the political chief of the nation, the Constitution charges him with its preservation, protection, and defense, and requires him to take care that the laws be faithfully executed. And in that character . . . he wages open war against armed rebellion, and arrests and holds in safe custody those whom, in the exercise of his political discretion, he believes to be friends of, and accomplices in, the armed insurrection, which it is his especial political duty to suppress. He has no judicial powers. And the judiciary department has no political powers, . . . therefore . . . no court or judge can take cognizance of the political acts of the President, or undertake to revise and reverse his political decisions. . . .[53]

. . . [S]hall it be said that when he has fought and captured the insurgent army, and has seized their secrete spies and emissaries, he is bound to bring their bodies before any judge who may send him a writ of habeas corpus, "to do, submit to, and receive whatever the said judge shall consider in that behalf?"

I deny that he is under any obligation to obey such a writ.[54]

General Bates made clear in his opinion that the Presidency, in times of peace and in war, is the branch of government that, by the Constitution, is to take the initiative to make sure that the laws are faithfully executed as well as to support, preserve, protect and defend the Constitution of the United States. The Constitution, General Bates asserted, "in a time like the present, when the very existence of the nation is assailed, by a great and dangerous insurrection, the President has the lawful discretionary power to arrest and hold in custody persons known to have criminal intercourse with the insurgents, or persons against whom there is probable cause for suspicion of such criminal complicity."[55] General Bates makes a very interesting, and as we will discover in later chapters, a familiar assertion of Presidential power based on the Constitution.

The last clause of the oath is peculiar to the President. All the other officers of the Government are required to swear only "to *support* this Constitution;" while the President must swear to "*preserve, protect* and *defend*" it, which implies the power to perform what he is required in so solemn a manner to undertake. And then follows the broad and compendious injunction to "take care that the laws be faithfully executed." And this injunction, embracing as it does all the laws—Constitution, treaties, statutes—is addressed to the President alone, and not to any other department or officer of the government. And this constitutes him, in a particular manner, and above all other officers, the guardian of the Constitution—its *preserver, protector,* and *defender*.[56]

. . . It is plainly impossible for him to perform this duty without putting down rebellion, insurrection and all unlawful combinations. . . .

The end, the suppression of the insurrection, is required of him; the means and the instruments to suppress it are lawfully in his hands; but the manner in which he shall use them is not prescribed . . . He is, therefore, necessarily,

thrown upon his discretion, as to the manner in which he will use his means
to meet the varying exigencies as they arise.[57]

The President, not Congress or the Judiciary, is the protector and defender
of the Constitution, its principles and its institutions. Lincoln shared this
perception of the Presidency. In February 1861 during a debate with some
New York representatives to a peace conference in New York City, the President said the following in regard to his perception of the duty of one who
is President of the United States:

> I shall take an oath. I shall swear that I will faithfully execute the office of
> President of the United States, of all the United States, and that I will, to the best
> of my ability, preserve, protect, and defend the Constitution of the United States.
> This is a great and solemn duty. With the support of the people and the assis-
> tance of the Almighty I shall undertake to perform it. I have full faith that I shall
> perform it. It is not the Constitution as I would like to have it, but as it is, that is
> to be defended. The Constitution will not be preserved and defended until it is
> enforced and obeyed in every part of every one of the United States. It must be
> so respected, obeyed, enforced, and defended, let the grass grow where it may.[58]

General Bates agreed with the Chief Justice that those who are in rebellion could be brought to court for trial but there is another interest in the
detention of those who support insurrection and rebellion during open
civil war. That interest is to arrest and imprison them in order to place them
"in custody for the milder end of rendering them powerless for mischief,
until the exigency is past."[59] General Bates would not be the last Attorney
General to make this argument. For slightly less than a century and a half
later the Bush Administration would argue that the President, as Commander-in-Chief, had the power to detain "enemy unlawful combatants"
for the purpose of gathering intelligence and removing them from the war
on terror. General Bates was not without legal precedence for his opinion,
for he cited *Martin v. Mott, Fleming v. Page* and *Luther v. Borden*, for the
general proposition that the president has the power to call out the military and decisions made by him for the preservation of the Union in time
of war or rebellion are binding on Judiciary. The proposition by General
Bates that the President is "the guardian of the Constitution—its preserver,
protector and defender" is the antecedent to the current view of Presidential power which President Bush and Vice President Cheney advocated;
that the President is empowered as Commander-in-Chief to act to protect
the people of the United States and this broad power carries various inherent powers to act in the pursuit of that protection. General Bates, almost
a century and a half ago, through to the modern Presidents of today have
all asserted that the Constitution, in regard to Presidential power, specifically grants the power to protect American interests. As Bates asserted and

modern Presidents have agreed, in times of war and national security crisis, "the President must, of necessity, be the sole judge, both of the exigency, which requires him to act, and of the manner in which it is most prudent for him to employ the powers entrusted to him, to enable him to discharge his Constitutional and legal duty. . . . And this discretionary power of the President is fully admitted by the Supreme Court."[60]

As to the obligation of the President to obey a court-issued writ of habeas corpus, General Bates did "not understand how it can be legally possible for a judge to issue a command to the President to come before him *ad subjiciendum*—that is, to submit implicitly to his judgment."[61] After all, "the President and the judiciary are co-ordinate departments . . . and the one not subordinate to the other"[62] and in a case of dealing with a military rebellion, the judiciary has no place under the Constitution to act. After conceding that the answer to his question is based on the meaning of the habeas corpus clause and that the *Habeas Corpus* mentioned in the Constitution is the *Great Writ* under English Common law, Bates concluded that the "Constitution is silent as to who may suspend it when the contingency happens."[63] In answering the Chief Justice that suspension of the writ is for the legislature to do and not the President, General Bates opined,

> If by the phrase *the suspension of the privilege of the writ of habeas corpus*, we must understand a repeal of all power to issue the writ, then I freely admit that none but Congress can do it. But if we are at liberty to understand the phrase to mean, that, in case of a great and dangerous rebellion, like the present, the public safety requires the arrest and confinement of persons implicated in the rebellion, I as freely declare the opinion, that the President has lawful power to suspend the privilege of persons arrested under such circumstances. For he is especially charged by the Constitution with the "public safety," and he is the sole judge of the emergency which requires his prompt action. . . .[64]
>
> For, not doubting the power of the President to capture and hold by force insurgents in open arms against the Government, and to arrest and imprison their suspected accomplices, I never thought of first suspending the writ of *habeas corpus*, any more than I thought of first suspending the writ of *replevin*, before seizing arms and munitions destined for the enemy.
>
> The power to do these things is in the hand of the President, placed there by the Constitution . . . to be used by him, in his best discretion, in the performance of his great first duty—to preserve, protect, and defend the Constitution.[65]

Notice the proposition, the suspension of habeas corpus is a matter for Congress alone, if what is proposed is to prevent the courts from issuing the writ *in toto* but the writ can be suspended by Presidential order if applied only to those involved in open acts of rebellion and to those who provide support to those in rebellion. Thus General Bates proposes two types of suspension of the writ, a general suspension and a specific suspension. The former case requires Congress because it takes an act of Congress to change or eliminate the powers of the judiciary to issue the writ since it is Congress who gave the judiciary the power in the first place.[66] But in the latter case, the President is acting in a "political" matter in which he has determined that specific individuals are in rebellion and/or support rebellion and such individuals can be arrested and held under the Constitutional powers of the President to "preserve, protect, and defend" the Constitution.

In the annuls of research and writing on the growth of the President and his powers to act under times of war and national security, not enough notice is paid to General Bates. But his opinion has lived on in every President's assertion of power in times of crisis ever since. President Bush, for more than two years after the attacks of September 11, 2001, asserted that his detention of enemy combatants and the refusal of those so held to have access to the courts through habeas corpus[67] and his position on Presidential power in general was totally in line with the opinion of General Bates. It is said that there is nothing new under the sun, and the opinions of General Bates and Chief Justice Taney are antecedent to the arguments on the powers asserted by the Bush Administration in the post–September 11 world. As we will discuss in more detail in part 2 of this volume, the arguments of the Chief Justice have prevailed.

THE SUPREME COURT AND THE CIVIL WAR CASES

In 1866 the Court observed,

> During the late wicked Rebellion, the temper of the times did not allow that calmness in deliberation and discussion so necessary to a correct conclusion of a purely judicial question. Then, considerations of safety were mingled with the exercise of power; and feelings and interests prevailed which are happily terminated. Now that the public safety is assured, this question, as well as all others, can be discussed and decided without passion or the admixture of any element not required to form a legal judgment. We approach the investigation of this case, fully sensible of the magnitude of the inquiry and the necessity of full and cautious deliberation.[68]

Here, Justice Davis voiced a common observation in regard to the Judiciary in times of war or national security threat—that when "the temper of the times d[o] not allow . . . calmness in deliberation and discussion [and when] considerations of [public] safety [are] mingled with the exercise of [Constitutional] power" the Judiciary will be muted and a "conclusion of a purely judicial question" will not occur until "public safety is assured." It is only when the fervor for security from danger is settled can questions of law "be discussed and decided without passion or the admixture of any element not required to form a legal judgment."[69]

Is Justice Davis correct that in times of war or national security crisis, the Constitution provides no boundaries that the President cannot cross? Is the muse of the law subdued and unable to offer a defense of the rule of law or civil liberties until after the crisis has passed? Is General Bates correct that in times of war, the President is supreme, accountable only to himself? The question is not that simple. In times of war and national security crisis, the judiciary places a focus on the Madisonian model and enforcement of checks and balances between the Executive and Legislative departments. The Court does not adhere to the Latin proverb *Inter Arma Enim Silent Leges*, but focuses on the nature of the law as it changes in times of war as compared to times of peace. As we will discuss through the rest of this book, the Court has developed a jurisprudence that focuses on the boundaries of Presidential power as checked by the powers of Congress and the Constitution itself, but does not, in times of crisis, conduct a *de novo* assessment of measures used if those measures are within the boundaries of Presidential power. The development of this jurisprudence began to take shape with the Civil War cases.

With the exception of Chief Justice Taney in *Ex parte Merryman*, the Court did not rule on the habeas corpus issue and only heard one case involving President Lincoln's use of his Commander-in-Chief powers during the war—and in that case, the *Prize Cases*, the President prevailed. In the *Prize Cases* the Supreme Court ratified many of the assertions of power made by the President and only after the war ended did the Court take the opportunity in *Ex parte Milligan* to propose some limitations of the powers of the President. To these last two Civil War cases we now turn our attention.

On April 19, 1861, President Lincoln, five days after the surrender of Fort Sumter, issued orders to blockade the Confederate States as follows:

BY THE PRESIDENT OF THE UNITED
STATES OF AMERICA: A PROCLAMATION:

Whereas an insurrection against the Government of the United States has broken out in the States of South Carolina, Georgia, Alabama, Florida, Mississippi, Louisiana, and Texas, and the laws of the United States for the collection of the revenue cannot be effectually executed therein conformably to that provision of the Constitution which requires duties to be uniform throughout the United States:

And whereas a combination of persons engaged in such insurrection, have threatened to grant pretended letters of marque to authorize the bearers thereof to commit assaults on the lives, vessels, and property of good citizens of the country lawfully engaged in commerce on the high seas, and in waters of the United States: And whereas an Executive Proclamation has been already issued, requiring the persons engaged in these disorderly proceedings to desist therefrom, calling out a militia force for the purpose of repressing the same, and convening Congress in extraordinary session, to deliberate and determine thereon:

Now, therefore, I, Abraham Lincoln, President of the United States, with a view to the same purposes before mentioned, and to the protection of the public peace, and the lives and property of quiet and orderly citizens pursuing their lawful occupations, until Congress shall have assembled and deliberated on the said unlawful proceedings, or until the same shall ceased, have further deemed it advisable to set on foot a blockade of the ports within the States aforesaid, in pursuance of the laws of the United States, and of the law of Nations, in such case provided. For this purpose a competent force will be posted so as to prevent entrance and exit of vessels from the ports aforesaid. If, therefore, with a view to violate such blockade, a vessel shall approach, or shall attempt to leave either of the said ports, she will be duly warned by the Commander of one of the blockading vessels, who will endorse on her register the fact and date of such warning, and if the same vessel shall again attempt to enter or leave the blockaded port, she will be captured and sent to the nearest convenient port, for such proceedings against her and her cargo as prize, as may be deemed advisable.

And I hereby proclaim and declare that if any person, under the pretended authority of the said States, or under any other pretense, shall molest a vessel of the United States, or the persons or cargo on board of her, such person will be held amenable to the laws of the United States for the prevention and punishment of piracy.

In witness whereof, I have hereunto set my hand, and caused the seal of the United States to be affixed.

Done at the City of Washington, this nineteenth day of April, in the year of our Lord one thousand eight hundred and sixty-one, and of the Independence of the United States the eighty-fifth.

Abraham Lincoln
By the President:
William H. Seward, Secretary of State

On April 27, 1861, Virginia and North Carolina were added to the list of southern states whose ports were placed under a blockade. By April 30, 1861, the Blockade was in place. Subsequent to the blockade four ships were seized for attempts to break the blockade. The owners of the ships, in part, asserted that the President did not have the power to institute a blockade. It was asserted that a blockade is an act of war and only Congress had the power to declare war and thus commit acts of war. Since Congress had not declared war, the President was without authority to institute the blockade and the actions of taking the ships were thus illegal. The *Prize Cases*,[70] as they have come to be known, is one of the key cases that clarify the inherent powers of the President as Commander-in-Chief to meet threats to the nation and his Constitutional obligation to do so.

Justice Robert Grier wrote for the majority of the Court. Reflecting the opinions in *Martin v. Mott* and *Luther v. Borden* as well as those by General Bates, the Court concluded, in regard to issuing a public notification of the blockade, that "the President, as the Executive Chief of the Government and Commander-in-Chief of the Army and Navy, [is] the proper person to make such notification, has not been, and cannot be disputed."[71] The Court asserted that to establish the legality of the blockade the issue was whether there was, *de facto*, a war and was notice provided of the establishment of a naval blockade.[72] The Court acknowledged and took judicial notice of the existence of the southern rebellion and its taking arms against the United States, and in a hostile manner held territory of the United States, and by force of arms sought to disrupt the authority of the national government in order to establish a counter government; all of which was resisted by the national government by the force of arms. The Court concluded that these facts clearly establish that a war exists.

> It is not the less a civil war, with belligerent parties in hostile array, because it may be called an "insurrection" by one side, and the insurgents be considered as rebels or traitors. It is not necessary that the independence of the revolted province or State be acknowledged in order to constitute it a party belligerent in a war according to the law of nations. Foreign nations acknowledge it as war by a declaration of neutrality.[73]

"The true test of its existence, as found in the writings of the sages of the common law, may be thus summarily stated: 'When the regular course of justice is interrupted by revolt, rebellion, or insurrection, so that the Courts of Justice cannot be kept open, civil war exists and hostilities may be prosecuted on the same footing as if those opposing the Government were foreign enemies invading the land.'"[74] The Court held that a formal declaration of war is not required for the recognition that a war, especially a civil war, is in fact being waged. Citing common law principles the Court concluded,

> Whether the hostile party be a foreign invader, or States organized in rebellion, it is none the less a war, although the declaration of it be "unilateral." Lord Stowell (1 Dodson, 247) observes, "It is not the less a war on that account, for war may exist without a declaration on either side. It is so laid down by the best writers on the law of nations. A declaration of war by one country only, is not a mere challenge to be accepted or refused at pleasure by the other."[75]

The Court held that in times of *de facto* war, in which the President is confronted by armed insurrection, rebellion or invasion,

> The President is not only authorized but bound to resist force by force. He does not initiate the war, but is bound to accept the challenge without waiting for any special legislative authority. . . .[76]

This greatest of civil wars was not gradually developed by popular commotion, tumultuous assemblies, or local unorganized insurrections. However long may have been its previous conception, it nevertheless sprung forth suddenly from the parent brain, a Minerva in the full panoply of war. The President was bound to meet it in the shape it presented itself, without waiting for Congress to baptize it with a name; and no name given to it by him or them could change the fact.[77]

Having acknowledged that an armed rebellion was imposed upon the President, the Court focused on the power of the President to deal with the rebellion and the discretion that was to be accorded to him to deal with the threat and the deference the judiciary owes to those decisions made by the President in times of war.

This Court must be governed by the decisions and acts of the political department of the Government to which this power was entrusted. He must determine what degree of force the crisis demands. The proclamation of blockade is itself official and conclusive evidence to the Court that a state of war existed which demanded and authorized a recourse to such a measure, under the circumstances peculiar to the case.[78]

Justice Grier concluded, as President Bush would more than a century later, that the President does not require the Congress to act in case of insurrection, rebellion, or invasion of the United States for the President is empowered by the Constitution as Commander-in-Chief to address such circumstances. But, the Court observed,

If it were necessary to the technical existence of a war, that it should have a legislative sanction, we find it in almost every act passed at the extraordinary session of the Legislature of 1861, which was wholly employed in enacting laws to enable the Government to prosecute the war with vigor and efficiency. And finally, in 1861, we find Congress *ex majore cautela* and in anticipation of such astute objections, passing an act "approving, legalizing, and making valid all the acts, proclamations, and orders of the President, &c., as if they had been issued and done under the previous express authority and direction of the Congress of the United States."

Without admitting that such an act was necessary under the circumstances, it is plain that if the President had in any manner assumed powers which it was necessary should have the authority or sanction of Congress, that on the well known principle of law, *omnis ratihabitio retrotrahitur et mandato equiparatur*,[79] this ratification has operated to perfectly cure the defect.[80]

Concluding on Congressional authorization of Presidential power, the Court observed that "by the Acts of Congress of February 28th, 1795, and 3d of March, 1807, the President is authorized to call out the militia and use the military and naval forces of the United States in case of invasion by foreign nations, and to suppress insurrection against the government of a State or of the United States."[81]

Justice Samuel Nelson writing for the minority[82] did not accept that a "legal" war was engaged when President Lincoln issued his proclamation of the blockade. Thus the seizure of the ships was not justified. The dissent asserted, that the "legality" of the war which could authorize a blockade could only be established by an Act of Congress. The minority rejected the view that the *de facto* presence of war was sufficient. The minority asserted, that for a war to have legal affect under the law of nations—thus allowing the authority of blockades and seizures—the war must be declared and recognized as such under international law. Justice Nelson asserted that

> a contest by force between independent sovereign States is called a public war; and, when duly commenced by proclamation or otherwise, it entitles both of the belligerent parties to all the rights of war against each other, and as respects neutral nations. . . .[83]
>
> War also effects a change in the mutual relations of all States or countries. . . .[84]
>
> This great and pervading change in the existing condition of a country, and in the relations of all her citizens or subjects, external and internal, from a state of peace, is the immediate effect and result of a state of war. . . .
>
> This power in all civilized nations is regulated by the fundamental laws or municipal Constitution of the country.
>
> By our Constitution this power is lodged in Congress. . . .
>
> In the case of a rebellion or resistance of a portion of the people of a country against the established government, there is no doubt, if in its progress and enlargement the government thus sought to be overthrown sees fit, it may by the competent power recognize or declare the existence of a state of civil war, which will draw after it all the consequences and rights of war between the contending parties as in the case of a public war. . . .
>
> But before this insurrection against the established Government can be dealt with on the footing of a civil war, within the meaning of the law of nations and the Constitution of the United States, and which will draw after it belligerent rights, it must be recognized or declared by the war-making power of the Government. No power short of this can change the legal status of the Government or the relations of its citizens from that of peace to a state of war, or bring into existence all those duties and obligations of neutral third parties growing out of a state of war. The war power of the Government must be exercised before this changed condition of the Government and people and of neutral third parties can be admitted. There is no difference in this respect between a civil or a public war. . . .[85]
>
> For we find there that to constitute a civil war in the sense in which we are speaking . . . it must be recognized or declared by the sovereign power of the State, and which sovereign power by our Constitution is lodged in the Congress of the United States—civil war, therefore, under our system of government, can exist only by an act of Congress. . . .[86]

The minority did not accept that Congress, in providing the President with the power to address insurrections and rebellions through the Acts of 1795 and 1805, provided the President with the power to declare war on states in rebellion. The minority made a distinction between meeting the military challenge of a rebellion, which it accepted, and the power to declare war on the rebellious states.

> The Acts of 1795 and 1805 did not, and could not under the Constitution, confer on the President the power of declaring war against a State of this Union, or of deciding that war existed, and upon that ground authorize the capture and confiscation of the property of every citizen of the State whenever it was found on the waters. The laws of war, whether the war be civil or *inter gents*, as we have seen, convert every citizen of the hostile State into a public enemy, and treat him accordingly, whatever may have been his previous conduct. This great power over the business and property of the citizen is reserved to the legislative department by the express words of the Constitution. It cannot be delegated or surrendered to the Executive. Congress alone can determine whether war exists or should be declared; and until they have acted, no citizen of the State can be punished in his person or property, unless he has committed some offence against a law of Congress passed before the act was committed, which made it a crime, and defined the punishment. The penalty of confiscation for the acts of others with which he had no concern cannot lawfully be inflicted.[87]

Drawing an analogy from English common law, the minority asserted that in the case of civil rebellion against the authority of the king, the ensuing civil war is considered a "personal" war against him, and he has the power to engage in that war, but until the parliament recognizes the rebellion and declares war on those engaged in it, the seizure of ships and the property of the enemy cannot occur.

> So the war carried on by the President against the insurrectionary districts in the Southern States, as in the case of the King of Great Britain in the American Revolution, was a personal war against those in rebellion, and with encouragement and support of loyal citizens with a view to their co-operation and aid in suppressing the insurgents, with this difference, as the war-making power belonged to the King, he might have recognized or declared the war at the beginning to be a civil war, which would draw after it all the rights of a belligerent, but in the case of the President no such power existed: the war therefore from necessity was a personal war, until Congress assembled and acted upon this state of things.[88]
>
> Congress assembled on the call for an extra session the 4th of July, 1861, and among the first acts passed was one in which the President was authorized by proclamation to interdict all trade and intercourse between all the inhabitants of States in insurrection and the rest of the United States. . . . The 4th section also authorized the President to close any port in a Collection District

obstructed so that the revenue could not be collected, and provided for the capture and condemnation of any vessel attempting to enter.

The President's Proclamation was issued on the 16th of August following, and embraced Georgia, North and South Carolina, part of Virginia, Tennessee, Alabama, Louisiana, Texas, Arkansas, Mississippi and Florida.

This Act of Congress, we think, recognized a state of civil war between the Government and the Confederate States, and made it territorial.[89]

Thus, the minority concluded,

> Here the captures were without any Constitutional authority, and void; and, on principle, no subsequent ratification could make them valid.
>
> Upon the whole, after the most careful consideration of this case which the pressure of other duties has admitted, I am compelled to the conclusion that no civil war existed between this Government and the States in insurrection till recognized by the Act of Congress 13th of July, 1861; that the President does not possess the power under the Constitution to declare war or recognize its existence within the meaning of the law of nations, which carries with it belligerent rights, and thus change the country and all its citizens from a state of peace to a state of war; that this power belongs exclusively to the Congress of the United States, and, consequently, that the President had no power to set on foot a blockade under the law of nations, and that the capture of the vessel and cargo in this case, and in all cases before us in which the capture occurred before the 13th of July, 1861, for breach of blockade, or as enemies' property, are illegal and void, and that the decrees of condemnation should be reversed and the vessel and cargo restored.[90]

Upon first read, one could conclude that Justice Nelson was asserting form over substance or at worst executing one law and letting the government go to pieces lest that one be violated. But Justice Nelson's observation that a declared state of war and the resulting domestic actions to conduct such a war require various changes in domestic law and only Congress has the power, as Madison argued in Helvidius 1, to change the laws from peace to war and from war to peace. It is no small technicality to defend the Congressional prerogative to make law or claim that the President, by military action, does not have the power to make *de facto* changes to domestic law. His power only allows him to meet acts of rebellion by force, not implement acts of *de jure* war as if sanctioned by Congress.

Justice Nelson was defending a significant Constitutional principle, namely that the Presidential power even in a time of great Constitutional crisis or full military rebellion and insurrection is not without constraints. Justice Nelson emphasized that a declaration of war has consequences on the legal rights of those on each side of a civil war and the President by fiat can't separate a citizen from his rights. "Certainly it cannot rightfully be said that the President has the power to convert a loyal citizen into a belliger-

ent enemy or confiscate his property as enemy's property."[91] By holding on
to legal distinctions and requirements, the minority struggled to maintain
that the rule of law must govern even in times of crisis. The Constitution requires the Congress to declare war and without that declaration, the aspects
of domestic and international law acting under peace cannot be changed
to those of war on the proclamation of the President alone. Congress must
be included.

> [W]e admit the President who conducts the foreign relations of the Govern-
> ment may fitly recognize or refuse to do so, the existence of civil war in the
> foreign nation under the circumstances stated.
> But this is a very different question from the one before us, which is whether
> the President can recognize or declare a civil war, under the Constitution,
> with all its belligerent rights, between his own Government and a portion of
> its citizens in a state of insurrection. That power, as we have seen, belongs to
> Congress. *We agree when such a war is recognized or declared to exist by the war-
> making power, but not otherwise, it is the duty of the Courts to follow the decision of
> the political power of the Government.*[92]

What separated the minority from the majority was not that the President
was obligated to act, nor that he could not act with force against the rebellious southern states or that a blockade was not an appropriate measure to
bring the south to heal. The minority asserted that the President could not
institute a blockade and seize the property of American citizens without a
declaration of war from Congress because a declaration of war is needed to
change the legal standing of the nation. A formal declaration of war provides
lawful notice to the nations of the world under international law as well as
provides lawful authorization for the legal seizure of property of those providing support to the enemy under domestic law. The majority disagreed and
maintained that the presence of *de facto* war caused by the armed insurrection
of the south was sufficient legal basis, under domestic law, for the imposition of the blockade as well as subsequent seizures. The proclamation of the
blockade and the recognition of the blockade by the foreign powers satisfied
international law requirements for notice of hostilities. What is significant in
both arguments is that the disagreement was on what was the governing law
on the President—not whether the President was governed by law.

The Court was unanimous on the issue of deference to the decisions of
the President in times of crisis, when those actions are made within his
Constitutional and or statutory authority. As Justice Grier wrote for the
majority, "Whether the President in fulfilling his duties, as Commander-in-
Chief, in suppressing an insurrection, has met with such armed hostile resistance, and a civil war of such alarming proportions as will compel him to
accord to them the character of belligerents, is a question to be decided by
him, and this Court must be governed by the decisions and acts of the po-

litical department of the Government to which this power was entrusted."[93] To which Justice Nelson answered for the minority, "We agree when such a war is recognized or declared to exist by the war-making power, but not otherwise, it is the duty of the Courts to follow the decision of the political power of the Government."[94] As this case demonstrates, the jurisprudence of judicial deference in times of war or national security crisis requires the Court is to be bound by Presidential and Congressional measures as long as those actions are within the boundaries of the Constitution. The Court in the *Prize Cases* split on whether the action of the President in establishing a blockade before July 13, 1861, was within those boundaries. The Court never assessed if the blockade itself was appropriate because once the fact of war was established, *de facto* or *de jure*, the range of actions of the President and Congress to address the successful pursuit of the war was for them to determine and not for the Court to review.

A year after the end of the war, with "the public safety . . . assured," the Court was presented with the second of the Civil War cases dealing with Presidential power in times of war and national crisis. In *Ex parte Milligan*[95] the Court was presented with the question of the power of the President to arrest and put on trial citizens accused of supporting the Confederacy in a military commission when the civilian court was operational and acting under the Constitution.

Lambdin P. Milligan petitioned the Circuit Court of Indiana for a writ of habeas corpus challenging his arrest, trial and conviction in a military commission for providing support to the confederacy. On October 21, 1864, Milligan was brought before the commission, convicted and sentenced to be hanged on May 19, 1865. He appealed to the Circuit Court on January 2, 1865. The authority of the trial and Milligan's appeal was based on the Habeas Corpus Act of 1863 which (1) allowed for the suspension of the writ throughout the United States; (2) required the military to submit a list of all persons held under military arrest to the jurisdiction of the federal courts in which such a person was being held and if a grand jury adjourned without indicting any person so held, such individuals were entitled to be released; and (3) provided that if twenty-four days elapsed between the arrest and the adjournment of the grand jury and no indictment was made by the grand jury, such individuals were also entitled to release. The Act further authorized and directed the district court that it was duty bound to grant the release. Thus the President had at least twenty-four days to hold an individual without the concern of answering a writ of habeas corpus and such a person could be held longer under indictment of a federal grand jury. Furthermore, the Congress struck a balance with the interest of liberty, by requiring actual notice to the courts so that, as Chief Justice Taney discussed in *Ex parte Merryman*, a person so arrested and held would not be held indefinitely due to malice or such a person being forgotten.

The Circuit Court could not agree on the issues argued by Milligan and the case was certified to the Supreme Court to address three questions:

- 1st. "On the facts stated in said petition and exhibits, ought a writ of habeas corpus to be issued?"
- 2d. "On the facts stated in said petition and exhibits, ought the said Lambdin P. Milligan to be discharged from custody as in said petition prayed?"
- 3d. "Whether, upon the facts stated in said petition and exhibits, the military commission mentioned therein had jurisdiction legally to try and sentence said Milligan in manner and form as in said petition and exhibits as stated?"[96]

Writing for the majority, Justice David Davis summarized the issue as follows:

> Milligan, not a resident of one of the rebellious states, or a prisoner of war, but a citizen of Indiana for twenty years past, and never in the military or naval service, is, while at his home, arrested by the military power of the United States, imprisoned, and, on certain criminal charges preferred against him, tried, convicted, and sentenced to be hanged by a military commission, organized under the direction of the military commander of the military district of Indiana. Had this tribunal the legal power and authority to try and punish this man?[97]

The reference to the fact that Milligan was not a member of the armed forces of the United States is the key to the majority opinion. The Court held that the fundamental tenet of the guarantees of the Constitution and the "provisions of that instrument on the administration of criminal justice are too plain and direct, to leave room for misconstruction or doubt of their true meaning. Those applicable to this case are found in that clause of the original Constitution which says, 'That the trial of all crimes, except in case of impeachment, shall be by jury;' and in the fourth, fifth, and sixth articles of the amendments."[98]

The Court focused on the fact that the protections of the Fourth, Fifth, and Sixth Amendments govern the trial of an American citizen and that they are required for all such trials of citizens not subject to the military by virtue of being members in the military. These rights, the Court asserted, require that an American citizen tried on federal charges is entitled to indictment of a federal grand jury, after which, if so indicted, to be tried before an impartial jury with the protections of the right to protection from self-incrimination, a speedy trial and the right against unlawful search and seizure as well as the right to counsel in a federal civil court having jurisdiction over the location of the offense.[99] The Court concluded that an American citizen, not subject to military law due to membership in the armed forces, could not be tried by a military commission when such an individual was in a state in which the federal courts were open and unrestricted by rebellion or invasion.

> [F]rom what source did the military commission that tried him derive their authority? . . . . They cannot justify on the mandate of the President; because he is controlled by law, and has his appropriate sphere of duty, which is to execute, not to make, the laws; and there is "no unwritten criminal code to which resort can be had as a source of jurisdiction."
>
> But it is said that the jurisdiction is complete under the "laws and usages of war." It can serve no useful purpose to inquire what those laws and usages are, whence they originated, where found, and on whom they operate; *they can never be applied to citizens in states which have upheld the authority of the government, and where the courts are open and their process unobstructed.* This court has judicial knowledge that in Indiana the Federal authority was always unopposed, and its courts always open to hear criminal accusations and redress grievances; and *no usage of war could sanction a military trial there for any offence whatever of a citizen in civil life, in nowise connected with the military service. Congress could grant no such power;* and to the honor of our national legislature be it said, it has never been provoked by the state of the country even to attempt its exercise. *One of the plainest Constitutional provisions was, therefore, infringed when Milligan was tried by a court not ordained and established by Congress, and not composed of judges appointed during good behavior.*[100]

The Court continued,

> Why was he not delivered to the Circuit Court of Indiana to be proceeded against according to law? No reason of necessity could be urged against it; because Congress had declared penalties against the offences charged, provided for their punishment, and directed that court to hear and determine them. [T] he Circuit Court . . . needed no bayonets to protect it, and required no military aid to execute its judgments. [Indiana was] a state, eminently distinguished for patriotism, by judges commissioned during the Rebellion, who were provided with juries, upright, intelligent, and selected by a marshal appointed by the President. *The government had no right to conclude that Milligan, if guilty, would not receive in that court merited punishment; for its records disclose that it was constantly engaged in the trial of similar offences, and was never interrupted in its administration of criminal justice.* If it was dangerous, in the distracted condition of affairs, to leave Milligan unrestrained of his liberty, because he "conspired against the government, afforded aid and comfort to rebels, and incited the people to insurrection," *the law said arrest him, confine him closely, render him powerless to do further mischief; and then present his case to the grand jury of the district, with proofs of his guilt, and, if indicted, try him according to the course of the common law.* If this had been done, the Constitution would have been vindicated, the law of 1863 enforced, and the securities for personal liberty preserved and defended.[101]
>
> The provisions of [the Constitution] on the administration of criminal justice are too plain and direct, to leave room for misconstruction or doubt of

their true meaning. Those applicable to this case are found in that clause of the original Constitution which says, "That the trial of all crimes, except in case of impeachment, shall be by jury;" and in the fourth, fifth, and sixth articles of the amendments.[102]

"Until recently" the Court wrote, "no one ever doubted that the right of trial by jury was fortified in the organic law against the power of attack. It is now assailed; but if ideas can be expressed in words, and language has any meaning, this right—one of the most valuable in a free country—is preserved to every one accused of crime who is not attached to the army, or navy, or militia in actual service."[103] The Court, in asserting the absolute right of the Sixth Amendment right to a jury trial, concluded that all "citizens of states where the courts are open, if charged with crime, are guaranteed the inestimable privilege of trial by jury. This privilege is a vital principle, underlying the whole administration of criminal justice; it is not held by sufferance, and cannot be frittered away on any plea of state or political necessity."[104]

The Court also rejected the assertion that in time of war or civil war, the military has the power to implement martial law and replace the civil courts. The Court concluded that if such a power were in fact true, republican government would cease. The Court explained,

It is claimed that martial law covers with its broad mantle the proceedings of this military commission. The proposition is this: that in a time of war the commander of an armed force (if in his opinion the exigencies of the country demand it, and of which he is to judge), has the power, within the lines of his military district, to suspend all civil rights and their remedies, and subject citizens as well as soldiers to the rule of his will; and in the exercise of his lawful authority cannot be restrained, except by his superior officer or the President of the United States.

If this position is sound to the extent claimed, then when war exists, foreign or domestic, and the country is subdivided into military departments for mere convenience, the commander of one of them can, if he chooses, within his limits, on the plea of necessity, with the approval of the Executive, substitute military force for and to the exclusion of the laws, and punish all persons, as he thinks right and proper, without fixed or certain rules.

The statement of this proposition shows its importance; for, if true, *republican government is a failure*, and there is an end of liberty regulated by law. *Martial law, established on such a basis, destroys every guarantee of the Constitution, and effectually renders the "military independent of and superior to the civil power"*—the attempt to do which by the King of Great Britain was deemed by our fathers such an offence, that they assigned it to the world as one of the causes which impelled them to declare their independence. *Civil liberty and this kind of martial law cannot endure together; the antagonism is irreconcilable; and, in the conflict, one or the other must perish.*[105]

The Court then provided this warning and practical observation about the nature of war and the need for obedience to the law during war.

> This nation, as experience has proved, cannot always remain at peace, and has no right to expect that it will always have wise and humane rulers, sincerely attached to the principles of the Constitution. Wicked men, ambitious of power . . . may fill the place once occupied by Washington and Lincoln; and if this right is conceded, and the calamities of war again befall us, the dangers to human liberty are frightful to contemplate. If our fathers had failed to provide for just such a contingency, they would have been false to the trust reposed in them. They knew—the history of the world told them—the nation they were founding, be its existence short or long, would be involved in war; how often or how long continued, human foresight could not tell; and that unlimited power, wherever lodged at such a time, was especially hazardous to freemen. For this, and other equally weighty reasons, they secured the inheritance they had fought to maintain, by incorporating in a written Constitution the safe-guards which time had proved were essential to its preservation. Not one of these safeguards can the President, or Congress, or the Judiciary disturb, except the one concerning the writ of habeas corpus.
>   *It is essential to the safety of every government that, in a great crisis, like the one we have just passed through, there should be a power somewhere of suspending the writ of habeas corpus.*
>   . . . Unquestionably, there is then an exigency which demands that the government, if it should see fit in the exercise of a proper discretion to make arrests, should not be required to produce the persons arrested in answer to a writ of habeas corpus. *The Constitution goes no further. It does not say after a writ of habeas corpus is denied a citizen, that he shall be tried otherwise than by the course of the common law;* if it had intended this result, it was easy by the use of direct words to have accomplished it.[106]

The Court defended the application of Constitutional rights, such as the right of trial by jury, even in times of war.

> The illustrious men who framed that instrument were guarding the founda-tions of civil liberty against the abuses of unlimited power; they were full of wisdom, and the lessons of history informed them that a trial by an estab-lished court, assisted by an impartial jury, was the only sure way of protect-ing the citizen against oppression and wrong. Knowing this, *they limited the suspension to one great right, and left the rest to remain forever inviolable.* But, it is insisted that the safety of the country in time of war demands that this broad claim for martial law shall be sustained. If this were true, it could be well said that *a country, preserved at the sacrifice of all the cardinal principles of liberty, is not worth the cost of preservation.* Happily, it is not so.[107]

The presence of war and the organization of the nation into military districts for the protection of the nation from insurrection or invasion, by itself, does not constitute the establishment of military law which allows for the substitution of military for civilian judicial proceedings. The Court, rejecting the proposition that subjugation of civilian for military government occurs during states of war or insurrection, held that "[m]artial law cannot arise from a threatened invasion. The necessity must be actual and present; the invasion real, such as effectually closes the courts and deposes the civil administration."[108] "Martial rule can never exist where the courts are open, and in the proper and unobstructed exercise of their jurisdiction. It is also confined to the locality of actual war. Because, during the late Rebellion it could have been enforced in Virginia, where the national authority was overturned and the courts driven out, it does not follow that it should obtain in Indiana, where that authority was never disputed, and justice was always administered."[109] This principle, that only specific obstruction of civil justice by invasion or rebellion would provide lawful justification for the imposition of martial law and military justice in the place of civil justice, would be affirmed by the Court in *Duncan v. Kahanamoku* (1944) and the Japanese internment cases less than a century later during the war of the Greatest Generation.

The Court concluded that when civilians in a state in which the federal courts are in operation and are in a state which is not in rebellion against the government, the Constitution (1) requires that all civilians charged by the federal government must be accorded the full protections of the Fourth, Fifth, and Sixth amendments and (2) prevents the substitution of military justice for civil justice. The presence of war does not negate the application of Constitutional protections when a citizen is charged with a capital offense or substitute military for civilian judicial proceedings. The Court held that the Military Commission had no authority to try, convict and sentence Milligan to death. As to his petition for release:

> The suspension of the privilege of the writ of habeas corpus does not suspend the writ itself. The writ issues as a matter of course; and on the return made to it the court decides whether the party applying is denied the right of proceeding any further with it.
> If the military trial of Milligan was contrary to law, then he was entitled, on the facts stated in his petition, to be discharged from custody by the terms of the act of Congress of March 3d, 1863.[110]

The dissent,[111] led by Chief Justice Salmon Chase, concurred with the majority that Milligan should be released because he was entitled to release under the provisions of the Habeas Corpus Act of 1863 but dissented on the proposition that Congress could not authorize military commissions to put on trial American citizens for crimes although the civilian courts were fully functional.[112]

We assent, fully, to all that is said, in the opinion, of the inestimable value of the trial by jury, and of the other Constitutional safeguards of civil liberty. And we concur, also, in what is said of the writ of habeas corpus, and of its suspension, with two reservations: (1.) That, in our judgment, when the writ is suspended, the Executive is authorized to arrest as well as to detain; and (2.) *that there are cases in which, the privilege of the writ being suspended, trial and punishment by military commission, in states where civil courts are open, may be authorized by Congress, as well as arrest and detention.*

We think that Congress had power, though not exercised, to authorize the military commission which was held in Indiana.[113]

The Chief Justice wrote that

the Constitution itself provides for military government as well as for civil government. And we do not understand it to be claimed that the civil safeguards of the Constitution have application in cases within the proper sphere of the former.

What, then, is that proper sphere? Congress has power to raise and support armies; to provide and maintain a navy; to make rules for the government and regulation of the land and naval forces; and to provide for governing such part of the militia as may be in the service of the United States. . . .[114]

And is it impossible to imagine cases in which citizens conspiring or attempting the destruction or great injury of the national forces may be subjected by Congress to military trial and punishment in the just exercise of this undoubted Constitutional power?

Congress has the power not only to raise and support and govern armies but to declare war. It has, therefore, the power to provide by law for carrying on war. This power necessarily extends to all legislation essential to the prosecution of war with vigor and success, except such as interferes with the command of the forces and the conduct of campaigns. That power and duty belong to the President as Commander-in-Chief. Both these powers are derived from the Constitution, but neither is defined by that instrument. *Their extent must be determined by their nature, and by the principles of our institutions.*[115]

The Chief Justice, evoking the theory of inherent powers, held that the "power to make the necessary laws is in Congress; the power to execute in the President. *Both powers imply many subordinate and auxiliary powers. Each includes all authorities essential to its due exercise.*"[116] The minority affirmed that the President has no power to institute military commissions without the express authorization of Congress[117] and that it was for Congress to determine if military commissions should be used to place on trial citizens alleged to have committed criminal acts against the nation in times of war.

We by no means assert that Congress can establish and apply the laws of war where no war has been declared or exists.

Where peace exists the laws of peace must prevail. What we do maintain is, that when the nation is involved in war, and some portions of the country are invaded, and all are exposed to invasion, it is within the power of Congress to determine in what states or districts such great and imminent public danger exists as justifies the authorization of military tribunals for the trial of crimes and offences against the discipline or security of the army or against the public safety.[118]

The Chief Justice answered the majority observation that because the federal court remained open and did not need "bayonets to protect it, and required no military aid to execute its judgments" with the proverbial response "that's not the point."

The fact that the Federal courts were open was regarded by Congress as a sufficient reason for not exercising the power; but that fact could not deprive Congress of the right to exercise it. Those courts might be open and undisturbed in the execution of their functions, and yet wholly incompetent to avert threatened danger, or to punish, with adequate promptitude and certainty, the guilty conspirators.

In Indiana, the judges and officers of the courts were loyal to the government. But it might have been otherwise. In times of rebellion and civil war it may often happen, indeed, that judges and marshals will be in active sympathy with the rebels, and courts their most efficient allies.[119]

The Chief Justice concluded,

We have confined ourselves to the question of power. It was for Congress to determine the question of expediency. And Congress did determine it. That body did not see fit to authorize trials by military commission in Indiana, but by the strongest implication prohibited them. With that prohibition we are satisfied, and should have remained silent if the answers to the questions certified had been put on that ground. . . .[120]

We think that the power of Congress, in such times and in such localities, to authorize trials for crimes against the security and safety of the national forces, may be derived from its Constitutional authority to raise and support armies and to declare war, if not from its Constitutional authority to provide for governing the national forces.[121]

Thus both the majority and minority agreed that Congress did not authorize military commissions to be used to put American citizens on trial for criminal offenses against the security of the United States even during a time of war and as such, the President as Commander-in-Chief could not institute such commissions on his own authority. A principle, as we will discuss later, that the Court enforced against President Bush in *Hamdan v. Rumsfeld* in 2006.[122] The Court, in *Ex parte Milligan*, was unanimous on the point that Milligan should be granted release and his conviction was unlawful. The majority maintained that Congress did not give the President the authorization to create military commissions to try American citizens and that it could not do so. The minority agreed that Congress did not authorize the President but that it could do so.

The Majority had the better argument. It does not follow that because Congress has the power to raise the armed forces of the United States, to declare war and is empowered to provide for the national defense, that Congress can institute military law to place on trial citizens charged with criminal activity while the civilian courts are functional within a military district. The Constitution, as the majority asserted, provides for the methods in which criminal trials are to be conducted and Congress cannot violate those specific requirements by using "implied powers" from the general power to raise and support the military and to declare war. The Constitution specifically guarantees the right of citizens to a jury trial, right to counsel, federal indictment, freedom from unreasonable search and seizure, and protection against self-incrimination. *Specific prohibitions cannot be disregarded and violated by the use of implied powers.* But even if Congress could establish military commissions to take the place of civilian courts, the Constitution would still require those commissions to provide the same basic rights when such commissions are used to place American citizens on trial. In subsequent chapters of this book we will revisit these issues.

These civil war cases were not the only cases in which the Court broadly discussed the powers of the President in times of war. In 1874 the Court was presented with a case dealing with that validity of an act of congress that authorized the President to set fees for licenses to trade with the states in rebellion. Although arguably *dicta*, the Court continued its broad reading of the Constitutional powers of both Presidential and Congressional power in time of war. The court unanimously observed:

In England this power to remit the restrictions on commercial intercourse with a hostile nation is exercised by the crown. Lord Stowell says: "By the law and constitution of this country, the sovereign alone has the power of declaring war and peace. He alone, therefore, who has the power of entirely removing a state of war, has the power of removing it in part, by permitting, where he sees proper, that commercial intercourse which is a partial suspension of the war." . . . By the Constitution of the United States the power to declare war is confided to Congress. The executive power and the command of the military and naval forces is vested in the President. Whether, in the absence of Congressional action, the power of permitting partial intercourse with a public enemy may or may not be exercised by the President alone, who is constitutionally invested with the entire charge of hostile operations, it is not now necessary to decide, although it would seem that little doubt could be raised on the subject. In the case of *Cross v. Harrison* [16 Howard, 164, 190], it was held that the President, as commander-in-chief, had power to form a temporary civil government for California as a conquered country, and to impose duties on imports and tonnage for the support of the government and for aiding to sustain the burdens of the war, which were held valid until Congress saw fit to supersede them; and an action brought to recover back duties paid under such regulation was adjudged to be not maintainable. . . .

But without pursuing this inquiry, and whatever view may be taken as to the precise boundary between the legislative and executive powers in reference to the question under consideration, there is no doubt that a concurrence of both affords ample foundation for any regulations on the subject.[123]

Although *dicta*, the Court's observation that when Congress and the President act together to implement the sovereign power of the nation in time of war "there is no doubt that the concurrence of both affords ample foundation for any regulations on the subject" was echoed almost eighty years later by Justice Jackson in the famous steel seizure case.[124] As discussed in chapter 4, the Court would define the sole power of the President "who is constitutionally invested with the entire charge of hostile operations" and the source of the national government foreign policy power in 1936 in the *United States v. Curtiss-Wright Export* case.

The last case, in the nineteenth century, in which the Court provided commentary and interpretation of Presidential power, was in 1890 in *Cunningham v. Neagle*[125] which involved the inherent powers of the President to faithfully execute the laws when Congress had not specifically authorized a method selected by the President. On August 14, 1889, David Neagle, a Deputy U.S. Marshall, shot and killed David S. Terry after Terry attempted to shoot Justice Stephen J. Field. Neagle was then arrested and detained on a charge of murder by Thomas Cunningham, sheriff of Joaquin County, California, upon a warrant issued by H. V. J. Swain, Justice of the Peace. Neagle, through a writ of habeas corpus, challenged his arrest and confinement in the United States Circuit Court for the Northern District of California, in which Judge Sawyer and District Judge Sabib ruled, on August 16, that Neagle acted in accordance to the laws of the United States and was unlawfully held by Cunningham and was ordered released. The state of California appealed to the Supreme Court.

The Court was presented with the assertion that Congress had not authorized the U.S. Marshall to protect individual justices of the Supreme Court and as such the Attorney General, exercising Presidential Power to faithfully execute the laws, could not order the U.S. Marshall to do so. The Court summarized the issue as follows:

The Constitution, 3, art. 2, declares that the President "shall take care that the laws be faithfully executed." . . . Is this duty limited to the enforcement of acts of Congress or of treaties of the United States according to their express terms; or does it include the rights, duties, and obligations growing out of the Constitution itself, our international relations, and all the protection implied by the nature of the government under the Constitution?[126]

After approvingly recounting a case in which a U.S. naval ship prevented an Austrian ship from arresting and carrying off by force an individual who had papers establishing citizenship application to the United States, an action that was not specifically authorized by an act of Congress, the Court asked rhetorically:

> So, if the President or the postmaster general is advised that the mails of the United States, possibly carrying treasure, are liable to be robbed, and the mail carriers assaulted and murdered, in any particular region of country, who can doubt the authority of the President, or of one of the executive departments under him, to make an order for the protection of the mail, and of the persons and lives of its carriers, by doing exactly what was done in the case of Mr. Justice Field, namely, providing a sufficient guard, whether it be by soldiers of the army or by marshals of the United States, with a posse comitatus properly armed and equipped, to secure the safe performance of the duty of carrying the mail wherever it may be intended to go?[127]

The Court concluded,

> We cannot doubt the power of the President to take measures for the protection of a judge of one of the courts of the United States who, while in the discharge of the duties of his office, is threatened with a personal attack which may probably result in his death; and we think it clear that where this protection is to be afforded through the civil power, the department of justice is the proper one to set in motion the necessary means of protection. The correspondence, already recited in this opinion, between the marshal of the northern district of California and the Attorney General and the District Attorney of the United States for that district, although prescribing no very specific mode of affording this protection by the Attorney General, is sufficient, we think, to warrant the marshal in taking the steps which he did take, in making the provisions which he did make, for the protection and defense of Mr. Justice Field.[128]

The Court also cited the case of *Wells v. Nickles*[129] in which the Secretary of the Interior was authorized to allow for the hiring of agents to protect U.S. forests from "timber thieves" who would illegally cut down trees on U.S. lands even though there was no specific act of Congress that allowed for the hiring of these agents. The Court in *Nickles* upheld the authority of the Secretary to employ these agents in the commission of his duty to protect the federal lands. The Court also cited *U.S. v. Tin Co.*[130] in which the Attorney General brought a civil suit to nullify a patent which he claimed was secured fraudulently. The Court in *Tin Co.* admitted that no act of Congress authorized the Attorney General to file such a suit but responded,

"How, then, can it be argued that if the United States has been deceived, entrapped, or defrauded into the making, under the forms of law, of an instrument which injuriously affects its rights of property, or other rights, it cannot bring a suit to avoid the effect of such instrument thus fraudulently obtained without a special act of Congress in each case, or without some special authority applicable to this class of cases?"[131]

The Court in *Neagle* asserted that the President and through him the officers of the government can take specific action not authorized by legislation if such action flows from the specific powers and duties imposed upon them through the Constitution, acts of Congress or treaties of the United States. Chief Justice Salmon Chase said as much in *Milligan*; the "power to make the necessary laws is in Congress; the power to execute in the President. *Both powers imply many subordinate and auxiliary powers. Each includes all authorities essential to its due exercise."*[132] Attorney General Bates similarly concluded that "the President must swear to *'preserve, protect* and *defend'* it, which implies the power to perform what he is required in so solemn a manner to undertake."[133] The Court, in *Martin v. Mott*, wrote that the President "whose duty it is to 'take care that the laws be faithfully executed,' and whose responsibility for an honest discharge of his official obligations is secured by the highest sanctions. *He is necessarily constituted the judge of the existence of the exigency in the first instance, and is bound to act according to his belief of the facts"*[134]

What did the Supreme Court, after the first century of the drafting of the Constitution, provide to the growth of Presidential power—not to mention Congressional power—in times of war and crisis? The Court concurred that the President has inherent powers that emanate from specific powers granted to him by the Constitution. The Court supported the view that the President as Commander-in-Chief has the power to act decisively in times of crisis and when he acts within the discretion granted to him by the Constitution or by Acts of Congress, he is not bound by contrary determinations by Congress. But regardless of the crisis or action, the President is not authorized to act in opposition to specific laws passed by Congress. The President can act when the laws require his action, when they give him discretion to act, or when his actions can be inferred from his inherent powers under the Constitution or by Congressional statute. But he cannot exercise such discretion when Congress has specifically passed legislation restricting his action or establishing, by law, what the President cannot do. In *Little v. Berreme* the Court made clear that misinterpretation of a law restricting Presidential action will not indemnify actions made by the chief executive or his officers, although such interpretation and action were committed in good faith.

In *Mott*, the Court wrote, "We are all of opinion, that the authority to decide whether the exigency has arisen, belongs exclusively to the President, and that his decision is conclusive upon all other persons. We think that this construction necessarily results from the nature of the power itself, and from the manifest object contemplated by the act of Congress." In *Fleming v. Page*, the Court made clear that Presidential powers were not unlimited upon the declaration of war: "The United States, it is true, may extend its boundaries by conquest or treaty, and may demand the cession of territory as the condition of peace, in order to indemnify its citizens for the injuries they have suffered, or to reimburse the government for the expenses of the war. But this can be done only by the treaty-making power or the legislative authority, and is not a part of the power conferred upon the President by the declaration of war." In the *Chinese Exclusion Case*, the Court wrote of the limits of the power of the President as Commander-in-Chief to commit the use of the armed forces of the United States in foreign policy. The Court wrote:

> England requested of the President . . . to authorize our naval and political authorities to act in concert with the allied forces [in China]. *As this proposition involved a participation in existing hostilities, the request could not be acceded to, and the secretary of state in his communication to the English government explained that the war-making power of the United States was not vested in the President, but in Congress, and that he had no authority, therefore, to order aggressive hostilities to be undertaken.*[135]

In *U.S. v. Smith*, Justice Paterson made it clear to the jury that only "in the Congress . . . solely and exclusively, . . . [is] the power of making war. As it is the people who are to endure the fatigues and calamities, and sustain the waste of blood and treasure inseparable from war, they have confided the power of making it to their immediate representatives."

But by the dawn of the Civil War, it was also clear that the Presidency was accepted as the branch of government with the primary role of determining foreign policy and protecting American lives outside of the United States. In *Durand v. Hollins*, Supreme Court Justice Samuel Nelson wrote in the strongest terms that "[a]s the Executive head of the nation, the President is made the only legitimate organ of the General Government, to open and carry on correspondence or negotiations with foreign nations, in matters concerning the interests of the country or of its citizens. It is to him, also, the citizens abroad must look for protection of person and of property, and for the faithful execution of the laws existing and intended for their protection. For this purpose, the whole executive power of the country is placed in his hands, under the Constitution, and the laws passed in pursuance thereof." The Civil War itself clarified that the President as Commander-in-Chief was free to meet military challenges to the United States without the need for Congress to recognize the military challenge. The majority in the *Prize Cases* held that "the President is not only authorized but bound to resist force by force. He does not initiate the war, but is bound to accept the challenge without waiting for any special legislative authority."

Although the President is not only empowered, but is duty bound, to address military and threats of insurrection, his powers to address such threats are not without limit. As Chief Justice Taney explained, the presence of Constitutional limits is not merely academic; "I can only say that if the authority which the Constitution has confided to the judiciary department and judicial officers, may thus, upon any pretext or under any circumstances, be usurped by the military power, at its discretion, the people of the United States are no longer living under a government of laws, but every citizen holds life, liberty and property at the will and pleasure of the army officer in whose military district he may happen to be found." Chief Justice Taney's observations were affirmed by the majority in *Ex parte Milligan* in which the Court wrote "It is claimed that . . . in a time of war the commander of an armed force (if in his opinion the exigencies of the country demand it, and of which he is to judge), has the power, within the lines of his military district, to suspend all civil rights and their remedies, and subject citizens as well as soldiers to the rule of his will. . . . If this position is sound . . . republican government is a failure, and there is an end of liberty regulated by law. Martial law, established on such a basis, destroys every guarantee of the Constitution, and effectually renders the military independent of and superior to the civil power."

In *Ex parte Milligan*, the Court held that Congress in the Habeas Corpus Act of 1863 did not authorize military commissions for the trial of citizens who were not members of the armed forces of the United States or for citizens of states that were not in rebellion in a time of civil war. Thus the President, through his military commanders, could not conduct such a trial. The majority made clear that Congress could not have granted the President such a power under the Constitution even if it was so inclined. "But it is said that the jurisdiction [of military commissions] is complete under the 'laws and usages of war.' It can serve no useful purpose to inquire what those laws and usages are, whence they originated, where found, and on whom they operate; they can never be applied to citizens in states which have upheld the authority of the government, and where the courts are open and their process unobstructed . . . no usage of war could sanction a military trial there for any offence whatever of a citizen in civil life, in nowise connected with the military service. Congress could grant no such power." Why? Because the Constitution in the Fourth, Fifth, and Sixth Amendments provides that a trial of a citizen for crimes must be provided a trial by civil jury with certain protections, among them being the right to counsel, federal indictment and freedom from self incrimination. The Court defended the Constitutional boundaries on Congressional power, even in times of war and national crisis, with the observation that it is possible that "[w]icked men, ambitious of power . . . may fill the place once occupied by Washington and Lincoln. [Our Founding Fathers knew our nation] would be involved in war . . . and that unlimited power, wherever lodged at such a time, was especially hazardous to freemen. For this, and other equally weighty reasons, they secured the inheritance they had fought to maintain, by incorporating in a written Constitution the safeguards which time had proved were essential to its preservation." The Court maintained that although it "is essential to the safety of every government that, in a great crisis, like the one we have just passed through, there should be a power somewhere of suspending the writ of habeas corpus. . . . The Constitution goes no further. It does not say after a writ of habeas corpus is denied a citizen, that he shall be tried otherwise than by the course of the common law; if it had intended this result, it was easy by the use of direct words to have accomplished it."

By the end of the nineteenth century the Supreme Court had established the foundations of its jurisprudence in the area of national security. It would defend the limits on Presidential power and would grant due deference to decisions made by the President when those decisions are made within his specified or implied powers. But the Court would also hold the President and Congress to the limits of their powers under the Constitution regardless of the utility of acting beyond those limits.

According to the Court's early jurisprudence, the Congress is responsible for the declaration of war and the President acts outside of his powers by initiating war but is not required to have Congress declare war when such a war is imposed upon the United States. Both political branches are restrained in their actions by the specific prohibitions of the Fourth, Fifth, and Sixth Amendments of the Constitution even in times of war and national crisis.

EPILOGUE

By the dawn of the twentieth century the President was acknowledged as the lead branch, if not the sole authority, to implement foreign policy and the primary protector of American interests throughout the world. Within twenty years of the beginning of the American Century the United States would be a world power but threats of insurrection at the hands of communism would raise new questions of Congressional power to protect the nation domestically. These issues would be raised again after a second world war which left the United States a super power in a worldwide cold war with a one-time ally. The red scare of 1917–1920, followed by the red scare and McCarthyism of 1947–1957, raised questions of free speech, freedom of association, and loyalty oaths. The rise of civil rights and civil liberty protection would engulf the Supreme Court for much of the second half of twentieth century. How the Court dealt with these issues and the post–September 11 claims of executive power to address the new war on terrorism will be the subjects for the remainder of this book.

NOTES

1. *Martin v. Mott* 25 U.S. (12 Wheat.) 19 (1827).
2. Ibid., 29.
3. Ibid.
4. Ibid.
5. Ibid., 30 (emphasis added).
6. Ibid.
7. Ibid., 31.
8. Ibid. (emphasis added).
9. Ibid., 31–32 (emphasis added).
10. Ibid., 32.
11. Ibid., 32–33.
12. *Luther v. Borden*, 48 U.S. 1 (How) (1849).
13. Ibid., 44.
14. Ibid., 42.
15. Ibid., 43.
16. Ibid.
17. Ibid., 44.
18. *Fleming v. Page* 50 U.S. 603, 614–15 (1850) (emphasis added).
19. *United States v. Smith* 27 Fed. Cas. 1192 (C.C.N.Y. 1806) (No. 16,342).
20. Ibid., 1210.
21. Ibid., 1211.
22. Ibid.
23. Ibid., 1228.
24. Ibid., 1230–31.
25. *United States v. Smith* 27 Fed. Cas. 1233, 1243 (C.C.N.Y. 1806) (No. 16,342a).
26. *Little v. Barreme* 6 U.S. 70 (1804).
27. *Durand v. Hollins*, 8 Fed. Cas. 111, 112 (Cir. Ct. S.D.N.Y. 1860) (Case no. 4,186).
28. South Carolina (December 20, 1860), Mississippi (January 9, 1861), Florida (January 10, 1861), Alabama (January 11, 1861), Georgia (January 19, 1861), Louisiana (January 26, 1861) and Texas (February 1, 1861).
29. Virginia (April 17, 1861), Arkansas (May 6, 1861), Tennessee (May 7, 1861) and North Carolina (May 20, 1861).
30. 12 U.S. Statute 755.
31. *Ex parte Bollman and Swartwout* 8 U.S. 75 (1807).
32. Ibid., 101 (emphasis added).
33. Ibid., 95 (emphasis added).

34. *Ex parte Merryman* 17 Fed. Cas. 144 (C.C. Md. 1861) (Case no. 9,487). See also Arthur T. Downey, "The Conflict between the Chief Justice and the Chief Executive: *Ex parte Merryman*," *Journal of Supreme Court History* 31, no. 3 (2006): 262–78.

35. *Ex parte Merryman* 17 Fed. Cas. 144, 148 (1861).

36. Ibid.

37. Ibid., 149.

38. Ibid.

39. Ibid., 152 (emphasis added).

40. Ibid., 149.

41. Ibid.

42. Ibid., 150.

43. Ibid., 151.

44. Ibid., 152 (emphasis added).

45. Ibid., 153.

46. Lucius Wilmerding, Jr., "Seizure of Industry under War Powers: Truman and the Steel Mills," in *The President's War Powers: From the Federalists to Reagan*, ed. Demetrios Caraley (New York: Academy of Political Science, 1984).

47. Arthur H. Garrison, "*Hamdi, Padilla*, and *Rasul*: The War on Terrorism on the Judicial Front," *American Journal of Trial Advocacy* 27, no. 1 (2003): 99–148.

48. Benjamin Franklin, Pennsylvania Assembly: Reply to the Governor, Tue., Nov 11, 1755. Leonard W. Labaree, ed., *The Papers of Benjamin Franklin*, vol. 6 (New Haven, CT: Yale University Press, 1963), 242. Thomas Jefferson is known for making a similar quote: "Those who are willing to sacrifice a little freedom for a little security will lose both and deserve neither."

49. James Madison, June 20, 1788 (speech on the *Power of the Judiciary* at the Virginia Constitutional Convention). See Gaillard Hunt, ed., *The Writings of James Madison*, vol. 5 (1787–1790) (New York: Putnam, 1900), 223.

50. Benjamin Franklin, April 17, 1789, letter To Messrs. The Abbes Chalut and Arnaud. Albert Henry Smyth, ed., *The Writings of Benjamin Franklin*, vol. 9 (1783–1788) (New York: Macmillan, 1906), 569.

51. Edward Bates, "Suspension of the Privilege of the Writ of Habeas Corpus," 10 Op. Att'y Gen. 74 (1861).

52. One hundred and forty-one years later, the Bush administration would argue the same thing. The Supreme Court, agreeing with Justice Taney, ruled against the Bush Administration and held that the issues of suspension of the writ, or limitations on the judiciary to issue the writ, were judicial matters, not political and military ones regardless of the President using his powers as Commander-in-Chief after the events of 9/11." See Part II of this book, and Arthur Garrison, "The Bush Administration and the War on Terrorism on the Judicial Front II: The Courts Strike Back," *American Journal of Trial Advocacy* 27, no. 3 (2004): 473–516 and Arthur Garrison, "The Judiciary in Times of National Security Crisis and Terrorism: *Ubi Inter Arma Enim Silent Leges, Quis Custodiet Ipso Custodies? American Journal of Trial Advocacy* 30, no. 1 (2006): 165–230.

53. Bates, "Suspension of the Privilege of the Writ of Habeas Corpus," 86.

54. Ibid., 90.

55. Ibid., 81.

56. Ibid., 82.

57. Ibid., 82–83.

58. Lucius E. Chittenden, *Recollections of President Lincoln and His Administration* (New York: Harper & Brothers, 1904), 75.

59. Bates, "Suspension of the Privilege of the Writ of Habeas Corpus," 84.

60. Ibid., 84.

61. Ibid., 85.

62. Ibid.

63. Ibid., 88.

64. Ibid., 90.

65. Ibid., 91.

66. Ibid., 89.

67. Garrison, "The Bush Administration and the War on Terrorism on the Judicial Front II."

68. *Ex parte Milligan*, 71 U.S. 2, 109 (1866).

69. For a modern example of this view of judicial decision making in times of war and national crisis, see William Brennan, "The Quest to Develop a Jurisprudence of Civil Liberties in Times of Security Crises," *Israel Yearbook on Human Rights* 18, no. 11 (1988): 17–18. But see Garrison, "The Judiciary in Times of National Security Crisis and Terrorism."

70. *The Prize Cases* 67 U.S. 635 (1863).

71. Ibid., 666.

72. Ibid.

73. Ibid., 669.

74. Ibid., 668.

75. Ibid.

76. Ibid.

77. Ibid., 668–69.

78. Ibid., 670.

79. Retroactive forgiveness for past actions at the express command of the sovereign power.

80. Ibid., 670–71.

81. Ibid., 668.

82. Justice Nelson was joined by Chief Justice Taney, Justice Catron, and Justice Clifford.

83. *The Prize Cases* 67 U.S., 686.

84. Ibid., 687.

85. Ibid., 688–89.

86. Ibid., 690.

87. Ibid., 693.

88. Ibid., 694–95.

89. Ibid., 695.

90. Ibid., 698–99.

91. Ibid., 695.

92. Ibid., 696–97 (emphasis added).

93. Ibid., 670.

94. Ibid., 697.

95. *Ex parte Milligan* 71 U.S. 2 (1866).

96. Ibid., 108–09.

97. Ibid., 118.

98. Ibid., 119.

99. Ibid., 119–20.

100. Ibid., 121–22 (emphasis added).

101. Ibid., 122 (emphasis added). See also *Ex parte Merryman*, in which Chief Justice Taney wrote, "Up to that time, there had never been the slightest resistance or obstruction to the process of any court or judicial officer of the United States, in Maryland. . . . There was no danger of any obstruction or resistance to the action of the civil authorities, and therefore no reason whatever for the interposition of the military" (17 Fed. Cas., 152 (emphasis added)).

102. *Ex parte Milligan* 71 U.S. 2, 120–21.

103. Ibid., 123.

104. Ibid.

105. Ibid., 124–25. Chief Justice Taney came to the same conclusion, reasoning that if the protections of the Fourth, Fifth, and Sixth Amendments and the right to habeas corpus could be brushed aside during times of crisis, "the people of the United States are no longer living under a government of laws" (*Ex parte Merryman* 17 Fed. Cas., 152). The Chief Justice wrote in regard to the protections of the Fourth, Fifth, and Sixth Amendments: "These great and fundamental laws, which Congress itself could not suspend, have been disregarded and suspended, like the writ of habeas corpus, by a military order, supported by force of arms. Such is the case now before me, and I can only say that if the authority which the Constitution has confided to the judiciary department and judicial officers, may thus, upon any pretext or under any circumstances, be usurped by the military power, at its discretion, the people of the United States are no longer living under a government of laws, but every citizen holds life, liberty and property at the will and pleasure of the army officer in whose military district he may happen to be found" (Ibid).

106. Ibid., 125–26.

107. Ibid., 126 (emphasis added).

108. Ibid., 127.

109. Ibid.

110. Ibid., 130–31.

111. Chief Justice Chase was joined by Justices Wayne, Swayne, and Miller.

112. "But the opinion . . . as we understand it, asserts not only that the military commission held in Indiana was not authorized by Congress, but that it was not in the power of Congress to authorize it; from which it may be thought to follow, that Congress has no power to indemnify the officers who composed the commission against liability in civil courts for acting as members of it. We cannot agree to this" (Ibid., 136).

113. Ibid., 137.

114. Ibid.

115. Ibid., 139.

116. Ibid. (emphasis added).

117. "Congress cannot direct the conduct of campaigns, nor can the President, or any commander under him, without the sanction of Congress, institute tribunals for the trial and punishment of offences, either of soldiers or civilians, unless in cases of a controlling necessity, which justifies what it compels, or at least insures acts of indemnity from the justice of the legislature" (Ibid., 139–40).

118. Ibid., 140.

119. Ibid., 140–41.

120. Ibid., 141.

121. Ibid., 142. "And we are unwilling to give our assent by silence to expressions of opinion which seem to us calculated, though not intended, to cripple the Constitutional powers of the government, and to augment the public dangers in times of invasion and rebellion" (Ibid.).

122. *Hamdan v. Rumsfeld* 126 S.Ct. 2749 (2006).

123. *Hamilton v. Dillin* 88 U.S. 73, 87–88 (1874).

124. See Arthur H. Garrison, "National Security and Presidential Power: Judicial Deference and Establishing Constitutional Boundaries in World War II and the Korean War," *Cumberland Law Review* 39, no. 3 (2008–2009): 609–84.

125. *Cunningham v. Neagle* 135 U.S. 1 (1890).

126. Ibid., 63–64.

127. Ibid., 65.

128. Ibid., 67–68.

129. *Wells v. Nickles*, 104 U.S. 444.

130. *U.S. v. Tin Co.*, 125 U.S. 273.

131. *Cunningham v. Neagle* 135 U.S., 67 citing *U.S. v. Tin Co.*, 125 U.S. 273.

132. *Ex parte Milligan* 71 U.S. 2, 139 (emphasis added).

133. Bates, "Suspension of the Privilege of the Writ of Habeas Corpus," 82.

134. *Martin v. Mott* 25 U.S. (12 Wheat.) (1827), 31.

135. *Chinese Exclusion Case*, 130 U.S. 581, 591 (1889) (emphasis added).

Communism, Red Scares, National Security, Free Speech, and the Supreme Court

3

World Wars, the Red Scare, and Free Speech I: World War I, the First Red Scare (1917–1920), and Free Speech

The first red scare was conceived with the entry of the United States into World War I, delivered to the dual parents of the radical left and the conservatism of the right and came to age on the milk of fear of international communism and radicalism and on the meat of public fears of socialist and anarchist immigration forming a fifth column in the domestic politics of America. The Supreme Court during the period of the Alien and Sedition Acts of 1798 was not a factor in the debates on free speech in times of war and the nature of the power of government to curtail civil and political liberties in such times. But more than a century later the Supreme Court had established itself as a co-equal branch of government and during the first red scare the Supreme Court began to define its jurisprudence of deference and establishment of Constitutional boundaries of government power in times of crisis to regulate civil liberties, specifically those involving political speech and dissent in times of war.

The beginning of the red scare came in the spring of 1917 when the United States entered World War I to make the world safe for democracy. By the time the United States entered the war more than four hundred thousand European soldiers were dead. Within three weeks after Congress declared war on Germany, Congress entered debate on the Espionage Act of 1917. The act made it unlawful to gather, copy or otherwise secure military information for the purpose of providing it to the enemy or otherwise using such information to the detriment of the United States or the military. Section 3 of the act made it unlawful to willfully make or convey false reports or false statements with intent to interfere with the operation or success of the military or naval forces of the United States or to promote the success of its enemies and whoever, when the United States is at war, shall willfully cause or attempt to cause insubordination, disloyalty, mutiny, refusal of duty, in the military or naval forces of the United States, or shall willfully obstruct the recruiting or enlistment service of the United States, to the injury of the service or of the United States.

The violation of Section 3 of the Espionage Act was punishable by a fine of not more than $10,000 or imprisonment for not more than twenty years, or both. A year after the passage of the Espionage Act of 1917 Congress passed the Sedition Act of 1918. The Sedition Act expanded Section 3 of the Espionage Act, broadly focusing on limiting dissenting speech on the war, by making it unlawful to

make or convey false reports or false statements with intent to interfere with the operation or success of the military or naval forces of the United States, or to promote the success of its enemies, or . . . willfully make or convey false reports or false statements, or . . . to obstruct the sale by the United States of bonds or other securities of the United States or . . . [to] willfully cause or attempt to cause, or incite or attempt to incite, insubordination, disloyalty, mutiny, or refusal of duty, in the military or naval forces of the United States, or . . . willfully obstruct or attempt to obstruct the recruiting or enlistment services of the United States, [or] when the United States is at war [to]. . . willfully utter, print, write or publish any disloyal, profane, scurrilous, or abusive language about the form of government of the United States or the Constitution of the United States, or the military or naval forces of the United States . . . , or [to] willfully utter, print, write, or publish any language intended to incite, provoke, or encourage resistance to the United States, or to promote the cause of its enemies, or . . . [to] willfully by utterance, writing, printing, publication, or language spoken, urge, incite, or advocate any curtailment of production in this country of any thing or things, product or products, necessary or essential to the prosecution of the war . . . with intent by such curtailment to cripple or hinder the United States in the prosecution of war, [or] and [to] willfully advocate, teach, defend, or suggest the doing of any of the acts or things in this section enumerated, [or] by word or act support or favor the cause of any country with which the United States is at war or by word or act oppose the cause of the United States therein.

Conviction carried a penalty of a fine not to exceed $10,000 and imprisonment not to exceed twenty years or both. The powers asserted by the Postmaster General to enforce the Espionage Act were formally sanctioned and codified in Section 4 of the Sedition Act. History has judged[1] that with the "passage of the Sedition Act in the summer of 1918, the government had put into place the perfect instrument to suppress dissent"[2] during the war and that these two laws were subsequently used to deal with those who advocated principles of socialism, communism and anarchism both during and after the conclusion of the war to end all wars.

Congress also passed legislation instituting the draft, preventing labor strikes, nationalizing the rail system, and enforcing prohibition as well as regulating domestic relations down to the level of rent control. All of these actions were claimed by the government to be within the power of Congress as measures to successfully deal with the implementation of the war. Collectively, the Court affirmed these measures by accepting the proposition they were a proper exercise of police and inherent powers to control domestic policy in time of war. The Court during this period *began* to develop a judicial philosophy of not invalidating Congressional action in times of war if those actions are within the boundaries of their Constitutional powers, while maintaining the Constitutional principle that action by Congress must be within its Constitutional boundaries.

THE ESPIONAGE AND SEDITION ACTS: THE RISE OF THE FREE SPEECH CIVIL LIBERTIES MOVEMENT

On June 5, 1917, Congress made it unlawful (1) to obtain military information on the national defense with the intent to use such information to the injury of the United States, or to the advantage of any foreign nation, (2) to willfully make or convey false reports or false statements with intent to interfere with the operation or success of the military or naval forces of the United States, (3) to promote the success of its enemies, (4) to cause or attempt to cause insubordination, disloyalty, mutiny, refusal of duty, in the military or naval forces of the United States, or (5) to willfully obstruct the recruiting or enlistment service of the United States.

The Espionage Act was passed during a heightened time of national fear of disloyalty and the desire to get the whole nation behind the war. Dissent on America's entry into the war was not well tolerated by the Wilson Administration. Even before America's entrance into the war, Wilson was lamenting the lack of unanimity of loyalty among the population. In a speech to the Daughters of the American Revolution in 1915 he claimed that he was in "a hurry for an opportunity to have a line-up and let the men who are thinking first of other countries stand on one side and all those that are for America first, last and all the time on the other."[3] In his December 7, 1915, Annual Message to Congress President Wilson echoed the sentiment of the Federalists in 1798. He explained to Congress that

> I am sorry to say that the gravest threats against our national peace and safety have been uttered within our own borders. There are citizens of the United States, I blush to admit, born under other flags but welcomed under our gener-

ous naturalization laws to the full freedom and opportunity of America, who have poured the poison of disloyalty into the very arteries of our national life; who have sought to bring the authority and good name of our Government into contempt, to destroy our industries . . . to debase our politics to the uses of foreign intrigue. Their number is not great . . . but it is great enough . . . to have made it necessary that we should promptly make use of processes of law by which we may be purged of their corrupt distempers. . . . But the ugly and incredible thing has actually come about and we are without adequate federal laws to deal with it. I urge you to enact such laws at the earliest possible moment and feel that in doing so I am urging you to do nothing less than save the honor and self-respect of the nation. Such creatures of passion, disloyalty, and anarchy must be crushed out. They are not many, but they are infinitely malignant, and the hand of our power should close over them at once. They have formed plots to destroy property, they have entered into conspiracies against the neutrality of the Government, they have sought to pry into every confidential transaction of the Government in order to serve interests alien to our own.

The Wilson Administration in June 1916 submitted to Congress legislation that would later become the substance of the Espionage Act, although the passage of the act would not come until the declaration of war a year later.[4]

When war was declared, Wilson made it clear that disloyalty or dissent on America's entry into the conflict was no longer a subject on which there was room for debate and the disloyal by their actions would be considered to have sacrificed their rights to civil liberty protection.[5] In his war message to Congress on April 2, 1917, Wilson continued to lay the foundation for the Espionage Act by stating that Germany had

filled our unsuspecting communities and even our offices of government with spies and set criminal intrigues everywhere afoot against our national unity of counsel, our peace within and without our industries and our commerce. Indeed it is now evident that its spies were here even before the war began; and it is unhappily not a matter of conjecture but a fact proved in our courts of justice that the intrigues which have more than once come perilously near to disturbing the peace and dislocating the industries of the country have been carried on at the instigation, with the support, and even under the personal direction of official agents of the Imperial Government accredited to the Government of the United States.

Four days later, Congress declared war on Germany and within three weeks started debate on the Espionage Act.

The secondary background to the passage of the act was the growing socialist, anarchist and pacifist forces in the United States. While all three had differing political philosophies, they were united in the opposition of the United States entering World War I. While the socialists sought to gain political power for the proletariat and opposed the war as a war to make millionaires richer, the anarchists advocated the destruction of the governmental structures altogether so as to free mankind from all social and moral restraints. Pacifists, while supportive of the government, sought to keep the United States out of the war and opposed the draft. The entry into the war was not greatly popular and many feared that the advocacy of the pacifists and avoiders of the draft presented a threat of reducing national resolve to prevail in the war in Europe. Fears of a fifth column were justified in the eyes of many by the passionate and persistent advocacy of socialists and anarchists who were promoting the destruction of the American capitalistic system of government. The socialists and anarchists were well organized, funded and articulate in their views and openly published newspapers and gave speeches across the nation. To make their advocacy even less tolerable, many of the socialists and anarchists were immigrants to the United States, further exacerbating a growing anti-immigrant sentiment. To many Americans in 1917, President Wilson was prophetic in his warning two years earlier when in his Annual speech to Congress in 1915 he warned that

> there are some men among us, and many resident abroad who, though born and bred in the United States and calling themselves Americans, have so forgotten themselves and their honor as citizens as to put their passionate sympathy with one or the other side in the great European conflict above their regard for the peace and dignity of the United States. They also preach and practice disloyalty. No laws, I suppose, can reach corruptions of the mind and heart; but I should not speak of others without also speaking of these and expressing the even deeper humiliation and scorn which every self-possessed and thoughtfully patriotic American must feel when he thinks of them and of the discredit they are daily bringing upon us.

The rise of the labor union movement in the late 1800s, labor strikes, the Bolshevik revolution in 1917, and socialist and communist influence in the labor movement all added to the general fear that there were forces in the nation that were designed to destroy the capitalistic, free property, pro-business, Christian social framework of the nation. The American Socialist Party (ASP) was the third largest political party in the country by 1904 and Eugene Debs, the leader of ASP, won a million votes in the 1912 Presidential election. The violence, bombings, and assassinations of European kings and nobles and an American President by anarchist cells and individuals between the middle nineteenth century and the first decade and a half of the twentieth century[6] solidified fears of a worldwide threat to Western democracy that were similar in intensity at the beginning of the American Century as the threat of Islamist terrorism was at the start of the twenty-first century.

The Wilson Administration determined that the nation needed to be unified in its support of the war as well as unified in its opposition to the vocal and organized pacifist, socialist, and anarchist left.

As the war began, government agencies such as the Committee on Public Information (CPI) and citizen groups like the American Protective League (APL) began a wholesale campaign to create fear of German agents, disloyal immigrants, and political subversives as well as to create positive support for the war throughout the nation. These public and private organizations sought out those who opposed the war, those who did not support the war to a satisfactory level, as well as purported German agents for public exposure. The CPI published movies, articles, speeches and pamphlets extolling the virtues of the war, the evil of Imperial Germany and requested popular support of the war through enlistment and the purchasing of war bonds. The work of the CPI achieved its goal and "united most of the public in common cause and common hatred."[7] The Department of Justice was an equal player in the creation of both fear and heightened patriotism in regard to the war by requesting citizens to report suspicious activity. Thomas Gregory, then Attorney General, asked Americans to report directly to the Justice Department suspicious activity and each day "thousands of accusations of disloyalty flooded into the department" and the CPI asked citizens to form associations for this purpose.[8] In addition to the APL, the largest of these citizen groups with two hundred thousand members, other groups including the Knights of Liberty, the National Security League, the American Defense Society, the Boy Spies of America, the Sedition Slammers, and the Terrible Threateners engaged in wiretaps and other illegal surveillance as well as examination of financial and medical records of those they believed to be disloyal.[9] These groups were not above physical violence against those who did not support the war to a satisfactory level. As a cultural and political matter, dissent was not viewed in a favorable light. Dissent was viewed as disloyal, if not outright treasonous, rather than disagreement by the loyal opposition. Such it was in 1798–1800 and such it was in 1917–1918.

Within this atmosphere the judiciary was presented with federal arrests and prosecutions under the Espionage Act of 1917. Attorney General Gregory was by no means weak handed in his prosecution of the Espionage Act. Although Attorney General Gregory thought the Act as passed by Congress in 1917 was weak[10] the Justice Department indicted 2,168 people and convicted 1,055 of them.[11] The federal bench proved not to be a significant hindrance to the act. Lower court judges applied the "bad tendency" theory to support broad interpretation and application of the Espionage Act, setting the stage for the Supreme Court development of the "clear and present danger" doctrine when applying First Amendment protection to political dissent. It was also during this period that the civil liberties movement within the American legal profession was born. It was out of this period that both the first red scare and the American Civil Liberties Union entered the pages of American history.

By the beginning of the twentieth century, the judiciary had not yet fully defined the First Amendment in times of war or crisis. Blackstone's commentary that freedom of the press and speech were not absolute and a seditious and a libelous editor could be punished after an utterance was still the accepted principle in the law. During this early period, the courts accepted the theory that speech in times of war was legitimately more restricted than in times of peace. In the September 1917 prosecution of the leaders of the Industrial Workers of the World (IWW) labor union, U.S. District Judge Kenesaw Landis declared in his sentence of William D. "Big Bill" Haywood, "When the country is at peace, it is a legal right of speech to oppose going to war. . . . But when once war is declared, this right ceases."[12] Prosecutions for violation of the Espionage Act included Socialist party leaders, communists, anarchists, as well as ordinary people. In November 1917 the movie *The Spirit of '76* was seized[13] because it historically depicted the infamous Wyoming massacre by the British and Hessian army during the revolutionary war.[14] Robert Goldstein, the producer of the movie, moved the court to release the film which was in the possession of the District U.S. Marshall. U.S. District Judge Bledsoe held that although "history is history, and fact is fact," the more significant issue is that the country is "engaged in a war in which Great Britain is an ally [and] this is no time . . . for the exploitation of those things that may have the tendency or effect of sowing dissension among our people, and of creating animosity or want of confidence between us and our allies."[15]

The court took great pains in explaining why it mattered that Great Britain not be shown in a historically deficient light. To place an ally in the Great War in such a light "weakens our efforts, weakens the chance of our success, impairs our solidarity, and renders less useful the lives we are giving, to the end that this war may soon be over."[16] But more importantly for the limits of free speech, Judge Bledsoe concluded that "in ordinary times [such a movie] might be clearly permissible . . . [but] in this hour of national emergency [it] may be as clearly treasonable, and therefore properly subject to review and repression. The Constitutional guarantee of 'free speech' carries with it no right to subvert the purposes and destiny of the nation."[17] Clearly believing Goldstein to have made the movie with the objected scenes in order to create excitement in the audience against Great Britain, Judge Bledsoe wrote, "The United States is confronted with what I conceive to be the greatest emergency we have ever been confronted with. . . . [and] as a necessary consequence no man should be permitted, by deliberate act, or even unthinkingly, to do that which will in any way detract from the efforts which the United States is putting forth or to postpone for a single moment the early coming of the day when. . . the righteousness of our cause shall have been demonstrated."[18]

This was not the end of Goldstein's problems for he was later arrested and prosecuted for violation of the Espionage Act.[19] Specifically he was charged with violation of Section 3 of the act. He was convicted and sentenced to ten years. In *Goldstein v. United States* the Ninth Circuit Court of Appeals heard his appeal and he encountered similar views of his movie and the First Amendment that he found with Judge Bledsoe during his criminal trial and in his motion to have his movie released. Dismissing the classical defense of sedition, truth, Circuit Judge Hunt held that the "question of the truth or falseness of the thing done . . . to cause disloyalty of any of the conditions enumerated, is not the essence of the inquiry. [The] purpose of [Section 3 is] to prevent any willful attempt to engender feelings of lack of fidelity to the United States among the military or naval forces."[20] In broadly interpreting the reach of Section 3 Judge Hunt ruled that Goldstein's criminal violation of the act was established by (1) the showing of the movie and (2) the circumstances and timing of the showing. The Court ruled that the "circumstances surrounding the exhibition thereof, the time, the occasions when the public exhibitions are had, [will] tend to show whether the picture . . . be clearly calculated to foment disloyalty or insubordination among the naval or military forces."[21] The Court of Appeals affirmed Judge Bledsoe's determination that Goldstein specifically inserted the Wyoming massacre footage implying rape and the mass murder of children and babies by British soldiers in order to cause a reaction in the audience. This act, the Court of Appeals held, established guilt under Section 3. The Court reasoned that at a time when the United States was at war and allied with British soldiers, to show them in such a light in public was "calculated to arouse antagonism and to raise hatred in the minds of some . . . as a *probable effect* to put obstruction in the way of the necessary co-operation between the allied countries against the enemy, and to undermine an undivided sentiment for the United States and to encourage disloyalty and refusal of duty or insubordination among the military and naval forces."[22]

In *Shaffer v. United States*, the Ninth Circuit Court of Appeals held that under Section 3 of the Espionage Act vocal advocacy of peace is not made criminal. The question of conviction, the Court asserted, under Section 3 is not whether the speech is opinion or established fact (again the rejection of truth as a defense) but "whether the natural and probable tendency and effect of the words quoted therefrom are such as are calculated to produce the result condemned by the statute."[23] Reminiscent of Justice Chase in the sedition cases, Circuit Judge Gilbert wrote, "The hostile attitude of his mind against the prosecution of the war . . . must be presumed to have intended the natural and probable consequences of what he knowingly did."[24] As did Judge Hunt in the *Goldstein* case, Judge Gilbert focused on the inevitable or probable results of the speech: "The service may be obstructed by attacking the justice of the cause for which the war is waged, and by undermining the spirit of loyalty which inspires men to enlist. . . . The greatest inspiration for entering into such service is patriotism, the love of country. To teach that patriotism is murder and the spirit of the devil, and that the war against Germany was wrong and its prosecution a crime, is to weaken patriotism and the purpose to enlist or to render military service in the war."[25] A result "condemned by the statute."

In these and other cases[26] the lower federal courts were almost uniform and unanimous in the use of the "bad tendency" test. With judicial focus on the time and place of the utterance and the unlawful probable result of the speech, the courts read into Section 3 a strict liability not intended by Congress.[27] Guilt was established not by specific criminal intent or action to cause insubordination or disloyalty in the military but by the "probable" result of such an event based on the speech or writing itself. As Justice Chase and other members of the Federalist federal bench did in the days of the Sedition Act of 1798, the courts bypassed the Constitutional issues raised by punishing speech itself and applied the Espionage Act to read out a key protection of free speech, truth, and to read into the statute a strict liability of presumed evil intent from the probable bad result of the speech or the nature of the speech.

The majority of the federal bench informed juries that it was for them to determine if in fact the speech violated Section 3 under the totality of the circumstances of the speech and the potential of that speech resulting in violation of the act. They "repeatedly announced the basic rule that one is presumed to intend the natural and usual consequences of his acts and that all relevant surrounding circumstances should be taken into account."[28] With such a jury instruction, almost all of the prosecutions led to guilty verdicts.[29] There were a few courts that took seriously considerations of the fairness of trials in times of war and the threat of jury instructions that all but guaranteed conviction based on the circumstances and character of the charge.[30] In *Wolf v. United States* Judge Stone of the Court of Appeals observed:

> The greatest danger to justice from a jury is through a confusion of the real issues in the case. This is peculiarly true when the times or circumstances or character of crime are such as to make jurymen lose sight of the questions of fact actually involved. It is natural, in times of war, when patriotic sentiment is high, that it is particularly difficult to secure a fair trial for men accused of crimes connected with the war. At such times the task of the court becomes especially difficult and requires great care to prevent miscarriages of justice. These are practical considerations, which must be constantly borne in mind, or the verdicts of juries in such cases will mistakenly become expressions of their hatred for unpatriotic acts in general, instead of their careful judgment on the facts shown by the evidence in the particular case. Patriotism must not become, even innocently, a cloak for injustice. The right of an accused in the courts of this nation to a fair trial must not vary with the character of the crime. The variation permitted is in the punishment, but that comes only *after* a fair trial.[31]

There was a small minority of judges on the federal bench that did not apply the "bad tendency" test to asserted violations of the Espionage Act and gave Section 3 a more restrictive interpretation and application.[32] In *United States v. Hall*,[33] Judge George Bourquin directed a verdict of acquittal for Ves Hall who was accused of saying in public that Germany would whip the United States and that the war was being fought for the Wall Street rich.[34] Judge Bourquin, as did the courts discussed above, based his decision on the statute itself rather than on an open discussion of the protections of the First Amendment for those opposing the war. Judge Bourquin, on the other hand, differed from some of his fellow judges on the meaning of Section 3. The Espionage Act, according to the judge, "is not intended to suppress criticism or denunciation, truth or slander, oratory or gossip, argument or loose talk, but only facts, willfully put forward as true, and broadly, with the specific intent to interfere with army or navy operations."[35] Judge Bourquin wrote that Hall's statements (which he noted Hall denied making) that the United States would lose to Germany, that the President was the tool of Wall Street, that he was a crook, that the United States entered the war by British dictation, and Germany had a right to attack U.S. ships and kill Americans without warning were made sixty miles away from the train station where men departed for military service and hundreds of miles away from military personnel. The point being the "defendant's beliefs, opinions, and hopes are not within the statute [and] the impossibility of far-distant military and naval forces hearing or being affected by the slanders, and, all else, render the inference [of guilt of violating Section 3] unjustified, absurd, and without support in the evidence."[36] More importantly to the point of conviction, the inference that his statements interfered with the military or supported insubordination fail because "interference with the operation or success of the military or naval forces is not the natural and ordinary consequences of said slanders, but [a] breach of the peace [charge] and a broken head for the slanderer are."[37]

Judge Bourquin throughout his opinion rejected the proposition that the probable bad result theory met the requirement for conviction under Section 3. "Nor does the evidence sustain the charge of 'willfully obstructing the recruitment or enlistment service of the Unites States. . . .' To sustain the charge, actual obstruction and injury must be proven, not mere attempts to obstruct. The Espionage Act does not create the crime of attempting to obstruct, but only the crime of actual obstruction, and when causing injury to the service."[38] Judge Bourquin concluded that Congress had not made "disloyal utterances, nor any slander or libel of the President or any other officer of the United States" illegal and that "since the sedition law had its share in the overthrow of the Federalists and in the elevation of Jefferson to the Presidency and his party to power, Congress has not ventured to denounce as crimes slanders and libels of government and its officers."[39]

Judge Bourquin's observation that Congress did not, and his implication, that it would not make the same mistake as the Federalists in making slander of the U.S. government a crime, was half right. Congress had not made it illegal to slander the government or to advocate against the war, an oversight it would remedy four months later.

A year before the *Hall* case Judge Learned Hand of the Southern District Court of New York issued an injunction against the Postmaster General of New York for not delivering the mail from a publishing company that he determined produced materials that violated the Espionage Act of 1917.[40] *Masses Publishing Co. v. Patten* involved the determination of the Postmaster that the August issue of the *Masses* was nonmailable[41] because four poems and four items of text violated the "false statements with intent to interfere with the operations or success of the military" clause and that the passages provide "counsel and advises resistance to existing law, especially to the draft."[42] As with the approach by Judge Bourquin a year later, Judge Hand did not assess the power of Congress to control political speech—for that matter he specifically maintained that the case did not raise issues of First Amendment protections or its subjugation to the war powers of Congress. Judge Hand rather interpreted Section 3 and wrote that the poems and text found nonmailable by the Postmaster were political opinion, not false statements. He assumed that even if Congress could use its war powers to restrict adverse "political agitation . . . I am confident that by [the] language [of Section 3] Congress had no such revolutionary purpose in view."[43]

Judge Hand did however, address the theory that "the general tenor and animus of the paper as a whole were subversive to authority and [thus] seditious in effect" under Section 3.[44] "The tradition" the Judge wrote, "of English-speaking freedoms [requires] that the state point with exactness to just that conduct which violates the law. It is difficult and often impossible to meet the charge that one's general ethos is treasonable; such a latitude . . . contradicts the normal assumption that law shall be embodied in general propositions capable of some measure of definition."[45] Again, while not addressing the power of Congress "to establish a personal censorship of the press under the war power," Judge Hand wrote, "I am quite satisfied that it has not as yet chosen to create one."[46] Judge Hand held that for the Postmaster to deem the August issue of the *Masses* nonmailable the text must be more than political opinion. Judge Hand explained that the conclusion that the cartoon and the text clearly attacked the virtues of the war and such advocacy may have an effect on military "is beside the question [of] whether such an attack is a willfully false statement." Judge Hand asserted the distinction between opinion and fact. Opinions and statements on the virtue and justness of America entering the war against Germany are political judgments and opinions and by definition, the Judge wrote, political opinions are not open to objective analysis of truth and political opinions "are all certainly believed to be true by the utterer."[47] For statements to be liable for punishment within Section 3 they must be false and known to be false to the utterer.

As to the provision to "willfully cause or attempt to cause insubordination, disloyalty, mutiny, refusal of duty, in the military or naval forces" Judge Hand wrote that to interpret the word 'cause' to include speech "to arouse discontent and disaffection among the people . . . and with the draft" would "involve necessarily as a consequence the suppression of all hostile criticism, and of all opinion except what encouraged and supported the existing policies, or which fell within the range of temperate argument."[48] To this point of Congressional power Judge Hand stated, "The power to repress such opinion may rest in Congress in the throes of a struggle for the very existence of the state [but] only the clearest expression of such a power justifies the conclusion that it was intended" under Section 3.[49]

The Government argued that the cartoons and text in the *Masses* provided actual counsel and advised resistance to the draft. Judge Hand rejected the argument explaining that "to assimilate agitation . . . with direct incitement to violent resistance, is to disregard the tolerance of all methods of political agitation which in normal times is a safeguard of free government. . . . If one stops short of urging upon others that it is their duty or their interest to resist that law, it seems to me one should not be held to have attempted to cause its violation."[50] Judge Hand reasoned that if that is not the test, then under Section 3 "every political agitation which can be shown to be apt to create a seditious temper is illegal."[51] The text and cartoons, Judge Hand observed, although showing contempt for the war, aversion to the draft, admiration for those who opposed the draft on principle, did not rise to the level of implication, much less outright advocacy, that it is the reader's duty to oppose the draft. Thus it "would be too strong a doctrine to say that any who openly admire their fortitude or even approved their conduct was willfully obstructing the draft."[52]

Since the power of the Postmaster was premised on his power to deem nonmailable any material that violated Section 3 and having held that the text and cartoons in the August *Masses* were political opinion and not false statements and they did not openly advocate willful disloyalty and avoidance of the draft, the publishers were entitled to an injunction against the Postmaster's determination not to deliver the publication.

Although Judge Hand and Bourquin stood against the tide of judicial enforcement of the Espionage Act, their decisions should not be romanticized as bulwarks against a pro-war, politically captured judiciary as some have asserted.[53] Both judges acted with proper, but not extraordinary, judicial temperament. Neither compared the Espionage Act to the First Amendment head on and determined that the act itself violated the principles of free speech. Nor did they write decisions bravely protecting the rights of the minority against a war-fevered majority. Nor should they have. They simply applied better and more reasonable interpretation of Section 3 than other members of the bench. They both asserted simply that speech, especially political speech, cannot be made criminal based on what *could* theoretically happen as a result of making the utterance. It was not enough that a speech could theoretically result in avoidance of the draft or insubordination or reduce fidelity to an ally. As Judge Hand wrote, for an utterance or printed word to be a criminal violation of Section 3 there must be direct advocacy to specifically break the law and the statements made must be false with the utterer knowing they are false. As Judge Bourquin concluded, Section 3 was not intended to restrict and outlaw political discourse and debate but to prevent false statements and direct interference with the operations of the military. Both agreed that Congress did not make advocacy against the war itself a criminal offense.

Although the "Bad Tendency" doctrine had prevailed with the majority of the federal bench, the rulings by Judges Bourquin and Hand that the Espionage Act did not directly criminalize speech against the war itself or the draft, was seen by many as something to be addressed. In the spring of 1918 Attorney General Gregory submitted to Congress amendments to make such speech covered by the Act. By this time the nation was fully engulfed by the need for unity and loyalty in regard to the war and had little sympathy for immigrant socialists, pacifists and anarchists advocating disruption to the war effort. The Senate took it upon itself to change Attorney General Gregory's amendments and produced the Sedition Act of 1918. The Senate amended Section 3 of the Espionage Act, to include the criminalization of willfully uttering or printing any disloyal, or abusive language about the American form of government or to promote the cause of its enemies, including the advocacy of curtailment of production of anything essential to the prosecution of the war. After some cantankerous as well as some serious debate on the value of and the limits on free speech,[54] the Senate and House passed the Sedition Act with clear majorities and on May 16, 1918, President Wilson signed it into law.

With the passage of the Sedition Act, the Supreme Court was presented with a series of cases that formed the first set of significant decisions on the First Amendment since its adoption in 1791. Leading the advocacy on behalf of pacifists, conscientious objectors, opponents to the war and later defendants charged under the amended Espionage Act were a cadre of lawyers cooperating with the newly formed Civil Liberties Bureau (opened on July 2, 1917, just two weeks after the passage of the Espionage Act), the forerunner of the National Civil Liberties Bureau which in 1920 became the American Civil Liberties Union.[55]

The first case, *Schenck v. United States*,[56] involved the activities of Charles Schenck, the General Secretary of the Socialist Party who implemented a resolution of the Executive Committee on August 13, 1917, that fifteen thousand leaflets should be mailed to men who were on the draft eligibility lists. Justice Oliver Wendell Holmes described the leaflets as follows:

> The document in question upon its first printed side recited the first section of the Thirteenth Amendment, said that the idea embodied in it was violated by the conscription act and that a conscript is little better than a convict. In impassioned language it intimated that conscription was despotism in its worst form and a monstrous wrong against humanity in the interest of Wall Street's chosen few. It said, "Do not submit to intimidation," . . . The other and later printed side . . . stated reasons for alleging that any one violated the Constitution when he refused to recognize "your right to assert your opposition to the draft," and went on, "If you do not assert and support your rights, you are helping to deny or disparage rights which it is the solemn duty of all citizens and residents of the United States to retain." It described the arguments on the other side as coming from cunning politicians and a mercenary capitalist press, and even silent consent to the conscription law as helping to support an infamous conspiracy. It denied the power to send our citizens away to foreign shores to shoot up the people of other lands, and added that words could not express the condemnation such cold-blooded ruthlessness deserves. . . . "You must do your share to maintain, support and uphold the rights of the people of this country."[57]

The Court concluded that "the document would not have been sent unless it had been intended to have some effect, and we do not see what effect it could be expected to have upon persons subject to the draft except to influence them to obstruct the carrying of it out."[58] Schenck did not dispute that the pamphlet violated the Espionage Act prohibiting the publishing of materials in order to obstruct the draft. Rather his defense was that the pamphlet was protected by the First Amendment right to free speech. The *Schenck* case is considered the first case in which the right to free speech was directly asserted to protect a political viewpoint asserted by the defendant against government action. Previous cases, as we have discussed, focused on the applicability of the statute, not its facial unconstitutionality as a defense in a criminal trial.

The Supreme Court, affirming the majority views of the lower courts as exampled by Judges Landis, Bledsoe, Hunt and Gilbert, observed that "in many places and in ordinary times the defendants in saying all that was said in the circular would have been within their Constitutional rights. But the character of every act depends upon the circumstances in which it is done. . . . When a nation is at war many things that might be said in time of peace are such a hindrance to its effort that their utterance will not be endured so long as men fight and no Court could regard them as protected by any Constitutional right."[59] Justice Holmes proposed that the line between free speech and criminal avocation "depends upon the circumstances in which it is done" and proceeded to write one of the most famous statements in Supreme Court jurisprudence:

> The most stringent protection of free speech would not protect a man in falsely shouting fire in a theatre and causing a panic. It does not even protect a man from an injunction against uttering words that may have all the effect of force. *The question in every case is whether the words used are used in such circumstances and are of such a nature as to create a clear and present danger that they will bring about the substantive evils that Congress has a right to prevent.* It is a question of proximity and degree. . . . If the act, (speaking, or circulating a paper,) its tendency and the intent with which it is done are the same, we perceive no ground for saying that success alone warrants making the act a crime.[60]

Judges Bourquin and Hand, in the *Hall* and *Masses* cases, proposed that heated and boisterous advocacy against the draft and the war does not equate with direct advocacy of violation of compliance with the draft. The Court in *Schenck* endorsed the views of Judges Bledsoe, Hunt and Gilbert expressed in the *Spirit of 76*, *Goldstein*, and *Shaffer* cases that political speech and advocacy, in times of war that has the probable result or "bad tendency" to interfere with the successful operation of national interests, such as the draft and recruitment, creates the violation of Section 3. Justice Holmes held that the First Amendment does not protect words that present a "clear and present danger" of bringing about that which Congress has a right to prohibit, in this case interference with the draft. Although the Court agreed with Judge Hand that "the natural and ordinary consequences" of the speech must be the evil Congress sought to prevent, Justice Holmes, speaking for the Court, accepted the proposition that the line between protected speech and criminal advocacy is drawn at what could happen as a result of speech rather than specific intent to cause the evil result. Criminal intent was determined by the tendency of the speech to result in the evil, not that the evil was intended by the speech.

On March 10, 1919, seven days after its issuance of the *Schenk* decision, Justice Holmes in *Frohwerk v. U.S.*[61] rejected the absolutist theory of free speech under the First Amendment, writing that "we think it necessary to add to what has been said in *Schenck v. United States*, only that the First Amendment while prohibiting legislation against free speech as such cannot have been, and obviously was not, intended to give immunity for every possible use of language."[62] Justice Holmes had said as much in at least one case predating the war and the advocacy of those opposing the war. In 1915 the Justice upheld the conviction of a pamphleteer who advocated resistance to a state law against public nudity in *Fox v. Washington*.[63] Fox was arrested and convicted for violation of a Washington law that made it unlawful to willfully publish a paper "advocating, encouraging or inciting, or having a tendency to encourage or incite the commission of any crime . . . or which shall tend to encourage or advocate disrespect for law."[64] To the challenge that the law was unconstitutionally vague and in violation of the First Amendment, Justice Holmes wrote, "In this present case the disrespect for law that was encouraged was disregard of it—an overt breach and technically criminal act. It would be in accord with the usages of English to interpret disrespect as manifested disrespect, as active disregard going beyond the line drawn by the law."[65] In 1897 the Supreme Court came to a similar conclusion when it held that "the freedom of speech and of the press (article 1) does not permit the publication of libels, blasphemous or indecent articles, or other publications injurious to public morals or private reputation."[66]

Frohwerk v. U.S. involved the indictment and conviction of Jacob Frohwerk and co-defendant Carl Gleeser for conspiracy to violate Section 3 by the preparation and publication of the socialist newspaper the *Missouri Staats Zeitung* in 1917. The various articles in the newspaper mirrored the statements in the *Schenk* leaflet: that the war was a rich man's war fought by poor men's sons, that the draft was a criminal act, and those who opposed it were committing a lesser sin than those who instituted it. The case involved various defenses including attacks on the sufficiency of the evidence of a conspiracy and legal sufficiency of the indictment. Justice Holmes affirmed the holding of *Schenk* and echoed the "bad tendency" test, observing that "on that record it is impossible to say that it might not have been found that the circulation of the paper was in quarters where a little breath would be enough to kindle a flame and that the fact was known and relied upon by those who sent the paper out. Small compensation would not exonerate the defendant if it were found that he expected the result, even if pay were his chief desire."[67]

On the same day Justice Holmes released the *Frohwerk* decision, he also published *Debs v. United States.*[68] Eugene Debs was arrested and convicted for violation of the Espionage Act as amended by the Sedition Act of 1918 for a speech he gave on June 16, 1918, in Canton Ohio. The speech was a basic dissertation on the virtues of socialism and the inevitable fall of capitalism. His speech also attacked the war and the draft with the standard complaints. Justice Holmes wrote, the "main theme of the speech was Socialism, its growth, and a prophecy of its ultimate success. With that we have nothing to do, but if a part or the manifest intent of the more general utterances was to encourage those present to obstruct the recruiting service and if in passages such encouragement was directly given, the immunity of the general theme may not be enough to protect the speech."[69] After affirming his conviction on First Amendment and sufficiency of the evidence grounds, citing *Schenck* and *Frohwerk*, Justice Holmes addressed the Socialists' *Anti-War Proclamation and Program*, which Debs endorsed in his speech.

The *Anti-War Proclamation and Program* "alleged that the war of the United States against Germany could not 'be justified even on the plea that it is a war in defense of American rights or American 'honor.' It said: 'We brand the declaration of war by our Government as a crime against the people of the United States and against the nations of the world. In all modern history there has been no war more unjustifiable than the war in which we are about to engage.'"[70] Debs, endorsing the proclamation, explained that "first recommendation was, 'continuous, active, and public opposition to the war, through demonstrations, mass petitions, and all other means within our power.'" Concurring with the holdings in the *Spirit of '76, Goldstein* and *Shaffer* cases, Justice Holmes observed:

> Evidence that the defendant accepted this view and this declaration of his duties at the time that he made his speech is evidence that *if in that speech he used words tending to obstruct the recruiting service he meant that they should have that effect.* The principle is too well established and too manifestly good sense to need citation of the books. We should add that the jury were most carefully instructed that they could not find the defendant guilty for advocacy of any of his opinions unless the words used had as their natural tendency and reasonably probable effect to obstruct the recruiting service, &c., and unless the defendant had the specific intent to do so in his mind.[71]

Reverting back to the "bad tendency" theory, Justice Holmes wrote that the "principle is too well established and too manifestly good sense to need citation of the books" that if the defendant spoke with words "tending to obstruct the draft" such speech was not protected by the First Amendment. Here is where Justice Holmes was in error because conviction under the Espionage Act required that the speaker have the "specific intent" to achieve the criminal result, not simply that a criminal result could occur resulting from the speech. But Justice Holmes affirmed the prevailing view of the law that the speaker is presumed to have that intent by the mere utterance of the speech and its probable "bad tendency" to create the unlawful result.

On November 10, 1919, the unanimity of the Court on the Espionage Act was lost in *Abrams v. U.S.*[72] Jacob Abrams was arrested and convicted for conspiracy to violate the Sedition Act, specifically unlawfully publishing abusive language about the form of the United States government, language to bring the United States government into contempt and disrepute, inciting to provoke interference with the United States during its war with Germany, and urging curtailment of production of materials necessary to the war effort. The defendants admitted during the trial that they were anarchists and socialists who were opposed to the American form of government and had written and distributed five thousand copies of two leaflets on August 22, 1918, in New York City which contained attacks on the American system of government, attacked the President as a coward, advocated the loss of the United States so as to aid the Russian revolution as well as other anarchist and socialist political desires to create a socialist world if not an anarchist world without government at all.

Justice Clark, for the majority, summarized the intent and the specific result of the leaflets drafted and published by the defendants as follows:

> It will not do to say, as is now argued, that the only intent of these defendants was to prevent injury to the Russian cause. Men must be held to have intended, and to be accountable for, the effects which their acts were likely to produce. Even if their primary purpose and intent was to aid the cause of the Russian Revolution, the plan of action which they adopted necessarily involved, before it could be realized, defeat of the war program of the United States, for the obvious effect of this appeal, if it should become effective, as they hoped it might, would be to persuade persons of character such as those whom they regarded themselves as addressing, not to aid government loans and not to work in ammunition factories, where their work would produce 'bullets, bayonets, cannon' and other munitions of war, the use of which would cause the 'murder' of Germans and Russians.
>
> Again, the spirit becomes more bitter as it proceeds to declare that— "America and her Allies have betrayed [the Workers]. Their robberish aims are clear to all men. The destruction of the Russian Revolution, that is the politics of the march to Russia. "Workers, our reply to the barbaric intervention has to be a general strike! An open challenge only will let the government know that not only the Russian Worker fights for freedom, but also here in America lives the spirit of Revolution."
>
> This is not an attempt to bring about a change of administration by candid discussion, for no matter what may have incited the outbreak on the part of the defendant anarchists, the manifest purpose of such a publication was to create an attempt to defeat the war plans of the government of the United States, by bringing upon the country the paralysis of a general strike, thereby arresting the production of all munitions and other things essential to the conduct of the war.[73]

Justice Clark concluded that "the interpretation we have put upon these articles, circulated in the greatest port of our land, from which great numbers of soldiers were at the time taking ship daily, and in which great quantities of war supplies of every kind were at the time being manufactured for transportation overseas, is not only the fair interpretation of them, but that it is the meaning which their authors consciously intended."[74]

Clearly the Court found the advocacy of the virtues of the Russian revolution and the advocacy of nationwide strikes by the workers to obstruct the production of war materials and the intent of the advocacy of the strike for the curtailment of success of the United States in the war with Germany sufficient for conviction. But the case itself did not add to the development of the meaning of the First Amendment in time of war because it was a clear application of the principles of *Schenck* and *Frohwerk*. The historical significance of *Abrams* is the dissent and the purported change of heart of Justices Holmes and Brandeis on the First Amendment.

In his dissent, Justice Holmes affirmed his opinions in *Schenck, Frohwerk,* and *Debs,* writing,

> The United States Constitutionally may punish speech that produces or is intended to produce a clear and imminent danger that it will bring about forthwith certain substantive evils that the United States Constitutionally may seek to prevent. The power undoubtedly is greater in time of war than in time of peace because war opens dangers that do not exist at other times. But as against dangers peculiar to war, as against others, the principle of the right to free speech is always the same. *It is only the present danger of immediate evil or an intent to bring it about that warrants Congress in setting a limit to the expression of opinion where private rights are not concerned.*[75]

Justice Holmes asserted that the First Amendment protection of free speech requires the showing of a close time and space link between the speech and the danger of achieving that harm as well as a "specific intent" to cause the illegal result. He asserted that "nobody can suppose that the surreptitious publishing of a silly leaflet by an unknown man, without more, would present any *immediate danger* that its opinions would hinder the success of the government arms or have any appreciable tendency to do so."[76] Justice Holmes reemphasized the "proximity and degree" aspects of his "clear and present danger" test in *Schenck* by defining the "proximity and degree" as an "immediate danger" of occurrence of the unlawful result Congress had a right to prevent and make unlawful. His observation that the First Amendment does not protect a man "falsely shouting fire in a theatre and causing a panic" takes on more meaning with his dissent in *Abrams* because in *Schenck* he says that the "panic" is the "immediate" result when the false statement of "fire" is made due to the "circumstances" surrounding the utterances. According to Holmes "the surreptitious publishing of a silly leaflet by an unknown man" such as Abrams did not create an "imminent danger" of mutiny and draft dodging under the circumstances of the publication of the leaflets.

But the dissent of Justice Holmes is mostly remembered for his conclusions on the value of open debate and limits of the utility of preventing speech of those who are on the fringe of political discourse. Again writing one of the most famous passages of Supreme Court jurisprudence, Justice Holmes spoke of the value of open speech in a democracy. Justice Holmes wrote,

> Persecution for the expression of opinions seems to me perfectly logical. If you have no doubt of your premises or your power and want a certain result with all your heart you naturally express your wishes in law and sweep away all opposition. . . . But when men have realized that time has upset many fighting

faiths, they may come to believe even more than they believe the very foundations of their own conduct that *the ultimate good desired is better reached by free trade in ideas—that the best test of truth is the power of the thought to get itself accepted in the competition of the market.* . . . That at any rate is the theory of our Constitution. . . . I think that we should be eternally vigilant against attempts to check the expression of opinions that we loathe and believe to be fraught with death, unless they so *imminently threaten immediate interference with the lawful and pressing purposes of the law* that an immediate check is required to save the country. I wholly disagree with the argument of the Government that the First Amendment left the common law as to seditious libel in force. History seems to me against the notion. I had conceived that the United States through many years had shown its repentance for the Sedition Act of 1798. . . . *Only the emergency that makes it immediately dangerous to leave the correction of evil counsels to time* warrants making any exception to the sweeping command, 'Congress shall make no law abridging the freedom of speech.' . . . I regret that I cannot put into more impressive words my belief that in their conviction upon this indictment the defendants were deprived of their rights under the Constitution of the United States.[77]

One of the more significant aspects of the *Abrams* case is that the Supreme Court was in total agreement with the basic assertion that Congress could place more constraints on political speech in times of war and national crisis than in times of peace. The nature and circumstances of the national emergency and war, alone, enabled Congress, under its war powers, to act in ways that would be unconstitutional in times of peace. Although the boundaries and contours of this principle would be adjusted by history, law and by the limitations of politics, the principle itself has remained accepted ever since. The debate in the lower courts pre-*Schenck* and in the Supreme Court post-*Abrams* (some of which we will discuss in later chapters) involved the means and ends selected in regard to the criminalization of politically motivated speech. The fact that Congress could criminalize such speech was taken by the Courts as a given.

But the advent of World War I did not only involve Congressional power over seditious speech or advocates of disloyalty during the war. The Supreme Court also addressed the powers of Congress to organize private industry and society in order to wage and successfully win the war. The power of Congress to act in domestic areas of American life in times of crisis is where we turn next.

CONGRESS AND ITS WAR POWER

On March 19, 1917, the Court, in *Wilson v. New*[78] addressed the power of Congress to "prevent the interruption of interstate commerce, to exert its will to supply the absence of a wage scale resulting from the disagreement as to wages between the employers and employees, and to make its will on that subject controlling for the limited period provided for."[79] The railroad workers and owners of the railroads were in dispute as to the number of hours in a work day and the wage for a work day. The union threatened a nationwide strike if its demands for an eight-hour work day were not accepted. To stave off a strike President Wilson asked Congress for powers to deal with the railroad strike and to establish a commission to deal with labor disputes. Congress obliged and passed the Adamson Act of 1916. The owners of the railroads claimed that the power of Congress to regulate interstate commerce did not give it the power to regulate labor disputes and set minimum wage standards.

Chief Justice Edward White wrote for the Court that Congress has the power to act when an emergency is such that imminent danger to the public welfare is at risk due to the failure of the parties to meet a national need, that is, to keep the railway system open and keep the transportation of food and goods across the nation free from disruption. As the Court did with the speech cases, the Court focused on the imminent result of the failure of the parties to agree as justification for Congress to act. The Court affirmed that Congress has the power to act preemptively to prevent the manifestation of an imminent threat from actualizing. The Court concluded that "although an emergency may not call into life a power which has never lived, nevertheless the emergency may afford a reason for the exertion of a living power already enjoyed. If acts which, if done, would interrupt, if not destroy, interstate commerce, may be by anticipation legislatively prevented, by the same token the power to regulate may be exercised to guard against the cessation of interstate commerce, threatened by a failure of employers and employees to agree as to the standard of wages, such standard being an essential prerequisite to the uninterrupted flow of interstate commerce."[80]

During the war period the Supreme Court held that the Selective Service Act of 1917, which instated the draft, was Constitutional because the power to raise an army necessarily includes the power to compel service when needed.[81] Additionally, the Court would not second guess Congressional determinations of security determinations. In *Hamilton v. Kentucky Distilleries*,[82] with no independent determination, the Court accepted that Congress, under its war powers, could govern the production of distilled spirits under the theory that the prohibition of liquors increases war efficiency by preventing the consumption of liquor by members of military forces. In *Ruppert v. Caffey*[83] the Court held that Congress, under its war powers, could prevent the use of certain foods for the production of spirits as a measure to maintain and protect the food supply during the war. The Court, affirming *Hamilton*, upheld Congressional inherent powers to implement its expressed powers. The Court, exercising its jurisprudence of judicial deference to the political branches when acting within their Constitutional authority, concluded in *Caffey* that "whether it be for purposes of national defense [or for some other purpose] Congress has the power 'to make all laws which shall be necessary and proper for carrying into execution' the duty so reposed in the federal government. While this is a government of enumerated powers, it has full attributes of sovereignty within the limits of those powers. . . . For the power conferred by Clause 18 of Section 8 'to make all laws which shall be necessary and proper for carrying into execution' powers specifically enumerated is also an express power. Since Congress has power to increase war efficiency by prohibiting the liquor traffic, no reason appears why it should be denied the power to make its prohibition effective."[84]

With similar logic the Court affirmed Congressional power in the establishment of railroad rates,[85] confiscation of property by those doing business with the enemy[86] and establishment of rent control in Washington, D.C.[87] In *Block v. Hirsh*, the Court, in upholding a rent control statute for housing in Washington, D.C. wrote, "Assuming that the end in view otherwise justified the means adopted by Congress, we have no concern of course with the question whether those means were the wisest, whether they may not cost more than they come to, or will effect the result desired. It is enough that we are not warranted in saying that legislation that has been resorted to for the same purpose all over the world, is futile or has no reasonable relation to the relief sought."[88] The Court, applying the rational basis test, concluded that the rent control was a rational act in the face of a legitimate governmental need, that is, preventing renters from taking advantage of the large influx of people moving into Washington, D.C. to serve the national government as a result of the war. According to the Court, the rent control measure designed by Congress had a "limit in time" and was designed "to tide over a passing trouble" and Congress "well may justify a law that could not be upheld as a permanent change. Machinery is provided to secure to the landlord a reasonable rent. It may be assumed that the interpretation of 'reasonable' will deprive him in part at least of the power of profiting by the sudden influx of people of Washington caused by the needs of Government and the war."[89] But the loss of such profits, the Court reasoned, is a small thing considered against the price paid by the American soldiers in Europe for the successful completion of the war.

During the war to end all wars, the Court began to develop the principle of deference to Congress in times of war and national crisis. During this period the Court did not restrict the means selected by Congress to successfully implement the war effort against Germany. The Court not only refused to independently assess the means selected to achieve the ends, the Court interpreted Congressional statutes to provide even broader use of government power to achieve those ends than Congress had intended. The Court, as did the country in 1918–1919, saw the successful prosecution of the war as paramount and the need for implementation of laws to achieve that success justified laws that in times of peace would not be Constitutional.

THE RED SCARE

The United States, like all nations, tend to react with social restriction and suspicion of political minority groups in times of national distress due to war or uncontrolled social integration. During World War I, most of those who opposed the war were "political" immigrants—socialists, pacifists, communists, and anarchists—as well as geographic immigrants—Germans and Eastern Europeans. Their views and presence were perceived as "un-American" at best and threatening to the social order at worst. They were seen by the establishment as threats to free business and the American way of doing things. The red scare simply carried the negative fears and backlash towards these political groups resulting from the need to win the war to the need to protect the American way of life interrupted by the needs of war. This coupled with the economic recession of 1918, the return of young men from the war and their inability to find work, the deregulation of industry, the general uncertainty of America's place in the world after its rejection of the League of Nations, and the ascendancy of the isolationist approach to foreign policy, a policy that remained predominant in both academic and political circles until December 7, 1941—all fostered an environment that sought to find and remove all those who opposed the "normal" order of things.

The shot heard around the world that started the red scare occurred on May 1, 1919, when the *New York Times* and other newspapers published articles disclosing a bomb plot in which thirty-six bombs were mailed to prominent social and political leaders, with the authorities blaming the plot on the International Workers of the World (IWW) labor union.[90] The country erupted in fear and demanded that the anarchists, socialists and others who sought to destroy the American way of life be sought out and destroyed. As one popular journal demanded, "Every true lover of God and his country should hit with an axe whenever and wherever appears this evil head of anarchy."[91] In addition to the May Day Bombs, newspapers were filled with stories of labor riots in major U.S. cities and many "citizens thought it more than accidental that such violent disturbances should coincide with the bombing attempts and on International Labor Day."[92] Then on June 2, 1919, nine bombs actually exploded at the homes of prominent American political leaders including the home of Attorney General Mitchell Palmer. To add to the growing fears of Americans there was the memory of anarchists Leon Czolgosz, a protégé of the anarchist leader Emma Goldman, who assassinated President McKinley in 1901, the arrest of Pietro Pierre on February 12, 1919, on charges of conspiracy to assassinate President Wilson and the January 15, 1918, arrest of members of the IWW for the bombing of the home of the Governor of California.[93] The trial and conviction of the top leadership of the IWW in 1917 was not long lost on the minds of Americans who considered the IWW as the leading communist organization in the nation.[94]

After the May bombing plot Attorney General Palmer created the General Intelligence Division (GID) within the Justice Department in August 1919 and placed J. Edgar Hoover as its chief with the objective of gathering intelligence on subversive organizations within the United States. Hoover coordinated Justice Department subversive investigations and worked closely with various intelligence and investigative agencies including the Justice Department Bureau of Investigation (BI) (created by Attorney General Charles Bonaparte in July 1908), of which Hoover would be named director in May 1924, which became the FBI in 1935.[95] On November 7, 1919, Attorney General Palmer initiated the first of two national raids (the second occurred in January 1920) by federal and local law enforcement on IWW offices and immigrant clubs, meeting houses, and private residences in search of illegal aliens, anarchists, socialists, communists as well as communist and socialist papers, articles and membership lists. Attorney General Palmer ordered the BI to work with Department of Labor immigration hearing officers to secure evidence of membership with the Communist Party which the government asserted advocated the violent overthrow of the United States. Proof of membership in an organization with such objectives authorized the deportation of such members under the Alien Deportation Act of 1918. The raid selected eleven cities and resulted in the arrest of seven hundred and fifty people, resulting in the deportation of two hundred and forty-nine to Russia on the Army transport *Buford* on December 21, 1919.[96] Those arrested and deported included the famous anarchists Emma Goldman and Alex Berkman as well as the leaders of the IWW and Russian labor and social clubs.

Although the raids were initially well approved of by the public, by May 1920 the red scare had run its course. By the early spring of 1920 a political backlash had occurred against the tactics of the Justice Department. Part of the backlash occurred due to the publication of national reports by politically respectable academics, scholars, former government officials and agents condemning the government actions, like the National Popular Government League and its report, *To the American People: Report on the Illegal Activities of the United States Department of Justice* (May 1920) and the publication of the Commission on the Church and Social Service, Federal Council of the Churches of Christ in America report, *The Deportation Cases of 1919–1920* (1921). Attorney General Palmer was finally discredited by Assistant Secretary of Labor Louis Post who overrode his order to deport more than two thousand aliens after the second raid in January 1920 along with the nonmaterializing of Palmer's prediction of additional anarchist bombings on the second anniversary of the May Day Bombings along with Congressional rejection of his proposed peacetime sedition act.[97] In addition to these factors there was another factor that led to the end of the red scare—judicial blowback to the extreme actions of Palmer and the BI.

In *Ex parte Jackson*[98] Judge George Bourquin, the same judge who rejected the application of the bad tendency doctrine to the espionage act, heard the habeas case of John Jackson who had been arrested in the first Palmer raids (November 1919) and it was through his habeas action that details were revealed on how Justice Department BI agents conducted raids on IWW and other Russian organizations and how Labor Department immigration inspectors conducted deportation hearings.

John Jackson was the assistant secretary of the Butte union of the IWW and was found to be deportable under the Alien Deportation Act of 1918. Sections 1 and 2 of the Alien Deportation Act authorized the Department of Labor to arrest and deport

> aliens who are anarchists; aliens who believe in or advocate the overthrow by force or violence of the Government of the United States or of all forms of law; aliens who disbelieve in or are opposed to all organized government; aliens who advocate or teach the assassination of public officials; aliens who advocate or teach the unlawful destruction of property; aliens who are members of or affiliated with any organization that entertains a belief in, teaches, or advocates the overthrow by force or violence of the Government of the United States or of all forms of law, or that entertains or teaches [the same].

Jackson was arrested and was found to have been in possession of and sold pamphlets that advocated the destruction of private property during a raid conducted by federal BI agents, Army personnel and local police officers along with agents of the Butte, Montana, mining industry. Judge Bourquin ruled that the raids were conducted without warrants and with excessive violence on the level of riot and unnecessary assault. He further held that the process engaged by the immigration inspector violated due process by refusing to allow Jackson to cross-examine government witnesses of his alleged support and advocacy of destruction of private property and the refusal of the hearing officer to permit him to access an attorney during questioning. After finding that the procedures of the arrest and deportation were in violation of due process, Judge Bourquin wrote, reminiscent of Chief Justice Taney, on the threat of unlawful actions on the part of the executive in times of war.

Judge Bourquin wrote that protection of "the inalienable rights of personal security and safety, orderly and due process of law, are the fundamentals of the social compact, the basis of organized society, the essence and justification of government, the foundation, key, and capstones of the Constitution."[99] Reminiscent of Madison and his concerns of frailty of civil liberties and law within a Constitutional republic in times of crisis, Judge Bourquin warned of the ends justifying the means.

> Assuming petitioner is of the so-called 'Reds' and of the evil practice charged against him, he and his kind are less a danger to America than are those who indorse or use the methods that brought him to deportation. These latter are the mob and the spirit of violence and intolerance incarnate, the most alarming manifestation in America today. . . .[100]
>
> They are breeders of suspicion, fear, anger, revenge, riot, crime, class hatred, . . . and they and the government by hysteria that they stimulate are more to be feared than all the miserable, baited, bedeviled 'Reds' that are their ostensible occasion and whose sins they exaggerate.[101]

In defending Constitutional principles of law and due process, the Judge warned:

> No emergency in war or peace warrants their violation, for in emergency, real or assumed, tyrants in all ages have found excuse for their destruction. Without them, democracy perishes, autocracy reigns, and the innocent suffer with the guilty. Without them is no safety, peace, content, happiness, and they must be vindicated, defended, and maintained in the face of every assault by government or otherwise.[102]

A deportation process "based upon evidence and procedures that violate the search and seizure and due process clauses of the Constitution," the Judge held, "the law and courts [could] no more sanction such evidence than such methods, and no more approve either than the thumbscrew and the rack."[103] With impassioned language, Judge Bourquin explained why it is important to stand against government use of raw power in violation of the law. He wrote that unrestricted government violation of due process and Constitutional law will "undermine the morale of the people, excite the latter's fears, distrust of our institutions, . . . incline the people toward arbitrary power, which for protection cowards too often seek, and knaves too readily grant, and subject to which the people cease to be courageous and free, and become timid and enslaved."[104] After citing the history of fear and violation of law by the English government in an effort to control those who opposed government action during the Napoleonic wars by creating a state of fear within the country and then falsely arresting dissenters for treason and accusing them of being supporters of France with no opposition from the bench of justice as an analogy of the red scare and the actions of the government, Judge Bourquin concluded "[e]ven as the 'Reds,' the advocates of arbitrary power, whether within or without law, will in due time pass away. *It is for the courts to restrain both, when brought within jurisdiction.*"[105] The restraint is found in the application of justice by punishing the guilty, releasing the innocent and requiring the government to act within the requirements of the rule of law and due process. This must occur in either times of peace or war.

Attorney General Palmer initiated the second set of raids of communist organizations and alien deportation hearings on January 2, 1920, and the resulting district court case, *Colyer v. Skeffington*[106] resulted in the release order of twenty-eight petitioners who asserted that the process of the raids violated their due process rights through a habeas corpus petition. With less eloquence on legal principle than Judge Bourquin, but more in detail, on June 23, 1920, Judge George Anderson, in a sixty-three-pages-long opinion, detailed the various unconstitutional methods utilized during the preparation and implementation of the raids, interviews of "Russian peasants" and preparation of cases for Department of Labor deportation hearings after the raids. Judge Anderson took judicial notice that the arrests and searches of the second set of Palmer raids occurred without warrants, that arrested individuals were held for days without access to attorneys, that cases for deportation were prepared by BI agents (under federal law deportation and immigration was to be investigated by officers of the Department of Labor), that the right to call witnesses in one's defense and cross-examination of government evidence and witnesses were denied in hearings until the evidentiary "interests" of the government were established in deportation hearings first, and the nature and manner of interviews of non-English-speaking aliens all resulted in systemic violation of due process. Judge Anderson further held that membership in the Communist Party, by itself, was not sufficient to authorize deportation under the Alien Deportation Act of 1918. But even if it was, concluded the Court, more was required than a simple showing of names on a membership list. The Court held that actual and knowing knowledge and support of the Communist Party was required. Holding that membership alone was not sufficient he ordered all but four petitioners released and that if the Court of Appeals reversed on the holding of membership in the Communist Party alone was insufficient to establish lawful deportation (which it did), the Secretary of Labor must conduct *de novo* hearings for the petitioners due to the illegal activities and procedures of the Department of Justice and Labor.

⁂

During World War I the federal bench was in congruence with the government in having concern for the safety of society as a whole and the successful prosecution of the war. As one court concluded, "This court at this time is in no mood to weigh the financial losses of a few individuals as against possible detriment to the United States of America. If it be that some will have to suffer loss, yet it is only a financial loss, and, at worse, will be only a fractional part of the loss that others are going to have to suffer—some even of their lives—because of the war in which we are now engaged."[107] Nor were the interests of those renting apartments to make a profit from their property beyond regulation and control when such profits are made from a "national misfortune."[108]

The Federalists' position on political opposition, during the Alien and Sedition era, found support in the initial key cases decided by the Supreme Court during the World War I era. As Attorney General Lee explained in his legal opinion to Secretary of State Jefferson that under the law as explained by Blackstone the protection of speech only prohibits prior restraint and the utterer is fully liable for the words spoken and the effect of his words, Justice Holmes ruled that "when a nation is at war many things that might be said in time of peace are such a hindrance to its effort that their utterance will not be endured so long as men fight and . . . no Court could regard them as protected by any Constitutional right." The majority of the District Courts and the Courts of Appeals pre-*Schenck* drew the line of free speech at the probability of the danger occurring and established intent to cause the harm by the intent to make the utterance. The Supreme Court in *Schenck, Frohwerk,* and *Debs* affirmed that speech that seeks to interfere or obstruct a legitimate governmental interest (the raising of an army in time of war and preventing disloyalty and insubordination of military forces) is not protected by the First Amendment. The dissent of Holmes and Brandeis in *Abrams* was not over this principle, but the application of the "Bad Tendency" principle to the facts of the case. Holmes and Brandeis came to define the "clear and present danger" test to only prohibit speech that under the circumstances had an "immediate threat" of creating the danger Congress had a right to prevent.

The judiciary was correct in enforcing statutes that prohibited speech that obstructed the discipline and recruitment of the military in times of war. The predominant view dating from the founding of the First Amendment, was adopted by the Supreme Court in the first set of cases specifically addressing the boundaries of Congressional power and executive enforcement to prohibit certain types of speech. In times of wholesale war, like World War I, the power of government naturally increases to achieve the ends of successful completion of the war. But as Judges Anderson and Bourquin made clear, the presence of war and the need to protect the nation and enforce legitimate government interests (whether the protection and enforcement of a military draft or control of immigration), the means used by the political branches (Congress and the office of the President) are constrained by the text of the Constitution. The Fourth, Fifth, Sixth, and Eighth Amendments are the boundaries on both branches regardless of the presence of war and administrative hearings must adhere to and satisfy the requirements of due process. The presence of war does not shift these boundaries and the judiciary is required to enforce these requirements regardless of the presence of war. As we will review in later chapters the Court continued to defend the principle of Constitutional boundaries as well as enforce those boundaries in the terrorism cases post-9/11.

As World War I ended, the seeds of the red scare were planted. During the war the government took great pains and efforts to make the nation afraid of the "Barbaric Huns" and the infestation of the nation with German spies as well as subversives who sought to attack and destroy the American way of life. With the end of the war but the rise of the Bolshevik revolution, the corresponding civil war in Russia and the advent of communism as the governing theory of the Soviet Union, the nation was now threatened with the spread of an anticapitalist anti-Christian movement with serious and vocal proponents in the United States. This combined with a post-war economic downturn; the rise of labor unions led by socialists, anarchists, communists (or at least that is how they were viewed in many quarters of society); the resurgence of business and corporate owners demanding full restoration of their rights to run their companies and labor relations without government interference; the ascendancy of American isolationists; demobilization of the military with a corresponding high unemployment rate; and high rates of immigration and nativism all combined to create the first red scare and the famous Palmer raids.

Although praised in the general press at the time, various contemporary witnesses and history have condemned the Palmer raids.[109] Congressional failure to impeach Assistant Secretary Post, initiated at Palmer's urging, and the revelations of the violations of Constitutional prohibitions by the BI and the GID by the Post as well as by Judges Anderson and Bourquin added to the end of the red scare and the further condemnation of Palmer. As it has been said, Lord, let me not fall into the hands of men; the nation that once extolled Palmer as the savior of the nation had now placed him in ridicule and political descendancy. The cooling of the red scare occurred due to the reduction of fear of immigration, business support of importing cheap labor, the improvement of the economy, the fall of socialist and communist influence in the labor movement, the fall of progressive policies, and the rise of an established and publicly supported civil liberties advocacy movement. By 1920 the ACLU had come into being and was recognized as a civil liberties organization that had fought the excesses of government power. The nation wanted peace and order which allowed for the tempering of the left and right of the political spectrum. Warren Harding's Presidential campaign to "return to normalcy" and his references to "political prisoners" resulting from Palmer's actions found resonance with the American people who elected Harding in a landslide popular and electoral majority in the 1920 Presidential election.

Unlike the period of the Sedition Act of 1798,[110] the federal bench was now a fully recognized co-equal branch of government and the litigation of the sedition cases during World War I had *begun the development* of the Courts as a Constitutional institution to appeal to for protection from government action. The *Colyer v. Skeffington* and *Ex parte Jackson* cases provided judicial recognition and remedy of unlawful activities of Attorney General Palmer and went a long way in adding to the growing political and social rejection of the red scare. These cases provided much needed research on the actions of the Departments of Justice and Labor for other organizations to publish reports on the tactics of the government. Judge Anderson's detailed decision also upheld an important principle regarding judicial deference and executive boundaries. The Court affirmed and defended the principle that although executive administrative determinations of facts authorized by statute are dispositive on the courts, the application of the law to those facts is within judicial review.

The cases of the World War I era and the first red scare birthed the beginning of civil liberties and individual rights jurisprudence in times of crisis and the development of jurisprudence on the boundaries of government power to infringe on those rights in times of crisis. Within thirty years the red scare would return and new questions of freedom of association, loyalty, and the power of Congress to investigate the presence of communists in government and entertainment would bring to maturity judicial enforcement of Constitutional protection of civil liberties and the establishment of boundaries of governmental power to impede First Amendment rights of association and speech. To this part of the story we now turn.

NOTES

1. For example, see Geoffrey R. Stone, *Perilous Times: Free Speech in Wartime from the Sedition Act of 1798 to the War on Terrorism* (New York: Norton, 2004); Robert K. Murray, *Red Scare: A Study in National Hysteria, 1919–1920* (New York: McGraw-Hill, 1955); Christopher M. Finan, *From the Palmer Raids to the Patriot Act: A History of the Fight for Free Speech in America* (Boston: Beacon, 2007).

2. Stone, *Perilous Times*, 191.

3. Finan, *From the Palmer Raids to the Patriot Act*, 7–8, citing Wilson.

4. Ibid., 8.

5. Stone, *Perilous Times*, 137.

6. Arthur H. Garrison, "Terrorism: The Nature of Its History," *Criminal Justice Studies* 16, no. 1 (2003): 39–52.

7. Stone, *Perilous Times*, 156.

8. Ibid.

9. Ibid, 156–57. See also Alan Brinkley, "Civil Liberties in Times of Crisis," *Bulletin of the American Academy* (Winter 2006): 26–29.

10. Stone, *Perilous Times*, 184.

11. Finan, *From the Palmer Raids to the Patriot Act*, 11.

12. Ibid., citing Judge Landis.

13. *United States v. Motion Picture Film "The Spirit of '76,"* 252 Fed. 946, S.D., California, 1917.

14. Ronald Schaffer, *America in the Great War: The Rise of the War Welfare State* (New York: Oxford University Press, 1994), 15.

15. *United States v. Motion Picture Film "The Spirit of '76,"* 252 Fed., 947–48.

16. Ibid., 948.

17. Ibid.

18. Ibid., 947.

19. *Goldstein v. United States*, 258 Fed. 908 (9th Cir. 1919).

20. Ibid., 910.

21. Ibid.

22. Ibid., (emphasis added).

23. *Shaffer v. United States*, 255 Fed. 886, 887 (9th Cir. 1919).

24. Ibid., 889.

25. Ibid., 888.

26. Stone, *Perilous Times*, 593n141. See also David M. Rabban, *Free Speech in Its Forgotten Years* (New York: Cambridge University Press, 1997).

27. For a contrary view that Congress full well intended the Espionage Act to make unlawful and to put down the political speech of radicals, socialists, communists, and anarchists and other antiwar materials, see Rabban, *Free Speech in Its Forgotten Years*, 249–55, 265.

28. Ibid., 257.

29. "Of the approximately two thousand Espionage Act prosecutions, the overwhelming majority were brought and won under title I, section 3" (Ibid., 256). "Federal district judges generally let juries decide as a question of fact whether a defendant's language violated the law. Whatever the offending language, surrounding circumstances, or jury instructions, almost all prosecutions led to guilty verdicts" (Ibid., 257).

30. Ibid., 269.

31. *Wolf v. United States*, 259 F. 388, 394 (8th Cir. 1919) (emphasis in original).

32. Stone, *Perilous Times*, 593n133. See also Rabban, *Free Speech in Its Forgotten Years*, 267–69.

33. *U.S. v. Ves Hall*, 248 Fed. 150 (1918).

34. Arnon Gutfeld, "The Ves Hall Case, Judge Bourquin, and the Sedition Act of 1918," *The Pacific Historical Review* 37, no. 2 (May 1968): 163–78. See also Arnon Gutfeld, "Western Justice and the Rule of Law: Bourquin on Loyalty, the 'Red Scare,' and Indians," *The Pacific Historical Review* 65, no. 1 (February 1996): 85–106.

35. *U.S. v. Ves Hall*, 248 Fed., 153.

36. Ibid., 152–53.

37. Ibid. at 152.

38. Ibid., 153.

39. Ibid., 152, 154.

40. *Masses Publishing Co. v. Patten* 244 F. 535 (SD NY 1917).

41. See *In re Rapier*, 143 U.S. 110, 133–35 (1892) and *Ex parte Jackson*, 96 U.S. 727, 736–37 (1877) on the power of the Postmaster General to exclude obscene and indecent materials from the mail.

42. *Masses Publishing Co. v. Patten* 244 F. at 539–40.

43. Ibid., 540.

44. Ibid., 543.

45. Ibid.

46. Ibid.
47. Ibid., 539.
48. Ibid.
49. Ibid., 540.
50. Ibid.
51. Ibid.
52. Ibid. at 542.
53. Stone, *Perilous Times*, 160–70.
54. Ibid., 184–91.
55. Finan, *From the Palmer Raids to the Patriot Act*, 21, 37.
56. 249 U.S. 47 (1919).
57. Ibid., 50–51.
58. Ibid., 51.
59. Ibid., 52.
60. Ibid. (emphasis added).
61. 249 U.S. 204 (1919).
62. Ibid., 206.
63. *Fox v. Washington*, 236 U.S. 273 (1915).
64. Ibid., 275.
65. Ibid., 277.
66. *Robertson v. Baldwin*, 165 U.S. 275, 281 (1897).
67. *Frohwerk v. United States*, 249 U.S., 209.
68. *Debs v. United States*, 249 U.S. 211 (1919).
69. Ibid., 212–13.
70. Ibid., 215–16.
71. Ibid., 216 (emphasis added).
72. 250 U.S. 616 (1919).
73. Ibid., 621.
74. Ibid.
75. Ibid., 627–28 (emphasis added).
76. Ibid.
77. Ibid., 630–31 (emphasis added).
78. 243 U.S. 332 (1917).
79. Ibid., 346.
80. Ibid., 348.
81. *Arver v. United States* (Selective Draft Law Cases), 245 U.S. 366 (1918).
82. 251 U.S. 146 (1919).
83. 251 U.S. 264 (1920).
84. Ibid., 301.
85. *Northern Pacific v. North Dakota*, 250 U.S. 135 (1919).
86. *Stoehr v. Wallace*, 255 U.S. 239 (1921).
87. *Block v. Hirsh*, 256 U.S. 135 (1921).
88. Ibid., 158.
89. Ibid., 157.
90. Harlan Grant Cohen, "The (Un)Favorable Judgment of History: Deportation Hearings, the Palmer Raids, and the Meaning of History," *New York University Law Review* 78 (2003):1431–71, 1453.

91. Robert K. Murray, *Red Scare: A Study in National Hysteria, 1919–1920* (New York: McGraw-Hill, 1964), 72.

92. Ibid., 73.

93. Cohen, "The (Un)Favorable Judgment of History," 1455.

94. Patrick Renshaw, "The IWW and the Red Scare of 1917–1924," *Journal of Contemporary History* 3, no. 4 (1968): 63–72.

95. Athan G. Theoharis, "Dissent and the State: Unleashing the FBI, 1917–1985," *The History Teacher* 24, no. 1(1990): 42–52 and David Williams, "The Bureau of Investigation and Its Critics, 1919–1921: The Origins of Federal Political Surveillance," *The Journal of American History* 68, no. 3 (1981): 560–79.

96. Cohen, "The (Un)Favorable Judgment of History," 1460; Murray, *Red Scare*, 207.

97. David H. Bennett, *The Party of Fear: The American Far Right from Nativism to the Militia Movement* (Chapel Hill: University of North Carolina Press, 1988); Cohen, "The (Un)Favorable Judgment of History"; Theoharis, "Dissent and the State"; Williams, "The Bureau of Investigation and Its Critics, 1919–1921"; and Murray, *Red Scare*.

98. *Ex parte Jackson*, 236 Fed. 110 (1920).

99. Ibid., 113.

100. Ibid.

101. Ibid., 114.

102. Ibid., 113.

103. Ibid., 112–13.

104. Ibid., 113.

105. Ibid., 114 (emphasis added).

106. *Colyer v. Skeffington*, 265 F. 17 (1920) rev'd sub nom *Skeffington v. Katzeff* 277 F. 129 (1922).

107. *United States v. Motion Picture Film "The Spirit of '76,"* 252 Fed., 947.

108. *Block v. Hirsh*, 256 U.S. 135 (1921).

109. Theoharis, "Dissent and the State"; Williams, "The Bureau of Investigation and Its Critics, 1919–1921"; Murray, *Red Scare*; Cohen, "The (Un)Favorable Judgment of History"; Rabban, *Free Speech in Its Forgotten Years*; Roberta Strauss Feuerlicht, *America's Reign of Terror: World War I, the Red Scare, and the Palmer Raids* (New York: Random House, 1971).

110. Arthur H. Garrison, "The Internal Security Acts of 1798: The Founding Generation and the Judiciary during America's First National Security Crisis," *Journal of Supreme Court History* 34, no. 1 (2009): 1–27.

4

World Wars, the Red Scare, and Free Speech II: World War II, the Second Red Scare (1947–1957), Free Speech, and the Loyalty Oath Cases

In a letter to Thomas Jefferson on October 17, 1788, during the debates on the final ratification of the Constitution and the drafting of a Bill of Rights as a condition for ratification in many state ratification conventions, Madison made the following observation of the utility of a Bill of Rights in the face of national crisis.

> My own opinion has always been in favor of a Bill of Rights. . . . At the same time I have never thought the omission a material defect, nor been anxious to supply it. . . . I have favored it because I supposed it might be of use, and if properly executed could not be of disservice. I have not viewed it in an important light: . . . because *experience proves the inefficacy of a Bill of Rights on those occasions when its control is most needed.* Repeated violations of these parchment barriers have been committed by overbearing majorities in every state. . . . Wherever the real power in a government lies, there is the danger of oppression. In our governments the real power lies in the majority of the community, and *the invasion of private rights is chiefly to be apprehended, not from acts of government contrary to the sense of its constituents but from acts in which the government is the mere instrument of the major number of the constituents.* This is a truth of great importance but not yet sufficiently attended to; and is probably more strongly impressed on my mind by facts, and reflections suggested by them, than on yours, which has contemplated abuses of power issuing from a very different quarter. *Wherever there is an interest and power to do wrong, wrong will generally be done, and not less readily by a powerful and interested party than by a powerful and interested prince.* . . . [I]n a popular government, the political and physical power may be considered as vested in the same hands, that is, in a majority of the people; and consequently the tyrannical will of the sovereign

125

is not to be controlled by the dread of an appeal to any other force within the community. What use then, it may be asked, can a Bill of Rights serve in popular governments? . . . 1. *The political truths declared in that solemn manner acquire by degrees the character of fundamental maxims of free government, and, as they become incorporated with the national sentiment, counter-act the impulses of interest and passion.* 2. Although it be generally true, as above stated, that the danger of oppression lies in the interested majorities of the people rather than in usurped acts of the government, yet there may be occasions on which the evil may spring from the latter source; and, on such, a Bill of Rights will be a good ground for an appeal to the sense of the community. . . .

The restrictions, however strongly marked on paper, will never be regarded when opposed to the decided sense of the public; and, after repeated violations, in extraordinary cases they will lose even their ordinary efficacy. Should a rebellion or insurrection alarm the people as well as the government, and a suspension of the habeas corpus be dictated by the alarm, no written prohibitions on earth would prevent the measure.[1]

In his letter to Jefferson, Madison was prophetic regarding the nature of governmental power and how nations react in times of crisis, sometimes contrary to their most cherished maxims. At the same time those maxims stand as a mirror in which acts of a government can be viewed in times of crisis. As we have discussed in previous chapters, Madison was confirmed in his observation that "[s]hould a rebellion or insurrection alarm the people as well as the government, and a suspension of the habeas corpus be dictated by the alarm, no written prohibitions on earth would prevent the measure." And in times of war or crisis without defenders "experience proves the inefficacy of a Bill of Rights on those occasions when its control is most needed." But because the principles of the Bill of Rights have been defended, they have become the "fundamental maxims of [our] free government" and have been "incorporated with[in] the national sentiment [to] counteract the impulses of interest and passion [forming] good ground for an appeal" in the face of government oppression. As discussed in chapter 3, the first red scare birthed the institutionalization of organizations and associations, including within the legal community, dedicated to the preservation of the rule of law and the principles of the Bill of Rights. Through this period, social acceptance of those who defended individual civil liberties became part of the American social and legal framework. Through the work of the American Civil Liberties Bureau and others, the Bill of Rights itself was seen as a protection of individual rights.

The principles of freedom and individual liberty from government oppression embedded in the Constitution and the Bill of Rights has found advocates in the judiciary during times of crisis. Chief Justice Taney held that a citizen can not be separated from his right to civil protection in times of war. Both defending individual rights protecting the individual from government and the limitations of governmental power in times of crisis, he warned that if the courts could be closed or disregarded for military necessity, then no citizen had any freedoms beyond the power of the government at its say so in times of crisis.[2] Justice Nelson wrote that the President can't by declaration declare citizens and their property subject to seizure because they find themselves on the wrong geographic side of a civil war.[3] Affirming these principles, writing for the Court, Justice Davis wrote that a citizen could not be taken by the military and tried by a military commission when the courts were in full operation and he could not be tried without the protections of the Fourth, Fifth, Sixth, and Eighth Amendments.[4] Judge Stone wrote that it was the duty of the judiciary to make sure that a trial was fair and the jury was not led to conviction based on political emotions or passions that were not germane to the case but only on facts proving guilt.[5] Judge Anderson held that an administrative hearing that was devoid of due process could not be sanctioned by the courts.[6] Judge Bourquin impassionedly wrote "the inalienable rights of personal security and safety, orderly and due process of law, are the . . . capstones of the Constitution. . . . No emergency in war or peace warrants their violation."[7]

But despite these defenses of civil liberties, Madison's observation that "the invasion of private rights is chiefly to be apprehended, not from acts of government contrary to the sense of its constituents but from acts in which the government is the mere instrument of the major number of the constituents" has proven correct. Such was true in the rise and fall of the first red scare and so it was with the rise and fall of the second red scare. Neither event could be said to have been imposed by the government against the will of the nation as a whole. Both resulted from the politics of some, acquiescence of most, and the opposition by the few. Societal fear, like injustice and oppression, does not affect all evenly; only the few suffer under the lash of measures implemented to comfort and allay the fears of the many. It is through the actions of those who suffer under the lash and those who fight the lash in our Constitutional history that the boundaries of what can be done are developed. Before the end of World War I the judiciary was a secondary player to the history of the development of the boundaries of Presidential and Congressional power and civil liberties protected by the Bill of Rights. As the first half of the twentieth century came to an end, the judiciary finally came into its own as the chief battlefield for the protection of what Madison called the "character of [the] fundamental maxims of [our] free government."

PRESIDENTIAL AND CONGRESSIONAL POWER: WAR POWERS BEFORE MCCARTHY AND THE SECOND RED SCARE

The period between the first red scare and the second revolutionized American society socially, politically, and militarily. The Stock Market crash of

1929 and the resulting times of economic social stress under the Great Depression forever institutionalized a demand in the American people to expect the national government to act and provide remedies in times of social and economic crisis. The New Deal policies of FDR not only met this new demand but increased the power of the national government to regulate the economy and provide for the social welfare of American citizens on a level never before witnessed in American history. By the dawn of World War II, President Roosevelt had created a national government that governed the prices of food, regulated the banking industry, provided social security and created a wide range of social programs to create work for thousands of out-of-work Americans. It was during this period that the rise of the national government as the paramount government within our federal system came into full blossom. The role of the President changed as well. The President was now what Teddy Roosevelt and Woodrow Wilson had envisioned at the beginning of the twentieth century, a man who could form and make the nation into whatever he had enough political will and skill to make it into. The Great Depression and the era of the New Deal truly ushered in a significant revolution in the roles of government that has remained intact to this day. The Supreme Court, at first, opposed this revolution but in 1937 surrendered its opposition[8] in *West Coast Hotel Co. v. Parrish*, in what has been called the case of the switch in time that saved nine.[9] This case marked the end of economic substantive due process and judicial scrutiny of government economic regulation.[10]

But the national government and the President did not increase their influence in domestic peacetime economic matters alone. The rise of the Third Reich and Fascism in Germany and Italy, the establishment of communism in the Soviet Union, along with the growth of organizations supporting both Marxism and Nazism in the United States, led to the increased power of the national government to deal with the internal security threats of Marxism and Nazism. Additionally, the power of the national government grew to meet the public expectations of the national government to prevail when World War II came to America's doorstep on the day that would live in infamy.

As with the first red scare, the seeds of the second red scare were sown in the ground of the lead-up to war and the successful implementation of the war. As with World War I, dissent was not only not to be tolerated, but was to be feared as a serious threat to the success of the United States in World War II. The powers of the national government, both Congress and the President, increased in order to meet this fear. The Supreme Court during this period facilitated this increase in power through a jurisprudence of deference to the political branches.

As we have discussed in chapters 1 and 2, the Presidency has grown from the limitations of Madison into an institution that has adopted the Hamiltonian view and has developed into the primary political figure envisioned by Wilson and Roosevelt. Although the Supreme Court provided support for this growth in the Civil War cases, the development of Presidential hegemony over foreign policy and predominance in domestic policy resulted from historical and political events in the nineteenth and early twentieth centuries. But in the times leading to and during World War II, the Court would provide its stamp of approval on the primacy of the President in foreign policy but would continue to develop the outer boundaries of Congressional and Presidential domestic powers to maintain security and place infringements on civil liberties in times of war.

In 1936 in *United States v. Curtiss-Wright Export* Justice Sutherland wrote the seminal case on Presidential power over foreign affairs and affirmed the Sole Organ theory.[11] The case involved the indictment of individuals of the Curtiss-Wright Export Company who were alleged to have sold weapons in violation of a Presidential order enforcing a Congressional joint resolution authorizing the President to prohibit such weapons sales if in his determination the ban would bring peace in the war between Bolivia and Paraguay over the Gran Chaco region of South America. The indicted appellees contended that the resolution provided the President with unfettered discretion. Justice Sutherland wrote that the powers of the national government involve powers to address domestic and foreign policy. "The broad statement that the federal government can exercise no powers except those specifically enumerated in the Constitution, and such implied powers as are necessary and proper to carry into effect the enumerated powers, is categorically true only in respect of our internal affairs. In that field, the primary purpose of the Constitution was to carve from the general mass of legislative powers then possessed by the states such portions as it was thought desirable to vest in the federal government, leaving those not included in the enumeration still in the states."[12] But the powers over foreign affairs, the Court reasoned, do not originate in the domestic powers of the several states but from the foreign policy powers of the Crown, which transferred to the Continental Congress of the United States when the colonies gained independence and international recognition as a sovereign power under the peace treaty of 1783.[13]

The power to implement foreign policy passed from the Continental Congress to the national government under the Articles of Confederation and to the national government under the Constitution.[14] Concluding that the foreign policy power belongs to the national government, Justice Sutherland wrote that the nature of foreign policy is such that the formation of that policy is an Executive function belonging to the President. As Hamilton wrote more than a century and a half before, the Court held that the nature of foreign policy requires a single actor representing the nation who possesses, and can act quickly with, information that is not open to the legislative process or deliberative action. Congressional power, Justice Sutherland wrote, over domestic affairs under the Constitution is different than

> the federal power over external affairs in origin and essential character . . . [and Congressional] participation in the exercise of the power is significantly limited. *In this vast external realm, with its important, complicated, delicate and manifold problems, the President alone has the power to speak or listen as a representative of the nation.* He makes treaties with the advice and consent of the Senate; but he alone negotiates. Into the field of negotiation the Senate cannot intrude; and Congress itself is powerless to invade it. As Marshall said in his great argument of March 7, 1800, in the House of Representatives, *"The President is the sole organ of the nation in its external relations, and its sole representative with foreign nations."* The Senate Committee on Foreign Relations at a very early day in our history (February 15, 1816), reported to the Senate, among other things, as follows:
>
> > 'The President is the Constitutional representative of the United States with regard to foreign nations. He manages our concerns with foreign nations and must necessarily be most competent to determine when, how, and upon what subjects negotiation may be urged with the greatest prospect of success. For his conduct he is responsible to the Constitution. The committee considers this responsibility the surest pledge for the faithful discharge of his duty. They think the interference of the Senate in the direction of foreign negotiations calculated to diminish that responsibility and thereby to impair the best security for the national safety. The nature of transactions with foreign nations, moreover, requires caution and unity of design, and their success frequently depends on secrecy and dispatch.'
>
> It is important to bear in mind that we are here dealing not alone with an authority vested in the President by an exertion of legislative power, but with such an authority plus the very delicate, *plenary and exclusive power of the President as the sole organ of the federal government in the field of international relations—a power which does not require as a basis for its exercise an act of Congress,* but which, of course, like every other governmental power, must be exercised in subordination to the applicable provisions of the Constitution. . . . [T]he President [has] a degree of discretion and freedom from statutory restriction which would not be admissible were domestic affairs alone involved. Moreover, he, not Congress, has the better opportunity of knowing the conditions which prevail in foreign countries, and especially is this true in time of war. He has his confidential sources of information. He has his agents in the form of diplomatic, consular and other officials. Secrecy in respect of information gathered by them may be highly necessary, and the premature disclosure of it productive of harmful results.[15]

While the *Curtiss-Wright* case is considered the seminal case establishing the President as the sole organ of foreign policy, the case was neither novel nor original. For as discussed in chapter 2, the Supreme Court, in the *Mott* and *Luther* cases, almost a century before had held that the President had the sole authority to determine when the use of the military was appropriate in both invasion and civil rebellion. The Court in the *Prize Cases* established that it was for the President to determine if war was inflicted upon the nation and if so it was for him to act and determine both military and foreign policy based on his determination of the state of war. Regarding Congressional legislative power in the area of foreign policy, the Court held that

> when the President is to be authorized by legislation to act in respect of a matter intended to affect a situation in foreign territory, the legislator properly bears in mind the important consideration that the form of the President's action—or, indeed, whether he shall act at all—may well depend, among other things, upon the nature of the confidential information which he has or may thereafter receive, or upon the effect which his action may have upon our foreign relations. This consideration, in connection with what we have already said on the subject discloses the unwisdom of requiring Congress in this field of governmental power to lay down narrowly definite standards by which the President is to be governed.[16]

While affirming the Hamiltonian and Wilsonian view of Presidential power in the area of foreign policy, the Court also broadly interpreted the foreign policy powers granted to Congress.

In *Lichter v. United States* Justice Burton provided a broad reading of Congressional power in time of war to raise and support the armed forces of the United States.[17] The case involved the Constitutionality of the Renegotiation Act which authorized the Under Secretary of War or the War Contracts Price Adjustment Board to file actions with the U.S. Tax Court to tax excessive profits due to war material contracts during World War II. In determining the Constitutionality of the Act, the Court assessed the Constitutional authority of Congress to regulate and if necessary, negatively impact profits during times of war. Echoing the sentiments of the Court in *Ruppert v. Caffey, Block v. Hirsh,* and Judge Bledsoe in *U.S. v. Motion Picture Film "The Spirit of 76,"* Justice Burton wrote

> the Renegotiation Act was developed as a major wartime policy of Congress comparable to that of the Selective Training and Service Act. The authority of Congress to authorize each of them sprang from its war powers. Each was a part of a national policy adopted in time of crisis in the conduct of total global warfare by a nation dedicated to the preservation, practice and development of the maximum measure of individual freedom consistent with the unity of effort essential to success.
>
> With the advent of such warfare, mobilized property in the form of equipment and supplies became as essential as mobilized manpower. Mobilization of effort extended not only to the uniformed armed services but to the entire population. Both Acts were a form of mobilization. The language of the Constitution authorizing such measures is broad rather than restrictive. It says,

"The Congress shall have Power. . . . To raise and support Armies. . . ." This
places emphasis upon the supporting as well as upon the raising of armies. The
power of Congress as to both is inescapably express, not merely implied. The
conscription of manpower is a more vital interference with the life, liberty and
property of the individual than is the conscription of his property or his profits
or any substitute for such conscription of them. For his hazardous, full-time
service in the armed forces a soldier is paid whatever the Government deems to
be a fair but modest compensation. Comparatively speaking, the manufacturer
of war goods undergoes no such hazard to his personal safety as does a frontline soldier and yet the Renegotiation Act gives him far better assurance of a
reasonable return for his wartime services than the Selective Service Act and all
its related legislation give to the men in the armed forces. The Constitutionality
of the conscription of manpower for military service is beyond question. The
Constitutional power of Congress to support the armed forces with equipment
and supplies is no less clear and sweeping.[18]

In regard to the role of the judiciary in times of war and assessing Congressional power in such times the Court held that after recognition of "this
power 'To raise and support Armies . . .' and the power granted in the same
Article of the Constitution 'To make all Laws which shall be necessary
and proper for carrying into Execution the foregoing Powers . . . ' the only
question remaining is whether the Renegotiation Act was a law 'necessary
and proper for carrying into Execution' the war powers of Congress and
especially its power to support armies."[19] To which the Court concluded
that it was "'necessary and proper' for Congress to provide for [the] production [of materials] in the successful conduct of the war, . . . [and] [t]he
only questions are whether the particular method of renegotiation and the
administrative procedure prescribed conformed to the Constitutional limitations under which Congress was permitted to exercise its basic powers."[20]
The Court concluded that an administrative process in which excessive war
profits during war were open to tax proceedings was a permitable means to
implement its legitimate governmental ends.

The Court continued to develop its jurisprudence of deference to decisions made by the political branches when made within their Constitutional spheres by deciding that the Enemy Aliens Act of 1798 was Constitutional and that the judiciary had no power to pass judgment on a
Presidential decision to remove an enemy alien from the United States in
Ludecke v. Watkins.[21] Justice Frankfurter held that a "power of the President
not subject to judicial review is not transmuted into a judicially reviewable
action because the President chooses to have that power exercised within
narrower limits than Congress authorized." The Court refused to accept the
proposition that the determination of when a war is ended for the purposes
of enforcing war measures is for a court to determine. After observing that
"[w]ar does not cease with a cease-fire order"[22] the Court made clear that

the decision of whether hostilities had ended was a political determination to be made by the President and Congress, not the judiciary. Justice Frankfurter reasoned that to decided otherwise,

> The Court would be assuming the functions of the political agencies of the Government to yield to the suggestion that the unconditional surrender of Germany and the disintegration of the Nazi Reich have left Germany without a government capable of negotiating a treaty of peace. It is not for us to question a belief by the President that enemy aliens who were justifiably deemed fit subjects for internment during active hostilities do not lose their potency for mischief during the period of confusion and conflict which is characteristic of a state of war even when the guns are silent but the peace of Peace has not come. These are matters of political judgment for which judges have neither technical competence nor official responsibility.[23]

The Court concluded that the Enemy Alien Act

> is almost as old as the Constitution, and it would savor of doctrinaire audacity now to find the statute offensive to some emanation of the Bill of Rights. The fact that hearings are utilized by the Executive to secure an informed basis for the exercise of summary power does not argue the right of courts to retry such hearings, nor bespeak denial of due process to withhold such power from the courts.
> Such great war powers may be abused, no doubt, but that is a bad reason for having judges supervise their exercise, whatever the legal formulas within which such supervision would nominally be confined. In relation to the distribution of Constitutional powers among the three branches of the Government, the optimistic Eighteenth Century language of Mr. Justice Iredell, speaking of this very Act, is still pertinent:

> > 'All systems of government suppose they are to be administered by men of common sense and common honesty. In our country, as all ultimately depends on the voice of the people, they have it in their power, and it is to be presumed they generally will choose men of this description; but if they will not, the case, to be sure, is without remedy. If they choose fools, they will have foolish laws. If they choose knaves, they will have knavish ones. But this can never be the case until they are generally fools or knaves themselves, which, thank God, is not likely ever to become the character of the American people.' (Case of Fries, supra, 9 Fed. Cas., 836, No. 5,126)

> Accordingly, we hold that full responsibility for the just exercise of this great power may validly be left where the Congress has Constitutionally placed it—on the President of the United States. The Founders in their wisdom made him not only the Commander-in-Chief but also the guiding organ in the conduct of our foreign affairs. He who was entrusted with such vast powers in relation to the outside world was also entrusted by Congress, almost throughout the whole life of the nation, with the disposition of alien enemies during a state of war.[24]

In *Chicago and Southern Air Lines v. Waterman S.S. Corp.* Justice Jackson writing on Congressional and Presidential power over foreign affairs, explained that "Congress may of course delegate very large grants of its power over foreign commerce to the President. The President also possesses in his own right certain powers conferred by the Constitution on him as Commander-in-Chief and as the Nation's organ in foreign affairs."[25] The case involved the interpretation of the Civil Aeronautics Act and its provision that allowed for judicial review of decisions made by the Civil Aeronautics Board. The Court affirmed the Circuit Court holding that judiciary had no authority to review the actions of the President in determining the correctness of a Board decision before it was published. Justice Jackson concluded that it was not for the judiciary to make independent decisions regarding the political matters of foreign policy; such determinations are left to Congress and the President.

> The court below considered, and we think quite rightly, that it could not review such provisions of the order as resulted from Presidential direction. The President, both as Commander-in-Chief and as the Nation's organ for foreign affairs, has available intelligence services whose reports neither are nor ought to be published to the world. It would be intolerable that courts, without the relevant information, should review and perhaps nullify actions of the Executive taken on information properly held secret. Nor can courts sit in camera in order to be taken into executive confidences. But even if courts could require full disclosure, the very nature of executive decisions as to foreign policy is political, not judicial. Such decisions are wholly confided by our Constitution to the political departments of the government, Executive and Legislative. They are delicate, complex, and involve large elements of prophecy. They are and should be undertaken only by those directly responsible to the people whose welfare they advance or imperil. They are decisions of a kind for which the Judiciary has neither aptitude, facilities nor responsibility and have long been held to belong in the domain of political power not subject to judicial intrusion or inquiry. We therefore agree that whatever of this order emanates from the President is not susceptible of review by the Judicial Department.[26]

In *United States ex rel Knauff v. Shaughnessy* the Court was presented with the question of "May the United States exclude without hearing, solely upon a finding by the Attorney General that her admission would be prejudicial to the interests of the United States, the alien wife of a citizen who had served honorably in the armed forces of the United States during World War II?"[27] To which Justice Minton answered in the affirmative. The Court held that the President, both under Congressional delegation and under his own authority as Commander-in-Chief, has the power to make determinations as to alien entry into the United States. "The exclusion of aliens is a fundamental act of sovereignty. The right to do so stems not alone from legislative power but is inherent in the executive power to control the foreign affairs of the nation. When Congress prescribes a procedure concerning the admissibility of aliens, it is not dealing alone with a legislative power. It is implementing an inherent executive power."[28] The Court, continuing its jurisprudence of deference to the decisions of the political branches when acting within their Constitutional boundaries, through Justice Minton, held that

> the decision to admit or to exclude an alien may be lawfully placed with the President, who may in turn delegate the carrying out of this function to a responsible executive officer of the sovereign, such as the Attorney General. The action of the executive officer under such authority is final and conclusive. Whatever the rule may be concerning deportation of persons who have gained entry into the United States, it is not within the province of any court, unless expressly authorized by law, to review the determination of the political branch of the Government to exclude a given alien. Normally Congress supplies the conditions of the privilege of entry into the United States. But because the power of exclusion of aliens is also inherent in the executive department of the sovereign, Congress may in broad terms authorize the executive to exercise the power, e. g., as was done here, for the best interests of the country during a time of national emergency. Executive officers may be entrusted with the duty of specifying the procedures for carrying out the Congressional intent.[29]

The Court affirmed both the need and authority of the President, through his subordinate officers, in this case the Attorney General, to take actions with intelligence only available to him and its use to protect the interests of the United States. The Court held that

> the Attorney General, exercising the discretion entrusted to him by Congress and the President, concluded upon the basis of confidential information that the public interest required that petitioner be denied the privilege of entry into the United States. He denied her a hearing on the matter because, in his judgment, the disclosure of the information on which he based that opinion would itself endanger the public security. We find no substantial merit to petitioner's contention that the regulations were not "reasonable" as they were required to be by the 1941 Act. We think them reasonable in the circumstances of the period for which they were authorized, namely, the national emergency of World War II.[30]

The Court concluded that "[w]hatever the procedure authorized by Congress is, [that] is [the] due process [that is due] as far as an alien denied entry is concerned."[31]

Before the development of the Cold War, the Supreme Court had established the broad boundaries of the powers of Congress and the President to deal with war and national security issues. The Court made clear in *U.S. v. Curtiss-Wright* that the President, under his powers as Commander-in-Chief, is the sole organ of American foreign policy and that Congress has a supportive role limited to the specific powers listed in the Constitution. In

Lichter v. United States the Court read broadly the powers that the Constitution did grant to Congress in the area of foreign policy—the power to raise and support the armed forces of the United States—in times of war. In such circumstances, the Court would not second-guess Congressional choices on how to accomplish its Constitutional responsibilities so long as the means were rationally related to achieving those responsibilities. Further the Court made clear that in times of total war, the loss or limiting of profits through war contracts with the national government is well within the boundaries of Congressional power to support the military in times of war. In *Ludecke v. Watkins, Chicago and Southern Air Lines v. Waterman S.S. Corp* and *United States ex rel Knauff v. Shaughnessy* the Court continued to show deference to decisions made by the President when those decisions were within his discretion under statutory powers granted by Congress or under his inherent powers as Commander-in-Chief.

In addition to supporting the power of the President as the sole organ of foreign policy through his powers as Commander-in-Chief, the Court also expounded on his powers to detain unlawful combatants and subject them to trial by military commission rather than by civilian federal courts. In *Ex parte Quirin* Chief Justice Stone wrote "the detention and trial of petitioners—ordered by the President in the declared exercise of his powers as Commander-in-Chief of the Army in time of war and of grave public danger—are not to be set aside by the courts without the clear conviction that they are in conflict with the Constitution or laws of Congress Constitutionally enacted."[32]

The *Quirin* case involved eight German agents who were trained in sabotage by the German Army who boarded two German submarines in France, transferred to landing zones in Long Island, New York, and Vedra Beach, Florida, on June 17, 1942, with the mission of committing sabotage in the United States. Upon entering the United States they changed into civilian clothes from military uniforms as part of their plan to fit into the United States population and later commit sabotage operations. They were captured in New York and Chicago by the FBI before they could complete their mission. On July 2, 1942, President Roosevelt ordered that the captured agents be tried by a military commission for violations of the law of war and the Articles of War.[33] The President also issued a Presidential Proclamation declaring that all persons, citizens or residents of nations at war with the United States that enter the United States with the attempt to commit sabotage, espionage or other warlike acts in violation of the law of war would be subject to the jurisdiction of military tribunals.[34] After summarily holding that the "Commission has jurisdiction to try the charge preferred against the petitioners. . . . We pass at once to the consideration of the basis of the Commission's authority."[35]

The Constitution, the Court observed, "invests the President as Commander-in-Chief with the power to wage war which Congress has declared, and to carry into effect all laws passed by Congress for the conduct of war and for the government and regulation of the Armed Forces, and all laws defining and punishing offences against the law of nations, including those which pertain to the conduct of war."[36] Congress had properly exercised its Constitutional powers, the Court held, by enacting the Articles of War statute which provides the rules of war for the American military and provides sanction for the violation of those articles. The articles "also recognize the 'military commission' appointed by military command as an appropriate tribunal for the trial and punishment of offenses against the law of war not ordinarily tried by court martial" and the Congress has authorized the President "with certain limitations, to proscribe the procedure for military commissions." Under Articles 81 and 82, the Court concluded, "those charged with relieving, harboring or corresponding with the enemy and those charged with spying" were subject to trial by military Commissions.[37]

The Court proceeded to hold that since it was well within the power of Congress and the President to create military commissions for the trial and punishment of violations of the law of war and the Articles of War, the only question is "whether it is within the Constitutional power of the national government to place petitioners upon trial before a military commission for the offenses with which they are charged."[38]

The Common law of the law of war, the Court asserted, was incorporated by reference into the Articles of War passed by Congress and that under the common law of war there is a difference between those who are lawful and unlawful combatants and as such have different protections due in times of war by all belligerent parties. These distinctions were not lost to the Bush administration decades later.

> Lawful combatants are subject to capture and detention as prisoners of war by opposing military forces. Unlawful combatants are likewise subject to capture and detention, but in addition they are subject to trial and punishment by military tribunals for acts which render their belligerency unlawful. *The spy* who secretly and without uniform passes the military lines of a belligerent in time of war, seeking to gather military information and communicate it to the enemy, *or an enemy combatant who without uniform* comes secretly through the lines for the purpose of waging war by destruction of life or property, *are familiar examples of belligerents who are generally deemed not to be entitled to the status of prisoners of war,* but to be offenders against the law of war subject to trial and punishment by military tribunals.[39]

After citing international law on the definition of unlawful combatants, the Court cited the rules of war as promulgated by the War Department which defined the lawful belligerent as one who is found carrying arms openly with fixed emblems or some other identifying uniform as compared to the unlawful belligerents who conduct belligerent acts without having such identification. Such men are punishable as war criminals and are not entitled to prisoner of war status and thus are subject to trial by military commission.[40] Citing War Department guidelines, the Court wrote that "persons of the enemy territory who steal within the lines of the hostile army for the purpose of robbing, killing, or of destroying bridges, roads or canals, of robbing or destroying the mail, or of cutting the telegraph wires, are not entitled to be treated as prisoners of war."[41] Thus, the Court concluded "our Government has likewise recognized that those who during time of war pass surreptitiously from enemy territory into our own, discarding their uniforms upon entry, for the commission of hostile acts involving destruction of life or property, have the status of unlawful combatants punishable as such by military commission."[42]

For our purposes of reviewing how the judiciary in times of war and crisis define the powers and limits of Congressional and Presidential power we will bypass the Court's view that the petitioners were not required to have a federal indictment and jury trial under the Fifth and Sixth amendments.[43] Suffice it to say that the Court reasoned that the right to a jury trial was never granted to those that violated the law of war in times of war when the Fifth Amendment was drafted and ratified, thus it could not be expected that the Founders intended such unlawful combatants to receive such protections with the ratification of the Fifth Amendment. But can Congress and the President subject an American citizen to the procedures of a military commission when the Courts are open? The petitioners cited *Ex parte Milligan* for the proposition that regardless of the charge an American citizen cannot be subjected to a military commission when the courts are open. Quirin, one of the German saboteurs, claimed U.S. citizenship.

The Court answered Quirin's proposition that "citizenship . . . does not relieve him from the consequences of a belligerency which is unlawful. . . . Citizens who associate themselves with the military arm of the enemy government, and with its aid, guidance and direction enter this country bent on hostile acts are enemy belligerents within the meaning of the Hague Convention and the law of war."[44] From which the Court concluded that since *Milligan* placed significant focus on the fact that Milligan was not a member of any rebellion against the national government and was never a member of the armed forces of the Union—*Milligan* is "inapplicable to the case presented by the present record."[45] Thus *Milligan* was not overturned. The Court, *correctly*, observed that the significance of *Milligan* is the principle that a citizen cannot be subjected to military commissions, bared from the civilian court jurisdiction and the protections of the Bill of Rights when such a citizen is not a member of the armed forces of the United States and has not engaged in military activities on behalf of another government or has not provided support to the military forces of another government in a state of war with the United States. The military may not place its hands on a civilian not within its lawful jurisdiction. Military justice jurisdiction is only established through membership in the Armed Forces of the United States or by active belligerent action against the United States in time of war.

But can the President, in a state of military emergency, authorize the institution of martial law over part of the United States, close its courts and impose military justice during the time of military emergency? On the same day of the Japanese attacks on December 7 Governor Joseph B. Poindexter issued a proclamation suspending the writ of habeas corpus and placed Hawaii under martial law.[46] President Roosevelt responded to the Governor on December 9 with a telegram approving his suspension of habeas corpus and placing Hawaii under martial law.[47] The "Military Governor" then issued orders taking military command of the territory, temporarily closing the civilian courts and issuing orders creating provost courts to handle criminal cases. Although the civilian courts were reopened on December 16, 1941, they were restricted from handling criminal jury trials. Full restoration of civilian and judicial authority was established by Presidential Proclamation on October 19, 1944.[48] During this period Harry E. White and Lloyd Duncan were arrested, tried and convicted of embezzlement and assault respectively by the standing Provost Court. Both cases involved petitions for writ of habeas corpus filed on their behalf asserting that the Provost Courts had no legal authority to hold, try and convict them.[49] The two cases were heard and decided together by the Supreme Court.

The government argued in the District Court, upon a show cause motion for an issuance of a writ of habeas corpus, that "Hawaii had become part of an active theatre of war constantly threatened by invasion from without; that the writ of habeas corpus had therefore properly been suspended and martial law had validly been established in accordance with the provisions of the Organic Act; that consequently the District Court did not have jurisdiction to issue the writ; and that the trials of petitioners by military tribunals pursuant to orders by the Military Governor issued because of military necessity were valid."[50] The District Court, in two separate trials held that since the civilian judiciary would have been open and able to function but for the military closing them and since the military was without authority to do so, ordered White and Duncan released. The Ninth Circuit Court of Appeals reversed.[51] The Court of Appeals in part held that the term "martial law" provided authorization to provide all government operations including judicial and as such had the power to create provost courts. White and Duncan appealed to the Supreme Court.

In *Duncan v. Kahanamoku* Justice Black, writing for the majority, held that when Hawaii was annexed into the United States it was not done so under circumstances and laws that limited the application of the Constitution. Justice Black wrote that the civilians in Hawaii are entitled to the Constitutional guarantee of a fair trial to the same extent as those who live in any other part of our country. We are aware that conditions peculiar to Hawaii might imperatively demand extraordinarily speedy and effective measures in the event of actual or threatened invasion. But this also holds true for other parts of the United States. Extraordinary measures in Hawaii, however necessary, are not supportable on the mistaken premise that Hawaiian inhabitants are less entitled to Constitutional protection than others. For here Congress did not in the Organic Act exercise whatever power it might have had to limit the application of the Constitution. . . . And Congress did not . . . authorize the military trials of petitioners. Whatever power the Organic Act gave the Hawaiian military authorities, such power must therefore be construed in the same way as a grant of power to troops stationed in any one of the states.[52]

Asking rhetorically if "the principles and practices developed during the birth and growth of our political institutions [have] been such as to persuade us that Congress intended that loyal civilians in loyal territory should have their daily conduct governed by military orders substituted for criminal laws, and that such civilians should be tried and punished by military tribunals," Justice Black wrote that Congress could not have intended the term "martial law" as used in Section 67 of the Organic Act to authorize the closing of civilian courts and the imposition of military tribunals for punishment of crimes otherwise tried in civilian courts.

In an impassioned review of American Constitutional history and tradition, Justice Black wrote that "[p]eople of many ages and countries have feared and unflinchingly opposed the kind of subordination of executive, legislative and judicial authorities to complete military rule which according to the government Congress has authorized here. In this country that fear has become part of our cultural and political institutions."[53] After reviewing the historical use of the military to assist civilian authority to put down armed resistance in the cases of Shay's Rebellion, the Whiskey Rebellion and the summer of 1892 riots at the Coeur-d'Alene mines, the Court explained that in each case the military was ordered to respect civilian and judicial authority and not to supplant it. Leaving aside the glaring omission of the actions of General Zachary Taylor and his suspension of civilian authority and outright defiance of the courts during the War of 1812 in New Orleans, Justice Black concluded that under the American Constitutional system, even in times of military threat or rebellion, the "[c]ourts and their procedural safeguards are indispensable to our system of government. They were set up by our founders to protect the liberties they valued."[54]

Justice Black wrote,

Our system of government clearly is the antithesis of total military rule and the founders of this country are not likely to have contemplated complete military dominance within the limits of a Territory made part of this country and not recently taken from an enemy. They were opposed to governments that placed in the hands of one man the power to make, interpret and enforce the laws. Their philosophy has been the people's throughout our history. For that reason we have maintained legislatures chosen by citizens or their representatives and courts and juries to try those who violate legislative enactments. We have always been especially concerned about the potential evils of summary criminal trials and have guarded against them by provisions embodied in the Constitution itself. See *Ex parte Milligan*. Legislatures and courts are not merely cherished American institutions; they are indispensable to our government.

Military tribunals have no such standing.[55]

The Court reversed the Court of Appeals and affirmed the District Court. Citing *Ex parte Milligan*, the Court concluded that civil liberty and martial law "cannot endure together; the antagonism is irreconcilable; and, in the conflict, one or the other must perish."[56] Chief Justice Taney had won the argument.

Having settled the Constitutional principle that the President may not separate a civilian or a civilian population from their Constitutional protections by closing the civilian courts in times of war by replacing them with military tribunals, the Court addressed the question of whether Congress can authorize the arrest of a civilian for crimes alleged to have been committed while such a person was in the military. Can the military lay its hands upon former servicemen and subject them to military courts-martial? The Supreme Court, as it did in *Duncan*, focused on the Constitutional protections of civilian justice and the limits of reach of military justice in *Toth v. Quarles*.[57]

In *Toth*, a former serviceman of the United States Air Force was arrested by military authority and transferred to Korea for court-marshal for murder and conspiracy to commit murder while he was a member of the Air Force. He was convicted and his conviction was affirmed by the District of Columbia Court of Appeals. The Supreme Court held that Article 3(a) of the Uniform Code for Military Justice that allowed for the seizure and conviction of Toth could not be sustained under Congressional powers to raise and support the armed forces, conduct war, govern the armed forces or punish crimes on the land and the high seas. Nor could such a conviction be sustained upon Presidential power as Commander-in-Chief or by the power to maintain martial law. The Court held that the powers of Congress to raise and govern the armed forces, including the power to maintain discipline in such forces, "restrict court-martial jurisdiction to persons who are actually members or part of the armed forces. There is a compelling reason for construing the clause this way: any expansion of court-martial jurisdiction like that in the 1950 Act necessarily encroaches on the jurisdiction of federal courts set up under Article III of the Constitution, where persons on trial are surrounded with more Constitutional safeguards than in military tribunals."[58]

The Court held that the Constitution constellation only has one judicial system that is coequal with the other two branches of government and Article III courts have a higher purpose than military courts-martial. The Court explained the difference in stature and purpose of Article III courts and military courts-martial as follows:

> It is the primary, indeed the sole, business of [Article III] courts to try cases and controversies between individuals and between individuals and the Government. This includes trial of criminal cases. . . .
> We find nothing in the history or Constitutional treatment of military tribunals which entitles them to rank along with Article III courts as adjudicators of the guilt or innocence of people charged with [criminal] offenses. . . . And conceding to military personnel that high degree of honesty and sense of justice which nearly all of them undoubtedly have, it still remains true that military tribunals have not been and probably never can be constituted in such way that they can have the same kind of qualifications that the Constitution has deemed essential to fair trials of civilians in federal courts.[59]

Although history would prove Justice Black wrong that military justice "probably never can be constituted in such way that they can have the same kind of qualifications that the Constitution has deemed essential to fair trials of civilians," the Court correctly held that to allow the military to lay hold of civilians and place them on trial "encroaches on the jurisdiction of federal courts set up under Article III of the Constitution." To allow Congress to extend military judicial jurisdiction to cover former servicemen would be not only a significant extension of Congressional authority contrary to Article III judicial jurisdiction, it would create an ever increasing population of civilians without Article III judicial protection. As Justice Black observed, "The 1950 Act here considered deprives of jury trial and sweeps under military jurisdiction over 3,000,000 persons who have become veterans since the Act became effective. That number is bound to grow from year to year; there are now more than 3,000,000 men and women in uniform. These figures point up what would be the enormous scope of a holding that Congress could subject every ex-serviceman and woman in the land to trial by court-martial for any alleged offense committed while he or she had been a member of the armed forces."[60]

Justice Black concluded that since it was undisputed that Congress has the power to subject civilians charged with crimes committed while in the military to trial in federal courts, there "can be no valid argument, therefore, that civilian ex-servicemen must be tried by court-martial or not tried at all."[61] The Court concluded that the rights to trial by jury and the procedures of civilian justice can not be circumvented by Congressional use of its Article I power over the military nor through Presidential power as Commander-in-Chief In similar fashion the Court held in *Reid v. Covert* that civilian dependants of active military personnel could not be subjected to court-martial[62] but in *Wilson v. Girard* the Court held that the United States was within its rights under international agreements with Japan to cede its jurisdiction over a current member of the armed forces to Japan for trial for murder.[63]

So what principles were affirmed? Neither the Congress nor President in times of war or peace can allow the military to close the courts or otherwise separate a civilian from Article III justice and the protections of the Constitution and the Bill of Rights. Although in *Quirin* the Court held that the German agents were lawfully tried in a military commission, the Court by hearing the case on the merits made clear that the agents had access to the civilian Constitutional review. In *Toth*, the Court entertained and ruled on the merits of the military actions of the Executive through the writ of habeas corpus, again allowing a citizen to have access to the Article III review even though Toth was not within the United States.

The Court also made clear that judicial review of Congressional or Presidential actions would be governed by Constitutional as well as statutory law. In *Duncan*, the Court accepted that in times of war or national crisis, as it did in World War I, Congress and the President can exercise broadened powers to successfully prosecute the war but they could not do so by violating Constitutional principles. The need for martial law is for the President and Congress to decide, the need to govern profits from war contracts is for Congress to control, the assessment of immigration of aliens is for the President to determine as governed by law, but Congress cannot close the Courts of the United States and the President cannot impose military justice in a state or territory not in rebellion. In *Toth* the Court defended its place as the branch of government to protect the rights of citizens against actions by the government, and especially in criminal matters, the judiciary was the branch to ensure that the protections of the Constitution are not circumvented. As the Court held in *Milligan*, in *Toth* the principle that the military could not place its hands on civilians when the civilian courts were in full operation, and could be called upon by the government for justice, found continued judicial annunciation. The Court made clear that the military necessities of war or peace may not separate a civilian from his Constitutional rights, especially those guaranteed by the Bill of Rights in cases of criminal adjudication. The protection of those rights is for the Supreme Court and the Article III Judiciary.

PRESIDENTIAL AND CONGRESSIONAL POWER: FREE SPEECH CASES BEFORE MCCARTHY AND THE SECOND RED SCARE

As we discussed in chapter 3, the Supreme Court had ruled that the Sedition Act of 1918 was Constitutional and that "if in [a] speech [the utterer] used words tending to obstruct" the recruitment for servicemen with intent to have that result[64] the First Amendment would provide no protection from prosecution for "the First Amendment while prohibiting legislation against free speech as such cannot have been, and obviously was not, intended to give immunity for every possible use of language."[65] The "most stringent protection of free speech," the Court held, "would not protect a man in falsely shouting fire in a theatre and causing a panic."[66] The line between protected political free speech and criminal incitement is "whether the words used are used in such circumstances and are of such a nature as to create a clear and present danger that will bring about the substantive evils that Congress has a right to prevent."[67]

Although the first red scare ended and the nation entered a period of normalcy and economic prosperity in the 1920s, the fear of subversive organizations was not completely eradicated. The need to control the advocacy of anti-American and pro-communistic speech had survived the fall of Attorney General Palmer and the ascendancy of J. Edgar Hoover. In 1927 the Court was confronted with a California law which made criminal syndicalism a felonious offense.[68] Specifically the California law made it unlawful to advocate or teach or to aid and abet "the commission of crime, sabotage (which word is hereby defined as meaning willful and malicious physical damage or injury to physical property), or unlawful acts of force and violence or unlawful methods of terrorism as a means of accomplishing a change in industrial ownership or control or effecting any political change."[69] The law also made it criminal for any person to organize or to assist in the "organizing, or is or knowingly becomes a member of, any organization, society, group or assemblage of persons organized or assembled to advocate, teach or aid and abet criminal syndicalism."[70] In *Whitney v. California*, the question was whether the law violated the Fourteenth Amendment "providing that no state shall deprive any person of life, liberty, or property, without due process of law, and that all persons shall be accorded the equal protection of the laws."[71]

Anita Whitney was a member of the Oakland, California, branch of the Socialist party who allied with the "radical" socialists in the 1919 split of the party at its convention and joined the "radical" wing which became the Communist Labor Party of America.[72] It was undisputed that Whitney was not only a member of the Communist Labor Party of California but that she was a major leader in the formation of the party. The party adhered to the basic tenets of the Communist Party and communism as defined and advocated from the Communist International in Moscow. Justice Sanford, writing for the Court, first discarded the claims by Whitney that the more "radical" views of the organization were agreed to over her objections as both noncredible and not within review of the Court since such claims were masked arguments against the sufficiency of the evidence and such claims are not covered by the Due Process Clause. The Court held that the due process clause protection against vagueness was not violated by the law because the law was clear in the type of organization that was outlawed and that the equal protection clause was not violated due to arbitrariness because the state has wide discretion in establishing its criminal laws. Justice Sanford wrote,

> A statute does not violate the equal protection clause merely because it is not all-embracing. A state may properly direct its legislation against what it deems an existing evil without covering the whole field of possible abuses. The statute must be presumed to be aimed at an evil where experience shows it to be most felt, and to be deemed by the Legislature coextensive with the practical need; and is not to be overthrown merely because other instances may be suggested to which also it might have been applied; that being a matter for the Legislature to determine unless the case is very clear.[73]

Justice Sanford rejected the proposition that the First Amendment is without limits. He wrote that the right of free speech does not protect the "absolute right to speak, without responsibility . . . giving immunity for every possible use of language and preventing the punishment of those who abuse this freedom," and the government's right to "punish those who abuse this freedom by utterances inimical to the public welfare, tending to incite to crime, disturb the public peace, or endanger the foundations of organized government and threaten its overthrow by unlawful means, is not open to question."[74] The Court concluded that California had the right to determine that an organization that advocated violence or terrorism was a threat to peace and order and as such was well with the police powers of California, and any reasonable inference to the statute must be made in favor of the statute.[75]

Whitney was the high-water mark on restrictive reading of the protections of the First Amendment and the expansive application of antisedition laws. With the economic upturn of the nation, followed by the depression and the almost uniform support of America in World War II the passion to stamp down politically divergent groups and views saw a gradual decrease as well as the flourishing of the acceptance of stronger protections of the First Amendment in the legal and academic professions. Many of the post-*Whitney* speech cases changed focus from Constitutional analysis to sufficiency of the evidence.[76] These and other cases gradually laid the groundwork for the complete repudiation of the "bad tendency" theory by making clear that intent to willfully obstruct the draft or inspire mutiny would not be presumed by the nature of the speech itself. Specific intent to cause the unlawful act would need to be proved in sedition cases. Mere advocacy of a political view, even one that was impassioned and unreasoned and volatile, would no longer alone establish guilt. Judges Hand and Bourquin would finally prevail.

In *Hartzel v. United States,* the Supreme Court all but officially by name overruled the "bad tendency" theory. In *Hartzel* the Court was presented with challenges to a conviction under the Espionage Act of 1917.[77] Hartzel published three articles in 1942 which in essence stated that the war with Germany was wrong and that only a German victory would provide stability for the West. Hartzel, both a racist and anti-Semite, published his articles and mailed them to more than six hundred people from a list he compiled from various public association master mailing lists and individuals listed in the phonebook. Justice Murphy summarized the views and the intent of Hartzel as follows:

> Shortly after being taken into custody, petitioner signed a statement in which he claimed that "the prime motive which impelled me in writing and distributing the articles discussed above, was the hope that they might tend to create sentiment against war amongst the white races and in diverting the war from them, to unite the white races against what I consider to be the more dangerous enemies, the yellow races." At the trial . . . [h]e said he thought his articles might improve the morale of persons available and eligible for recruiting and enlistment in the armed forces, though he retracted this statement on cross-examination. His efforts, he thought, "were political in character" and "the effect on the troops of saying that America was betrayed would be for them to consider whether it was or not and if so, to fight for Americans."[78]

Although Justice Murphy conceded that no claim was made that the Espionage Act of 1917 was unconstitutional, he observed that "such legislation, being penal in nature and restricting the right to speak and write freely, must be construed narrowly."[79] The Court held that the clause "willfully cause . . . insubordination . . ." must be read to mean "deliberately and with a specific purpose to do the acts proscribed" and the clause "willfully obstruct the recruiting or enlistment . . ." must, citing *Schenck v. United States*, present "a clear and present danger that the activities in question will bring about the substantive evils which Congress has a right to prevent."[80] Justice Murphy held that the circumstances of the facts alone require a reversal of the conviction because they did not establish that Hartzel had the required specific intent "to cause insubordination, disloyalty, mutiny or refusal of duty in the military forces or to obstruct the recruiting and enlistment service. . . . They contain, instead, vicious and unreasoning attacks on one of our military allies, flagrant appeals to false and sinister racial theories and gross libels of the President. . . . [T]hey cannot by themselves be taken as proof beyond a reasonable doubt that petitioner had the narrow intent requisite to a violation of this statute."[81]

In a complete repudiation of the World War I "bad tendency" theory cases Justice Murphy concluded,

> We are not unmindful of the fact that the United States is now engaged in a total war for national survival and that total war of the modern variety cannot be won by a doubtful, disunited nation in which any appreciable sector is disloyal. For that reason our enemies have developed psychological warfare

to a high degree in an effort to cause unrest and disloyalty. Much of this type of warfare takes the form of insidious propaganda in the manner and tenor displayed by petitioner's three pamphlets. Crude appeals to overthrow the government or to discard our arms in open mutiny are seldom made. Emphasis is laid, rather, on such matters as the futility of our war aims, the vices of our allies and the inadequacy of our leadership. But *the mere fact that such ideas are enunciated by a citizen is not enough by itself to warrant a finding of a criminal intent to violate Section 3 of the Espionage Act. Unless there is sufficient evidence* from which a jury could infer beyond a reasonable doubt *that he intended to bring about the specific consequences prohibited by the Act,* an American citizen has *the right to discuss these matters either by temperate reasoning or by immoderate and vicious invective without running afoul of the Espionage Act of 1917.* Such evidence was not present in this case.[82]

Judge Bourquin could not have said it better himself. But, Justice Murphy's repudiation was not lost on the minority. Justice Reed wrote that

> Congress has made it an offense willfully to attempt to cause insubordination and likewise willfully to obstruct the recruiting and enlistment service of the Nation. It does not commend itself to us to hold that thereby Congress was merely concerned with crude attempts to undermine the war effort but gave free play to less obvious and more skillful ways of bringing about the same mischievous results. Papers or speeches may contain incitements for the military to be insubordinate or to mutiny without a specific call upon the armed forces so to act. *If circulated for the purpose of undermining military discipline, scurrilous articles, attacking an ally, a minority of our citizens and the President, may contain, without words of solicitation, indications of purpose sufficient, if accepted as true, from which to draw an intent to accomplish the unlawful results.*[83]

"We are at a loss" Justice Reed wrote, "to know what other intent is to be attributed to the dissemination of these documents to our soldiery. To adapt the language of Mr. Justice Holmes speaking for a unanimous Court in *Schenck v. United States,* of course the documents would not have been sent unless they had been intended to have some effect, and we do not see what effect they could be expected to have upon persons in the military service except to influence them to obstruct the carrying on of the war against Germany when petitioner deemed that a betrayal of our country."[84]

PRESIDENTIAL AND CONGRESSIONAL POWER: DENATURALIZATION AND FREEDOM OF THOUGHT BEFORE THE SECOND RED SCARE

In *Schneiderman v. United States*[85] the Court was presented with "the first case to come before us in which the Government has sought to set aside a decree of naturalization years after it was granted on a charge that the finding of attachment was erroneous. Accordingly for the first time we have had to consider the nature and scope of the Government's right in a denaturalization proceeding to re-examine a finding and judgment of attachment upon a charge of illegal procurement."[86] Justice Murphy began his opinion affirming the value of individual civil rights protection and the rejection of the proposition that support of communism, per se, was a dispositive factor in a denaturalization case. "We agree with our brethren of the minority that our relations with Russia, as well as our views regarding its government and the merits of Communism are immaterial to a decision of this case. . . . [W]e should have a jealous regard for the rights of petitioner. We should let our judgment be guided so far as the law permits by the spirit of freedom and tolerance in which our nation was founded, and by a desire to secure the blessings of liberty in thought and action to all those upon whom the right of American citizenship has been conferred by statute, as well as to the native born."[87] In an eloquent defense of doing justice, applying the law and advocating the particular value of the First Amendment, Justice Murphy wrote,

> We are directly concerned only with the rights of this petitioner and the circumstances surrounding his naturalization, but we should not overlook the fact that we are a heterogeneous people. In some of our larger cities a majority of the school children are the offspring of parents only one generation, if that far, removed from the steerage of the immigrant ship, children of those who sought refuge in the new world from the cruelty and oppression of the old, where men have been burned at the stake, imprisoned, and driven into exile in countless numbers for their political and religious beliefs. Here they have hoped to achieve a political status as citizens in a free world in which men are privileged to think and act and speak according to their convictions, without fear of punishment or further exile so long as they keep the peace and obey the law.[88]

Justice Murphy wrote that although the Court assumed, without deciding, that Congress has authorized denaturalization on the grounds of a certificate of citizenship being illegally procured, the government must prove illegal conduct by "clear, unequivocal, and convincing [evidence] because rights once conferred should not be lightly revoked. And more especially is this true when the rights are precious and when they are conferred by solemn adjudication, as is the situation when citizenship is granted."[89]

Schneiderman received citizenship from the U.S. District Court for the Southern District of California on June 10, 1927, and on June 30, 1939, the government began proceedings to revoke the citizenship on the grounds that Schneiderman was a member of the socialist party and as such falsely affirmed allegiance to the United States and the protection to the same. "The claim that petitioner was not in fact attached to the Constitution and well disposed to the good order and happiness of the United States at the time of his naturalization and for the previous five year period is twofold: First, that he believed in such sweeping changes in the Constitution that he simply could not be attached to it; Second, that he believed in and advocated the overthrow by force and violence of the Government, Constitution and laws of the United States."[90] The District Court agreed and was affirmed by the Court of Appeals.

Justice Murphy, defending the right of association and rejecting the proposition by the government that association proves guilt of infidelity to the Constitution, held "[a]t this point it is appropriate to mention what will be more fully developed later—that under our traditions beliefs are personal and not a matter of mere association, and that men in adhering to a political party or other organization notoriously do not subscribe unqualifiedly to all of its platforms or asserted principles."[91] "The Constitutional fathers" wrote Justice Murphy "did not forge a political strait-jacket for the generations to come. . . . Instead they wrote Article V and the First Amendment, guaranteeing freedom of thought . . . [And that Article V and the First Amendment] refute the idea . . . that one who advocates radical changes is necessarily not attached to the Constitution."[92] Concluding, "criticism of, and the sincerity of desires to improve the Constitution should not be judged by conformity to prevailing thought because, if there is any principle of the Constitution that more imperatively calls for attachment than any other it is the principle of free thought—not free thought for those who agree with us but freedom for the thought that we hate."[93]

> In view of our tradition of freedom of thought, it is not to be presumed that Congress in the Act of 1906, or its predecessors of 1795 and 1802, intended to offer naturalization only to those whose political views coincide with those considered best by the founders in 1787 or by the majority in this country today. Especially is this so since the language used, posing the general test of "attachment" is not necessarily susceptible of so repressive a construction. The Government agrees that an alien "may think that the laws and the Constitution should be amended in some or many respects" and still be attached to the principles of the Constitution within the meaning of the statute.[94]

Justice Murphy, both defending the right of thought as well as the insufficiency of the government's case, explained that the belief that the people should use government as a vehicle to direct their own destinies and that government should be used to compensate for the excesses of capitalism are not necessarily views that are incapable with the government's own test of fidelity to the basic philosophy of the Constitution.[95] Nor did the Court accept the proposition that membership in the Communist Party, per se, established that Schneiderman by clear, unequivocal, and convincing evidence did not hold fidelity to the Constitution when he was naturalized.[96]

The Court accepted that the Communist Party sought to impose a dictatorship of the proletariat on the ruins of the old bourgeois state but observed that the term was both fluid in its use and meaning and that it did not require violence as the only tool to achieve this new world order. Justice Murphy throughout his opinion stressed the following principle; "Our concern is with the extent of the allowable area of thought under the statute. We decide only that it is possible to advocate such changes and still be attached to the Constitution within the meaning of the Government's minimum test."[97] The Court rejected that it is a settled fact that the Communist Party, per se, advocates violence to achieve its objectives as either optional or inevitable. In any event, the Court observed that as far as the First Amendment is concerned "[t]here is a material difference between agitation and exhortation calling for present violent action which creates a clear and present danger of public disorder or other substantive evil, and mere doctrinal justification or prediction of the use of force under hypothetical conditions at some indefinite future time—prediction that is not calculated or intended to be presently acted upon, thus leaving opportunity for general discussion and the calm processes of thought and reason."[98] The Court concluded that Congress intended the lack of "attachment" to the Constitution was designed for agitation and exhortation of the first category and not the second. "We conclude that the Government has not carried its burden of proving by 'clear, unequivocal, and convincing' evidence which does not leave 'the issue in doubt', that petitioner obtained his citizenship illegally."[99]

The *Schneiderman* case, although not acknowledged by those who claim the Court was passive, if not complicit, in Congressional and Executive actions to curb freedom of thought and speech in the days of World War II, clearly stands for the Court setting clear boundaries for Executive action. The Court accepted that Congress under the Constitution could govern naturalization standards and rules for eligibility as well as executive power to revoke such naturalization. The Court also strongly defended freedom of political thought supporting socialism and communism—in 1943! Justice Murphy wrote of those who held views supporting socialism, "If room is allowed, as we think Congress intended, for the free play of ideas, none of the foregoing principles which might be held to stand forth with sufficient clarity to be imputed to petitioner on the basis of his membership and activity in the League and the Party and his testimony that he subscribed to the principles of those organizations, is enough, whatever our opinion as to their merits, to prove that he was necessarily not attached to the Constitution when he was naturalized."[100]

In *Baumgartner v. United States*[101] Justice Frankfurter concluded in a similar case of a denaturalization of a German national who being naturalized after World War I began to support the virtues of Hitler and the German Reich. Defending the right to think, be wrong and even to hold the views of fools,

Justice Frankfurter wrote "American citizenship is the right to criticize public men and measures—and that means not only informed and responsible criticism but the freedom to speak foolishly and without moderation. Our trust in the good sense of the people on deliberate reflection goes deep. For such is the contradictoriness of the human mind that the expression of views which may collide with cherished American ideals does not necessarily prove want of devotion to the Nation. It would be foolish to deny that even blatant intolerance toward some of the presuppositions of the democratic faith may not imply rooted disbelief in our system of government."[102]

The Court also made clear that the rights of citizenship granted upon naturalization are to be protected with greater diligence than review of loyalty before citizenship is granted. Justice Frankfurter wrote,

> But relaxation in the vigor appropriate for scrutinizing the intensity of the allegiance to this country embraced by an applicant before admitting him to citizenship is not to be corrected by meagre standards for disproving such allegiance retrospectively. New relations and new interests flow, once citizenship has been granted. All that should not be undone unless the proof is compelling that that which was granted was obtained in defiance of Congressional authority. Non-fulfillment of specific conditions, like time of residence or the required number of supporting witnesses, are easily established, and when established leave no room for discretion because Congress has left no area of discretion. But where the claim of "illegality" really involves issues of belief or fraud, proof is treacherous and objective judgment, even by the most disciplined minds, precarious. That is why denaturalization on this score calls for weighty proof, especially when the proof of a false or fraudulent oath rests predominantly not upon contemporaneous evidence but is established by later expressions of opinion argumentatively projected, and often through the distorting and self-deluding medium of memory, to an earlier year when qualifications for citizenship were claimed, tested and adjudicated.[103]

The Court concluded that the government did not meet its burden that Baumgartner achieved his naturalization illegally.[104] "The evidence in the record before us is not sufficiently compelling to require that we penalize a naturalized citizen for the expression of silly or even sinister-sounding views which native-born citizens utter with impunity."[105]

In *Knauer v. United States*[106] Justice Douglas affirmed *Schneiderman* and *Baumgartner* holding that

> Citizenship obtained through naturalization is not a second-class citizenship. It has been said that citizenship carries with it all of the rights and prerogatives of citizenship obtained by birth in this country "save that of eligibility to the Presidency." There are other exceptions of a limited character. But it is plain that citizenship obtained through naturalization carries with it the privilege of full participation in the affairs of our society, including the right to speak

freely, to criticize officials and administrators, and to promote changes in our laws including the very Charter of our Government. Great tolerance and caution are necessary lest good faith exercise of the rights of citizenship be turned against the naturalized citizen and be used to deprive him of the cherished status. Ill-tempered expressions, extreme views, even the promotion of ideas which run counter to our American ideals, are not to be given disloyal connotations in absence of solid, convincing evidence that that is their significance. Any other course would run counter to our traditions and make denaturalization proceedings the ready instrument for political persecutions.[107]

In *Girouard v. United States* the Court held that sincerely held religious views against the taking of arms does not establish the false taking of the oath of citizenship.[108] In *Bridges v. Wixon*[109] Justice Douglas further developed the protection of freedom of thought and association by making significant distinctions between membership and active participation to bring about the evil that is proscribed by law. Reminiscent of Judge Anderson's holding in *Colyer v. Skeffington*, and the deportation hearings under the Alien Deportation Act of 1918, that mere membership in the Communist Party per se was not sufficient for deportation, Justice Douglas wrote the following:

So Congress declared in the case of an alien who contributed to the treasury of an organization whose aim was to overthrow the government by force and violence. But he who cooperates with such an organization only in its wholly lawful activities cannot by that fact be said as a matter of law to be "affiliated" with it. Nor is it conclusive that the cooperation was more than intermittent and showed a rather consistent course of conduct. Common sense indicates that the term "affiliation" in this setting should be construed more narrowly. Individuals, like nations, may cooperate in a common cause over a period of months or years though their ultimate aims do not coincide. Alliances for limited objectives are well known. Certainly those who joined forces with Russia to defeat the Nazis may not be said to have made an alliance to spread the cause of Communism. An individual who makes contributions to feed hungry men does not become "affiliated" with the Communist cause because those men are Communists. A different result is not necessarily indicated if aid is given to or received from a proscribed organization in order to win a legitimate objective in a domestic controversy. Whether intermittent or repeated the act or acts tending to prove *"affiliation" must be of that quality which indicates an adherence to or a furtherance of the purposes or objectives of the proscribed organization as distinguished from mere co-operation with it in lawful activities.* The act or acts must evidence a working alliance to bring the program to fruition.[110]

In *Bridges* the government sought to deport Henry Bridges under the Immigration Act of 1918 as amended in 1940, which authorized the deportation of aliens who were or are "affiliated" with the Communist Party which was asserted by the government to have advocated the violent overthrow of the government. Justice Douglas affirmed that to be deportable under the amended statute the government must prove Bridges has "conducted himself [so as to show] that he has brought about a status of mutual recognition that he may be relied on to cooperate with the Communist Party on a fairly permanent basis. He must be more than merely in sympathy with its aims or even willing to aid it in a casual intermittent way."[111] Regarding the activity of Bridges the Court concluded "when we turn to the facts of this case we have little more than a course of conduct which reveals cooperation with Communist groups for the attainment of wholly lawful objectives."[112]

"It is clear that Congress desired" Justice Douglas explained "to have the country rid of those aliens who embraced the political faith of force and violence. But we cannot believe that Congress intended to cast so wide a net as to reach those whose ideas and program, though coinciding with the legitimate aims of such groups, nevertheless fell far short of overthrowing the government by force and violence. Freedom of speech and of press is accorded aliens residing in this country. So far as this record shows the literature published by Harry Bridges, the utterances made by him were entitled to that protection. They revealed a militant advocacy of the cause of trade unionism. But they did not teach or advocate or advise the subversive conduct condemned by the statute."[113] Aside from the meaning of "affiliated" to establish membership and advocacy of violence against the United States, the Court found that the procedures of the deportation hearing were not Constitutionally sound. Explaining why the procedures of a deportation hearing were significant to their lawfulness, Justice Douglas observed,

> Here the liberty of an individual is at stake. Highly incriminating statements are used against him—statements which were unsworn and which under the governing regulations are inadmissible. We are dealing here with procedural requirements prescribed for the protection of the alien. Though deportation is not technically a criminal proceeding, it visits a great hardship on the individual and deprives him of the right to stay and live and work in this land of freedom. That deportation is a penalty—at times a most serious one—cannot be doubted. Meticulous care must be exercised lest the procedure by which he is deprived of that liberty not meet the essential standards of fairness.[114]

The Court concluded that since "Harry Bridges has been ordered deported on a misconstruction of the term 'affiliation' as used in the statute and by reason of an unfair hearing on the question of his membership in the Communist Party, his detention under the warrant is unlawful" and the dismissal of his Habeas Corpus petition was reversed.[115]

By the end of the 1940s the Court had clearly rejected the red scare view that membership in the Communist Party per se established violation of federal law that criminalized the advocacy of violent overthrow of the government. Neither in criminal trials or deportation could the government paint individuals as communists, with nothing more, and then deport them or imprison them. As discussed in chapter 3, the decisions by Judges Bourquin and Anderson helped bring about the end of the first red scare through judicial determinations that deportations based on improper procedures and assertions of membership in the Communist Party per se were unlawful. Twenty years later, the Court required the government to prove beyond a reasonable doubt ("clear, unequivocal, and compelling evidence") that an alien engaged in membership of an organization which advocated violence and that the alien had engaged in activity to bring about such advocacy. Mere membership, mere ideological agreement, or participation in legal activities of an organization that advocated the virtues of communism, without more, would not establish engagement in activity that Congress had made criminal or deportable.

Acting within its sphere, the Court in these denaturalization cases maintained the Constitutional boundaries of the Executive branch by requiring it present evidence of falsehood during the naturalization process on the highest level of scrutiny—beyond reasonable doubt—because to revoke naturalization involved both the loss of citizenship and the overturning of a judicial finding of fidelity and attachment to the Constitution and loyalty to the United States. More importantly, the Court held that membership in the Communist Party, by itself, did not meet the test of false declaration of attachment. The Court defended the right of speech, association and political thought. Membership in a party, that may indeed advocate violence, was not enough alone, because one could be a member of a party and not subscribe to all of its tenets and could be a member seeking lawful social change. Guilt by association was not acceptable under First Amendment protection.

The Court also made clear that the procedures of a denaturalization hearing must be such that they meet the standards of due process. Here again, the Court enforced the boundaries on the Executive by rejecting the proposition that the Executive is free to make determinations that adversely affect Constitutionally protected rights, U.S. citizenship being one of these rights, with procedures of its own choosing. In *United States ex rel Knauff v. Shaughnessy* the Court held that the Executive has the power to prevent the entrance of an alien into the United States and such decisions and the process for making such decisions are based on executive power in foreign affairs and are not subject to judicial scrutiny; but once entry is allowed and once citizenship is granted the Executive is to be limited to much more stringent standards and open to judicial review when action is taken to deport a legal alien or to denaturalize a United States citizen. The difference being that an alien does not have a Constitutional right to enter the United States, but a legal alien and a naturalized citizen have Constitutional rights worthy of high judicial protection. Though an alien can be barred entry due to his political thoughts, a legal alien can not be deported and a citizen can not be denaturalized because of theirs.

PRESIDENTIAL AND CONGRESSIONAL POWER: THE COLD WAR, MCCARTHY, AND THE SECOND RED SCARE

The only thing we have to fear is fear itself.

The close of World War II, the rise of the Soviet Union as a direct worldwide political and military threat as well as the rise of fears of communist infiltration in American society and government rekindled fears of fifth columns and the need to protect the American way of life from ideological assault. These fears of communism fostered the rise of loyalty oaths, Congressional investigations and the assumption of guilt by association and innuendo. During the second red scare, the Supreme Court would play its most significant role in the review of the domestic security policies of Congress than it ever had before. With the denaturalization cases and second red scare cases, along with the battles over civil rights for African Americans and criminal procedure protections for criminal defendants, the Court entered into its third judicial era[116]—individual civil liberty protection—which would govern its jurisprudence for the majority of the last half of the twentieth century.

The Second Red Scare

Dissent and fears of a fifth column along with desires to unify the nation helped develop the seeds for the first red scare. These seeds found fertile ground in the fears of communist infiltration of American society in the American public. The same fears provided fertile ground for the second red scare. The alliance of World War II between the United States and the Soviet Union had collapsed into a cold war in which an iron curtain had fallen dividing Europe into east and west political blocks in which the United States and the Soviet Union led efforts to bring democracy and communism to the rest of the world. On June 24, 1948, the Soviet Union blockaded the railways and roads into West Germany and war was averted through the famous Berlin Airlift in which food and other supplies maintained the city of Berlin until the Soviet Union ended the blockade May 11, 1949. Two months after the Soviet blockade of Berlin began, China, another ally of the United States during the war "fell" to the communists in August 1948.

In response to the growing military threat of the Soviet Union to the Western democracies NATO was born on April 4, 1949. On August 29, 1949, the Soviets successfully exploded their first atomic bomb and on August 12, 1953, they successfully exploded a hydrogen bomb. On June 25, 1950, North Korea crossed the 38th parallel and invaded South Korea, igniting a war that involved a multinational force of fifteen nations led by the United States to force the North Korean forces back across the 38th parallel. The entrance of a Chinese armed force of three hundred thousand

men with air support from the Soviet Union on the side of the North Koreans on November 26, 1950, proved to many in the United States that
the forces of communism were both politically and militarily ready to
confront and threaten the United States and its allies both at home and
abroad. Before the Korean armistice was signed on July 27, 1953, more
than 150,000 American servicemen were killed and wounded in what many
saw as America's first direct war with the realities of communism and the
communist menace.

In response to NATO the Soviet Union unified Central and Eastern
Europe under the Warsaw Pact on May 14, 1955. On October 24, 1956,
Soviet tanks invaded Hungary to aid its communist government in putting
down an armed rebellion led by students and journalists supported in part
by Hungarian soldiers. The rebellion was put down. In the eyes of many
Americans, the military actions in Korea and Hungary along with the Polish
uprising that was put down by the Soviet Union–backed Polish government in June 1956, all demonstrated that the United States was engulfed
in a battle between good and evil and its adversary was willing and able to
destroy America and western democracy. Ten years after the complete victory of the United States in World War II, it was in a political war, had fin-
ished a hot war by proxy, and was now in a world divided by a worldwide
ideological battle between itself and supporters of communism.

On the domestic side, many sought to make sure that the American political, social, and moral fabric was not similarly divided with equal forces on
both sides. Although tempered between the World Wars, America had never
fully withdrawn from its domestic fears of communist sympathizers in American society. In 1938 the first special Committee on Un-American Activities
was created to address the strength of anti-American groups like the Communist Party and the German-American Bund. In May 1940 President Roosevelt
asserted that there were organizations who sought to destroy the American
way of life and Congress responded by passing the Alien Registration Act (the
Smith Act)—the nation's first peacetime antisedition act[117] which President
Roosevelt signed on June 28, 1940. The President then ordered FBI director
Hoover to initiate investigations into subversive organizations and individuals—"American fascists, Trotskyites and members of the CPUSA would soon
feel the lash of the 'cat-o'-nine-tails' known as the Smith Act."[118] The government initiated more than two hundred prosecutions including the famous
"Great Sedition Trial" of twenty-six American fascists including William Dud-
ley Pelley, who referred to himself as "the American Hitler" in July 1942.[119]

With the end of World War II and the birth of the Cold War many believed that part of the reason for the success of the world communist movement and the Soviet Union was the result of duplicity and outright support
from communists in the American government and social society. But
the fears were not without practical evidence. Soon after the war evidence

of Soviet espionage came to light and fostered continued belief that the United States had communist traitors in its government. In 1945 Elizabeth Bentley told the FBI and later the House Un-American Activities Committee (HUAC) that dozens of federal employees had provided her with documents that she in turn provided to the Soviet Union.[120] With the election of a Republican Congress in 1946 and growing fears of communist infiltration the HUAC found new life and direction. In July 1946 a subcommittee of the House Civil Service Committee issued a report recommending that a complete and unified system be created to ferret out those in government who had loyalty to governments other than their own and in October 1946 the U.S. Chamber of Commerce similarly issued a report asserting that communists had well infiltrated various U.S. government agencies including the State Department.[121] In 1945 HUAC became a standing committee and in January 1947 announced that its new function was to expose communists and communist sympathizers in the federal government.[122]

On March 25, 1947, President Truman, through executive order 9835, ordered investigations on the loyalty of federal government employees, resulting in dismissals and resignations of more than ten thousand federal employees. In 1948 HUAC held public hearings on soviet espionage and showcased Elizabeth Bentley and Whittaker Chambers as public witnesses to evidence that government employees were aiding the Soviet Union; the capstone testimony was Chambers testifying that Alger Hiss was his state department contact that provided him with government documents. The proving of these charges by the discovery of classified state department documents in Hiss's handwriting and from his typewriter[123] caused a firestorm, especially since Secretary of State Dean Acheson and President Truman publicly supported Hiss.[124] In March 1948 the FBI arrested Judith Coplon for copying FBI documents and providing them to the Soviet Union. In January 1950 a British scientist confessed to providing Manhattan Project atomic bomb secrets to the Soviets between 1943 and 1947 and named various coconspirators including Julius and Ethel Rosenberg. In February 1950 both Senator McCarthy and FBI Director Hoover claimed that communists were rampant in society, Hoover claiming there were as many as half a million communists and ideological supporters of communism in the United States and McCarthy asserting that the State department was full of such people.[125]

The HUAC also took aim at private organizations and specifically took aim at Hollywood. In 1947 a series of hearings occurred in which friendly witnesses testified of communistic infiltration of the movie industry, followed by hearings with hostile witnesses who refused to cooperate with the committee. These original ten witnesses—the "Hollywood Ten"—were later blacklisted from work for the next decade. But worse for Hollywood, "eight of the ten had [in fact] been communists" and those who defended them felt betrayed because they "had signed on to protect free speech, not to defend communists."[126] Many actors, writers and producers in Hollywood subsequently supported the HUAC through friendly testimony or by providing names. The Hollywood establishment from then to this day has a cultural, intellectual and political hostility against those who supported the HUAC communist investigations, enforced the blacklists, provided names to the HUAC and supported U.S. national security concerns. The entertainment industry and academic left took its most public, cultural and institutional assaults during the HUAC Hollywood investigations and the Hollywood enforcement of the blacklists; and these events still resonate today.

In 1950 Congress passed the Internal Security Act (McCarran Act) which required the Communist Party to register with the Subversive Activities Control Board and declared members of the party ineligible for government employment as well as authorized the President to detain any person he has reasonable ground to believe will engage in or conspire to engage in espionage or sabotage during a declared internal security emergency.[127] The first wave of the Red Scare culminated in the 1952 elections in which the Republicans swept the elections and took both Houses of Congress and the Presidency in large part on the growing anticommunist sentiment. The Republicans, including the rise of Nixon and McCarthy, painted Democrats as soft on communism if not being under its control. To this day it has been a staple of Republican election rhetoric that the Democratic Party, by definition, cannot be trusted with American security and foreign policy. "By 1953, the federal government was investigating 10,000 citizens for possible denaturalization and 12,000 for possible deportation [and] Eisenhower signed the Communist Control Act of 1954 which 'outlawed' the Communist Party and declared that it was 'not entitled to any . . . rights, privileges and immunities.'"[128] The government employee loyalty investigations were intensified by Eisenhower under executive order 10450 in May 1953, resulting in the resignation or dismissal of well over twelve thousand employees. Not to be outdone, the HUAC between "1947 and 1948 . . . compiled dossiers on 25,591 individuals and 1,786 organizations and created a list of 363,119 persons who at some time in the past had signed a Communist Party election petition."[129] It would not be until 1954 with the famous McCarthy Army hearings in June 1954 and the Democrats regaining control of the Congress in the 1954 midterm elections that the fate of the second red scare and the fall of McCarthy would be sealed.

As in the first red scare the Court both deferred and enforced Constitutional limits on the activities of Congress and the President in addressing the crisis of communists in the government and the need to find and control fifth column organizations. In the second red scare the Court was not without voice on the power of the Executive to address issues of government loyalty investigations or those conducted by Congressional committees. Although supporting certain measures, the Court continued its expanding protection of First Amendment rights of free speech and association that it began in the 1940s. This protection and enforcement of Constitutional boundaries culminated in a series of cases in 1957 which provided a capstone to the end of the second red scare and laid the groundwork for the final triumph of First Amendment protection against the criminalization of political speech.

PRESIDENTIAL AND CONGRESSIONAL POWER: THE SUPREME COURT, COLD WAR, MCCARTHY, AND THE SECOND RED SCARE

Emergency, crisis, always the plea of those who would give dictatorial powers to rulers.[130]

In 1944 the Court held in *Hartzel v. United States* that under the Sedition Act of 1917 speech, although incendiary, could not be criminally punished because such speech, without more, did not present "a clear and present danger that the activities in question will bring about the substantive evils which Congress has a right to prevent."[131] A year earlier in *Schneiderman v. United States*[132] the Court defended the purpose of the First Amendment and the limitations on the government to deport a citizen for his political views; "if there is any principle of the Constitution" the Court held, "that more imperatively calls for attachment than any other it is the principle of free thought—not free thought for those who agree with us but freedom for the thought that we hate."[133] In 1946 Justice Douglas affirmed *Schneiderman* in *Knauer v. United States*,[134] holding that the First Amendment includes "the right to speak freely, to criticize officials and administrators, and to promote changes in our laws including the very Charter of our Government."[135] In *Bridges v. Wixon*[136] Justice Douglas wrote for the Court that mere membership in the Communist Party, without direct evidence in support of unlawful activity or advocacy of unlawful activity by the party, could not form sufficient evidence for deportation. The Court further held that the procedures of a deportation hearing must provide basic due process and the failure to provide procedures of fairness was fatal to those hearings upon judicial review. The "bad tendency" view of sedition had been all but officially abandoned and political speech was protected so long as it did not present a clear and present danger of producing the event that Congress has a legitimate power to prevent. The rights of naturalized citizenship were held to be equal to those of native-born citizenship and denaturalization as well as deportation could not be justified and accomplished by proof of unpopular political speech alone. Such were the views and holdings of the Court shortly after the dawn of the second red scare.

Dennis v. United States: **Conspiracy to Be a Clear and Present Danger**

In 1951 the Court was presented with the convictions of twelve members of the national board of the Communist Party including Eugene Dennis, the general secretary of the party. The members were indicted on July 28, 1948, for violation of the Alien Registration Act (the Smith Act) passed by Congress and signed by the President on June 28, 1940. The Smith Act, which was more narrowly tailored than the Espionage Act of 1917, made it unlawful to "knowingly or willfully advocate, abet, advise, or teach the duty, necessity, desirability, or propriety of overthrowing or destroying any government in the United States by force or violence" or to organize any organization to do the same. In what was to be the second longest criminal trial in American legal history[137] all twelve of the defendants were convicted. The convictions were affirmed by Chief Judge Learned Hand of the Second Circuit Court of Appeals[138] and by a divided Supreme Court.[139] Chief Justice Vinson wrote the plurality opinion for the Court joined by Justices Reed, Burton and Minton with concurring opinions by Frankfurter and Jackson. Justices Black and Douglas dissented. Justice Clark recused himself since he initiated the prosecution while Attorney General for President Truman.[140]

The petitioners asserted that the Smith Act violated the First Amendment prohibition against free speech and association as well as violated the Fifth Amendment due to the indefiniteness of the Smith Act provisions. The plurality first addressed the jury instruction by the trial judge that the jury could only convict the defendants if they found that the defendants had an actual specific intent to overthrow the government. Rejecting the assertion that the Smith Act does not require such a specific intent, the plurality ruled that Congress intended to make such intent required for conviction.[141]

The Chief Justice made clear from the beginning of his analysis that Congress acted in order to protect the nation from violent destruction. The plurality held that such action is Constitutional on its face and required little validation.[142] The Chief Justice wrote that the Act did not affect academic discussion of communism and its purported virtues as the petitioners claimed. The plurality held that the Act sought to address advocacy of an illegal activity, not discussion of a political point of view.[143] Approvingly citing the instructions by the trial judge, Chief Justice Vinson held that the principle of academic freedom and First Amendment protection of that freedom was not threatened by the Act.

> Thus, the trial judge properly charged the jury that they could not convict if they found that petitioners did "no more than pursue peaceful studies and discussions or teaching and advocacy in the realm of ideas." He further charged that it was not unlawful "to conduct in an American college or university a course explaining the philosophical theories set forth in the books which have been placed in evidence." Such a charge is in strict accord with the statutory

language, and illustrates the meaning to be placed on those words. Congress did not intend to eradicate the free discussion of political theories, to destroy the traditional rights of Americans to discuss and evaluate ideas without fear of governmental sanction.[144]

The plurality cited the general understanding that the First Amendment has a utility as well as a social value but the right is not without its own boundaries. Free speech, the Chief Justice asserted, is not an unbridled right to say and advocate anything, anywhere at anytime. Free speech is a political tool to create discourse to improve the nation and its policies, but no more than that. It is this understanding, the Chief Justice explained, that provides the First Amendment and judicial interpretation of the amendment's actual meaning.

> The basis of the First Amendment is the hypothesis that speech can rebut speech, propaganda will answer propaganda, free debate of ideas will result in the wisest governmental policies. It is for this reason that this Court has recognized the inherent value of free discourse. An analysis of the leading cases in this Court which have involved direct limitations on speech, however, will demonstrate that both the majority of the Court and the dissenters in particular cases have recognized that this is not an unlimited, unqualified right, but that the societal value of speech must, on occasion, be subordinated to other values and considerations.[145]

After reviewing the cases of sustaining the convictions in *Frohwerk v. United States, Debs v. United States, Abrams v. United States, Schaefer v. United States,* and *Pierce v. United States* through the application of the "clear and present danger" doctrine of *Schenck v. United States* the Court correctly concluded that "where an offense is specified by a statute in nonspeech or nonpress terms, a conviction relying upon speech or press as evidence of violation may be sustained only when the speech or publication created a 'clear and present danger' of attempting or accomplishing the prohibited crime, e. g., interference with enlistment."[146]

The plurality, by implication, overturned the approach of *Gitlow v. New York* (1925) and *Whitney v. California* (1927) in which the Court did not apply the "clear and present" danger doctrine.[147] "Although no case" the Chief Justice wrote "subsequent to *Whitney* and *Gitlow* has expressly overruled the majority opinions in those cases, there is little doubt that subsequent opinions have inclined toward the Holmes-Brandeis rationale."[148] Citing *American Communications Assn. v. Douds*[149] the plurality held that although the "clear and present" danger doctrine was the governing principle in cases involving statutes that directly implicated freedom of speech, it was not without elasticity and limits to cases involving the power of Congress to prevent violence to the government. The Chief Justice explained that neither Justice Holmes nor Justice Brandeis ever envisioned that a shorthand phrase should be crystallized into a rigid rule to be applied inflexibly without regard to the circumstances of each case. Speech is not an absolute, above and beyond control by the legislature when its judgment, subject to review here, is that certain kinds of speech are so undesirable as to warrant criminal sanction. Nothing is more certain in modern society than the principle that there are no absolutes, that a name, a phrase, a standard has meaning only when associated with the considerations which gave birth to the nomenclature. To those who would paralyze our Government in the face of impending threat by encasing it in a semantic straitjacket we must reply that all concepts are relative.[150]

Moving to the case of the petitioners the plurality held that since it was obvious that the harm of advocacy of violent overthrow of the government is a legitimate government end, "the literal problem which is presented is what has been meant by the use of the phrase 'clear and present danger' of the utterances bringing about the evil within the power of Congress to punish."[151]

The trial court instructed the jury that they could not convict unless they concluded that the defendants had specifically intended to overthrow the government and that they intended to do so as speedily as circumstances would permit.[152] Starting here, the plurality began to adjust the "clear and present danger" test. For they moved further away from the dissent of Justice Holmes in *Abrams v. United States* and his definition that speech that presents a "clear and present danger" of the evil Congress has a right to prevent must be an "immediate interference with the lawful and pressing purposes of the law that an immediate check is required to save the country."[153] The plurality held that these "words cannot mean that before the Government may act, it must wait until the putsch is about to be executed."[154] Nor is the government limited to act only when the success of the defendants is apparent. "[T]his analysis," the plurality concluded, "disposes of the contention that a conspiracy to advocate, as distinguished from the advocacy itself, cannot be Constitutionally restrained, because it comprises only the preparation. It is the existence of the conspiracy which creates the danger."[155] The plurality adopted the formulation developed by Chief Judge Hand in *U.S. v. Dennis* that the application of the "clear and Present Danger" doctrine involves an assessment of "whether the gravity of the 'evil,' discounted by its improbability, justifies such invasion of free speech as is necessary to avoid the danger."[156] "The mere fact that from the period 1945 to 1948 petitioners' activities did not result in an attempt to overthrow the Government by force and violence is of course no answer to the fact that there was a group that was ready to make the attempt. The formation by petitioners of such a highly organized conspiracy, with rigidly disciplined members subject to call when the leaders, these petitioners, felt that the time had come for action, coupled with the inflammable nature of world conditions . . ., convince us that their convictions were justified on this score. . . . If the ingredients of the reaction are present, we cannot bind the Government to wait until the catalyst is added."[157]

Addressing the ability of Congress to punish the organizing of a group to advocate and teach the overthrow of the government, the plurality affirmed the trial court explanation to the jury.[158] In defending the jury instructions of the trial court, the Plurality defended the Judicial Branch's own prerogatives regarding First Amendment jurisprudence. The plurality held that when "facts are found that establish the violation of a statute, the protection against conviction afforded by the First Amendment is a matter of law. The doctrine that there must be a clear and present danger of a substantive evil that Congress has a right to prevent is a judicial rule to be applied as a matter of law by the courts. The guilt is established by proof of facts. Whether the First Amendment protects the activity which constitutes the violation of the statute must depend upon a judicial determination of the scope of the First Amendment applied to the circumstances of the case."[159] Chief Justice Vinson concluded that the Smith Act, as a matter of law, may be Constitutionally applied when there is a clear and present danger that the evil that Congress intended to prevent is alleged and proven to a jury.

Justice Frankfurter viewed the case as a balancing of interests, both supported by the Constitution. The petitioners have the right to speak and advocate their views, the Justice reasoned, but the government has an equal right to protect the national security of the nation and protect the nation from violent overthrow. Justice Frankfurter asked rhetorically who is to decide on whose side the balance should ally to. In his classic academic approach he defended the Constitutional boundaries on the judiciary to weigh and balance political matters that are both supported by the text of the Constitution. In the balancing of such interest, it is not for the Judicial Department to choose one over the other in opposition to the decisions of the political departments.

> Full responsibility for the choice cannot be given to the courts. Courts are not representative bodies. They are not designed to be a good reflex of a democratic society. Their judgment is best informed, and therefore most dependable, within narrow limits. Their essential quality is detachment, founded on independence. History teaches that the independence of the judiciary is jeopardized when courts become embroiled in the passions of the day and assume primary responsibility in choosing between competing political, economic and social pressures. Primary responsibility for adjusting the interests which compete in the situation before us of necessity belongs to the Congress. The nature of the power to be exercised by this Court has been delineated in decisions not charged with the emotional appeal of situations such as that now before us. We are to set aside the judgment of those whose duty it is to legislate only if there is no reasonable basis for it.[160]

Frankfurter asserted that after the judiciary determines that a statute meets the requirements of due process, that it complies with principles of separation of powers, that procedures of determination of fact are fair and free from unfair government discretion and the facts meet the standard of beyond a reasonable doubt in criminal proceeding, the judiciary has completed its work and is at the end of its judicial powers. "Beyond these powers we must not go; we must scrupulously observe the narrow limits of judicial authority even though self-restraint is alone set over us. Above all we must remember that this Court's power of judicial review is not 'an exercise of the powers of a super-legislature.'"[161]

Justice Frankfurter lamented judicial abandonment of self-restraint, its creation of judicial principles like the "clear and present danger" doctrine and judicial interpretation of statutes that involve the First Amendment differently than any other statute. Because of judicial policy making, Frankfurter complained, the Court has to create adjustments to various judicially created principles and doctrines to enforce them as it did in the present case.[162] "Free-speech cases" wrote Justice Frankfurter "are not an exception to the principle that we are not legislators, that direct policymaking is not our province. How best to reconcile competing interests is the business of legislatures, and the balance they strike is a judgment not to be displaced by ours, but to be respected unless outside the pale of fair judgment."[163]

Justice Frankfurter concurred that the conviction of the petitioners was lawful and that the Smith Act was within the power of Congress to balance national security against the impact of that legislation on free speech. He counseled that when the Judiciary affirmatively defers to Congressional determinations it makes no permanent error if the act of Congress is in political error.

> But it is relevant to remind that in sustaining the power of Congress in a case like this nothing irrevocable is done. The democratic process at all events is not impaired or restricted. Power and responsibility remain with the people and immediately with their representatives. All the Court says is that Congress was not forbidden by the Constitution to pass this enactment and that a prosecution under it may be brought against a conspiracy such as the one before us. . . . In finding that Congress has acted within its power, a judge does not remotely imply that he favors the implications that lie beneath the legal issues.[164]

The Constitutional principle that Justice Frankfurter was defending is that once the Court holds that Congress cannot make the political scales weigh in a particular direction, only a contrary decision by the Court or a Constitutional amendment can alter the political result of the decision. However, if the Court makes a decision on which the result is that Congress is not forbidden to make the scale move in a particular direction, later acts of Congress can make the change with little fear of implicating the Constitution. Justice

Frankfurter's point being the political scales, which belong to the political branches of national and state governments, should not be confused with the scales of justice held by the state and federal Judicial Departments which govern the boundaries of the discretion within the political scales.

Justice Frankfurter concluded that those who have expertise in assessing the threat of communism have determined that the threat is real and that Congress must act to meet the threat. On that ground he concurred with the plurality decision to affirm the convictions. He maintained a general distrust of the tendency to use the Judiciary as a break on the political branches and the utility of judicially created principles like the "clear and present danger" doctrine to enforce Constitutional requirements.

On the broader issue of judicial power and the establishing of Constitutional boundaries of Congress and the President in times of war and national crisis and the development of judicial deference to decisions made within those boundaries, Justice Frankfurter makes both an interesting and prophetic observation on the development of civil liberty jurisprudence in American law.

> Civil liberties draw at best only limited strength from legal guaranties. Preoccupation by our people with the Constitutionality, instead of with the wisdom, of legislation or of executive action is preoccupation with a false value. Even those who would most freely use the judicial brake on the democratic process by invalidating legislation that goes deeply against their grain, acknowledge, at least by paying lip service, that Constitutionality does not exact a sense of proportion or the sanity of humor or an absence of fear. Focusing attention on Constitutionality tends to make Constitutionality synonymous with wisdom. When legislation touches freedom of thought and freedom of speech, such a tendency is a formidable enemy of the free spirit. Much that should be rejected as illiberal, because repressive and envenoming, may well be not unconstitutional. The ultimate reliance for the deepest needs of civilization must be found outside their vindication in courts of law; apart from all else, judges, howsoever they may conscientiously seek to discipline themselves against it, unconsciously are too apt to be moved by the deep undercurrents of public feeling.[165]

In the abstract Justice Frankfurter is correct; but the individual who loses his or her liberty in the short run, to be restored in the long run, takes no comfort in the short-term loss. The battle of civil liberties jurisprudence in the end is over who loses rights in the short run. Only those who are not losing in the short run talk about in the long run there will be rectification of injustice or that in the short run the loss is for the greater good. But, conversely, although it is true that the power of the Judiciary to equalize the powers of parties in conflict make it an ideal sanctuary of the weak seeking redress for injustice, not every injustice is for the Judiciary to provide rectification. One of the ironies of a functioning republic governed by the rule of law is that although the law applies to all; the law does not correct all wrongs, for all people, all the time.

Justice Frankfurter wrote in *Ludecke v. Watkins* that although Presidential and Congressional "powers may be abused, no doubt, . . . that is a bad reason for having judges supervise their exercise." It is an often less acknowledged but unfortunate truth that the Constitution does not provide an answer to all injustice. In a Constitutional republic some injustices are for Congress, the President, the electorate and the political process—and no one else—to address. As the Court wrote in *Martin v. Mott* in the earliest days of the republic, "the frequency of elections, and the watchfulness of the representatives of the nation, carry with them all the checks which can be useful to guard against usurpation or wanton tyranny."

Although the Founders may have indeed expected the nature of politics and elections to right that which was wrong, history has placed her own mark on our Constitutional system. Frankfurter's observation that the "ultimate reliance for the deepest needs of civilization must be found outside their vindication in courts of law" have been put aside and the American preoccupation with the "Constitutionality" of legislative and executive action and the failure to view civil liberties beyond legal guarantees has ushered in the victory of "those who would most freely use the judicial brake on the democratic process by invalidating legislation that goes deeply against their grain." In today's civil liberties arguments, regardless of the position taken, each side of the many political debates are prepared to use the courts to prevail in the body politic if they are defeated in the political stadiums of debate.

Justice Jackson concurred with the conviction of the petitioners because, in his view, there is no Constitutional right to conspire to advocate the destruction of the nation. He would have sustained the conviction based on the Smith Act itself rather than on the use of the "clear and present danger" doctrine as a Constitutional background to its enforcement.

Justice Black dissented, summarizing that the "petitioners were not charged with an attempt to overthrow the Government. They were not charged with overt acts of any kind designed to overthrow the Government. They were not even charged with saying anything or writing anything designed to overthrow the Government. The charge was that they agreed to assemble and to talk and publish certain ideas at a later date: The indictment is that they conspired to organize the Communist Party and to use speech or newspapers and other publications in the future to teach and advocate the forcible overthrow of the Government. No matter how it is worded, this is a virulent form of prior censorship of speech and press, which I believe the First Amendment forbids. I would hold [section] 3 of the Smith Act authorizing this prior restraint unConstitutional on its face and as applied."[166]

In defending the "clear and present danger doctrine" and its importance to the First Amendment Justice Black asserted that the "First Amendment is the keystone of our Government, that the freedoms it guarantees provide the best insurance against destruction of all freedom. At least as to speech in the realm of public matters, I believe that the 'clear and present danger' test does not 'mark the furthermost Constitutional boundaries of protected expression' but does 'no more than recognize a minimum compulsion of the Bill of Rights.' "[167] To the proposition of Justice Frankfurter that statutes involving First Amendment rights should be viewed as any other statute, Justice Black answered,

> So long as this Court exercises the power of judicial review of legislation, I cannot agree that the First Amendment permits us to sustain laws suppressing freedom of speech and press on the basis of Congress' or our own notions of mere "reasonableness." Such a doctrine waters down the First Amendment so that it amounts to little more than an admonition to Congress. The Amendment as so construed is not likely to protect any but those "safe" or orthodox views which rarely need its protection. . . . Public opinion being what it now is, few will protest the conviction of these Communist petitioners. There is hope, however, that in calmer times, when present pressures, passions and fears subside, this or some later Court will restore the First Amendment liberties to the high preferred place where they belong in a free society.[168]

Justice Douglas, one of the most eloquent defenders of the principles and values underlying the First Amendment made it clear that if the present case involved the teaching or advocacy of the techniques of terror, assassination or other violence he would clearly support the proposition that the First Amendment provides no protection to such speech.[169] "But the fact is that no such evidence was introduced at the trial."[170] Justice Douglas took issue with the fact that the crime involved the teaching of the philosophies of communism. He viewed the case of criminalizing those who taught material that was readily available in books that were not themselves criminal to be in possession of as illogical. "The Act, as construed, requires the element of intent—that those who teach the creed believe in it. The crime then depends not on what is taught but on who the teacher is. That is to make freedom of speech turn not on what is said, but on the intent with which it is said. Once we start down that road we enter territory dangerous to the liberties of every citizen."[171]

In his characteristic defense of the First Amendment, why it should be defended, why acts of Congress that intrude on the exercise of free speech should be voided by the Court, Justice Douglas warned of the danger of using conspiracy to prove sedition:

> The vice of treating speech as the equivalent of overt acts of a treasonable or seditious character is emphasized by a concurring opinion, which, by involving the law of conspiracy, makes speech do service for deeds which are dangerous to society. . . . But never until today has anyone seriously thought that the

ancient law of conspiracy could Constitutionally be used to turn speech into seditious conduct. Yet that is precisely what is suggested. I repeat that we deal here with speech alone, not with speech plus acts of sabotage or unlawful conduct. Not a single seditious act is charged in the indictment. To make a lawful speech unlawful because two men conceive it is to raise the law of conspiracy to appalling proportions. That course is to make a radical break with the past and to violate one of the cardinal principles of our Constitutional scheme.

Free speech has occupied an exalted position because of the high service it has given our society. Its protection is essential to the very existence of a democracy. The airing of ideas releases pressures which otherwise might become destructive. When ideas compete in the market for acceptance, full and free discussion exposes the false and they gain few adherents. Full and free discussion even of ideas we hate encourages the testing of our own prejudices and preconceptions. Full and free discussion keeps a society from becoming stagnant and unprepared for the stresses and strains that work to tear all civilizations apart.

Full and free discussion has indeed been the first article of our faith. We have founded our political system on it. It has been the safeguard of every religious, political, philosophical, economic, and racial group amongst us. We have counted on it to keep us from embracing what is cheap and false; we have trusted the common sense of our people to choose the doctrine true to our genius and to reject the rest. This has been the one single outstanding tenet that has made our institutions the symbol of freedom and equality. We have deemed it more costly to liberty to suppress a despised minority than to let them vent their spleen. We have above all else feared the political censor.[172]

His eloquence continued in conceding that freedom of speech is not an absolute in the pantheon of Constitutional rights and responsibilities.

There comes a time when even speech loses its Constitutional immunity. Speech innocuous one year may at another time fan such destructive flames that it must be halted in the interests of the safety of the Republic. That is the meaning of the clear and present danger test. When conditions are so critical that there will be no time to avoid the evil that the speech threatens, it is time to call a halt. Otherwise, free speech which is the strength of the Nation will be the cause of its destruction.

Yet free speech is the rule, not the exception. The restraint to be Constitutional must be based on more than fear, on more than passionate opposition against the speech, on more than a revolted dislike for its contents. There must be some immediate injury to society that is likely if speech is allowed.[173]

Justice Douglas dissented that the issue of whether the teachings of the Communist Party presented a clear and present danger was a question of law for the court and not a question of fact for the jury, but stated that regardless of whether the issue is for the court or jury — it must be proved. He accepted that communism is a force to be reckoned with on the world stage but not in the United States. He took issue with the plurality assertion that the fact that the Communist Party in the United States, having limited potency, is no answer to its dangerousness and ability to prepare others to conduct violence through advocacy and education. "Communists in this country have never made a respectable or serious showing in any election. . . . Communism has been so thoroughly exposed in this country that it has been crippled as a political force. Free speech has destroyed it as an effective political party."[174] Justice Douglas concluded: "How it can be said that there is a clear and present danger that this advocacy will succeed is, therefore, a mystery. Some nations less resilient than the United States, where illiteracy is high and where democratic traditions are only budding, might have to take drastic steps and jail these men for merely speaking their creed. But in America they are miserable merchants of unwanted ideas; their wares remain unsold. The fact that their ideas are abhorrent does not make them powerful."[175]

Such was the Court at the dawn of the rise of McCarthy, the unleashing of the HUAC, the widespread use of loyalty oaths and government investigations into communist infiltration of the government and Hollywood. In the short term the Court would provide support to the Congress in both its power to investigate communism and enact legislation authorizing the dismissal of those who refused to take loyalty oaths or cooperate with Congressional investigations. But by the late 1950s the Court shifted and in 1957 issued four cases that placed the capstone on the grave of the second red scare. To these cases we will turn our attention.

LOYALTY BOARDS, OATHS, AND INVESTIGATIONS: YE SHALL KNOW THEM BY THEIR WORKS: THE HUNT FOR THE DISLOYAL

In 1950, a year before the decision in *Dennis*, the Court in *American Communications Association v. Douds*[176] was presented with the Constitutionality of Section 9 (h) of the National Labor Relations Act, as amended by the Labor Management Relations Act in 1947 which prevented the National Labor Relations Board from conducting investigations or otherwise providing services to an employee labor dispute if the directors of the union did not submit an affidavit that its officers were not members of the Communist Party, supporters of the Communist Party or otherwise supporters of the violent overthrow of the government. In finding the Labor Management Relations Act Constitutional Chief Justice Vinson, writing for the Court, applied a rational basis test and concluded,

> There can be no doubt that Congress may, under its Constitutional power to regulate commerce among the several States, attempt to prevent political strikes and other kinds of direct action designed to burden and interrupt

the free flow of commerce. We think it is clear, in addition, that the remedy provided by 9 (h) bears reasonable relation to the evil which the statute was designed to reach. Congress could rationally find that the Communist Party is not like other political parties in its utilization of positions of union leadership as means by which to bring about strikes and other obstructions of commerce for purposes of political advantage, and that many persons who believe in the overthrow of the Government by force and violence are also likely to resort to such tactics when, as officers, they formulate union policy.

The fact that the statute identifies persons by their political affiliations and beliefs, which are circumstances ordinarily irrelevant to permissible subjects of government action, does not lead to the conclusion that such circumstances are never relevant.[177]

Asserting that in time of war or national security danger measures otherwise unsustainable can be justified and be Constitutional, the Chief Justice wrote that the Court has "held that aliens may be barred from certain occupations because of a reasonable relation between that classification and the apprehended evil, even though the Constitution forbids arbitrary banning of aliens from the pursuit of lawful occupations. Even distinctions based solely on ancestry, which we declared 'are by their very nature odious to a free people,' have been upheld under the unusual circumstances of wartime. *Hirabayashi v. United States.* If accidents of birth and ancestry under some circumstances justify an inference concerning future conduct, it can hardly be doubted that voluntary affiliations and beliefs justify a similar inference when drawn by the legislature on the basis of its investigations."[178]

The Chief Justice, as Justice Frankfurter would advocate a year later in *Dennis,* applied the principle of deference to the decisions within the boundaries of the political branches: "It should be emphasized that Congress, not the courts, is primarily charged with determination of the need for regulation of activities affecting interstate commerce. This Court must, if such regulation unduly infringes personal freedoms, declare the statute invalid under the First Amendment's command that the opportunities for free public discussion be maintained. But insofar as the problem is one of drawing inferences concerning the need for regulation of particular forms of conduct from conflicting evidence, this Court is in no position to substitute its judgment as to the necessity or desirability of the statute for that of Congress."[179]

Accepting the view that in times of crisis the balance between Constitutional rights and national security needs can bring the political scales on the side of security, the Chief Justice held, "When the effect of a statute or ordinance upon the exercise of First Amendment freedoms is relatively small and the public interest to be protected is substantial, it is obvious that a rigid [application of the clear and present danger] test requiring a showing of imminent danger to the security of the Nation is an absurdity."[180] To the contention that "this Court must find that political [labor] strikes create a clear and present danger to the security of the Nation or of widespread industrial strife in order to sustain 9 (h)" the Chief Justice answered that the clear and present danger doctrine had not been conceived or applied subsequent to *Schenck v. United States* to contradict the recognition that when "particular conduct is regulated in the interest of public order, and the regulation results in an indirect, conditional, partial abridgment of speech, the duty of the courts is to determine which of these two conflicting interests demands the greater protection under the particular circumstances presented."[181]

In *Garner v. Board of Public Works*[182] and *Adler v. Board of Education*[183] the Court supported the enforcement of government loyalty oaths. In *Garner* the Court defended such oaths, explaining that "[p]ast conduct may well relate to present fitness; past loyalty may have a reasonable relationship to present and future trust. Both are commonly inquired into in determining fitness for both high and low positions in private industry and are not less relevant in public employment."[184] In *Adler* the Court upheld *Garner* and held that there is no Constitutional right to work for the state, or an arm of the state, in this case a school district. Justice Minton, writing for the Court, held that the balance between the First Amendment and the right of the government to prevent teachers who supported communism or the violent overthrow of the government from having access to children is not violated by the dismissal of such a teacher.

> It is clear that such persons have the right under our law to assemble, speak, think and believe as they will. *Communications Assn. v. Douds.* It is equally clear that they have no right to work for the State in the school system on their own terms. *United Public Workers v. Mitchell.* They may work for the school system upon the reasonable terms laid down by the proper authorities of New York. If they do not choose to work on such terms, they are at liberty to retain their beliefs and associations and go elsewhere. Has the State thus deprived them of any right to free speech or assembly? We think not. Such persons are or may be denied, under the statutes in question, the privilege of working for the school system of the State of New York because, first, of their advocacy of the overthrow of the government by force or violence, or, secondly, by unexplained membership in an organization found by the school authorities, after notice and hearing, to teach and advocate the overthrow of the government by force or violence, and known by such persons to have such purpose.[185]

The Court concluded that under a loyalty system in which membership of an organization listed by the school system as subversive results in the determination that "a person is found to be unfit and is disqualified from employment in the public school system because of membership in a listed organization, he is not thereby denied the right of free speech and assembly. His freedom of choice between membership in the organization and employment in the school system might be limited, but not his freedom of speech or assembly, except in the remote sense that limitation is inherent in every choice. Certainly such limitation is not one the state may not make in the exercise of its police power to protect the schools from pollution and thereby to defend its own existence."[186]

With the principle established that the states and by extension Congress can require oaths to be taken by prospective and current employees of their loyalty and requiring them not to be members of subversive organizations, the Court held that the process of taking such oaths was of Constitutional significance. In *Gerende v. Election Board*[187] the Court upheld the Maryland requirement that elected officials take an oath when the State Attorney General conceded during oral arguments that he would advise the state that an affidavit stating non-membership and that the candidate has not engaged in violent activity to overthrow the government would meet the state statute. But in *Wieman v. Updegraff*[188] Justice Clark, writing for the majority, reviewed the Courts' decisions in *Garner, Adler,* and *Gerende* and concluded that they all assumed that the requirement for an oath and/or affidavit required specific knowledge of subversive goals and objectives of the organization or they advocated the use of violence to overthrow the government. The Court overruled the Oklahoma Supreme Court affirmance of the dismissal of Wieman because the court had refused to allow Wieman to take the oath based on his membership alone.[189]

The State of Oklahoma, correctly, asserted that under *Adler* the Court had made clear that there was no Constitutional right to state employment: "It is equally clear that they have no right to work for the State in the school system on their own terms" to which the Court not very convincingly answered that to "draw from this language the facile generalization that there is no Constitutionally protected right to public employment is to obscure the issue."[190] The Court, citing *United Public Workers v. Mitchell*[191] as an example of how to apply *Adler,* held that its holding that a person could be bared for engaging in certain political activities "thought inimical to the interests of the Civil Service" should be read in like manner to the "perspective . . . that Congress could not 'enact a regulation providing that no Republican, Jew or Negro shall be appointed to federal office, or that no federal employee shall attend Mass or take any active part in missionary work.' We need not pause to consider whether an abstract right to public employment exists. It is sufficient to say that Constitutional protection does extend to the public servant whose exclusion pursuant to a statute is patently arbitrary or discriminatory."[192]

The Court, backing away from the import of *Adler,* analogized that innocent membership in an organization was akin to race. As it would be arbitrary to not hire a Negro or Catholic, it would be arbitrary not to hire a person who is a member of an association which is innocent of disloyalty or a person who is innocent of the knowledge of the disloyalty of the organization. The point the Court was trying to make is that the government could not prevent the hiring of a citizen based on membership in a non-subversive organization any more than it could prevent hiring based on race, but it could do so upon failure of a citizen to take an oath or submit an affidavit that he/she is not a knowing member of a subversive organization and has not engaged in advocacy or activity to violently overthrow the government.

The Court, during the Red Scare, accepted the proposition that in times of war and domestic threats Congressional prioritization of national security against minor infringement of First Amendment rights is within the powers of Congress and it is not for the judiciary to substitute its judgment for that of Congress. In *Tenney v. Brandhove* the Court held that in times of political discourse legislative investigative committees could abuse their power and become vindictive, but vindictiveness alone does not establish civil liability.[193] Justice Frankfurter wrote,

> This Court has not hesitated to sustain the rights of private individuals when it found Congress was acting outside its legislative role. . . .
> Investigations, whether by standing or special committees, are an established part of representative government. Legislative committees have been charged with losing sight of their duty of disinterestedness. *In times of political passion, dishonest or vindictive motives are readily attributed to legislative conduct and as readily believed. Courts are not the place for such controversies. Self-discipline and the voters must be the ultimate reliance for discouraging or correcting such abuses.*[194] *The courts should not go beyond the narrow confines of determining that a committee's inquiry may fairly be deemed within its province.* To find that a committee's investigation has exceeded the bounds of legislative power it must be obvious that there was a usurpation of functions exclusively vested in the Judiciary or the Executive.[195]

Although the Court deferred to the legislative branch determinations when made within their Constitutional prerogatives, the Court in a series of cases held fast to enforcement of the boundaries of those prerogatives. The Court in a series of cases protected the Fifth Amendment right not to provide testimony to Congressional investigative committees without fear of criminal charges of contempt.[196] The boundaries on Executive action established by due process and procedural principles found enforcement by the Court in cases dealing with national security determinations made by the President regarding the listing of subversive organizations and dismissal of employees on the grounds of membership with such organizations. In *Wieman* the Court held that the failure to require a person to have active knowledge of subversive goals in an organization to which he belongs violates due process. In *Joint Anti-Fascist Refuge Committee v. McGrath*[197] the Court reversed the U.S. Court of Appeals affirmance of placing the petitioner groups on the U.S. Attorney General list of subversive organizations due to the lack of reasonable due process in the determination of the Attorney General that these groups should be placed on his list.[198]

In *Cole v. Young*[199] the Court addressed the dismissal of Cole who was an inspector for the Food and Drug Administration, Department of Health, Education and Welfare due to a finding by the Secretary that he had close relations with communists in the past and had demonstrated sympathy with them through financial donations and attendance at meetings. Cole brought suit and the District Court, on a motion for judgment on the pleadings and dismissal, dismissed Cole's complaint. The Court of Appeals affirmed. The Court reviewed Presidential Order 10450 which implemented the Congressional Act of August 26, 1950, which provided each agency head of government with the power to suspend and/or dismiss any person who the head determines such dismissal is necessary for the protection of national security. The Court reversed the District Court and the Court of Appeals on due process and procedural grounds. The Court held that because Order 10450 did not provide what factual determinations an agency head was to make in order to authorize dismissal, due to threats upon "national security" or evidence of lack of loyalty, an order of dismissal violated due process because it failed to provide the agency head or the employee fair notice of what behavior triggered dismissal.[200]

In *Peters v. Hobby*[201] the Court addressed the power of the Civil Service Commission's Loyalty Review Board, established under President Truman's Executive Order 9835 issued on March 21, 1947, which was authorized to review agency loyalty review board determinations on the disloyalty of federal employees. Peters was a doctor at Yale medical school and "a Special Consultant in the United States Public Health Service of the Federal Security Agency. On April 10, 1953, the functions of the Federal Security Agency were transferred to the Department of Health, Education, and Welfare."[202] After being found loyal by two investigations, one by the Federal Security Agency in January 1949 and by the Loyalty Review Board in May 1952, Peters was subjected to an audit investigation in April 1953 which determined that he was to be barred from further government service. The District Court on a motion for judgment on the pleading decided in favor of the government and was affirmed by the U.S. Court of Appeals for the District of Columbia.[203]

Chief Justice Warren, writing for the Court, bypassed the Constitutional claims made by Peters and decided that his removal was in violation of Executive Order 9835 by concluding that the Civil Service Commission Loyalty Review Board was without authority to debar Peters. The Court admitted that it specifically bypassed the Constitutional issues due to the difficulties that they raised,[204] citing the principle of Constitutional avoidance, and determined that the case could be decided on other grounds. The Court ruled that the Civil Service Commission's Loyalty Review Board acted outside of its authority in Peters' case because the Board only had authority to act when appealed to in cases of decision of disloyalty. The Court ruled that the Civil Service Commission's Loyalty Review Board overstepped its authority by passing a regulation which empowered it to independent review and reverse decisions of loyalty made by an agency review board. The Court ordered the records of Peters cleared of the Civil Service Commission's Loyalty Review Board finding of a reasonable doubt to Peters' loyalty.

Both Justice Black and Douglas would have reversed on Constitutional grounds. Justice Douglas found the procedures of the Board unconstitutional because they allowed for secret evidence and denial of compulsory cross-examination of documents and testimony. Justice Black wrote that he doubted the President had the power to issue the executive order in its current form because it read more like a statute than an executive order and that Congress did not authorize the President to conduct widespread loyalty investigations of federal employees.

Although the Court required due process protections in Executive procedures to enforce loyalty oaths and dismissal of "disloyal" employees, the Court enforced the supremacy of the national government to deal with the threat of sedition. In *Pennsylvania v. Nelson*, the Court overruled the Supreme Court of Pennsylvania and its enforcement of a state law that criminalized the violent overthrow of the United States. The Court held that Congress had legislated in the area of sedition and had exercised plenary jurisdiction; therefore, "a state sedition statute is superseded regardless of whether it purports to supplement the federal law."[205]

By 1956–1957 the mood of the nation had changed and the heightened fear of communist infiltration into the government and fabric of American society had abated. This fact, along with changes to the membership of the Court also marked the end of the Smith Act and loyalty oaths.[206] With Earl Warren replacing Fred Vinson as Chief Justice in 1953, William Brennan replacing Sherman Minton in 1956, Charles Whittaker replacing Stanley Reed in 1957 and John Marshall Harlan replacing Robert Jackson in 1955, the "four justices who had taken a deferential approach to anti-Communist programs and policies were succeeded by four" justices who had alternative views.[207] The difference was felt on June 17, 1957, when the new Court issued four cases, a day that many called "Red Monday."

LOYALTY BOARDS, OATHS, AND INVESTIGATIONS: RED MONDAY

Two months before Red Monday the Court issued three opinions that would provide a preview of what was to come. In *Schware v. Board of Bar Examiners*, Justice Black wrote for the majority that membership in the Communist Party in the 1930s "cannot be said to raise substantial doubts about [the] present good moral character" of Schware to justify New Mexico from barring him from the practice of law.[208] On the same day the Court in *Konigsberg v. State Bar of California* reversed the decision of the California Bar Examiners for failure to admit Raphael Konigsberg to the bar.[209] The California Committee of Bar Examiners during a fitness hearing repeatedly inquired into the political beliefs of Konigsberg who repeatedly objected, claiming that such questions were in violation of the First and Fourteenth Amendment rights. The Court bypassed the Constitutional implications of the Bar Examiners making inquiries into the political beliefs of Konigsberg and affirmed that membership in the Communist Party, per se, was not evidence of the lack of moral character. But more importantly, the Court made clear that membership in a political group that subsequently comes into disfavor cannot be used as evidence to deprive citizens of their rights.[210] Justice Black, writing for the Court, also rejected the use of political articles written by Konigsberg as evidence of his lack of moral character. The Court also affirmed the principle that political writings that simply criticize government policy cannot be used to presume the lack of moral character. Defending the right of free political speech Justice Black wrote,

> Because of the very nature of our democracy such expressions of political views must be permitted. Citizens have a right under our Constitutional system to criticize government officials and agencies. Courts are not, and should not be, immune to such criticism. Government censorship can no more be reconciled with our national Constitutional standard of freedom of speech and press when done in the guise of determining "moral character," than if it should be attempted directly.[211]

The Court held that the refusal of Konigsberg to answer questions of his membership in the Communist Party did not establish evidence of bad character. Justice Black wrote that Konigsberg had a good faith belief that such questions violated his Constitutional rights and that such belief was not improper or frivolous based on Supreme Court jurisprudence.[212] In any event, "the State could not draw unfavorable inferences as to his truthfulness, candor or his moral character in general if his refusal to answer was based on a belief that the United States Constitution prohibited the type of inquiries which the Committee was making."[213] Although victorious, Konigsberg was not admitted to the bar due to his continued refusal to answer questions regarding his membership in the Communist Party.[214]

One month before Red Monday, the Court continued to provide a preview of what was to come in the case of *Jencks v. United States* which involved the prosecution of perjury of Clinton Jencks.[215] The government prosecution was based on undercover FBI informants who testified that Jencks was an active member of the Communist Party of New Mexico when he had declared through affidavit that he was not a member in compliance with the Smith Act. The FBI informants under cross-examination admitted that they had submitted written and oral reports to the FBI regarding the activities of Jencks. Counsel for Jencks moved for government production of the reports by the FBI informants. The trial judge refused and Jencks was convicted. The Court of Appeals affirmed the convictions and the Court reversed. In a broad opinion protecting the right of the defendant to have access to government documents pertinent to his defense and to the testimony of government witnesses, the Court concluded that

> we hold that the criminal action must be dismissed when the Government, on the ground of privilege, elects not to comply with an order to produce, for the accused's inspection and for admission in evidence, relevant statements or reports in its possession of government witnesses touching the subject matter of their testimony at the trial. The burden is the Government's not to be shifted to the trial judge, to decide whether the public prejudice of allowing the crime to go unpunished is greater than that attendant upon the possible disclosure of state secrets and other confidential information in the Government's possession.[216]

The Court accepted, as a truism, that the government has the right to protect national security by withholding documents in its possession, but held that in criminal cases the government does not have the right to withhold such documents in prosecutions based on those papers. The Court held that the government is entitled to secure its papers but "the Government can invoke its evidentiary privileges only at the price of letting the defendant go free. The rationale of the criminal cases is that, since the Government which prosecutes an accused also has the duty to see that justice is done, it is unconscionable to allow it to undertake prosecution and then invoke its governmental privileges to deprive the accused of anything which might be material to his defense."[217]

Although the Court held that membership in the Communist Party was not per se proof of immoral character for admission to the bar and that the government could not withhold evidence under national security concerns while at the same time using such documents in criminal trials, the Court supported absolute Congressional power over sedition as well as its power to deport legal resident aliens because of membership in the Communist Party, even though such membership terminated before Congress made such membership cause for deportation,[218] and that proven membership without evidence of avocation of violent overthrow of the government was sufficient to authorize deportation.[219] The Court ruled that as "long as aliens fail to obtain and maintain citizenship by naturalization, they remain subject to the plenary power of Congress to expel them under the sovereign right to determine what noncitizens shall be permitted to remain within our borders. . . . [Congress] according to any theory of reasonableness or arbitrariness [may] expel known alien communists under its power to regulate the exclusion, admission and expulsion of aliens."[220] The Court further concluded that the Attorney General's refusal to allow bail "in these cases is not arbitrary or capricious, or an abuse of power. There is no denial of the due process of the Fifth Amendment under circumstances where there is reasonable apprehension of hurt from aliens charged with a philosophy of violence against this Government."[221] The power of Executive authority over entry into the United States was affirmed by the Court which held that the permanent exclusion and detention on Ellis Island of a returning resident alien without a hearing did not amount to unlawful detention and that under the Passport Act passed by Congress the President was not obligated to provide reasons or justifications for his exclusion of the alien.[222]

But despite these pro-anticommunist decisions, the Court as an institution had by 1954 become politicized and had formed the ground for its conservative and original intent detractors who have ever since claimed that the Supreme Court is an institution against God, states' rights, the original intent and text of the Constitution, national security and a political activist agent against the morals and values of the nation. By 1954 the Court, asserting federal power over local and states' rights, had ruled that the states could not mandate schoolchildren to salute the flag and recite the pledge of allegiance,[223] nor could religious instruction be mandated in public schools,[224] that a state may not ban a film on the basis of a censor's conclusion that it is "sacrilegious,"[225] that more than half a century of white supremacy and racial segregation under the doctrine of "separate but equal" was no longer protected by the law of the land,[226] followed by a pronouncement in 1955 that the Federal Courts have the authority to dictate to the local and state governments how they would comply with judicial orders.[227] And now, at the dawn of Red Monday, to the horror of many, the Court was seen as allowing communists to become members of the bar, elevating due process procedures over the removal of communists from government and unions, allowing communists in criminal trials to have access to FBI files and providing aid to subversive agents and organizations by ruling that mere membership in the Communist Party, without more, was not enough to dismiss people from government service. All this before the Supreme Court would enter the decade of judicial protection and expansion of voting rights and being in the vanguard of the federal civil rights enforcement against asserted states' rights[228] and the criminal and juvenile justice revolutions of the 1960s.

After the Court issued its decisions in the *Konigsberg* and *Schware* cases on May 6, 1957, one scholar at the time observed that "while the Senate last week was burying McCarthy, the United States Supreme Court buried McCarthyism."[229] If so, the Court on June 17, 1957, in *Yates v. United States*,[230] *Watkins v. United States*,[231] *Sweezy v. New Hampshire*,[232] and *Service v. Dulles*[233] wrote its epitaph. The two lead cases were *Yates* in which the

Court addressed the resulting Smith Act trials of the second tier of communist leaders after the *Dennis* case and *Watkins* in which the Court addressed the activities of the HUAC.

On July 26, 1951, the FBI arrested Oleta Yates and thirteen other members of the Communist Party in California, charging that the defendants conspired "to advocate and teach the duty and necessity of overthrowing the Government of the United States by force and violence, and to organize, as the Communist Party of the United States, a society of persons who so advocate and teach, all with the intent of causing the overthrow of the Government by force and violence as speedily as circumstances would permit."[234] The majority decision, written by Justice Harlan, through statutory constriction, issued the death knell to the Smith Act. The Smith Act by its terms punished "whoever organizes or helps or attempts to organize any society, group, or assembly of persons who teach, advocate, or encourage the overthrow or destruction" of the United States. Justice Harlan wrote that the word "organizes" was key to conviction. Since the Congress did not define the word, the Court was obliged to interpret the word strictly regarding meaning and concluded that "the word refers only to acts entering into the creation of a new organization, and not to acts thereafter performed in carrying on its activities, even though such acts may loosely be termed 'organizational.' . . . . We conclude, therefore, that since the Communist Party came into being in 1945, and the indictment was not returned until 1951, the three-year statute of limitations had run on the 'organizing' charge, and required the withdrawal of that part of the indictment from the jury's consideration"[235] Thus the Court held that prosecutions under the Smith Act for "organizing" the Communist Party to "advocate" the violent overthrow of the government could only be brought three years after the formation of the Communist Party in 1945. Thus no prosecutions could be brought after 1947, effectively ending subsequent trials.

But more significant was the Court's treatment of the "advocacy" of violence against the United States requirement of the Smith Act. Justice Harlan wrote that the question is "whether the Smith Act prohibits advocacy and teaching of forcible overthrow as an abstract principle, divorced from any effort to instigate action to that end, so long as such advocacy or teaching is engaged in with evil intent. We hold that it does not."[236] Echoing the positions of Judge Hand in the *Masses* case, Judge Bourquin in the *Hall* case, Justice Holmes in the *Schenck* case and his dissent in the *Abrams* case, Justice Harlan wrote of the First Amendment that the "distinction between advocacy of abstract doctrine and advocacy directed at promoting unlawful action is one that has been consistently recognized in the opinions of this Court."[237]

The Court distinguished *Dennis* from *Yates* on the ground that *Dennis* stands for the proposition that speech that actively advocates for violent action and for that action to be carried out has no Constitutional protection but mere advocacy without any assertion that action is required or to be initiated has Constitutional protection.[238] In other words, speech for its own sake is protected but speech to achieve a specific action, if illegal, has no First Amendment protection. Justice Harlan concluded that the jury instruction was in error because it did not make clear the distinction between advocacy with nothing more in mind and advocacy with direction to action.[239] Although without saying so, Justice Harlan affirmed Justice Holmes in his dissent in *Abrams* that "only the emergency that makes it immediately dangerous to leave the correction of evil counsels to time warrants any exception to the sweeping command, Congress shall make no law abridging the freedom of speech." Justice Harlan further clarified the meaning of *Dennis* by explaining that the applicability of the Smith Act to the actions in *Dennis* involved a group that was organized with leaders providing advocacy to its members for violent action against the United States at some point in the future. "*Dennis* was thus not concerned with a conspiracy to engage at some future time in seditious advocacy, but rather with a conspiracy to advocate presently the taking of forcible action in the future. It was action, not advocacy, that was to be postponed until 'circumstances' would 'permit.'"[240] Justice Harlan concluded that the trial court error in *Yates* was in that it "did not consider the urging of action for forcible overthrow as being a necessary element of the proscribed advocacy, but rather considered the crucial question to be whether the advocacy was uttered with a specific intent to accomplish such overthrow.[241]

While in *Yates* the Court assumed that Congress did not intend to cross the boundaries of free speech, in *Watkins* the Court was presented with deciding on the outer boundaries of the power of Congressional investigative committees and in the furtherance of their inherent power to conduct investigations and gather information for legislative purposes. Chief Justice Warren, writing for the Court, held that Congressional investigative committees were not unbounded and were subject to due process requirements.

Watkins v. United States involved the conviction of John T. Watkins for contempt of Congress based on his refusal to answer questions regarding his knowledge of other individuals whom he associated with in the past.[242] In April 1954 Watkins was called before a subcommittee of the HUAC to answer allegations that he attended meetings reserved for members of the Communist Party and that he was a communist while an officer of a local union in Illinois. The Court opened its opinion with an acknowledgement that Watkins' refusal was based on the principled belief that the HUAC subcommittee inquiries regarding other people he was associated with was beyond the authority of the committee. Chief Justice Warren wrote the case "rests upon fundamental principles of the power of the Congress and the limitations upon that power."[243]

Watkins freely admitted that between 1942 and 1947 he had provided support to the Communist Party by signing petitions and providing financial support for communist activities and could understand why two prior witnesses had testified that he was a member but that he had never formally joined the party. He further testified that he ceased all cooperation with the party in 1947 over a dispute regarding union compliance with the Taft-Hartley Act which he had advocated for.[244] Satisfied with his candor the committee moved to inquire about other individuals in the Communist Party, to which Watkins refused to answer under the following statement:

> I am not going to plead the [F]ifth [A]mendment, but I refuse to answer certain questions that I believe are outside the proper scope of your committee's activities. I will answer any questions which this committee puts to me about myself. I will also answer questions about those persons whom I knew to be members of the Communist Party and whom I believe still are. I will not, however, answer any questions with respect to others with whom I associated in the past. I do not believe that any law in this country requires me to testify about persons who may in the past have been Communist Party members or otherwise engaged in Communist Party activity but who to my best knowledge and belief have long since removed themselves from the Communist movement.
>
> I do not believe that such questions are relevant to the work of this committee nor do I believe that this committee has the right to undertake the public exposure of persons because of their past activities. I may be wrong, and the committee may have this power, but until and unless a court of law so holds and directs me to answer, I most firmly refuse to discuss the political activities of my past associates.[245]

The Chairman submitted the refusal to the House which certified the refusal to the United States Attorney who brought an indictment and later secured a conviction of contempt. The Court of Appeals reversed but after a rehearing en banc affirmed the conviction. The Supreme Court took the case "because of the very important questions of Constitutional law presented."[246]

The Chief Justice first acknowledged the obligation of a witness to cooperate with a Congressional investigation and the broad powers of Congress to conduct investigations regarding fraud and abuse as well as compliance with statutes and the need for new or adjustments to existing laws.

> But, broad as is this power of inquiry, it is not unlimited. There is no general authority to expose the private affairs of individuals without justification in terms of the functions of the Congress. . . . Nor is the Congress a law enforcement or trial agency. . . . No inquiry is an end in itself; it must be related to, and in furtherance of, a legitimate task of the Congress. Investigations conducted solely for the personal aggrandizement of the investigators or to "punish" those investigated are indefensible.

It is unquestionably the duty of all citizens to cooperate with the Congress. . . . It is their unremitting obligation to respond to subpoenas. . . . This, of course, assumes that the Constitutional rights of witnesses will be respected by the Congress as they are in a court of justice. The Bill of Rights is applicable to investigations as to all forms of governmental action. Witnesses cannot be compelled to give evidence against themselves. They cannot be subjected to unreasonable search and seizure. Nor can the First Amendment freedoms of speech, press, religion, or political belief and association be abridged.[247]

Speaking directly to the right to invoke the First Amendment in the face of Congressional investigative committee inquiries, the Chief Justice wrote,

Clearly, an investigation is subject to the command that the Congress shall make no law abridging freedom of speech or press or assembly. While it is true that there is no statute to be reviewed, and that an investigation is not a law, nevertheless an investigation is part of lawmaking. It is justified solely as an adjunct to the legislative process. The First Amendment may be invoked against infringement of the protected freedoms by law or by lawmaking.[248]

The Court, without explicitly saying so, reversed *Tenney v. Brandhove* by defending the outer boundaries on Congressional investigative powers and the protection of individual rights, when it held that legitimate legislative functions do not include intentionally subjecting individuals to humiliation[249] or procedures that do violence to individual liberties protected by the Bill of Rights. Chief Justice Warren concluded,

The critical element is the existence of, and the weight to be ascribed to, the interest of the Congress in demanding disclosures from an unwilling witness. We cannot simply assume, however, that every Congressional investigation is justified by a public need that overbalances any private rights affected. To do so would be to abdicate the responsibility placed by the Constitution upon the judiciary to insure that the Congress does not unjustifiably encroach upon an individual's right to privacy nor abridge his liberty of speech, press, religion or assembly.[250]

But equally clear the Court held that it was not for the judiciary to determine the validity of Congressional proceedings based on the motives of the committee or on Congress, especially when the investigation serves a legitimate Congressional purpose. It was on the assumption that a committee of Congress or a subcommittee thereof is limited to the tasks and purposes provided to it and that those tasks and purposes must be to achieve a Congressional purpose that the Court hinged its reversal of the contempt conviction.

The Court held that a Congressional committee or its subcommittee is governed as to purpose and scope of investigative power by its charter and the "more vague the committee's charter is, the greater becomes the possibility that the committee's specific actions are not in conformity with the will of the parent House of Congress."[251] The Court found that the authorizing charter for the HUAC was drafted in very broad and undefined terms and acknowledged that those very inexact terms had been approved on multiple occasions dating back to its creation in 1938. The Government asserted that the Court should uphold the authority of the subcommittee by negative inference that the actions were not barred by the charter. In the alternative, the Government argued that the Court should hold that if legitimate legislative purposes "might have been furthered by the kind of disclosure sought" the conviction for contempt should be upheld.[252] The Court rejected this argument because it would allow unfettered access into cherished Constitutional freedoms.

> The Government contends that the public interest at the core of the investigations of the Un-American Activities Committee is the need by the Congress to be informed of efforts to overthrow the Government by force and violence so that adequate legislative safeguards can be erected. From this core, however, the Committee can radiate outward infinitely to any topic thought to be related in some way to armed insurrection. The outer reaches of this domain are known only by the content of "un-American activities." Remoteness of subject can be aggravated by a probe for a depth of detail even farther removed from any basis of legislative action. A third dimension is added when the investigators turn their attention to the past to collect minutiae on remote topics, on the hypothesis that the past may reflect upon the present. . . .
>
> Protected freedoms should not be placed in danger in the absence of a clear determination by the House or the Senate that a particular inquiry is justified by a specific legislative need.
>
> It is, of course, not the function of this Court to prescribe rigid rules for the Congress to follow in drafting resolutions establishing investigating committees. That is a matter peculiarly within the realm of the legislature, and its decisions will be accepted by the courts up to the point where their own duty to enforce the constitutionally protected rights of individuals is affected. An excessively broad charter, like that of the House Un-American Activities Committee, places the courts in an untenable position if they are to strike a balance between the public need for a particular interrogation and the right of citizens to carry on their affairs free from unnecessary governmental interference.[253]

This problem of an overly broad charter and almost no Congressional oversight of the HUAC and its subcommittee raised the problem of the validity of the conviction of contempt because the federal statute making the failure to answer questions by the subcommittee a criminal offense requires the witness to fail to answer "any question pertinent to the question under inquiry."[254] If a question is posed in which it is not clear why the question is pertinent to the purpose of the committee hearing, a contempt charge cannot be maintained. "That knowledge must be available with the same degree of explicitness and clarity that the Due Process Clause requires in the expression of any element of a criminal offense."[255] The Court reversed the contempt conviction because Watkins was not provided with a detailed explanation of the purpose of the hearing and how the questions posed were germane to that purpose.[256]

After its decision in *Yates* that the conviction of communist leaders for their advocacy could not be sustained unless it was proven that they advocated for the overthrowing of the government through specific violent action and that simple advocacy of that overthrow, even with evil intent, was not enough, the Court in *Watkins* was now seen as providing a former communist sympathizer with the right to avoid Congressional questions about other former sympathizers—this during the cold war in 1957! Social conservatives and other anticourt observers used these two cases as further evidence of a judiciary "out of control" which was "setting social policy" and "acting beyond what the founders intended." The remaining Red Monday cases only added to this perception, which would grow and find a permanent intellectual home in the Republican Party over the next few decades. The demonization of the Court by social conservatives continued to grow with the civil liberties and the desegregation cases[257] of the 1960s and fully metastasized as a permanent theory of political discourse by conservatives and Republican politicians with the Court support of abortion and forced integration through bussing and affirmative action in the early 1970s.

In *Sweezy v. New Hampshire* Paul M. Sweezy was found guilty of contempt for his failure to answer questions posed by the New Hampshire Attorney General who was authorized by the state legislature in 1953 under the "Joint Resolution Relating to the Investigation of Subversive Activities" to investigate subversive individuals and groups as well as hold hearings into the activities of such groups and individuals. "Under state law, this was construed to constitute the Attorney General as a one-man legislative committee."[258] Sweezy was called before the Attorney General's committee on two occasions and in both refused to answer questions dealing with his activities in the Progressive Party as well as those who were members of the party. During his second hearing he refused to provide information about a lecture he had presented or his political beliefs regarding communism, although he testified during his first committee hearing that he was a "classic Marxist" and that he believed in socialism. The Attorney General sought a contempt citation against Sweezy which he achieved. The New Hampshire Supreme Court affirmed the contempt conviction.

Writing for a plurality,[259] the Chief Justice wrote that the case raised the issue of the power of legislative investigative committees as did *Watkins*, but with the difference of the applicability of the Fourteenth Amendment Due Process Clause as applied to the state legislative investigations. The Chief Justice, echoing his decision in *Watkins*, wrote,

There is no doubt that legislative investigations, whether on a federal or state level, are capable of encroaching upon the Constitutional liberties of individuals. It is particularly important that the exercise of the power of compulsory process be carefully circumscribed when the investigative process tends to impinge upon such highly sensitive areas as freedom of speech or press, freedom of political association, and freedom of communication of ideas, particularly in the academic community. Responsibility for the proper conduct of investigations rests, of course, upon the legislature itself. If that assembly chooses to authorize inquiries on its behalf by a legislatively created committee, that basic responsibility carries forward to include the duty of adequate supervision of the actions of the committee. This safeguard can be nullified when a committee is invested with a broad and ill-defined jurisdiction. The authorizing resolution thus becomes especially significant in that it reveals the amount of discretion that has been conferred upon the committee.[260]

The Attorney General was instructed in 1953 to enforce the provisions of the New Hampshire Subversive Activities Act of 1951. The Plurality took issue with both the State Supreme Court interpretation of the act which affirmed the labeling of a person as subversive based on the membership of an organization determined to be subversive regardless of individual knowledge of and agreement with the subversive aspects of the organization's beliefs—thus in violation of *Wieman v. Updegraff*—in addition to the inquiries into the personal beliefs and academic lectures made by Sweezy. The Plurality was joined by Justices Frankfurter and Harlan in the defense of the First Amendment in academia and aversion to government intrusion into academic freedom of thought and debate. Chief Justice Warren, for the plurality, wrote,

> Merely to summon a witness and compel him, against his will, to disclose the nature of his past expressions and associations is a measure of governmental interference in these matters. These are rights which are safeguarded by the Bill of Rights and the Fourteenth Amendment. We believe that there unquestionably was an invasion of petitioner's liberties in the areas of academic freedom and political expression—areas in which government should be extremely reticent to tread.
>
> The essentiality of freedom in the community of American universities is almost self-evident. No one should underestimate the vital role in a democracy that is played by those who guide and train our youth. To impose any strait jacket upon the intellectual leaders in our colleges and universities would imperil the future of our Nation. No field of education is so thoroughly comprehended by man that new discoveries cannot yet be made. Particularly is that true in the social sciences, where few, if any, principles are accepted as absolutes. Scholarship cannot flourish in an atmosphere of suspicion and distrust. Teachers and students must always remain free to inquire, to study and to evaluate, to gain new maturity and understanding; otherwise our civilization will stagnate and die.[261]

Equally manifest as a fundamental principle of a democratic society is political freedom of the individual. Our form of government is built on the premise that every citizen shall have the right to engage in political expression and association. This right was enshrined in the First Amendment of the Bill of Rights. Exercise of these basic freedoms in America has traditionally been through the media of political associations. Any interference with the freedom of a party is simultaneously an interference with the freedom of its adherents. All political ideas cannot and should not be channeled into the programs of our two major parties. History has amply proved the virtue of political activity by minority, dissident groups, who innumerable times have been in the vanguard of democratic thought and whose programs were ultimately accepted. Mere unorthodoxy or dissent from the prevailing mores is not to be condemned. The absence of such voices would be a symptom of grave illness in our society.[262]

The plurality found the New Hampshire Supreme Court failure to address the First Amendment rights of Sweezy and its conclusion that "the need for the legislature to be informed on so elemental a subject as the self-preservation of government outweighed the deprivation of Constitutional rights that occurred in the process" unsupportable.[263] But the Plurality held that they need not decide the case on these Constitutional principles (Justices Frankfurter and Harlan not agreeing)[264] and, echoing *Watkins*, held that the act authorizing the Attorney General to conduct investigations was so broad as not to provide the judiciary with any guidance as to what information the legislature had empowered the Attorney General to find and what the relevancy any of the questions posed to Sweezy had to the legislature.[265]

The last case of Red Monday was *Service v. Dulles*[266] which involved the dismissal of a Foreign Service officer by order of the Secretary of Defense upon the recommendation of the Civil Service Commission Loyalty Review Board after it conducted a review, on its own motion, of prior determinations of loyalty by the State Department Loyalty Review Board. The District Court held that under *Peters v. Hobby* the actions of the Civil Service Commission Loyalty Review Board were invalid and ordered the service record of Service to be cleared of any finding of reasonable doubt of his loyalty but sustained the dismissal under the "absolute discretion" of the Secretary to "terminate the employment of any officer or employee . . . whenever he shall deem such termination necessary" under the McCarran Rider to the Espionage Act of 1917.[267] The Court of Appeals affirmed and the Court reversed. Justice Harlan, writing for the majority, held that federal regulations required the Secretary to complete a review of the total record before deciding and not simply affirm the decision of the Civil Service Commission Loyalty Review Board without reading and reviewing the entire record.

In 1788 Madison, having doubts of the power of a Bill of Rights to stand up to the popular will in times of crisis, also believed that the validity of the Bill of Rights would lay in the ability of people to appeal to it as a standard of free government. As we have seen Madison was right on both counts. Although the First Amendment did not save many from prosecution for what they believed during the Red Scare both before and after World War II, the presence of the First Amendment provided the foundation for the civil liberties movement and the final placing of freedom of thought and association at the pantheon of political values in Supreme Court jurisprudence and popular culture. The Court supported the government in times of war but settled that the powers of government during war were not absolute and freedom from forced confessions, criminal prosecutions based on implied evil intent, freedom from military dictatorship, and the sanctity of the judiciary were not to be breached. Justices Douglas, Black, Murphy, Frankfurter, and Warren continued the defense of freedom of speech, thought and association, as well as judicial authority to protect these rights, started by Judges Hand and Bourquin along with Justices Holmes and Brandeis.

But the Court is not without critics of its jurisprudence during World War II and the Cold War. The Court has ever since been saddled with a decision seen as the *Dred Scott* of the twentieth century as well as praised for determining that as Commander-in-Chief the President cannot act to meet what he determines as a military necessity in the face of limiting legislation. To these two cases we will now turn.

NOTES

1. Robert A. Rutland and Charles F. Hobson, eds., *The Papers of James Madison*, vol. 11. (Charlottesville: University Press of Virginia, 1977), 296–300 (emphasis added).

2. *Ex parte Merryman*, 17 Fed. Cas. 144 (1861).

3. *The Prize Cases*, 67 U.S. 635 (1863) (dissenting opinion).

4. *Ex parte Milligan*, 71 U.S. 2 (1866).

5. *Wolf v. United States*, 259 F. 388, 394 (8th Cir. 1919).

6. *Colyer v. Skeffington*, 265 F. 17 (1920) rev'd sub nom *Skeffington v. Katzeff*, 277 F. 129 (1922).

7. *Ex parte Jackson*, 236 Fed. 110, 113 (1920).

8. See Christopher Wolf, *The Rise of Modern Judicial Review: From Judicial Interpretation to Judge-Made Law*, rev. ed. (Lanham, MD: Rowman & Littlefield, 1994).

9. 300 U.S. 379 (1937). *West Coast Hotel v. Parrish* overruled *Adkins v. Children's Hospital*, 261 U.S. 525 (1923).

10. See Gerald Gunther, *Constitutional Law*, 11th ed. (Mineola, NY: The Foundation Press, 1985) and William B. Lockhart, Yale Kamisar, and Jesse H. Choper (1970), *The American Constitution: Cases, Comments and Questions*, 3rd ed. (St Paul, MN: West, 1970). The expressed renunciation of the economic due process theory was announced in *Olsen v. State of Nebraska ex rel Western Reference & Bond Association*, 313 U.S. 236, 246–47 (1941) in its explicit overruling of *Ribnik v. McBride*, 277 U.S. 350 (1928). See also *Williamson v. Lee Optical Co.*, 348 U.S. 483, 487–88 (1955).

11. 299 U.S. 304 (1936). See also chap. 1.

12. Ibid., 315–16.
13. Ibid., 316–18.
14. Ibid.
15. Ibid., 319–20 (emphasis added).
16. Ibid., 321–22.
17. 334 U.S. 742 (1948).
18. Ibid., 754–56.
19. Ibid., 757.
20. Ibid., 765–66.
21. 335 U.S. 160, 164–65 (1948).
22. Ibid., 166–67.
23. Ibid., 170.
24. Ibid., 171–73.
25. 333 U.S. 103, 109 (1948) citing *Norwegian Nitrogen Products Co. v. United States,* 288 U.S. 294 (1933) and *United States v. George S. Bush & Co.,* 310 U.S. 371 (1940).
26. 333 U.S. 103, 111–12 (1948) citing *Coleman v. Miller,* 307 U.S. 433 (1939), *United States v. Curtiss-Wright Corporation,* 299 U.S. 304 (1936), 319–21, 220, 221; *Oetjen v. Central Leather Co.,* 246 U.S. 297 (1918).
27. 338 U.S. 537, 539 (1950).
28. Ibid., 542, citing *United States v. Curtiss-Wright Export Corp., Fong Yue Ting v. United States,* 149 U.S. 698 (1893).
29. *United States ex rel Knauff v. Shaughnessy,* 338 U.S., 542–43.
30. Ibid., 544.
31. Ibid.
32. *Ex parte Quirin,* 317 U.S. 18,25 (1942).
33. Ibid., 21–22.
34. Ibid., 22–23.
35. Ibid., 25.
36. Ibid., 26.
37. Ibid., 27.
38. Ibid., 29.
39. Ibid., 31 (emphasis added).
40. Ibid., 34.
41. Ibid.
42. Ibid., 35.
43. The Court held that "we conclude that the Fifth and Sixth Amendments did not restrict whatever authority was conferred by the Constitution to try offenses against the law of war by military commission, and that petitioners, charged with such an offense not required to be tried by jury at common law, were lawfully placed on trial by the Commission without a jury" (Ibid., 45).
44. Ibid., 37–38.
45. Ibid., 45.
46. *Duncan v. Kahanamoku,* 327 U.S. 304, 346–47 (1946) (Justice Burton, joined by Justice Frankfurter, dissenting).
47. "Your Telegram of December Seventh Received and Your Action in Suspending the Writ of Habeas Corpus and Placing the Territory of Hawaii Under Martial Law in Accordance with U.S.C., Title 48, Section 532 Has My Approval" (Ibid., 348).

48. Ibid., 354–55.

49. *Duncan v. Kahanamoku*, 327 U.S. 304. See also Luis Fisher, *Military Tribunals: Historical Patterns and Lessons* (Washington, DC: Congressional Research Service, 2004).

50. *Duncan v. Kahanamoku*, 327 U.S. at 311.

51. 146 F2d 576 (9th Cir., 1944). See also *Ex parte Zimmerman*, 132 F2d 442 (9th Cir., 1943).

52. *Duncan v. Kahanamoku*, 327 U.S., 318–19.

53. Ibid., 319.

54. Ibid., 322.

55. Ibid.

56. Ibid., 324.

57. 350 U.S. 11 (1955).

58. Ibid., 15.

59. Ibid., 15, 17.

60. Ibid., 19.

61. Ibid., 21–22.

62. 354 U.S. 1 (1957). See also, *Kinsella v. United States ex rel Singleton*, 361 U.S. 234 (1960).

63. 345 U.S. 524 (1957).

64. *Debs v. United States*, 249 U.S. 211, 216 (1919).

65. *Frohwerk v. United States*, 249 U.S. 204, 206 (1919).

66. *Schenck v. United States*, 249 U.S. 47, 52 (1919).

67. Ibid.

68. *Whitney v. California*, 274 U.S. 377 (1927) reversed by *Brandenburg v. Ohio*, 345 U.S. 444 (1969).

69. Ibid., 359.

70. Ibid.

71. Ibid., 361.

72. Ibid., 363.

73. Ibid., 370.

74. Ibid., 371.

75. "By enacting the provisions of the Syndicalism Act the State has declared, through its legislative body, that to knowingly be or become a member of or assist in organizing an association to advocate, teach or aid and abet the commission of crimes or unlawful acts of force, violence or terrorism as a means of accomplishing industrial or political changes, involves such danger to the public peace and the security of the State, that these acts should be penalized in the exercise of its police power. That determination must be given great weight. Every presumption is to be indulged in favor of the validity of the statute, and it may not be declared unconstitutional unless it is an arbitrary or unreasonable attempt to exercise the authority vested in the State in the public interest" (Ibid).

76. For example, see *Schaefer v. United States*, 251 U.S. 468 (1920), *Pierce v. United States*, 252 U.S. 239 (1920), *U.S. ex rel Milwaukee Social Demographic Publishing Co. v. Burleson*, 255 U.S. 407 (1921), *Viereck v. United States*, 318 U.S. 236 (1943), *Keegan v. United States*, 325 U.S. 478 (1945).

77. 322 U.S. 680 (1944) (Justice Roberts concurring in the judgment).

78. Ibid., 685.

79. Ibid., 686.
80. Ibid., 686–87.
81. Ibid., 687–89.
82. Ibid., 689 (emphasis added).
83. Ibid., 691. Justice Reed was joined by Justices Frankfurter, Douglas, and Jackson.
84. Ibid., 693.
85. 320 U.S. 119 (1943).
86. Ibid., 123.
87. Ibid., 119–20.
88. Ibid., 120.
89. Ibid., 125.
90. Ibid., 135.
91. Ibid., 136.
92. Ibid., 137.
93. Ibid., 138 (internal citations omitted).
94. Ibid., 139.
95. Ibid., 141.
96. Ibid., 142.
97. Ibid., 144.
98. Ibid., 157–58.
99. Ibid., 158.
100. Ibid., 146.
101. 322 U.S. 665 (1944).
102. Ibid., 674.
103. Ibid., 675.
104. Ibid., 676. "The insufficiency of the evidence to show that Baumgartner did not renounce his allegiance to Germany in 1932 need not be labored. Whatever German political leanings Baumgartner had in 1932, they were to Hitler and Hitlerism, certainly not to the Weimar Republic. Hitler did not come to power until after Baumgartner foreswore his allegiance to the then German nation" (Ibid).
105. Ibid., 677.
106. 328 U.S. 654 (1946).
107. Ibid., 658.
108. 328 U.S. 1 (1946).
109. 326 U.S. 135 (1945).
110. Ibid., 143–44 (emphasis added).
111. Ibid., 142 (internal citation omitted).
112. Ibid., 145.
113. Ibid., 147–48.
114. Ibid., 154.
115. Ibid., 157.
116. The first era, the nation-state conflict—the establishment of both horizontal and vertical federalism—lasted from 1789–1865. The second era—the rise and fall of economic substantive due process—lasted from 1865–1937. See generally Robert G. McCloskey, *The American Supreme Court* (Chicago: University of Chicago Press, 1960).

117. Christopher M. Finan, *From the Palmer Raids to the Patriot Act: A History of the Fight for Free Speech in America* (Boston: Beacon, 2007), 139.

118. Brian E. Birdnow, "Communism, Anti-Communism, and the Federal Courts in Missouri, 1952–1958: The Trial of the St. Louis Five," *Studies in American History, vol. 58* (Lewiston, NY: Edwin Mellon, 2005), 17.

119. Finan, *From the Palmer Raids to the Patriot Act*, 142 and Geoffrey R. Stone, *Perilous Times: Free Speech in Wartime: From the Sedition Act of 1798 to the War on Terrorism* (New York: Norton, 2004), 272–75.

120. Finan, *From the Palmer Raids to the Patriot Act*, 146.

121. Stone, *Perilous Times*, 325.

122. Ibid., 325, 354.

123. Finan, *From the Palmer Raids to the Patriot Act*, 146.

124. Stone, *Perilous Times*, 328.

125. Ibid., 331 and Finan, *From the Palmer Raids to the Patriot Act*, 146.

126. Finan, *From the Palmer Raids to the Patriot Act*, 153.

127. Ibid., 155.

128. Stone, *Perilous Times*, 340.

129. Ibid., 355.

130. Justice Hugo Black's written notation on his copy of the draft opinion by Chief Justice Vinson in *Dennis v. United States*; Stone, *Perilous Times*, 407.

131. *Hartzel v. United States*, 322 U.S. 680, 686–87 (1944) citing *Schenck v. United States*, 249 U.S. 47 (1919).

132. 320 U.S. 119 (1943).

133. Ibid., 138 (internal citations omitted).

134. 328 U.S. 654 (1946).

135. Ibid., 658.

136. 326 U.S. 135 (1945).

137. The trial began on January 17, 1949, and ended with convictions on October 21, 1949—a total of 279 days (nine months and four days). The O. J. Simpson trial began on January 24, 1995, and ended with acquittal of all charges on October 3, 1995—a total of 254 days (eight months and nine days). The longest trial in American legal history was the first McMartin Preschool child molestation trial of Peggy and Ray Buckey, which began on July 14, 1987, and ended with the acquittal of Peggy Buckey on all counts and a hung jury on Ray Buckey on January 18, 1990—a total of 918 days (two and a half years).

138. *U.S. v. Dennis*, 183 F 2d 201 (1950).

139. *Dennis v. United States*, 341 U.S. 494 (1951).

140. Stone, *Perilous Times*, 653n346.

141. "The structure and purpose of the statute demand the inclusion of intent as an element of the crime. Congress was concerned with those who advocate and organize for the overthrow of the Government. Certainly those who recruit and combine for the purpose of advocating overthrow intend to bring about that overthrow. We hold that the statute requires as an essential element of the crime proof of the intent of those who are charged with its violation to overthrow the Government by force and violence" (*Dennis v. United States*, 341 U.S., 499).

142. Ibid., 501.

143. Ibid., 502.

144. Ibid.
145. Ibid., 503.
146. Ibid., 505.
147. Ibid., 506.
148. Ibid., 507.
149. 339 U.S. 382 (1950).
150. *Dennis v. United States*, 341 U.S., 508.
151. Ibid., 509.
152. Ibid., 510.
153. 250 U.S. 616, 630–31 (1919).
154. *Dennis v. United States*, 341 U.S., 509.
155. Ibid., 511.
156. Ibid., 510.
157. Ibid.
158. Ibid., 511–12.
159. Ibid., 513.
160. Ibid., 525.
161. Ibid., 526. "The Framers of the Constitution chose to keep the judiciary dissociated from direct participation in the legislative process. In asserting the power to pass on the Constitutionality of legislation, Marshall and his Court expressed the purposes of the Founders. But the extent to which the exercise of this power would interpenetrate matters of policy could hardly have been foreseen by the most prescient. The distinction which the Founders drew between the Court's duty to pass on the power of Congress and its complementary duty not to enter directly the domain of policy is fundamental. But in its actual operation it is rather subtle, certainly to the common understanding. Our duty to abstain from confounding policy with Constitutionality demands perceptive humility as well as self-restraint in not declaring unconstitutional what in a judge's private judgment is deemed unwise and even dangerous" (Ibid., 552).
162. Justice Frankfurter observed that "in all fairness, the argument cannot be met by reinterpreting the Court's frequent use of 'clear' and 'present' to mean an entertainable 'probability.' In giving this meaning to the phrase 'clear and present danger,' the Court of Appeals was fastidiously confining the rhetoric of opinions to the exact scope of what was decided by them. We have greater responsibility for having given Constitutional support, over repeated protests, to uncritical libertarian generalities" (Ibid., 527).
163. Ibid., 539.
164. Ibid., 552–53.
165. Ibid., 555–56.
166. Ibid., 579.
167. Ibid., 580.
168. Ibid., 580–81.
169. "If this were a case where those who claimed protection under the First Amendment were teaching the techniques of sabotage, the assassination of the President, the filching of documents from public files, the planting of bombs, the art of street warfare, and the like, I would have no doubts. The freedom to speak is not absolute, the teaching of methods of terror and other seditious conduct should be beyond the pale along with obscenity and immorality" (Ibid., 581).

170. Ibid.
171. Ibid., 583.
172. Ibid., 584–85.
173. Ibid., 585.
174. Ibid., 588.
175. Ibid., 588–89.
176. 339 U.S. 382 (1950).
177. Ibid., 390–91.
178. Ibid., 391 (internal citation omitted).
179. Ibid., 400–01.
180. Ibid., 397. See also Ibid., 394–96.
181. Ibid., 399. "The right of the public to be protected from evils of conduct, even though First Amendment rights of persons or groups are thereby in some manner infringed, has received frequent and consistent recognition by this Court" (Ibid., 398). The Chief Justice concluded, "In essence, the problem is one of weighing the probable effects of the statute upon the free exercise of the right of speech and assembly against the Congressional determination that political strikes are evils of conduct which cause substantial harm to interstate commerce and that Communists and others identified by 9 (h) pose continuing threats to that public interest when in positions of union leadership. We must, therefore, undertake the 'delicate and difficult task . . . to weigh the circumstances and to appraise the substantiality of the reasons advanced in support of the regulation of the free enjoyment of the rights'" (Ibid., 400).
182. 341 U.S. 716 (1951).
183. 342 U.S. 485 (1952).
184. 341 U.S., 720. "We adhere to [*Garner*]. A teacher works in a sensitive area in a schoolroom. There he shapes the attitude of young minds towards the society in which they live. In this, the state has a vital concern. It must preserve the integrity of the schools. That the school authorities have the right and the duty to screen the officials, teachers, and employees as to their fitness to maintain the integrity of the schools as a part of ordered society, cannot be doubted. One's associates, past and present, as well as one's conduct, may properly be considered in determining fitness and loyalty. From time immemorial, one's reputation has been determined in part by the company he keeps. In the employment of officials and teachers of the school system, the state may very properly inquire into the company they keep, and we know of no rule, Constitutional or otherwise, that prevents the state, when determining the fitness and loyalty of such persons, from considering the organizations and persons with whom they associate" (*Adler v. Board of Education*, 342 U.S., 493).
185. 342 U.S., 492.
186. Ibid., 493.
187. 341 U.S., 56 (1951).
188. 344 U.S. 183 (1952).
189. Ibid., 190–91.
190. Ibid.
191. 330 U.S. 75 (1947).
192. *Wieman*, 344 U.S., 191–92.
193. 341 U.S. 367 (1951).

194. Justice Frankfurter, reminiscent of Justice Story's holding in *Martin v. Mott* more than a century before, addressed the assertion that executive power must not be absolute in execution:

> It is no answer that such a power may be abused, for there is no power which is not susceptible of abuse. The remedy for this, as well as for all other official misconduct, if it should occur, is to be found in the Constitution itself. In a free government, the danger must be remote, since in addition to the high qualities which the Executive must be presumed to possess, of public virtue, and honest devotion to the public interests, the frequency of elections, and the watchfulness of the representatives of the nation carry with them all the checks which can be useful to guard against usurpation or wanton tyranny.

Martin v. Mott, 25 U.S. (12 Wheat) 19, 32 (1827).

195. 341 U.S., 377–78 (emphasis added).

196. *Blau v. United* States, 340 U.S. 159 (1950). Justice Black wrote for the Court:

> Petitioner refused to answer these questions on the ground that the answers might tend to incriminate her. She was then taken before the district judge where the questions were again propounded and where she again claimed her Constitutional privilege against self-incrimination and refused to testify. The district judge found petitioner guilty of contempt of court and sentenced her to imprisonment for one year. . . .
>
> At the time petitioner was called before the grand jury, the Smith Act was on the statute books making it a crime among other things to advocate knowingly the desirability of overthrow of the Government by force or violence; to organize or help to organize any society or group which teaches, advocates or encourages such overthrow of the Government; to be or become a member of such a group with knowledge of its purposes. These provisions made future prosecution of petitioner far more than "a mere imaginary possibility. . . ."*Mason v. United States*, 244 U.S. 362, 366; she reasonably could fear that criminal charges might be brought against her if she admitted employment by the Communist Party or intimate knowledge of its workings. Whether such admissions by themselves would support a conviction under a criminal statute is immaterial. Answers to the questions asked by the grand jury would have furnished a link in the chain of evidence needed in a prosecution of petitioner for violation of (or conspiracy to violate) the Smith Act. Prior decisions of this Court have clearly established that under such circumstances, the Constitution gives a witness the privilege of remaining silent. The attempt by the courts below to compel petitioner to testify runs counter to the Fifth Amendment as it has been interpreted from the beginning.

Ibid., 160–61.

See also *Quinn v. United States*, 349 U.S. 155 (1955), *Emspak v. United States*, 349, U.S. 190 (1955), *Bart v. United States*, 349 U.S. 219 (1955), *Slochower v. Board of Education*, 350 U.S. 513 (1956).

197. 341 U.S. 123 (1951).

198. Ibid., 126.

199. 351 U.S. 536 (1956).

200. Ibid., 556–57.

201. 349 U.S. 331 (1955).

202. Ibid., 333.

203. The Court of Appeals affirmed based on its decision in *Bailey v. Richardson*, 86 U.S. App. D.C. 248, 182 F.2d 46 (1950), which was sustained by the Supreme Court by a four-to-four vote. *Bailey v. Richardson*, 341 U.S. 918 (1951).

204. 349 U.S. at 338.

205. *Pennsylvania v. Nelson*, 350 U.S. 497, 504–05 (1956).

206. Stone, *Perilous Times*, 413–16.

207. Ibid., 413.

208. 353 U.S. 232, 246 (1957).

209. 353 U.S. 252 (1957).

210. Ibid., 267–68.

211. Ibid., 269.

212. Ibid., 270.

213. Ibid.

214. Although Justice Black, joined by Douglas, Brennan, Burton, and Chief Justice Warren, held the majority that inferences could not be made by refusal to answer (Justices Frankfurter, Harlan, and Clark dissenting—Justice Whittaker not participating), the majority shifted in 1961 when Konigsberg was again before the Court. In *Konigsberg v. State of Bar of California*, 366 U.S. 36 (1961) (*Konigsberg II*), the majority lined up Frankfurter, Clark, Whittaker, Harlan, and Potter Stewart (who replaced Burton), leaving Black, Douglas, Brennan, and Chief Justice Warren in dissent. See also *Barsky v. Board of Regents*, 347 U.S. 442 (1954), in which the Court upheld a New York statute that made conviction of contempt of Congress grounds for suspension of a medical license. In this case the doctor failed to provide documents to the HUAC.

215. 353 U.S. 757 (1957).

216. Ibid., 672.

217. Ibid., 671 (internal citations omitted).

218. *Harisiades v. Shaughnessy*, 342 U.S. 524 (1952).

219. *Galvan v. Press*, 347 U.S. 522 (1954).

220. *Carlson v. Landon*, 342 U.S. 524, 534, 536 (1952).

221. Ibid., 542.

222. *Shaughnessy v. Mezei*, 345 U.S. 206 (1953).

223. *West Virginia State Board of Education v. Barnette*, 319 U.S. 624 (1943). Two decades later in *Engle v. Vitale*, 370 U.S. 421 (1962), the Court held that a school-district-drafted prayer that was required to be read each day was a violation of the establishment clause of the First Amendment. In *Abington School District v. Schempp*, 374 U.S. 203 (1963), with *Murray v. Curlett* decided in the same opinion, the Court held no state law or school board may require that passages from the Bible be read or that the Lord's Prayer be recited in the public schools of a State at the beginning of each school day—even if individual students may be excused from attending or participating in such exercises upon written request of their parents.

224. *State of Illinois ex rel McCollum v. Board of Education*, 333 U.S. 203 (1948).

225. *Burstyn, Inc. v. Wilson*, 343 U.S. 495 (1952).

226. *Brown v. Board of Education*, 347 U.S. 483 (1954).

227. *Brown v. Board of Education, II* 349 U.S. 294 (1955).

Full implementation of [*Brown v. Board of Education*] may require solution of varied local school problems. School authorities have the primary responsibility for elucidating, assessing, and solving these problems; courts will have to consider whether the action of school authorities constitutes good faith implementation of the governing Constitutional principles. . . .

In fashioning and effectuating the decrees, the courts will be guided by equitable principles. . . . At stake is the personal interest of the plaintiffs in admission to public schools
as soon as practicable on a nondiscriminatory basis. . . .

While giving weight to these public and private considerations, the courts will require
that the defendants make a prompt and reasonable start toward full compliance with our
May 17, 1954, ruling. . . .

. . . [T]he cases are remanded to the District Courts to take such proceedings and enter
such orders and decrees consistent with this opinion as are necessary and proper to admit to public schools on a racially nondiscriminatory basis with all deliberate speed the
parties to these cases.

Ibid., 299–301.

228. For example, see *Holmes v. City of Atlanta*, 350 U.S. 877 (1955) (desegregation of municipal golf courses), *Mayor of Baltimore v. Dawson*, 350 U.S. 877 (1955)
(desegregation of public beaches and bathhouses), *Gayle v. Browder*, 352 U.S. 903
(1956) (desegregation of buses—ending the Montgomery Bus Boycott), *New Orleans City Park Improvement Association v. Detiege*, 358 U.S. 54 (1958) (desegregation
of public parks), and *State Athletic Commission v. Dorsey*, 359 U.S. 533 (1959) (desegregation of athletic competitions).

229. Arthur J. Sabin, *Calmer Times: The Supreme Court and Red Monday* (Philadelphia: University Pennsylvania Press, 1999), 141 citing I. F. Stone.

230. 354 U.S. 298 (1957).

231. 354 U.S. 178 (1957).

232. 354 U.S. 234 (1957).

233. 354 U.S. 363 (1957).

234. Yates, 354 U.S. 298, 300 (1957).

235. Ibid., 310, 312.

236. Ibid., 318.

237. Ibid. The Court cited *Gitlow v. New York*, 268 U.S. 652, 664–69.

238. Ibid., 321–22 (internal citation omitted).

239. "In failing to distinguish between advocacy of forcible overthrow as an
abstract doctrine and advocacy of action to that end, the District Court appears to
have been led astray by the holding in Dennis that advocacy of violent action to
be taken at some future time was enough. It seems to have considered that, since
'inciting' speech is usually thought of as something calculated to induce immediate
action, and since Dennis held advocacy of action for future overthrow sufficient,
this meant that advocacy, irrespective of its tendency to generate action, is punishable, provided only that it is uttered with a specific intent to accomplish overthrow.
In other words, the District Court apparently thought that Dennis obliterated the
traditional dividing line between advocacy of abstract doctrine and advocacy of action" (Ibid., 320).

240. Ibid., 324.

241. Ibid., 324–25.

242. Sabin, *In Calmer Times*, 156.

243. *Watkins*, 354 U.S., 182.

244. Ibid., 184.

245. Ibid., 185.

246. Ibid., 186.

247. Ibid., 187–88.

248. Ibid., 197. Regarding the right to invoke the Fifth Amendment in the face of Congressional investigative committees the Court concluded that the "Fifth Amendment privilege against self-incrimination was frequently invoked and recognized as a legal limit upon the authority of a committee to require that a witness answer its questions. Some early doubts as to the applicability of that privilege before a legislative committee never matured. When the matter reached this Court, the Government did not challenge in any way that the Fifth Amendment protection was available to the witness, and such a challenge could not have prevailed" (Ibid., 195–96).

249. "Abuses of the investigative process may imperceptibly lead to abridgment of protected freedoms. The mere summoning of a witness and compelling him to testify, against his will, about his beliefs, expressions or associations is a measure of governmental interference. And when those forced revelations concern matters that are unorthodox, unpopular, or even hateful to the general public, the reaction in the life of the witness may be disastrous. This effect is even more harsh when it is past beliefs, expressions or associations that are disclosed and judged by current standards rather than those contemporary with the matters exposed. Nor does the witness alone suffer the consequences. Those who are identified by witnesses and thereby placed in the same glare of publicity are equally subject to public stigma, scorn and obloquy. Beyond that, there is the more subtle and immeasurable effect upon those who tend to adhere to the most orthodox and uncontroversial views and associations in order to avoid a similar fate at some future time. That this impact is partly the result of non-governmental activity by private persons cannot relieve the investigators of their responsibility for initiating the reaction" (Ibid., 197–98).

250. Ibid., 198.

251. Ibid., 201.

252. Ibid., 204.

253. Ibid., 204–06.

254. Ibid., 208.

255. Ibid.

256. Ibid., 214–15. "Petitioner was thus not accorded a fair opportunity to determine whether he was within his rights in refusing to answer, and his conviction is necessarily invalid under the Due Process Clause of the Fifth Amendment" (Ibid., 215).

257. For example, see *Turner v. City of Memphis*, 369 U.S. 350 (1962) (desegregation of airport restaurants), *Johnson v. Virginia*, 373 U.S. 61 (1963) (desegregation of courtrooms), and *Schiro v. Bynum*, 375 U.S. 395 (1964) (desegregation of municipal auditoriums).

258. *Sweezy v. New Hampshire*, 354 U.S. 234, 237 (1957).

259. Chief Justice Warren was joined by Justices Black, Douglas, and Brennan. Justice Frankfurter joined by Justice Harlan concurred in the result. Justice Clark joined by Justice Burton dissented.

260. Ibid., 245.

261. Ibid., 250. Justice Frankfurter, joined by Justice Harlan wrote,

Progress in the natural sciences is not remotely confined to findings made in the laboratory. Insights into the mysteries of nature are born of hypothesis and speculation. The more so is this true in the pursuit of understanding in the groping endeavors of what are called the social sciences, the concern of which is man and society. The problems that are the respective preoccupations of anthropology, economics, law, psychology, sociology and related areas of scholarship are merely departmentalized dealing, by way of manageable division of analysis, with interpenetrating aspects of holistic perplexities.

For society's good—if understanding be an essential need of society—inquiries into these problems, speculations about them, stimulation in others of reflection upon them, must be left as unfettered as possible. Political power must abstain from intrusion into this activity of freedom, pursued in the interest of wise government and the people's well-being, except for reasons that are exigent and obviously compelling.

These pages need not be burdened with proof, based on the testimony of a cloud of impressive witnesses, of the dependence of a free society on free universities. This means the exclusion of governmental intervention in the intellectual life of a university. It matters little whether such intervention occurs avowedly or through action that inevitably tends to check the ardor and fearlessness of scholars, qualities at once so fragile and so indispensable for fruitful academic labor.

Ibid., 261–62.

262. Ibid., 250–51.

263. Ibid., 251.

264. Justice Frankfurter wrote the following: "The Supreme Court of New Hampshire justified this intrusion upon his freedom on the same basis that it upheld questioning about the university lecture, namely, that the restriction was limited to situations where the Committee had reason to believe that violent overthrow of the Government was being advocated or planned. . . . For a citizen to be made to forego even a part of so basic a liberty as his political autonomy, the subordinating interest of the State must be compelling. . . . But the inviolability of privacy belonging to a citizen's political loyalties has so overwhelming an importance to the well-being of our kind of society that it cannot be Constitutionally encroached upon on the basis of so meagre a countervailing interest of the State as may be argumentatively found in the remote, shadowy threat to the security of New Hampshire allegedly presented in the origins and contributing elements of the Progressive Party and in petitioner's relations to these" (Ibid., 265).

265. Ibid., 253–55.

266. 354 U.S. 363 (1957).

267. Ibid., 370–71.

Case Studies in Presidential
Power and the Judiciary

5

Mr. Roosevelt and His Camps[1]

Although the World War II internment camps held thousands of Italians, Germans, and Japanese Americans for the duration of the war, the relocation and internment policy is mostly condemned because it included the complete relocation of the Japanese population from the West Coast of the United States. In addition to the 110,000 Japanese citizens and aliens,[2] an estimated eleven thousand German citizens and aliens[3] together with 1,500 Italian citizens and aliens were arrested.[4] The result was that 250 of these individuals were interned with dozens of Hungarians, Romanians, and Bulgarians during World War II. It is the judgment of history that the policy was developed, at least partially, as a result of racism against the Japanese and fear of German and Italian fifth columns. It is conventional wisdom that the Supreme Court in the internment cases not only acquiesced but supported the policy. Leaving the first judgment aside, this chapter will demonstrate that the Supreme Court in *Hirabayashi v. United States*,[5] *Korematsu v. United States*,[6] and *Ex parte Mitsuye Endo*,[7] did not simply sanction a racist policy; rather, it accepted the Government's assertions that the presence of a large Japanese population on the West Coast created a national security threat and failed to apply the proper judicial standard to those assertions. In both *Hirabayashi* and *Korematsu*, the Court held that the President had the power to authorize a policy of curfew and exclusion followed by detention in time of war. However, the Court held in *Ex parte Mitsuye Endo* that the internment of loyal Japanese Americans could not be supported by the fact that proposed relocation communities refused to accept the released Japanese Americans. The

Court further held that military necessity may justify the policy but political expediency does not.

The error in *Hirabayashi* and *Korematsu* rests not in the Court accepting the rationalization of the Government imposing a policy of curfew, exclusion, and detention on the Japanese, but with subjecting those rationalizations to a rational basis review rather than a strict scrutiny review. Since the wholesale removal of a people, determined by race, is not narrowly tailored to meet the compelling governmental interest of coastal safety in time of war, the curfew, exclusion, and detention policies should have been held overly broad and thus unconstitutional. The Court itself in *Hirabayashi* held that racial classification had no place in public policy and that it would apply a strict standard in reviewing the policy. The problem with the *Hirabayashi* and later the *Korematsu* case is that the Court failed to apply the very standard it said would apply. If the Court had applied the correct standard of review, the rule of law would have prevailed without the Court having to assess the rationality or reasonableness of the policy. Under strict scrutiny review, the Court could have observed that regardless of whether the curfew and exclusion policies were rational under the circumstances, they were not cognizable under a Constitution that prevents classification and exclusion of a population based on race and cultural assumptions based on race alone. Because the Court failed to apply strict scrutiny review, the *Korematsu* decision has left the Court with the "black eye" of sanctioning seriously flawed policy.

> It's only a human right if it applies to all human beings. It's only a rule of law if it applies all the time.[8]

In 1950 Chief Justice Vinson observed that although the distinction in the treatment of citizens based on ancestry is "odious to a free people,"[9] distinctions can be upheld in times of war and inferences of future behavior can be justified based on race alone.[10]

On December 7, 1941, the Empire of Japan attacked the U.S. Pacific Military and Naval Base at Pearl Harbor. The nation was not only astonished that its Pacific fleet was attacked and almost destroyed, but was outraged that it had been attacked without a formal declaration of war. Adding to the outrage of the attacks was the systemic racism against the Japanese. The Japanese had been members of the California and West Coast communities for more than half a century, beginning in 1890, when Japanese laborers came to California and Hawaii to work the fruit plantations. In May of 1892, California newspapers began to reflect anti-Japanese sentiment. On June 10, 1893, the San Francisco School Board banned the integration of Japanese children into public schools. After an official protest by the Japanese government, the ban was lifted. On May 14, 1905, the Asiatic Exclusion League, the first of many formal anti-Japanese associations, was formed in San Francisco. On March

14, 1907, President Theodore Roosevelt issued an Executive Order stopping the migration of Japanese laborers from Hawaii and Mexico—functionally ending all immigration of Japanese laborers from Japan. By 1913 anti-Japanese sentiment produced fruit in California with the passage of the California Alien Land Law which barred Japanese ownership of land. The Supreme Court in *Takao Ozawa v. United States*[11] affirmed a district court holding that, under federal law, a Japanese national born in Japan could not receive U.S. citizenship. In 1924, Congress passed the Immigration Act of 1924, which outlawed Japanese immigration to the United States. On July 25, 1941, President Roosevelt froze all Japanese assets in the United States. One day after the day that will live in infamy, the U.S. entered World War II against Japan.

On February 19, 1942, two months after Pearl Harbor, President Roosevelt signed Executive Order 9066. This order authorized the Secretary of War and his designated military commanders to exclude certain individuals from military areas as they deemed it necessary. Although the Executive Order was developed with Japanese nationals and citizens in mind to exclude them from most of the West Coast of the United States, the Executive Order was drafted broadly to authorize the military to exclude any individual from any military area. The Executive Order signed by President Roosevelt on February 19, 1942, in part, reads as follows:

EXECUTIVE ORDER NO. 9066
Authorizing the secretary of war to prescribe military areas. . . .

NOW, THEREFORE, by virtue of the authority vested in me as President of the United States, and Commander in Chief of the Army and Navy, *I hereby authorize and direct the Secretary of War*, and the Military Commanders whom he may from time to time designate, whenever he or any designated Commander deems such actions necessary or desirable, *to prescribe military areas in such places and of such extent as he or the appropriate Military Commanders may determine, from which any or all persons may be excluded, and with such respect to which, the right of any person to enter, remain in, or leave shall be subject to whatever restrictions the Secretary of War or the appropriate Military Commander may impose in his discretion.* . . .

I hereby further authorize and direct the Secretary of War and the said Military Commanders to take such other steps as he or the appropriate Military Commander may deem advisable to enforce compliance with the restrictions applicable to each Military area herein above authorized to be designated, including the use of Federal troops and other Federal Agencies, with authority to accept assistance of state and local agencies.[12]

On March 18, 1942, President Roosevelt issued Executive Order 9102, which established the War Relocation Authority (WRA). The WRA was tasked with the responsibility for "the removal, from areas designated from time to time by the Secretary of War or appropriate military commander under the authority of Executive Order No. 9066 of February 19, 1942, of the persons or classes of persons designated under such Executive Order, and for their relocation, maintenance, and supervision."[13] In addition, the WRA was responsible for providing food and shelter and for organizing labor and compensation on behalf of those relocated and evaluated through the War Relocation Work Corps.[14] On March 21, 1942, Congress passed legislation, affirming the Executive Order, which established that failure to comply with the Order was a crime punishable by up to one year imprisonment and/or a $5,000 fine.[15]

Between March 24 and July 22, 1942, General DeWitt, Military Commander of the Western Defense Command, issued orders first declaring a curfew for all Japanese citizens and foreign nationals in the area of California and later orders excluding all such individuals from the entire Western District, which included all of California, western Washington, western Oregon, and southern Arizona.[16]

THE DISTRICT COURTS AND THE CURFEW CASES

The Government found early support for the curfew policies from the federal courts. In *Ex parte Ventura*,[17] Mary Asaba Ventura, a Japanese American citizen by birth, residing in Seattle, Washington, brought suit against the enforcement of the curfew restrictions issued by General DeWitt on March 27, 1942.[18] She argued that the curfew interfered with her right to liberty and filed a habeas corpus petition requiring the Government to produce her in court and justify the interference with her right to free movement in her home under military curfew. After hearing arguments on the habeas corpus petition from both the petitioner and the government, Judge Black held the petition was at the very "least, very premature" because the petitioner was not unlawfully restrained or in custody, but merely placed on a curfew: "She wishes to be relieved of an imprisonment before any such occurs."[19]

Aside from the premature filing of the habeas petition, the court took the opportunity to justify the necessity and the constitutionality of the Act of March 21, 1942, and Executive Order 9066. Judge Black concluded that under the circumstances of war and the threat of additional attacks upon the United States, the curfew is not an unreasonable military act.[20] Judge Black bypassed—apparently it was not argued to the court—the racial selection and application of the curfew and exclusion and wrote in broad terms of necessity to justify the policy.

> The question here should be viewed with common sense consideration of the situation that confronts this nation now—that confronts this coast today. These are critical days. To strain some technical right of [the petitioner] to

defeat the military needs in this vital area during this extraordinary time could mean perhaps that the "constitution, laws, institutions" of this country . . . would be for a time destroyed . . . by an invading army.

In the Civil War when Milligan was tried . . . no invasion could have been expected. . . . They never imagined the possibility of flying lethal engines hurtling through the air. . . . They never visioned the possibility of far distant forces dispatching an air armada that would rain destroying parachutists from the sky and invade and capture far distant territory overnight. They never had to think then of fifth columnists . . . successfully pretending loyalty to the land where they were born, who, in fact, would forthwith guide or join any such invaders. The past few months in the Philippines . . . establish that apparently peaceful residents may become enemy soldiers overnight. The orders and commands of our President and the military forces, as well as the laws of Congress, must, if we secure that victory that this nation intends to win, be made and applied with realistic regard for the speed and hazards of lightning war. . . .

I do not believe the Constitution of the United States is so unfitted for survival that it unyieldingly prevents the President and the Military, pursuant to law enacted by the Congress, from restricting the movements of civilians such as petitioner, regardless of how actually loyal they perhaps may be, in critical military areas desperately essential for national defense.

Aside from any rights involved it seems to me that if petitioner is as loyal and devoted as her petition avers she would be glad to conform to the precautions which Congress, the President, the armed forces, deem so requisite to preserve the Constitution, laws and institutions for her and all Americans, born here or naturalized.[21]

Judge Black's decision is reminiscent of the views of Lincoln and Bates during the Civil War and of the courts in the early speech cases during World War I in which the necessity to win the war was almost presumed to trump temporary abridgement of civil liberties.[22] As Judge Bledsoe reasoned in the 1917 *The Spirit of '76* case,[23] protected speech in times of peace can become an act subject to repression when it subverts the purposes and destiny of the nation in times of war. Judge Black reasoned in 1942 that the right to freedom of movement, protected in peace, can be restrained when it becomes a strain against the need of the military to protect the nation from possible invasion.[24] Of course such a balance places the individual rights on the light end of the political scales. Judge Black's decision was not an isolated one, although decided on April 15, 1942, it was the first[25] but not the last.

On July 29, 1942, District Judge Duffy ruled in the case of Lincoln Seiichi Kanai, who violated the May 20, 1942, Executive Order that placed San Francisco under an evacuation order, that "[t]his court will not constitute itself as a board of strategy, and declare what is a necessary or proper military area."[26] Echoing the sentiments of Judge Black in *Ex parte Ventura*, Judge Duffy observed:

The field of military operation is not confined to the scene of actual physical combat. Our cities and transportation systems, our coastline, our harbors, and even our agricultural areas are all vitally important in the all-out war effort in which our country must engage if our form of government is to survive. The coast of California has already been under fire from a Japanese vessel of war. . . . Neither the general public nor the judges of our courts have any information upon which they can properly base a conclusion as to the proper necessary area to be included in military areas or defense zones. The theater of war is no longer limited to any definite geographical area. Saboteurs have already landed on our coasts. This court can take judicial notice of the extensive manufacturing facilities for airplanes and other munitions of war which are located on or near our West Coast.

Rights of the individual, under our federal Constitution and its amendments, are not absolute. When such rights come into conflict with other rights granted for the protection and safety and general welfare of the public, they must at times give way. There is no individual right so absolute that it may be exercised under any and all circumstances, and without any qualification. At the present time, the right of our citizens to come and go as they please may be somewhat restricted by the necessity of protecting this nation from our enemies in time of war. . . .

That there is nothing about the executive order or the designation of the military areas, which is unconstitutional, is very certain, considering the necessities and the exigencies of war which has already struck upon our Pacific coast.[27]

On November 16, 1942, in *United States v. Yasui*,[28] District Judge James Fee upheld the conviction of Minoru Yasui, an American born Japanese citizen, for violation of the March 24, 1942, curfew order by General DeWitt.[29] At the same time, Judge Fee held that the constitutionality of the Executive Order was not as certain as Judges Duffy and Black believed, at least so far as it was applied to American citizens.[30] Judge Fee wrote broadly in defense of individual freedom, the validity of *Ex parte Milligan*, the supremacy of civilian justice in times of war, and the limits of executive and military power over civilians even in times of war and crisis. Eleven months after Pearl Harbor, Judge Fee wrote as follows:

It must be remembered, however, when dealing with claims made by writers who are not charged with the responsibility of maintaining the structure of the fundamental law and the guarantees of the liberty of the individual, that the perils which now encompass the nation, however imminent and immediate, are not more dreadful than those which surrounded the people who fought the Revolution and at whose demand shortly thereafter, the ten amendments containing the very guarantees now at issue were written into the Federal Constitution; nor those perils which threatened the country in the War of 1812, when its soil was in the hands of the invader and the Capital itself was violated; nor those perils which engulfed the belligerents in the war between the states, when each was faced with disaffection and disloyalty in the territory in its control. Yet each maintained the liberty of the individual.[31]

Judge Fee, in defending constitutional liberties in time of war and maintaining constitutional boundaries on government power, wrote that "the war power of the federal government is not created by the emergency of war, but it is a power given to meet that emergency. It is a power to wage war successfully. . . . But even the war power does not remove constitutional limitations safeguarding essential liberties."[32] Defending the principle that the rights of citizenship once gained by birth or granted by law cannot be easily disregarded, Judge Fee concluded that "[i]f Congress attempted to classify citizens based upon color or race and to apply criminal penalties for a violation of regulations, founded upon that distinction, the action is insofar void,"[33] but such protections are not as applicable to noncitizens or enemy aliens.

Judge Fee wrote that although race-based curfew and exclusion policies and criminal punishment for violations of such policies are inapplicable to U.S. citizens, the

> power of Congress, however, during time of war over aliens of a country which is hostile to the United States is almost plenary. . . . While in ordinary times such persons are entitled to the equal protection of the laws, when their country is at war with the United States, Congress or the President may intern, take into custody, restrain and control all enemy aliens . . . and neither are restrained by any constitutional guarantees from such action.[34]

That being the case, Judge Fee reasoned that the only issue before the court was whether Yasui was a citizen or an enemy alien.[35] Judge Fee held that Yasui was an enemy alien and subject to the exclusion order of General DeWitt.[36] The Court reasoned that Yasui, due to his employment in the Japanese Consulate and performing duties to advance the goals of the Consulate up until the outbreak of hostilities between the United States and Japan, had demonstrated a renouncement of his U.S. citizenship and the maintenance of his Japanese citizenship by virtue of his parents.[37] Although the Supreme Court ultimately reversed this holding,[38] it would, with its companion case *Hirabayashi*, also overrule the distinction Judge Fee made between the power of the President and the military to impose a curfew on Japanese American citizens and aliens alike. *Yasui* is generally remembered for the Supreme Court reversal of the district court decision that Yasui renounced his citizenship; thus, the significance of Judge Fee's early defense of individual rights in times of war, the inability of the military to interfere with civil justice, and the primacy of civil justice in times of national crisis as advanced in *Ex parte Milligan*[39] has been shamefully overlooked.

Notwithstanding the *Yasui* decision, West Coast courts provided support for the curfew and exclusion policies throughout the war and even after its conclusion. In *Labedz v. Kramer*,[40] the District Court for the District of Oregon held that Carl Labedz, a German American, could not challenge the Constitutionality of the exclusion order applied to him until he was indicted and brought to trial for failure to comply.[41] Although the Government had not submitted the merits of the exclusion process challenged by Labedz, Judge McColloch noted that if the merits were brought before him he would hold that "the action of the military authorities are not arbitrary or capricious and that there were rational bases for their action."[42] The West Coast courts supported the power of the Western Military Command to enforce evacuation orders[43] and found the Western Military Command immune to economic losses resulting from force or acquiescence to its evacuation orders.[44]

HIRABAYASHI V. UNITED STATES: THE COURT'S RATIONALIZATION OF THE CURFEW

In October 1942, Gordon Kiyoshi Hirabayashi was convicted for failure to comply with the curfew order of May 9, 1942, and failure to report to the Civil Control Station on May 11–12, 1942, to register for evacuation in compliance with the military orders.[45] Hirabayashi appealed his conviction, and in the Supreme Court's October Term of 1942, the Government filed its brief justifying Executive Order 9066 and the Act of March 21, 1942, passed by Congress authorizing the exclusion of Japanese Americans from the West Coast.

The Government's argument was two-fold. First, the Government argued that "Article I grants comprehensive powers to the Congress, and Article II independently confers sweeping authority directly upon the President as Commander in Chief."[46] The

> Japanese, during the winter of 1942, were at the crest of their military fortunes. . . . The condition of our temporarily crippled Pacific fleet and the course of the war at that time rendered it imperative that those charged with the defense of our shores take adequate protective measures against a possible invasion of the West Coast.[47]

Secondly, the Government argued the majority of the Japanese population was concentrated on the West Coast.[48] One-third of this population consisted of aliens. The majority, not American-born, some of whom held joint citizenship,[49] were young and educated in Japan where they learned to revere the Emperor.[50] The Government asserted that the Japanese population of more than 110,000 on the West Coast was not well-integrated and assimilated into American culture and society.[51] Specifically, the Government noted that members of the population had instituted Japanese language schools, formed civil organizations that were loyal to Japan and Japanese culture, and held religious views asserting that the Emperor was a deity.[52] Children were raised to hold the views and values of their parents, and these social factors together, along with the possibility of the risk of violence against the Japanese due to the attack on Pearl Harbor, presented the military with a situation that established a threat to the war effort.[53] Although the Government asserted to the Court that "it may be assumed that the majority of the Japanese . . . were loyal[,] . . . the very presence of the entire group presented grave danger because that group comprehended an unknown number of unidentified persons who constituted a serious threat."[54] The Government concluded:

> Prompt and decisive action was necessary, and it cannot be said that it was unreasonable to determine to exclude the Japanese as a whole from these vital areas, and to adopt such supplementary measures as the curfew.
> The action thus taken did not result in any denial of due process. The exercise of governmental power generally interferes with one's liberty to a greater or lesser degree, and the only question is whether that interference is wholly unreasonable or arbitrary.[55]

Leaving aside the sociological justifications for the curfew and exclusion, the Government concluded that the measures taken were "certainly less drastic than compulsory military service," which it is well conceded the Government can compel, and that in the "field of foreign relations, the war power admits of far wider latitude of authority delegable to the executive branch than is permissible in the case of ordinary domestic affairs."[56] Thus, the Government believed that it was well within its powers to impose curfews upon the Japanese on the West Coast.

Although much has been and continues to be said on the curfew, exclusion, and later the internment policies, the focus of this chapter is to demonstrate how the federal district courts and the Supreme Court reviewed the policy and determined that the policy was within the powers of the national government to impose. Although history has made its determination on the policy—a judgment with which this author has no serious debate—the popular judgment that the Supreme Court failed to defend civil liberty in these cases will be challenged insofar as it will be presented that the Court maintained its historical deference to the political branches but failed to apply the correct judicial standard to the policy. The Court's reasoning was wrong, for it failed to hold the policy to a higher standard due to its specific application to a people based on race and culture rather than objective factors. Further, the Court inflicted upon itself a "black eye" by focusing on the justification for the policy, thus leaving itself open to the popular assessment that the Court tacitly approved of a discriminatory policy based on race.

On June 21, 1943, Chief Justice Stone, writing for a unanimous Court,[57] held that "it was within the constitutional power of Congress and the executive arm of the Government[58] to prescribe this curfew order for the period under consideration and that its promulgation by the military commander involved no unlawful delegation of legislative power."[59] The Chief Justice wrote in broad language that in times of war the Court has historically provided great deference to the executive power to implement strategies to successfully conduct hostilities. The Chief Justice concluded:

> The war power of the national government is "the power to wage war successfully." It extends to every matter and activity so related to war as substantially to affect its conduct and progress. The power is not restricted to the winning of victories in the field and the repulse of enemy forces. It embraces every phase of the national defense, including the protection of war materials and the members of the armed forces from injury and from the dangers which attend the rise, prosecution and progress of war. *Since the Constitution commits to the Executive and to Congress the exercise of the war power in all the vicissitudes and conditions of warfare, it has necessarily given them wide scope for the exercise of judgment and discretion in determining the nature and extent of the threatened injury or danger and in the selection of the means for resisting it.* Where, as they did here, the conditions call for the exercise of judgment and discretion and for the choice of means by those branches of the Government on which the Constitution has placed the responsibility of warmaking, it is not for any court to sit in review of the wisdom of their action or substitute its judgment for theirs.[60]

The Court affirmed the test advocated by the Government[61] that the "actions taken must be appraised in the light of the conditions with which the President and Congress were confronted in the early months of 1942, many of which since disclosed, were then peculiarly within the knowledge of the military authorities."[62] Accepting the assertion that the early months of 1942 were militarily dangerous for the United States and that invasion was more than an abstract possibility,[63] the Court concluded that "reasonably prudent men charged with the responsibility of our national defense had ample ground for concluding that they must face the danger of invasion, take measures against it, and in making the choice of measures consider our internal situation, cannot be doubted."[64]

The Chief Justice accepted the sociological as well as the military justifications of the Government verbatim and, with no independent assessment of their validity, concluded:

> Whatever views we may entertain regarding the loyalty to this country of the citizens of Japanese ancestry, we cannot reject as unfounded the judgment of the military authorities and of Congress that there were disloyal members of that population, whose number and strength could not be precisely and quickly ascertained. We cannot say that the war-making branches of the Government did not have ground for believing that in a critical hour such persons could not readily be isolated and separately dealt with, and constituted a menace to the national defense and safety, which demanded that prompt and adequate measures be taken to guard against it. . . .

Like every military control of the population of a dangerous zone in war time, it necessarily involves some infringement of individual liberty, just as does the police establishment of fire lines during a fire, or the confinement of people to their houses during an air raid alarm—neither of which could be thought to be an infringement of constitutional right. Like them, the validity of the restraints of the curfew order depends on all the conditions which obtain at the time the curfew is imposed and which support the order imposing it.[65]

On the issue of racial discrimination and the specific application of the curfew to the Japanese, the Court confirmed that "[d]istinctions between citizens solely because of their ancestry are by their very nature odious to a free people whose institutions are founded upon the doctrine of equality,"[66] and government action based on racial classifications is a denial of due process. However, the threat of sabotage and espionage and possible invasion provided justification for the distinction which resulted in the specific targeting of the Japanese:

The alternative, which appellant insists must be accepted is for the military authorities to impose the curfew on all citizens within the military area, or on none. In a case of threatened danger requiring prompt action, it is a choice between inflicting obviously needless hardship on the many or sitting passive and unresisting in the presence of the threat. We think that constitutional government, in time of war, is not so powerless and does not compel so hard a choice if those charged with the responsibility of our national defense have reasonable ground for believing that the threat is real.[67]

Because racial discriminations are in most circumstances irrelevant and therefore prohibited, it by no means follows that, in dealing with the perils of war, Congress and the Executive are wholly precluded from taking into account those facts and circumstances . . . which may, in fact, place citizens of one ancestry in a different category from others.[68]

The adoption by Government, in the crisis of war and of threatened invasion, of measures for the public safety, based upon the recognition of facts and circumstances which indicate that a group of one national extraction may menace that safety more than others, is not wholly beyond the limits of the Constitution, and is not to be condemned merely because, in other and in most circumstances, racial distinctions are irrelevant.[69]

Thus, the Court concluded that the "fact alone that attack on our shores was threatened by Japan rather than another enemy power set these citizens apart from others who have no particular associations with Japan. . . . [T]he challenged orders and statute afforded a reasonable basis for the action taken in imposing the curfew."[70]

The Court was correct in its holding that it was not for the Court to second-guess the military determinations of risk to the nation, for such is exclusively a military and political assessment that belongs to the Congress and the President. Although the Court held "that the curfew order as applied, and at the time it was applied, was within the boundaries of the war power,"[71] is the legitimate tool of a curfew in time of war justified against the mirror of the Due Process Clause of the Fifth Amendment when the tool is applied to a specific race? Is the test of reasonableness under the circumstances enough to protect Constitutional civil liberties?

The fact that the military, assuming the truth of the justifications on their face, had a "rational basis for the decision which they made"[72] is beside the point. Because the use of racial classifications is "odious" and "irrelevant" in government policymaking, their use should not be reviewed on the lowest level of Constitutional analysis. Otherwise, the fact the classifications are "odious" is without meaning or relevancy. Civil liberty rights, especially due process rights granted by the Fifth Amendment, cannot be subjected to the rational basis test because such a test is easily met—the reasonableness of the justifications only needs to surpass total arbitrary conjecture. Under such a low threshold, Constitutional due process rights maintain verbal allegiance but lose all meaning and relevancy as well as superiority over ordinary governmental policy determinations.

The *Hirabayashi* case itself shows why the use of the reasonableness under the circumstances test is inadequate to protect due process protections. Leaving aside the assessed military threat, the Court accepted the Government's assertion that because the Japanese were an isolated population with cultural, religious, and social differences compared to other members of the society, those differences justified the identification of the Japanese as different and dangerous. The Court assumed the validity of the assertion that these social differences in conjunction with the concentration of the Japanese population on the West Coast created a military threat of espionage and sabotage. Under a more stringent test, simple sociological assumptions could not support evidence of a threat. Cultural and racial distinctions are not Constitutionally "irrelevant" or "odious" if their presence supports the conclusion that such distinctions create a military threat of sabotage or espionage per se. The mere presence of the Japanese on the West Coast, alone, provided enough evidence of threats to national security according to the Government. Had the Court applied a more stringent test it could have, as it did, assume the truth of the Government's assertions regarding military need and nevertheless held that, although the Government had a reasonable and rational basis for its determination, the Constitution demands more when a specific race of people are selected for government interference with civil liberties. Such a decision would have affirmed the proper role for the Judiciary while at the same time protecting and enforcing the outer boundaries on the powers of the Congress and the President by protecting Constitutional principles and the civil liberties of American citizens.

Although *Korematsu* is the main World War II internment case attacked as the *Dred Scott* of the Twentieth Century, *Korematsu* merely applied the lowest test of Constitutional scrutiny to the exclusion policy of the Executive Order 9066 and the Act of March 21, 1942, approved in *Hirabayashi*.[73] Seventeen months after submitting its brief in *Hirabayashi* (May 1943) defending the curfew policy, the Government returned to the Court in the October 1944 term to defend the exclusion policies in *Korematsu*:

> The authority for the removal of persons of Japanese ancestry . . . has been determined by this Court in [*Hirabayashi*]. . . . The removal was a valid exercise of the war power because the military situation which this Court noticed in the *Hirabayashi* case, coupled with the danger from a disloyal minority and the difficulty of segregating these from other persons of Japanese ancestry, constituted a substantial basis for the military decision that the exclusion was a necessary protective measure. . . .
>
> We submit that there was a substantial basis for concluding that the Exclusion Order, equally with the curfew which was sustained in the *Hirabayashi* case, was such a necessary measure.[74]
>
> Although the Court in *Hirabayashi* held that the curfew was within the war powers of Congress and the President, the Court established the imminent threat of sabotage, espionage and invasion as the judicial threshold for its implementation.[75] It was this threshold of imminent danger that placed significant limits on the applicability of Executive Order 9066 as a national policy.

THE DISTRICT COURTS POST-
HIRABAYASHI: PROVE THE IMMINENT THREAT

Two months after *Hirabayashi* was decided, the U.S. District Court for the Eastern District of Pennsylvania held that the military finding that Olga Schueller posed a military threat was not sufficient to "warrant the abridgement of [her] constitutional rights"[76] by issuing an individual exclusion order in April 1943 prohibiting her from entering the Eastern Military District. Judge Ganey fully agreed that, under the Constitution, in time of war, the President must have the power to act swiftly, and Congress must have the power "to see that war is successfully waged." However, Judge Ganey emphasized that "it does not follow that all actions taken by the Executive are conclusive," and the question of "'what are the allowable limits of military discretion, and whether or not they have been overstepped in a particular case, are judicial questions,'"[77] a conclusion the Bush administration would fight for years after the events of 9/11. The district court, defending the boundaries of executive power, even in times of war, wrote that the government's exercise of power to exclude a citizen from one's home is "of no ordinary magnitude and its exercise by Military Authorities engenders the jealousy of a free people."[78]

Citing *Milligan*, Judge Ganey observed that if the military can take actions against citizens at the order of the President with no review, "republican government is a failure."[79] To prevent this "it is of the very essence of the rule of law that the executive's ipse dixit is not of itself conclusive of the necessity."[80] Defending the power of the civil courts to deal with those who would cause violence to society, Judge Ganey concluded that the evidence provided to the court did not "warrant denial to the petitioner of her right to due process of law."[81] Judge Ganey, echoing Chief Justice Taney in *Ex parte Milligan* on the ability and authority of the civil courts to deal with those who threaten the peace in an area loyal to the nation and free from rebellion, wrote that

> the normal civilian life of the area was being pursued; commercial and industrial activities, their tempo heightened by the demand for greater production, were in private ownership; the courts both federal and state were open and functioning as well as all the administrative and executive departments of government, and it could not be honestly said that ordinary law did not adequately secure public safety and private rights. Accordingly, it would seem to me that Congress cannot authorize the executive to establish by conclusive proclamation the very thing which, upon familiar principle, would have been the subject of judicial scrutiny. . . .
>
> [W]hile I am not unmindful that the issuance of a proclamation by the Commander of the area is some evidence of the finding of the necessity for his assuming control of the functions of civil government, yet where there is a direct interference as here with one's liberty and property, conduct normally beyond the scope of governmental power, such action could only be justified, a constitutional guarantee of freedom can only be abridged, when the danger to the government is real, impending and imminent.[82]

Judge Ganey concluded with the observation that although the "proper adjustment between judicial power and administrative action, in time of war, is extremely delicate in nature," the test of whether an action by the Executive is valid is determined by the "nearness or proximity of the danger to government, as against the particular constitutional guarantee trespassed," and it is for the Judiciary to make that determination.[83]

One month after the *Schueller* decision, the District Court for the District of Massachusetts held that the "individual Exclusion Order" issued to Maximilian Franz Joseph Ebel on April 23, 1943, was invalid because "the order at the time it was applied was an excessive exercise of authority and invalid."[84] Judge Ford concluded:

> I do not believe in the light of conditions prevailing in the Eastern Military Area in April of this year, the time when the exclusion order was applied, there was present a reasonable and substantial basis for the judgment the military authorities made, i.e., that the threat of espionage and sabotage to our military resources was real and imminent. Consequently, the order at the time it was applied was an excessive exercise of authority and invalid.[85]

More importantly to the issue of the role of the Judiciary in times of war and national crisis, in 1943, in the middle of a "hot" World War with the military forces of the United States in combat on almost every continent on the globe, when Ebel challenged the designation that he was a danger to national security and was thus excluded from the Eastern Military District, "[n]o question [was] raised by the defendants with respect to the jurisdiction of this court concerning the matters in the present case."[86] This is no small point. While the Roosevelt Administration did not resist judicial review of military designation of individuals as threats to national and military security during the war of the Greatest Generation, the Bush Administration fought against any judicial review of its designation of individuals, citizens or not, as enemy combatants for more than three years during his declared "war on terrorism."

Judge Ford summarized that in times of war Congress and the President can impose restraints on the personal liberty of citizens,[87] but in such times the judicial question to be determined is whether the restraints instituted are appropriate in time and place.[88] Judge Ford defended the role of the judiciary in times of war when civil liberties are restrained by executive power to meet military or national security threats. Judge Ford wrote,

> This order must be judged as of the date when it was made, and . . . whether its issuance at the time and place . . . was made was within the boundaries of the war power . . . and the question whether such military necessity existed, is subject to judicial review. . . .
>
> Agreeing unequivocally that the authorities should be given wide latitude in the exercise of the power authorized and realizing full well I have no right to substitute my judgment for theirs as to the appropriateness of the order at the time it was imposed, yet, *in the light of the constitutional questions presented, it is finally for the court, considering the nature of the power exercised and with knowledge that the war power does not remove limitations safeguarding essential liberties, to determine the question* as to whether the action taken was appropriate to the situation in April of 1943.[89]

Judge Ford, fully acceding to the power of Congress to enact legislation that could have the impact of restraining liberties in times of war,[90] also made clear that the war power was not without limits:

> True, Congress by the Act of 1942 passed an act broad enough to embrace all designated military areas with no distinction as to race, yet, with its knowledge of the limitations of governmental war power, it did not—nor could it constitutionally—authorize the imposition of such drastic restrictions as are here involved upon the right guaranteed our citizens under the Fifth Amendment to be free from physical restraint in moving freely from state to state, unless the exercise of the war power was reasonable and necessary at the time and place of its application.[91]

The court concluded that the evidence presented to justify the imposition of the exclusion order in April 1943 did not rise to the level of imminent threat and danger as to justify its application.[92] The court, although citing *Hirabayashi* as an example of what an appropriate imminent threat was, rejected the proposition that *Hirabayashi* governed the outcome of Ebel's case.[93] The court reasoned,

> [*Hirabayashi*] is of little help to us in this case [because] [e]ach case must be bottomed on its own facts, especially when dealing with the nature of the power exercised here by the military authorities. Appropriate action with respect to one type of restriction in a situation at a certain time and place is not at all helpful in determining the appropriateness of action at another time and place unless the conditions and degree of restraint upon personal liberty imposed are reasonably comparable.[94]

Almost a year after his decision in *Schueller*, on July 24, 1944, Judge Ganey held in *Scherzberg v. Madeira*[95] that the exclusion order placed against a German-American citizen based on evidence showing that he "seems more imbued with Nazi principles than with American ideals" is not enough to justify the interference with his due process rights:

> There must be existing in the area some immediacy of danger to the welfare of the country. An order such as here under scrutiny, must be laid in a society, engaged in a war, whose setting and background is, either already in a disturbed status . . . or one in which there is every immediate likelihood of such a happening, as opposed to a society engaged in a war, having, what one might term a static equilibrium such as exists in the instant case, with a normal home-front, where discipline under civil law is ample to cope with every emergency arising under the war effort.[96]

Reading *Hirabayashi* in a similar manner as Judge Ford, Judge Ganey explained that *Hirabayashi* was

> factually different, in that the court in that case had under construction the validity of a curfew order and here an evacuation order, but further that the court was in no wise attempting to define the ultimate limits of the war power, but merely the narrow question of the validity of a curfew in its attendant setting.[97]

Affirming that the determination of "the allowable limits of military discretion are . . . still a judicial question," Judge Ganey wrote that "it is for the judicial power to say whether or not the decisions made by the Executive through the Military Commander backed by legislative authority had a rational basis under given circumstances."[98] Citing his decision in *Schueller*, Judge Ganey concluded that, although the exclusion orders are within the war powers of Congress and the President and are appropriate means for the protection of military areas, the circumstances in November 1943 were not "fraught with some degree of immediate danger to the welfare of the country" to justify the "infringement of [the] inherent rights and liberties [provided to] the individual guaranteed by the constitution."[99] "Here, every normal phase of civilian life was being engaged in, and in addition, the record is barren of any actual instance of espionage or sabotage in the particular area in which the plaintiff is situated."[100]

KOREMATSU V. UNITED STATES: GOVERNMENT POWER TO IMPOSE EXCLUSION AND RELOCATION

The Supreme Court issued its unanimous decision in *Hirabayashi* on June 21, 1943.[101] The Court held that Executive Order 9066 and the March 21, 1942, Act of Congress were within the war powers of the President and Congress due to the imminent military threat of possible invasion as well as sabotage and espionage immediately after the attacks on Peal Harbor.[102] The Court held that it would not second-guess the possibility of invasion and the methods to prevent such an invasion—the imposition of a curfew on all those of Japanese ancestry.[103]

But time has a way of making that which is Constitutional, unconstitutional. With the mounting military success of the allied forces in the Atlantic and Pacific and the threat of imminent invasion waning in 1943, the East Coast district courts limited the applicability of *Hirabayashi* to its facts in time and space and held that Executive Order 9066 was Constitutional only to the extent that the Government could prove that the threat to the East Coast in 1943 was equal to the state of military danger during the first few months of 1942. With the military situation never as grave on the East Coast as it was purported to be on the West Coast, the practical result became that the East Coast district courts limited the application of the Executive Order 9066 to the Western Military Command.

While *Hirabayashi* was being used on the east coast as the standard to limit the applicability of Executive Order 9066, the Government returned to the Supreme Court in 1944 to defend the exclusion and the detention of the Japanese from the West Coast. The Government continued to find a sympathetic Court to its arguments of necessity and deference to military determinations made at the time of the making of the exclusion policy; however, the Court was less deferential and agreeable on the defense of long-term detention of loyal Americans because the Government could not find hospitable communities for the Japanese who were excluded from West Coast states.

The Court, led by Chief Justice Stone and joined by Justices Roberts, Black, Reed, Frankfurter, and Jackson, with concurring opinions by Justices

Douglas, Murphy, and Rutledge, held in *Hirabayashi* that Executive Order 9066 and the Act of March 21, 1942, were within the congressional and presidential war powers and that the forced curfew was not a violation of the Fifth Amendment Due Process Clause.[104] A year and half later on December 18, 1944, a divided Court, led by Justice Black and joined by Chief Justice Stone and Justices Reed, Douglas, Rutledge, and Frankfurter, with separate dissenting opinions from Justices Roberts, Murphy, and Jackson, held in *Korematsu* that the exclusion and temporary detention policies implemented under Executive Order 9066 and the Act of March 21, 1942, were also within the war powers of Congress and the President.[105]

Justice Black at the very beginning of his opinion asserted that the Constitution requires a higher level of scrutiny when a government policy singles out a specific racial group.[106] He wrote that

> it should be noted, to begin with, that all legal restrictions which curtail the civil rights of a single racial group are immediately suspect. That is not to say that all such restrictions are unconstitutional. It is to say that *courts must subject them to the most rigid scrutiny.* Pressing public necessity may sometimes justify the existence of such restrictions; racial antagonism never can.[107]

But the Court abandoned this "most rigid scrutiny" in the very next passage, for *Korematsu* affirmed the enforcement of the exclusion and relocation policies strictly on the reasoning of the *Hirabayashi* decision:

> In the light of the principles we announced in the *Hirabayashi* case, we are unable to conclude that it was beyond the war power of Congress and the Executive to exclude those of Japanese ancestry from the West Coast war area at the time they did. True, exclusion from the area in which one's home is located is a far greater deprivation than constant confinement to the home from 8 p.m. to 6 a.m. Nothing short of apprehension by the proper military authorities of the gravest imminent danger to the public safety can constitutionally justify either. But exclusion from a threatened area, no less than curfew, has a definite and close relationship to the prevention of espionage and sabotage. The military authorities, charged with the primary responsibility of defending our shores, concluded that curfew provided inadequate protection and ordered exclusion. They did so, as pointed out in our *Hirabayashi* opinion, in accordance with Congressional authority to the military to say who should, and who should not, remain in the threatened areas.[108]

Justice Black, as Chief Justice Stone did in *Hirabayashi*, assumed the truth of imminent threat of sabotage and espionage and as such held that the policy of moving an entire people from their homes, rather than using the military and law enforcement to secure the disloyal to protect the war effort, was reasonable.[109] The Government argued in *Hirabayashi* that hearings and investigations would not be practical or efficient in the face of the possibility of invasion, sabotage, and espionage by disloyal Japanese residents on the West Coast. The Government argued that it was easier to move them all rather than find the disloyal. The Court affirmed the Government in *Hirabayashi* and *Korematsu*:

> Like curfew, exclusion of those of Japanese origin was deemed necessary because of the presence of an unascertained number of disloyal members of the group, most of whom we have no doubt were loyal to this country. It was because we could not reject the finding of the military authorities that it was impossible to bring about an immediate segregation of the disloyal from the loyal that we sustained the validity of the curfew order as applying to the whole group. In the instant case, temporary exclusion of the entire group was rested by the military on the same ground. The judgment that exclusion of the whole group was for the same reason a military imperative answers the contention that the exclusion was in the nature of group punishment based on antagonism to those of Japanese origin. That there were members of the group who retained loyalties to Japan has been confirmed by investigations made subsequent to the exclusion. Approximately five thousand American citizens of Japanese ancestry refused to swear unqualified allegiance to the United States and to renounce allegiance to the Japanese Emperor, and several thousand evacuees requested repatriation to Japan.
>
> We uphold the exclusion order as of the time it was made and when the petitioner violated it.[110]

The Court bypassed Korematsu's assertion that, since the imminent threat of invasion, sabotage, and espionage had waned by the time of his arrest for violation of the exclusion order, May 1942, the order was invalid[111] and held that

> because we could not reject the finding of the military authorities that it was impossible to bring about an immediate segregation of the disloyal from the loyal that we sustained the validity of the curfew order as applying to the whole group. In the instant case, temporary exclusion of the entire group was rested by the military on the same ground.[112]

The Court reasoned that this "impossibility" justified the policy, and although admitting that this burden was harsh,

> Hardships are part of war, and war is an aggregation of hardships. All citizens alike, both in and out of uniform, feel the impact of war in greater or lesser measure. Citizenship has its responsibilities as well as its privileges, and in time of war the burden is always heavier.[113]

So as not to belabor the point, the deserved "black eye" that the Court received due to the *Korematsu* and *Hirabayashi* decisions was well-deserved for its acceptance of the Government's argument that the inconvenience of searching out the disloyal from among the loyal justified the wholesale population extraction and relocation of a specific race of citizens. Even accepting the claim of military threat, due process and individual civil liberties cannot be disregarded on such a grand scale because it is inconvenient to support such rights in time of war. The true error of the Court was not in rejecting the Government's assertion of imminent threat; it was the application of a weak judicial standard in the protection of Constitutional rights so as to allow the policy to be held within the war powers of Congress and the President. The error was in the application of a Constitutional tool—not the justification of the tool. The imposition of a curfew or exclusion in time of war is Constitutional, but the application of these policies on a specific race for no other reason except that it would be too inconvenient to withdraw the disloyal from the loyal in that population is not. Such a distinction would have provided the political branches with the proper deference they are due in times of war but would have enforced the boundaries that the Constitution places on the Government even in times of war.

Justice Roberts, who joined the majority in *Hirabayashi*, issued a strong dissent in *Korematsu* and asserted that the facts of the case in *Korematsu* were fundamentally different:

> This is not a case of keeping people off the streets at night, as was *Kiyoshi Hirabayashi v. United States* . . . nor a case of temporary exclusion of a citizen from an area for his own safety or that of the community, nor a case of offering him an opportunity to go temporarily out of an area where his presence might cause danger to himself or to his fellows. On the contrary, it is the case of convicting a citizen as a punishment for not submitting to imprisonment in a concentration camp, based on his ancestry, and solely because of his ancestry, without evidence or inquiry concerning his loyalty and good disposition towards the United States. If this be a correct statement of the facts disclosed by this record, and facts of which we take judicial notice, I need hardly labor the conclusion that Constitutional rights have been violated.[114]

Justice Roberts summarized that the situation in *Korematsu* was untenable and that it was clear that the intention of the Government "was to drive all citizens of Japanese ancestry into Assembly Centers within the zones of their residence, under pain of criminal prosecution."[115]

> The predicament in which the petitioner thus found himself was this: He was forbidden, by Military Order, to leave the zone in which he lived; he was forbidden, by Military Order, after a date fixed, to be found within that zone unless he were in an Assembly Center located in that zone. General DeWitt's report to the Secretary of War concerning the programme of evacuation and relocation of Japanese makes it entirely clear, if it were necessary to refer to that document—and, in the light of the above recitation, I think it is not—that

an Assembly Center was a euphemism for a prison. No person within such a center was permitted to leave except by Military Order.

In the dilemma that he dare not remain in his home, or voluntarily leave the area, without incurring criminal penalties, and that the only way he could avoid punishment was to go to an Assembly Center and submit himself to military imprisonment, the petitioner did nothing.[116]

Justice Roberts rejected the Government's assertion that the power to issue a curfew or to exclude a group from an area due to military need is of the same type as forced evacuation and placement of evacuees into detention centers with the power to apply sanctions for the failure to comply with such policies.[117] "[T]he facts," Justice Roberts wrote,

> show that the exclusion was but a part of an over-all plan for forceable detention. This case cannot, therefore, be decided on any such narrow ground as the possible validity of a Temporary Exclusion Order under which the residents of an area are given an opportunity to leave and go elsewhere in their native land outside the boundaries of a military area. To make the case turn on any such assumption is to shut our eyes to reality.[118]

Justice Roberts, rejecting the proposition "that the detention was a necessary part of the process of evacuation,"[119] contended that Korematsu was caught between two military orders that were contradictory to his Constitutional rights; Military Proclamation No. 1 required him to stay within the Military Area No. 1, but Civilian Exclusion Order No. 34 informed him that the only lawful area for him within Military Area No. 1 was the general assembly area under penalty of the Act of March 21, 1942.[120] Thus, he was provided with the choice of surrendering his rights to liberty by being placed in a "concentration camp" or remaining in the area to which he was restricted without entering in the "concentration camp" under pain of criminal penalty. Justice Roberts reasoned that this dichotomy is what made the conviction of Korematsu unconstitutional.[121] Justice Roberts concluded that it is no answer to

> [suggest] . . . [that] it is lawful to compel an American citizen to submit to illegal imprisonment on the assumption that he might, after going to the Assembly Center, apply for his discharge by suing out a writ of habeas corpus. . . . The answer, of course, is that . . . he was not bound, in order to escape violation of one or the other, to surrender his liberty for any period.[122]

Justice Murphy began his dissent by asserting that

> This exclusion of "all persons of Japanese ancestry, both alien and nonalien," from the Pacific Coast area on a plea of military necessity in the absence of martial law ought not to be approved. Such exclusion goes over "the very brink of constitutional power," and falls into the ugly abyss of racism.[123]

Justice Murphy wrote that although the military determinations of military risk are due great "respect and consideration," "it is essential that there be definite limits to military discretion," and the questions of "[w]hat are the allowable limits of military discretion, and whether or not they have been overstepped in a particular case, are judicial questions."[124] Justice Murphy recognized the racial application of the exclusion policy and asserted that the policy violated the Equal Protection Clause and the forced relocation and interference with the right to live and move about the nation freely violated the Fifth Amendment Due Process Clause.[125] Yet "no reasonable relation to an 'immediate, imminent, and impending' public danger is evident to support this racial restriction, which is one of the most sweeping and complete deprivations of constitutional rights in the history of this nation in the absence of martial law."[126] Justice Murphy concluded:

> It must be conceded that the military and naval situation in the spring of 1942 was such as to generate a very real fear of invasion of the Pacific Coast, accompanied by fears of sabotage and espionage in that area. The military command was therefore justified in adopting all reasonable means necessary to combat these dangers. In adjudging the military action taken in light of the then apparent dangers, we must not erect too high or too meticulous standards; it is necessary only that the action have some reasonable relation to the removal of the dangers of invasion, sabotage and espionage. But the exclusion, either temporarily or permanently, of all persons with Japanese blood in their veins has no such reasonable relation. And that relation is lacking because the exclusion order necessarily must rely for its reasonableness upon the assumption that all persons of Japanese ancestry may have a dangerous tendency to commit sabotage and espionage and to aid our Japanese enemy in other ways. It is difficult to believe that reason, logic, or experience could be marshaled in support of such an assumption.[127]

But notice the discrepancy in his dissent. First he asserted that the test should be "whether the deprivation is reasonably related to a public danger that is so 'immediate, imminent, and impending' as not to admit of delay and not to permit the intervention of ordinary constitutional processes to alleviate the danger,"[128] but in actual application, all this test requires is that "the action have some reasonable relation to the removal of the dangers of invasion, sabotage and espionage."[129] Although the policy is overbroad, an issue that only matters using higher judicial scrutiny, there is a rational relationship between the removal of the Japanese and ending the threat of espionage and sabotage. Clearly the removal of enemy aliens and citizens from the West Coast will result in a reduction of people who could pose a military threat of espionage and sabotage. The rational relation is clear on its face. The problem is not that the military action had no rational relationship to its policy; the problem is that such a low test was used to justify the policy. When Constitutional rights are directly infringed, especially when they are specifically and intentionally burdensome on a specific race, those Constitutional rights require a higher level of Constitutional review than rational basis. It's not enough that because the military had a reasonable fear, that fear justified the wholesale destruction of a community based on race and cultural opinions about that race.

The flaw in Justice Murphy's dissent is that he had no compulsion against imposing a curfew on the freedom of Japanese Americans to move about their homes and community based on race. He found it objectionable to impose a policy excluding the Japanese from their homes and community for the exact same reasons as the curfew. But the Government was correct in its assertion that the exclusion was a logical development and growth of the curfew policy. Both were rationally related to the legitimate governmental interest to protect the West Coast from invasion, sabotage, and espionage in 1942. Justice Murphy's dissent simply did not like the logical result of approving the military in *Hirabayashi*. The problem with Justice Murphy's dissent is that it is not the role of the Court to make independent assessments of a military security policy in time of war; it is the Court's role to make sure that the policy is within Constitutional bounds. His dissent would have been better delivered in *Hirabayashi*.

Justice Roberts's dissent was little better. Justice Roberts defended *Hirabayashi* in *Korematsu* by asserting that the curfew was analogous to a fire line while the exclusion policy was outside of public safety protection analogy.[130] To assert that a curfew enforced along the lines of race is just as acceptable as the imposition of a "fire line"[131] is disingenuous on its face because no fire line in the history of public safety has been imposed on a specific racial group, excluding all other groups from compliance. A fire line excludes all from entering a specific area for reasons of public safety—it does not block only those of a specific race from a specific area. More importantly, the wording of Executive Order 9066[132] makes clear that exclusion was not only contemplated but intended. If the curfew was within Constitutional boundaries, exclusion could scarcely be held to be outside of those same Constitutional boundaries.

Justice Jackson, echoing the dissent of Justice Roberts, observed that Korematsu was convicted for being where he was prohibited as well as not being where he was ordered to be:

> Korematsu, however, has been convicted of an act not commonly a crime. It consists merely of being present in the state whereof he is a citizen, near the place where he was born, and where all his life he has lived.
>
> Even more unusual is the series of military orders which made this conduct a crime. They forbid such a one to remain, and they also forbid him to leave. They were so drawn that the only way Korematsu could avoid violation was to

give himself up to the military authority. This meant submission to custody, examination, and transportation out of the territory, to be followed by indeterminate confinement in detention camps.

A citizen's presence in the locality, however, was made a crime only if his parents were of Japanese birth. Had Korematsu been one of four—the others being, say, a German alien enemy, an Italian alien enemy, and a citizen of American-born ancestors, convicted of treason but out on parole—only Korematsu's presence would have violated the order. The difference between their innocence and his crime would result, not from anything he did, said, or thought, different than they, but only in that he was born of different racial stock.[133]

But like Justice Murphy, Justice Jackson balked at affirming the exclusion policy when it was the logical result of affirming the curfew policy. The same reasons that were sufficient for curfew were now racist on their face when used to support forced exclusion and relocation. "Now, if any fundamental assumption underlies our system," Justice Jackson wrote, "it is that guilt is personal and not inheritable. Even if all of one's antecedents had been convicted of treason, the Constitution forbids its penalties to be visited upon him."[134] Totally true! But this truism was not applied in June 1943 in *Hirabayashi*—what changed in December 1944? Why was it rational in June 1943 to place a curfew on all Japanese but rank racism to exclude them in December 1944 for the same reasons in both time periods? It is more reasonable to place an exclusion order on a suspected people in times of war to end the threat of espionage and sabotage than to place a dawn to dusk curfew on them and let them remain in the sensitive area as a possible threat.

Justice Jackson wrote, "[I]f we cannot confine military expedients by the Constitution, neither would I distort the Constitution to approve all that the military may deem expedient. This is what the Court appears to be doing, whether consciously or not."[135] True, but the time for such an observation was in *Hirabayashi* when the Government's argument of expediency over the individual rights of the Japanese citizens was first asserted, as the Government admitted in *Korematsu*, based upon opinion and views of tendencies of behavior.[136] The rejection of a race-based policy, in application if not on its face, should not be rejected on the grounds that the Court does not approve of the logical result of its prior approval. Hirabayashi had as much right to be allowed to walk the streets of California after dark as Korematsu had the right to live in California. Executive Orders 9066[137] and 9102[138] as well as the Act of March 21, 1942,[139] involved the power to impose an exclusion order as deemed necessary by the military and relocation of the Japanese; in *Hirabayashi* the Court, including the three dissents, fully acknowledged this fact and affirmed it. Having affirmed the interference of civil liberties with the curfew under the Act of March 21, 1942, and Executive Orders 9066 and 9102 in *Hirabayashi*, there was no logical reason not to affirm the actual purpose of these policies—the expulsion and relocation of the Japanese from the West Coast. Again the error of the Court was to let these two orders and the Act of Congress stand in the first instance in *Hirabayashi*.

Ex parte Endo[140] involved an entirely different issue. *Ex parte Endo* involved the long-term detention of the Japanese in relocation centers because, as the Government fully admitted in its *Korematsu* brief,[141] there was nowhere for the relocated Japanese internees to go.[142] Curfew and exclusion with temporary detention for organized relocation was one thing, the Court would observe, but the forced long-term internment due to the prejudice of targeted relocation communities is another. It was on this distinction that the Court held the detention programs of the War Relocation Authority unconstitutional.[143]

The Court, led by Justice Douglas and joined by Chief Justice Stone and Justices Black, Reed, Frankfurter, Rutledge, and Jackson, with concurring opinions by Justices Murphy and Roberts, wrote: "We approach the construction of Executive Order No. 9066 as we would approach the construction of legislation in this field."[144] The "broad powers," Justice Douglas wrote, "granted to the President or other executive officers by Congress so that they may deal with the exigencies of wartime problems . . . gave them wide scope for the exercise of judgment and discretion so that war might be waged effectively and successfully."[145] Justice Douglas wrote that the Court would review Executive and Congressional actions in times of war with the assumption

> that their purpose was to allow for the greatest possible accommodation between those liberties and the exigencies of war. We must assume, when asked to find implied powers in a grant of legislative or executive authority, that the law makers intended to place no greater restraint on the citizen than was clearly and unmistakably indicated by the language they used.[146]

Concluding that it would "approach the construction of Executive Order No. 9066 as [it] would approach the construction of legislation in this field,"[147] the Court held that

> neither the Act nor the orders use the language of detention. The Act says that no one shall "enter, remain in, leave, or commit any act" in the prescribed military areas. . . . Executive Order No. 9066 subjects the right of any person "to enter, remain in, or leave" those prescribed areas to such restrictions as the military may impose. And, apart from those restrictions, the Secretary of War is only given authority to afford the evacuees "transportation, food, shelter, and other accommodations." Executive Order No. 9102 authorizes and directs the War Relocation Authority "to formulate and effectuate a program for the removal" of the persons covered by Executive Order No. 9066 from the prescribed military areas, and "for their relocation, maintenance, and supervision." And power is given the Authority to make regulations "necessary or de-

sirable to promote effective execution of such program." Moreover, unlike the case of curfew regulations (*Hirabayashi v. United States*), the legislative history of the Act of March 21, 1942, is silent on detention. And that silence may have special significance in view of the fact that detention in Relocation Centers was no part of the original program of evacuation, but developed later to meet what seemed to the officials in charge to be mounting hostility to the evacuees on the part of the communities where they sought to go.[148]

The Court concluded that "whatever power the War Relocation Authority may have to detain other classes of citizens, it has no authority to subject citizens who are concededly loyal to its leave procedure."[149] Justice Douglas reasoned that since Executive Order 9066 and the March 21 Act of Congress were instituted specifically to address the need to protect the West Coast from sabotage and espionage, any exercise of power by the military or the War Relocation Authority must be measured against that specific purpose.[150]

Throughout the decision the Court sought to make clear that the justification for the curfew (*Hirabayashi*) and exclusion (*Korematsu*) did not justify detention based on racial considerations. "A citizen" like Endo, the Court asserted,

who is concededly loyal presents no problem of espionage or sabotage. Loyalty is a matter of the heart and mind, not of race, creed, or color. He who is loyal is by definition not a spy or a saboteur. When the power to detain is derived from the power to protect the war effort against espionage and sabotage, detention which has no relationship to that objective is unauthorized.[151]

The Court rejected the proposition that, under Executive Order 9066, the WRA could detain concededly loyal Americans as a natural extension of exclusion or due to the hostility of communities that were to be the sites for relocation:[152]

The authority to detain a citizen or to grant him a conditional release as protection against espionage or sabotage is exhausted at least when his loyalty is conceded. If we held that the authority to detain continued thereafter, we would transform an espionage or sabotage measure into something else. That was not done by Executive Order No. 9066 or by the Act of March 21, 1942, which ratified it. What they did not do we cannot do. Detention which furthered the campaign against espionage and sabotage would be one thing. But detention which has no relationship to that campaign is of a distinct character. Community hostility even to loyal evacuees may have been (and perhaps still is) a serious problem. But if authority for their custody and supervision is to be sought on that ground, the Act of March 21, 1942, Executive Order No. 9066, and Executive Order No. 9102, offer no support.[153]

The majority, although rejecting the argument made by the Government in its brief in *Korematsu*, found that the detention could be viewed as a logical result of the exclusion order and continued to reject the proposition that the entire policy of curfew, exclusion, and relocation was the result of racism against the Japanese.[154] While acknowledging that the detention program, developed due to community hostility to the relocation of the Japanese, was based on race, Justice Douglas wrote that the policies of curfew and exclusion that led to the detention had no racial undertones.[155]

Although Justice Douglas and the majority would not admit race was a factor in the exclusion policies, Justice Murphy in his concurring opinion, as he wrote in *Korematsu*, had no such reservations: "I join in the opinion of the Court, but I am of the view that detention in Relocation Centers of persons of Japanese ancestry regardless of loyalty is not only unauthorized by Congress or the Executive, but is another example of the unconstitutional resort to racism inherent in the entire evacuation program."[156] Justice Roberts concurred in the result of the decision but dissented to the continued avoidance of the Court to address the Constitutional issues raised by the exclusion and relocation policies.[157] Justice Roberts rejected the proposition that the executive branch did not authorize the detention, since it was fully aware of the actions and policies of the WRA, or that Congress did not approve of those policies since it specifically funded the WRA.[158] Justice Roberts concluded with the following statements:

> I conclude, therefore, that the court is squarely faced with a serious constitutional question—whether [Endo's] detention violated the guarantees of the Bill of Rights of the federal Constitution and especially the guarantee of due process of law. There can be but one answer to that question. An admittedly loyal citizen has been deprived of her liberty for a period of years. Under the Constitution she should be free to come and go as she pleases. Instead, her liberty of motion and other innocent activities have been prohibited and conditioned. She should be discharged.[159]

SUMMARY

In *Hirabayashi, Yasui, Korematsu,* and *Endo* the Court bypassed the Constitutional question of whether the curfew, exclusion, relocation, and detention policies were violations of the Constitution per se. The Court held, and only held, that in times of war the Government would be provided wide discretion in the measures it utilized to both protect the nation and effectively prosecute the war. The Court accepted the rationale for the policies and failed to apply a more stringent test to the policies in the face of assertions that they violated individual and group civil liberties guaranteed by the U.S. Constitution. History has judged the exclusion and internment policies as racially motivated; thus, the Court has been harshly judged for accepting racially biased policies at the expense of the Japanese.

It is proposed here that the significance of the Court's error was not that it accepted racially biased and suspect rationalizations in times of national crisis and war, but that it failed to review those policies against a judicial standard of review equal to the Constitutional rights that were affected by the policies. Again, assuming the truth of the Government's arguments concerning threats of invasion, espionage, and sabotage at the time the policies were instituted, the tools designed to address these threats were not equal to the rights that they abridged. The tools of curfew, exclusion, and detention specifically applied to an entire race based on cultural assumptions and the inconvenience of extracting the disloyal from the loyal is not acceptable when measured against individual rights of liberty, due process of law, and equal protection under the law. In times of war and crisis, as well as in times of peace, it is the role of the Judiciary to make sure the boundaries of the Constitution and the rule of law are adhered to and defended regardless of the inconvenience of obedience to those boundaries.[160] Only when the Government makes policy within those boundaries is it entitled to great deference from the Judiciary.

As Judge Marilyn Patel wrote in *Korematsu* when she vacated Korematsu's conviction:

> *Korematsu.* . . . As historical precedent it stands as a constant caution that in times of war or declared military necessity our institutions must be vigilant in protecting constitutional guarantees. It stands as a caution that in times of distress . . . military necessity and national security must not be used to protect government action from close scrutiny and accountability. It stands as a caution that in times of international hostility and antagonisms our institutions, legislative, executive and judicial, must be prepared to exercise their authority to protect all citizens from the petty fears and prejudices that are so easily aroused.[161]

Although history has observed that national crisis exposes the "frailty of our civil rights, the fallibility of our wisest leaders, [and] the timidity of the Supreme Court in a time of crisis,"[162] it has also observed that the American system of justice and its institutions, both public and private, are designed to protect Constitutional rights and to ensure that past failures are not easily repeated. The legacy of the *Hirabayashi, Yasui, Korematsu,* and *Endo* cases is the historical rejection of the rationale for the curfew policies during World War II.

It is written, blessed are those who "executeth justice for the oppressed."[163] One of the enduring legacies of the World War II cases is the embracement of individuals that defend individual civil liberties, and in subsequent decades they have taken center stage in American political discourse, both at the Supreme Court Bar and on the bench of the Supreme Court itself. Another legacy of World War II is the development of limitations on Presidential power in domestic affairs even during times of war.

During World War II the Supreme Court held that the President could order the detainment of Japanese citizens. The nation regretted the policy, and the Supreme Court took a less deferential view of executive power when President Truman ordered the seizure of the nation's steel industry to maintain steel production during the Korean War.[164] In 1952 the Court issued what has become the seminal case on limiting, regulating, and defining the boundaries of domestic Presidential power.

NOTES

1. First published and adapted from *Cumberland Law Review* 39 (2009): 609–84 by permission; © 2009 by *Cumberland Law Review*.

2. See generally Maisie Conrat and Richard Conrat, *Executive Order 9066: The Internment of 110,000 Japanese Americans* (Los Angeles: UCLA Asian American Studies Center Press, 1992).

3. Arndt Peltner, "Unforgettable Injustice," *Atlantic Times*, May 2007, http://www.atlantic-times.com/archive_detail.php?recordID=864. For additional information, see German American Internee Coalition website, http://www.gaic.info.

4. Lawrence DiStasi and Sandra Gilbert, *Una Storia Segreta: The Secret History of Italian American Evacuation and Internment During World War II* (Berkeley, CA: Heyday Books, 2001); see also FBI, "1521 Italian Aliens Taken Into Custody by FBI, June 30, 1942," FBI Custodial Detention Files, 1999, http://foia.fbi.gov/foiaindex/custodet.htm.

5. *Hirabayashi v. United States*, 320 U.S. 81 (1943).

6. *Korematsu v. United States*, 323 U.S. 214 (1944).

7. *Ex parte* Mitsuye Endo, 323 U.S. 283 (1944).

8. "The Legal Rights of Guantanamo Detainees: What Are They, Should They Be Changed, and Is an End in Sight?" (hearing Before the Subcomm. on Terrorism, Tech. and Homeland Sec. of the S. Judiciary Comm., 110th Cong. 1 [December 11, 2007], Serial no. J-110-66 [statement of Rear Adm. John D. Hutson (Ret.), Dean, Franklin Pierce Law Center]), http://www.fas.org/irp/congress/2007_hr/gtmo-legal.pdf.

9. *Am. Commc'ns Ass'n. v. Douds*, 339 U.S. 382, 391 (1950) (citing *Hirabayashi*, 320 U.S., 100).

10. *Douds*, 339 U.S., 391.

11. *Takao Ozawa v. United States*, 260 U.S. 178 (1922).

12. Exec. Order No. 9066, 7 Fed. Reg. 1407, 1407 (Feb. 19, 1942) (emphasis added).

13. Exec. Order No. 9102, 7 Fed. Reg. 2165, 2165 (Mar. 18, 1942).

14. Exec. Order No. 9102, 7 Fed. Reg. at 2165.

15. 18 U.S.C. § 97a (Supp. 1943).

16. Nanette Dembitz, "Racial Discrimination and the Military Judgment: The Supreme Court's *Korematsu* and *Endo* Decisions," *Columbia Law Review* 45 (1945): 175–239.

17. *Ex parte Ventura*, 44 F. Supp. 520 (W.D. Wash. 1942).

18. Ibid.

19. Ibid., 522.

20. Ibid.

21. Ibid., 522–23.

22. His observation that if the petitioner were the loyal American she claimed to be, she would comply with the orders of her government and bear the burden on her civil liberties in time of war, is a classic response to times of crisis. The same sentiment can be heard by those who say that extra scrutiny at airports applied to those who are Arab or Muslim is the price they must pay for the safety of the nation as a whole. It is easy to demand the sacrifice of liberty when it's not your liberty being sacrificed.

23. *United States v. Motion Picture Film "The Spirit of '76,"* 252 F. 946 (S.D. Cal. 1917).

24. See *Ventura,* 44 F. Supp. at 522.

25. See Ibid.

26. *Ex parte* Kanai, 46 F. Supp. 286, 288 (E.D. Wis. 1942).

27. Ibid.; see *infra,* note 85.

28. *United States v. Yasui,* 48 F. Supp. 40 (D. Or. 1942), *vacated,* 320 U.S. 115 (1943).

29. Ibid., 44.

30. Ibid.

31. Ibid., 45 (footnote omitted).

32. Ibid., 50 (citing *Home Builders & Loan Ass'n. v. Blaisdell,* 290 U.S. 398, 426, [1934]).

33. Ibid., 53.

34. *Yasui,* 48 F. Supp. at 53–54 (quotation marks omitted) (footnotes omitted).

35. Ibid., 54.

36. Ibid., 55.

37. Ibid.

38. *United States v. Yasui,* 320 U.S. 115 (1943).

39. *Yasui,* 48 F. Supp. at 40, 44–53; see also *Ex parte* Milligan, 71 U.S. (4 Wall.) 2 (1866). The crisis referred to by the *Milligan* Court was the American Civil War. See generally *Ex parte* Milligan, 71 U.S. (4 Wall.) 2 (1866).

40. *Labedz v. Kramer,* 55 F. Supp. 25 (D. Or. 1944).

41. Ibid., 27 (citing *Falbo v. United States,* 320 U.S. 549, [1944]).

42. *Labedz,* 55 F. Supp. at 27.

43. See, for example, *DeWitt v. Wilcox,* 161 F.2d 785 (9th Cir. 1947).

44. See *Alexander v. DeWitt,* 141 F.2d 573 (9th Cir. 1944); *Wilcox v. Emmons,* 67 F. Supp. 339 (S.D. Cal. 1946).

45. *Hirabayashi v. United States,* 320 U.S. 81, 84 (1943).

46. Brief for the United States at 33, *Hirabayashi v. United States,* 320 U.S. 81 (1943) (No. 870).

47. Ibid.

48. See Ibid., 18–31.

49. Ibid.

50. Ibid.

51. Ibid., 18.

52. Brief for the United States at 18, *Hirabayashi v. United States,* 320 U.S. 81 (1943) (No. 870).

53. Ibid.

54. Ibid., 34.

55. Ibid.

56. Ibid., 35–36, 58.

57. Chief Justice Stone's opinion was joined by Justices Roberts, Black, Reed, Frankfurter, and Jackson, with concurring opinions by Justices Douglas, Murphy, and Rutledge. Each of the concurrences were in complete agreement on the decision that the Government had a rational basis for the curfew and that it was well within the war powers of the Congress to pass the Act of March 21, 1942, and for the President to issue Executive Order 9066. For this reason the Court is considered unanimous.

58. The Court held that

[w]e have no occasion to consider whether the President, acting alone, could lawfully have made the curfew order in question, or have authorized others to make it. For the President's action has the support of the Act of Congress, and we are immediately concerned with the question whether it is within the constitutional power of the national government, through the joint action of Congress and the Executive, to impose this restriction as an emergency war measure.

Hirabayashi, 320 U.S. at 92.

59. Ibid.

60. Ibid., 93 (emphasis added) (internal citations omitted).

61. Brief for the United States at 60, *Hirabayashi v. United States*, 320 U.S. 81 (1943) (No. 870).

62. *Hirabayashi*, 320 U.S., 93–94.

63. During the early months of 1942, the Japanese military launched various attacks against the West Coast and the American mainland. On February 23, 1942, a Japanese submarine fired thirteen shells at an oil refinery at Goleta, California, crippling one oil well. "The Shelling of Elwood, California State Military Museum," http://www.militarymuseum.org/Ellwood.html (accessed April 13, 2009).

The Japanese also sought to ignite forest fires through incendiary bombing. A Japanese warplane, launched from a specially refitted submarine, dropped incendiary bombs on Oregon, on September 9 and 29, 1942, which ignited some fires. Larry Bingham, "Oregon Coast Trail Dedicated for World War Two Bombing," *Oregonian*, October 2, 2008, http://www.oregonlive.com/news/index.ssf/2008/10/a_bomb_a_ peace_tree_and_now_a.html. Additional forest fires in the Midwest were started by thousands of incendiary balloons launched from Japan, carried by the jet stream, to explode in the United States. John McPhee, "Balloons of War," *New Yorker*, January 29, 1996.

Although the damage was minimal in all these attempts, the fact that they were made lent some credence to the general fear that the Japanese had the desire, if not the capacity, to attack the mainland United States in the early months of 1942 (Ibid). Although it is acknowledged that the Battle of Midway, June 4–7, 1942, ended the offensive power of the Japanese Fleet and placed Japan on the defensive in the Pacific for the remainder of the war, this fact was not so clear in June 1942, and the Midway victory occurred well after the curfew and exclusion policies had been implemented. The same submarine that attacked Goleta in February 1942 also launched seventeen shells at a naval base at Fort Stevens, Oregon, on June 22, 1942. "The Shelling of Elwood," *supra.*

64. *Hirabayashi*, 320 U.S., 94.

65. Ibid., 99.

66. Ibid., 100.

67. Ibid., 95.

68. Ibid., 100.

69. Ibid., 101.

70. *Hirabayashi*, 320 U.S. at 101.

71. Ibid., 102.

72. Ibid.

73. Arthur H. Garrison, "The Judiciary in Times of National Security Crisis and Terrorism: Ubi Inter Arma Enim Silent Leges, Quis Custodiet Ipso Custodes?" *American Journal of Trial Advocacy Law Review* 30, no. 1 (2006): 169–87n90.

74. Brief for the United States at 16–17, 20, *Korematsu v. United States*, 324 U.S. 885 (1945) (No. 22) (petition for rehearing).

75. This judicial threshold resulted from the arguments of the Government in *Hirabayashi*:

> It was learned that Japanese espionage had supplied the Japanese forces with precise information as to the disposition of the vessels of the fleet at Pearl Harbor. . . . Great apprehension was felt that . . . a number of [Japanese], citizens and aliens alike, might be disposed to assist the enemy, particularly in the case of an attack. . . . It is in the light of these circumstances that the validity of the Act of March 21, 1942, and the related orders must be examined under the war powers.

Brief for the United States at 45–47, *Hirabayashi v. United States*, 320 U.S. 81 (1943, No. 870).

76. *Schueller v. Drum*, 51 F. Supp 383, 388 (E.D. Pa. 1943).

77. Ibid., 386 (quoting *Sterling v. Constantin*, 287 U.S. 378, 401, 1932).

78. Ibid.

79. Ibid., 387.

80. Ibid.

81. Ibid.

82. *Schueller*, 51 F. Supp., 387.

83. Ibid., 387–88.

84. *Ebel v. Drum*, 52 F. Supp. 189, 197 (D. Mass. 1943).

85. Ibid.

86. Ibid., 190.

87. Ibid., 194.

88. Ibid., 195.

89. Ibid., 195, 196–97 (emphasis added) (internal citations omitted).

90. *Ebel*, 52 F. Supp., 194–95.

91. Ibid., 196.

92. Ibid., 196–97.

93. Ibid., 196.

94. Ibid.

95. *Scherzberg v. Madeira*, 57 F. Supp. 42 (E.D. Pa. 1944).

96. Ibid., 47–48.

97. Ibid., 46.

98. Ibid. (citing *Sterling v. Constantin*, 287 U.S. 378, 399–401, 1932). The *Sterling* Court explained:

The nature of the [war] power [of the President] also necessarily implies that there is a permitted range of honest judgment as to the measures to be taken in meeting force with force, in suppressing violence and restoring order, for, without such liberty to make immediate decisions, the power itself would be useless. Such measures, conceived in good faith, in the face of the emergency, and directly related to the quelling of the disorder or the prevention of its continuance, fall within the discretion of the executive in the exercise of his authority to maintain peace.

It does not follow from the fact that the executive has this range of discretion . . . that every sort of action . . . no matter how unjustified by the exigency or subversive of private right and the jurisdiction of the courts, otherwise available, is conclusively supported by mere executive fiat. The contrary is well established. What are the allowable limits of military discretion, and whether or not they have been overstepped in a particular case, are judicial questions. Thus, in the theatre of actual war, there are occasions in which private property may be taken or destroyed. . . . "But we are clearly of opinion," said the Court speaking through Chief Justice Taney, "that in all of these cases the danger must be immediate and impending; or the necessity urgent for the public service, such as will not admit delay, and where the action of the civil authority would be too late in providing the means which the occasion calls for. Every case must depend on its own circumstances. It is the emergency that gives the right, and the emergency must be shown to exist before the taking can be justified."

Sterling, 287 U.S., 399–401 (quoting *Mitchell v. Harmony*, 54 U.S. 115, 134, 1851).

99. *Scherzberg*, 57 F. Supp., 47.

100. Ibid.

101. *Hirabayashi v. United States*, 320 U.S. 81 (1943).

102. Ibid., 104–05.

103. Ibid., 105.

104. *Hirabayashi*, 320 U.S., 104–05.

105. *Korematsu*, 323 U.S., 223–24.

106. Ibid., 216.

107. Ibid. (emphasis added).

108. Ibid., 217–18.

109. Ibid., 217.

110. Ibid., 218–19 (footnote and citations omitted).

111. *Korematsu*, 323 U.S., 218.

112. Ibid., 219.

113. Ibid.

114. Ibid., 225–26 (Roberts, J., dissenting) (internal citation omitted).

115. Ibid., 229 (Roberts, J., dissenting).

116. Ibid. (Roberts, J., dissenting).

117. *Korematsu*, 323 U.S., 225–26 (Roberts, J., dissenting).

118. Ibid., 232 (Roberts, J., dissenting).

119. Ibid., 233 (Roberts, J., dissenting).

120. Ibid., 230–32 (Roberts, J., dissenting).

121. Ibid., 233 (Roberts, J., dissenting).

122. Ibid. (Roberts, J., dissenting). Justice Roberts concluded,

Again it is a new doctrine of constitutional law that one indicted for disobedience to an unconstitutional statute may not defend on the ground of the invalidity of the statute but must obey it though he knows it is no law and, after he has suffered the disgrace of conviction and lost his liberty by sentence, then, and not before, seek, from within prison walls, to test the validity of the law.

Korematsu, 323 U.S., 233 (Roberts, J., dissenting). But see *Labedz v. Kramer*, 55 F. Supp. 25 (D. Or. 1944) (citing *Falbo v. United States*, 320 U.S. 549 [1944] holding that Labedz could challenge the exclusion policy only upon indictment for failure to comply with it).

123. *Korematsu*, 323 U.S., 233 (Murphy, J., dissenting).

124. Ibid., 233–34 (Murphy, J., dissenting) (citing *Sterling v. Constantin*, 287 U.S. 378, 401, 1932).

125. Ibid., 234–35 (Murphy, J., dissenting).

126. Ibid., 235 (Murphy, J., dissenting).

127. Ibid. (Murphy, J., dissenting).

128. Ibid., 234 (Murphy, J., dissenting).

129. *Korematsu*, 323 U.S., 235 (Murphy, J., dissenting).

130. Ibid., 231 (Roberts, J., dissenting).

131. Ibid. (Roberts, J., dissenting).

132. Exec. Order No. 9066, 7 Fed. Reg. 1407 (Feb. 19, 1942).

133. *Korematsu*, 323 U.S., 243 (Jackson, J., dissenting).

134. Ibid. (Jackson, J., dissenting).

135. Ibid., 244–45 (Jackson, J., dissenting).

136. Brief for the United States at 57–58, *Korematsu v. United States*, 323 U.S. 214 (1944) (No. 22).

137. Exec. Order No. 9066, 7 Fed. Reg. 1407 (Feb. 19, 1942).

138. Exec. Order No. 9102, 7 Fed. Reg. 2165 (Mar. 18, 1942).

139. Act of March 21, 1942, 56 Stat. 173 (1942).

140. *Ex parte* Endo, 323 U.S. 283 (1944).

141. Brief for the United States, *Korematsu v. United States*, 323 U.S. 214 (1944) (No. 22).

142. *Endo*, 323 U.S., 291.

143. Ibid., 302–04, 305.

144. Ibid., 298.

145. Ibid., 298–99.

146. Ibid., 300.

147. Ibid., 298.

148. *Endo*, 323 U.S., 300–01.

149. Ibid., 297.

150. Ibid., 300.

151. Ibid., 302.

152. Ibid.

153. Ibid., 302–03.

154. *Endo*, 323 U.S., 302–03.

155. See Ibid., 302.

156. Ibid., 307 (Murphy, J., concurring).

157. Ibid., 308–10 (Roberts, J., concurring).

158. Ibid. (Roberts, J., concurring).

159. Ibid., 310 (Roberts, J., concurring).

160. See Arthur H. Garrison, "Enemy Combatants, Detention and the War on Terror: Why This Is Any of the Court's Business" (address at the University of Central Missouri Conference on Terrorism and Justice: The Balance for Civil Liberties Conference, February 18, 2008).

161. *Korematsu v. United States*, 584 F. Supp. 1406, 1420 (N.D. Cal. 1984).

162. Lorraine K. Bannai and Dale Minami, "Internment During World War II and Litigations," in *Asian Americans and the Supreme Court: A Documentary History*, ed. Hyung-chan Kim (Santa Barbara, CA: Greenwood, 1992),756, 780.

163. *Psalms* 146:7.

164. See *Youngstown Sheet & Tube Co. v. Sawyer* (*Steel Seizure*), 343 U.S. 579 (1952).

6

President Truman and His Steel[1]

In times of national crisis and war democracies can rise to the occasion and meet the threat without violating the civil liberties of some to save the whole. In other times a democracy can fall prey to its base instincts and make critical mistakes. But can the rule of law and its muse, the Judiciary, be depended upon to assist in meeting the better parts of our angels or is Madison correct that no Bill of Rights will "be regarded when opposed to the decided sense of the public." In 1952 President Truman seized the American steel industry to avert a national strike which he determined would adversely affect the efforts in the Korean War. The Supreme Court ruled the seizure of the steel industry unconstitutional. The Supreme Court in the *Steel Seizure Case*, as it did in the Internment cases, both ratified and overruled the overreach of Presidential power in the face of assertions of national security necessity. As discussed in the previous chapter, *Korematsu* is significant in what was not done in maintaining the boundaries of Presidential power in time of war, *Youngstown Sheet & Tube v. Sawyer* is significant in what was done and how the Court defined the boundaries of Presidential power and how the Judiciary would determine when those boundaries had been breached.

PRESIDENTIAL POWER IN TIME OF WAR:
TRUMAN AND HIS STEEL

Rex non debet esse sub homine sed sub Deo et lege[2]

It has been said of the American Constitutional republican system that

[w]ith all its defects, delays and inconveniences, men have discovered no technique for long preserving free government except that the Executive be under the law, and that the law be made by parliamentary deliberations. Such institutions may be destined to pass away. But it is the duty of the Court to be last, not first, to give them up.[3]

And "[w]hile historical graveyards are littered with bones of nations that tried to short-cut consensus, democratic governments have survived."[4]

While the World War II internment cases involved the Constitutional limits on *what* can be done in a time of war, the government seizure of the steel industry in 1952 involved the question of *who* decides what can be done. Although President Truman was not the first, he raised the question of whether the President can use his powers as Commander-in-Chief to form domestic policy in order to support the needs of national security on his own authority exclusive of Congress. In *Youngstown Sheet & Tube Co. v. Sawyer*[5] the Supreme Court reaffirmed that the President does not have unencumbered exclusive power to effect domestic policy through his powers as Commander-in-Chief, and, more importantly, the President is bound to the laws that are duly passed by Congress.[6]

On June 25, 1950, the armed forces of North Korea sent forces across the 38th parallel and invaded South Korea. On June 27, the United Nations Security Council passed Resolution 82 which required North Korea to withdraw from South Korea. On July 5, 1950, the United States Army engaged the North Koreans for the first time at Osan, South Korea, to enforce the United Nations resolution. The Korean "police action" had begun.

During World War II, inflation was controlled through direct price controls instituted through the use of Congressional and Presidential war powers. Many of the price controls were still in effect when Truman committed American forces to Korea, and he wanted to maintain the current price controls on the economy in order to control inflation. Leaving aside that President Truman did not request from Congress a declaration of war and committed American military forces under his authority as Commander-in-Chief to enforce a United Nations resolution, President Truman did not want to declare a national emergency and implement economic policies similar to those used during World War II to support the effort in Korea. At the beginning of the war Truman sought to use "political" means to control the economy while engaging in what he thought would be a limited police action, not a protracted war.[7] The advent of the Chinese entering the war in November 1950, President Truman's determination that the steel production capacity of the nation had to remain stable and uninterrupted during the war, and the labor dispute over wages for steel workers all culminated in President Truman seizing the steel industry and the issuance of one of the most significant cases on Presidential power in the second half of the twentieth century.

HISTORICAL BACKGROUND

With the Chinese entering the war on behalf of the North Koreans in November 1950, the Korean War took on a new seriousness, and the materials to support the war effort, in this case steel, were a high priority to the Truman Administration. During World War II, both wages and prices in the steel industry were under national controls to prevent inflation, and after the war ended the steel companies enjoyed high profits due to the caps on wages for steel workers. By 1952 the steelworkers union was set to defend its claim, with a national strike if necessary, that the workers were entitled to a significant wage increase. After the first steel strike of 1946,[8] the Truman Administration was hesitant to become directly involved in another labor dispute between the steel industry and labor. After being forced to increase price control limits for the steel industry to compensate for wage increases for labor in 1946, the President sought to remain out of negotiations for the next labor contract in 1952. While the Administration may have wanted to remain outside of the negotiations, both sides of the labor dispute had other plans. Both viewed the price control power of Washington as the definitive factor in the negotiations; labor wanted to increase the wages of steel workers and the steel companies were willing to increase wages only if government controls on the price of steel were increased.[9] The steel companies also sought increases in price controls in order to avoid losses as the demand for steel decreased at the conclusion of the war.

The current labor contract between the United Steelworkers of America and the steel companies was set to expire on December 31, 1951, and the Truman Administration was standing firm that it would not raise the price controls on steel. The Administration further argued that it was sure that, even with a wage increase, the steel companies could still maintain a reasonable profit.[10] With a strike becoming a serious possibility, President Truman referred the dispute to the War Stabilization Board (WSB).[11] In the meantime it was made known to the steel companies that the Office of Price Stabilization (OPS) would review controls on the price of steel only after wage negotiations had been completed through the WSB.[12] With the union requesting a pay increase of 18.5 cents per hour and the steel companies looking for a price cap increase of $6 to $9 per ton to compensate for the wage increase, the threat of a strike looked even more probable because the OPS was considering only a $3 per ton increase.[13] On March 20, 1952, a divided WSB issued its report and recommended an 18-month contract with a wage increase of 12.5 cents per hour with an additional 2.5 cents per hour effective June 30, 1952, and again on January 1, 1953.[14] Needless to say, the union took the WSB recommendation of a 17.5 cents per hour increase as the floor rather than the ceiling for future negotiations and refused the offer of 14.4 cents per hour made by the steel companies on April 3, 1952.[15]

Although some backdoor negotiations were being conducted to provide a price increase as high as $4.50 per ton, the Truman Administration was preparing options for avoiding a national strike, which the Administration was unified in concluding could not be tolerated.[16] The options open to the Administration were to (1) seek an injunction under the Taft-Hartley Act, (2) seize the steel mills under § 18 of the Selective Service Act, (3) seize the steel mills through the use of the inherent powers of the President, (4) seek legislation from Congress to seize the steel industry, or (5) requisition the steel industry under the Defense Production Act.[17] After a series of discussions between the White House staff and Justice and Defense Department attorneys, it was decided that the best course of action to avert the loss of steel production in the event of a strike would be for the President to seize the steel companies under his inherent powers as Commander-in-Chief.[18] On April 8, 1952, in a radio address, President Truman announced his seizure of the steel industry.[19] In his address the President blamed the labor dispute on the steel companies.[20] President Truman asserted that, during the war, labor had sacrificed wage increases in the interests of the nation and that they were due the reasonable increase in wages they were requesting; the demands of the steel companies for increases in price caps on steel would cause a recession; the steel companies knew their demands would cause economic disruption to the United States economy, and they did not care; steel companies, with their current profits, could afford to negotiate and provide a wage increase to labor without demanding increases in prices; and as President, it was his duty to stand against disruption to the American economy and interference with the needed supply of military materials posed by the actions of the steel companies.[21] The die was cast and the steel companies—first, affronted by the President placing blame for the labor dispute squarely on them and, second, wanting to turn the debate against the Administration—claimed that the action of the President was unconstitutional.[22]

President Truman thought that the seizure was both lawful and politically acceptable.[23] He correctly argued, both in public and later before the Supreme Court, that there was clear precedent for his actions as a President in time of war. The assertion of plenary, if not absolute, policy making authority in foreign affairs and in times of war did not originate with Truman. Lincoln, Wilson, Theodore Roosevelt, Franklin D. Roosevelt, and subsequent Presidents, including Clinton, George H.W. Bush, and George W. Bush, all have made similar assertions of power. Truman was correct that the Government under Wilson nationalized and took control of almost every major industry for the successful mobilization of the nation for conducting World War I. Under Wilson, government control was on such a micro level that it addressed rent prices in Washington, D.C. President Truman's predecessor during World War II had the entire nation mobilized for conducting the war. President Franklin D. Roosevelt's belief in his absolute powers as Commander-in-Chief was such that on September 7, 1942, he informed Congress that, if it did not pass economic legislation to control the cost of living that he recommended in April 1942, he would by executive order institute the increase in taxes and place a cap on prices for farm products.[24] President Roosevelt, in his message to Congress, asserted that

> war calls for sacrifice. War makes sacrifice a privilege. That sacrifice will have to be expressed in terms of a lack of many of the things to which we all have become accustomed. Workers, farmers, white collar people and businessmen must expect that. No one can expect that, during the war, he will always be able to buy what he can buy today.
>
> If we are to keep wages effectually stabilized, it becomes imperative, in fairness to the worker, to keep equally stable the cost of food and clothing and shelter and other articles used by workers.
>
> Prices and rents should not be allowed to advance so drastically ahead of wage rates that the real wages of workers as of today—their ability to buy food and clothing and medical care—will be cut down. For if the cost of living goes up as fast as it is threatening to do in the immediate future, it will be unjust, in fact impossible, to deny workers rises in wages which would meet at least a part of that increase.[25]

True as this may be, how is it that the control of inflation and the justice of sacrifice in time of war are for the President to define, impose, and demand? His answer was not without precedent and is important in understanding why Truman believed he had the authority to seize the steel industry. President Roosevelt, in 1942, appealed to Congress with the following address:

> I ask the Congress to take this action by the first of October. Inaction on your part by that date will leave me with an inescapable responsibility to the people of this country to see to it that the war effort is no longer imperiled by threat of economic chaos.
>
> In the event that the Congress should fail to act, and act adequately, I shall accept the responsibility, and I will act.
>
> At the same time that farm prices are stabilized, wages can and will be stabilized also. This I will do.
>
> *The President has the powers, under the Constitution and under Congressional Acts, to take measures necessary to avert a disaster which would interfere with the winning of the war.*
>
> I have given the most thoughtful consideration to meeting this issue without further reference to the Congress. I have determined, however, on this vital matter to consult with the Congress.
>
> There may be those who will say that, if the situation is as grave as I have stated it to be, I should use my powers and act now. I can only say that I have approached this problem from every angle, and that I have decided that the

course of conduct which I am following in this case is consistent with my sense of responsibility as President in time of war, and with my deep and unalterable devotion to the processes of democracy.

The responsibilities of the President in war time to protect the Nation are very grave. This total war, with our fighting front all over the world, makes the use of executive power far more essential than in any previous war.

If we were invaded, the people of this country would expect the President to use any and all means to repel the invader.

The Revolution and the War Between The States were fought on our own soil but today this war will be won or lost on other continents and remote seas.

I cannot tell what powers may have to be exercised in order to win this war.

The American people can be sure that I will use my powers with a full sense of my responsibility to the Constitution and to my country. The American people can also be sure that *I shall not hesitate to use every power vested in me to accomplish the defeat of our enemies in any part of the world where our own safety demands such defeat.*

When the war is won, the powers under which I act automatically revert to the people—to whom they belong.[26]

Leaving aside that Congress acquiesced to such a direct frontal assault on its Constitutional power to determine domestic economic policy by passing the requested legislation under threat, President Roosevelt was prepared to exercise power he himself admitted was for Congress to exercise under his powers as Commander-in-Chief for the safety and security of America as he saw the need.[27] In his fireside chat that very evening, President Roosevelt restated his view that, on his own authority, he had the power to implement policies which required legislation to successfully conduct the war, but he decided nonetheless to seek Congressional action before taking action on his own. The point is not that Congress acted on his proposals but that he would have acted on his own if Congress did not comply. "In the event that the Congress should fail to act," FDR said, "and act adequately, I shall accept the responsibility, and I will act."[28] This was Truman's example.[29]

During World War II the nation mobilized and sacrificed as Roosevelt requested and expected. Ladies during the war painted their legs to compensate for government restriction of civilian use of oil and rubber which reduced the production of stockings. The nation was mobilized from victory gardens and food and gas rationing to the complete coordination of America's industrial strength to meet the needs of war production. What was different for Truman was that the war in Korea in 1952 was not World War I in 1917 or World War II in 1941. Those wars fully absorbed American culture and politics. World War I was seen as the war to end all wars and one in which America would make the world safe for democracy. World War II was seen as the war to rid the earth of fascism and totalitarianism by the Greatest Generation.

The Korean War, unlike the World Wars, was not a declared war. Truman entered the war under a resolution of the United Nations. President Truman did not discuss the war in classical warlike terms. Initially he called the war a "police action" under the United Nations, not a war the United States had to win and intended to win at all costs, which was the policy of the two World Wars, thus justifying the governmental demands for individual and societal sacrifice. The Korean War was seen by many as a war in which the western powers were taking sides in a civil war in order to face down communists in a country few people could find on a map, while the two World Wars were viewed as righteous and even "holy" in purpose. What would come to be referred to as the "forgotten war" was perceived as a war of limited scope and purpose; but even more importantly, America was a different place in 1952 than it was in 1917 and 1941.

By 1952 the nation was not prone to allow the President, as a political matter, to take powers that were used by the Presidents of the two great and significant World Wars. Gone were the days when a President was seen as almost omnipotent in times of war. The nation was no longer prone to surrender all in the conducting of war as it had in the two World Wars. The nation was at the dawn of the civil rights and civil liberties era. The lessons of unrestricted use of executive power exposed by the Nuremberg Trials, the growing unpopularity of the dropping of the atomic bomb by Presidential authority, and the Japanese curfew and exclusion policies of World War II had tempered American acceptance of unbridled executive power in times of war much less during a military "police action" not declared or authorized by Congress. The exercise of free speech and association judicial battles of World War I, the first red scare, the Palmer Raids, and the denaturalization and deportation cases of the post–World War I era, and the current battles during the second red scare and McCarthyism to restrict individual rights were now opposed by an established civil liberties legal community. The nation was tempering its acceptance of Roosevelt's and Wilson's views of the Presidency. This tempering was reflected in the Supreme Court's reception to the Government's assertion of power to act without Congressional concurrence in the formation of domestic policy.

INHERENT PRESIDENTIAL POWER: THE GOVERNMENT'S BRIEF

The Government argued that President Truman's seizure of the steel industry was lawful because he acted under the combined powers of the President under Article II. The Government argued that his power under Article II, Section I—that "the executive power shall be vested in a President of the United States of America"—in addition to Article II, Section 2—that the President "shall be Commander in Chief of the Army and Navy"—supplemented by Article II, Section 3—that the President "shall take care that the laws be faithfully executed"—and the history of Presidential power to act in cases of emergency all supported the lawfulness of President Truman seizing the steel industry in order to prevent the loss of steel production during a time of war. The Government proposed that the use of Presidential powers must be judged by the circumstances of the action taken. The Government argued that in understanding Presidential power and its application to a specific event and measuring the act against the Constitution, "from the beginning of the Republic, it has been recognized that presidential power to act on a particular occasion may derive from more than one of the grants contained in Article II."[30] The Government cited then-Attorney General Murphy and his 1939 opinion in response to the U.S. Senate as follows:

> It is universally recognized that the constitutional duties of the executive carry with them the constitutional powers necessary for their proper performance. These constitutional powers have never been specifically defined, and in fact cannot be, since their extent and limitations are largely dependent upon conditions and circumstances. In a measure this is true with respect to most of the powers of the executive, both constitutional and statutory. The right to take specific action might not exist under one state of facts, while under another it might be the absolute duty of the Executive to take such action.[31]

Thus the inherent powers of the President are not based "upon a single provision of Article II but upon the combined force of the several provisions."[32] The power to execute the laws, the Government asserted, arises "not only on the provision that 'he shall take care that the laws be faithfully executed' but also upon his authority as Chief Executive, as Commander in Chief, and as the organ of foreign relations."[33]

The Government asserted that history also makes clear that the President has, and has been understood to have, broad executive power in times of economic and national security crisis. The Government summed up the history of Presidential power to address threats to the military and/or economy through domestic policy with or without specific Congressional authority by listing the following incidents:

1. President Washington's Neutrality Proclamation of 1793
2. President Washington's suppression of the Whiskey Rebellion in 1794
3. President Jackson's Proclamation of 1832 that he would use force against the execution of the Ordinance of Nullification by South Carolina
4. President Tyler sending military forces into Texas in 1844
5. The actions of President Lincoln during the Civil War 1861–1863
6. President Hayes use of troops in the Railway strike of 1877
7. President Cleveland's dispatch of troops in 1894 to prevent a strike at the Pullman company and the interference with the U.S. Mail

8. President McKinley's dispatch of troops to Idaho in 1899 to suppress a strike of lead and silver miners
9. President Roosevelt considered seizure of the Pennsylvania coal mines during the strike of 1902
10. President Wilson's seizure of the Smith & Wesson Company in 1918
11. President Harding's use of troops to quell the West Virginia coal miner's strike of 1921.
12. President Roosevelt, who on twelve different occasions between 1941–1943, seized private property in order to prevent work stoppage.[34]

The Government concluded that these historical incidents together prove that the President, without statutory authority, has the power to seize private property or otherwise intercede in disputes between labor and business if such intervention will protect the national interests.

The Government further argued that the power of the President to act and seize property is lawful during a time of war. The Government cited the actions of Lincoln, Wilson, and Roosevelt for the proposition that, in time of war, the Government can take property for its use either to bring itself aid or to prevent its use by the enemy. "By the close of the War of 1812, it was firmly established that property could be taken in wartime emergencies as an exercise of independent executive power."[35] The Government cited Lincoln as follows:

> I think the Constitution invests its Commander-in-Chief with the law of war in time of war. The most that can be said—if so much—is that slaves are property. Is there—has there ever been—any question that by the law of war, property, both of enemies and friends, may be taken when needed? And is it not needed whenever taking it will help us, or hurt the enemy?[36]

The Government also cited Wilson's explanation of the seizure of the Smith & Wesson Company on August 31, 1918:

> The Smith & Wesson Company . . . engaged in government work, has refused to accept the mediation of the National War Labor Board. . . . With my consent the War Department has taken over the plant and business of the Company to secure continuity in production and to prevent industrial disturbance.[37]

Additionally, the Government referenced the opinion of Attorney General Biddle regarding the legality of President Roosevelt's seizure of the facilities of the Montgomery Ward & Company in Chicago in 1944:

> As Chief Executive and as Commander-in-Chief of the Army and Navy, the president possesses an aggregate of powers that are derived from the Constitution and from various statutes enacted by the Congress for the purpose of carrying on the war. . . . In time of war when the existence of the nation is at

stake, this aggregate of powers includes authority to take reasonable steps to prevent nation-wide labor disturbances that threaten to interfere seriously with the conduct of the war. The fact that the initial impact of these disturbances is on the production or distribution of essential civilian goods is not a reason for denying the Chief Executive and the Commander-in-Chief of the army and Navy the power to take steps to protect the nation's war effort. . . . I believe that by the exercise of the aggregate of your powers as Chief Executive and Commander-in-Chief, you could lawfully take possession of and operate the plants and facilities of Montgomery Ward and Company if you found it necessary to do so to prevent injury to the Country's war effort.[38]

During oral argument, the Government explained that the reason the seizure of the steel industry was necessary was "to prevent injury to the Country's war effort" was due to the nature of how the steel industry operated and how a strike could cripple the production of steel for weeks, if not months.[39] The loss of a constant and consistent supply of steel in time of war, the Government concluded, created a necessity for the President to seize the steel industry in order to protect the successful implementation of the war effort in Korea.

The Government concluded that the Court has long recognized the power of the Executive to act in times of crisis and war: "[D]irect judicial recognition of executive power to seize property to avert a crisis in time of war or national emergency is not lacking,"[40] and in cases addressing Presidential taking of property, the "judicial controversy . . . has not been over the question whether the power to take exists but whether just compensation was required in view of the circumstances of the taking."[41] The Government concluded that as long as the President could establish that an emergency threatened the safety of the nation, the President, under his aggregate powers as Chief Executive and Commander-in-Chief, had the authority to seize the steel industry to ensure the uninterrupted supply of steel.

THE COURT AND JUSTICE JACKSON'S CONCURRENCE

Justice Black, joined by separate concurring opinions by Justices Frankfurter, Douglas, Jackson, Burton, and Clark, held that

> we cannot with faithfulness to our constitutional system hold that the Commander in Chief of the Armed Forces has the ultimate power as such to take possession of private property in order to keep labor disputes from stopping production. This is a job for the Nation's lawmakers, not for its military authorities.[42]

Justice Black rejected the Government's assertion that the seizure was lawful under the aggregate powers of the President and stated: "It is clear that if the

President had authority to issue the order he did, it must be found in some provision of the Constitution."[43] More importantly, the Court rejected the assertion that Congressional legislation was not required before a seizure could be issued:

> It is said that other Presidents without congressional authority have taken possession of private business enterprises in order to settle labor disputes. But even if this be true, Congress has not thereby lost its exclusive constitutional authority to make laws necessary and proper to carry out the powers vested by the Constitution "in the Government of the United States, or any Department or Officer thereof."[44]

Justice Black wrote that the Congress, not the President, has lawmaking power under the Constitution and thus concluded that Truman's Executive Order to seize the steel industry read and functioned like a statute creating policy rather than an order implementing law passed by Congress. Defending the role of Congress in domestic policy determination and the limits of Presidential power to act without Congress, Justice Black held that it was for Congress to adopt

> policies as those proclaimed by the [Executive] order. . . . It can authorize the taking of private property for public use. It can make laws regulating the relationships between employers and employees, prescribing rules designed to settle labor disputes, and fixing wages and working conditions in certain fields of our economy. The Constitution does not subject this lawmaking power of Congress to Presidential or military supervision or control. . . .
>
> The Founders of this Nation entrusted the lawmaking power to the Congress alone in both good and bad times.[45]

While the Court decision has come to be cited for the principle that the President has limited domestic powers in times of peace or war, the concurring opinion by Justice Jackson has come to be recognized as the seminal decision defining Presidential power within the separation of powers context.[46] It is Justice Jackson's justifications for why the powers of the President are divided and how these divisions support the Constitutional structure of separation of powers, in addition to the practicality and applicability of the three-tiered test, that has endured. For this reason only Justice Jackson's concurring opinion will be reviewed in detail below.

In his beginning paragraph Justice Jackson makes a very interesting observation about how the power of the Presidency is viewed and advanced. He wrote that

> [t]he opinions of judges, no less than executives and publicists, often suffer the infirmity of confusing the issue of a power's validity with the cause it is invoked to promote, of confounding the permanent executive office with

its temporary occupant. The tendency is strong to emphasize transient results upon policies—such as wages or stabilization—and lose sight of enduring consequences upon the balanced power structure of our Republic.[47]

This astute observation that the use of Presidential power is judged through the prism of partisan politics and advocacy of policy outcomes, rather than through the values of the Republic and why the Constitution creates a system of limited and separated powers, is, in the first place, not a small academic issue of civics. Issues regarding the operation of a Constitutional system are about the system, not the transient policies and individuals who are entrusted with its operation. But as Hamilton, Madison, Jefferson, and Adams proved during the very founding of our Constitutional republic, the total separation of partisan politics from the discussion and the use of Presidential power has never been attained nor will it be. The inevitable fact of the merging of the issue of the use of power with the achievement of a political policy does not negate the fact that there is a difference between the "validity" of the use of Presidential power and the "cause" for which it is evoked; this difference should be recognized, asserted, and defined, with "validity" being the more important issue to the institution of the Presidency.

Echoing President Wilson's views in *Constitutional Government in the United States* that the government is an organism with various parts that need to function together as a unit,[48] Justice Jackson explained that "[w]hile the Constitution diffuses power . . . it also contemplates that practice will integrate the dispersed powers into a workable government. It enjoins upon its branches separateness but interdependence, autonomy but reciprocity."[49] It is within this dynamic of interdependence while protecting the principle of separateness to "better . . . secure liberty" that Presidential powers are to be understood and defined.[50] Justice Jackson explained that "[p]residential powers are not fixed but fluctuate, depending upon their disjunction or conjunction with those of Congress."[51] It is with this background of seeing the Presidency as a part of a working interrelated system of powers all working to make government functional as well as making sure that government does not get out of hand[52] that Justice Jackson developed the categories of Presidential power. In defining the use of Presidential power Justice Jackson wrote the following:

> We may well begin by a somewhat over-simplified grouping of practical situations in which a President [uses] . . . his powers, and by distinguishing roughly the legal consequences of this factor of relativity.
>
> 1. *When the President acts pursuant to an express or implied authorization of Congress, his authority is at its maximum, for it includes all that he possesses in his own right plus all that Congress can delegate. In these circum-*

stances, and in these only, may he be said (for what it may be worth) to personify the federal sovereignty. If his act is held unconstitutional under these circumstances, it usually means that the federal Government as an undivided whole lacks power . . .

2. *When the President acts in absence of either a congressional grant or denial of authority,* he can only rely upon his own independent powers, but there is a zone of twilight *in which he and Congress may have concurrent authority,* or in which its distribution is uncertain. Therefore, congressional inertia, indifference or quiescence may sometimes, at least, as a practical matter, enable, if not invite, measures on independent Presidential responsibility. In this area, any actual test of power is likely to depend on the imperatives of events and contemporary imponderables, rather than on abstract theories of law.

3. *When the President takes measures incompatible with the expressed or implied will of Congress, his power is at its lowest ebb, for then he can rely only upon his own constitutional powers minus any constitutional powers of Congress over the matter.* Courts can sustain exclusive Presidential control in such a case only by disabling the Congress from acting upon the subject. Presidential claim to a power at once so conclusive and preclusive must be scrutinized with caution, for what is at stake is the equilibrium established by our constitutional system.[53]

Although Justice Jackson thought these categories simplistic, they have captured the main areas of argument over Presidential authority throughout American history. Justice Jackson observed that since it was uncontested that President Truman was not implementing an Act of Congress when he seized the steel industry and that there were at least three statutes that the President could have used to address the possible strike, it was clear that the first two categories could not be relied upon to support President Truman's seizures.[54] The remainder of Jackson's opinion expanded on the third category and why the President was not authorized to seize the steel industry under the third category—use of Presidential powers in the face of contrary Congressional action based on his own expressed and inherent powers.

Justice Jackson wrote that, although the powers of the Presidency should not be controlled by "rigidity dictated by a doctrinaire textualism" but given "scope and elasticity afforded by what would seem to be reasonable,"[55] he rejected the Government's assertion that Article II, Section 1 grants to the President "all the executive powers of which the Government is capable" of using because, if such were "true[,] . . . why [would] the founders [have] bothered to add [the] several specific items" listed in Article II?[56] Keeping in mind why the Constitution created a limited government and did not create an American version of King George,[57] Justice Jackson reminded that

[t]he example of such unlimited executive power that must have most impressed the forefathers was the prerogative exercised by George III, and the description of its evils in the Declaration of Independence leads me to doubt that they were creating their new Executive in his image. Continental European examples were no more appealing. And, if we seek instruction from our own times, we can match it only from the executive powers in those governments we disparagingly describe as totalitarian. I cannot accept the view that this clause is a grant in bulk of all conceivable executive power, but regard it as an allocation to the Presidential office of the generic powers thereafter stated.[58]

Justice Jackson was equally suspect of the Government's broad assertion of power under Article II, Section 2. Justice Jackson agreed with the Government that the authority of Commander-in-Chief was not "an empty title."[59] But he rejected the Government's assertion that, under this title, "the President having, on his own responsibility, sent American troops abroad derives from that act 'affirmative power' to seize the means of producing a supply of steel for them."[60] Defending the principle that executive power in foreign policy does not create concurrent domestic power to the exclusion of Congress, Justice Jackson observed that no court had ever held that the President is plenary in domestic affairs when such affairs impact his foreign policy initiatives in either peace or war.[61]

Defending the boundaries of the Constitutional structure of the republic and recognizing the borders on the expressed but limited powers of one branch in order to protect the system of checks and balances by the other branches, Justice Jackson's observations on the Commander-in-Chief's power deserve extended citation. Justice Jackson wrote the following:

Assuming that we are in a war de facto, whether it is or is not a war de jure, does that empower the Commander in Chief to seize industries he thinks necessary to supply our army? The Constitution expressly places in Congress power "to raise and *support* Armies" and "to *provide* and *maintain* a Navy." (Emphasis supplied.) This certainly lays upon Congress primary responsibility for supplying the armed forces. Congress alone controls the raising of revenues and their appropriation, and may determine in what manner and by what means they shall be spent for military and naval procurement. I suppose no one would doubt that Congress can take over war supply as a Government enterprise. On the other hand, if Congress sees fit to rely on free private enterprise collectively bargaining with free labor for support and maintenance of our armed forces, can the Executive, because of lawful disagreements incidental to that process, seize the facility for operation upon Government-imposed terms?

There are indications that the Constitution did not contemplate that the title Commander in Chief *of the Army and Navy* will constitute him also Commander in Chief of the country, its industries and its inhabitants. He has no monopoly of "war powers," whatever they are. While Congress cannot deprive the President of the command of the army and navy, only Congress can provide him an army or navy to command. It is also empowered to make rules for the "Government and Regulation of land and naval Forces," by which it may, to some unknown extent, impinge upon even command functions.

That military powers of the Commander in Chief were not to supersede representative government of internal affairs seems obvious from the Constitution and from elementary American history. Time out of mind, and even now, in many parts of the world, a military commander can seize private housing to shelter his troops. Not so, however, in the United States, for the Third Amendment says, "No Soldier shall, in time of peace be quartered in any house, without the consent of the Owner, nor in time of war, but in a manner to be prescribed by law." Thus, even in war time, his seizure of needed military housing must be authorized by Congress. It also was expressly left to Congress to "provide for calling forth the Militia to execute the Laws of the Union, suppress Insurrections and repel Invasions. . . ." Such a limitation on the command power, written at a time when the militia, rather than a standing army, was contemplated as the military weapon of the Republic, underscores the Constitution's policy that Congress, not the Executive, should control utilization of the war power as an instrument of domestic policy. Congress, fulfilling that function, has authorized the President to use the army to enforce certain civil rights. On the other hand, Congress has forbidden him to use the army for the purpose of executing general laws except when expressly authorized by the Constitution or by Act of Congress.[62]

As important as the principle of separation of powers is in our Constitutional framework, the acknowledgement of the outer boundaries of those powers, and the defense of those boundaries which define the limited powers of the President, is even more important. Although Presidential powers should not be arbitrarily limited, the power of the Commander-in-Chief, in a limited government, does not support the proposition that "any Presidential action, internal or external, involving use of force . . . vests [in the President the] power to do anything, anywhere, that can be done with an army or navy."[63] While Justice Jackson contended that the power of the President should be given broad interpretation in his use of the military "at least when turned against the outside world for the security of our society," it is a different matter

when it is turned inward, not because of rebellion but because of a lawful economic struggle between industry and labor . . . . His command power is not such an absolute as might be implied from that office in a militaristic system, but is subject to limitations consistent with a constitutional Republic whose law and policymaking branch is a representative Congress.[64]

What[ever] the power of command may include . . . it is not a military prerogative, without support of law, to seize persons or property because they are important or even essential for the military and naval establishment.[65]

As to the assertion that Article II, Section 3 authorized the seizure, Justice Jackson reminded the Government that "government authority . . . reaches [only] so far as there is law" and the right to seize property is protected by the Fifth Amendment which "gives a private right" to property, which can be taken only under law.[66] "These signify about all there is of the principle that ours is a government of laws, not of men, and that we submit ourselves to rulers only if under rules."[67] Although Justice Jackson disposed of the Government's Article II, Section III assertion with quick dispatch, he broadly considered the "nebulous, inherent [Presidential] powers never expressly granted but said to have accrued to the office from the customs and claims of preceding administrations."[68]

Madison lamented that in the event of public danger no bill of rights would be able to prevent those with power from acting to address the danger.[69] During the first national security debate in American history, over the Neutrality Proclamation issued by Washington in 1798, Madison opposed President Washington's proclamation for both political and Constitutional reasons, asserting that the Constitution gave no such power to the Presidency.[70] Hamilton, defending the issuance of the proclamation, argued that it was an inherent power of the President to determine if a treaty required the nation to remain neutral and to so inform the nation and dictate individual behavior regarding activity on the high seas.[71] Such was born the concept of inherent and implied Presidential powers. Justice Jackson's rejection of the Government's construction of these powers was based on what he called the "[l]oose and irresponsible use of adjectives . . . often [used] interchangeably and without fixed or ascertainable meanings."[72] Justice Jackson asked rhetorically, if these powers existed and were needed in times of emergency, why didn't the founders approve of them by placing them into Article II, for they were fully aware the nation would face a day of national crisis and war?[73] With this knowledge, "they made no express provision for exercise of extraordinary authority because of a crisis."[74] Justice Jackson, the former prosecutor at the Nuremburg Trials, observed that it was the granting of unlimited power to the executive in times of crisis that lead to Hitler, the fall of the First French Republic, and a "temporary dictatorship created by legislation" in Great Britain.[75] To Justice Jackson, the use of emergency powers can be instituted only through the rule of law:

> [E]mergency powers are consistent with free government only when their control is lodged elsewhere than in the Executive who exercises them. That is the safeguard that would be nullified by our adoption of the "'inherent powers' formula. Nothing in my experience convinces me that such risks are warranted by any real necessity, although such powers would, of course, be an executive convenience."[76]

Justice Jackson's opinion reminds that the point of discussions concerning Presidential power are not about the particular policy or the occupant of the White House, but rather the Constitutional republic that will last long after a specific debate is long forgotten. Defending that system, Justice Jackson reminded that in times of crisis and war, if emergency measures are required, it is for Congress to implement such measures:

> Congress may and has granted extraordinary authorities which lie dormant in normal times but may be called into play by the Executive in war or upon proclamation of a national emergency. . . . Under this procedure, we retain Government by law—special, temporary law, perhaps, but law nonetheless. The public may know the extent and limitations of the powers that can be asserted, and persons affected may be informed from the statute of their rights and duties.
>
> In view of the ease, expedition and safety with which Congress can grant and has granted large emergency powers, certainly ample to embrace this crisis, I am quite unimpressed with the argument that we should affirm possession of them without statute. Such power either has no beginning or it has no end. If it exists, it need submit to no legal restraint. I am not alarmed that it would plunge us straightway into dictatorship, but it is at least a step in that wrong direction.[77]

Continuing to have astute practical reasons for requiring that the President be restrained by the rule of law and be constrained to work with Congress in the development of domestic policy, Justice Jackson wrote the following on the nature of the Presidency and the Constitutional system of government as it exists:

> As to whether there is imperative necessity for such powers, it is relevant to note the gap that exists between the President's paper powers and his real powers. The Constitution does not disclose the measure of the actual controls wielded by the modern presidential office. That instrument must be understood as an Eighteenth-Century sketch of a government hoped for, not as a blueprint of the Government that is. Vast accretions of federal power, eroded from that reserved by the States, have magnified the scope of presidential activity. Subtle shifts take place in the centers of real power that do not show on the face of the Constitution.
>
> Executive power has the advantage of concentration in a single head in whose choice the whole Nation has a part, making him the focus of public hopes and expectations. In drama, magnitude and finality, his decisions so far overshadow any others that, almost alone, he fills the public eye and ear. No other personality in public life can begin to compete with him in access to the public mind through modern methods of communications. By his prestige as head of state and his influence upon public opinion, he exerts a leverage upon those who are supposed to check and balance his power which often cancels their effectiveness.
>
> Moreover, rise of the party system has made a significant extra-constitutional supplement to real executive power. No appraisal of his necessities is realistic which overlooks that he heads a political system, as well as a legal system. Party loyalties and interests, sometimes more binding than law, extend his ef-

fective control into branches of government other than his own, and he often may win, as a political leader, what he cannot command under the Constitution. Indeed, Woodrow Wilson, commenting on the President as leader both of his party and of the Nation, observed, "If he rightly interpret the national thought and boldly insist upon it, he is irresistible. . . . His office is anything he has the sagacity and force to make it." I cannot be brought to believe that this country will suffer if the Court refuses further to aggrandize the presidential office, already so potent and so relatively immune from judicial review, at the expense of Congress.[78]

Wilson and Theodore Roosevelt could not have described the Presidency better themselves nor would Madison and Jefferson have been surprised by such a revelation. With an echo of Wilson's views on Congress, Justice Jackson concluded:

> But I have no illusion that any decision by this Court can keep power in the hands of Congress if it is not wise and timely in meeting its problems. A crisis that challenges the President equally, or perhaps primarily, challenges Congress. . . . We may say that power to legislate for emergencies belongs in the hands of Congress, but only Congress itself can prevent power from slipping through its fingers.[79]

Madison assumed that institutions of power seek to increase power at the expense of other institutions. He counted on this fact and created a system of checks and balances to make sure that power was not concentrated in such a way as to jeopardize liberty. Justice Jackson rejected the Government's assertion that President Truman had lawfully used his inherent powers as President, Commander-in-Chief, and as the Chief Executive responsible to make sure that the laws were faithfully executed, because the President

> except for recommendation and veto, has no legislative power. The executive action we have here originates in the individual will of the President, and represents an exercise of authority without law. . . . With all its defects, delays and inconveniences, men have discovered no technique for long preserving free government except that the Executive be under the law, and that the law be made by parliamentary deliberations.[80]

In time of war and national crisis, can society depend upon the Supreme Court to protect civil liberties and the Constitutional system of limited powers and checks and balances? It can be said that, in the case of Japanese Americans during the war of the Greatest Generation, the answer was no; and, in the case of the steel industry during the Forgotten War, the answer was yes. But this would be too simplistic of an answer. The *Youngstown* Court, to a better degree than in the internment cases, maintained the Constitutional boundaries of the Executive and Legislative branches and maintained its role of focusing on the asserted powers and Constitutional parameters of policy making rather than focusing on the underlying policies. As Justice Jackson observed, the importance of judicial determination of the actions of the elected branches of government reaches beyond the underlying policies themselves, extending to the very nature of the Constitutional Republic. The "rightness" of policy and its correction is for the Congress, the people, elections, and, if necessary, impeachment to resolve. The antimajoritarian nature of judicial review and reversing Presidential or Congressional action is justified only when it is used to protect the rule of law, as established by the Constitution. The implementation of "bad" policy is not for the judiciary to remedy.

Youngstown Sheet & Tube Company v. Sawyer established that the President has different categories of acceptable action in relation to Congress. He may act in concert with Congress; he may act in an area in which he shares power with Congress; and he may act under his own authority. Within the third category, the President is at his weakest point and subject to challenge; and he may not act contrary to Constitutional or statutory law. Following the Al Qaeda terrorist attacks of September 11, 2001, President George W. Bush initiated military attacks on Afghanistan and those who supported Al Qaeda. President Bush, acting under his own authority as Commander-in-Chief, established procedures for detaining, interrogating, and trying members of Al Qaeda and the Taliban. Citing Justice Jackson's concurring opinion, the Supreme Court in *Rasul v. Bush* (2004),[81] *Hamdi v. Rumsfeld* (2004),[82] *Hamdan v. Rumsfeld* (2006),[83] and *Boumediene v. Bush* (2008),[84] held collectively that the President faced Constitutional restraints on his authority to address the post-9/11 world and both Congress and the Judiciary had a role in how the nation will respond in the "war on terror." Justice Jackson's principle that, in the American Constitutional republic, the President is under the law has prevailed.

Kings, princes, governors, and judges have always ruled over men. But before Paul laid claim to Roman citizenship[85] and demanded his rights under Roman Justice in the face of his accusers,[86] the police,[87] and a judge as well as a king,[88] and even before the Greek Republic became the cradle of democracy, there was an ancient principle of justice: no one—subject or citizen, man or woman, slave or king!—is above the law.[89]

NOTES

1. First published and adapted from *Cumberland Law Review* 39 (2009): 609–84 by permission; © 2009 by *Cumberland Law Review*.
2. Let not the King be under any man, but he is under God and the Law.
3. *Youngstown*, 343 U.S., 655 (Jackson, J., concurring).

4. John P. Roche, "Executive Power and Domestic Emergency: The Quest for Prerogative," *Western Political Quarterly* 5 (1952): 592–618.

5. *Youngstown*, 343 U.S., 579.

6. Ibid., 591–92.

7. See Maeva Marcus, *Truman and the Steel Seizure Case: The Limits of Presidential Power* (Durham, NC: Duke University Press, 1994).

8. See Barton J. Bernstein, "The Truman Administration and the Steel Strike of 1946," *Journal of American History* 52, no. 4 (1966): 791–803.

9. Marcus, *supra* 56n221.

10. Ibid., 59.

11. Ibid.

12. Ibid., 60.

13. Ibid., 62–63.

14. Ibid., 65.

15. Marcus, *supra* 73n221.

16. Ibid., 74.

17. Ibid., 75.

18. Ibid., 78.

19. Ibid., 80.

20. Ibid.

21. President Harry S. Truman, radio and television address to the American people on the need for government operation of the steel mills, April 8, 1952, Truman Library, http://trumanlibrary.org/calendar/viewpapers.php?pid=965.

22. Marcus, *supra* 83n221.

23. Ibid.

24. President Franklin D. Roosevelt, message to Congress, September 7, 1942, http://www.ibiblio.org/pha/policy/1942/420907a.html.

25. Ibid.

26. Ibid. (emphasis added).

27. Ibid.

28. Ibid.

29. Ibid. Truman was not the first or the last President to assert that he had the power to act regardless of Congressional approval. See Arthur H. Garrison, "Hamiltonian and Madisonian Democracy, the Rule of Law and Why the Courts Have a Role in the War on Terror," *Journal of the Institute of Justice & International Studies* 8 (2008): 120; Arthur H. Garrison, "The Internal Security Acts of 1798: The Founding Generation and the Judiciary During America's First National Security Crisis," *Journal of Supreme Court History* 34, no. 1 (2009): 1–27.

During the first Bush Administration then Secretary of Defense Cheney advised the President that if Congress did not pass the authorization to use force to reverse the Iraqi invasion of Kuwait, the President could and should engage in military actions regardless of the Congressional vote. *Frontline: Cheney's Law*, PBS television documentary, October 16, 2007, http://www.pbs.org/wgbh/pages/frontline/cheney/etc/script.html.

When Congress passed the authorization, President George H. W. Bush in his signing statement made clear that, although he appreciated Congress acting, as Commander-in-Chief he did not need the authorization to take military action against Iraq:

As I made clear to Congressional leaders at the outset, my request for Congressional support did not, and my signing this resolution does not, constitute any change in the longstanding positions of the executive branch on either the President's Constitutional authority to use the Armed Forces to defend vital U.S. interests or the Constitutionality of the War Powers Resolution.

Statement on Signing the Resolution Authorizing the Use of Military Force Against Iraq, 1 Pub. Papers 40, January 14, 1991, The American Presidency Project, http://www.presidency.ucsb.edu/ws/index.php?pid=19217.

President George W. Bush similarly asserted that, although he appreciated Congressional authorization to use force against those who implemented and supported those who committed the attacks of 9/11, he did not need the authorization to act:

Senate Joint Resolution 23 recognizes the seriousness of the terrorist threat to our Nation and the authority of the President under the Constitution to take action to deter and prevent acts of terrorism against the United States. In signing this resolution, I maintain the longstanding position of the executive branch regarding the President's constitutional authority to use force, including the Armed Forces of the United States and regarding the constitutionality of the War Powers Resolution.

Press Release, Office of the Press Secretary of George W. Bush, President Signs Authorization for Use of Military Force Bill, September 18, 2001, Yale Law School, http://avalon.law.yale.edu/sept11/president_022.asp.

30. Brief for the United States at 99, *Youngstown Sheet & Tube Co. v. Sawyer*, 343 U.S. 579 (1952) (Nos. 744, 745).

31. Ibid., 120–21; 39 Op. Att'y. Gen. 343, 347–48 (1939).

32. Brief for the United States at 99, *Youngstown Sheet & Tube Co. v. Sawyer*, 343 U.S. 579 (1952) (Nos. 744, 745).

33. Ibid., 100.

34. Ibid., 100–01, 105, 107, 109, 110–12.

35. Ibid., 105.

36. Ibid., 106.

37. Ibid., 99.

38. Brief for the United States at 119–20, *Youngstown Sheet & Tube Co. v. Sawyer*, 343 U.S. 579 (1952) (Nos. 744, 745); 40 Op. Att'y Gen. 312, 319–20 (1944).

39. Transcript of Oral Argument, *Youngstown Sheet & Tube Co. v. Sawyer* 343 U.S. 579 (1952) (Nos. 744, 745), in *Landmark Briefs and Arguments of the Supreme Court of the United States: Constitutional Law* 48 (1975): 877, 909–10.

40. Brief for the United States at 121, *Youngstown Sheet & Tube Co. v. Sawyer*, 343 U.S. 579 (1952) (Nos. 744, 745).

41. Ibid., 123.

42. *Youngstown Sheet & Tube Co. v. Sawyer (Steel Seizure)*, 343 U.S. 579, 587 (1952).

43. Ibid.

44. Ibid., 588–89.

45. Ibid.

46. In *Medellin v. Texas*, 128 S. Ct. 1346 (2008), Chief Justice Roberts, joined by Justices Scalia, Kennedy, Thomas, and Alito and Justice Stevens (concurring in the result), citing *Youngstown* as the framework for assessing assertions of Presidential

power, wrote the following regarding Presidential power to enforce international treaty obligations on state criminal justice procedures without Congressional enabling legislation:

> In this case, the President seeks to vindicate United States interests in ensuring the reciprocal observance of the Vienna Convention, protecting relations with foreign governments, and demonstrating commitment to the role of international law. These interests are plainly compelling.
>
> Such considerations, however, do not allow us to set aside first principles. The President's authority to act, as with the exercise of any governmental power, "must stem either from an act of Congress or from the Constitution itself." *Justice Jackson's familiar tripartite scheme provides the accepted framework for evaluating executive action in this area.* First, "[w]hen the President acts pursuant to an express or implied authorization of Congress, his authority is at its maximum, for it includes all that he possesses in his own right plus all that Congress can delegate." Second, "[w]hen the President acts in absence of either a congressional grant or denial of authority, he can only rely upon his own independent powers, but there is a zone of twilight in which he and Congress may have concurrent authority, or in which its distribution is uncertain." In this circumstance, Presidential authority can derive support from "congressional inertia, indifference or quiescence." Finally, "[w]hen the President takes measures incompatible with the expressed or implied will of Congress, his power is at its lowest ebb," and the Court can sustain his actions "only by disabling the Congress from acting upon the subject." . . .
>
> Once a treaty is ratified without provisions clearly according it domestic effect, however, whether the treaty will ever have such effect is governed by the fundamental constitutional principle that "[t]he power to make the necessary laws is in Congress; the power to execute in the President." As already noted, the terms of a non-self-executing treaty can become domestic law only in the same way as any other law—through passage of legislation by both Houses of Congress, combined with either the President's signature or a congressional override of a Presidential veto. Indeed, "the President's power to see that the laws are faithfully executed refutes the idea that he is to be a lawmaker." . . .
>
> [G]iving domestic effect to an international treaty obligation under the Constitution—for making law—requires joint action by the Executive and Legislative Branches: The Senate can ratify a self-executing treaty "ma[de]" by the Executive, or, if the ratified treaty is not self-executing, Congress can enact implementing legislation approved by the President. It should not be surprising that our Constitution does not contemplate vesting such power in the Executive alone. As Madison explained in *The Federalist* No. 47, under our constitutional system of checks and balances, "[t]he magistrate in whom the whole executive power resides cannot of himself make a law." That would, however, seem an apt description of the asserted executive authority unilaterally to give the effect of domestic law to obligations under a non-self-executing treaty. . . .
>
> [T]he Executive cannot unilaterally execute a non-self-executing treaty by giving it domestic effect. That is, the non-self-executing character of a treaty constrains the President's ability to comply with treaty commitments by unilaterally making the treaty binding on domestic courts. The President may comply with the treaty's obligations by some other means, so long as they are consistent with the Constitution. But he may not rely upon a non-self-executing treaty to "establish binding rules of decision that preempt contrary state law."

Medellin v. Texas, 128 S. Ct. 1346, 1367–71 (2008) (emphasis added) (internal citations omitted).

In *Hamdan v. Rumsfeld*, 548 U.S. 557 (2006), Justice Stevens wrote for the Court, joined by Justices Kennedy, Souter, Ginsburg, and Breyer, that "[w]hether or not the

President has independent power, absent congressional authorization, to convene military commissions, he may not disregard limitations that Congress has, in proper exercise of its own war powers, placed on his powers. . . . The Government does not argue otherwise" (Ibid., 593n23). Justice Kennedy, in his concurrence, joined by Justices Souter, Ginsburg, and Breyer, contended that "[t]he proper framework for assessing whether Executive actions are authorized is the three-part scheme used by Justice Jackson in his opinion in *Youngstown*" (Ibid., 638 [Kennedy, J., concurring]). Writing in dissent, both Justices Thomas and Scalia cited Justice Jackson's concurrence as authoritative in the determination of the proper use of Presidential power. See also *Hamdi v. Rumsfeld*, 542 U.S. 507 (2004); Sarah H. Cleveland, "*Hamdi* meets *Youngstown*: Justice Jackson's Wartime Security Jurisprudence and the Detention of 'Enemy Combatants,'" *Albany Law Review* 68 (2005): 1127–28.

47. *Youngstown*, 343 U.S. at 634 (Jackson, J., concurring).

48. Woodrow Wilson, *Constitutional Government in the United States* (New York: Columbia University Press, 5th ed., 1917), 199–200.

49. *Youngstown*, 343 U.S. at 635 (Jackson, J., concurring).

50. Ibid. (Jackson, J., concurring).

51. Ibid. (Jackson, J., concurring).

52. Ibid., 640 (Jackson, J. concurring).

53. Ibid., 635–38 (Jackson, J., concurring) (emphasis added) (footnotes omitted).

54. Ibid., 638–39 (Jackson, J., concurring).

55. *Youngstown*, 343 U.S., 640 (Jackson, J., concurring).

56. Ibid., 640–41 (Jackson, J., concurring).

57. One is reminded that many within the Revolutionary Army had offered to make George Washington king after the defeat of England, to which he is said to have responded, "I did not defeat George the Third to become George the First." On his death bed, lamenting his actions during his rule of France, Napoleon is remarked to have said, "They wanted me to be another Washington."

58. *Youngstown*, 343 U.S. at 641 (Jackson, J., concurring).

59. Ibid. (Jackson, J., concurring).

60. Ibid., 642 (Jackson, J., concurring).

61. Ibid. (Jackson, J., concurring).

62. Ibid., 643–44 (Jackson, J., concurring) (footnotes omitted).

63. Ibid., 641–42 (Jackson, J., concurring).

64. *Youngstown*, 343 U.S., 645–46 (Jackson, J., concurring).

65. Ibid., 646 (Jackson, J., concurring).

66. Ibid. (Jackson, J., concurring).

67. Ibid. (Jackson, J., concurring).

68. Ibid. (Jackson, J., concurring).

69. See "Letter from James Madison to Thomas Jefferson (Oct. 17, 1788)," in *The Papers of James Madison*, vol. 11, ed. Robert A. Rutland and Charles F. Hobson (Chicago: University of Chicago Press 1977), 296–300.

70. See Garrison, "Hamiltonian and Madisonian Democracy," *supra* 129–30n243.

71. See Ibid.

72. *Youngstown*, 343 U.S., 646–47 (Jackson, J., concurring).

73. See Ibid., 648–50 (Jackson, J., concurring).

74. Ibid., 650 (Jackson, J., concurring).
75. Ibid., 651 (Jackson, J., concurring).
76. Ibid., 652 (Jackson, J., concurring) (citations omitted).
77. Ibid., 653–54 (Jackson, J., concurring).
78. *Youngstown*, 343 U.S. at 653–54 (Jackson, J., concurring).
79. Ibid., 654.
80. Ibid., 655.
81. *Rasul v. Bush*, 542 U.S. 466 (2004).
82. *Hamdi v. Rumsfeld*, 542 U.S. 507 (2004).
83. *Hamdan v. Rumsfeld*, 548 U.S. 557 (2006).
84. *Boumediene v. Bush*, 128 S. Ct. 2229 (2008).
85. *Acts* 22:27–28.
86. *Acts* 24–25.
87. *Acts* 22:24–26.
88. *Acts* 25:11; 26:32.
89. Legendary Pictures, *300*, DVD (Burbank, CA: Warner Home Video, 2007).

II

September 11, 2001, Terrorism, and the Vindication of the Rule of Law

7

September 11, the War on Terrorism, and the Judiciary

Although the mark of September 11, 2001, on the history of the United States will not soon be forgotten or erased, it was not the first time that America has faced a crisis of a defining nature. The assertions of President Bush on the powers and prerogatives of the presidency in times of international threat are not new or novel. Nor is American law or history without reference and guidance on how to deal with the current threat of violent Islamist fundamentalism. Before Al Qaeda, before the Cold War, before Hitler and Tojo, before the Kaiser, before the bombs of the anarchists, before the rebellion of the liberty-loving slave owners of the south and before the army of King George III almost burned the U.S. Capital building to the ground, the Presidency was acknowledged as the Constitutional branch responsible for the safety of the nation.

Although the Presidency has always been acknowledged as having the power and responsibility to answer the initiation of war, both the law and American traditions have established that the President even in times of war is governed by the rule of law. Madison's warnings that "it is a universal truth that the loss of liberty at home is to be charged to the provisions against danger, real or imagined, from abroad"[1] and "If tyranny and oppression come to this land, it will be in the guise of fighting a foreign enemy"[2] should not be taken lightly.

> Of all the enemies to public liberty war is, perhaps, the most to be dreaded, because it comprises and develops the germ of every other. War is the parent of armies; from these proceed debts and taxes; and armies, and debts, and taxes

are the known instruments for bringing the many under the domination of the few. In war, too, the discretionary power of the Executive is extended; its influence in dealing out offices, honors, and emoluments is multiplied; and all the means of seducing the minds, are added to those of subduing the force of the people. The same malignant aspect in republicanism may be traced in the inequality of fortunes, and the opportunities of fraud, growing out of a state of war, and in the degeneracy of manners and of morals engendered by both. No nation could preserve its freedom in the midst of continual warfare.[3]

But, Madison's fear that in times of war and national security crisis, the demand of the people and government for safety would negate the rule of law[4] has not materialized.

Through American history the rule of law has prevailed over the dogs of war and the power of government. Lincoln and Roosevelt submitted to the will of the people and the dictates of the Constitution during the two greatest wars of American history. Truman submitted to the rule of law as announced by the Supreme Court which maintained that the President is not the Commander-in-Chief of domestic society. During the most violent and bitter war in American history, which was fought on the shores of this nation, Presidential elections required by the Constitution were not suspended. It is no small accomplishment in the history of the world for a nation in the middle of a civil war (initiated by the results of the previous election) to hold open and free elections which all acknowledged would determine the conduct of the war thereafter. Lincoln assumed many powers onto himself to wage the war, but it did not occur to him or to the nation to suspend elections required by the Constitution and declare the Constitution suspended due to civil rebellion; an unrivaled event in the annuls of government.

President Bush was not the first President to assert expanded inherent powers over domestic and international affairs as a result of military aggression upon the United States. Nor was President Bush the first to assert that as President, he alone was empowered by the Constitution to be the protector of the American people. The assertion that the President, and the President alone, as the "preserver, protector and defender" of the Constitution and the American people originates first in the Constitution,[5] and as discussed in chapter 2, secondly with President Lincoln and Attorney General Bates. Presidential power in times of war, as we have discussed, has developed far beyond what the founding generation may have envisioned. Congress has surrendered much of its national security policy making power to the President[6] and the nation has come to expect the President to provide the primary leadership and direction in times of military or economic crisis. It was to President Bush, not Congress, which the nation turned when Al Qaeda achieved an attack on the shores of the United States only equaled in scope and execution by the attack on Pearl Harbor. The terrorist attack on 9/11 killed an estimated three thousand people; the attack on Pearl Harbor killed an estimated 2,400 people.

President Bush was not without voice or determination to meet these obligations. President Bush, along with Vice President Cheney, asserted that as a "war time" Commander-in-Chief he had the inherent powers to seize and detain "enemy combatants" indefinitely as he determined with no accountability to the Judiciary or Congress. The President maintained that he had the power to order the electronic surveillance of American citizens to investigate and subdue additional terrorist plans being developed within the United States without court issued warrants. The President maintained that as Commander-in-Chief he had the power to detain "enemy combatants" at the U.S. Naval bases at Guantanamo Bay, Cuba, immune from judicial review of the legality of their capture, treatment or trial. The President asserted that as Commander-in-Chief in time of war, he had the power to use physical and psychological methods, bordering on torture if not actual torture, to secure information from suspected terrorists. He asserted that it was within his powers as Commander-in-Chief and Chief Executive to determine that international law did not govern the capture and treatment of suspected terrorists and enemy combatants.

Madison feared that in times of crisis nothing would prevent the people and the government from acting as they wished, violating the law if required. President Bush asserted that his actions were within the boundaries of his powers as a President engaged in war, both at home and abroad. The voice of the law, the Supreme Court, would soon prove that the Commander-in-Chief powers during the "war on terror" were not as broad as asserted by the Bush Administration and President Bush would be held to the limitations established by the Constitution, the rule of law and American traditions established in both peace and war. Although the Supreme Court would draw the Constitutional line on the assertion that the President could detain individuals without any judicial review and that both Congress and the Judiciary had a role in the development of post-9/11 policies, President Bush's assertion that as Commander-in-Chief he enjoyed wide latitude in dealing with military threats and utilizing American military power to deal with those threats was not without precedent and was well in line with the prevailing history of legal opinions by the Attorneys General from the Washington Administration to Clinton Administration.

THE JUSTICE DEPARTMENT AND PRESIDENTIAL POWER: THE POWER OF THE COMMANDER AND CHIEF

The assertion of inherent Presidential power to act in times of crisis or in the protection of the national interests hardly began with the Bush Administration. Almost without waver from the Washington Administration to the present, all Presidents and their legal advisors have similarly asserted a primary, if not an exclusive and plenary, view of Presidential power in foreign affairs and the ability to use the military to implement foreign policy for the public good and defense of the nation with or without prior Congressional approval.[7] In 1794 Attorney General William Bradford informed President Washington that as President he was not obligated to provide Congress with diplomatic and other communications that he deemed inappropriate to provide. Attorney General Bradford asserted that communications developed during the conduct of foreign affairs belong to the President as the Chief Executive who is responsible for foreign policy.[8] In 1838 Attorney General Benjamin F. Butler asserted in his legal opinion to the Secretary of War that "there are indeed, cases in which a war between the United States and a public enemy may exist without sanction of Congress—as where an unexpected war is commenced against the United States, and waged before Congress acts upon the subject."[9] From the very earliest period of the Constitution it was understood that not all wars or use of military force required a declaration of war for the President to act. Attorney General Butler wrote in his opinion to the Secretary of War that a "public war" had existed with the Seminoles since January 1836 regardless of the fact that "no formal declaration of war has been made, (probably because deemed unnecessary)" by Congress. He concluded that since Congress had provided funds for the suppression of the Indians "the war, on our part has been waged by authority of the legislative department, to whom the power of making war has been given by the Constitution."[10]

At the dawn of the Civil War, Attorney General Jeremiah S. Black opined in 1860 on the plenary power of the President to control, deploy and assign duties and functions to the armed forces exclusive of Congress. He opined to the President that

> as Commander-in-Chief of the army it is your right to decide according to your own judgment what officer shall perform any particular duty, and as the supreme executive magistrate you have power to appoint. Congress could not, if it wanted, take away from the President, or in any way diminish the authority conferred upon him by the Constitution.[11]

As discussed in chapter 2, Attorney General Bates continued to reflect the established belief that the President, as Commander-in-Chief, is obligated to use his powers to preserve, protect and defend the Constitution and the people of the United States against domestic rebellion as well as foreign aggression.[12] Soon after the civil war Attorney General Charles Devens provided President Rutherford Hayes an opinion in 1877 regarding the power of the President to convene courts-martial in the absence of Congressional authorization. In explaining how to define the powers of the President acting as Commander-in-Chief, General Devens opined as follows:

As has been already observed, the Constitution, while it declares that the President shall be Commander-in-Chief of the Army, does not define the functions of that office, but these are left to be ascertained by reference to the law and usage of our military service as it existed when the Constitution was formed. On examination of the history of this service down to that period, it is found that the Commander-in-Chief, among the duties of whose office, as set forth in his commission, was that of causing "strict discipline and order to be observed in the Army," from time to time exercised authority to appoint general courts-martial without any formal or specific grant of the authority, but nevertheless with the tacit sanction of Congress and the acquiescence of the Army; and thus it became the established law and usage of the military service of the United States for the Commander-in-Chief to exercise such authority. The conclusion to which this directly leads is, that, as Commander-in-Chief of the Army, the President is by the Constitution invested with authority to constitute general courts-martial, and, consequently, can legally exercise such authority without a legislative grant.[13]

In 1898 Acting Attorney General John Richards opined on the Presidential powers as Commander-in-Chief as follows:

The preservation of our territorial integrity and the protection of our foreign interests is instructed, in the first instance, to the President. The Constitution, established by the people of the United States as a fundamental law of the land, has conferred upon the President the executive power; has made him the commander in chief of the Army and Navy . . . and has made it his duty to take care that the laws be faithfully executed. In protection of these fundamental rights, which are based upon the Constitution and grow out of the jurisdiction of this nation over its own territory and its international rights and obligations as a distinct sovereignty, the President is not limited to the enforcement of specific acts of Congress. He takes a solemn oath to faithfully execute the office of President, and to preserve, protect, and defend the Constitution of the United States. To do this he must preserve, protect, and defend those fundamental rights which flow from the Constitution itself and belong to the sovereignty it created.

The President has charge of our relations with foreign powers. It is his duty to see that in the exchange of comities among nations we get as much as we give.[14]

Affirming the views of his nineteenth-century colleagues, Attorney General T.W. Gregory opined in 1914 that the President had the power to order the censorship of domestic radio transmissions. In a very matter of fact reasoning, Attorney General Gregory explained that the exercise of the Commander-in-Chief powers of the President rests on the assumption of proper use.

The President of the United States is at the head of one of the three great coordinate departments of the Government. He is Commander in Chief of the Army and the Navy. In the preservation of the safety and integrity of the United States and the protection of its responsibilities and obligations as a sovereignty, his powers are broad. In the words of Mr. Justice Miller in *In re Neagle* (1890), 135 U.S. 64, his power includes the enforcement of "the rights, duties, and obligations growing out of the Constitution itself, our international relations, and all the protection implied by the nature of the Government under the Constitution."

If the President is of the opinion that the relations of this country with foreign nations are, or are likely to be, endangered by actions deemed by him inconsistent with a due neutrality, it is his right and duty to protect such relations; and in doing so, in the absence of any statutory restriction, he may act through such executive officer or department as appears best adapted to effectuate the desired end. . . .

The powers above outlined are not novel; they have been exercised in numerous emergencies by Presidents of the United States; and, whenever their exercise has been attacked in legal proceedings, their validity has, with hardly an exception, been upheld by the courts. Such powers intrusted to the President are of a fundamental nature, exerted to maintain or preserve the security of the Nation, and subject to that high responsibility to which the Executive is held by the American people; they are not likely to be abused, and not without the gravest reasons are the courts likely to withhold their sanction.[15]

In 1940 Attorney General Robert Jackson opined on the power of the President to make arrangements with Great Britain to exchange naval vessels for the rights to establish military bases on territories held by the British without making such agreements formal treaties subject to Senate approval.[16] Attorney General Jackson opined that the answer to the question "involves consideration of two powers which the Constitution vests in the President."[17]

One of these is the power of the Commander in Chief of the Army and Navy of the United States, which is conferred upon the President by the Constitution but is not defined or limited. . . . But it will hardly be open to controversy that the vesting of the [Commander-in-Chief] function in the President also places upon him a responsibility to use all constitutional authority which he may possess to provide adequate bases and stations for the utilization of the naval and air weapons of the United States at their highest efficiency in our defense. . . . .

The Second power to be considered is that control of foreign relations which the Constitution vests in the President as part of the Executive function.[18]

As a constitutional matter, Attorney General Jackson concluded that the negotiations for the locations of the bases did not require Senate approval because the negotiations did not involve future expenditures of funds nor did they involve establishing obligations by the United States at present or in the future. While acknowledging that the power of the President in foreign relations is not unlimited he provided a very restrictive interpretation on the need for Senate involvement in foreign policy negotiations.

Some negotiations involve commitments as to the future which would carry an obligation to exercise powers vested in the Congress. Such Presidential arrangements are customarily submitted for ratification by a two-thirds vote of the Senate before the future legislative power of the country is committed. However, the acquisitions which you are proposing to accept are without express or implied promises on the part of the United States to be performed in the future. The consideration, which we later discuss, is completed upon the transfer of the special items. The Executive agreement obtains an opportunity to establish naval and air bases for the protection of our coastline but it imposes no obligation upon Congress to appropriate money to improve the opportunity. It is not necessary for the Senate to ratify an opportunity that entails no obligation.[19]

In 1941 Attorney General Robert Jackson expanded on his opinion on the President's responsibility to protect American interests and that the President was at liberty to use the military to this end.

Article II, section 2 of the Constitution provides that the President 'shall be Commander in Chief of the Army and Navy of the United States.' By virtue of this constitutional office he has supreme command over the land and naval forces of the country and may order them to perform such military duties as, in his opinion, are necessary or appropriate for the defense of the United States. These powers exist in time of peace as well as in time of war.[20]

On the question of whether the President had the power to authorize the training of British pilots within the United States as well as by military personnel, Attorney General Jackson concluded that no statute precluded such use of military personnel, but as a Constitutional matter the President had the authority to authorize such use regardless of Congressional approval. Citing two treatises on Constitutional law, one of which concluded that by "virtue of his rank as head of forces, he has certain powers and duties with which Congress cannot interfere" of which included how the President "may direct the movements of the army and the stationing of them at various posts [or the direction of] the movements of the vessels of the navy, sending them wherever in his judgment it is expedient," Attorney General Jackson concluded,

Thus the President's responsibility as Commander in Chief embraces the authority to command and direct the armed forces in their immediate movements and operations designed to protect the security and effectuate the defense of the United States. . . . Indeed the President's authority has long been recognized as extending to the dispatch of armed forces outside of the United States, either on missions of good will or rescue, or for the purpose of protecting American lives or property or American interests. . . .
. . . I have no doubt of the President's authority to utilize forces under his command to instruct others in matters of defense which are vital to the security of the United States.[21]

In 1944 Attorney General Francis Biddle informed President Roosevelt that he had the power as Commander-in-Chief in times of war to seize the mail order, production plants, and facilities of the Montgomery Ward and Company because they were suffering from a labor strike that was interfering with the commerce of the nation in a time of war. Attorney General Biddle informed the President that he had the power to order the seizure of the company. He opined that

> as Chief Executive and as Commander-in-Chief of the Army and Navy, the President possesses an aggregate of powers that are derived from the Constitution and from various statutes enacted by the Congress for the purpose of carrying on the war. The Constitution lays upon the President the duty "to take care that the laws be faithfully executed." The Constitution also places on the President the responsibility and invests in him the powers of Commander-in-Chief of the Army and Navy. In time of war when the existence of the nation is at stake, this aggregate of powers includes authority to take reasonable steps to prevent nation-wide labor disturbances that threaten to interfer seriously with the conduct of the war. The fact that the initial impact of these disturbances is on the production or distribution of essential civilian goods is not a reason for denying the Chief Executive and the Commander-in-Chief of the Army and Navy the power to take steps to protect the nation's war effort. In modern war the maintenance of a healthy, orderly, and stable civilian economy is essential to successful military effort . . . , therefore, I believe that by the exercise of the aggregate of your powers as Chief Executive and Commander-in-Chief, you could lawfully take possession of and operate the plants and facilities of Montgomery Ward and Company if you found it necessary to do so to prevent injury to the country's war effort.[22]

During the Vietnam War, Assistant Attorney General William H. Rehnquist, Chief of the Office of Legal Counsel (OLC),[23] continued to support the broad assertion of Presidential power to dictate military policy in time of war. In a May 1970 opinion to Charles W. Colson, Special Counsel to the President, Rehnquist echoed the view of Hamilton in *Pacificus*:

> Because of the nature of the President's power as Commander-in-chief and because of the fact that it is frequently exercised in external affairs . . . the designation of the President as Commander-in-Chief of the Armed Forces is a substantive grant of power, and not merely a commission which entitles him to precedence in a reviewing stand.[24]

The majority of the opinion actually focused the meaning of "declare war" as opposed to "make war" to which Rehnquist concluded that

> [i]t is well to first dispel any notion that the United States may lawfully engage in armed hostilities with a foreign power only if Congress has declared war. From the earliest days of the republic, all three branches of the federal

government have recognized that this is not so, and that not every armed conflict between forces of two sovereigns is "War."[25] . . .

The questions of how far the Chief Executive may go without Congressional authorization . . . have arisen repeatedly throughout the Nation's history. The Executive has asserted and exercised at least three different varieties of authority under his power as Commander-in-Chief:

    i.   Authority to commit military forces of the United States to armed conflict, at least in response to enemy attack or to protect the lives of American troops in the field;

    ii.   Authority to deploy United States troops throughout the world, both to fulfill United States' treaty obligations and to protect American interests; and

    iii.   Authority to conduct or carry on armed conflict once it is instituted, by making and carrying out the necessary strategic and tactical decisions in connection with such conflict.[26]

"Congress has on some of these occasions acquiesced . . . ; on others it has ratified . . . ; and on still others it has taken no action at all. [A] long continued practice on the Part of the Executive, acquiescence in by the Congress, is itself some evidence of the existence of constitutional authority to support such a practice."[27] A legal position that was not unheard of before or since. Defending President Nixon's authority to use military force to expel Vietnamese forces from Cambodia, in part to protect American forces in Vietnam, Rehnquist concluded,

> Since even those authorities least inclined to a broad construction of the Executive power concede that the Commander-in-Chief provision does confer substantive authority over the manner in which hostilities are conducted, the President's decision to invade and destroy the border sanctuaries in Cambodia was authorized under even a narrow reading of his power as Commander-in-Chief.[28]

After the Vietnam War and the revelations of the Gulf of Tonkin incident and abuses by the FBI and other law enforcement and intelligence agencies of civil liberties combined with the Watergate scandal, Congress sought to reassert itself and place controls and limitations on the Commander-in-Chief powers of the President by passing the War Powers Resolution in 1973. Five years after its passage the Carter Administration requested an opinion on the power of the President to authorize "warrantless foreign intelligence surveillance using certain specific techniques" to which Assistant Attorney General John M. Harmon, Chief of the Office of Legal Counsel (OLC), answered,

> We conclude that the President may, in a proper case, invoke his constitutional powers to regulate foreign affairs [and] authorize warrantless electronic surveillance of an agent of a foreign power, pursuant to his constitutional

power to gather foreign intelligence. This Office has taken the position that the same constitutional power authorizes limited physical entries and seizures incident to installation of such devices.[29]

On November 4, 1979, a mob of students stormed the American Embassy in Iran and took sixty-three members of the embassy staff hostage. Three days after the seizure Harman provided Attorney General Benjamin Civiletti a detailed assessment of the diplomatic options open to the President, concluding that it "is well established that the President has the constitutional power as Chief Executive and Commander-in-Chief to protect the lives and property of Americans abroad [and] the War Powers Resolution does not limit the President's power to act in this instance."[30] In a supplemental opinion, Harmon asserted that the reporting requirements of the War Powers Resolution, *properly read*, are not, per se, an unconstitutional interference with the power of the President to protect Americans abroad.[31]

By early 1980 President Carter was considering using force to free the hostages. On February 12, 1980, Harmon provided an answer to the Attorney General regarding the power of the President to use military force without special Congressional authorization as required by the War Powers Resolution. Not wanting to assert the act was unconstitutional on its face, Harman asserted that "the War Powers Resolution has neither the purpose nor the effect of modifying the President's power" to deploy military forces into the Persian Gulf, use military force to rescue the hostages or retaliate against Iran for harm inflicted upon the hostages, or repel an assault against American interest in the region.[32]

Harmon continued to support the general proposition maintained by the previous Attorneys General by making clear "that the framers contemplated that the President might use force to repel sudden invasions or rebellions without first seeking congressional approval" and the President has "broad foreign policy powers [to] support deployment of the armed forces abroad" to which any "substantive constitutional limits on the exercise of these inherent powers by the President are, at any particular time, a function of historical practice and the political relationship between the President and Congress."[33] Harmon concluded his defense of broad Presidential power with an observation that would be echoed by the Bush Administration OLC post 9/11.[34]

> Our history is replete with instances of presidential use of military force abroad in the absence of prior congressional approval. This pattern of presidential initiative and congressional acquiescence may be said to reflect the implicit advantage held by the executive over the legislative under our constitutional scheme in situations calling for immediate action. Thus, constitutional practice over two centuries, supported by the nature of the functions exercised and by the few legal benchmarks that exist, evidences the existence of broad constitutional power.

The power to deploy troops abroad without the initiation of hostilities is the most clearly established exercise of the President's general power as a matter of historical practice.[35]

In answering the policy assertion of the War Powers Resolution that "while Presidents have exercised their authority to introduce troops . . . without prior congressional authorization, those troops remained only with the approval of Congress,"[36] Harmon rejected one of the key methods of the War Powers Resolution to achieve its objective.

The Resolution requires the President to terminate any use of the armed forces in hostilities after 60 days unless Congress has authorized his action. It also requires termination whenever Congress so directs by concurrent resolution.[37]

We believe that Congress may terminate presidentially initiated hostilities through the enactment of legislation, but that it cannot do so by means of a legislative veto device such as a concurrent resolution.[38]

Congress may regulate the President's exercise of his inherent powers by imposing limits *by statute*. We do not believe that Congress may, on a case-by-case basis, require the removal of our armed forces by passage of a concurrent resolution which is not submitted to the President for his approval or disapproval pursuant to Article I, § 7 of the Constitution.[39]

Although Harmon's defense of Presidential power in foreign affairs was in line with previous Attorneys General, his defense was more deferential to the power of Congress to place some limits on broad Commander-in-Chief powers than previous Attorneys General.

The Practical effect of the 60-day limit is to shift the burden to the President to convince the Congress of the continuing need for the use of our armed forces abroad. We cannot say that placing that burden on the President unconstitutionally intrudes upon his executive powers.[40]

"The important provisions of the Resolution concern consultation and reporting requirements [which] apply not only when hostilities are taking place or are imminent, but also when armed forces are sent to a foreign country . . . within 48 hours from the time that they are introduced"[41] to which Harmon concluded,

There may be constitutional considerations involved in the consultation requirement. . . . No Administration has taken the position that these requirements are unconstitutional on their face. Nevertheless, there may be applications which raise constitutional questions.[42]

To escape these "constitutional considerations" Harmon affirmed the State Department Legal Advisor, whom he asserted spoke for the Carter Administration, who testified before Congress that the consultation clause leaves to the President [how] to determine precisely how consultation is to be carried out . . . unless the President determines that such consultation is inconsistent with his constitutional obligation. In the latter event the President's decision could not as a practical matter be challenged but he would have to be prepared to accept the political consequences of such action, which might be heavy.[43]

Such was the most deferential and positive reception of the War Powers Resolution received by any Presidential administration. Even with the concession that the 60-day termination and the reporting requirements were not unconstitutional per se, the President was at liberty as Commander-in-Chief not to comply with the provisions. The next administration would not be so conciliatory.

In 1984 Theodore Olsen, Chief of the OLC, opined to Attorney General William French Smith that the "Executive Branch has taken the position from the very beginning that § 2(c) of the WPR does not constitute a legally binding definition of Presidential authority to deploy our armed forces."[44] Olsen provided a list of situations categorizing the types of situations that would allow the President to deploy military forces without Congressional prior approval. These included the deployment of forces

1. To rescue Americans;
2. To rescue foreign nationals where doing so facilitates the rescue of Americans;
3. To protect U.S. Embassies and legations;
4. To suppress civil insurrection in the United States;
5. To implement and administer the terms of an armistice or cease fire designed to terminate hostilities involving the United States; and
6. To carry out the terms of security commitments contained in treaties.[45]

In 1986 the Reagan OLC asserted that "any statute infringing upon the President's inherent authority to conduct foreign policy would be unconstitutional and void" on its face.[46] Assistant Attorney General Charles J. Cooper, Head of the OLC, in his opinion submitted to Attorney General Edwin Meese addressed "the legality of the President's decision to postpone notifying Congress of a recent series of actions that he took with respect to Iran [to pursue] a multifaceted secret diplomatic effort aimed at bringing about better relations between the United States and Iran."[47] Cooper concluded,

On these facts, we conclude that the President was within his authority in maintaining the secrecy of this sensitive diplomatic initiative from Congress until such time as he believed that disclosure to Congress would not interfere with the success of the operation.[48]

Cooper not only continued to support the view of the Justice Department that the President as Commander-in-Chief had plenary authority to utilize the military as he deemed appropriate to protect American interests, he also added to the modern assertion of plenary Presidential power to determine American foreign policy. He asserted that "the President possesses inherent and plenary constitutional authority in the field of international relations" and that his power is "subject only to limits specifically set forth in the Constitution itself and to such statutory limitations as the Constitution permits Congress to impose by exercising one of its enumerated powers."[49] "The President's executive power," Cooper explained, "includes, at minimum, all the discretion traditionally available to any sovereign in its external relations."[50] Thus the President's power to develop and implement policy is limited only by the text of the Constitution itself and Congress has only a role so far as it can justify it by a specific enumerated power within Article I. Such a view asserts in practicality that as a Constitutional matter Congress has no significant role in foreign policy after confirming the Secretary of State and Defense, the sub-cabinet officers in the State and Defense departments, confirmation of senior military commanders, and funding the departments of State and Defense. Cooper, citing Alexander Hamilton, explained that Congress is the legislative department and as such is responsible for establishing the rules for the regulation of society while the President is the head of the executive department which is responsible for employing the common strength of the society for its common defense—which includes the formation and implementation of foreign policy. As discussed in detail in chapter 2, although an aggressive reader of Hamilton, Cooper was not without grounding on his assertion of the distinctions that Hamilton drew regarding the difference between Congress and the Presidency during America's birth and within its first Presidential Administration.

Cooper wrote that whatever the outer limits of a President's authority over foreign policy were, "the conduct of secret negotiations and intelligence operations lies at the very heart of the President's executive power,"[51] a theme that the Bush Administration would later assert with great emphasis. After citing, among other sources, *In re Neagle*, *Curtis-Wright*, John Jay's Federalist 64, *Durand v. Hollins*, and *Marbury v. Madison*,[52] Cooper advanced three principles that govern the protection of the President's foreign policy powers.

First, decisions and actions by the President and his immediate staff in the conduct of foreign policy are not subject to direct review by Congress.

Second, while Congress unquestionably possesses the power to make decisions as to the appropriation of public funds, it may not attach conditions to executive Branch appropriations that require the President to relinquish any of his constitutional discretion in foreign affairs.

Third, any statute that touches on the President's inherent authority in foreign policy must be interpreted to leave the President as much discretion as the language of the statute will allow.[53]

In case one would try to interpret principles two and three as conservative conciliatory acceptance of Congressional involvement in foreign policy as an important but junior partner, Cooper explained his third principle as follows:

Because the President's constitutional authority in international relations is by its very nature virtually as broad as the national interest and as indefinable as the exigencies of unpredictable events, almost *any* congressional attempt to curtail his discretion raises questions of constitutional dimension. Those questions can, and must, be kept to a minimum the only way possible: by resolving all statutory ambiguities in accord with the presumption that recognizes the President's constitutional independence in international affairs.[54]

Cooper concluded that Section 501(B) of the National Security Act, which required the President to report to Congress "in a timely fashion" any intelligence operations that were not reported prior to initiation, must be interpreted to mean when the President determines that the information regarding the operation can be disclosed without risk of disrupting the operation.

The Bush I Administration continued the aggressive defense and assertion of plenary power of the President to develop and implement foreign and intelligence policy. On July 31, 1989, William Barr, Chief of the OLC, provided Attorney General Dick Thornburgh with an opinion answering his question "on the constitutionality of a proposed amendment to section 502 of the National Security Act [that] would prohibit the expenditure or obligation of any funds from the "Reserve for Contingencies" for any covert action in a foreign country . . . if the President has not first notified the appropriate congressional committees of the proposed expenditure."[55]

Building on Cooper's absolutist position, Barr informed the Attorney General that "we believe such a requirement is an unconstitutional condition on the President's authority to conduct covert activities abroad pursuant to the President's constitutional responsibilities, including his responsibility to safeguard the lives and interests of Americans abroad."[56] Focusing on the operational nature of the President's Constitutional power to conduct foreign policy as well as the Constitutional limits placed on Congressional appropriations powers, Barr asserted that

we believe that because the Constitution permits the President, where necessary, to act secretly to achieve vital national security objectives abroad, a rigid requirement of prior notice for covert operations impermissibly intrudes upon his constitutional authority. . . .

Congress's authority incident to its power over the purse is broad, and generally includes the power to attach conditions to appropriations, but its power is by no means limitless. For example, Congress appropriates money for all federal agencies in all three branches of government. But the fact that Congress appropriates money for the Army does not mean that it can constitutionally condition an appropriation on allowing its armed services committees to have tactical control of the armed forces. . . . Interpreting the appropriations power in this manner would in effect transfer to Congress all powers of the branches of government. . . . Accordingly, however broad the Congress's appropriations powers may be, the power may not be exercised in ways that violate constitutional restrictions on its own authority or that invade the constitutional prerogatives of other branches.[57]

In summary, Barr asserted that "the President cannot be compelled to give up the authority of his Office as a condition of receiving the funds necessary to carry out the duties of his office."[58]

On December 4, 1992, Timothy Flanigan, Chief of the OLC, citing the absolutist OLC opinions by Cooper and Rehnquist as well as Attorney General Jackson's 1941 opinion and the *Durand v. Hollins* case, informed Attorney General William Barr that

in our opinion, the President's role under our Constitution as Commander in Chief and Chief Executive vests him with the constitutional authority to order United States troops abroad to further national interests such as protecting the lives of Americans overseas. Accordingly, where, as here, United States government personnel and private citizens are participating in a lawful relief effort in a foreign nation, we conclude that the President may commit United States troops to protect those involved in the relief effort.[59]

While Cooper and Barr focused on the Constitutional justification for the President's actions, Flanigan focused on defending the policy of the President to support the United Nations as well as protect American lives—that is, aid workers and military personnel to ensure that food and other humanitarian supplies were protected during relief work to stave off starvation in Somalia.

In case one would think that the aggressive defense of Presidential power to use the foreign policy, intelligence, and military resources of the United States to defend American interests without Congressional prior approval is a Republican Party concept, one is quickly disappointed by the OLC legal opinions issued during the Clinton Administration. In 1994 William Dellinger, Head of OLC, provided an opinion to Senators Dole, Simpson, Thurmond, and Cohen defending the Clinton Administration deployment of troops to Haiti.[60] Although the Clinton Administration continued the action of sending military forces overseas without specific authorization of Congress, Dellinger defended the actions on a much more conciliatory tone by defending the policy itself and asserting that (1) Congress authorized the action through a Department of Defense Appropriation Act of 1994, (2) that the action was in obedience with the War Powers Resolution reporting requirements, and (3) the scope of the deployment did not engage the Article I War Declaration Clause. Although Dellinger was justifying classical Presidential action without prior Congressional support in a much less confrontational method, his opinion cited Cooper for the proposition that historically Presidents have deployed American military force to protect American interests on their own authority as Commander-in-Chief.

In 1995 Dellinger in an opinion to the General Counsel of the President[61] responded to an inquiry as to the power of the President to use force in Bosnia.

> This is to provide you with our analysis of whether the President, acting without specific statutory authorization, lawfully may introduce United States ground troops into Bosnia and Herzegovina ("Bosnia") to help the North Atlantic Treaty organization ("NATO") ensure compliance with the recently negotiated peace agreement. We believe that the President may act unilaterally in the circumstances here.[62]

Citing Harmon's opinion, *Presidential Power to Use the Armed Forces Abroad Without Statutory Authorization*, Dellinger observed that "American soldiers are deployed at many places around the world . . . in some instances they deal with conditions of appreciable danger. Indeed, continuously for the last forty years, American forces have been deployed under [hostile] conditions."[63] In an opinion that would be echoed by John Yoo, Dellinger cited Attorney General Jackson's *Training of British Flying Students in the United States* opinion that the President has the power to dispense the Armed Forces of the United States as he deems fit to protect the safety of the nation and that this view was in line with "Historical practice" which

> supplies numerous cases in which Presidents, acting on the claim of inherent power, have introduced armed forces into situations in which they encountered, or risked encountering, hostilities, but which were not "wars" in either the common meaning or the constitutional sense. . . . In at least 125 instances, the President acted without express authorization from Congress.[64]

After approvingly citing Flanigan's *Authority to use United States Military Forces in Somalia* opinion, Dellinger concluded that historical "practice reinforces the most natural reading of the constitutional [declare war] language: at the least, the President may deploy United States forces here without authorization to protect the national interests, even if the deployment is not without some risk."[65] As Harmon attempted during the Carter Administration, Dellinger sought to defend the inherent power of the President as Commander-in-Chief without making a frontal assault on the War Powers Resolution.

> The Resolution necessarily presupposes the President's authority, even in the absence of express authorization by Congress, to deploy troops in circumstances such as those here. Where (as here) the President would be ordering United

States forces into foreign territory while equipped for combat, the Resolution requires a report to Congress. The Resolution thus assumes that the President sometimes may order such deployments without prior statutory authorization. . . . At the least, even if the Resolution does not add to the President's authority, it takes for granted that he may make deployments in situations where hostilities are not actual or imminent, without purporting to limit the circumstances in which such deployments may be made, and without placing any restrictions on the time during which the deployments may continue.

In our view, the Resolution lends support to the broader conclusion that the President has authority, without specific statutory authorization, to introduce troops into hostilities in a substantial range of circumstances.[66]

By May 1996, Dellinger took a much more aggressive position supporting the use of Presidential power in foreign affairs in the face of Congressional assertions of its authority over military and foreign policy. In his 1996 memo, *Placing of United States Armed Forces Under United Nations Operational or Tactical Control*, he asserted that a proposed Congressional act that would prevent funds from being obligated or allocated that supported placing American armed forces under United Nations operational or tactical control

unconstitutionally constrains the President's exercise of his constitutional authority as Commander-in-Chief. Further, it undermines his constitutional role as the United States' representative in foreign relations. While '[t]he constitutional power of Congress to raise and support armies and to make all laws necessary and proper to that end is broad and sweeping,' Congress may not deploy that power so as to exercise functions constitutionally committed to the Executive alone, . . . Nor may Congress legislate in a manner that 'impermissibly undermine[s]' the powers of the Executive Branch.[67]

In 1793 Hamilton asserted that it was within the exclusive province of the powers exercised by President Washington to determine if the new French government was to be recognized and the treaty of alliance between the United States and France was to be honored. Madison disagreed. In 1996 Dellinger, backed by two hundred years of history, affirmed Hamilton and asserted the recognition power was exclusive to the Chief Executive and Commander-in-Chief. As did Rehnquist, Dellinger echoed Hamilton when he asserted that "[e]ven though there are areas in which Congress and the President have a constitutional voice . . . [Congress] may not impose constraints in the areas that the Constitution commits exclusively to the President."[68] Those exclusive powers include the power to determine how and by whom American military forces will be lead and under what circumstances. "[T]here can be no room to doubt that the Commander-in-Chief Clause commits to the President alone the power to select the particular personnel who are to exercise tactical and operational control over U.S. forces."[69] As had previous Attorneys General and heads of the OLC, Dellinger made clear that the Commander-in-Chief power not only provides the President with plenary power to determine military tactical policy but also to direct foreign policy. The proposed act, Dellinger asserted, "impermissibly undermin[ed] the President's constitutional authority with respect to the conduct of diplomacy."[70] In absolutist language worthy of the Reagan and Bush I Administrations, Dellinger, citing an opinion[71] by Eisenhower's first Attorney General Herbert Brownell, concluded as follows:

> Congress cannot, however, burden or infringe the President's exercise of a core constitutional power by attaching conditions precedent to the exercise of that power. . . .
> That Congress has chosen to invade the President's authority indirectly, through a condition on an appropriation, rather than through a direct mandate, is immaterial. Broad as Congress's spending power undoubtedly is, it is clear that Congress may not deploy it to accomplish unconstitutional ends. 'Congress may not use its power over appropriations of the public funds to attach conditions to Executive Branch appropriations requiring the President to relinquish his constitutional discretion in foreign affairs.'[72]

One month later Dellinger again forcefully defended the President's powers as Commander-in-Chief against Congressional legislative action. In an echo of the debate between Hamilton and Madison, discussed in chapter 1, on the power of the President to be the lead branch in determining the meaning and applicability of a treaty, Dellinger advised that a proposed appropriation stating that the "United States shall not be bound to any international agreement entered by the President that would substantially modify the ABM Treaty" unless it was submitted to the Senate as a treaty "raises serious constitutional questions."[73] Dellinger concluded that the proposed appropriation amendment "intrudes on two exclusively Executive prerogatives: the power to interpret and execute treaties, and the power of recognition."[74]

> It belongs exclusively to the President to interpret and execute treaties. This is a direct corollary of his constitutional responsibility to 'take care' that the laws are faithfully executed. . . .
> The responsibility to interpret and carry out a treaty necessarily includes the power to determine whether, and how far, the treaty remains in force.[75]

Citing a Congressional Research Service report, which asserted that "there is clear judicial recognition that the President may without consulting Congress validly determine the question whether specific treaty provisions have lapsed," Dellinger made clear that "Congress may not interfere with or direct the President's interpretation and execution of a treaty any more than it may do so in the case of a statute."[76] Which is a more conservative position than was taken by Rehnquist in his 1970 memo in which he acquiesced that "Congress undoubtedly has the power in certain situations to restrict the President's power as Commander-in-Chief to a narrower scope than it would have had in the absence of legislation. . . . Congress, exercising its constitutional authority to 'make rules concerning captures on land and water' may thus constrict the President's power to direct the manner of proceeding with such captures."[77] Moreover, during the Nixon Administration "Congress has enacted legislation providing that United States forces shall not be dispatched to Laos or Thailand in connection with the Vietnam conflict. This proviso was accepted by the executive." Constitutional doubt on Congressional appropriation direction of foreign and military policy rises when "Congress attempt[s] by detailed instructions as to the use of American forces already in the field to supersede the President as Commander-in-Chief of the armed forces."[78] A more liberal and limited position than that taken by Dellinger.

∽

Whether the defense has been more confrontational or conciliatory, the result is the same—no modern President and as we have discussed, no President post–World War II, has not defended his right to engage in foreign policy or use of military force to protect American interests with or without Congressional support. The Carter, Reagan, Bush, and Clinton Administrations all defended the inherent power of the President to use military force as deemed necessary by the President and that he alone had the final authority to determine the needs of the nation in the area of foreign policy. The assertions made by the George W. Bush Administration after 9/11 simply continued the Presidential line of asserting plenary power in the realm of foreign affairs.

The Bush Administration general perspective that the Office of the Presidency has been under continuous attack by the press and the Congress since the 1970s resulting in a delusion of Presidential power and that delusion was to be opposed, if not reversed, did not originate with the Bush Administration but started with the Reagan Administration followed by the first Bush Administration. As we will discuss in the remainder of this book, although the opinions of John Yoo regarding plenary Presidential power in foreign affairs were not dissimilar to the OLC positions by Rehnquist, Harmon, Flanigan, Dellinger, Cooper, or Barr, where the proverbial wheels came of the train was in the extent the Bush administration took its views of plenary Presidential power in times of war after 9/11.

THE BUSH ADMINISTRATION AND THE ASSERTION OF INHERENT EXECUTIVE POWER

More than six decades before President George W. Bush asserted that the events of September 11 required him to take on powers as Commander-in-Chief that were closed to him on September 10 because the nation was not at war, Attorney General Frank Murphy answered a Congressional inquiry as to what was the extent of the powers of the President after he has declared a national emergency. Although maintaining that under law and tradition the Attorney General was not authorized to provide legal opinions to Congress, in 1939 the Attorney General provided this conclusion on the powers of the Presidency:

> You are aware, of course, that the Executive has powers not enumerated in the statutes—powers derived not from statutory grants but from the Constitution. It is universally recognized that the Constitutional duties of the Executive carry with them the Constitutional powers necessary for their proper performance. These Constitutional powers have never been specifically defined, and in fact cannot be, since their extent and limitations are largely dependent upon conditions and circumstances. In a measure this is true with respect to most of the powers of the Executive, both Constitutional and statutory. The right to take specific action might not exist under one state of facts, while under another it might be the absolute duty of the Executive to take such action.[79]

Three score and two years later, the U.S. Justice Department would inform President George W. Bush that the "state of facts" due to the attacks of 9/11 not only gave him the "right to take specific action" but an "absolute duty . . . to take such action," and the specific actions he could take had no Congressional or Judicial limits or constraints.[80]

On September 25, 2001, John Yoo, Deputy Assistant Attorney General within the OLC, released a memo describing the powers that had been released due to the state of war that resulted from 9/11. This memo and others would authorize the President to take any and all actions he determined were required to defend the United States against additional terrorist attacks both at home and abroad. During the initial months of post 9/11 the OLC and John Yoo specifically became the single point of contact for the White House to secure legal approval of its post-9/11 domestic and military operations.

∽

After the attacks of 9/11 the Bush Administration viewed the attacks not as an international criminal act but an act of war warranting a complete military response. On September 12, 2001, during the first National Security Council (NSC) meeting after the attacks, discussions on how the government would track down those responsible for the attacks occurred and FBI Director Robert Mueller commented that if some of the tactics being discussed were used "it may impair our ability to prosecute" to which Attorney General John Ashcroft replied, "This is different."[81] Ashcroft continued,

We simply can't let this happen again. Prosecution cannot be our priority. If we lose the ability to prosecute, that's fine; but we have to prevent the next attack. Prevention has to be our top priority. The chief mission of U.S. law enforcement is to stop another attack and apprehend any accomplices and terrorists before they hit us again. If we can't bring them to trial, so be it.[82]

On November 8 Attorney General Ashcroft publically announced that the "attacks of September 11 have redefined the mission of the Department of Justice. . . . Defending our nation and defending the citizens of America against terrorist attacks is now our first and overriding priority."[83] In a June 2002 press conference Secretary Rumsfeld echoed the Bush Administration view that captured terrorists would be treated differently than criminals.

If you think about it, the task we have is to try to protect the American people, and our friends and allies around the world from terrorist acts and we, we—to do that one has to gather as much as intelligence information as is humanly possible. Here is an individual who has intelligence information, and it is, in answer to the last part of your question—will be submitted to a military court, or something like that—our interest really in his case is not law enforcement, it is not punishment because he was a terrorist or working with the terrorists. Our interest at the moment is to try and find out everything he knows so that hopefully we can stop other terrorist acts.

It seems to me that the problem in the United States is that we have—we are in a certain mode. Our normal procedure is that if somebody does something unlawful, illegal against our system of government, that the first thing we want to do is apprehend them, then try them in a court and then punish them. In this case that is not our first interest.

Our interest is to—we are not interested in trying him at the moment; we are not interested in punishing him at the moment. We are interested in finding out what he knows. Here is a person who unambiguously was interested in radiation weapons and terrorist activity, and was in league with al Qaeda. Now our job, as responsible government officials, is to do everything possible to find out what that person knows, and see if we can't help our country or other countries.

If you think about it, we found some material in Kandahar that within a week was used—information, intelligence information—that was used to prevent a least three terrorist attacks in Singapore—against a U.S. ship, against a U.S. facility and against a Singaporean facility.

Now if someone had said when we found that information or person, well now let's us arrest the person and let's start the process of punishing that person for having done what he had did, we never would have gotten that information. People would have died.

So I think what our country and other countries have to think of is, what is your priority today? And given the power of weapons and given the number of terrorists that exist in the world, our approach has to be to try to protect the American people, and provide information to friendly countries and allies, and protect deployed forces from those kind of attacks.

I think the American people understand that, and that not withstanding the fact that some people are so locked into the other mode that they seem not able to understand it, I suspect that overwhelming that the American people will.[84]

Less than three months after the attacks, during a Senate Judiciary Committee hearing, some members of Congress were voicing concern on how the Bush Administration was advocating for increased domestic powers to prevent additional terrorist attacks and investigate American citizens within the United States. During that hearing General Ashcroft continued to advocate the view that terrorists were different than mere criminals and should be treated as such.

The war crimes commission ordered by the president, now being developed by the Department of Defense, is designed to say that attacks on innocent civilians that are not military targets, taking hostages and killing them, are acts of war. Now, when we come to those responsible for this, say who are in Afghanistan, are we supposed to read them the Miranda rights, hire a flamboyant defense lawyer, bring them back to the United States to create a new cable network of Osama TV or what have you, provide a worldwide platform from which propaganda can be developed? We have judges in the United States that are constantly protected because of their prior involvement in terrorist trials. Can you imagine making a courthouse in a city a target for terrorist activity as a result of focusing the world's attention on some trial in the normal setting for these war crimes?[85]

During this time the Bush Administration was not taking kindly to those who questioned the powers that the Bush Administration was asserting to protect the nation or calling for establishing judicial oversight over FBI and Justice Department operations to deal with terrorist threats. During the same hearing Senator Cantwell voiced concerns on who was guarding the guardians, to which General Ashcroft responded,

You remind me of a spate of cartoons that has appeared in the last week, and it's generally a kid sitting on Santa's knee, and Santa saying, "I know when you've been sleeping, I know when you've been awake, I know when you've been bad or good"—and the kid looks up and says, "Who are you, John Ashcroft?"[86]

Although those in the hearing room found the comment humorous, Senator Cantwell did not. Echoing the general dissatisfaction with the criminal justice process to address the post–September 11 world, Secretary Rumsfeld remarked four years later:

In the years leading up to September 11th, the United States dealt with terrorism primarily as a law enforcement issue. Terrorists who had already killed Americans were investigated, they were arrested, and then they were put on trial, and then they were punished. When terrorists committed an act of war against our country on September 11th, killing 3,000 people, the United States and our allies responded by using military force against al Qaeda and its Taliban sponsors in Afghanistan. In this new era, it became clear that prosecuting terrorists after they strike was an inadequate approach, particularly given the lethal threats posed by violent extremists.[87]

President Bush a year before would defend this same view during his 2004 State of the Union address: "After the chaos and carnage of September the 11th, it is not enough to serve our enemies with legal papers. The terrorists and their supporters declared war on the United States, and war is what they got."[88] The Bush Administration assertion that the attacks of 9/11 were an act requiring a military and not a law enforcement response was not an act of political sophistry or rhetoric. As Jack Goldsmith, former head of the OLC, would observe:

> The government's decision to embrace a war framework was not only, or even primarily, about using the military in battle. The war lens also carries with it important legal powers. . . . The most obvious such power is the power to kill enemy soldiers with impunity. The United States actually started asserting this war power long before 9/11. [During the Clinton Administration the] OLC determin[ed] that the United States was in an "armed conflict" with al Qaeda in 1998 [so those] involved in the capture-and-kill mission for Bin Laden didn't have to worry about violating murder laws or the ban on assassination.
>
> After 9/11 the . . . government settled on another traditional wartime authority: the power to detain captured enemy soldiers, without charge or trial, until the conflict is over. . . . When the U.S. military and allies started capturing hundreds of Taliban and al Qaeda fighters . . . it detained them on precisely the same basis as it detained enemy fighters in past wars.[89]

The Bush Administration's perception that terrorism in the post-9/11 world required a military response rather than a traditional law enforcement response is only part of the background to its assertion of broad, exclusive and plenary Presidential power. John Yoo, along with Vice President Dick Cheney and his General Counsel, David Addington, believed that the power of the President had been fundamentally weakened by the Congress[90] and the courts during the 1970s and 1980s. The Church investigations, Watergate, President Ford appearing before Congress, the War Powers Act, the Foreign Intelligence Surveillance Act (FISA), the Iran-Contra hearings, and Congressional formation of permanent committees to oversee foreign and military policy were all considered by this new administration as successful systemic attempts to limit the power of the President to exercise his Constitutional powers as Commander-in-Chief as he deemed necessary. John Yoo, David Addington, and the Vice President were not only determined not to allow any additional erosion of Presidential authority, they intended to reassert and restore the lost powers and prerogatives of the President.

Yoo, Addington, and the Vice President believed that the President, especially when he acted as Commander-in-Chief in time of war, was not subject
to the desires, dictates or approval of Congress. The Vice President explained
in an interview in 1996 after the first Iraq war that, when he was Secretary
of Defense for the first Bush Administration, he opposed President Bush
going to Congress to seek authorization to use force against Iraq to compel
its withdrawal from Kuwait because he believed that Congressional authorization was not required, that he was afraid it would not be provided and
that if Congress did not approve military action he would have advised the
President to initiate hostilities against Iraq anyway.[91] After thanking Congress for passing the authorization for the use of force in Iraq, President Bush
reflected the sentiments of his Secretary of Defense in his signing statement
(January 14, 1991). In his statement the President made clear that he was
of the view that he did not need the approval Congress had provided; "As I
made clear to Congressional leaders at the outset, my request for Congressional support did not, and my signing this resolution does not, constitute
any change in the longstanding positions of the executive branch on either
the President's Constitutional authority to use the Armed Forces to defend
vital U.S. interests or the Constitutionality of the War Powers Resolution."[92]
On April 12, 2002, the Senate Judiciary Committee, Subcommittee on the
Constitution, Federalism and Property Rights held a hearing on the powers
of the President to deal with terrorism in light of the War Powers Resolution.[93] Testifying for the Administration, John Yoo asserted that

> under Article 2, Section 1 of the Constitution, the President is a locus of the
> entire executive power of the United States and thus, in the Supreme Court's
> words, is the sole organ of the Federal Government in the field of international
> relations. Under Article 2, Section 2, he is the Commander in Chief of the
> armed forces.
>   These two provisions give the President the Constitutional authority to in-
> troduce U.S. armed forces into hostilities when appropriate, with or without
> specific Congressional authorization.
>   Notably, nothing in the text of the Constitution requires the advice and con-
> sent of the Senate or the authorization of Congress before the President may
> exercise the executive power and his authority as Commander in Chief.[94]

When Senator Feingold asked Mr. Yoo, "Why, as a practical matter,
would any administration ever seek a Congressional authorization for committing military troops abroad, if there is no military necessity to do so?"
Mr. Yoo responded, "You are quite right that the administration's position
has been that the Congressional authorization [to use force against the terrorists who committed the attacks of 9/11] was not necessary, but it was
welcome. And I think it goes to the administration's preference, as a practical matter, as a political matter, as a matter of prudence and good policy, to

seek cooperation with the legislature in matters involving the use of armed forces abroad. That said, the administration does not consider the negotiations that led to the drafting of that authorization and the signature of it to cede any of the executive branch's Constitutional authorities."[95]

Advocating an absolutist version of the "Sole Organ" theory of Presidential power, the Bush Administration maintained that the President has exclusive and plenary policy-making jurisdiction in the areas of foreign policy and the use of military force. Led by the Vice President, the primary policy of the Bush Administration was to assert at every opportunity and to defend, against any challenge or assertion of oversight power by Congress, the Presidential plenary power as Commander-in-Chief as well as the "unitary executive" power of the President in domestic policy making and implementation. In its mildest form, the theory of the "unitary executive" asserts that the President has final authority over the operations of the Executive Branch and that the departments, agencies and offices within the Executive Branch of government are subject to the policy determinations of the President. In its more masculine form, it is asserted that actions taken by the President within his powers as Chief Executive are not subject to review or contestation by Congress and require complete deference from the Judiciary. It is through this assertion of prerogatives and inherent "unitary executive" power that the assertion of "executive privilege" is asserted to refuse the release of documents or other Presidential papers or proceedings to Congress. Under separation of powers, the assertion goes, the President as a co-equal is not bound to release internal papers or deliberations due to Congressional request because the President is entitled to keep confidential advice or papers provided to him in his role as Chief Executive and Commander-in-Chief. Congressional desire to know what information is provided to the President, per se, does not require the release. The ability of the President to withhold information under the theory of "executive privilege" dates back to the opinion of Attorney General William Bradford who opined to President Washington on January 28–31, 1794, "The Attorney General has the honour to report, . . . that it is the duty of the Executive to withhold such parts of the said correspondence as in the judgment of the Executive shall be deemed unsafe and improper to be disclosed. . . . The Attorney General is therefore of the opinion, That it will be advisable for the President to communicate to the Senate such parts of the said Correspondence as upon examination he shall deem safe & proper to disclose; withholding all such, as any circumstances may render improper to be communicated."[96]

These twin views, that 9/11 was an act of war, not a crime to be prosecuted in the courts, and that as Commander-in-Chief the President was plenary in the area of foreign policy, provide the context for the legal opinions sought by the White House and provided by Yoo during the first few months after 9/11. Within months of the attacks the government of Afghanistan, which provided a sanctuary and support for Al Qaeda, was deposed and the Bush Administration initiated a worldwide covert military operation to find and capture the major members of Al Qaeda. The memos written by John Yoo would form the legal basis for all of the Bush Administration's initial activities in the War on Terror.

The first Yoo memo, *President's Constitutional Authority to Conduct Military Operations against Terrorists and Nations Supporting Them*, was submitted to the White House on September 25, 2001. Yoo, citing recent uses of military force by the first Bush and the Clinton Administrations broadly concluded that the "President has broad Constitutional powers to take military action in response to the terrorist attacks on the United States on September 11 [and the] President has [the] Constitutional power not only to retaliate against any person, organization, or state suspected of involvement in the terrorist attacks . . . [t]he President may deploy military force preemptively against terrorist organizations or the States that harbor or support them, whether or not they can be linked to the specific terrorist incidents of September 11."[97] With reference to both history and various legal opinions by previous Attorneys General he asserted that the "text, structure and history of the Constitution establishes that the Founders entrusted the President with the primary responsibility, and therefore the power, to use military force in situations of emergency."[98] Article II, Section 2 provides the President with the power "to use military force in response to threats to the national security and foreign policy of the United States" but more importantly up to the period of the drafting of the Constitution "the power to initiate hostilities and to control the escalation of conflict had been long understood to rest in the hands of the executive branch."[99]

Although Yoo is correct as to the principle of executive power to control the military and to use it in times of crisis to maintain and execute the law, it is a debatable statement, to say the least, to assert that the Founders intended to provide in the President the sole and plenary authority to "initiate hostilities and to control the escalation of conflict." As we discussed in chapter 1, Jefferson and Madison would certainly have objected to such a sweeping statement and even Hamilton admitted that only the Congress had the power to declare that the laws of war had replaced the laws of peace. But Yoo's observation that the "historical record [of the United States and Presidential use of the military] demonstrates that the power to initiate military hostilities, particularly in response to the threat of an armed attack, rests exclusively with the president"[100] is correct. As discussed in previous chapters, from threats of fifth columns sympathetic to France to the Barbary pirates; from the various wars with Indian tribes to the invasion of the British; from the rebellion of Southern slave owners to threats from Spain and Mexico; from the anarchists to the fascists; from the Japanese to the communists; and to today's Islamic terrorists, history has made it clear that in times of crisis it is the President who has been expected to protect national security when confronted by domestic and foreign belligerents with military force regardless of Congressional recognition of the threat or prior approval of military action. In recent history Truman ordered military troops into Korea, Kennedy ordered a naval "quarantine" around Cuba with orders to interdict the Soviet navy from entering Cuban waters, Nixon ordered the military into Cambodia, Ford ordered military action against the Cambodian Island Koh Tang to force the release of the S.S. *Mayaguez* and her crew captured by the Cambodian Navy, Carter sent the Delta Force into Iran, Reagan send the Marines into Lebanon and invaded Granada, and Clinton sent military forces to Somalia, Haiti, and initiated an air bombing campaign in Kosovo, all without Congressional prior approval. As Yoo noted, on at least 125 occasions "the President acted without prior express authorization from Congress" to deploy military force to achieve American political ends.[101] It is a historical and political reality that although Congress has had a role in the implementation of policies to protect America through history, it has been the President who has had the plenary position in the determination of initial military action. Although Congress may agree or disagree with the policy, that agreement or disagreement has become a secondary check, not a primary one on foreign and war policy initiation.[102] The truth is that the proposition that the founders intended Congress to control the initiation and pace of hostilities is not synonymous with whom history and practice has determined has such control. As Yoo correctly observed, as Attorney General Devens asserted more than a century before, "governmental practice plays a highly significant role in establishing the contours of the Constitutional separation of powers."[103] Regardless of whether the President was intended to be plenary, the fact remains that he is plenary in the area of foreign affairs and the use of the military to achieve his policy objectives. As President Wilson observed, only the political will of the President and the level of political support of his policies by the people place limits upon his power.

Two months after the attacks of 9/11 President Bush issued *Presidential Military Order of November 13, 2001: Detention, Treatment and Trial of Certain Non Citizens in the War Against Terrorism*, which created a military commission to try non citizens who had committed or would in the future commit terrorist attacks on the United States. Specifically, President Bush justified his conclusion that the establishment of the commissions and the inapplicability of "principles of law and the rules of evidence generally recognized in the trial of criminal cases" as follows:

> By the authority vested in me as President and as Commander in Chief . . . it is hereby ordered as follows:

I. FINDINGS

(a) International terrorists, including members of al Qaida, have carried out attacks on the United States . . . on a scale that has created a state of armed conflict that requires the use of the United States Armed Forces. . . .

(d) The ability of the United States to protect the United States and its citizens, and to help its allies and other cooperating nations protect their nations and their citizens, from such further terrorist attacks depends in significant part upon using the United States Armed Forces to identify terrorists and those who support them, to disrupt their activities, and to eliminate their ability to conduct or support such attacks.

(e) To protect the United States and its citizens, and for the effective conduct of military operations and prevention of terrorist attacks, it is necessary for individuals subject to this order pursuant to section 2 hereof to be detained, and, when tried, to be tried for violations of the laws of war and other applicable laws by military tribunals.

(f) Given the danger to the safety of the United States and the nature of international terrorism, and to the extent provided by and under this order, *I find* consistent with section 836 of title 10, United States Code, *that it is not practicable to apply in military commissions under this order the principles of law and the rules of evidence generally recognized in the trial of criminal cases* in the United States district courts.

(g) Having fully considered the magnitude of the potential deaths, injuries, and property destruction that would result from potential acts of terrorism against the United States, and the probability that such acts will occur, I have determined that an extraordinary emergency exists for national defense purposes, that this emergency constitutes an urgent and compelling government interest, and that issuance of this order is necessary to meet the emergency.[104]

As we will discuss later in detail in chapter 8 it was the Bush Administration's assertion that since "an extraordinary emergency exists for national defense purposes" post 9/11, not only was he authorized as Commander-in-Chief to "identify terrorists and those who support them, to disrupt their activities, and to eliminate their ability to conduct or support such attacks," but he also had the power, independent and exclusive of Congress, to order the detainment of such individuals and to order them "tried for violations of the laws of war and other applicable laws by military tribunals" under procedures not "generally recognized" in and outside of established civilian and military judicial establishments, that the Supreme Court would reject in *Hamdan v. Rumsfeld*.[105]

Subsequent to the issuance of the Presidential order Yoo submitted a second memo to the Defense Department regarding the selection of the U.S. Naval Base at Guantanamo Bay, Cuba, as the location to detain captured suspected terrorists and Taliban fighters. On December 28, 2001, John Yoo and Patrick F. Philbin submitted a memo, *Possible Habeas Jurisdiction over*

Aliens Held in Guantanamo Bay, Cuba, to the Defense Department General Counsel. They concluded that "the great weight of legal authority indicates that a federal district court could not properly exercise habeas jurisdiction over an alien detained at [the U.S. Naval Base at Guantanamo Bay, Cuba] GBC. Nonetheless, we cannot say with absolute certainty that any such petition would be dismissed for lack of jurisdiction. . . . While we believe that the correct answer is that federal courts lack jurisdiction . . . there remains some litigation risk that a district court might reach the opposite result."[106]

Needless to say there was litigation opposing the assertions of power by the Bush Administration and as it did during the early days after Pearl Harbor, the judiciary initially supported the President's assertions of power as Commander-in-Chief and limitations on its own power to independently review the decisions of the Commander-in-Chief in time of war.[107] Subsequent to the initial successes the Supreme Court held that the President had no authority to prohibit judicial jurisdiction over those detained at GBC in *Rasul v. Bush.*[108] But the Court upheld the President's power to detain "enemy combatants" with the limitation that such detained individuals were entitled to a hearing before a neutral decision maker to contest the designation in *Hamdi v. Rumsfeld.*[109] In chapter 8 the Supreme Court's review of the assertion by the Bush Administration that as Commander-in-Chief, President Bush had plenary authority to detain and classify both citizens and noncitizens as enemy combatants will be discussed in detail. We will also review the Court's answer to the Bush Administration's assertion that the judiciary owed the Executive a high level of deference to decisions relating to measures taken to address the post-9/11 war on terrorism and that it did not have jurisdiction to hear habeas cases brought by those detained at GBC. To these landmark Supreme Court cases we will now turn.

NOTES

1. Letter to Thomas Jefferson, May 13, 1798, in *The Papers of James Madison,* vol. 17, ed. Thomas A. Mason, Robert A. Rutland, and Jeanne K. Sisson (*The Papers of James Madison,* vol. 17, ed. Thomas A. Mason, Robert A. Rutland, and Jeanne K. Sisson (Charlottesville: University Press of Virginia, 1985), 130.

2. Quote attributed to James Madison as a U.S. Congressman.

3. "Political Observations—April 20, 1795," in Mason, Rutland, and Sisson, *The Papers of James Madison,* vol. 17, 511, 518.

4. Discussed in chapter 4.

5. "I do solemnly swear . . . to preserve, protect and defend the Constitution of the United States." U.S. Constitution Article II, Section 1, Clause 7. Compare to "The Senators and Representatives before mentioned . . . and all executive and judicial Officers, both of the United States and of the several states, shall be bound

by Oath or Affirmation, to support this Constitution" (U.S. Constitution). Article VI, Clause 3. All members of Congress, the Vice President, and the judiciary, in part, take an oath to "support and defend the Constitution of the United States against all enemies, foreign or domestic." 5 USC 3331, 23 Stat 22 (1884). See 28 USC 453 for the oath of office for the federal judiciary.

6. Arthur H. Garrison, "Hamiltonian and Madisonian Democracy, the Rule of Law, and Why the Courts Have a Role in the War on Terror," *The Journal of the Institute of Justice & International Studies* 8:120–38.

7. H. Jefferson Powell, *The Constitution and the Attorneys General* (Durham, NC: Carolina Academic Press, 1999).

8. Ibid., 10–11.

9. *Existence of War with the Seminoles* 3 Op. Att'y Gen. 307 (March 9, 1838).

10. Ibid., 307.

11. *Memorial of Captain Meigs* 9 Op. Att'y Gen. 462, 468 (July 31, 1860).

12. For a contrary opinion see *Power of the President in Executing the Laws* 9 Op. Att'y Gen. 516 (November 20, 1860) in which Attorney General Black asserted that while the national government had the power to defend itself against a foreign aggression, it was without power to compel states to remain in the union and that if the national government acted offensively to subdue rebellious states it would effectively dissolve the union and the Constitution. But see *President's Power to use Federal Troops to Suppress Resistance to Enforcement of Federal Court Orders—Little Rock, Arkansas* 41 Op. Att'y Gen. 313 (November 7, 1957) in which Attorney General Herbert Brownell opined that the President has the power to enforce judicial orders against state resistance with the military if necessary.

13. *Approval of Court-Martial Sentence* 15 Op. Att'y Gen. 290, 299–300 (June 6, 1877).

14. *Foreign Cables* 22 Op. Att'y Gen. 13, 25–26 (January 18, 1898).

15. *Censorship of Radio* 30 Op. Att'y Gen. 291, 292 (September 16, 1914).

16. *Acquisition of Naval and Air Bases in Exchange for Over-Age Destroyers* 39 Op. Att'y Gen. 484 (August 27, 1940).

17. Ibid., 486.

18. Ibid.

19. Ibid., 487.

20. *Training of British Flying Students in the United States* 40 Op. Att'y Gen. 58, 61 (May 23, 1941).

21. Ibid., 61–63.

22. *Powers of the President under the War Labor Disputes Act to Seize Properties Affected by strikes*, 40 Op. Att'y Gen. 312, 319–20 (April 22, 1944).

23. The OLC is the Justice Department office that provides legal opinions to the White House and other federal government agencies and departments as to the legality of proposed initiatives and provides advice on the power of the President to initiate a specific policy or the Constitutionality of proposed legislation.

24. *Memorandum on Presidential Power: The President and the War Power: South Vietnam and the Cambodian Sanctuaries* (May 22, 1970), 4–5.

25. Ibid., 2–3.

26. Ibid., 8.

27. Ibid.

28. Ibid., 27.

29. *Memorandum Opinion for the Attorney General: Warrantless Foreign Intelligence Surveillance—Use of Television-Beepers* 2 Op. OLC 14 (January 25, 1978), 15.

See also J. Michael Luttig, *Military Use of Infrared Radars Technology to assist Civilian Law Enforcement Agencies* 15 Op. OLC 36 (February 19, 1991) and *Fourth Amendment Implications of Military Use of Forward Looking Infrared Radars Technology for Civilian Law Enforcement* 16 Op. OLC 41 (March 4, 1992) in which Timothy Flanigan, chief of the OLC under the Bush I Administration, opined to the General Counsel of the Department of Defense that

> DoD may assist civilian law enforcement agencies to identify or confirm suspected illegal drug production within structures located on private property by conducting aerial reconnaissance that uses [Forward Looking Infrared Radars] FLIR technology. . . . A memorandum that you made available to us preliminarily concludes that FLIR reconnaissance of structures on private lands does constitute [a search under the Fourth Amendment and] we conclude that it does not.

Fourth Amendment Implications of Military Use of Forward Looking Infrared Radars Technology for Civilian Law Enforcement 16 OP OLC 41, 41.

The Courts have disagreed. See *People v. Deutsch* 44 Cal. App. 4th 1224 (1996) and *Kyllo v. U.S.* 533 U.S. 27 (2001).

30. *Presidential Powers Relating to the Situation in Iran* 4A Op OLC 115, 121 (November 7, 1979).

31. *Supplemental Discussion of the President's Powers Relating to the Seizure of the American Embassy in Iran* 4A Op OLC 123 (November 11, 1979).

32. *Presidential Power to Use the Armed Forces Abroad Without Statutory Authorization* 4A Op. O.L.C.185 (February 12, 1980), 185–86.

33. Ibid., 186.

34. See chapter 8 for detailed discussion of Justice Department assertions of Presidential power.

35. *Presidential Power to Use the Armed Forces Abroad Without Statutory Authorization* 4A Op. O.L.C.185 (February 12, 1980), 187.

36. Ibid., 188.

37. Ibid., 191.

38. Ibid., 186.

39. Ibid., 196.

40. Ibid.

41. Ibid., 190.

42. Ibid., 195.

43. Ibid.

44. *Overview of the War Powers Act*, 8 Op. O.L.C. 271(October 30, 1984), 274.

45. Ibid.

46. *The President's Compliance with "Timely Notification" Requirement of Section 501(B) of the National Security Act* 10 Op. O.L.C. 159 (December 17, 1986), 167.

47. Ibid., 159.

48. Ibid., 160.

49. Ibid., 160–61.

50. Ibid., 161.

51. Ibid., 165.

52. "By the constitution of the United States, the President is invested with certain important political powers, in the exercise of which he is to use his own discretion, and is accountable only to his country in his political character, and to his own conscience" (*Marbury v. Madison*, 5 U.S. (1 Cranch) 137, 164, 1803).

53. Ibid., 169–70.

54. Ibid., 170 (emphasis in original).

55. *Constitutionality of Proposed Statutory Provision Requiring Prior Congressional Notification for Certain CIA covert Activities* 13 Op. O.L.C. 258 (July 31, 1989).

56. Ibid., 258.

57. Ibid., 260, 261.

58. Ibid., 262.

59. *Authority to Use United States Military Force in Somalia* 16 Op. O.L.C. 8 (December 4, 1992), 8.

60. *Deployment of United States Armed Forces into Haiti* 18 Op. O.L.C. 173 (September 27, 1994).

61. *Proposed Deployment of United States Armed Forces into Bosnia* 19 Op OLC 327 (November 30, 1995).

62. Ibid., 327.

63. Ibid., 330.

64. Ibid., 330–31.

65. Ibid., 334.

66. Ibid., 334–35.

67. *Placing of United States Armed Forces Under United Nations Operational or Tactical Control* 20 Op. OLC 182 (May 8, 1996), 183 (internal citations omitted).

68. Ibid., 184.

69. Ibid.

70. Ibid., 186.

71. *Authority of Congressional Committees to Disapprove Action of Executive Branch* 41 Op. Atty. Gen. 230 (1955).

72. *Placing of United States Armed Forces under United Nations Operational or Tactical Control* 20 Op. OLC, 187–88 (international citations omitted).

73. *Constitutionality of Legislative Provision Regarding ABM Treaty* 20 Op. OLC 246 (June 26, 1996), 246.

74. Ibid.

75. Ibid., 248–49.

76. Ibid., 249–50.

77. *Memorandum on Presidential Power: The President and the War Power: South Vietnam and the Cambodian Sanctuaries* (May 22, 1970), 21.

78. Ibid.

79. *Request of the Senate for an Opinion as to the Powers of the President "In Emergency or State of War"* 39 Op. Att'y Gen. 343, 347–48 (October 4, 1939).

80. John C. Yoo, "The President's Constitutional Authority to Conduct Military Operations Against Terrorists and Nations Supporting Them" (memorandum opinion for Timothy Flannigan, Deputy Counsel to the President, September 25, 2001), in *The Torture Papers: The Road to Abu Ghraib*, ed. Karen J. Greenburg and Joshua L. Dratel (New York: Cambridge University Press: New York, 2005), at 11 citing Attorney General Frank Murphy.

81. John Ashcroft, *Never Again: Securing America and Restoring Justice* (New York: Center Street, 2006), 133.

82. Ibid.

83. Ibid., 135–36.

84. U.S. Department of Defense, Office of the Assistant Secretary of Defense (Public Affairs), News Conference Transcript, *Secretary Rumsfeld Media Availability in Qatar*, June 11, 2002, http://www.defenselink.mil/transcripts/transcript.aspx?transcriptid=3502.

85. Senate Judiciary Committee Hearing, *The Department of Justice and Terrorism*, December 6, 2001, http://www.law.uchicago.edu/tribunals/doj_hearinghtml.htm.

86. Ibid.

87. U.S. Department of Defense, Office of the Assistant Secretary of Defense (Public Affairs), News Conference Transcript, *DoD News Briefing with Secretary Rumsfeld and General Pace*, June 14, 2005, http://www.globalsecurity.org/military/library/news/2005/06/mil-050614-dod01.htm.

88. Arthur H. Garrison, "The War on Terrorism on the Judicial Front, Part II: The Courts Strike Back," *American Journal of Trial Advocacy* 27, no. 3 (2004): 473, 506.

89. Jack Goldsmith, *The Terror Presidency* (New York: Norton, 2007), 106–07.

90. The view that Congress had weakened the Office of the Presidency was not a new assertion made by the second Bush Administration. Within months of inauguration the first Bush Administration asserted that Congress had unconstitutionally interfered with the operations of the Executive Branch. This view was articulated in July 1989 by then Assistant Attorney General William Barr in *Common Legislative Encroachments on Executive Branch Constitutional Authority* 13 Op. OLC 247 (July 27, 1989). This opinion was formally superseded by the opinion of Walter Dellinger, Attorney General, in *The Constitutional Separation of Powers between the President and Congress* 20 Op OLC ____ (May 7, 1996). Both opinions are reprinted in H. Jefferson Powell, *The Constitution and the Attorneys General* (Durham, NC: Carolina Academic Press, 1999).

91. "Cheney's Law," *Frontline*, 2007, PBS, http://www.pbs.org/wgbh/pages/frontline/cheney/etc/script.html.

92. "Statement on Signing the Resolution Authorizing the Use of Military Force against Iraq," 1 *Public Papers of George Bush* 40 (1991). See statement reprinted at http://www.presidency.ucsb.edu/ws/index.php?pid=19217.

93. Senate Judiciary Committee, Subcommittee on the Constitution, Federalism and Property Rights, *Applying the War Powers Resolution to the War on Terrorism*, April 17, 2002 S. HRG. 107–892 Serial no J-107-74.

94. Ibid., 9.

95. Senate Judiciary Committee, Subcommittee on the Constitution, Federalism and Property Rights, *Applying the War Powers Resolution to the War on Terrorism*, April 17, 2002 S. HRG. 107–892 Serial no J-107-74, p. 68.

96. Powell, *The Constitution and the Attorneys General*, 10–11.

97. Yoo, September 2001 memo, 3.

98. Ibid., 5.

99. Ibid.

100. Ibid., 15.

101. Ibid.

102. Arthur H. Garrison, "Hamiltonian and Madisonian Democracy, the Rule of Law and Why the Courts Have a Role in the War on Terror," *The Journal of the Institute of Justice & International Studies* 8:120.

103. Yoo, September 2001 memo, 15.

104. Karen J. Greenburg and Joshua L. Dratel, eds., *The Torture Papers: The Road to Abu Ghraib* (New York: Cambridge University Press, 2005), 25–26 (hereafter Presidential Military Order Number One) (emphasis added).

105. *Hamdan v. Rumsfeld*, 548 U.S. 557 (2006).

106. Greenburg and Dratel, *The Torture Papers*, 29.

107. Arthur H. Garrison, "*Hamdi, Padilla,* and *Rasul*: The War on Terrorism on the Judicial Front," *American Journal of Trial Advocacy* 27, no. 1 (2003): 99.

108. *Rasul v. Bush*, 542 U.S. 466 (2004).

109. *Hamdi v. Rumsfeld*, 542 U.S. 507 (2004).

8

Enemy Combatants: Is the President's Designation Enough?

After the events of 9/11 Congress required President Bush to seek Congressional authorization to respond with military force and on September 18th provided to the President a joint resolution to authorize the use of military force (AUMF) in response to the attacks on Washington, D.C. and New York. Senate Joint Resolution 23 read as follows:

AUTHORIZATION FOR USE OF MILITARY FORCE
SEPTEMBER 18, 2001
PUBLIC LAW 107-40 § 2(A), 115 STAT. 224 (2001)
107TH CONGRESS JOINT RESOLUTION

To authorize the use of United States Armed Forces against those responsible for the recent attacks launched against the United States.

Whereas, on September 11, 2001, acts of treacherous violence were committed against the United States and its citizens; and

Whereas, such acts render it both necessary and appropriate that the United States exercise its rights to self-defense and to protect United States citizens both at home and abroad; and

Whereas, in light of the threat to the national security and foreign policy of the United States posed by these grave acts of violence; and

Whereas, such acts continue to pose an unusual and extraordinary threat to the national security and foreign policy of the United States; and

Whereas, the President has authority under the Constitution to take action to deter and prevent acts of international terrorism against the United States: Now, therefore, be it

Resolved by the Senate and House of Representatives of the United States of America in Congress assembled,

SECTION 1. SHORT TITLE.

This joint resolution may be cited as the "Authorization for Use of Military Force."

SEC. 2. AUTHORIZATION FOR USE OF UNITED STATES ARMED FORCES.

(a) IN GENERAL—That the President is authorized to use all necessary and appropriate force against those nations, organizations, or persons he determines planned, authorized, committed, or aided the terrorist attacks that occurred on September 11, 2001, or harbored such organizations or persons, in order to prevent any future acts of international terrorism against the United States by such nations, organizations or persons.

(b) War Powers Resolution Requirements—

(1) SPECIFIC STATUTORY AUTHORIZATION—Consistent with section 8(a)(1) of the War Powers Resolution, the Congress declares that this section is intended to constitute specific statutory authorization within the meaning of section 5(b) of the War Powers Resolution.

(2) APPLICABILITY OF OTHER REQUIREMENTS—Nothing in this resolution supercedes any requirement of the War Powers Resolution.

Approved by Congress and signed by President Bush on September 18, 2001.

Echoing the signing statement of his father regarding the authorization to use force in Iraq, President Bush thanked Congress for its quick action in passing the resolution but made clear that the resolution was not required.

> Senate Joint Resolution 23 recognizes the seriousness of the terrorist threat to our Nation and the authority of the President under the Constitution to take action to deter and prevent acts of terrorism against the United States. In signing this resolution, I maintain the longstanding position of the executive branch regarding the President's Constitutional authority to use force, including the Armed Forces of the United States and regarding the Constitutionality of the War Powers Resolution.[1]

Subsequent to the passage of the AUMF President Bush initiated hostilities against the government of Afghanistan which was the host nation for Al Qaeda which implemented the attacks of 9/11. Yaser Esam Hamdi, an American-born citizen, was captured after his Taliban unit surrendered to Northern Alliance forces in November 2001.[2] The Northern Alliance was an alliance of Afghan tribes and anti-Taliban forces that allied with the United States to depose the Taliban government in Afghanistan. After Hamdi was captured he was interviewed by military officials whom he informed that he had joined the Taliban with the intent to fight for the Taliban government if necessary. Upon his initial declarations and upon subsequent affirmance of his capture within the Taliban unit and that he was armed and prepared to fight for the Taliban, the military classified him as an enemy combatant and transferred him to Guantanamo Bay, Cuba, in January 2002. Subsequent to his arrival at Guantanamo Bay and the determination that he held U.S. citizenship, Hamdi was transferred to the Norfolk Naval Station in Virginia in April 2002. On June 11, 2002, Hamdi's father filed a habeas corpus petition with the U.S. District Court for the Eastern District of Virginia claiming that the detention of his son violated the due process clause of the Fifth Amendment. The main issues argued in the District Court and the Court of Appeals for the Fourth Circuit was (1) the standard and process to classify Hamdi as an enemy combatant, (2) the authority of the President to declare Hamdi an enemy combatant, (3) the level of deference the judiciary owed the military in making the classification, and (4) did Hamdi have a right to counsel and the right to challenge the classification as an enemy combatant.

The government argued before both courts that (1) the government could provide "some evidence" to establish that Hamdi was an enemy combatant, (2) as long as the court was satisfied that "some evidence" existed for the classification and that evidence had been presented to the judiciary, the judiciary was obligated to show great deference to the military determination, (3) the power to classify Hamdi as an enemy combatant flowed from the Article II powers of the President as Commander-in-Chief and through the AUMF, (4) that the citizenship of Hamdi did not entitle him to protection against classification and detention as an enemy combatant, and (5) that Hamdi was not entitled to have access to an attorney or to challenge his confinement or classification because (a) the Constitution does not provide enemy combatants with due process rights and (b) the purpose of detention of enemy combatants is not criminal punishment—regulated by the Constitution—but intelligence gathering and preventing such combatants from returning to the battle against American and allied forces.

The District Court held on August 16, 2002, that the evidence submitted by the government of Hamdi's participation with the Taliban and his taking of arms against the United States was insufficient.[3] Additionally the court held that Hamdi was entitled to due process, including the right to an attorney and to challenge the legality of his confinement and his classification as an enemy combatant. The Court of Appeals reversed and held that "because it is undisputed that Hamdi was captured in a zone of active combat in a foreign theater of conflict, we hold that the submitted declaration is a sufficient basis upon which to conclude that the Commander-in-Chief has Constitutionally detained Hamdi pursuant to the war powers entrusted to him by the Constitution. No further factual inquiry is necessary or proper, and we remand the case with directions to dismiss the [habeas] petition."[4] The Court of Appeals accepted the assertion by the Bush Administration that Hamdi's citizenship did not immune him from classification as an enemy combatant but agreed that his citizenship granted him the right to file a habeas action. But since the government had established that Hamdi was captured on the field of battle, armed, and in support of enemies of the United States, there was no need for further assessment of his status, because his being armed and in the service of the declared military enemy of the United States was enough to be properly declared as an enemy combatant.

Hamdi, of course, appealed to the U.S. Supreme Court and on June 28, 2004, the Supreme Court held that "although Congress authorized the detention of combatants in the narrow circumstances alleged here, due process demands that a citizen held in the United States as an enemy combatant be given a meaningful opportunity to contest the factual basis for that detention before a neutral decision maker."[5] In an opinion by Justice O'Connor joined by Chief Justice Rehnquist and Justices Kennedy and Breyer with a concurring opinion by Justice Souter, joined by Justice Ginsburg, the Court rejected the Bush Administration's assertion that the determination of an individual as an enemy combatant was beyond judicial review. The plurality wrote,

> We necessarily reject the Government's assertion that separation of powers principles mandate a heavily circumscribed role for the courts in such circumstances. Indeed, the position that the courts must forgo any examination of the individual case and focus exclusively on the legality of the broader detention scheme cannot be mandated by any reasonable view of separation of powers, as this approach serves only to *condense* power into a single branch of government. We have long since made clear that a state of war is not a blank check for the President when it comes to the rights of the Nation's citizens. . . . Likewise, we have made clear that, unless Congress acts to suspend it, the Great Writ of habeas corpus allows the Judicial Branch to play a necessary role in maintaining this delicate balance of governance, serving as an important judicial check on the Executive's discretion in the realm of detentions.[6]

Justice O'Connor asserted that "it would turn our system of checks and balances on its head to suggest that a citizen could not make his way to court with a challenge to the factual basis for his detention by his government, simply because the Executive opposes making available such a challenge."[7] "We therefore hold that a citizen-detainee seeking to challenge his classification as an enemy combatant must receive notice of the factual basis for his classification, and a fair opportunity to rebut the Government's factual assertions before a neutral decision maker."[8]

Justice Souter, joined by Justice Ginsburg, concurred in the judgment of vacating the decision by the Fourth Circuit Court of Appeals. Justice Souter agreed with Justice O'Connor regarding the rejection of the limited judicial role the government advocated in reviewing the classification and detention of those designated as "Enemy Combatants" by the President. Justice Souter dissented from O'Connor's opinion regarding the government's power to detain Hamdi under the AUMF and the Non-Detention Act of 1950.

> The plurality does, however, accept the Government's position that if Hamdi's designation as an enemy combatant is correct, his detention (at least as to some period) is authorized by an Act of Congress as required by §4001(a), that is, by the Authorization for Use of Military Force, 115 Stat. 224 (hereinafter Force Resolution). Here, I disagree and respectfully dissent. The Government has failed to demonstrate that the Force Resolution authorizes the detention complained of here even on the facts the Government claims. If the Government raises nothing further than the record now shows, the Non-Detention Act entitles Hamdi to be released.[9]

Justice Scalia, joined by Justice Stevens, dissented from the plurality opinion that the President had the power to declare and detain an American citizen as an enemy combatant without the suspension of the Great Writ.[10]

> Where the Government accuses a citizen of waging war against it, our Constitutional tradition has been to prosecute him in federal court for treason or some other crime. Where the exigencies of war prevent that, the Constitution's Suspension Clause, Art. I, §9, cl. 2, allows Congress to relax the usual protections temporarily. Absent suspension, however, the Executive's assertion of military exigency has not been thought sufficient to permit detention without charge. No one contends that the Congressional Authorization for Use of Military Force, on which the Government relies to justify its actions here, is an implementation of the Suspension Clause. Accordingly, I would reverse the decision below.[11]

In an impassioned opinion on the value, purpose and utility of the Great Writ and how it protects the interest of due process, Justice Scalia wrote that "[i]t is unthinkable that the Executive could render otherwise criminal grounds for detention noncriminal merely by disclaiming an intent to prosecute, or by asserting that it was incapacitating dangerous offenders rather than punishing wrongdoing."[12] But as we have discussed in chapter 2, Lincoln did just that. Although Congress later authorized the detention through the Habeas Corpus Act, the idea of detention to prevent the enemy from returning or otherwise aiding the enemy is not unthinkable but has been a practical aspect of war. Justice Scalia observed that citizens who are found in arms against their own nation are not arrested and detained without charge but are "treated as traitors subject to the criminal process."[13] Justice Scalia also rejected the balancing approach of Justice O'Connor between the national security interest of the government and due process interests of Hamdi and then her subsequent development of procedures for a hearing before a "neutral decision maker" and the shifting burden of proof in such a hearing. Justice Scalia asserted that it was not for the Court to engage in such balancing of interests or the development of procedures because the Constitution requires that habeas corpus be granted to a U.S. citizen being held by executive authority for a criminal act without criminal charge. The fact that the government may have a "good" reason for doing so is irrelevant. What the Constitution requires, by its text, is sufficient for the Court to impose on the political branches.

Only with the dissent from Justice Thomas did the Bush Administration find complete support on the Court. "I agree with the plurality that the Federal Government has power to detain those that the Executive Branch determines to be enemy combatants. But I do not think that the plurality has adequately explained the breadth of the President's authority to detain enemy combatants, an authority that includes making virtually conclusive factual findings. In my view, the structural considerations [of the Constitution], as recognized in our precedent, demonstrate that we lack the capacity and responsibility to second-guess this determination."[14]

> The Government's asserted authority to detain an individual that the President has determined to be an enemy combatant, at least while hostilities continue, comports with the Due Process Clause. As these cases also show, the Executive's decision that a detention is necessary to protect the public need not and should not be subjected to judicial second-guessing. Indeed, at least in the context of enemy-combatant determinations, this would defeat the unity, secrecy, and dispatch that the Founders believed to be so important to the warmaking function.
>
> I therefore cannot agree with *Justice Scalia*'s conclusion that the Government must choose between using standard criminal processes and suspending the writ.[15]

Justice Thomas accepted the government arguments *in toto* and wrote "[t]he Executive Branch, acting pursuant to the powers vested in the President by the Constitution and with explicit Congressional approval, has determined that Yaser Hamdi is an enemy combatant and should be detained. This detention falls squarely within the Federal Government's war powers, and we lack the expertise and capacity to second-guess that decision. As such, petitioners' habeas challenge should fail, and there is no reason to remand the case."[16] Justice Thomas concluded that although the question of whether the President has the power to classify an American citizen as an enemy combatant is a judicially determinable question, it is not for the Court to determine if that classification is correctly made to an individual citizen.

According to Justice Thomas, "the Government's detention of Hamdi as an enemy combatant does not violate the Constitution. By detaining

Hamdi, the President, in the prosecution of a war and authorized by Congress, has acted well within his authority. Hamdi thereby received all the process to which he was due under the circumstances."[17] While Justice O'Connor would leave an individual classified and detained as an enemy combatant to judicial review or a neutral military review process to contest his detention and seek his freedom and Justice Scalia would leave such an individual to the criminal justice system to seek review or to the mercies of the government upon a formal suspension of the Great Writ by an Act of Congress, Justice Thomas would leave such an individual to his own devices and the mercies of the President with no meaningful appeal to the courts of justice or the rights protected by the Great Writ. "I therefore believe" the Justice concluded "that this is no occasion to balance the competing interests, as the plurality unconvincingly attempts to do."[18]

According to Justice Thomas and the Bush Administration, the nature of national security interests and the operation of war, as well as the needs for swift action by the President in times of war, allowed for the President to detain American citizens whom he determined aided the enemy. On this point he agreed with Justice O'Connor but he left her company by asserting that the President's power is plenary and the Constitution provides no role, and the judiciary has no role in imposing additional checks or limits on his power as Commander-in-Chief in times of war. It was on this last concept that the plurality led by Justice O'Connor, the concurring opinion by Justice Souter and the dissent by Justice Scalia concluded otherwise. Both Justice Scalia and Justice O'Connor held that the Constitution provided checks on the President's power. They disagreed on the mechanics of those checks. The plurality held that the requirements of Due Process required the President to sustain his determination to a neutral party while Justice Scalia held that the President can only detain citizens as enemy combatants through the suspension of the writ or through the criminal justice system because those are the checks the Constitution itself places on the national security powers of the national government. Justice Souter agreed that the President did not have the power to detain American citizens without an Act of Congress, but disagreed with O'Connor that the AUMF was such an Act of Congress. With the exception of Justice Thomas, the Court supported the assertion that the Constitution itself prevents indefinite confinement based on a Presidential declaration in times of war. History agreed with this conclusion. Although Lincoln ordered arrests and detention through the suspension of the writ, he did not assert that such detention could occur indefinitely and Congress, although doing so two years after Lincoln acted, authorized the suspension and imposed statutory and judicial action on the limits on the length of time such detention could occur.

The Court has historically approached national security cases by determining if the challenged act violates the Constitution by relying on assessing if the challenged act is within the boundaries of the Constitutional power granted to the government. Detention of enemy combatants for reasons of intelligence and incapacitation are acceptable during national security threats or in times of war. In *Hamdi*, the Court held that although the power to detain an enemy combatant is within the boundaries of the power of the President as Commander-in-Chief, citing *Ex parte Quirin*, the Court made clear that the tool of detaining an American citizen as an enemy combatant was limited by the Constitutional boundary of due process requirements that the citizen be provided a neutral forum to contradict the facts underlying the classification. The Court defended the Constitutional principle that American citizens cannot be detained without review or trial. The Court, aside from Justice Thomas, was unanimous in its agreement that the question of whether an American citizen can challenge his detention as an enemy combatant was a judiciable question and the Court has a role in determining if such a policy can be implemented. The Court split on the how and the boundaries on the implementation of that policy.

With the classification and the indefinite detention of American citizens as enemy combatants by Presidential fiat rejected by the Court, the Bush Administration instituted the Combatant Status Review Tribunals (CSRT) to review individual cases to determine if "enemy combatant" status should be maintained. Hamdi was released and transferred to Saudi Arabia on October 11, 2004, after agreeing to renounce his citizenship and "promising" not to engage in terrorist activity.

The detention of noncitizens detained by the Bush Administration in camp x-ray on the U.S. naval base at Guantanamo Bay, Cuba, and the power of aliens to have access to the courts to challenge their detention and classification was the next major issue for the court to address. To the assertion by the Bush Administration that the Judiciary had no authority to hear habeas petitions from non citizens held at Guantanamo Bay, Cuba, the Court turned next to *Rasul v. Bush*.

∽

HAMDI *ET AL.*
V.
RUMSFELD, SECRETARY OF DEFENSE, *ET AL.*
542 US 507, 124 S. CT 2633, 159 L. ED 2D 578 (2004)
ARGUED APRIL 28, 2004—DECIDED JUNE 28, 2004

[*Justice O'Connor*, joined by *Chief Justice Rehnquist, Justice Kennedy*, and *Justice Breyer*, wrote the plurality opinion. *Justice Souter*, joined by *Justice Ginsburg*, wrote a concurring opinion. *Justice Scalia*, joined by *Justice Stevens*, wrote a dissenting opinion. Justice *Thomas* issued a separate dissenting opinion.]
Justice *O'Connor* delivered the opinion of the Court

At this difficult time in our Nation's history, we are called upon to consider the legality of the Government's detention of a United States citizen on United States soil as an "enemy combatant" and to address the process that is constitutionally owed to one who seeks to challenge his classification as such. The United States Court of Appeals for the Fourth Circuit held that petitioner's detention was legally authorized and that he was entitled to no further opportunity to challenge his enemy-combatant label. We now vacate and remand. We hold that although Congress authorized the detention of combatants in the narrow circumstances alleged here, due process demands that a citizen held in the United States as an enemy combatant be given a meaningful opportunity to contest the factual basis for that detention before a neutral decision maker.

I
[Justice O'Connor reviewed the facts of the case and the lower court decisions].

II
The threshold question before us is whether the Executive has the authority to detain citizens who qualify as "enemy combatants." There is some debate as to the proper scope of this term, and the Government has never provided any court with the full criteria that it uses in classifying individuals as such. It has made clear, however, that, for purposes of this case, the "enemy combatant" that it is seeking to detain is an individual who, it alleges, was "'part of or supporting forces hostile to the United States or coalition partners'" in Afghanistan and who "'engaged in an armed conflict against the United States'" there. We therefore answer only the narrow question before us: whether the detention of citizens falling within that definition is authorized.

The Government maintains that no explicit congressional authorization is required, because the Executive possesses plenary authority to detain pursuant to Article II of the Constitution. We do not reach the question whether Article II provides such authority, however, because we agree with the Government's alternative position, that Congress has in fact authorized Hamdi's detention, through the AUMF.

Our analysis on that point, set forth below, substantially overlaps with our analysis of Hamdi's principal argument for the illegality of his detention. He posits that his detention is forbidden by 18 U. S. C. §4001(a). Section 4001(a) states that "[n]o citizen shall be imprisoned or otherwise detained by the United States except pursuant to an Act of Congress." Congress passed §4001(a) in 1971 as part of a bill to repeal the Emergency Detention Act of 1950, 50 U. S. C. §811 *et seq.*, which provided procedures for executive detention, during times of emergency, of individuals deemed likely to engage in espionage or sabotage. Congress was particularly concerned about the possibility that the Act could be used to reprise the Japanese internment camps of World War II. H. R. Rep. No. 92–116 (1971); *id.*, at 4 ("The concentration camp implications of the legislation render it abhorrent"). The Government again presses two alternative positions. First, it argues that §4001(a), in light of its legislative history and its location in Title 18, applies only to "the control of civilian prisons and related detentions," not to military detentions. Second, it maintains that §4001(a) is satisfied, because Hamdi is being detained "pursuant to an Act of Congress"—the AUMF. *Id.*, at 21–22. Again, because we conclude that the Government's second assertion is correct, we do not address the first. In other words, for the reasons that follow, we conclude that the AUMF is explicit congressional authorization for the detention of individuals in the narrow category we describe (assuming, without deciding, that such authorization is required), and that the AUMF satisfied §4001(a)'s requirement that a detention be "pursuant to an Act of Congress" (assuming, without deciding, that §4001(a) applies to military detentions).

The AUMF authorizes the President to use "all necessary and appropriate force" against "nations, organizations, or persons" associated with the September 11, 2001, terrorist attacks. There can be no doubt that individuals who fought against the United States in Afghanistan as part of the Taliban, an organization known to have supported the al Qaeda terrorist network responsible for those attacks, are individuals Congress sought to target in passing the AUMF. We conclude that detention of individuals falling into the limited category we are considering, for the duration of the particular conflict in which they were captured, is so fundamental and accepted an incident to war as to be an exercise of the "necessary and appropriate force" Congress has authorized the President to use.

The capture and detention of lawful combatants and the capture, detention, and trial of unlawful combatants, by "universal agreement and practice," are "important incident[s] of war." *Ex parte Quirin*, 317 U. S., at 28. The purpose of detention is to prevent captured individuals from returning to the field of battle and taking up arms once again. Naqvi, Doubtful

Prisoner-of-War Status, 84 Int'l Rev. Red Cross 571, 572 (2002) ("[C]aptivity in war is 'neither revenge, nor punishment, but solely protective custody, the only purpose of which is to prevent the prisoners of war from further participation in the war'" (quoting decision of Nuremberg Military Tribunal, reprinted in 41 Am. J. Int'l L. 172, 229 (1947)); W. Winthrop, Military Law and Precedents 788 (rev. 2d ed. 1920) ("The time has long passed when 'no quarter' was the rule on the battlefield. . . . It is now recognized that 'Captivity is neither a punishment nor an act of vengeance,' but 'merely a temporary detention which is devoid of all penal character.' . . . 'A prisoner of war is no convict; his imprisonment is a simple war measure.'" (citations omitted); cf. *In re Territo*, 156 F.2d 142, 145 (CA9 1946) ("The object of capture is to prevent the captured individual from serving the enemy. He is disarmed and from then on must be removed as completely as practicable from the front, treated humanely, and in time exchanged, repatriated, or otherwise released" (footnotes omitted)).

There is no bar to this Nation's holding one of its own citizens as an enemy combatant. In *Quirin*, one of the detainees, Haupt, alleged that he was a naturalized United States citizen. We held that "[c]itizens who associate themselves with the military arm of the enemy government, and with its aid, guidance and direction enter this country bent on hostile acts, are enemy belligerents within the meaning of . . . the law of war." While Haupt was tried for violations of the law of war, nothing in *Quirin* suggests that his citizenship would have precluded his mere detention for the duration of the relevant hostilities. . . . Nor can we see any reason for drawing such a line here. A citizen, no less than an alien, can be "part of or supporting forces hostile to the United States or coalition partners" and "engaged in an armed conflict against the United States"; such a citizen, if released, would pose the same threat of returning to the front during the ongoing conflict.

In light of these principles, it is of no moment that the AUMF does not use specific language of detention. Because detention to prevent a combatant's return to the battlefield is a fundamental incident of waging war, in permitting the use of "necessary and appropriate force," Congress has clearly and unmistakably authorized detention in the narrow circumstances considered here.

Hamdi objects, nevertheless, that Congress has not authorized the *indefinite* detention to which he is now subject. The Government responds that "the detention of enemy combatants during World War II was just as 'indefinite' while that war was being fought." We take Hamdi's objection to be not to the lack of certainty regarding the date on which the conflict will end, but to the substantial prospect of perpetual detention. We recognize that the national security underpinnings of the "war on terror," although crucially important, are broad and malleable. As the Government concedes, "given its unconventional nature, the current conflict is unlikely to end with a formal cease-fire agreement." The prospect Hamdi raises is therefore not far-fetched. If the Government does not consider this unconventional war won for two generations, and if it maintains during that time that Hamdi might, if released, rejoin forces fighting against the United States, then the position it has taken throughout the litigation of this case suggests that Hamdi's detention could last for the rest of his life.

It is a clearly established principle of the law of war that detention may last no longer than active hostilities. [Citations omitted]

Hamdi contends that the AUMF does not authorize indefinite or perpetual detention. Certainly, we agree that indefinite detention for the purpose of interrogation is not authorized. Further, we understand Congress' grant of authority for the use of "necessary and appropriate force" to include the authority to detain for the duration of the relevant conflict, and our understanding is based on longstanding law-of-war principles. If the practical circumstances of a given conflict are entirely unlike those of the conflicts that informed the development of the law of war, that understanding may unravel. But that is not the situation we face as of this date. Active combat operations against Taliban fighters apparently are ongoing in Afghanistan. . . . The United States may detain, for the duration of these hostilities, individuals legitimately determined to be Taliban combatants who "engaged in an armed conflict against the United States." If the record establishes that United States troops are still involved in active combat in Afghanistan, those detentions are part of the exercise of "necessary and appropriate force," and therefore are authorized by the AUMF.

Ex parte Milligan, 4 Wall. 2, 125 (1866) does not undermine our holding about the Government's authority to seize enemy combatants, as we define that term today. In that case, the Court made repeated reference to the fact that its inquiry into whether the military tribunal had jurisdiction to try and punish Milligan turned in large part on the fact that Milligan was not a prisoner of war, but a resident of Indiana arrested while at home there. That fact was central to its conclusion. Had Milligan been captured while he was assisting Confederate soldiers by carrying a rifle against Union troops on a Confederate battlefield, the holding of the Court might well have been different. The Court's repeated explanations that Milligan was not a prisoner of war suggest that had these different circumstances been present he could have been detained under military authority for the duration of the conflict, whether or not he was a citizen.[1]

Moreover, as *Justice Scalia* acknowledges, the Court in *Ex parte Quirin*, dismissed the language of *Milligan* that the petitioners had suggested prevented them from being subject to military process. Clear in this rejection was a disavowal of the New York State cases cited in *Milligan*, on which *Justice Scalia* relies. Both *Smith* v. *Shaw*, 12 Johns. *257 (N. Y. 1815), and *M'Connell* v. *Hampton*, 12 Johns. *234 (N. Y. 1815), were civil suits for false imprisonment. Even accepting that these cases once could have been viewed as standing for the sweeping proposition for which *Justice Scalia* cites them—that the military does not have authority to try an American citizen accused of spying against his country during wartime—*Quirin* makes undeniably clear that this is not the law today. Haupt, like the citizens in *Smith* and *M'Connell*, was accused of being a spy. The Court in *Quirin* found him "subject to trial and punishment by [a] military tribunal[ ]" for those acts, and held that his citizenship did not change this result.

Quirin was a unanimous opinion. It both postdates and clarifies *Milligan*, providing us with the most apposite precedent that we have on the question of whether citizens may be detained in such circumstances. Brushing aside such precedent—particularly when doing so gives rise to a host of new questions never dealt with by this Court—is unjustified and unwise.

To the extent that *Justice Scalia* accepts the precedential value of *Quirin*, he argues that it cannot guide our inquiry here because "[i]n *Quirin* it was uncontested that the petitioners were members of enemy forces," while Hamdi challenges his classification as an enemy combatant. But it is unclear why, in the paradigm outlined by *Justice Scalia*, such a concession should have any relevance. *Justice Scalia* envisions a system in which the only options are congressional suspension of the writ of habeas corpus or prosecution for treason or some other crime. He does not explain how his historical analysis supports the addition of a third option—detention under some other process after concession of enemy-combatant status—or why a concession should carry any different effect than proof of enemy-combatant status in a proceeding that comports with due process. To be clear, our opinion only finds legislative authority to detain under the AUMF once it is sufficiently clear that the individual is, in fact, an enemy combatant; whether that is established by concession or by some other process that verifies this fact with sufficient certainty seems beside the point.

Further, *Justice Scalia* largely ignores the context of this case: a United States citizen captured in a *foreign* combat zone. *Justice Scalia* refers to only one case involving this factual scenario—a case in which a United States citizen-POW (a member of the Italian army) from World War II was seized on the battlefield in Sicily and then held in the United States. The court in that case held that the military detention of that United States citizen was lawful. See *In re Territo*, 156 F. 2d, at 148.

Justice Scalia's treatment of that case—in a footnote—suffers from the same defect as does his treatment of *Quirin*: Because *Justice Scalia* finds the fact of battlefield capture irrelevant, his distinction based on the fact that the petitioner "conceded" enemy combatant status is beside the point. *Justice Scalia* can point to no case or other authority for the proposition that those captured on a foreign battlefield (whether detained there or in U. S. territory) cannot be detained outside the criminal process.

Moreover, *Justice Scalia* presumably would come to a different result if Hamdi had been kept in Afghanistan or even Guantanamo Bay. This creates a perverse incentive. Military authorities faced with the stark choice of submitting to the full-blown criminal process or releasing a suspected enemy combatant captured on the battlefield will simply keep citizen-detainees abroad. Indeed, the Government transferred Hamdi from Guantanamo Bay to the United States naval brig only after it learned that he might be an American citizen. It is not at all clear why that should make a determinative constitutional difference.

III

Even in cases in which the detention of enemy combatants is legally authorized, there remains the question of what process is constitutionally due to a citizen who disputes his enemy-combatant status. Hamdi argues that he is owed a meaningful and timely hearing and that "extra-judicial detention [that] begins and ends with the submission of an affidavit based on third-hand hearsay" does not comport with the Fifth and Fourteenth Amendments. Government counters that any more process than was provided below would be both unworkable and "constitutionally intolerable." Our resolution of this dispute requires a careful examination both of the writ of habeas corpus, which Hamdi now seeks to employ as a mechanism of judicial review, and of the Due Process Clause, which informs the procedural contours of that mechanism in this instance. . . .

1

It is beyond question that substantial interests lie on both sides of the scale in this case. Hamdi's "private interest . . . affected by the official action," is the most elemental of liberty interests—the interest in being free from physical detention by one's own government. *Foucha* v. *Louisiana*, 504 U. S. 71, 80 (1992) ("Freedom from bodily restraint has always been at the core of the liberty protected by the Due Process Clause from arbitrary governmental action"); see also *Parham* v. *J. R.*, 442 U. S. 584, 600 (1979) (noting the "substantial liberty interest in not being confined unnecessarily"). "In our society liberty is the norm," and detention without trial "is the carefully limited exception." *Salerno, supra,* at 755. "We have always been careful not to 'minimize the importance and fundamental nature' of the individual's right to liberty," *Foucha, supra,* at 80 (quoting *Salerno, supra,* at 750), and we will not do so today.

Nor is the weight on this side of the *Mathews* scale offset by the circumstances of war or the accusation of treasonous behavior, for "[i]t is clear that commitment for *any* purpose constitutes a significant deprivation of liberty that requires due process protection," *Jones* v. *United States*, 463 U. S. 354, 361 (1983) (emphasis added; internal quotation marks omitted), and at this stage in the *Mathews* calculus, we consider the interest of the *erroneously* detained individual. *Carey* v. *Piphus*, 435 U. S. 247, 259 (1978) ("Procedural due process rules are meant to protect persons not from the deprivation, but from the mistaken or unjustified deprivation of life, liberty, or property"); see also *id.*, at 266 (noting "the importance to organized society that procedural due process be observed," and emphasizing that "the right to procedural due process is 'absolute' in the sense that it does not depend upon the merits of a claimant's substantive assertions"). Indeed, as *amicus* briefs from media and relief organizations emphasize, the risk of erroneous deprivation of a citizen's liberty in the absence of sufficient process here is very real. Moreover, as critical as the Government's interest may be in detaining those who actually pose an immediate threat to the national security of the United States during ongoing international conflict, history and common sense teach us that an unchecked system of detention carries the potential to become a means for oppression and abuse of others who do not present that sort of threat. See *Ex parte Milligan*, ("[The Founders] knew—the history of the world told them—the nation they were founding, be its existence short or long, would be involved in war; how often or how long continued, human foresight could not tell; and that unlimited power, wherever lodged at such a time, was especially hazardous to freemen"). Because we live in a society in which "[m]ere public intolerance or animosity cannot constitutionally justify the deprivation of a person's physical liberty," *O'Connor* v. *Donaldson*, 422 U. S. 563, 575 (1975), our starting point for the *Mathews* v. *Eldridge* analysis is unaltered by the allegations surrounding the particular detainee or the organizations with which he is alleged to have associated. We reaffirm today the fundamental nature of a citizen's right to be free from involuntary confinement by his own government without due process of law, and we weigh the opposing governmental interests against the curtailment of liberty that such confinement entails.

2

On the other side of the scale are the weighty and sensitive governmental interests in ensuring that those who have in fact fought with the enemy during a war do not return to battle against the United States. As discussed above, the law of war and the realities of combat may render such detentions both necessary and appropriate, and our due process analysis need not blink at those realities. Without doubt, our Constitution recognizes that core strategic matters of war making belong in the hands of those who are best positioned and most politically accountable for making them. *Department of Navy* v. *Egan*, 484 U. S. 518, 530 (1988) (noting the reluctance of the courts "to intrude upon the authority of the Executive in military and national security affairs"); *Youngstown Sheet & Tube Co.* v. *Sawyer*, 343 U. S. 579, 587 (1952) (acknowledging "broad powers in military commanders engaged in day-to-day fighting in a theater of war").

The Government also argues at some length that its interests in reducing the process available to alleged enemy combatants are heightened by the practical difficulties that would accompany a system of trial-like process. In its view, military officers who are engaged in the serious work of waging battle would be unnecessarily and dangerously distracted by litigation half a world away, and discovery into military operations would both intrude on the sensitive secrets of national defense and result in a futile search for evidence buried under the rubble of war. To the extent that these burdens are triggered by heightened procedures, they are properly taken into account in our due process analysis.

3

Striking the proper constitutional balance here is of great importance to the Nation during this period of ongoing combat. But it is equally vital that our calculus not give short shrift to the values that this country holds dear or to the privilege that is American citizenship. It is during our most challenging and uncertain moments that our Nation's commitment to due process is most severely tested; and it is in those times that we must preserve our commitment at home to the principles for which we fight abroad. See *Kennedy* v. *Mendoza-Martinez*, 372 U. S. 144, 164–165 (1963) ("The imperative necessity for safeguarding these rights to procedural due process under the gravest of emergencies has existed throughout our constitutional history, for it is then, under the pressing exigencies of crisis, that there is the greatest temptation to dispense with guarantees which, it is feared, will inhibit government action"); see also *United States* v. *Robel*, 389 U. S. 258, 264 (1967) ("It would indeed be ironic if, in the name of national defense, we would sanction the subversion of one of those liberties . . . which makes the defense of the Nation worthwhile").

With due recognition of these competing concerns, we believe that neither the process proposed by the Government nor the process apparently envisioned by the District Court below strikes the proper constitutional balance when a United States citizen is detained in the United States as an enemy combatant. That is, "the risk of erroneous deprivation" of a detainee's liberty interest is unacceptably high under the Government's proposed rule, while some of the "additional or substitute procedural safeguards" suggested by the District Court are unwarranted in light of their limited "probable value" and the burdens they may impose on the military in such cases. *Mathews*, 424 U. S., at 335.

We therefore hold that a citizen-detainee seeking to challenge his classification as an enemy combatant must receive notice of the factual basis for his classification, and a fair opportunity to rebut the Government's factual assertions before a neutral decision maker. See *Cleveland Bd. of Ed.* v. *Loudermill*, 470 U. S. 532, 542 (1985) ("An essential principle of due process is that a deprivation of life, liberty, or property 'be preceded by notice and opportunity for hearing appropriate to the nature of the case'"). "For more than a century the central meaning of procedural due process has been clear: 'Parties whose rights are to be affected are entitled to be heard; and in order that they may enjoy that right they must first be notified.' It is equally fundamental that the right to notice and an opportunity to be heard 'must be granted at a meaningful time and in a meaningful manner.'" *Fuentes* v. *Shevin*, 407 U. S. 67, 80 (1972). These essential constitutional promises may not be eroded.

At the same time, the exigencies of the circumstances may demand that, aside from these core elements, enemy combatant proceedings may be tailored to alleviate their uncommon potential to burden the Executive at a time of ongoing military conflict. Hearsay, for example, may need to be accepted as the most reliable available evidence from the Government in such a proceeding. Likewise, the Constitution would not be offended by a presumption in favor of the Government's evidence, so long as that presumption remained a rebuttable one and fair opportunity for rebuttal were provided. Thus, once the Government puts forth credible evidence that the habeas petitioner meets the enemy-combatant criteria, the onus could shift to the petitioner to rebut that evidence with more persuasive evidence that he falls outside the criteria. A burden-shifting scheme of this sort would meet the goal of ensuring that the errant tourist, embedded journalist, or local aid worker has a chance to prove military error while giving due regard to the Executive once it has put forth meaningful support for its conclusion that the detainee is in fact an enemy combatant. In the words of *Mathews*, process of this sort would sufficiently address the "risk of erroneous deprivation" of a detainee's liberty interest while eliminating certain procedures that have questionable additional value in light of the burden on the Government. 424 U. S., at 335.[2]

We think it unlikely that this basic process will have the dire impact on the central functions of warmaking that the Government forecasts. The parties agree that initial captures on the battlefield need not receive the process we have discussed here; that process is due only when the determination is made to *continue* to hold those who have been seized. The Government has made clear in its briefing that documentation regarding battlefield detainees already is kept in the ordinary course of military affairs. Any fact finding imposition created by requiring a knowledgeable affiant to summarize these records to an independent tribunal is a minimal one. Likewise, arguments that military officers ought not have to wage war under the threat of litigation lose much of their steam when factual disputes at enemy-combatant hearings are limited to the alleged combatant's acts. This focus meddles little, if at all, in the strategy or conduct of war, inquiring only into the appropriateness of continuing to detain an individual claimed to have taken up arms against the United States. While we accord the greatest respect and consideration to the judgments of military authorities in matters relating to the actual prosecution of a war, and recognize that the scope of that discretion necessarily is wide, it does not infringe on the core role of the military for the courts to exercise their own time-honored and constitutionally mandated roles of reviewing and resolving claims like those presented here. Cf. *Korematsu* v. *United States,* 323 U. S. 214, 233–234 (1944) (Murphy, J., dissenting) ("[L]ike other claims conflicting with the asserted constitutional rights of the individual, the military claim must subject itself to the judicial process of having its reasonableness determined and its conflicts with other interests reconciled"); *Sterling* v. *Constantin,* 287 U. S. 378, 401 (1932) ("What are the allowable limits of military discretion, and whether or not they have been overstepped in a particular case, are judicial questions").

In sum, while the full protections that accompany challenges to detentions in other settings may prove unworkable and inappropriate in the enemy-combatant setting, the threats to military operations posed by a basic system of independent review are not so weighty as to trump a citizen's core rights to challenge meaningfully the Government's case and to be heard by an impartial adjudicator.

D

In so holding, we necessarily reject the Government's assertion that separation of powers principles mandate a heavily circumscribed role for the courts in such circumstances. Indeed, the position that the courts must forgo any examination of the individual case and focus exclusively on the legality of the broader detention scheme cannot be mandated by any reasonable view of separation of powers, as this approach serves only to *condense* power into a single branch of government. We have long since made clear that a state of war is not a blank check for the President when it comes to the rights of the Nation's citizens. *Youngstown Sheet & Tube,* 343 U. S., at 587. Whatever power the United States Constitution envisions for the Executive in its exchanges with other nations or with enemy organizations in times of conflict, it most assuredly envisions a role for all three branches when individual liberties are at stake. *Mistretta* v. *United States,* 488 U. S. 361, 380 (1989) (it was "the central judgment of the Framers of the Constitution that, within our political scheme, the separation of governmental powers into three coordinate Branches is essential to the preservation of liberty"); *Home Building & Loan Assn.* v. *Blaisdell,* 290 U. S. 398, 426 (1934) (The war power "is a power to wage war successfully, and thus it permits the harnessing of the entire energies of the people in a supreme cooperative effort to preserve the nation. But even the war power does not remove constitutional limitations safeguarding essential liberties"). Likewise, we have made clear that, unless Congress acts to suspend it, the Great Writ of habeas corpus allows the Judicial Branch to play a necessary role in maintaining this delicate balance of governance, serving as an important judicial check on the Executive's discretion in the realm of detentions. See *St. Cyr*, 533 U. S., at 301 ("At its historical core, the writ of habeas corpus has served as a means of reviewing the legality of Executive detention, and it is in that context that its protections have been strongest"). Thus, while we do not question that our due process assessment must pay keen attention to the particular burdens faced by the Executive in the context of military action, it would turn our system of checks and balances on its head to suggest that a citizen could not make his way to court with a challenge to the factual basis for his detention by his government, simply because the Executive opposes making available such a challenge. Absent suspension of the writ by Congress, a citizen detained as an enemy combatant is entitled to this process.

Because we conclude that due process demands some system for a citizen detainee to refute his classification, the proposed "some evidence" standard is inadequate. Any process in which the Executive's factual assertions go wholly unchallenged or are simply presumed correct without any opportunity for the alleged combatant to demonstrate otherwise falls constitutionally short. As the Government itself has recognized, we have utilized the "some evidence" standard in the past as a standard of review, not as a standard of proof. That is, it primarily has been employed by courts in examining an administrative record developed after an adversarial proceeding—one with process at least of the sort that we today hold is constitutionally mandated in the citizen enemy-combatant setting. See, *e.g.*, *St. Cyr*, *supra*; *Hill*, 472 U. S., at 455–457. This standard therefore is ill suited to the situation in which a habeas petitioner has received no prior proceedings before any tribunal and had no prior opportunity to rebut the Executive's factual assertions before a neutral decision maker.

Today we are faced only with such a case. Aside from unspecified "screening" processes, and military interrogations in which the Government suggests Hamdi could have contested his classification, Hamdi has received no process. An interrogation by one's captor, however effective an intelligence-gathering tool, hardly constitutes a constitutionally adequate fact finding before a neutral decision maker. Compare Brief for Respondents 42–43 (discussing the "secure interrogation environment," and noting that military interrogations require a controlled "interrogation dynamic" and "a relationship of trust and dependency" and are "a critical source" of "timely and effective intelligence") with *Concrete Pipe*, 508 U. S., at 617–618 ("one is entitled as a matter of due process of law to an adjudicator who is not in a situation which would offer a possible temptation to the average man as a judge . . . which might lead him not to hold the balance nice, clear and true" (internal quotation marks omitted). That even purportedly fair adjudicators "are disqualified by their interest in the controversy to be decided is, of course, the general rule." *Tumey* v. *Ohio*, 273 U. S. 510, 522 (1927). Plainly, the "process" Hamdi has received is not that to which he is entitled under the Due Process Clause.

There remains the possibility that the standards we have articulated could be met by an appropriately authorized and properly constituted military tribunal. Indeed, it is notable that military regulations already provide for such process in related instances, dictating that tribunals be made available to determine the status of enemy detainees who assert prisoner-of-war status under the Geneva Convention. In the absence of such process, however, a court that receives a petition for a writ of habeas corpus from an alleged enemy combatant must itself ensure that the minimum requirements of due process are achieved. Both courts below recognized as much, focusing their energies on the question of whether Hamdi was due an opportunity to rebut the Government's case against him. The Government, too, proceeded on this assumption, presenting its affidavit and then seeking that it be evaluated under a deferential standard of review based on burdens that it alleged would accompany any greater process. As we have discussed, a habeas court in a case such as this may accept affidavit evidence like that contained in the Mobbs Declaration, so long as it also permits the alleged combatant to present his own factual case to rebut the Government's return. We anticipate that a District Court would proceed with the caution that we have indicated is necessary in this setting, engaging in a fact finding process that is both prudent and incremental. We have no reason to doubt that courts faced with these sensitive matters will pay proper heed both to the matters of national security that might arise in an individual case and to the constitutional limitations safeguarding essential liberties that remain vibrant even in times of security concerns.

IV

Hamdi asks us to hold that the Fourth Circuit also erred by denying him immediate access to counsel upon his detention and by disposing of the case without permitting him to meet with an attorney. Since our grant of certiorari in this case, Hamdi has been appointed counsel, with whom he has met for consultation purposes on several occasions, and with whom he is now being granted unmonitored meetings. He unquestionably has the right to access to counsel in connection with the proceedings on remand. No further consideration of this issue is necessary at this stage of the case.

The judgment of the United States Court of Appeals for the Fourth Circuit is vacated, and the case is remanded for further proceedings.

It is so ordered.

NOTES

1. President George W. Bush Statement on Signing the Authorization to Use Military Force, The American Presidency Project, http://www.presidency.ucsb.edu/ws/index.php?pid=64595.

2. Arthur H. Garrison, "*Hamdi, Padilla*, and *Rasul*: The War on Terrorism on the Judicial Front," *American Journal of Trial Advocacy* 27, no. 1 (2003): 99, 100.

3. *Hamdi v. Rumsfeld*, 243 F. Supp. 2d 527 (E.D. Va. 2002).

4. *Hamdi v. Rumsfeld*, 316 F. 3rd 450, 459 (4th Cir. 2003).

5. *Hamdi v. Rumsfeld*, 542 US 507, 509 (2004).

6. Ibid., 535–56.

7. Ibid., 536.

8. Ibid., 533.

9. Ibid., 541.

10. "Hamdi is entitled to a habeas decree requiring his release unless (1) criminal proceedings are promptly brought, or (2) Congress has suspended the writ of habeas corpus" (Ibid., 573).

11. Ibid., 554.

12. Ibid., 556.

13. Ibid., 559.

14. Ibid., 589.

15. Ibid., 592.

16. Ibid., 579.

17. Ibid., 594.

18. Ibid.

HAMDI V. RUMSFELD NOTES

1. Here the basis asserted for detention by the military is that Hamdi was carrying a weapon against American troops on a foreign battlefield; that is, that he was an enemy combatant. The legal category of enemy combatant has not been elaborated upon in great detail. The permissible bounds of the category will be defined by the lower courts as subsequent cases are presented to them.

2. Because we hold that Hamdi is constitutionally entitled to the process described above, we need not address at this time whether any treaty guarantees him similar access to a tribunal for a determination of his status.

9

Captured Terrorists: Guantanamo
Bay, Military Commissions,
and Habeas Corpus

As discussed in more detail in the next chapter, the rule of law should be more than cavalierly acknowledged in assessing the boundaries of governmental power in general or the limitations placed on the power of the President by the rule of law in both times of crisis and peace. For the process of democracy does not by its own terms guarantee the supremacy of the rule of law over Presidential power. In our Constitutional system, as it functions today, there are only three external factors that control the Executive Department. The first factor involves the dynamics of Presidential political power. The dynamics of Presidential political power are comprised of three aspects: Constitutional limits, institutional power, and political power. The Constitutional limits on the Presidency involve the restrictions on the power of the President imposed by the text of the Constitution itself and by Congressional action—for example, the Twenty-second Amendment or Congressional statutes specifically prohibiting action. The institutional power of the Presidency includes the "inherent" or "executive" power to act. The theories of "executive privilege," "unitary President," "inherent powers," and "sole organ" all reflect the range of asserted institutional power of the chief executive. Lastly, political power defines the ability of a specific President at any given time during his administration to achieve or prevent policy action.[1] Political power defines what the President wants to do and can do without and/or over "political" resistance. The second external control of the Executive Department is the support of the principles of separated and limited powers by the American people. The third is the supremacy of the rule of law (as defended by the

Judicial Department) and the assent of the American people to the results of the application of the rule of law.

In our Constitutional democracy Presidential power, even during times of war, is not without limits and it must be observed to submit to those limits even in times of crisis and war. At the same time, in times of war or crisis, the government must be able to act with powers reserved for such circumstances to preserve and protect the nation with force if necessary. Under such circumstances, the outer boundaries of governmental power are approached which otherwise would not be. While it is for the political branches to determine what policy choices weighed in the political scales will prevail, it is for the Courts to weigh the boundaries of available choices within the scales of justice, which is the rule of law. As we have reviewed, the Supreme Court has developed into the arbiter of the boundaries of Presidential power and although the President has extended powers in time of war those powers also have limitations.

After the events of 9/11 the Bush Administration asserted that it had the power to detain enemy combatants captured during the war in Afghanistan, the patron nation of Al Qaeda, at the U.S. Naval Base at Guantanamo Bay, Cuba without any concern of judicial interference through habeas corpus. In 1942 in *Ex parte Quirin*,[2] the Supreme Court held that the President had the authority to establish military commissions to deal with soldiers who acted in violation of the laws of war and establish policies for determining what soldiers would be subjected to the procedures of the commission. It is one thing for the President to declare a person an enemy combatant in times of war but it is another to assert sole authority to determine how they will be treated and what rights of due process they have after being detained in contradiction to Congressional statutory enactment—that is, the Uniform Code of Military Justice (UCMJ) and Senate ratification of the Geneva Convention protocols on treatment of captured combatants. Can the President order detainees to be held, theoretically for life, until the "War on Terrorism" ends and, if so, when and how will the end of the war be determined? On the same day the Court issued the *Hamdi* decision, the Supreme Court in *Rasul v. Bush* (2004)[3] rejected the Bush Administration assertion that the statutory right to habeas corpus was not applicable to the detainees and held that the detainees could not be separated from the courts by Presidential fiat.

In *Rasul* the Court held that under the federal habeas corpus act, the judiciary had the authority to hear the petitions of the detainees and decide the Constitutionality of their detention on the merits. Congress in 2005 passed the Detainee Treatment Act (DTA) which reversed, in part, the Court's decision in *Rasul* by removing habeas corpus jurisdiction of the Supreme Court and the lower courts to hear the petitions of the detainees until after the detainees had exhausted the procedures of the Combatant

Status Review Tribunals (CSRTs) which were created to comply with the Court decision in *Hamdi* that detainees were entitled to a hearing before a neutral decision maker to challenge their designations as enemy combatants. Subsequently, the Court held in *Hamdan v. Rumsfeld* (2006)[4] that the DTA did not remove its jurisdiction to hear pending detainee cases at the time of passage of the DTA. The Court also addressed the power of the President to create a military commission process which was constituted outside of the procedures of the UCMJ and the civil criminal justice system. The Bush Administration asserted that as Commander-in-Chief, the President had the power to create such commissions and establish the rules and procedures governing the commissions exclusive of Congressional approval. The Supreme Court held in *Hamdan* that although the President had the power to establish military commissions he could not do so in violation of statutory law governing the creation of such commissions and could not violate standing treaties ratified by the Senate which, in part, defined the laws of war.

In 2006 Congress passed the Military Commission Act (MCA) in response to the *Hamdan* decision and by statute created a military commission process to handle the determination of the status of detainees and to put selected detainees on trial for war crimes. The MCA reinstated the restriction of habeas jurisdiction of the federal courts and allowed appeals to the D.C. Court of Appeals and to the Supreme Court for review only after the procedures of the MCA were exhausted. In 2008 the Supreme Court held in *Boumediene v. Bush*[5] that Congress fully intended to deny the federal courts jurisdiction to hear habeas petitions pending before the courts at the time of its enactment and as such, section 7 of the MCA was an unconstitutional suspension of the writ of habeas corpus. Further, the Court held that the petitioners had a *Constitutional right* to file habeas actions to challenge their detention and designation as enemy combatants, that the DTA procedures to handle the petitioners' challenges were not an adequate substitute for a habeas hearing, and that the District of Columbia Court of Appeals had the authority to hear the habeas petitions and rule on the merits of those petitions.

Together these three cases continued in the tradition of judicial protection of the boundaries of executive power in times of crisis. Regardless of the crisis, the President is not authorized to disregard laws passed by Congress because they are encumbrances. Nor can the government create Constitutional law-free zones or separate individuals detained by the President from the courts in times of war. In a Constitutional democracy the law is supposed to frustrate the limitless use of governmental power to achieve its legitimate ends; and although the government has a right and duty to protect the nation against threats, both foreign and domestic, it is equally true that the obligation does not entitle the hand of government to withhold the protections of law and justice because the majority resents those who lay claim to them.

∽

RASUL v. BUSH AND HABEAS CORPUS: THE RIGHT TO BE HEARD

In 2002 twelve Kuwaiti, two Australian, and two British citizens, through their relatives filed a writ of habeas corpus in the U.S. District Court for the District of Columbia seeking to challenge the authority of the President to detain them at Guantanamo Bay, Cuba as enemy combatants.[6] The two British citizens Shafiq Rasul, the lead name on the petition, and Asif Iqbal were later released in 2003. The two Australian citizens, Madouh Habib and David Hicks also filed a petition for release as well as access to counsel and freedom from interrogation, while the Kuwaiti citizens, led by Fawzi Khalid Abdullah Al Odah, filed a petition demanding to be informed of the charges against them, to have access to counsel and family members, and to have access to the courts.[7] The District Court dismissed the petitions for lack of jurisdiction, in essence holding that Guantanamo Bay, Cuba was outside of the sovereign territory of the United States.[8] The Court of Appeals for the District of Columbia affirmed the District Court in *Al Odah v. United States*[9] and the Supreme Court granted certiorari to answer the question of "whether United States courts lack jurisdiction to consider challenges to the legality of the detention of foreign nationals captured [as a result of hostilities arising from the attacks of September 11, 2001, and the resulting war against Afghanistan and Al Qaeda] and incarcerated at Guantanamo Bay Naval Base, Cuba."[10] Justice Stevens, joined by Justices O'Connor, Souter, Ginsberg, Breyer and Kennedy (concurring in the judgment) held that the judiciary has the jurisdiction to entertain the petitions by the detainees because the base at Guantanamo is within exclusive and plenary control of the United States. Justice Scalia, joined by the Chief Justice and Justice Thomas, dissented.

The government asserted that the case was governed by the 1950 case of *Johnson v. Eisentrager*[11] which held that the federal courts had no jurisdiction to issue writs of habeas corpus to twenty-one German prisoners who had been tried and convicted of war crimes by a military commission in China. The Court reasoned in *Eisentrager* that since the trial and the prisoners were outside of the territorial jurisdiction of the United States, the court was without jurisdiction to issue the writ. The government argued that Guantanamo, like the military commission in China, was outside of the territory and sovereignty of the United States and as in *Eisentrager*, the Court should hold that the judiciary has no jurisdiction to entertain a habeas petition by the detainees in Cuba.

Justice Jackson in his opinion in *Eisentrager* stressed the historical significance of the various levels of status an alien had in the United States and the graduated increase in legal rights due to his/her status as an alien. Justice Jackson, in rejecting the Court of Appeals holding that the judiciary had jurisdiction to entertain the petition of the twenty-one German prisoners, wrote, "We are cited to no instance where a court, in this or any other country where the writ is known, has issued it on behalf of an alien enemy who at no relevant time and in no stage of his captivity has been within its territorial jurisdiction. Nothing in the text of the Constitution extends such a right, nor does anything in our statutes."[12] Justice Jackson continued, "We have pointed out that the privilege of litigation has been extended to aliens, whether friendly or enemy, only because permitting their presence in the country implied protection. No such basis can be invoked here, for these prisoners at no relevant time were within any territory over which the United States is sovereign, and the scenes of their offense, their capture, their trial and their punishment were all beyond the territorial jurisdiction of any court of the United States."[13] Justice Jackson concluded with his famous observation that "it would be difficult to devise more effective fettering of a field commander than to allow the very enemies he is ordered to reduce to submission to call him to account in his own civil courts and divert his efforts and attention from the military offensive abroad to the legal defensive at home."[14] The key to *Eisentrager* is the Court's determination that the judiciary had no authority to entertain habeas petition from twenty-one German prisoners because they were nonresident aliens, with no history of residency in the United States, who were captured in a foreign nation, engaged in hostilities with the United States and were captured, tried, convicted, sentenced and incarcerated outside of the sovereign territory of the United States. There was no dispute as to the nature of the alien status *and* the military status and behavior of the petitioners. It was these factual distinctions of *Eisentrager* that Justice Stevens focused on to hold that *Eisentrager* does not apply to the petitioners in *Rasul*.

In *Rasul* the government was asserting its right to detain and hold the petitioners as enemy combatants in the "War on Terror," not to detain them as convicted violators of the laws of war, which the twenty-one German soldiers were. These distinctions made all the difference to the Court in *Rasul*. Justice Stevens wrote,

> Petitioners in these cases differ from the *Eisentrager* detainees in important respects: They are not nationals of countries at war with the United States, and they deny that they have engaged in or plotted acts of aggression against the United States; they have never been afforded access to any tribunal, much

less charged with and convicted of wrongdoing; and for more than two years they have been imprisoned in territory over which the United States exercises exclusive jurisdiction and control.

Not only are petitioners differently situated from the *Eisentrager* detainees, but the Court in *Eisentrager* made quite clear that all six of the facts critical to its disposition were relevant only to the question of the prisoners' *Constitutional* entitlement to habeas corpus. *Id.*, at 777. The Court had far less to say on the question of the petitioners' *statutory* entitlement to habeas review.[15]

The Court rejected the assertion that *Eisentrager* was based on the alien status of the twenty-one German agents alone. More importantly, the Court held that *Eisentrager* answered the question of whether the German agents had a Constitutional right to habeas, not whether they had a statutory right to the writ. *Rasul*, the Court reasoned, raised the questions of the statutory right to a habeas hearing by the federal courts not the Constitutional right.

Although the Court's interpretation is plausible, it is not the only possible reading. The majority of the opinion in *Eisentrager* focused on the rights of aliens to have access to the federal courts. Justice Jackson made distinctions between resident, enemy, and naturalized aliens and the right each had to the courts in both times of peace and war. It is only close to the end of the opinion does he make note of the other factors that led to his conclusion that the twenty-one German agents did not have the right to have access to the courts in a habeas petition. A more plausible interpretation of *Eisentrager* is that the Court held that since the twenty-one German agents were enemy aliens, not even enemy resident aliens, who had never been inside of the United States, they had no right to have access to the courts. This fact, in addition to the other facts of time, place and circumstances of their detention only added to the reasons they did not have a right of access to the courts. Of course this interpretation would have resulted in the refusal to grant the petitions in *Rasul* the right to have access to the courts, a result the plurality, joined by Justice Kennedy, were not inclined to reach. The Bush Administration for more than two years had asserted in both public and before the lower federal courts as well as before the Supreme Court that the judiciary had no role in the determination or review of his actions as Commander-in-Chief to designate and detain individuals, regardless of American or foreign citizenship, as enemy combatants; a position only Justice Thomas supported. The Court was presented with a Presidential policy that held hundreds of individuals incarcerated for more than two years without any due process or independent review with impunity under a claim of plenary and absolute authority. The Court was not inclined to accept and sanction such a broad assertion of power when a plausible interpretation of precedent would allow it to place a check on such powers. The Court in *Hamdi* held that the President did not have absolute and plenary authority to detain an American citizen without any due process review regardless of the fact that he was alleged to have been captured on the field of war in the service of the enemy and detained as an enemy combatant. In *Rasul* the Court was equally disinclined to sanction the Bush Administration intentionally creating a Constitutional rights free zone off the continental territory of the United States in which it could detain foreign nationals indefinitely at its pleasure. Indulging in an arguably less plausible reading of *Eisentrager* allowed for the Court to place limits on the asserted powers of President Bush.

Aside from the Court's interpretation of *Eisentrager* on the issue of the right of aliens to have access to the federal courts, the Court in *Rasul* also distinguished the case on the grounds that *Eisentrager* focused on the Constitutional right to have access to the courts with a habeas petition, not the statutory right to such access. Justice Stevens reasoned that subsequent decisions to *Eisentrager* make clear that "persons detained outside the territorial jurisdiction of any federal district court no longer need rely on the Constitution as the source of their right to federal habeas review."[16] Citing *Braden v. 30th Judicial Circuit Court of Kentucky*[17] Justice Stevens held that under the federal habeas statute physical presence within the territorial jurisdiction of a district court is not a primary prerequisite to the exercise of jurisdiction but rather the statute requires that the court have jurisdiction over the person who holds the prisoner in custody.[18] Citing *Braden*, the Court held that as long as the custodian of the prisoner can be reached by service of process by the district court, the court has jurisdiction to address the merits of a habeas petition sought by the prisoner.[19]

The Court reasoned that aside from the question of jurisdiction to entertain the petitioners' application for the writ, the government's assertion that there is no extraterritorial application of statutory or Constitutional rights and that Cuba is outside of the sovereignty of the United States and thus outside of the jurisdiction of the federal courts regardless of its officers being subject to process service is void because the United States enjoys complete control and jurisdiction over the base and territory of Guantanamo Bay and as such is within the jurisdiction of the United States. The Court reasoned that

> respondents themselves concede that the habeas statute would create federal court jurisdiction over the claims of an American citizen held at the base. Tr. of Oral Arg. 27. Considering that the statute draws no distinction between Americans and aliens held in federal custody, there is little reason to think that Congress intended the geographical coverage of the statute to vary depending on the detainee's citizenship. Aliens held at the base, no less than American citizens, are entitled to invoke the federal courts' authority under §2241.[20]

Justice Stevens concluded that

petitioners contend that they are being held in federal custody in violation of the laws of the United States. No party questions the District Court's jurisdiction over petitioners' custodians. Cf. *Braden*, 410 U. S., at 495. Section 2241, by its terms, requires nothing more. We therefore hold that §2241 confers on the District Court jurisdiction to hear petitioners' habeas corpus challenges to the legality of their detention at the Guantanamo Bay Naval Base.[21]

Justice Scalia's dissent focused on what he called a "novel" reading of the federal habeas statute as well as a misreading of the history of the application of the writ of habeas corpus. In his characteristic style, Justice Scalia was blunt in what he thought the Court in *Rasul* had accomplished.

The reality is this: Today's opinion, and today's opinion alone, overrules *Eisentrager*; today's opinion, and today's opinion alone, extends the habeas statute, for the first time, to aliens held beyond the sovereign territory of the United States. . . . Today, the Court springs a trap on the Executive subjecting Guantanamo Bay to the oversight of the federal courts even though it has never before been thought to be within their jurisdiction—and thus making it a foolish place to have housed alien wartime detainees.[22]

Leaving aside Justice Scalia's erroneous view that the holding that federal courts could have jurisdiction over Guantanamo had "never been thought" before, for John Yoo's memo made clear that it was a real possibility that a court could conclude that it had authority to hear petitions from detainees, Justice Scalia's assertion that the Court overruled *Eisentrager* is simply wrong. Although the Court used a less plausible reading of the case to reject the absolutist position of the Bush administration, the reading was not completely beyond reason.

Justice Scalia argued that the federal habeas statute, reflecting the historical use of the writ, focused on judicial jurisdiction over the detained individual. Justice Stevens argued that the federal habeas statute focused on judicial jurisdiction over the detaining power, not the individual detained because the purpose of the writ was to provide judicial power over the governmental power to detain a person without due process. While the Court found that U.S. *de facto* sovereignty due to its "complete jurisdiction and control" over Guantanamo was sufficient to conclude that the federal courts could exert jurisdiction, Justice Scalia wrote that the lease retained sovereignty of the territory to Cuba and U.S. dominance over the base was beside the point.

The Court does not explain how "complete jurisdiction and control" without sovereignty causes an enclave to be part of the United States for purposes of its domestic laws. Since "jurisdiction and control" obtained through a lease is no different in effect from "jurisdiction and control" acquired by lawful force of arms, parts of Afghanistan and Iraq should logically be regarded as subject to our domestic laws. Indeed, if "jurisdiction and control" rather than sovereignty were the test, so should the Landsberg Prison in Germany, where the United States held the *Eisentrager* detainees.[23]

Of course Landsberg Prison was under the joint command of the allies and was not subject to total control of the United States. The point Justice Scalia rejects, by implication, is the distinction made by the Court that in *Eisentrager* the petitioners received a full trial with due process to determine their status. In *Eisentrager* the petitioners had their day in court and were seeking to use a U.S. judiciary to circumvent their military trial and sentence. In *Rasul*, the petitioners asserted their innocence to the designation as enemy combatants and requested a judicial hearing to assert their erroneous detention. To which Scalia wrote,

> The consequence of this holding, as applied to aliens outside the country, is breathtaking. It permits an alien captured in a foreign theater of active combat to bring a §2241 petition against the Secretary of Defense. Over the course of the last century, the United States has held millions of alien prisoners abroad. A great many of these prisoners would no doubt have complained about the circumstances of their capture and the terms of their confinement. The military is currently detaining over 600 prisoners at Guantanamo Bay alone; each detainee undoubtedly has complaints—real or contrived—about those terms and circumstances. The Court's unheralded expansion of federal-court jurisdiction is not even mitigated by a comforting assurance that the legion of ensuing claims will be easily resolved on the merits. To the contrary, the Court says that the "[p]etitioners' allegations . . . unquestionably describe 'custody in violation of the Constitution or laws or treaties of the United States.'" From this point forward, federal courts will entertain petitions from these prisoners, and others like them around the world, challenging actions and events far away, and forcing the courts to oversee one aspect of the Executive's conduct of a foreign war.[24]

Justice Scalia in his dissent asserted that "[e]ven a cursory reading of the habeas statute shows that it presupposes a federal district court with territorial jurisdiction over the detainee."[25] He argued that under the application statute of Section 2241, Section 2242 requires that an application for a writ "addressed to the Supreme Court, a justice thereof or a circuit judge shall state the reasons for not making application to the district court of the district in which the applicant is held,"[26] thus concluding,

> No matter to whom the writ is directed, custodian or detainee, the statute could not be clearer that a necessary requirement for issuing the writ is that *some* federal district court have territorial jurisdiction over the detainee.[27]

Justice Scalia has a point. Section 2241 reads as follows:

(a) Writs of habeas corpus may be granted by the Supreme Court, any justice thereof, the district courts and any circuit judge within their respective jurisdictions. *The order of a circuit judge shall be entered in the records of the district court of the district wherein the restraint complained of is had.*

(b) The Supreme Court, any justice thereof, and any circuit judge may decline to entertain an application for a writ of habeas corpus and may transfer the application for hearing and determination to the district court having jurisdiction to entertain it.

(c) The writ of habeas corpus shall not extend to a prisoner unless—

> (1) He is in custody under or by color of the authority of the United States or is committed for trial before some court thereof; or
>
> (2) He is in custody for an act done or omitted in pursuance of an Act of Congress, or an order, process, judgment or decree of a court or judge of the United States; or
>
> (3) He is in custody in violation of the Constitution or laws or treaties of the United States[28]

Sections 2241(a) and 2242 arguably establish that the writ requires that judicial jurisdiction is established by the location of the detainee. To answer this conclusion Justice Stevens asserted that the Court in *Braden* made clear that section 2241 jurisdiction is established by the location of the detaining authority, not the location of the detainee. The Court in *Braden* held:

> The writ of habeas corpus does not act upon the prisoner who seeks relief, but upon the person who holds him in what is alleged to be unlawful custody. *Wales v. Whitney*, 114 U.S. 564, 114 U.S. 574 (1885). In the classic statement:

> "The important fact to be observed in regard to the mode of procedure upon this writ is that it is directed to, and served upon, not the person confined, but his jailer. It does not reach the former except through the latter. The officer or person who serves it does not unbar the prison doors and set the prisoner free, but the court relieves him by compelling the oppressor to release his constraint. The whole force of the writ is spent upon the respondent."

> *In the Matter of Jackson*, 15 Mich. 417, 439–440 (1867), quoted with approval in *Ex parte Endo*, 323 U. S. 283, 323 U. S. 306 (1944). *See also Ahrens v. Clark*, 335 U.S. at 335 U. S. 196–197 (Rutledge, J., dissenting).

> Read literally, the language of § 2241(a) requires nothing more than that the court issuing the writ have jurisdiction over the custodian. So long as the custodian can be reached by service of process, the court can issue a writ "within its jurisdiction" requiring that the prisoner be brought before the court for a hearing on his claim, or requiring that he be released outright from custody, even if the prisoner himself is confined outside the court's territorial jurisdiction.[29]

Justice Stevens concluded:

Because subsequent decisions of this Court have filled the statutory gap that had occasioned *Eisentrager*'s resort to "fundamentals," persons detained outside the territorial jurisdiction of any federal district court no longer need rely on the Constitution as the source of their right to federal habeas review.[30]

Braden thus established that *Ahrens* can no longer be viewed as establishing "an inflexible jurisdictional rule," and is strictly relevant only to the question of the appropriate forum, not to whether the claim can be heard at all. Because *Braden* overruled the statutory predicate to *Eisentrager*'s holding, *Eisentrager* plainly does not preclude the exercise of §2241 jurisdiction over petitioners' claims.[31]

Thus Justice Stevens's answer to Justice Scalia's statutory interpretation of section 2241 and 2242 is that section 2242 only addresses the "question of the appropriate forum, not whether the claim can be heard at all" and judicial jurisdiction over a petition under section 2241 has been understood since 1973 as being allowable if the detaining power can be served with the petition. Scalia answered that *Braden* was the case addressing a prisoner's challenge to an indictment filed in Kentucky while he was incarcerated in Alabama and that *Braden*

> stands for the proposition, and only the proposition, that where a petitioner is in custody in multiple jurisdictions within the United States, he may seek a writ of habeas corpus in a jurisdiction in which he suffers legal confinement, though not physical confinement, if his challenge is to that legal confinement. Outside that class of cases, *Braden* did not question the general rule of *Ahrens* (much less that of *Eisentrager*). Where, as here, present physical custody is at issue, *Braden* is inapposite, and *Eisentrager* unquestionably controls.[32]

Rasul would not be the last case in which the Court would address the range and limitations of judicial power to hear habeas petitions from the detainees at Guantanamo nor would it be the last case that a majority of the Court would reject the Bush Administration assertion that the detainees had not statutory or Constitutional rights to assert they had a right to a hearing regarding their detention.

In *Rasul* the Court held that the federal habeas statute made no distinctions between citizens and non citizens and only required that a district court have subject matter jurisdiction over the detaining power. It was this reading of the habeas statute that Congress sought to overturn with the DTA of 2005. Congress sought to change the text of the statute to make a distinction in "geographical coverage" and to make a distinction between American citizens and aliens held at Guantanamo regarding the availability of the habeas statute to those detained at the base. It was this issue along with the question of whether President Bush had the authority to establish procedures for military commissions that conflicted with the UCMJ and the Geneva Convention that the Court addressed in *Hamdan*.

EXECUTIVE POWER, NOT EXCLUSIVE POWER:
HAMDAN V. RUMSFELD AND PRESIDENTIAL POWER TO
ESTABLISH PROCEDURES TO PUT TERRORISTS ON TRIAL

Hamdan was captured during military operations in Afghanistan and transferred to Guantanamo Bay. The Government alleged that he conspired with Osama Bin Laden in the implementation of terrorism and was declared an enemy combatant.[33] The Court issued a total of 176 pages encompassing the opinion of the Court; concurring and dissenting opinions in *Hamdan* and space limitations preclude a detailed review of all the issues and reasoning in the opinions. The Court addressed three issues: first whether the case should be dismissed for want of jurisdiction due to the DTA; second, whether the President has the authority to establish procedures for trials conducted by military commissions that are contrary to the UCMJ; and third, whether the Geneva Convention on treatment of captured enemy combatants is judicially enforceable and do they apply to the commissions established by President Bush. As to the first issue the Court held that the case would not be dismissed because, although the DTA did restrict judicial jurisdiction to entertain petitions from detainees outside of the procedures established by the DTA, the DTA did not restrict judicial jurisdiction over cases currently pending before the courts at the time of its passage. Thus the Supreme Court had jurisdiction to hear and decide the remaining issues in *Hamdan* and concluded that the District Court for the District of Columbia had subject matter jurisdiction to hear the merits of the Constitutional claims raised by the petitioners.

Justice Stevens, joined by Justices Souter, Ginsburg, Breyer and Kennedy (concurring in part and in the judgment) briefly reviewed the history of military commissions and observed that "exigency alone, of course, will not justify the establishment and use of penal tribunals not contemplated by Article I, § 8 and Article III, § 1 of the Constitution unless some other part of that document authorizes a response to the felt need. And that authority, if it exists, can derive only from the powers granted jointly to the President and Congress in time of war."[34] Citing *Ex parte Milligan*, the Court held that as the Congress has no authority to direct military operations during war, nor can the President as Commander-in-Chief create military tribunals without an act of Congress as a general rule. Justice Stevens held that whether the Court in *Milligan* was correct that in times of "controlling necessity" the President can act "without the sanction of Congress" to create such commissions it would not decide because Congress in Article 21 of the UCMJ authorized the formation of military commissions and determined that they shall have "concurrent jurisdiction in respect of offenders or offenses that by statute or by the law of war may be tried by such commissions."[35]

Justice Stevens held that although the AUMF "activated the President's war powers" and that the war powers of the President include "the authority to convene military commissions in appropriate circumstances," neither the AUMF nor the DTA authorized the President to use these powers outside of the UCMJ which regulates the procedures of all military tribunals.[36] As discussed in chapter 5, two months after 9/11 the President issued the *Presidential Military Order of November 13, 2001: Detention, Treatment and Trial of Certain Non Citizens in the War Against Terrorism* which created the military commission system and declared that the procedures of the commission would not apply "principles of law and the rules of evidence generally recognized in the trial of criminal cases" because they would be impractical to implement. The UCMJ is an act of Congress signed into law by the President and as such he is obligated to carry out the law as written. "The UCMJ" Justice Stevens wrote "conditions the President's use of military commissions on compliance not only with the American common law of war, but also with the rest of the UCMJ itself."[37] The Court concluded that the procedures established by the military commission, including the exclusion of the defendant and his counsel from reviewing evidence submitted to the tribunal, the admission of hearsay evidence, the ability to admit evidence secured through coercion, the admission of non sworn testimony, a non unanimous vote to sustain a defendant's conviction, appeal to a panel which is not comprised of military judges, regulations asserting that the disregarding of any procedures that do not materially affect the outcome of the trial will not form a justification for appeal or reversal of conviction, final remand or sustaining of a verdict is at the sole discretion of the Secretary of Defense and, if forwarded, the President, were not in compliance with the requirements of military justice, which included military commissions, as required under the UCMJ.

Citing section 36 of the UCMJ, the Court held that although the procedures, including the modes of proof, used in military commissions can be determined by the President, as a general rule, they must comply with the principles of law and rules of evidence generally recognizable in the trial of criminal cases in the United States district courts and may not be contrary to or inconsistent with the UCMJ unless doing so proves to be impractical.[38] The Government asserted essentially that the declaration by the President as Commander-in-Chief that it would be impractical to apply the principles of the UCMJ and that to do so would place the United States at risk of addition terrorist attacks by itself was sufficient for the Court to hold that the impractibility exception to the implantation of regular UCMJ procedures was established. The Court rejected this assertion and held that the Government is required to submit evidence to support the declaration. The "absence of any showing of impracticability," the Court concluded, "is particularly disturbing when considered in light of the clear and admitted failure to apply one of the most fundamental protections afforded not just by the Manual for Courts-Martial but also by the UCMJ itself: the right to be present . . . the jettisoning of so basic a right cannot lightly be excused as 'practicable.'"[39] The Court reasoned that since the rules of the military commission were not supported by a proffer of evidence of impractibility, the rules of the UCMJ were to prevail. Since the rules of the UCMJ were not applied to the military commission system, the commission trial of Hamdan is illegal.[40]

Justice Scalia, joined by Justices Thomas and Alito dissented on the preliminary issue that the Court had jurisdiction to hear Hamdan's case. Justice Scalia correctly[41] rejected the Court's negative inference of section (e)(1) and its conclusion that it did not remove judicial jurisdiction to entertain habeas cases that were pending at the time of passage of the DTA because section (e)(10) was not applied to the specific enactment date in section (h)(1).[42] But statutory interpretation aside, all of the dissenting justices raised important separation of powers and judicial competence arguments regarding which branch of government is tasked by the Constitution to determinate military necessity. Justice Scalia, as did General Bates in his opinion, wrote that there are other considerations and purposes to judicial abstaining from interfering with military operations and the application of justice under the UCMJ. Justice Scalia agreed with the Court that Hamdan was not a member of the U.S. armed forces and as a result the abstention of civilian judicial interference with military justice to further the interest of maintaining military discipline did not apply.

> But for some reason, the Court fails to make any inquiry into whether military commission trials might involve *other* "military necessities" or "unique military exigencies" comparable in gravity. . . .[43]
>
> The reason . . . is not hard to fathom. The principal opinion on the merits makes clear that it does not believe that the trials by military commission involve any "military necessity" *at all*. . . . This is quite at odds with the views on this subject expressed by our political branches.[44]

Justice Scalia wrote that the Congress through the AUMF authorized the President to use all necessary force to deal with the attacks of 9/11 and those who were responsible and a military commission tribunal is one tool to achieve that directive. The directive of the AUMF along with the determination by the President that the rules of evidence used in such tribunals may not comply with those regularly observed in civil trials is enough to meet the UCMJ authority to deviate from rules of evidence otherwise required by the UCMJ. "It is not clear where the Court derives the authority—or the audacity—to contradict this determination."[45]

Justice Stevens answered Justice Scalia and the government on the applicability of the AUMF and the DTA, asserting that neither of these congressional Acts, however, expands the President's authority to convene military commissions. First, while we assume that the AUMF activated the President's war powers, see *Hamdi* v. *Rumsfeld*, 542 U. S. 507 (2004) (plurality opinion), and that those powers include the authority to convene military commissions in appropriate circumstances, see *id.*, at 518; *Quirin*, 317 U. S., at 28–29; see also *Yamashita*, 327 U. S., at 11, there is nothing in the text or legislative history of the AUMF even hinting that Congress intended to expand or alter the authorization set forth in Article 21 of the UCMJ. . . .[46]

[W]e conclude that the "practicability" determination the President has made is insufficient to justify variances from the procedures governing courts-martial.[47]

Nothing in the record before us demonstrates that it would be impracticable to apply court-martial rules in this case. There is no suggestion, for example, of any logistical difficulty in securing properly sworn and authenticated evidence or in applying the usual principles of relevance and admissibility. Assuming *arguendo* that the reasons articulated in the President's Article 36(a) determination ought to be considered in evaluating the impracticability of applying court-martial rules, the only reason offered in support of that determination is the danger posed by international terrorism. Without for one moment underestimating that danger, it is not evident to us why it should require, in the case of Hamdan's trial, any variance from the rules that govern courts-martial.

The absence of any showing of impracticability is particularly disturbing when considered in light of the clear and admitted failure to apply one of the most fundamental protections afforded not just by the Manual for Courts-Martial but also by the UCMJ itself: the right to be present. Whether or not that departure technically is "contrary to or inconsistent with" the terms of the UCMJ, 10 U. S. C. §836(a), the jettisoning of so basic a right cannot lightly be excused as "practicable."

Under the circumstances, then, the rules applicable in courts-martial must apply. Since it is undisputed that Commission Order No. 1 deviates in many significant respects from those rules, it necessarily violates Article 36(b).

The Government's objection that requiring compliance with the court-martial rules imposes an undue burden both ignores the plain meaning of Article 36(b) and misunderstands the purpose and the history of military commissions. The military commission was not born of a desire to dispense a more summary form of justice than is afforded by courts-martial; it developed, rather, as a tribunal of necessity to be employed when courts-martial lacked jurisdiction over either the accused or the subject matter. Exigency lent the commission its legitimacy, but did not further justify the wholesale jettisoning of procedural protections. That history explains why the military commission's procedures typically have been the ones used by courts-martial.[48]

Justice Thomas, joined by Justices Scalia and Alito, supported Justice Scalia's dissent by reiterating his opinion in *Hamdi* that "the Constitution vests in the President . . . broad constitutional authority to protect the Nation's security in the manner he deems fit."[49] Thus "the President's decision to try Hamdan before a military commission for his involvement with al

Qaeda is entitled to a heavy measure of deference."[50] Aside from the doctrine of separation of powers and judicial deference to the President, Justice Thomas asserted that on the merits of the case, Common Article 3 of the Geneva Convention did not limit the power of the President to create and implement military commissions. Article 3, section 1 of the Third Geneva Convention reads as follows:

> *In the case of armed conflict not of an international character* occurring in the territory of one of the High Contracting Parties, each party to the conflict shall be bound to apply, as a minimum, the following provisions:
>   1. Persons taking no active part in the hostilities, including members of armed forces who have laid down their arms and those placed hors de combat by sickness, wounds, detention, or any other cause, shall in all circumstances be treated humanely, without any adverse distinction founded on race, colour, religion or faith, sex, birth or wealth, or any other similar criteria.
> *To this end the following acts are and shall remain prohibited* at any time and in any place whatsoever with respect to the above-mentioned persons:
>   (a) Violence to life and person, in particular murder of all kinds, mutilation, cruel treatment and torture;
>   (b) Taking of hostages;
>   (c) Outrages upon personal dignity, in particular, humiliating and degrading treatment;
>   (d) *The passing of sentences and the carrying out of executions without previous judgment pronounced by a regularly constituted court affording all the judicial guarantees which are recognized as indispensable by civilized peoples.*[51]

Justice Stevens rejected the government's assertion that section 1(d) did not apply to Hamdan because the conflict with al Qaeda is one of international scope and does not qualify as a conflict not of an international character. The Court held that the phrase "conflict not of an international character" is a distinction between conflicts between signatories which bring in the full panoply of protections under the Geneva Convention—conflicts of an international character—and those conflicts involving one signatory which provides a minimal level of protection when the conflict is in the territory of at least one signatory.

> Common Article 3, by contrast, affords some minimal protection, falling short of full protection under the Conventions, to individuals associated with neither a signatory nor even a non-signatory "Power" who are involved in a conflict "in the territory of" a signatory. The latter kind of conflict is distinguishable from the conflict described in Common Article 2 chiefly because it does not involve a clash between nations (whether signatories or not). In context, then, the phrase "not of an international character" bears its literal meaning. See, *e.g.*, J. Bentham, *Introduction to the Principles of Morals and Legislation* 6, 296 (J. Burns & H. Hart eds., 1970) (using the term "international law" as a "new though not inexpressive appellation" meaning "betwixt nation

and nation"; defining "international" to include "mutual transactions between sovereigns as such"); Commentary on the Additional Protocols to the Geneva Conventions of 12 August 1949, p. 1351 (1987) ("[A] non-international armed conflict is distinct from an international armed conflict because of the legal status of the entities opposing each other").[52]

Justice Thomas accepted the assertion made by the government that since al Qaeda was an international organization waging a worldwide attack it was waging a war of international scope; and by its terms Common Article 3 did not apply to such situations.

> Hamdan's claim under Common Article 3 of the Geneva Conventions is meritless. Common Article 3 applies to "armed conflict not of an international character occurring in the territory of one of the High Contracting Parties." 6 U.S.T., at 3318. "Pursuant to [his] authority as Commander in Chief and Chief Executive of the United States," the President has "accept[ed] the legal conclusion of the Department of Justice . . . that common Article 3 of Geneva does not apply to . . . al Qaeda . . . detainees, because, among other reasons, the relevant conflicts are international in scope and common Article 3 applies only to 'armed conflict not of an international character.'" App. 35.[53]

More importantly, he asserted that even if one accepted that Common Article 3 of the Geneva Convention governed the actions of the President, the principles of separation of powers and judicial deference to Presidential decisions on war strategy precluded the Court from providing Hamdan with relief.

> Under this Court's precedents, "the meaning attributed to treaty provisions by the Government agencies charged with their negotiation and enforcement is entitled to great weight." *Sumitomo Shoji America, Inc.* v. *Avagliano*, 457 U.S. 176, 184–185 (1982); *United States* v. *Stuart*, 489 U.S. 353, 369 (1989). Our duty to defer to the President's understanding of the provision at issue here is only heightened by the fact that he is acting pursuant to his constitutional authority as Commander in Chief and by the fact that the subject matter of Common Article 3 calls for a judgment about the nature and character of an armed conflict. See generally *United States* v. *Curtiss-Wright Export Corp.*, 299 U. S. 304, 320 (1936).
>
> The President's interpretation of Common Article 3 is reasonable and should be sustained. The conflict with al Qaeda is international in character in the sense that it is occurring in various nations around the globe. Thus, it is also "occurring in the territory of" more than "one of the High Contracting Parties." The Court does not dispute the President's judgments respecting the nature of our conflict with al Qaeda, nor does it suggest that the President's interpretation of Common Article 3 is implausible or foreclosed by the text of the treaty. Indeed, the Court concedes that Common Article 3 is principally concerned with "furnish[ing] minimal protection to rebels involved in . . . a

civil war," *ante*, at ____, 165 L. Ed. 2d, at 777, precisely the type of conflict the President's interpretation envisions to be subject to Common Article 3. Instead, the Court, without acknowledging its duty to defer to the President, adopts its own, admittedly plausible, reading of Common Article 3. But where, as here, an ambiguous treaty provision ("not of an international character") is susceptible of two plausible, and reasonable, interpretations, our precedents require us to defer to the Executive's interpretation.[54]

Justice Thomas concluded that even if the Common Article 3 fully applied in Hamdan's case, the military commission was in compliance with the requirements of the treaty. He explained that

> the procedures to be employed by Hamdan's commission afford "all the judicial guarantees which are recognized as indispensable by civilized peoples." Neither the Court nor petitioner disputes the Government's description of those procedures. . . .
> . . . If petitioner is found guilty, the judgment will be reviewed by a review panel, the Secretary of Defense, and the President, if he does not designate the Secretary as the final decision-maker. 32 C.F.R. 9.6(h). The final judgment is subject to review in the Court of Appeals for the District of Columbia Circuit and ultimately in this Court.[55]

Justice Alito's dissent, joined by Justices Thomas and Scalia, focused on the assertion that the military commissions were not regularly constituted courts because they did not comply with all of the rules and procedures of a regular court martial under the UCMJ.[56] Justice Alito argued that a regularly constituted court under Common Article 3 "is a court that has been appointed, set up, or established in accordance with the domestic law of the appointing country."[57] This is true "because I am not aware of any international law standard regarding the way in which such a court must be appointed, set up, or established, and because different countries with different government structures handle this matter differently."[58] Echoing an observation made by Justice Thomas, Justice Alito wrote that

> I see no basis for the Court's holding that a military commission cannot be regarded as "a regularly constituted court" unless it is similar in structure and composition to a regular military court or unless there is an "evident practical need" for the divergence. There is no reason why a court that differs in structure or composition from an ordinary military court must be viewed as having been improperly constituted. Tribunals that vary significantly in structure, composition, and procedures may all be "regularly" or "properly" constituted. Consider, for example, a municipal court, a state trial court of general jurisdiction, an Article I federal trial court, a federal district court, and an international court, such as the International Criminal Tribunal for the Former Yugoslavia. Although these courts are "differently constituted" and differ substantially in many other respects, they are all "regularly constituted."[59]

But more importantly, if "Common Article 3 had been meant to require trial before a country's military courts or courts that are similar in structure and composition, the drafters almost certainly would have used language that expresses that thought more directly."[60] Justice Alito concluded that if one were to accept that some of the procedures of the military commission were questionable or unlawful, that fact does not make the commission unlawful. The commissions are lawful if created under domestic law, and any unlawful procedures used by the commission are appealable and reversible under the normal due process protected by the DTA. By analogy Justice Alito explained,

> Even if it is assumed for the sake of argument that some of the procedures specified in Military Commission Order No. 1 impermissibly deviate from court-martial procedures, it does not follow that the military commissions created by that order are not "regularly constituted" or that trying petitioner before such a commission would be inconsistent with the law of war. If Congress enacted a statute requiring the federal district courts to follow a procedure that is unconstitutional, the statute would be invalid, but the district courts would not. Likewise, if some of the procedures that may be used in military commission proceedings are improper, the appropriate remedy is to proscribe the use of those particular procedures, not to outlaw the commissions. I see no justification for striking down the entire commission structure simply because it is possible that petitioner's trial might involve the use of some procedure that is improper.[61]

Justice Alito concluded that the complaints by the Court about the DTA procedures that allow rules of trial to be changed during the trial, that allow proceedings to occur without the defendant being present and that allow the admission of evidence that is prohibited from being shared with the defendant will result in unfair trials is speculative. In any event, it "makes no sense to strike down the entire commission structure based on speculation that some evidence might be improperly admitted in some future case."[62]

> In sum, I believe that Common Article 3 is satisfied here because the military commissions (1) qualify as courts, (2) were appointed and established in accordance with domestic law, and (3) any procedural improprieties that might occur in particular cases can be reviewed in those cases.[63]
> Whatever else may be said about the system that was created by Military Commission Order No. 1 and augmented by the Detainee Treatment Act, §1005(e)(1), 119 Stat. 2742, this system—which features formal trial procedures, multiple levels of administrative review, and the opportunity for review by a United States Court of Appeals and by this Court—does not dispense "summary justice."[64]

From a separation of power perspective, the dissenting opinions had the better argument. Although President Bush pushed the limits of his power to determine how suspected terrorists would be tried, the UCMJ does allow for the changing of procedures. The law itself does not require the President to prove that the applications of procedures familiar to those of a criminal proceeding in federal court are impractical. A Presidential declaration, without more, is not statutorily required. Furthermore, the DTA does not prohibit judicial review but requires judicial review after the DTA process of review is completed. The Court preserved its authority to have a role in the judicial procedures involving trials of detainees—and for that matter that there would be independent review of detainee status and trials in the first place—in *Hamdi* and *Rasul*. *Ex Parte Milligan*, Article 36 of the UCMJ, and Common Article 3 together require that military commissions provide minimal due process and prevent the creation of kangaroo courts to rubber stamp convictions of enemy combatants—lawful or not. But as the dissent asserted, the military commissions under the DTA protected and implemented the minimal procedures and due process required. As Commander-in-Chief the President is entitled to enforce international treaties as he determines their meaning if such interpretation is reasonable and plausible, a principle that was asserted and defended at the very founding of the republic by Washington and Hamilton in 1793 to the chagrin of Madison and Jefferson.[65]

ᕦᑗᕤ

Justice Kennedy in his concurring opinion in *Hamdan* supported the decision by Justice Stevens and made clear that if the President wanted to adjust the UCMJ to meet the threats and needs of placing enemy combatants and violators of the law of war on trial through military commissions, he need only go to Congress to secure the appropriate legislation. Congress and the President took the advice of Justice Kennedy and passed the MCA of 2006. The legislation sought to address the *Hamdan* decision by correcting the Court's interpretation of the DTA that the habeas jurisdiction limitation did not apply to pending cases and address the procedural deficiencies that resulted in the Court striking down the military commissions created by President Bush's military order. The Court two years later reviewed these changes in *Boumediene v. Bush*.[66]

BOUMEDIENE V. BUSH AND HABEAS CORPUS: THE CONSTITUTIONAL RIGHT TO BE HEARD

In *Rasul* the Court held that the detainees had the statutory right to seek habeas relief from the federal courts. The Court specifically held that it did not address the petitioners' Constitutional right to habeas. Upon remand to the D.C. District Court the government argued that the detainees did not have cognizable rights under the Constitution and that the petitions should be dismissed. The detainee cases were consolidated in two groups and Judge Richard J. Leon in *Khalid v. Bush* held that the detainees had no rights protected by the Constitution,[67] but in the second set of cases, *In re Guantanamo Detainee Cases*, Judge Joyce Hens Green held that detainees did have cognizable rights under the due process clause of the Fifth Amendment of the U.S. Constitution.[68] Subsequent to both parties submitting appeals to the Court of Appeals of the District of Columbia, Congress passed the DTA and the government moved to have the appeals in both the Court of Appeals and the pending *Hamdan* case before the Supreme Court dismissed on the basis that the DTA had removed subject matter jurisdiction of the courts. Subsequent to the Supreme Court ruling in *Hamdan* that the DTA did not remove jurisdiction of pending detainee cases, Congress passed the MCA, which sought to correct the Supreme Court's interpretation of the DTA that habeas jurisdiction was maintained for pending cases. The Court of Appeals held in *Boumediene v. Bush* that the MCA did remove subject matter jurisdiction from the judiciary for both future and pending detainee habeas cases and that the petitioners did not have any cognizable rights under the Constitution to support the issuance of the habeas petition.[69] The petitioners appealed and after an initial refusal to hear the case (April 2, 2007), the Court accepted certiorari (June 29, 2007), heard arguments (December 5, 2007), and issued its decision on July 14, 2008, reversing the Court of Appeals.

Writing for the Court, Justice Kennedy (joined by Justices Stevens, Souter, Ginsburg, and Breyer) asserted that the Court of Appeals decision that the MCA did remove habeas jurisdiction from the Court was correct and the MCA provision that removed jurisdiction was "an unconstitutional suspension of the writ."[70] The government asserted, as it had in the District Court and the Court of Appeals, that the detainees being noncitizens and enemy combatants detained at Guantanamo Bay, Cuba, had no Constitutional rights to be enforced by the writ. Justice Kennedy approached the question from the vantage point that the writ, both historically and Constitutionally, is "one of the few safeguards of liberty specified in [the] Constitution" and interpreting the writ in light of a safeguard of liberty "must inform [the] proper interpretation of the Suspension Clause" of the Constitution.[71] The dissent had a different view. The dissent, led by the Chief Justice and Justice Scalia, explained that the writ is a procedural right that allows the judiciary to hear assertions of Constitutional rights. It was this distinction that governed the review of history that both Justice Kennedy and Justice Scalia gave to the history of the writ and the significance of its meaning on the application of the writ.

After painstaking review of the history of the writ and what the history of the development and application of the Great Writ provided to the question of its availability to enemy aliens detained abroad, Justice Kennedy held that the history is inconclusive and as such the Court would "decline . . . to infer too much, one way or the other, from the lack of historical evidence on point,"[72] although "at common law a petitioner's status as an alien was not a categorical bar to habeas corpus relief."[73] With history not providing a conclusive answer, Justice Kennedy held that the writ had a specific purpose in the minds of the founders. Justice Kennedy asserted that

> the Framers considered the writ a vital instrument for the protection of individual liberty is evident from the care taken to specify the limited grounds for its suspension. . . .
> Surviving accounts of the ratification debates provide additional evidence that the Framers deemed the writ to be an essential mechanism in the separation-of-powers scheme. . . . A resolution passed by the New York ratifying convention made clear its understanding that the Clause not only protects against arbitrary suspensions of the writ but also guarantees an affirmative right to judicial inquiry into the causes of detention. . . . Alexander Hamilton likewise explained that by providing the detainee a judicial forum to challenge detention, the writ preserves limited government.[74]

Explaining the value of the purpose of the writ, Justice Kennedy explained,

> In our own system the Suspension Clause is designed to protect against these cyclical abuses. The Clause protects the rights of the detained by a means consistent with the essential design of the Constitution. It ensures that, except during periods of formal suspension, the Judiciary will have a time-tested device, the writ, to maintain the "delicate balance of governance" that is itself the surest safeguard of liberty. See *Hamdi*, 542 U. S., at 536 (plurality opinion). The Clause protects the rights of the detained by affirming the duty and authority of the Judiciary to call the jailer to account. See *Preiser* v. *Rodriguez*, 411 U. S. 475, 484 (1973) ("[T]he essence of habeas corpus is an attack by a person in custody upon the legality of that custody"); cf. *In re Jackson*, 15 Mich. 417, 439–440 (1867) (Cooley, J., concurring) ("The important fact to be observed in regard to the mode of procedure upon this [habeas] writ is, that it is directed to, and served upon, not the person confined, but his jailer"). The separation-of-powers doctrine, and the history that influenced its design, therefore must inform the reach and purpose of the Suspension Clause.[75]

In any event the Court reasoned that regardless of the disputed and inconclusive common law history of whether the writ was ever applied to territory outside the sovereignty of the crown, it was without dispute that the United States enjoyed complete control over the territory and base at Guantanamo Bay. Justice Kennedy rejected the Government's assertion that *de jure* sovereignty was determinative because such a holding would be "inconsistent" with the principles of separation of powers within the American Constitutional structure.[76] The Court distinguished *Eisentrager*, as it did in *Rasul*, from the present case with the following observation,

> True, the Court in *Eisentrager* denied access to the writ, and it noted the prisoners "at no relevant time were within any territory over which the United States is sovereign, and [that] the scenes of their offense, their capture, their trial and their punishment were all beyond the territorial jurisdiction of any court of the United States." 339 U. S., at 778. The Government seizes upon this language as proof positive that the *Eisentrager* Court adopted a formalistic, sovereignty-based test for determining the reach of the Suspension Clause. We reject this reading for three reasons.
>
> First, we do not accept the idea that the above-quoted passage from *Eisentrager* is the only authoritative language in the opinion and that all the rest is dicta. The Court's further determinations, based on practical considerations, were integral to Part II of its opinion and came before the decision announced its holding. See 339 U. S., at 781.
>
> Second, because the United States lacked both *de jure* sovereignty and plenary control over Landsberg Prison, it is far from clear that the *Eisentrager* Court used the term sovereignty only in the narrow technical sense and not to connote the degree of control the military asserted over the facility. . . . . That the Court devoted a significant portion of Part II to a discussion of practical barriers to the running of the writ suggests that the Court was not concerned exclusively with the formal legal status of Landsberg Prison but also with the objective degree of control the United States asserted over it. Even if we assume the *Eisentrager* Court considered the United States' lack of formal legal sovereignty over Landsberg Prison as the decisive factor in that case, its holding is not inconsistent with a functional approach to questions of extraterritoriality. The formal legal status of a given territory affects, at least to some extent, the political branches' control over that territory. *De jure* sovereignty is a factor that bears upon which constitutional guarantees apply there.
>
> Third, . . . Nothing in *Eisentrager* says that *de jure* sovereignty is or has ever been the only consideration in determining the geographic reach of the Constitution or of habeas corpus. . . . A constricted reading of *Eisentrager* overlooks . . . that questions of extraterritoriality turn on objective factors and practical concerns, not formalism.[77]

Justice Kennedy reasoned that if the government's theory of *Eisentrager* were correct that *de jure* sovereignty was determinative in habeas petitions received from non citizens detained in a leased area by the United States in which the lease allowed for complete control over the leased area and the activities thereof, "it would be possible for the political branches to govern without legal constraint. Our basic charter cannot be contracted away like this. The Constitution grants Congress and the President the power to acquire . . . and govern territory, not the power to decide when and where [Constitutional] terms apply."[78]

Abstaining from questions involving formal sovereignty and territorial governance is one thing. To hold the political branches have the power to switch the Constitution on or off at will is quite another. The former position reflects this Court's recognition that certain matters requiring political judgments are best left to the political branches. The latter would permit a striking anomaly in our tripartite system of government, leading to a regime in which Congress and the President, not this Court, say "what the law is." *Marbury v. Madison*, 1 Cranch 137, 177 (1803).

These concerns have particular bearing upon the Suspension Clause question in the cases now before us, for the writ of habeas corpus is itself an indispensable mechanism for monitoring the separation of powers. The test for determining the scope of this provision must not be subject to manipulation by those whose power it is designed to restrain.[79]

The Court held that the determinative and relevant factors in *Eisentrager* were

(a) is an enemy alien; (b) has never been or resided in the United States; (c) was captured outside of our territory and there held in military custody as a prisoner of war; (d) was tried and convicted by a Military Commission sitting outside the United States; (e) for offenses against laws of war committed outside the United States; (f) and is at all times imprisoned outside the United States." 339 U. S., at 777.[80]

Justice Kennedy concluded that under *Eisentrager* three factors determine if the Suspension Clause reaches a specific location of detention; (1) the citizenship of the detainee and the adequacy of the process utilized to determine the status of the detainee, (2) the nature of the location of the apprehension and detention, and (3) the practical obstacles inherent to resolving the prisoner's exercising the writ.[81] The Court observed, even if the Government's reliance on and interpretation of *Eisentrager* governed, the case with the detainees is significantly different from the 21 German soldiers tried and convicted by a military tribunal in China. The petitioners in *Eisentrager* involved individuals who enjoyed a complete trial in which the minimal due process of having charges formally made, having access to counsel, having access to all of the evidence against them, having full ability to provide evidence in their defense, having the power to cross-examine all evidence and witnesses against them, and having the right to a tribunal requirement of unanimous voting of guilt all resulting in a conviction of war crimes, before they sought the protection of the federal courts—none of which were provided to the detainees at Guantanamo.[82] The CSRT system, which was designed to provide an independent review of enemy combatant designation, was not even instituted until the government assertion that the President had plenary authority to make such designations and the judiciary had no role at all in reviewing the detention of the detainees was rejected in *Hamdi*, three years after they were detained at Guantanamo.

In sum, the Court held that (a) the process to determine the enemy combatant designation of the detainees was well below the recognized principles of due process, (b) the United States holds *de facto* plenary and complete control over the location of the detainees, and (c) since the government is in complete control of the facility it can protect national security while allowing a judicial hearing to occur.[83] The Court concluded that because the United States enjoys *de facto* sovereignty over the territory of Guantanamo Bay, Cuba, it would hold for the first time that "noncitizens detained by our Government in territory over which another country maintains *de jure* sovereignty have . . . rights under our Constitution [because] Art. I, § 9, cl. 2, of the Constitution has full effect at Guantanamo Bay. . . . Petitioners, therefore, are entitled to the privilege of habeas corpus to challenge the legality of their detention."[84]

With the determination that the petitioners have a Constitutional right to protest their detention and that Congress has removed the habeas right, the MCA is in violation of the Suspension Clause unless Congress has provided an "adequate substitute procedures for habeas corpus."[85] As the Court explained,

> The Government submits there has been compliance with the Suspension Clause because the DTA review process in the Court of Appeals, see DTA §1005(e), provides an adequate substitute. Congress has granted that court jurisdiction to consider
> (i) whether the status determination of the [CSRT] . . . was "(i) consistent with the standards and procedures specified by the Secretary of Defense . . . and (ii) to the extent the Constitution and laws of the United States are applicable, whether the use of such standards and procedures to make the determination is consistent with the Constitution and laws of the United States." §1005(e)(2)(C), 119 Stat. 2742.

Rather than remanding the case back to the Court of Appeals for its determination, Justice Kennedy held that

> the gravity of the separation-of-powers issues raised by these cases and the fact that these detainees have been denied meaningful access to a judicial forum for a period of years render these cases exceptional. The parties before us have addressed the adequacy issue. While we would have found it informative to consider the reasoning of the Court of Appeals on this point, we must weigh that against the harms petitioners may endure from additional delay. And, given there are few precedents addressing what features an adequate substitute for habeas corpus must contain, in all likelihood a remand simply would delay ultimate resolution of the issue by this Court.[86]

In sum, Justice Kennedy concluded that the DTA was not an adequate substitute for habeas corpus because (1) "the DTA's jurisdictional grant

[to the Court of appeals] is quite limited. The Court of Appeals has jurisdiction not to inquire into the legality of the detention generally but only
to assess whether the CSRT complied with the 'standards and procedures
specified by the Secretary of Defense' and whether those standards are
lawful,"[87] (2) "the DTA does not explicitly empower the Court of Appeals
to order the applicant in a DTA review proceeding released should the
court find that the standards and procedures used at his CRST hearing
were insufficient to justify detention,"[88] (3) the DTA does not allow the
detainee to challenge the President's authority to detain him under his
powers as Commander-in-Chief or under the AUMF, (4) it was not clear
that the DTA allowed the Court of Appeals to make determinations of fact
because the DTA confines the Court of Appeals to a determination as to
whether the procedures of the CSRT were followed, (5) the DTA does not
allow "the detainee to present relevant exculpatory evidence that was not
made part of the record in the earlier proceedings," for on its face the DTA
prohibits the Court of Appeals to consider evidence outside of the CSRT
record,[89] (6) the DTA, even if it allowed evidence to be considered by the
Court of Appeals that was available during the CSRT hearing that was not
placed in the record, the DTA does not permit the detainee to "present
evidence discovered after the CSRT proceeding concluded,"[90] and (7) the
detainee has no ability to force the Deputy Defense Secretary to review
and/or order a new hearing based on new evidence secured after the
CSRT hearing has concluded.[91] In addition to these objections the Court
observed that the CSRT hearing, unlike a habeas hearing, is a closed and
accusatorial process, not an adversarial process in habeas hearings, thus
the detainee has no direct influence on the development of the hearing
record and the evidence submitted.[92] Justice Kennedy maintained that the
right to a judicial hearing on the law and facts, the ability to supplement
the record, to enjoy an adversarial process, to have the power to compel
government action if entitled under the law, to have the right to demand
release if required by the law are all paramount rights protected under a
habeas process and the DTA restriction of these rights make the DTA an
unacceptable substitute for the habeas hearing.

Since 9/11 the government resisted the idea that the judiciary had a
role in the review of the Presidential classification of detainees for three
years before it ruled in *Hamdi* and *Rasul,* and then argued for two years in
the courts and before the Supreme Court that the detainees did not have
Constitutional rights before the Court ruled in *Hamdan,* and then fought
judicial jurisdiction under the DTA and the MCA for two more years, leading to the present case in *Boumediene.* With this background the Court was
not sympathetic to the Government's assertion that the detainees should
seek CSRT review by the Court of Appeals before they seek a habeas hearing
before the district Court. Justice Kennedy wrote,

The cases before us, however, do not involve detainees who have been held for a short period of time while awaiting their CSRT determinations. Were that the case, or were it probable that the Court of Appeals could complete a prompt review of their applications, the case for requiring temporary abstention or exhaustion of alternative remedies would be much stronger. These qualifications no longer pertain here. In some of these cases six years have elapsed without the judicial oversight that habeas corpus or an adequate substitute demands. And there has been no showing that the Executive faces such onerous burdens that it cannot respond to habeas corpus actions. To require these detainees to complete DTA review before proceeding with their habeas corpus actions would be to require additional months, if not years, of delay. The first DTA review applications were filed over a year ago, but no decisions on the merits have been issued. While some delay in fashioning new procedures is unavoidable, the costs of delay can no longer be borne by those who are held in custody. The detainees in these cases are entitled to a prompt habeas corpus hearing.[93]

Although the Court held that the DTA was not an acceptable substitute to a habeas hearing, the Court made clear that the decision did not require a wholesale use of the District Courts to deal with the issue of detention at Guantanamo and affirmed that the D.C. District Court could be designated as the exclusive court to hear detainee habeas cases under the DTA. In an effort to limit the impact of his opinion, Justice Kennedy made clear that

our decision today holds only that the petitioners before us are entitled to seek the writ; that the DTA review procedures are an inadequate substitute for habeas corpus; and that the petitioners in these cases need not exhaust the review procedures in the Court of Appeals before proceeding with their habeas actions in the District Court. The only law we identify as unconstitutional is MCA §7, 28 U.S.C.A. §2241(e) (Supp. 2007). Accordingly, both the DTA and the CSRT process remain intact. Our holding with regard to exhaustion should not be read to imply that a habeas court should intervene the moment an enemy combatant steps foot in a territory where the writ runs. The Executive is entitled to a reasonable period of time to determine a detainee's status before a court entertains that detainee's habeas corpus petition. The CSRT process is the mechanism Congress and the President set up to deal with these issues. Except in cases of undue delay, federal courts should refrain from entertaining an enemy combatant's habeas corpus petition at least until after the Department, acting via the CSRT, has had a chance to review his status.

Although we hold that the DTA is not an adequate and effective substitute for habeas corpus, it does not follow that a habeas corpus court may disregard the dangers the detention in these cases was intended to prevent.[94]

Justice Souter (joined by Justices Ginsburg and Breyer) focused on the amount of time that had elapsed since 9/11 regarding the legal issues involving the detainees. Justice Souter challenged, as a hollow statement, the dissent assertion that the detainees would have adequate review under the DTA.

> A second fact insufficiently appreciated by the dissents is the length of the disputed imprisonments, some of the prisoners represented here today having been locked up for six years. Hence the hollow ring when the dissenters suggest that the Court is somehow precipitating the judiciary into reviewing claims that the military (subject to appeal to the Court of Appeals for the District of Columbia Circuit) could handle within some reasonable period of time. . . .
>
> It is in fact the very lapse of four years from the time *Rasul* put everyone on notice that habeas process was available to Guantanamo prisoners, and the lapse of six years since some of these prisoners were captured and incarcerated, that stand at odds with the repeated suggestions of the dissenters that these cases should be seen as a judicial victory in a contest for power between the Court and the political branches. The several answers to the charge of triumphalism might start with a basic fact of Anglo-American constitutional history: that the power, first of the Crown and now of the Executive Branch of the United States, is necessarily limited by habeas corpus jurisdiction to enquire into the legality of executive detention. And one could explain that in this Court's exercise of responsibility to preserve habeas corpus something much more significant is involved than pulling and hauling between the judicial and political branches. Instead, though, it is enough to repeat that some of these petitioners have spent six years behind bars. After six years of sustained executive detentions in Guantanamo, subject to habeas jurisdiction but without any actual habeas scrutiny, today's decision is no judicial victory, but an act of perseverance in trying to make habeas review, and the obligation of the courts to provide it, mean something of value both to prisoners and to the Nation.[95]

The Chief Justice was not moved. In his dissent (joined by Justices Scalia, Thomas, and Alito) the Chief Justice answered,

> The concurrence is wrong to suggest that I "insufficiently appreciat[e]" the issue of delay in these cases. This Court issued its decisions in *Rasul* v. *Bush*, and *Hamdi* v. *Rumsfeld* in 2004. The concurrence makes it sound as if the political branches have done nothing in the interim. In fact, Congress responded 18 months later by enacting the DTA. Congress cannot be faulted for taking that time to consider how best to accommodate both the detainees' interests and the need to keep the American people safe. Since the DTA became law, petitioners have steadfastly refused to avail themselves of the statute's review mechanisms. It is unfair to complain that the DTA system involves too much delay when petitioners have consistently refused to use it, preferring to litigate instead. Today's decision obligating district courts to craft new procedures to replace those in the DTA will only prolong the process—and delay relief.[96]

But more importantly, the Chief Justice complained that the Court mischaracterized the nature of the Great Writ and that its decision "is not really about the detainees at all, but about control of federal policy regarding enemy combatants."[97] The Great Writ, the Chief Justice explained,

> is most fundamentally a procedural right, a mechanism for contesting the legality of executive detention. The critical threshold question in these cases, prior to any inquiry about the writ's scope, is whether the system the political branches designed protects whatever rights the detainees may possess. If so, there is no need for any additional process, whether called "habeas" or something else.[98]

Thus,

> The only issue in dispute is the process the Guantanamo prisoners are entitled to use to test the legality of their detention. *Hamdi* concluded that American citizens detained as enemy combatants are entitled to only limited process, and that much of that process could be supplied by a military tribunal, with review to follow in an Article III court. That is precisely the system we have here. It is adequate to vindicate whatever due process rights petitioners may have.[99]

The majority of the dissent focused on how the DTA and the CSRT system vindicated the due process rights of the detainees and how they, as required by *Hamdi*, were "tailored to alleviate [the] uncommon potential to burden the Executive at a time of ongoing military conflict."[100] In an answer to Justice Kennedy's list of fatal flaws with the DTA, the Chief Justice observed (1) the D.C. Court is the second, not the first review of the decision to confine,[101] (2) the initial Executive determination is not a provisional decision made in haste,[102] (3) the CSRT process is a review of a classification, not part of the initial classification,[103] (4) the CSRT functions "much as habeas courts would if hearing the detainee's collateral challenge for the first time,"[104] and (5) the detainees have "full access to appellate counsel and the right to challenge the factual and legal bases of their detentions" before the Court of Appeals.[105] The Chief Justice considered the facts that the detainees could not introduce evidence to the D.C. Court of Appeals that was not in the CSRT record a small matter, noting that if "this is the most the Court can muster, the ice beneath its feet is thin indeed."[106] The Chief Justice noted that the DTA permits in the event of newly discovered evidence the remand of the case back to the CSRT for a new hearing by the D.C. Court as well as requires Defense Department review of all cases on an annual basis and Defense Department regulations authorize the Deputy Secretary of Defense to order new CSRT hearings when new evidence appears that was not available in the original CSRT review.[107] The Chief Justice was not as certain with the majority complaint that the DTA did not authorize release of detainees that the CSRT or the D.C. Court of Appeals determined should be released. He agreed with the majority that it is *possible* to read into the DTA that ability.[108]

Convinced that the DTA and CSRT provided adequate due process protections and independent review of the status of the detainees, he nevertheless asserted that as a procedural and subject-matter jurisdictional matter
the Court should have declined to intervene in the case "until the D. C. Circuit had assessed the nature and validity of the congressionally mandated
proceedings in a given detainee's case."[109]

Echoing the dissents in *Hamdan,* the Chief Justice observed that the DTA
and CSRT system provide for multiple reviews and provides for Article III
court review of determinations made by the CSRT. After making clear that a
Congressional determination that the detainees must exhaust the statutory
measures of the DTA before appealing and involving Article III courts is no
way a suspension of the writ,[110] the Chief Justice asserted that the majority
failed to show "what rights the detainees have that cannot be vindicated by
the DTA system."[111] The Chief Justice explained that a detainee's review of
a classification as an enemy combatant does not start at a CSRT hearing;
such a hearing is actually a review of an initial determination made by
the military.[112] The CSRT provides for the gathering of evidence, taking of
testimony, challenging evidence, and a rendering of a legal decision on the
legality of the detention of the detainee. After the CSRT makes its determination, the D.C. Court of Appeals is given the authority to review not only
the CSRT determination and process but is authorized to determine if the
process meets Constitutional standards of review. Further review is authorized by the Supreme Court. The Chief Justice concluded,

> The DTA system of military tribunal hearings followed by Article III review
> looks a lot like the procedure *Hamdi* blessed. If nothing else, it is plain from
> the design of the DTA that Congress, the President, and this Nation's military
> leaders have made a good-faith effort to follow our precedent.
>
> The Court, however, will not take "yes" for an answer.[113]

But aside from accusing the majority of a bait and switch on Congress,
the Chief Justice asserted that the Court answered the wrong question.

> The question is not how much process the CSRTs provide in comparison to
> other modes of adjudication. The question is whether the CSRT procedures—
> coupled with the judicial review specified by the DTA—provide the "basic
> process" *Hamdi* said the Constitution affords American citizens detained as
> enemy combatants.[114]

Whether the basic process required in *Hamdi* is met by the DTA and the
CSRT is for the D.C. Court of Appeals to determine first, after the basic
process is carried out in an individual detainee's case.

More importantly, as a Constitutional matter it is not an answer to say that
the detainees have a Constitutional right to habeas corpus in the face of the

DTA without the Court providing an explanation as to why the DTA does not protect the rights the detainees have to due process. "Because if the DTA provides a means for vindicating petitioners' rights, it is necessarily an adequate substitute for habeas corpus."[115] Citing *Hamdi*, the Chief Justice assumed

> that any due process rights petitioners may possess are no greater than those of American citizens detained as enemy combatants. It is worth noting again that the *Hamdi* controlling opinion said the Constitution guarantees citizen detainees only "basic" procedural rights, and that the process for securing those rights can "be tailored to alleviate [the] uncommon potential to burden the Executive at a time of ongoing military conflict." 542 U. S., at 533. The majority, however, objects that "the procedural protections afforded to the detainees in the CSRT hearings are ... limited." *Ante*, at ___, 171 L. Ed. 2d, at 78. . . . Contrary to the repeated suggestions of the majority, DTA review need not parallel the habeas privileges enjoyed by noncombatant American citizens, as set out in 28 U. S. C. §2241 (2000 ed. and Supp V). Cf. *ante*, at ___, 171 L. Ed. 2d, at 83–84. It need only provide process adequate for noncitizens detained as alleged combatants.[116]

Justice Scalia, joined by the Chief Justice and Justices Thomas and Alito, while concurring that the DTA and the CSRT "provide the essential protections that habeas corpus guarantees" asserted that the "writ of habeas corpus does not, and never has, run in favor of aliens abroad," thus "the Suspension Clause . . . has no application."[117] Justice Scalia explained that as an initial matter,

> As a court of law operating under a written Constitution, our role is to determine whether there is a conflict between that Clause and the Military Commissions Act. A conflict arises only if the Suspension Clause preserves the privilege of the writ for aliens held by the United States military as enemy combatants at the base in Guantanamo Bay, located within the sovereign territory of Cuba.
> We have frequently stated that we owe great deference to Congress's view that a law it has passed is constitutional. That is especially so in the area of foreign and military affairs. . . . Indeed, we accord great deference even when the President acts alone in this area.
> In light of those principles of deference, the Court's conclusion that "the common law [does not] yiel[d] a definite answer to the questions before us," *ante*, at ___, 171 L. Ed. 2d, at 68, leaves it no choice but to affirm the Court of Appeals. The writ as preserved in the Constitution could not possibly extend farther than the common law provided when that Clause was written. See Part III, *infra*. The Court admits that it cannot determine whether the writ historically extended to aliens held abroad, and it concedes (necessarily) that Guantanamo Bay lies outside the sovereign territory of the United States. See *ante*, at ___, 171 L. Ed. 2d at, 89; *Rasul* v. *Bush*, 542 U. S. 466, 500–501 (2004) (Scalia, J., dissenting). Together, these two concessions establish that it is (in the Court's view) perfectly ambiguous whether the common-law writ would have provided a remedy for these petitioners. If that is so, the Court has no ba-

sis to strike down the Military Commissions Act, and must leave undisturbed
the considered judgment of the coequal branches.[118]

Nor was the Court's assertion of enforcement of the principle of separation of powers persuasive to Justice Scalia. Justice Scalia agreed that the separation of powers principle has application but the principle itself is derived "from the sum total of the individual separation-of-powers provisions that the Constitution sets forth," not "from a judicially imagined matrix."[119] "It is nonsensical to interpret those provisions themselves in light of some general "separation-of-powers principles" dreamed up by the Court. Rather, they must be interpreted to mean what they were understood to mean when the people ratified them."[120] Justice Scalia asserted that

> the proper course of constitutional interpretation is to give the text the meaning it was understood to have at the time of its adoption by the people. That course is especially demanded when (as here) the Constitution limits the power of Congress to infringe upon a pre-existing common-law right. The nature of the writ of habeas corpus that cannot be suspended must be defined by the common-law writ that was available at the time of the founding.
>
> It is entirely clear that, at English common law, the writ of habeas corpus did not extend beyond the sovereign territory of the Crown.[121]

Justice Scalia concluded with a structural interpretation of the Suspension Clause, observing that

> what history teaches is confirmed by the nature of the limitations that the Constitution places upon suspension of the common-law writ. It can be suspended only "in Cases of Rebellion or Invasion." Art. I, §9, cl. 2. The latter case (invasion) is plainly limited to the territory of the United States; and while it is conceivable that a rebellion could be mounted by American citizens abroad, surely the overwhelming majority of its occurrences would be domestic. If the extraterritorial scope of habeas turned on flexible, "functional" considerations, as the Court holds, why would the Constitution limit its suspension almost entirely to instances of domestic crisis?[122]

୧ଓ

In *Hamdi, Rasul, Hamdan* and *Boumediene* collectively the Court demonstrated an aversion to allowing the Congress and the President, or the President on his own authority, to create and operate a zone in which neither habeas corpus or judicial review can be seen, and to allow the political branches to "switch the Constitution on or off at will" in that zone is not an academic observation for a high school civics class (as if we still had such things). For the founding generation considered the writ "a vital instrument for the protection of individual liberty" and reflected in the Constitution the protection of the writ by specifically limiting its suspension to cases of rebellion or invasion.[123] Justice Kennedy in *Boumediene* stressed that the history and purpose of the writ during the seventeenth and eighteenth centuries was to meet the need to restrain the power of the king and make him subject to the law. Both the courts of England in the early days of the development of control over the executive power of the king and the founding generation determined in the Constitution, it is for the judiciary to enforce the law and make the lawmakers subservient to the Law. In the American Constitutional system the subservience of the lawmakers to the rule of law is maintained structurally through the separation of powers dynamic. Part of that structure is made up of the assurance that "persons as well as citizens, foreign nationals who have the privilege of litigating in our courts can seek to enforce separation-of-powers principles"[124] through habeas corpus under the protection of the Suspension Clause in cases of government use of its ultimate power—that of taking away the liberty of the individual. So long as the Suspension Clause is applicable to a specific area, the right to seek its protection cannot be withheld short of formal suspension by Congress.

Although Justice Kennedy had a better argument on the purpose of the Great Writ, the Chief Justice was correct in his dissent that the Court had struck down the DTA without an actual case in which the process of the CSRT and its appeal to the Court of Appeals had occurred, thus providing an actual case to base a determination that the process did not meet the standards of a habeas hearing. Justice Kennedy's answer was that it has been six years and some of the detainees have not had a hearing and it has been four years since the *Hamdi* and *Rasul* decisions required a hearing. Further, if it had not been for the *Hamdi* and *Rasul* decisions, the detainees would not even have the CSRT as an option. Although the Bush administration never supported the concept that the detainees were entitled to a hearing, once the Court ordered the President and Congress to create a review process and the political branches complied—three times—the Court was not obliged to inject itself into the beginning of that process because the process placed Article III review at the end. Justice Alito was correct in *Hamdan* when he observed that the CSRT system is not made invalid because certain procedures within it are flawed.

∽

In *Boumediene*, Justice Kennedy concluded his opinion with the following defense of the rule of law, the separation of powers and why they matter even in times of war and crisis.

Officials charged with daily operational responsibility for our security may consider a judicial discourse on the history of the Habeas Corpus Act of 1679 and like matters to be far removed from the Nation's present, urgent concerns. Established legal doctrine, however, must be consulted for its teaching. Remote in time it may be; irrelevant to the present it is not. Security depends upon a sophisticated intelligence apparatus and the ability of our Armed Forces to act and to interdict. There are further considerations, however. Security subsists, too, in fidelity to freedom's first principles. Chief among these are freedom from arbitrary and unlawful restraint and the personal liberty that is secured by adherence to the separation of powers. It is from these principles that the judicial authority to consider petitions for habeas corpus relief derives.

. . . Within the Constitution's separation-of-powers structure, few exercises of judicial power are as legitimate or as necessary as the responsibility to hear challenges to the authority of the Executive to imprison a person. . . .

Because our Nation's past military conflicts have been of limited duration, it has been possible to leave the outer boundaries of war powers undefined. If, as some fear, terrorism continues to pose dangerous threats to us for years to come, the Court might not have this luxury. . . .

. . . We hold that petitioners may invoke the fundamental procedural protections of habeas corpus. The laws and Constitution are designed to survive, and remain in force, in extraordinary times. Liberty and security can be reconciled; and in our system they are reconciled within the framework of the law. The Framers decided that habeas corpus, a right of first importance, must be a part of that framework, a part of that law.[125]

The issue of why the rule of law matters and why the judiciary has a role in national security issues will be reviewed in the next chapter.

NOTES

1. See chapter 1, notes 8–10 for discussion on how the laws of politics, party politics, and cycles of Presidential elections affect the political powers of a specific President.

2. *Ex parte Quirin*, 317 U.S. 1 (1942).

3. *Rasul v. Bush* and *Al Odah v. United States*, 542 U.S. 466 124 S.Ct 2686, 159 L. Ed 2d 548 (2004).

4. *Hamdan v. Rumsfeld*, 548 U.S. 557 126, S.Ct 2749, 165 L. Ed 2d 723 (2006).

5. *Boumediene v. Bush* and *Al Odah v. United States*, 553 U.S. 723, 128 S.Ct 2229, 171 L. Ed 2d 41 (2008).

6. *Rasul v. Bush*, 542 U.S. 466, 470–73 (2004).

7. Ibid.

8. *Rasul v. Bush*, 215 F. Supp. 2d 55 (D.D.C. 2002).

9. *Al Odah v. United States*, 321 F.3d 1134 (D.C. Cir. 2003).

10. *Rasul v. Bush*, 542 U.S. 466, 470 (2004).

11. *Johnson v. Eisentrager*, 339 U.S. 763 (1950).

12. Ibid., 768.

13. Ibid., 777–78

14. Ibid., 779.

15. *Rasul v. Bush*, 542 U.S., 476 (emphasis in original).

16. Ibid., 478.

17. *Braden v. 30th Judicial Circuit Court of Kentucky*, 410 U.S. 484 (1973).

18. *Rasul v. Bush*, 542 U.S., 478–79.

19. Ibid., 479 citing *Braden v. 30th Judicial Circuit Court of Kentucky*, 410 U.S., 495.

20. Ibid., 481.

21. Ibid., 483–84.

22. Ibid., 497–98.

23. Ibid., 501.

24. Ibid., 498–99.

25. Ibid., 489.

26. U.S. Code Title 28, Part VI, chapter 153, section 2242 (2004).

27. *Rasul*, 542 U.S., 490.

28. U.S. Code Title 28, Part VI, chapter 153, section 2242 (2004) (emphasis added).

29. *Braden v. 30th Judicial Circuit Court of Kentucky*, 410 U.S. 484, 494–95 (1973).

30. *Rasul*, 542 U.S., 478.

31. Ibid., 479.

32. Ibid., 495.

33. Subsequent to the Court's ruling in his case, Hamdan was tried by a military commission under the MCA of 2006 and on August 6, 2008, was found guilty of five counts of providing material support to terrorism specifically through his actions of acting as Bin Laden's driver and bodyguard but was acquitted of charges that he conspired with bin Laden and other top al-Qaeda operatives to carry out the September 11 attacks, the 1998 bombings of the U.S. embassies in Kenya and Tanzania, and the 2000 attack on the USS *Cole* in Yemen. Hamdan was the first detainee to be tried under the MCA. Hamdan was sentenced to five and a half years in prison on August 7, 2008.

34. *Hamdan v. Rumsfeld* 548 U.S. 557, 126 S. Ct. _____, 165 L. Ed. 2d 723, 753 (2006) (internal citation omitted).

35. *Hamdan v. Rumsfeld*, 165 L. Ed. 2d, 754.

36. Ibid., 755.

37. Ibid., 766.

38. Ibid., 771.

39. Ibid., 773.

40. Ibid., 774.

41. See Arthur Garrison, "*Hamdan v. Rumsfeld*, Military Commissions, and Acts of Congress: A Summary," *American Journal of Trial Advocacy* 30, no. 2 (2006): 339–62.

42. *Hamdan v. Rumsfeld*, 165 L. Ed. 2d, 792–93.

43. Ibid., 804 (emphasis in original).

44. Ibid. (emphasis in original).

45. Ibid.

46. Ibid., 755.

47. Ibid., 772.

48. Ibid., 773.

49. Ibid., 807.

50. Ibid., 808.

51. Geneva Convention Relative to Treatment of Prisoners of War, August 12, 1949, 6 U.S.T. 3316 (emphasis added).

52. *Hamdan v. Rumsfeld*, 165 L. Ed. 2d, 777.

53. Ibid., 831.

54. Ibid., 831–32.

55. Ibid., 833.

56. Ibid., 768–74, 778, 787, 789–91.

57. Ibid., 836.

58. Ibid.

59. Ibid., 837.

60. Ibid.

61. Ibid., 839.

62. Ibid., 840.

63. Ibid.

64. Ibid., 841.

65. See chapter 1.

66. *Boumediene v. Bush* and *Al Odah v. United States*, 553 US 723, 128 S.Ct 2229, 171 L. Ed 2d 41 (2008).

67. *Khalid v. Bush*, 355 F. Supp. 2d 311 (DC 2005).

68. *In re Guantanamo Detainee Cases*, 355 F. Supp 2d 443 (DC 2005).

69. *Boumediene v. Bush*, 476 F. 3d 981 (CADC 2007).

70. *Boumediene v. Bush* and *Al Odah v. United States*, 553 US 723, 128 S.Ct 2229, 171 L. Ed 2d 41, 57 (2008).

71. Ibid., 61.

72. Ibid., 68.

73. Ibid., 65.

74. Ibid., 63–64.

75. Ibid., 64.

76. Ibid., 70.

77. Ibid., 75–76.

78. Ibid., 77.

79. Ibid.

80. Ibid., 77.

81. Ibid.

82. Ibid., 78.

83. Ibid., 78–80.

84. Ibid., 80–81.

85. Ibid., 81.

86. Ibid.

87. Ibid., 84.

88. Ibid., 91.

89. Ibid.

90. Ibid., 92.

91. Ibid., 93.

92. Ibid., 89, 90, 93.
93. Ibid., 95.
94. Ibid.
95. Ibid., 98–99.
96. Ibid., 103.
97. Ibid., 99.
98. Ibid.
99. Ibid., 104.
100. Ibid.
101. Ibid., 104.
102. Ibid.
103. Ibid.
104. Ibid.
105. Ibid., 110.
106. Ibid.
107. Ibid., 111.
108. Ibid., 113.
109. Ibid., 100.
110. Ibid., 102.
111. Ibid., 103.
112. Ibid., 104.
113. Ibid., 106.
114. Ibid., 107.
115. Ibid.
116. Ibid., 108.
117. Ibid., 115.
118. Ibid., 118–19.
119. Ibid., 119.
120. Ibid.
121. Ibid., 126.
122. Ibid., 128.
123. Ibid., 63. See Article I, Section 9, Clause 2 of the U.S. Constitution.
124. Ibid.
125. Ibid., 96–97.

Appendix to Chapter 9

SHAFIQ RASUL, *ET AL.,* PETITIONERS
GEORGE W. BUSH, PRESIDENT OF THE UNITED STATES, *ET AL.*
&
FAWZI KHALID ABDULLAH FAHAD AL ODAH, *ET AL.,*
PETITIONERS
UNITED STATES *ET AL.*
542 US 466 124 S. CT 2686, 159 L. ED 2D 548 (2004)
ARGUED APRIL 20, 2004—DECIDED JUNE 28, 2004

[*Stevens, J.,* joined by Justices *O'Connor, Souter, Ginsburg,* and *Breyer,* held that the judiciary can review the merits of habeas claims by individuals detained at Guantanamo Bay, Cuba, by Presidential designation of such individuals as enemy combatants. Justice *Kennedy* concurred in the judgment. Justice *Scalia,* joined by Chief Justice *Rehnquist* and Justice *Thomas* dissented.]

Justice *Stevens* delivered the opinion of the Court.

These two cases present the narrow but important question whether United States courts lack jurisdiction to consider challenges to the legality of the detention of foreign nationals captured abroad in connection with hostilities and incarcerated at the Guantanamo Bay Naval Base, Cuba.

I

On September 11, 2001, agents of the al Qaeda terrorist network hijacked four commercial airliners and used them as missiles to attack American targets. While one of the four attacks was foiled by the heroism of the plane's passengers, the other three killed approximately 3,000 innocent civilians, destroyed hundreds of millions of dollars of property, and severely damaged the U.S. economy. In response to the attacks, Congress passed a joint resolution authorizing the President to use "all necessary and appropriate force against those nations, organizations, or persons he determines planned, authorized, committed, or aided the terrorist attacks . . . or harbored such organizations or persons." Authorization for Use of Military Force, Pub. L. 107-40, §§1–2, 115 Stat. 224. Acting pursuant to that authorization, the President sent U.S. Armed Forces into Afghanistan to wage a military campaign against al Qaeda and the Taliban regime that had supported it.

Petitioners in these cases are 2 Australian citizens and 12 Kuwaiti citizens who were captured abroad during hostilities between the United States and the Taliban. Since early 2002, the U.S. military has held them—along with, according to the Government's estimate, approximately 640 other non-Americans captured abroad—at the Naval Base at Guantanamo Bay. Brief for United States 6. The United States occupies the Base, which comprises 45 square miles of land and water along the southeast coast of Cuba, pursuant to a 1903 Lease Agreement executed with the newly independent Republic of Cuba in the aftermath of the Spanish-American War. Under the Agreement, "the United States recognizes the continuance of the ultimate sovereignty of the Republic of Cuba over the [leased areas]," while "the Republic of Cuba consents that during the period of the occupation by the United States . . . the United States shall exercise complete jurisdiction and control over and within said areas." In 1934, the parties entered into a treaty providing that, absent an agreement to modify or abrogate the lease, the lease would remain in effect "[s]o long as the United States of America shall not abandon the . . . naval station of Guantanamo."

In 2002, petitioners, through relatives acting as their next friends, filed various actions in the U.S. District Court for the District of Columbia challenging the legality of their detention at the Base. All alleged that none of the petitioners has ever been a combatant against the United States or has ever engaged in any terrorist acts. They also alleged that none has been charged with any wrongdoing, permitted to consult with counsel, or provided access to the courts or any other tribunal. App. 29, 77, 108.

The two Australians, Mamdouh Habib and David Hicks, each filed a petition for writ of habeas corpus, seeking release from custody, access to counsel, freedom from interrogations, and other relief. *Id.*, at 98–99, 124–126. Fawzi Khalid Abdullah Fahad Al Odah and the 11 other Kuwaiti detainees filed a complaint seeking to be informed of the charges against them, to be allowed to meet with their families and with counsel, and to have access to the courts or some other impartial tribunal. *Id.*, at 34. They claimed that denial of these rights violates the Constitution, international law, and treaties of the United States. Invoking the court's jurisdiction under 28 U.S.C. §§1331 and 1350, among other statutory bases, they asserted causes of action under the Administrative Procedure Act, 5 U.S.C. §§555, 702, 706; the Alien Tort Statute, 28 U.S.C. §1350; and the general federal habeas corpus statute, §§2241-2243. App. 19.

Construing all three actions as petitions for writs of habeas corpus, the District Court dismissed them for want of jurisdiction. The court held, in reliance on our opinion in *Johnson* v. *Eisentrager*, 339 U.S. 763 (1950), that "aliens detained outside the sovereign territory of the United States [may not] invok[e] a petition for a writ of habeas corpus." 215 F. Supp. 2d 55, 68 (DC 2002). The Court of Appeals affirmed. Reading *Eisentrager* to hold that "'the privilege of litigation' does not extend to aliens in military custody who have no presence in 'any territory over which the United States is sovereign,'" 321 F.3d 1134, 1144 (CADC 2003) (quoting *Eisentrager*, 339 U.S., at 777–778), it held that the District Court lacked jurisdiction over petitioners' habeas actions, as well as their remaining federal statutory claims that do not sound in habeas. We granted certiorari, 540 U.S. 1003 (2003), and now reverse.

II

Congress has granted federal district courts, "within their respective jurisdictions," the authority to hear applications for habeas corpus by any person who claims to be held "in custody in violation of the Constitution or laws or treaties of the United States." 28 U.S.C. §§2241(a), (c)(3). The statute traces its ancestry to the first grant of federal court jurisdiction: Section 14 of the Judiciary Act of 1789 authorized federal courts to issue the writ of habeas corpus to prisoners "in custody, under or by colour of the authority of the United States, or committed for trial before some court of the same." Act of Sept. 24, 1789, ch. 20, §14, 1 Stat. 82. In 1867, Congress extended the protections of the writ to "all cases where any person may be restrained of his or her liberty in violation of the Constitution, or of any treaty or law of the United States." Act of Feb. 5, 1867, ch. 28, 14 Stat. 385. See *Felker* v. *Turpin*, 518 U.S. 651, 659–660 (1996).

Habeas corpus is, however, "a writ antecedent to statute, . . . throwing its root deep into the genius of our common law." *Williams* v. *Kaiser*, 323 U.S. 471, 484, n. 2 (1945) (internal quotation marks omitted). The writ appeared in English law several centuries ago, became "an integral part of our common-law heritage" by the time the Colonies achieved independence, *Preiser* v. *Rodriguez*, 411 U.S. 475, 485 (1973), and received explicit recognition in the Constitution, which forbids suspension of "[t]he Privilege of the Writ of Habeas Corpus . . . unless when in Cases of Rebellion or Invasion the public Safety may require it," Art. I, §9, cl. 2.

As it has evolved over the past two centuries, the habeas statute clearly has expanded habeas corpus "beyond the limits that obtained during the

17th and 18th centuries." *Swain* v. *Pressley*, 430 U.S. 372, 380, n. 13 (1977). But "[a]t its historical core, the writ of habeas corpus has served as a means of reviewing the legality of Executive detention, and it is in that context that its protections have been strongest." *INS* v. *St. Cyr*, 533 U.S. 289, 301 (2001). See also *Brown* v. *Allen*, 344 U.S. 443, 533 (1953) (Jackson, J., concurring in result) ("The historic purpose of the writ has been to relieve detention by executive authorities without judicial trial"). As Justice Jackson wrote in an opinion respecting the availability of habeas corpus to aliens held in U.S. custody:

> "Executive imprisonment has been considered oppressive and lawless since John, at Runnymede, pledged that no free man should be imprisoned, dispossessed, outlawed, or exiled save by the judgment of his peers or by the law of the land. The judges of England developed the writ of habeas corpus largely to preserve these immunities from executive restraint." *Shaughnessy* v. *United States ex rel. Mezei*, 345 U.S. 206, 218–219 (1953) (dissenting opinion).

Consistent with the historic purpose of the writ, this Court has recognized the federal courts' power to review applications for habeas relief in a wide variety of cases involving Executive detention, in wartime as well as in times of peace. The Court has, for example, entertained the habeas petitions of an American citizen who plotted an attack on military installations during the Civil War, *Ex parte Milligan*, 4 Wall. 2 (1866), and of admitted enemy aliens convicted of war crimes during a declared war and held in the United States, *Ex parte Quirin*, 317 U.S. 1 (1942), and its insular possessions, *In re Yamashita*, 327 U.S. 1 (1946).

The question now before us is whether the habeas statute confers a right to judicial review of the legality of Executive detention of aliens in a territory over which the United States exercises plenary and exclusive jurisdiction, but not "ultimate sovereignty."

III

Respondents' primary submission is that the answer to the jurisdictional question is controlled by our decision in *Eisentrager*. In that case, we held that a Federal District Court lacked authority to issue a writ of habeas corpus to 21 German citizens who had been captured by U.S. forces in China, tried and convicted of war crimes by an American military commission headquartered in Nanking, and incarcerated in the Landsberg Prison in occupied Germany. The Court of Appeals in *Eisentrager* had found jurisdiction, reasoning that "any person who is deprived of his liberty by officials of the United States, acting under purported authority of that Government, and who can show that his confinement is in violation of a prohibition of the Constitution, has a right to the writ." *Eisentrager* v. *Forrestal*, 174 F.2d

961, 963 (CADC 1949). In reversing that determination, this Court summarized the six critical facts in the case:

"We are here confronted with a decision whose basic premise is that these prisoners are entitled, as a constitutional right, to sue in some court of the United States for a writ of *habeas corpus*. To support that assumption we must hold that a prisoner of our military authorities is constitutionally entitled to the writ, even though he (a) is an enemy alien; (b) has never been or resided in the United States; (c) was captured outside of our territory and there held in military custody as a prisoner of war; (d) was tried and convicted by a Military Commission sitting outside the United States; (e) for offenses against laws of war committed outside the United States; (f) and is at all times imprisoned outside the United States." 339 U.S., at 777.

On this set of facts, the Court concluded, "no right to the writ of *habeas corpus* appears." *Id.*, at 781.

Petitioners in these cases differ from the *Eisentrager* detainees in important respects: They are not nationals of countries at war with the United States, and they deny that they have engaged in or plotted acts of aggression against the United States; they have never been afforded access to any tribunal, much less charged with and convicted of wrongdoing; and for more than two years they have been imprisoned in territory over which the United States exercises exclusive jurisdiction and control.

Not only are petitioners differently situated from the *Eisentrager* detainees, but the Court in *Eisentrager* made quite clear that all six of the facts critical to its disposition were relevant only to the question of the prisoners' *constitutional* entitlement to habeas corpus. *Id.*, at 777. The Court had far less to say on the question of the petitioners' *statutory* entitlement to habeas review. Its only statement on the subject was a passing reference to the absence of statutory authorization: "Nothing in the text of the Constitution extends such a right, nor does anything in our statutes." *Id.*, at 768.

Reference to the historical context in which *Eisentrager* was decided explains why the opinion devoted so little attention to question of statutory jurisdiction. In 1948, just two months after the *Eisentrager* petitioners filed their petition for habeas corpus in the U.S. District Court for the District of Columbia, this Court issued its decision in *Ahrens* v. *Clark*, 335 U.S. 188, a case concerning the application of the habeas statute to the petitions of 120 Germans who were then being detained at Ellis Island, New York, for deportation to Germany. The *Ahrens* detainees had also filed their petitions in the U.S. District Court for the District of Columbia, naming the Attorney General as the respondent. Reading the phrase "within their respective jurisdictions" as used in the habeas statute to require the petitioners' presence within the district court's territorial jurisdiction, the Court held that the District of Columbia court lacked jurisdiction to entertain the detainees' claims. *Id.*, at 192. *Ahrens* expressly reserved the question "of what process, if any, a person confined in an area not subject to the jurisdiction of any district court may employ to assert federal rights." *Id.*, 192, n. 4. But as the dissent noted, if the presence of the petitioner in the territorial juris-diction of a federal district court were truly a jurisdictional requirement, there could be only one response to that question. *Id.*, at 209 (opinion of Rutledge, J.).

When the District Court for the District of Columbia reviewed the Ger-man prisoners' habeas application in *Eisentrager*, it thus dismissed their action on the authority of *Ahrens*. See *Eisentrager*, 339 U.S., at 767, 790. Although the Court of Appeals reversed the District Court, it implicitly con-ceded that the District Court lacked jurisdiction under the habeas statute as it had been interpreted in *Ahrens*. The Court of Appeals instead held that petitioners had a constitutional right to habeas corpus secured by the Sus-pension Clause, U.S. Const., Art. I, §9, cl. 2, reasoning that "if a person has a right to a writ of habeas corpus, he cannot be deprived of the privilege by an omission in a federal jurisdictional statute." *Eisentrager* v. *Forrestal*, 174 F. 2d, at 965. In essence, the Court of Appeals concluded that the habeas statute, as construed in *Ahrens*, had created an unconstitutional gap that had to be filled by reference to "fundamentals." 174 F. 2d, at 963. In its review of that decision, this Court, like the Court of Appeals, proceeded from the premise that "nothing in our statutes" conferred federal-court jurisdiction, and accordingly evaluated the Court of Appeals' resort to "fundamentals" on its own terms. 339 U.S., at 768.

Because subsequent decisions of this Court have filled the statutory gap that had occasioned *Eisentrager*'s resort to "fundamentals," persons detained outside the territorial jurisdiction of any federal district court no longer need rely on the Constitution as the source of their right to federal habeas review. In *Braden* v. *30th Judicial Circuit Court of Ky.*, 410 U.S. 484, 495 (1973), this Court held, contrary to *Ahrens*, that the prisoner's presence within the territorial jurisdiction of the district court is not "an invariable prerequisite" to the exercise of district court jurisdiction under the federal habeas statute. Rather, because "the writ of habeas corpus does not act upon the prisoner who seeks relief, but upon the person who holds him in what is alleged to be unlawful custody," a district court acts "within [its] respective jurisdiction" within the meaning of §2241 as long as "the cus-todian can be reached by service of process." 410 U.S., at 494–495. *Braden* reasoned that its departure from the rule of *Ahrens* was warranted in light of developments that "had a profound impact on the continuing vitality of that decision." 410 U.S., at 497. These developments included, notably, decisions of this Court in cases involving habeas petitioners "confined overseas (and thus outside the territory of any district court)," in which the Court "held, if only implicitly, that the petitioners' absence from the district does not present a jurisdictional obstacle to the consideration of the claim." *Id.*, at 498 (citing *Burns* v. *Wilson*, 346 U.S. 137 (1953), rehearing denied, 346 U.S. 844, 851–852 (opinion of Frankfurter, J.); *United States ex rel. Toth* v. *Quarles*, 350 U.S. 11 (1955); *Hirota* v. *MacArthur*, 338 U.S. 197, 199 (1948) (Douglas, J., concurring)). *Braden* thus established that *Ahrens* can no longer be viewed as establishing "an inflexible jurisdictional rule," and is strictly relevant only to the question of the appropriate forum, not to whether the claim can be heard at all. 410 U.S., at 499–500.

Because *Braden* overruled the statutory predicate to *Eisentrager*'s holding, *Eisentrager* plainly does not preclude the exercise of §2241 jurisdiction over petitioners' claims.

IV

Putting *Eisentrager* and *Ahrens* to one side, respondents contend that we can discern a limit on §2241 through application of the "longstanding principle of American law" that congressional legislation is presumed not to have extraterritorial application unless such intent is clearly manifested. *EEOC* v. *Arabian American Oil Co.*, 499 U.S. 244, 248 (1991). Whatever traction the presumption against extraterritoriality might have in other contexts, it certainly has no application to the operation of the habeas statute with respect to persons detained within "the territorial jurisdiction" of the United States. *Foley Bros., Inc.* v. *Filardo*, 336 U.S. 281, 285 (1949). By the express terms of its agreements with Cuba, the United States exercises "complete jurisdiction and control" over the Guantanamo Bay Naval Base, and may continue to exercise such control permanently if it so chooses. 1903 Lease Agreement, Art. III; 1934 Treaty, Art. III. Respondents themselves concede that the habeas statute would create federal-court jurisdiction over the claims of an American citizen held at the base. Tr. of Oral Arg. 27. Considering that the statute draws no distinction between Americans and aliens held in federal custody, there is little reason to think that Congress intended the geographical coverage of the statute to vary depending on the detainee's citizenship. Aliens held at the base, no less than American citizens, are entitled to invoke the federal courts' authority under §2241.

Application of the habeas statute to persons detained at the base is consistent with the historical reach of the writ of habeas corpus. At common law, courts exercised habeas jurisdiction over the claims of aliens detained within sovereign territory of the realm, as well as the claims of persons detained in the so-called "exempt jurisdictions," where ordinary writs did not run, and all other dominions under the sovereign's control. As Lord Mansfield wrote in 1759, even if a territory was "no part of the realm," there was "no doubt" as to the court's power to issue writs of habeas corpus if the territory was "under the subjection of the Crown." *King* v. *Cowle*, 2 Burr. 834,

854–855, 97 Eng. Rep. 587, 598–599 (K. B.). Later cases confirmed that the reach of the writ depended not on formal notions of territorial sovereignty, but rather on the practical question of "the exact extent and nature of the jurisdiction or dominion exercised in fact by the Crown." *Ex parte Mwenya,* [1960] 1 Q. B. 241, 303 (C. A.) (Lord Evershed, M. R.).

In the end, the answer to the question presented is clear. Petitioners contend that they are being held in federal custody in violation of the laws of the United States. No party questions the District Court's jurisdiction over petitioners' custodians. Cf. *Braden,* 410 U.S., at 495. Section 2241, by its terms, requires nothing more. We therefore hold that §2241 confers on the District Court jurisdiction to hear petitioners' habeas corpus challenges to the legality of their detention at the Guantanamo Bay Naval Base.

V

In addition to invoking the District Court's jurisdiction under §2241, the *Al Odah* petitioners' complaint invoked the Court's jurisdiction under 28 U.S. C. §1331, the federal question statute, as well as §1350, the Alien Tort Statute. The Court of Appeals, again relying on *Eisentrager,* held that the District Court correctly dismissed the claims founded on §1331 and §1350 for lack of jurisdiction. . . .

As explained above, *Eisentrager* itself erects no bar to the exercise of federal court jurisdiction over the petitioners' habeas corpus claims. . . . The courts of the United States have traditionally been open to nonresident aliens. Cf. *Disconto Gesellschaft* v. *Umbreit,* 208 U.S. 570, 578 (1908) ("Alien citizens, by the policy and practice of the courts of this country, are ordinarily permitted to resort to the courts for the redress of wrongs and the protection of their rights"). And indeed, 28 U.S.C. §1350 explicitly confers the privilege of suing for an actionable "tort . . . committed in violation of the law of nations or a treaty of the United States" on aliens alone. The fact that petitioners in these cases are being held in military custody is immaterial to the question of the District Court's jurisdiction over their non habeas statutory claims.

VI

Whether and what further proceedings may become necessary after respondents make their response to the merits of petitioners' claims are matters that we need not address now. What is presently at stake is only whether the federal courts have jurisdiction to determine the legality of the Executive's potentially indefinite detention of individuals who claim to be wholly innocent of wrongdoing. Answering that question in the affirmative, we reverse the judgment of the Court of Appeals and remand for the District Court to consider in the first instance the merits of petitioners' claims.
It is so ordered.

SALIM AHMED HAMDAN, PETITIONER
V.
DONALD H. RUMSFELD, SECRETARY OF DEFENSE, *ET AL.*
548 US 557, 126 S.CT. 2749, 165 L. ED. 2D 723 (2006)
ARGUED MARCH 28, 2006—DECIDED JUNE 29, 2006

[Justice *Stevens*, joined by Justices *Souter, Ginsburg, Breyer* and *Kennedy*, announced the judgment of the Court and delivered the opinion of the Court with respect to Parts I through IV, Parts VI through VI–D–iii, Part VI–D–v, and Part VII. Part V of the opinion was joined by Justices *Souter, Ginsburg* and *Breyer*. Justice *Breyer* and *Kennedy* filed concurring opinions. Justices *Thomas, Scalia* and *Alito* all filed dissenting opinions.]

Justice *Stevens* announced the judgment of the Court.

Petitioner Salim Ahmed Hamdan, a Yemeni national, is in custody at an American prison in Guantanamo Bay, Cuba. In November 2001, during hostilities between the United States and the Taliban (which then governed Afghanistan), Hamdan was captured by militia forces and turned over to the U.S. military. In June 2002, he was transported to Guantanamo Bay. Over a year later, the President deemed him eligible for trial by military commission for then-unspecified crimes. After another year had passed, Hamdan was charged with one count of conspiracy "to commit . . . offenses triable by military commission."

Hamdan filed petitions for writs of habeas corpus and mandamus to challenge the Executive Branch's intended means of prosecuting this charge. He concedes that a court-martial constituted in accordance with the Uniform Code of Military Justice (UCMJ), 10 U.S.C. §801 *et seq.* (2000 ed. and Supp. III), would have authority to try him. His objection is that the military commission the President has convened lacks such authority, for two principal reasons: First, neither congressional Act nor the common law of war supports trial by this commission for the crime of conspiracy—an offense that, Hamdan says, is not a violation of the law of war. Second, Hamdan contends, the procedures that the President has adopted to try him violate the most basic tenets of military and international law, including the principle that a defendant must be permitted to see and hear the evidence against him.

The District Court granted Hamdan's request for a writ of habeas corpus. 344 F. Supp. 2d 152 (DC 2004). The Court of Appeals for the District of Columbia Circuit reversed. 415 F. 3d 33 (2005). Recognizing, as we did over a half-century ago, that trial by military commission is an extraordinary measure raising important questions about the balance of powers in our constitutional structure, *Ex parte Quirin*, 317 U.S. 1, 19 (1942), we granted certiorari.

For the reasons that follow, we conclude that the military commission convened to try Hamdan lacks power to proceed because its structure and procedures violate both the UCMJ and the Geneva Conventions. Four of us also conclude, see Part V, *infra*, that the offense with which Hamdan has been charged is not an "offens[e] that by . . . the law of war may be tried by military commissions." 10 U.S.C. §821.

. . .

I

. . .

On November 7, 2005, we granted certiorari to decide whether the military commission convened to try Hamdan has authority to do so, and whether Hamdan may rely on the Geneva Conventions in these proceedings.

II

On February 13, 2006, the Government filed a motion to dismiss the writ of certiorari. The ground cited for dismissal was the recently enacted Detainee Treatment Act of 2005 (DTA), Pub. L. 109–148, 119 Stat. 2739. We postponed our ruling on that motion pending argument on the merits and now deny it.

The DTA, which was signed into law on December 30, 2005, addresses a broad swath of subjects related to detainees. It places restrictions on the treatment and interrogation of detainees in U.S. custody, and it furnishes procedural protections for U.S. personnel accused of engaging in improper interrogation. DTA §§1002–1004, 119 Stat. 2739–2740. It also sets forth certain "procedures for status review of detainees outside the United States." §1005, *id.*, at 2740. Subsections (a) through (d) of §1005 direct the Secretary of Defense to report to Congress the procedures being used by CSRTs to determine the proper classification of detainees held in Guantanamo Bay, Iraq, and Afghanistan, and to adopt certain safeguards as part of those procedures.

Subsection (e) of §1005, which is entitled "Judicial Review of Detention of Enemy Combatants," supplies the basis for the Government's jurisdictional argument. The subsection contains three numbered paragraphs. The first paragraph amends the judicial code as follows:

In general.—Section 2241 of title 28, United States Code,

(1) is amended by adding at the end the following:

. . . .

(e)Except as provided in section 1005 of the Detainee Treatment Act of 2005, no court, justice, or judge shall have jurisdiction to hear or consider—

(1) an application for a writ of habeas corpus filed by or on behalf of an alien detained by the Department of Defense at Guantanamo Bay, Cuba; or

(2) any other action against the United States or its agents relating to any aspect of the detention by the Department of Defense of an alien at Guantanamo Bay, Cuba, who—

(A) is currently in military custody; or

(B) has been determined by the United States Court of Appeals for the District of Columbia Circuit in accordance with the procedures set forth in section 1005(e) of the Detainee Treatment Act of 2005 to have been properly detained as an enemy combatant. §1005(e), *id.*, at 2741–2742.

Paragraph (2) of subsection (e) vests in the Court of Appeals for the District of Columbia Circuit the "exclusive jurisdiction to determine the validity of any final decision of a [CSRT] that an alien is properly designated as an enemy combatant." Paragraph (2) also delimits the scope of that review. See §§1005(e)(2)(C)(i)–(ii), *id.*, at 2742.

Paragraph (3) mirrors paragraph (2) in structure, but governs judicial review of final decisions of military commissions, not CSRTs. It vests in the Court of Appeals for the District of Columbia Circuit "exclusive jurisdiction to determine the validity of any final decision rendered pursuant to Military Commission Order No. 1, dated August 31, 2005 (or any successor military order)." §1005(e)(3)(A), *id.*, at 2743. Review is as of right for any alien sentenced to death or a term of imprisonment of 10 years or more, but is at the Court of Appeals' discretion in all other cases. The scope of review is limited to the following inquiries:

(i) whether the final decision [of the military commission] was consistent with the standards and procedures specified in the military order referred to in subparagraph (A); and

(ii) to the extent the Constitution and laws of the United States are applicable, whether the use of such standards and procedures to reach the final decision is consistent with the Constitution and laws of the United States. §1005(e)(3)(D), *ibid.*

Finally, §1005 contains an "effective date" provision, which reads as follows:

(1) In general.—This section shall take effect on the date of the enactment of this Act.

(2) Review of Combatant Status Tribunal and Military Commission Decisions.—Paragraphs (2) and (3) of subsection (e) shall apply with respect to any claim whose review is governed by one of such paragraphs and that is pending on or after the date of the enactment of this Act." §1005(h), *id.*, at 2743–2744.

The Act is silent about whether paragraph (1) of subsection (e) "shall apply" to claims pending on the date of enactment.

The Government argues that §§1005(e)(1) and 1005(h) had the immediate effect, upon enactment, of repealing federal jurisdiction not just over detainee habeas actions yet to be filed but also over any such actions then pending in any federal court—including this Court. Accordingly, it argues, we lack jurisdiction to review the Court of Appeals' decision below.

Hamdan objects to this theory on both constitutional and statutory grounds. Principal among his constitutional arguments is that the Government's preferred reading raises grave questions about Congress' authority to impinge upon this Court's appellate jurisdiction, particularly in habeas cases. Support for this argument is drawn from *Ex parte Yerger*, 8 Wall. 85 (1869), in which, having explained that "the denial to this court of appellate jurisdiction" to consider an original writ of habeas corpus would "greatly weaken the efficacy of the writ," *id.*, at 102–103, we held that Congress would not be presumed to have effected such denial absent an unmistakably clear statement to the contrary. See *id.*, at 104–105; see also *Felker* v. *Turpin*, 518 U.S. 651 (1996); *Durousseau* v. *United States*, 6 Cranch 307, 314 (1810) (opinion for the Court by Marshall, C.J.) (The "appellate powers of this court" are not created by statute but are "given by the Constitution"); *United States* v. *Klein*, 13 Wall. 128 (1872). Cf. *Ex parte McCardle*, 7 Wall. 506, 514 (1869) (holding that Congress had validly foreclosed one avenue of appellate review where its repeal of habeas jurisdiction, reproduced in the margin, could not have been "a plainer instance of positive exception"). Hamdan also suggests that, if the Government's reading is correct, Congress has unconstitutionally suspended the writ of habeas corpus.

We find it unnecessary to reach either of these arguments. Ordinary principles of statutory construction suffice to rebut the Government's theory—at least insofar as this case, which was pending at the time the DTA was enacted, is concerned.

The Government acknowledges that only paragraphs (2) and (3) of subsection (e) are expressly made applicable to pending cases, see §1005(h) (2), 119 Stat. 2743–2744, but argues that the omission of paragraph (1) from the scope of that express statement is of no moment. This is so, we are told, because Congress' failure to expressly reserve federal courts' jurisdiction over pending cases erects a presumption against jurisdiction, and that presumption is rebutted by neither the text nor the legislative history of the DTA.

The first part of this argument is not entirely without support in our precedents. We have in the past "applied intervening statutes conferring or ousting jurisdiction, whether or not jurisdiction lay when the underlying conduct occurred or when the suit was filed." *Landgraf* v. *USI Film Products*, 511 U.S. 244, 274 (1994) (citing *Bruner* v. *United States*, 343 U.S. 112 (1952); *Hallowell* v. *Commons*, 239 U.S. 506 (1916)); see *Republic of Austria* v. *Altmann*, 541 U.S. 677, 693 (2004). But the "presumption" that these cases have applied is more accurately viewed as the nonapplication of another presumption—viz., the presumption against retroactivity—in certain limited circumstances. If a statutory provision "would operate retroactively" as applied to cases pending at the time the provision was enacted, then "our traditional presumption teaches that it does not govern absent clear congressional intent favoring such a result." *Landgraf*, 511 U.S., at 280. We have explained, however, that, unlike other intervening changes in the law, a jurisdiction-conferring or jurisdiction-stripping statute usually "takes away no substantive right but simply changes the tribunal that is to hear the case." *Hallowell*, 239 U.S., at 508. If that is truly all the statute does, no retroactivity problem arises because the change in the law does not "impair rights a party possessed when he acted, increase a party's liability for past conduct, or impose new duties with respect to transactions already completed." *Landgraf*, 511 U.S., at 280. And if a new rule has no retroactive effect, the presumption against retroactivity will not prevent its application to a case that was already pending when the new rule was enacted.

That does not mean, however, that all jurisdiction-stripping provisions—or even all such provisions that truly lack retroactive effect—must apply to cases pending at the time of their enactment. "[N]ormal rules of construction," including a contextual reading of the statutory language, may dictate otherwise. *Lindh* v. *Murphy*, 521 U.S. 320, 326 (1997). A familiar principle of statutory construction, relevant both in *Lindh* and here, is that a negative inference may be drawn from the exclusion of language from one statutory provision that is included in other provisions of the same statute. See *id.*, at 330; see also, *e.g.*, *Russello* v. *United States*, 464 U.S. 16, 23 (1983) ("'[W]here Congress includes particular language in one section of a statute but omits it in another section of the same Act, it is generally presumed that Congress acts intentionally and purposely in the disparate inclusion or exclusion'"). The Court in *Lindh* relied on this reasoning to conclude that certain limitations on the availability of habeas relief imposed by AE-DPA applied only to cases filed after that statute's effective date. Congress' failure to identify the temporal reach of those limitations, which governed noncapital cases, stood in contrast to its express command in the same legislation that new rules governing habeas petitions in capital cases "apply to cases pending on or after the date of enactment." §107(c), 110 Stat. 1226; see *Lindh*, 521 U.S., at 329–330. That contrast, combined with the fact that the amendments at issue "affect[ed] substantive entitlement to relief," *id.*, at 327, warranted drawing a negative inference.

A like inference follows *a fortiori* from *Lindh* in this case. "If . . . Congress was reasonably concerned to ensure that [§§1005(e)(2) and (3)] be applied to pending cases, it should have been just as concerned about [§1005(e) (1)], unless it had the different intent that the latter [section] not be applied to the general run of pending cases." *Id.*, at 329. If anything, the evidence of deliberate omission is stronger here than it was in *Lindh*. In *Lindh*, the provisions to be contrasted had been drafted separately but were later "joined together and . . . considered simultaneously when the language raising the implication was inserted." *Id.*, at 330. We observed that Congress' tandem review and approval of the two sets of provisions strengthened the presumption that the relevant omission was deliberate. *Id.*, at 331; see also *Field* v. *Mans*, 516 U.S. 59, 75 (1995) ("The more apparently deliberate the contrast, the stronger the inference, as applied, for example, to contrasting statutory sections originally enacted simultaneously in relevant respects"). Here, Congress not only considered the respective temporal reaches of paragraphs (1), (2), and (3) of subsection (e) together at every stage, but omitted paragraph (1) from its directive that paragraphs (2) and (3) apply to pending cases only after having *rejected* earlier proposed versions of the statute that would have included what is now paragraph (1) within the scope of that directive. Compare DTA §1005(h)(2), 119 Stat. 2743–2744, with 151 Cong. Rec. S12655 (Nov. 10, 2005) (S. Amdt. 2515); see *id.*, at S14257–S14258 (Dec. 21, 2005) (discussing similar language proposed in both the House and the Senate). Congress' rejection of the very language that would have achieved the result the Government urges here weighs heavily against the Government's interpretation. See *Doe* v. *Chao*, 540 U.S. 614, 621–623 (2004).

The Government nonetheless offers two reasons why, in its view, no negative inference may be drawn in favor of jurisdiction. First, it asserts that *Lindh* is inapposite because "Section 1005(e)(1) and (h)(1) remove jurisdiction, while Section 1005(e)(2), (3) and (h)(2) create an exclusive review mechanism and define the nature of that review." Reply Brief in Support of Respondents' Motion to Dismiss 4. Because the provisions being contrasted "address wholly distinct subject matters," *Martin* v. *Hadix*, 527 U.S. 343, 356 (1999), the Government argues, Congress' different treatment of them is of no significance.

This argument must fail because it rests on a false distinction between the "jurisdictional" nature of subsection (e)(1) and the "procedural" character of subsections (e)(2) and (e)(3). In truth, all three provisions govern jurisdiction over detainees' claims; subsection (e)(1) addresses jurisdiction in habeas cases and other actions "relating to any aspect of the detention," while subsections (e)(2) and (3) vest exclusive, but limited, *jurisdiction* in the Court of Appeals for the District of Columbia Circuit to review "final decision[s]" of CSRTs and military commissions.

That subsection (e)(1) strips jurisdiction while subsections (e)(2) and (e)(3) restore it in limited form is hardly a distinction upon which a negative inference must founder. Justice Scalia, in arguing to the contrary, maintains that Congress had "ample reason" to provide explicitly for application of subsections (e)(2) and (e)(3) to pending cases because "jurisdiction-stripping" provisions like subsection (e)(1) have been treated differently under our retroactivity jurisprudence than "jurisdiction-conferring" ones like subsections (e)(2) and (e)(3). *Post*, at 8 (dissenting opinion); see also Reply Brief in Support of Respondents' Motion to Dismiss 5–6. That theory is insupportable. Assuming *arguendo* that subsections (e)(2) and (e)(3) "confer *new* jurisdiction (in the D. C. Circuit) where there was none before," *post*, at 8 (emphasis in original); but see *Rasul* v. *Bush*, 542 U.S. 466

(2004), and that our precedents can be read to "strongly indicat[e]" that jurisdiction-creating statutes raise special retroactivity concerns not also raised by jurisdiction-stripping statutes, *post*, at 8, subsections (e)(2) and (e)(3) "confer" jurisdiction in a manner that cannot conceivably give rise to retroactivity questions under our precedents. The provisions impose no additional liability or obligation on any private party or even on the United States, unless one counts the burden of litigating an appeal—a burden not a single one of our cases suggests triggers retroactivity concerns. Moreover, it strains credulity to suggest that the desire to reinforce the application of subsections (e)(2) and (e)(3) to pending cases drove Congress to *exclude* subsection (e)(1) from §1005(h)(2).

The Government's second objection is that applying subsections (e)(2) and (e)(3) but not (e)(1) to pending cases "produces an absurd result" because it grants (albeit only temporarily) dual jurisdiction over detainees' cases in circumstances where the statute plainly envisions that the District of Columbia Circuit will have "*exclusive*" and immediate jurisdiction over such cases. Reply Brief in Support of Respondents' Motion to Dismiss 7. But the premise here is faulty; subsections (e)(2) and (e)(3) grant jurisdiction only over actions to "determine the validity of any final decision" of a CSRT or commission. Because Hamdan, at least, is not contesting any "final decision" of a CSRT or military commission, his action does not fall within the scope of subsection (e)(2) or (e)(3). There is, then, no absurdity.

The Government's more general suggestion that Congress can have had no good reason for preserving habeas jurisdiction over cases that had been brought by detainees prior to enactment of the DTA not only is belied by the legislative history, see n. 10, *supra*, but is otherwise without merit. There is nothing absurd about a scheme under which pending habeas actions—particularly those, like this one, that challenge the very legitimacy of the tribunals whose judgments Congress would like to have reviewed— are preserved, and more routine challenges to final decisions rendered by those tribunals are carefully channeled to a particular court and through a particular lens of review.

Finally, we cannot leave unaddressed Justice Scalia's contentions that the "meaning of §1005(e)(1) is entirely clear," *post*, at 6, and that "the *plain import* of a statute repealing jurisdiction is to eliminate the power to consider and render judgment—in an already pending case no less than in a case yet to be filed," *post*, at 3 (emphasis in original). Only by treating the *Bruner* rule as an inflexible trump (a thing it has never been, see n. 7, *supra*) and ignoring both the rest of §1005's text and its drafting history can one conclude as much. Congress here expressly provided that subsections (e)(2) and (e)(3) applied to pending cases. It chose not to so provide—after having been presented with the option—for subsection (e)(1). The omission is an integral part of the statutory scheme that muddies whatever "plain meaning" may be discerned from blinkered study of subsection (e)(1) alone. The dissent's speculation about what Congress might have intended by the omission not only is counterfactual, cf. n. 10, *supra* (recounting legislative history), but rests on both a misconstruction of the DTA and an erroneous view of our precedents, see *supra*, at 17, and n. 12.

For these reasons, we deny the Government's motion to dismiss.

III

Relying on our decision in *Councilman*, 420 U.S. 738, the Government argues that, even if we have statutory jurisdiction, we should apply the "judge-made rule that civilian courts should await the final outcome of on-going military proceedings before entertaining an attack on those proceedings." Brief for Respondents 12. Like the District Court and the Court of Appeals before us, we reject this argument.

In *Councilman*, an army officer on active duty was referred to a court-martial for trial on charges that he violated the UCMJ by selling, transferring, and possessing marijuana. 420 U.S., at 739–740. Objecting that the alleged offenses were not "'service connected,'" *id.*, at 740, the officer filed suit in Federal District Court to enjoin the proceedings. He neither questioned the lawfulness of courts-martial or their procedures nor disputed that, as a serviceman, he was subject to court-martial jurisdiction. His sole argument was that the subject matter of his case did not fall within the scope of court-martial authority. See *id.*, at 741, 759. The District Court granted his request for injunctive relief, and the Court of Appeals affirmed.

We granted certiorari and reversed. *Id.*, at 761. We did not reach the merits of whether the marijuana charges were sufficiently "service connected" to place them within the subject-matter jurisdiction of a court-martial. Instead, we concluded that, as a matter of comity, federal courts should normally abstain from intervening in pending court-martial proceedings against members of the Armed Forces, and further that there was nothing in the particular circumstances of the officer's case to displace that general rule. See *id.*, at 740, 758.

Councilman identifies two considerations of comity that together favor abstention pending completion of ongoing court-martial proceedings against service personnel. See *New* v. *Cohen*, 129 F. 3d 639, 643 (CADC 1997); see also 415 F. 3d, at 36–37 (discussing *Councilman* and *New*). First, military discipline and, therefore, the efficient operation of the Armed Forces are best served if the military justice system acts without regular interference from civilian courts. See *Councilman*, 420 U.S., at 752. Second, federal courts should respect the balance that Congress struck between military preparedness and fairness to individual service members when it created "an integrated system of military courts and review procedures, a critical element of which is the Court of Military Appeals, consisting of civilian judges 'completely removed from all military influence or persuasion. . . .'" *Id.*, at 758 (quoting H. R. Rep. No. 491, 81st Cong., 1st Sess., p. 7 (1949)). Just as abstention in the face of ongoing state criminal proceedings is justified by our expectation that state courts will enforce federal rights, so abstention in the face of ongoing court-martial proceedings is justified by our expectation that the military court system established by Congress—with its substantial procedural protections and provision for appellate review by independent civilian judges—"will vindicate servicemen's constitutional rights," 420 U.S., at 758. See *id.*, at 755–758.

The same cannot be said here; indeed, neither of the comity considerations identified in *Councilman* weighs in favor of abstention in this case. First, Hamdan is not a member of our Nation's Armed Forces, so concerns about military discipline do not apply. Second, the tribunal convened to try Hamdan is not part of the integrated system of military courts, complete with independent review panels, that Congress has established. Unlike the officer in *Councilman*, Hamdan has no right to appeal any conviction to the civilian judges of the Court of Military Appeals (now called the United States Court of Appeals for the Armed Forces, see Pub. L. 103–337, 108 Stat. 2831). Instead, under Dept. of Defense Military Commission Order No. 1 (Commission Order No. 1), which was issued by the President on March 21, 2002, and amended most recently on August 31, 2005, and which governs the procedures for Hamdan's commission, any conviction would be reviewed by a panel consisting of three military officers designated by the Secretary of Defense. Commission Order No. 1 §6(H)(4). Commission Order No. 1 provides that appeal of a review panel's decision may be had only to the Secretary of Defense himself, §6(H)(5), and then, finally, to the President, §6(H)(6).

We have no doubt that the various individuals assigned review power under Commission Order No. 1 would strive to act impartially and ensure that Hamdan receive all protections to which he is entitled. Nonetheless, these review bodies clearly lack the structural insulation from military influence that characterizes the Court of Appeals for the Armed Forces, and thus bear insufficient conceptual similarity to state courts to warrant invocation of abstention principles.

In sum, neither of the two comity considerations underlying our decision to abstain in *Councilman* applies to the circumstances of this case. Instead, this Court's decision in *Quirin* is the most relevant precedent. In *Quirin*, seven German saboteurs were captured upon arrival by submarine in New York and Florida. 317 U.S., at 21. The President convened a military commission to try the saboteurs, who then filed habeas corpus petitions in the United States District Court for the District of Columbia challenging their trial by commission. We granted the saboteurs' petition for certiorari to the Court of Appeals before judgment. See *id.*, at 19. Far from abstaining pending the conclusion of military proceedings, which were ongoing, we convened a special Term to hear the case and expedited our review. That course of action was warranted, we explained, "[i]n view of the public importance of the questions raised by [the cases] and of the duty which rests on the courts, in time of war as well as in time of peace, to preserve unimpaired the constitutional safeguards of civil liberty, and because in our opinion the public interest required that we consider and decide those questions without any avoidable delay." *Ibid.*

As the Court of Appeals here recognized, *Quirin* "provides a compelling historical precedent for the power of civilian courts to entertain challenges that seek to interrupt the processes of military commissions." 415 F. 3d, at 36. The circumstances of this case, like those in *Quirin*, simply do not implicate the "obligations of comity" that, under appropriate circumstances, justify abstention. *Quackenbush* v. *Allstate Ins. Co.*, 517 U.S. 706, 733 (1996) (Kennedy, J., concurring).

Finally, the Government has identified no other "important countervailing interest" that would permit federal courts to depart from their general "duty to exercise the jurisdiction that is conferred upon them by Congress." *Id.*, at 716 (majority opinion). To the contrary, Hamdan and the Government both have a compelling interest in knowing in advance whether Hamdan may be tried by a military commission that arguably is without any basis in law and operates free from many of the procedural rules prescribed by Congress for courts-martial—rules intended to safeguard the accused and ensure the reliability of any conviction. While we certainly do not foreclose the possibility that abstention may be appropriate in some cases seeking review of ongoing military commission proceedings (such as military commissions convened on the battlefield), the foregoing discussion makes clear that, under our precedent, abstention is not justified here. We therefore proceed to consider the merits of Hamdan's challenge.

IV

The military commission, a tribunal neither mentioned in the Constitution nor created by statute, was born of military necessity. See W. Winthrop, Military Law and Precedents 831 (rev. 2d ed. 1920) (hereinafter Winthrop). Though foreshadowed in some respects by earlier tribunals like the Board of General Officers that General Washington convened to try British Major John André for spying during the Revolutionary War, the commission "as such" was inaugurated in 1847. *Id.*, at 832; G. Davis, A Treatise on the Military Law of the United States 308 (2d ed. 1909) (hereinafter Davis). As commander of occupied Mexican territory, and having available to him no other tribunal, General Winfield Scott that year ordered the establishment of both "'*military commissions*'" to try ordinary crimes committed in the occupied territory and a "*council of war*" to try offenses against the law of war. Winthrop 832 (emphases in original).

When the exigencies of war next gave rise to a need for use of military commissions, during the Civil War, the dual system favored by General Scott was not adopted. Instead, a single tribunal often took jurisdiction over ordinary crimes, war crimes, and breaches of military orders alike. As further discussed below, each aspect of that seemingly broad jurisdiction was in fact supported by a separate military exigency. Generally, though, the need for military commissions during this period—as during the Mexican War—was driven largely by the then very limited jurisdiction of courts-martial: "The *occasion* for the military commission arises principally from the fact that the jurisdiction of the court-martial proper, in our law, is restricted by statute almost exclusively to members of the military force and to certain specific offences defined in a written code." *Id.*, at 831 (emphasis in original).

Exigency alone, of course, will not justify the establishment and use of penal tribunals not contemplated by Article I, §8 and Article III, §1 of the Constitution unless some other part of that document authorizes a response to the felt need. See *Ex parte Milligan*, 4 Wall. 2, 121 (1866) ("Certainly no part of the judicial power of the country was conferred on [military commissions]"); *Ex parte Vallandigham*, 1 Wall. 243, 251 (1864); see also *Quirin*, 317 U.S., at 25 ("Congress and the President, like the courts, possess no power not derived from the Constitution"). And that authority, if it exists, can derive only from the powers granted jointly to the President and Congress in time of war. See *id.*, at 26–29; *In re Yamashita*, 327 U.S. 1, 11 (1946).

The Constitution makes the President the "Commander in Chief" of the Armed Forces, Art. II, §2, cl. 1, but vests in Congress the powers to "declare War . . . and make Rules concerning Captures on Land and Water," Art. I, §8, cl. 11, to "raise and support Armies," *id.*, cl. 12, to "define and punish . . . Offences against the Law of Nations," *id.*, cl. 10, and "To make Rules for the Government and Regulation of the land and naval Forces," *id.*, cl. 14. The interplay between these powers was described by Chief Justice Chase in the seminal case of *Ex parte Milligan*:

> "The power to make the necessary laws is in Congress; the power to execute in the President. Both powers imply many subordinate and auxiliary powers. Each includes all authorities essential to its due exercise. But neither can the President, in war more than in peace, intrude upon the proper authority of Congress, nor Congress upon the proper authority of the President. . . . Congress cannot direct the conduct of campaigns, nor can the President, or any commander under him, without the sanction of Congress, institute tribunals for the trial and punishment of offences, either of soldiers or civilians, unless in cases of a controlling necessity, which justifies what it compels, or at least insures acts of indemnity from the justice of the legislature." 4 Wall., at 139–140.

Whether Chief Justice Chase was correct in suggesting that the President may constitutionally convene military commissions "without the sanction of Congress" in cases of "controlling necessity" is a question this Court has not answered definitively, and need not answer today. For we held in *Quirin* that Congress had, through Article of War 15, sanctioned the use of military commissions in such circumstances. 317 U.S., at 28 ("By the Articles of War, and especially Article 15, Congress has explicitly provided, so far as it may constitutionally do so, that military tribunals shall have jurisdiction to try offenders or offenses against the law of war in appropriate cases"). Article 21 of the UCMJ, the language of which is substantially identical to the old Article 15 and was preserved by Congress after World War II, reads as follows:

> "Jurisdiction of courts-martial not exclusive.
> "The provisions of this code conferring jurisdiction upon courts-martial shall not be construed as depriving military commissions, provost courts, or other military tribunals of concurrent jurisdiction in respect of offenders or offenses that by statute or by the law of war may be tried by such military commissions, provost courts, or other military tribunals." 64 Stat. 115.

We have no occasion to revisit *Quirin*'s controversial characterization of Article of War 15 as congressional authorization for military commissions. Cf. Brief for Legal Scholars and Historians as *Amici Curiae* 12–15. Contrary to the Government's assertion, however, even *Quirin* did not view the authorization as a sweeping mandate for the President to "invoke military commissions when he deems them necessary." Brief for Respondents 17. Rather, the *Quirin* Court recognized that Congress had simply preserved what power, under the Constitution and the common law of war, the President had had before 1916 to convene military commissions—with the express condition that the President and those under his command comply with the law of war. See 317 U.S., at 28–29. That much is evidenced by the Court's inquiry, *following* its conclusion that Congress had authorized military commissions, into whether the law of war had indeed been complied with in that case. See *ibid*.

The Government would have us dispense with the inquiry that the *Quirin* Court undertook and find in either the AUMF or the DTA specific, overriding authorization for the very commission that has been convened to try Hamdan. Neither of these congressional Acts, however, expands the President's authority to convene military commissions. First, while we assume that the AUMF activated the President's war powers, see *Hamdi* v. *Rumsfeld*, 542 U.S. 507 (2004) (plurality opinion), and that those powers include the authority to convene military commissions in appropriate circumstances, see *id.*, at 518; *Quirin*, 317 U.S., at 28–29; see also *Yamashita*, 327 U.S., at 11, there is nothing in the text or legislative history of the AUMF even hinting that Congress intended to expand or alter the authorization set forth in Article 21 of the UCMJ. Cf. *Yerger*, 8 Wall., at 105 ("Repeals by implication are not favored").

Likewise, the DTA cannot be read to authorize this commission. Although the DTA, unlike either Article 21 or the AUMF, was enacted after the President had convened Hamdan's commission, it contains no language authorizing that tribunal or any other at Guantanamo Bay. The DTA obviously "recognize[s]" the existence of the Guantanamo Bay commissions in the weakest sense, Brief for Respondents 15, because it references some of the military orders governing them and creates limited judicial review of their "final decision[s]," DTA §1005(e)(3), 119 Stat. 2743. But the statute also pointedly reserves judgment on whether "the Constitution and laws of the United States are applicable" in reviewing such decisions and whether, if they are, the "standards and procedures" used to try Hamdan and other detainees actually violate the "Constitution and laws." *Ibid.*

Together, the UCMJ, the AUMF, and the DTA at most acknowledge a general Presidential authority to convene military commissions in circumstances where justified under the "Constitution and laws," including the law of war. Absent a more specific congressional authorization, the task of this Court is, as it was in *Quirin*, to decide whether Hamdan's military commission is so justified. It is to that inquiry we now turn.

. . . .

VI

Whether or not the Government has charged Hamdan with an offense against the law of war cognizable by military commission, the commission lacks power to proceed. The UCMJ conditions the President's use of military commissions on compliance not only with the American common law of war, but also with the rest of the UCMJ itself, insofar as applicable, and with the "rules and precepts of the law of nations," *Quirin*, 317 U.S., at 28—including, *inter alia*, the four Geneva Conventions signed in 1949. See *Yamashita*, 327 U.S., at 20–21, 23–24. The procedures that the Government has decreed will govern Hamdan's trial by commission violate these laws.

A

The commission's procedures are set forth in Commission Order No. 1, which was amended most recently on August 31, 2005—after Hamdan's trial had already begun. Every commission established pursuant to Commission Order No. 1 must have a presiding officer and at least three other members, all of whom must be commissioned officers. §4(A)(1). The presiding officer's job is to rule on questions of law and other evidentiary and interlocutory issues; the other members make findings and, if applicable, sentencing decisions. §4(A)(5). The accused is entitled to appointed military counsel and may hire civilian counsel at his own expense so long as such counsel is a U.S. citizen with security clearance "at the level SECRET or higher." §§4(C)(2)–(3).

The accused also is entitled to a copy of the charge(s) against him, both in English and his own language (if different), to a presumption of innocence, and to certain other rights typically afforded criminal defendants in civilian courts and courts-martial. See §§5(A)–(P). These rights are subject, however, to one glaring condition: The accused and his civilian counsel may be excluded from, and precluded from ever learning what evidence was presented during any part of the proceeding that either the Appointing Authority or the presiding officer decides to "close." Grounds for such closure "include the protection of information classified or classifiable . . . ; information protected by law or rule from unauthorized disclosure; the physical safety of participants in Commission proceedings, including prospective witnesses; intelligence and law enforcement sources, methods, or activities; and other national security interests." §6(B)(3). Appointed military defense counsel must be privy to these closed sessions, but may, at the presiding officer's discretion, be forbidden to reveal to his or her client what took place therein. *Ibid.*

Another striking feature of the rules governing Hamdan's commission is that they permit the admission of *any* evidence that, in the opinion of the presiding officer, "would have probative value to a reasonable person." §6(D)(1). Under this test, not only is testimonial hearsay and evidence obtained through coercion fully admissible, but neither live testimony nor witnesses' written statements need be sworn. See §§6(D)(2)(b), (3). Moreover, the accused and his civilian counsel may be denied access to evidence in the form of "protected information" (which includes classified information as well as "information protected by law or rule from unauthorized disclosure" and "information concerning other national security interests," §§6(B)(3), 6(D)(5)(a)(v)), so long as the presiding officer concludes that the evidence is "probative" under §6(D)(1) and that its admission without the accused's knowledge would not "result in the denial of a full and fair trial." §6(D)(5)(b). Finally, a presiding officer's determination that evidence "would not have probative value to a reasonable person" may be overridden by a majority of the other commission members. §6(D)(1).

Once all the evidence is in, the commission members (not including the presiding officer) must vote on the accused's guilt. A two-thirds vote will suffice for both a verdict of guilty and for imposition of any sentence not including death (the imposition of which requires a unanimous vote). §6(F). Any appeal is taken to a three-member review panel composed of military officers and designated by the Secretary of Defense, only one member of which need have experience as a judge. §6(H)(4). The review panel is directed to "disregard any variance from procedures specified in this Order or elsewhere that would not materially have affected the outcome of the trial before the Commission." *Ibid.* Once the panel makes its recommendation to the Secretary of Defense, the Secretary can either remand for further proceedings or forward the record to the President with his recommendation as to final disposition. §6(H)(5). The President then, unless he has delegated the task to the Secretary, makes the "final decision." §6(H)(6). He may change the commission's findings or sentence only in a manner favorable to the accused. *Ibid.*

B

Hamdan raises both general and particular objections to the procedures set forth in Commission Order No. 1. His general objection is that the procedures' admitted deviation from those governing courts-martial itself renders the commission illegal. Chief among his particular objections are that he may, under the Commission Order, be convicted based on evidence he has not seen or heard, and that any evidence admitted against him need not comply with the admissibility or relevance rules typically applicable in criminal trials and court-martial proceedings.

The Government objects to our consideration of any procedural challenge at this stage on the grounds that (1) the abstention doctrine espoused in *Councilman*, 420 U.S. 738, precludes pre-enforcement review of procedural rules, (2) Hamdan will be able to raise any such challenge following a "final decision" under the DTA, and (3) "there is . . . no basis to presume, before the trial has even commenced, that the trial will not be conducted in good faith and according to law." Brief for Respondents 45–46, nn. 20–21. The first of these contentions was disposed of in Part III, *supra*, and neither of the latter two is sound.

First, because Hamdan apparently is not subject to the death penalty (at least as matters now stand) and may receive a sentence shorter than 10 years' imprisonment, he has no automatic right to review of the commission's "final decision" before a federal court under the DTA. See §1005(e)(3), 119 Stat. 2743. Second, contrary to the Government's assertion, there *is* a "basis to presume" that the procedures employed during Hamdan's trial will violate the law: The procedures are described with particularity in Commission Order No. 1, and implementation of some of them has already occurred. One of Hamdan's complaints is that he will be, and *indeed already has been*, excluded from his own trial. See Reply Brief for Petitioner 12; App. to Pet. for Cert. 45a. Under these circumstances, review of the procedures in advance of a "final decision"—the timing of which is left entirely to the discretion of the President under the DTA—is appropriate. We turn, then, to consider the merits of Hamdan's procedural challenge.

C

In part because the difference between military commissions and courts-martial originally was a difference of jurisdiction alone, and in part to protect against abuse and ensure evenhandedness under the pressures of war, the procedures governing trials by military commission historically have been the same as those governing courts-martial. See, *e.g.*, 1 The War of the Rebellion 248 (2d series 1894) (General Order 1 issued during the Civil War required military commissions to "be constituted in a similar manner and their proceedings be conducted according to the same general rules as courts-martial in order to prevent abuses which might otherwise arise"). Accounts of commentators from Winthrop through General Crowder—who drafted Article of War 15 and whose views have been deemed "authoritative" by this Court, *Madsen*, 343 U.S., at 353—confirm as much. As recently as the Korean and Vietnam wars, during which use of military commissions was contemplated but never made, the principle of procedural parity was espoused as a background assumption. See Paust, Antiterrorism Military Commissions: Courting Illegality, 23 *Mich. J. Int'l L.* 1, 3–5 (2001–2002).

There is a glaring historical exception to this general rule. The procedures and evidentiary rules used to try General Yamashita near the end of World War II deviated in significant respects from those then governing courts-martial. See 327 U.S. 1. The force of that precedent, however, has been seriously undermined by post–World War II developments.

Yamashita, from late 1944 until September 1945, was Commanding General of the Fourteenth Army Group of the Imperial Japanese Army, which had exercised control over the Philippine Islands. On September 3, 1945, after American forces regained control of the Philippines, Yamashita surrendered. Three weeks later, he was charged with violations of the law of war. A few weeks after that, he was arraigned before a military commission convened in the Philippines. He pleaded not guilty, and his trial lasted for two months. On December 7, 1945, Yamashita was convicted and sentenced to hang. See *id.*, at 5; *id.*, at 31–34 (Murphy, J., dissenting). This Court upheld the denial of his petition for a writ of habeas corpus.

The procedures and rules of evidence employed during Yamashita's trial departed so far from those used in courts-martial that they generated an unusually long and vociferous critique from two Members of this Court. See *id.*, at 41–81 (Rutledge, J., joined by Murphy, J., dissenting). Among the dissenters' primary concerns was that the commission had free rein to consider all evidence "which in the commission's opinion 'would be of assistance in proving or disproving the charge,' without any of the usual modes of authentication." *Id.*, at 49 (Rutledge, J.).

The majority, however, did not pass on the merits of Yamashita's procedural challenges because it concluded that his status disentitled him to any protection under the Articles of War (specifically, those set forth in Article 38, which would become Article 36 of the UCMJ) or the Geneva Convention of 1929, 47 Stat. 2021 (1929 Geneva Convention). The Court explained that Yamashita was neither a "person made subject to the Articles of War by Article 2" thereof, 327 U.S., at 20, nor a protected prisoner of war being tried for crimes committed during his detention, *id.*, at 21.

At least partially in response to subsequent criticism of General Yamashita's trial, the UCMJ's codification of the Articles of War after World War II expanded the category of persons subject thereto to include defendants in Yamashita's (and Hamdan's) position, and the Third Geneva Convention of 1949 extended prisoner-of-war protections to individuals tried for crimes committed before their capture. See 3 Int'l Comm. of Red Cross, Commentary: Geneva Convention Relative to the Treatment of Prisoners of War 413 (1960) (hereinafter GCIII Commentary) (explaining that Article 85, which extends the Convention's protections to "[p]risoners of war prosecuted under the laws of the Detaining Power for acts committed prior to capture," was adopted in response to judicial interpretations of the 1929 Convention, including this Court's decision in *Yamashita*). The most notorious exception to the principle of uniformity, then, has been stripped of its precedential value.

The uniformity principle is not an inflexible one; it does not preclude all departures from the procedures dictated for use by courts-martial. But any departure must be tailored to the exigency that necessitates it. See Winthrop 835, n. 81. That understanding is reflected in Article 36 of the UCMJ, which provides:

> (a) The procedure, including modes of proof, in cases before courts-martial, courts of inquiry, military commissions, and other military tribunals may be prescribed by the President by regulations which shall, so far as he considers practicable, apply the principles of law and the rules of evidence generally recognized in the trial of criminal cases in the United States district courts, but which may not be contrary to or inconsistent with this chapter.
>
> (b) All rules and regulations made under this article shall be uniform insofar as practicable and shall be reported to Congress. 70A Stat. 50.

Article 36 places two restrictions on the President's power to promulgate rules of procedure for courts-martial and military commissions alike. First, no procedural rule he adopts may be "contrary to or inconsistent with" the UCMJ—however practical it may seem. Second, the rules adopted must be "uniform insofar as practicable." That is, the rules applied to military commissions must be the same as those applied to courts-martial unless such uniformity proves impracticable.

Hamdan argues that Commission Order No. 1 violates both of these restrictions; he maintains that the procedures described in the Commission Order are inconsistent with the UCMJ and that the Government has offered no explanation for their deviation from the procedures governing courts-martial, which are set forth in the Manual for Courts-Martial, United States (2005 ed.) (Manual for Courts-Martial). Among the inconsistencies

Hamdan identifies is that between §6 of the Commission Order, which permits exclusion of the accused from proceedings and denial of his access to evidence in certain circumstances, and the UCMJ's requirement that "[a]ll . . . proceedings" other than votes and deliberations by courts-martial "shall be made a part of the record and shall be in the presence of the accused." 10 U.S.C. A. §839(c) (Supp. 2006). Hamdan also observes that the Commission Order dispenses with virtually all evidentiary rules applicable in courts-martial.

The Government has three responses. First, it argues, only 9 of the UCMJ's 158 Articles—the ones that expressly mention "military commissions"— actually apply to commissions, and Commission Order No. 1 sets forth no procedure that is "contrary to or inconsistent with" those 9 provisions. Second, the Government contends, military commissions would be of no use if the President were hamstrung by those provisions of the UCMJ that govern courts-martial. Finally, the President's determination that "the danger to the safety of the United States and the nature of international terrorism" renders it impracticable "to apply in military commissions ... the principles of law and rules of evidence generally recognized in the trial of criminal cases in the United States district courts," November 13 Order §1(f), is, in the Government's view, explanation enough for any deviation from court-martial procedures. See Brief for Respondents 43–47, and n. 22.

Hamdan has the better of this argument. Without reaching the question whether any provision of Commission Order No. 1 is strictly "contrary to or inconsistent with" other provisions of the UCMJ, we conclude that the "practicability" determination the President has made is insufficient to justify variances from the procedures governing courts-martial. Subsection (b) of Article 36 was added after World War II, and requires a different showing of impracticability from the one required by subsection (a). Subsection (a) requires that the rules the President promulgates for courts-martial, provost courts, and military commissions alike conform to those that govern procedures in Article III courts, "so far as *he considers* practicable." 10 U.S.C. §836(a) (emphasis added). Subsection (b), by contrast, demands that the rules applied in courts-martial, provost courts, and military commissions— whether or not they conform with the Federal Rules of Evidence—be "uniform *insofar as practicable.*" §836(b) (emphasis added). Under the latter provision, then, the rules set forth in the Manual for Courts-Martial must apply to military commissions unless impracticable.

The President here has determined, pursuant to subsection (a), that it is impracticable to apply the rules and principles of law that govern "the trial of criminal cases in the United States district courts," §836(a), to Hamdan's commission. We assume that complete deference is owed that determination. The President has not, however, made a similar official determination that it is impracticable to apply the rules for courts-martial. And even if subsection (b)'s requirements may be satisfied without such an official determination, the requirements of that subsection are not satisfied here.

Nothing in the record before us demonstrates that it would be impracticable to apply court-martial rules in this case. There is no suggestion, for example, of any logistical difficulty in securing properly sworn and authenticated evidence or in applying the usual principles of relevance and admissibility. Assuming *arguendo* that the reasons articulated in the President's Article 36(a) determination ought to be considered in evaluating the impracticability of applying court-martial rules, the only reason offered in support of that determination is the danger posed by international terrorism. Without for one moment underestimating that danger, it is not evident to us why it should require, in the case of Hamdan's trial, any variance from the rules that govern courts-martial.

The absence of any showing of impracticability is particularly disturbing when considered in light of the clear and admitted failure to apply one of the most fundamental protections afforded not just by the Manual for Courts-Martial but also by the UCMJ itself: the right to be present. See 10 U.S.C. A. §839(c) (Supp. 2006). Whether or not that departure technically is "contrary to or inconsistent with" the terms of the UCMJ, 10 U.S.C. §836(a), the jettisoning of so basic a right cannot lightly be excused as "practicable."

Under the circumstances, then, the rules applicable in courts-martial must apply. Since it is undisputed that Commission Order No. 1 deviates in many significant respects from those rules, it necessarily violates Article 36(b).

The Government's objection that requiring compliance with the court-martial rules imposes an undue burden both ignores the plain meaning of Article 36(b) and misunderstands the purpose and the history of military commissions. The military commission was not born of a desire to dispense a more summary form of justice than is afforded by courts-martial; it developed, rather, as a tribunal of necessity to be employed when courts-martial lacked jurisdiction over either the accused or the subject matter. See Winthrop 831. Exigency lent the commission its legitimacy, but did not further justify the wholesale jettisoning of procedural protections. That history explains why the military commission's procedures typically have been the ones used by courts-martial. That the jurisdiction of the two tribunals today may sometimes overlap, see *Madsen*, 343 U.S., at 354, does not detract from the force of this history; Article 21 did not transform the military commission from a tribunal of true exigency into a more convenient adjudicatory tool. Article 36, confirming as much, strikes a careful balance between uniform procedure and the need to accommodate exigencies that may sometimes arise in a theater of war. That Article not having been complied with here, the rules specified for Hamdan's trial are illegal.

D

The procedures adopted to try Hamdan also violate the Geneva Conventions. The Court of Appeals dismissed Hamdan's Geneva Convention challenge on three independent grounds: (1) the Geneva Conventions are not judicially enforceable; (2) Hamdan in any event is not entitled to their protections; and (3) even if he is entitled to their protections, *Councilman* abstention is appropriate. Judge Williams, concurring, rejected the second ground but agreed with the majority respecting the first and the last. As we explained in Part III, *supra*, the abstention rule applied in *Councilman*, 420 U.S. 738, is not applicable here. And for the reasons that follow, we hold that neither of the other grounds the Court of Appeals gave for its decision is persuasive.

i

The Court of Appeals relied on *Johnson* v. *Eisentrager*, 339 U.S. 763 (1950), to hold that Hamdan could not invoke the Geneva Conventions to challenge the Government's plan to prosecute him in accordance with Commission Order No. 1. *Eisentrager* involved a challenge by 21 German nationals to their 1945 convictions for war crimes by a military tribunal convened in Nanking, China, and to their subsequent imprisonment in occupied Germany. The petitioners argued, *inter alia*, that the 1929 Geneva Convention rendered illegal some of the procedures employed during their trials, which they said deviated impermissibly from the procedures used by courts-martial to try American soldiers. See *id.*, at 789. We rejected that claim on the merits because the petitioners (unlike Hamdan here) had failed to identify any prejudicial disparity "between the Commission that tried [them] and those that would try an offending soldier of the American forces of like rank," and in any event could claim no protection, under the 1929 Convention, during trials for crimes that occurred before their confinement as prisoners of war. *Id.*, at 790.

Buried in a footnote of the opinion, however, is this curious statement suggesting that the Court lacked power even to consider the merits of the Geneva Convention argument:

> "We are not holding that these prisoners have no right which the military authorities are bound to respect. The United States, by the Geneva Convention of July 27, 1929, 47 Stat. 2021, concluded with forty-six other countries, including the German Reich, an agreement upon the treatment to be accorded captives. These prisoners claim to be and are entitled to its protection. It is, however, the obvious scheme of the Agreement that responsibility for observance and enforcement of these rights is upon political and military authorities. Rights of alien enemies are vindicated under it only through protests and intervention of protecting powers as the rights of our citizens against foreign governments are vindicated only by Presidential intervention." *Id.*, at 789, n. 14.

The Court of Appeals, on the strength of this footnote, held that "the 1949 Geneva Convention does not confer upon Hamdan a right to enforce its provisions in court." 415 F. 3d, at 40.

Whatever else might be said about the *Eisentrager* footnote, it does not control this case. We may assume that "the obvious scheme" of the 1949 Conventions is identical in all relevant respects to that of the 1929 Convention, and even that that scheme would, absent some other provision of law, preclude Hamdan's invocation of the Convention's provisions as an independent source of law binding the Government's actions and furnishing petitioner with any enforceable right. For, regardless of the nature of the rights conferred on Hamdan, cf. *United States* v. *Rauscher*, 119 U.S. 407 (1886), they are, as the Government does not dispute, part of the law of war. See *Hamdi*, 542 U.S., at 520–521 (plurality opinion). And compliance with the law of war is the condition upon which the authority set forth in Article 21 is granted.

ii

For the Court of Appeals, acknowledgment of that condition was no bar to Hamdan's trial by commission. As an alternative to its holding that Hamdan could not invoke the Geneva Conventions at all, the Court of Appeals concluded that the Conventions did not in any event apply to the armed conflict during which Hamdan was captured. The court accepted the Executive's assertions that Hamdan was captured in connection with the United States' war with al Qaeda and that that war is distinct from the war with the Taliban in Afghanistan. It further reasoned that the war with al Qaeda evades the reach of the Geneva Conventions. See 415 F. 3d, at 41–42. We, like Judge Williams, disagree with the latter conclusion.

The conflict with al Qaeda is not, according to the Government, a conflict to which the full protections afforded detainees under the 1949 Geneva Conventions apply because Article 2 of those Conventions (which appears in all four Conventions) renders the full protections applicable only to "all cases of declared war or of any other armed conflict which may arise between two or more of the High Contracting Parties." 6 U.S. T., at 3318. Since Hamdan was captured and detained incident to the conflict with al Qaeda and not the conflict with the Taliban, and since al Qaeda, unlike Afghanistan, is not a "High Contracting Party"—*i.e.*, a signatory of the Conventions, the protections of those Conventions are not, it is argued, applicable to Hamdan.

We need not decide the merits of this argument because there is at least one provision of the Geneva Conventions that applies here even if the relevant conflict is not one between signatories. Article 3, often referred to as Common Article 3 because, like Article 2, it appears in all four Geneva Conventions, provides that in a "conflict not of an international character occurring in the territory of one of the High Contracting Parties, each Party to the conflict shall be bound to apply, as a minimum," certain provisions protecting "[p]ersons taking no active part in the hostilities, including members of armed forces who have laid down their arms and those placed *hors de combat* by . . . detention." *Id.*, at 3318. One such provision prohibits "the passing of sentences and the carrying out of executions without previous judgment pronounced by a regularly constituted court affording all the judicial guarantees which are recognized as indispensable by civilized peoples." *Ibid.*

The Court of Appeals thought, and the Government asserts, that Common Article 3 does not apply to Hamdan because the conflict with al Qaeda, being "'international in scope,'" does not qualify as a "'conflict not of an international character.'" 415 F. 3d, at 41. That reasoning is erroneous. The term "conflict not of an international character" is used here in contradistinction to a conflict between nations. So much is demonstrated by the "fundamental logic [of] the Convention's provisions on its application." *Id.*, at 44 (Williams, J., concurring). Common Article 2 provides that "the present Convention shall apply to all cases of declared war or of any other armed conflict which may arise between two or more of the High Contracting Parties." 6 U.S. T., at 3318 (Art. 2, ¶1). High Contracting Parties (signatories) also must abide by all terms of the Conventions vis-à-vis one another even if one party to the conflict is a nonsignatory "Power," and must so abide vis-à-vis the nonsignatory if "the latter accepts and applies" those terms. *Ibid.* (Art. 2, ¶3). Common Article 3, by contrast, affords some minimal protection, falling short of full protection under the Conventions, to individuals associated with neither a signatory nor even a nonsignatory "Power" who are involved in a conflict "in the territory of" a signatory. The latter kind of conflict is distinguishable from the conflict described in Common Article 2 chiefly because it does not involve a clash between nations (whether signatories or not). In context, then, the phrase "not of an international character" bears its literal meaning. See, *e.g.,* J. Bentham, *Introduction to the Principles of Morals and Legislation* 6, 296 (J. Burns & H. Hart eds. 1970) (using the term "international law" as a "new though not inexpressive appellation" meaning "betwixt nation and nation"; defining "international" to include "mutual transactions between sovereigns as such"); Commentary on the Additional Protocols to the Geneva Conventions of 12 August 1949, p. 1351 (1987) ("[A] non-international armed conflict is distinct from an international armed conflict because of the legal status of the entities opposing each other").

Although the official commentaries accompanying Common Article 3 indicate that an important purpose of the provision was to furnish minimal protection to rebels involved in one kind of "conflict not of an international character," *i.e.,* a civil war, see GCIII Commentary 36–37, the commentaries also make clear "that the scope of the Article must be as wide as possible," *id.*, at 36. In fact, limiting language that would have rendered Common Article 3 applicable "especially [to] cases of civil war, colonial conflicts, or wars of religion," was omitted from the final version of the Article, which coupled broader scope of application with a narrower range of rights than did earlier proposed iterations. See GCIII Commentary 42–43.

iii

Common Article 3, then, is applicable here and, as indicated above, requires that Hamdan be tried by a "regularly constituted court affording all the judicial guarantees which are recognized as indispensable by civilized peoples." 6 U.S. T., at 3320 (Art. 3, ¶1(d)). While the term "regularly constituted court" is not specifically defined in either Common Article 3 or its accompanying commentary, other sources disclose its core meaning. The commentary accompanying a provision of the Fourth Geneva Convention, for example, defines " 'regularly constituted' " tribunals to include "ordinary military courts" and "definitely exclud[e] all special tribunals." GCIV Commentary 340 (defining the term "properly constituted" in Article 66, which the commentary treats as identical to "regularly constituted"); see also *Yamashita*, 327 U.S., at 44 (Rutledge, J., dissenting) (describing military commission as a court "specially constituted for a particular trial"). And one of the Red Cross' own treatises defines "regularly constituted court" as used in Common Article 3 to mean "established and organized in accordance with the laws and procedures already in force in a country." Int'l Comm. of Red Cross, 1 Customary International Humanitarian Law 355 (2005); see also GCIV Commentary 340 (observing that "ordinary military courts" will "be set up in accordance with the recognized principles governing the administration of justice").

The Government offers only a cursory defense of Hamdan's military commission in light of Common Article 3. See Brief for Respondents, 49–50. As Justice Kennedy explains, that defense fails because "[t]he regular military courts in our system are the courts-martial established by congressional statutes." *Post*, at 8 (opinion concurring in part). At a minimum, a military commission "can be 'regularly constituted' by the standards of our military justice system only if some practical need explains deviations from court-martial practice." *Post*, at 10. As we have explained, see Part VI–C, *supra*, no such need has been demonstrated here.

iv

. . . .

v

Common Article 3 obviously tolerates a great degree of flexibility in trying individuals captured during armed conflict; its requirements are general ones, crafted to accommodate a wide variety of legal systems. But *requirements* they are nonetheless. The commission that the President has convened to try Hamdan does not meet those requirements.

. . .

VII

We have assumed, as we must, that the allegations made in the Government's charge against Hamdan are true. We have assumed, moreover, the truth of the message implicit in that charge—viz., that Hamdan is a dangerous individual whose beliefs, if acted upon, would cause great harm and even death to innocent civilians, and who would act upon those beliefs if given the opportunity. It bears emphasizing that Hamdan does not challenge, and we do not today address, the Government's power to detain him for the duration of active hostilities in order to prevent such harm. But in undertaking to try Hamdan and subject him to criminal punishment, the Executive is bound to comply with the Rule of Law that prevails in this jurisdiction.

The judgment of the Court of Appeals is reversed, and the case is remanded for further proceedings.

It is so ordered.

Justice *Breyer*, joined by Justices *Kennedy, Souter,* and *Ginsburg,* wrote a concurring opinion.

The dissenters say that today's decision would "sorely hamper the President's ability to confront and defeat a new and deadly enemy." They suggest that it undermines our Nation's ability to "preven[t] future attacks" of the grievous sort that we have already suffered. That claim leads me to state briefly what I believe the majority sets forth both explicitly and implicitly at greater length. The Court's conclusion ultimately rests upon a single ground: Congress has not issued the Executive a "blank check." Cf. *Hamdi* v. *Rumsfeld,* 542 U.S. 507, 536 (2004) (plurality opinion). Indeed, Congress has denied the President the legislative authority to create military commissions of the kind at issue here. Nothing prevents the President from returning to Congress to seek the authority he believes necessary.

Where, as here, no emergency prevents consultation with Congress, judicial insistence upon that consultation does not weaken our Nation's ability to deal with danger. To the contrary, that insistence strengthens the Nation's ability to determine—through democratic means—how best to do so. The Constitution places its faith in those democratic means. Our Court today simply does the same.

LAKHDAR BOUMEDIENE, *ET AL.*, PETITIONERS
V.
GEORGE W. BUSH, PRESIDENT OF THE UNITED STATES, *ET AL.*
&
KHALED A. F. AL ODAH, NEXT FRIEND OF FAWZI KHALID
ABDULLAH FAHAD AL ODAH, *ET AL.*, PETITIONERS
V.
UNITED STATES *ET AL.*
553 U.S. 723, 128 S. CT. 2229, 171 L. ED. 2D 41 (2008)
ARGUED DECEMBER 5, 2007—DECIDED JUNE 12, 2008

[Justice *Kennedy*, joined by Justices *Stevens*, *Souter*, *Ginsburg*, and *Breyer*, announced the opinion of the Court, which was joined by a concurring opinion by Justice *Souter*, which was joined by Justices *Ginsburg* and *Breyer*. Chief Justice *Roberts* filed a dissenting opinion, which was joined by Justices *Scalia*, *Thomas*, and *Alito*. Justice *Scalia* filed a dissenting opinion which was joined by the Chief Justice and Justices *Thomas* and *Alito*.]

Justice Kennedy delivered the opinion of the Court.

Petitioners are aliens designated as enemy combatants and detained at the United States Naval Station at Guantanamo Bay, Cuba. There are others detained there, also aliens, who are not parties to this suit.

Petitioners present a question not resolved by our earlier cases relating to the detention of aliens at Guantanamo: whether they have the constitutional privilege of habeas corpus, a privilege not to be withdrawn except in conformance with the Suspension Clause, Art. I, §9, cl. 2. We hold these petitioners do have the habeas corpus privilege. Congress has enacted a statute, the Detainee Treatment Act of 2005 (DTA), 119 Stat. 2739, that provides certain procedures for review of the detainees' status. We hold that those procedures are not an adequate and effective substitute for habeas corpus. Therefore §7 of the Military Commissions Act of 2006 (MCA), 28 U.S. C. A. §2241(e) (Supp. 2007), operates as an unconstitutional suspension of the writ. We do not address whether the President has authority to detain these petitioners nor do we hold that the writ must issue. These and other questions regarding the legality of the detention are to be resolved in the first instance by the District Court.

I

Under the Authorization for Use of Military Force (AUMF), §2(a), 115 Stat. 224, note following 50 U.S.C. §1541 (2000 ed., Supp. V), the President is authorized "to use all necessary and appropriate force against those nations, organizations, or persons he determines planned, authorized, committed, or aided the terrorist attacks that occurred on September 11, 2001, or harbored such organizations or persons, in order to prevent any future acts of international terrorism against the United States by such nations, organizations or persons."

In *Hamdi v. Rumsfeld*, 542 U.S. 507 (2004), five Members of the Court recognized that detention of individuals who fought against the United States in Afghanistan "for the duration of the particular conflict in which they were captured, is so fundamental and accepted an incident to war as to be an exercise of the 'necessary and appropriate force' Congress has authorized the President to use." *Id.*, at 518 (plurality opinion of O'Connor, J.), *id.*, at 588–589 (Thomas, J., dissenting). After *Hamdi*, the Deputy Secretary of Defense established Combatant Status Review Tribunals (CSRTs) to determine whether individuals detained at Guantanamo were "enemy combatants," as the Department defines that term. See App. to Pet. for Cert. in No. 06–1195, p. 81a. A later memorandum established procedures to implement the CSRTs. See App. to Pet. for Cert. in No. 06–1196, p. 147. The Government maintains these procedures were designed to comply with the due process requirements identified by the plurality in *Hamdi*. See Brief for Respondents 10.

Interpreting the AUMF, the Department of Defense ordered the detention of these petitioners, and they were transferred to Guantanamo. Some of these individuals were apprehended on the battlefield in Afghanistan, others in places as far away from there as Bosnia and Gambia. All are foreign nationals, but none is a citizen of a nation now at war with the United States. Each denies he is a member of the al Qaeda terrorist network that carried out the September 11 attacks or of the Taliban regime that provided sanctuary for al Qaeda. Each petitioner appeared before a separate CSRT; was determined to be an enemy combatant; and has sought a writ of habeas corpus in the United States District Court for the District of Columbia.

The first actions commenced in February 2002. The District Court ordered the cases dismissed for lack of jurisdiction because the naval station is outside the sovereign territory of the United States. See *Rasul v. Bush*, 215 F. Supp. 2d 55 (2002). The Court of Appeals for the District of Columbia Circuit affirmed. See *Al Odah v. United States*, 321 F. 3d 1134, 1145 (2003). We granted certiorari and reversed, holding that 28 U.S.C. §2241 extended statutory habeas corpus jurisdiction to Guantanamo. See *Rasul v. Bush*, 542 U.S. 466, 473 (2004). The constitutional issue presented in the instant cases was not reached in *Rasul. Id.*, at 476.

After *Rasul*, petitioners' cases were consolidated and entertained in two separate proceedings. In the first set of cases, Judge Richard J. Leon granted the Government's motion to dismiss, holding that the detainees had no rights that could be vindicated in a habeas corpus action. In the second set of cases Judge Joyce Hens Green reached the opposite conclusion, holding the detainees had rights under the Due Process Clause of the Fifth Amendment. See *Khalid v. Bush*, 355 F. Supp. 2d 311, 314 (DC 2005); *In re Guantanamo Detainee Cases*, 355 F. Supp. 2d 443, 464 (DC 2005).

While appeals were pending from the District Court decisions, Congress passed the DTA. Subsection (e) of §1005 of the DTA amended 28 U.S.C. §2241 to provide that "no court, justice, or judge shall have jurisdiction to hear or consider . . . an application for a writ of habeas corpus filed by or on behalf of an alien detained by the Department of Defense at Guantanamo Bay, Cuba." 119 Stat. 2742. Section 1005 further provides that the Court of Appeals for the District of Columbia Circuit shall have "exclusive" jurisdiction to review decisions of the CSRTs. *Ibid.*

In *Hamdan* v. *Rumsfeld,* 548 U.S. 557, 576–577 (2006), the Court held this provision did not apply to cases (like petitioners') pending when the DTA was enacted. Congress responded by passing the MCA, 10 U.S.C.A. §948a *et seq.* (Supp. 2007), which again amended §2241. The text of the statutory amendment is discussed below. See Part II, *infra.* (Four Members of the *Hamdan* majority noted that "[n]othing prevent[ed] the President from returning to Congress to seek the authority he believes necessary." 548 U.S., at 636 (Breyer, J., concurring). The authority to which the concurring opinion referred was the authority to "create military commissions of the kind at issue" in the case. *Ibid.* Nothing in that opinion can be construed as an invitation for Congress to suspend the writ.)

Petitioners' cases were consolidated on appeal, and the parties filed supplemental briefs in light of our decision in *Hamdan.* The Court of Appeals' ruling, 476 F. 3d 981 (CADC 2007), is the subject of our present review and today's decision.

The Court of Appeals concluded that MCA §7 must be read to strip from it, and all federal courts, jurisdiction to consider petitioners' habeas corpus applications, *id.,* at 987; that petitioners are not entitled to the privilege of the writ or the protections of the Suspension Clause, *id.,* at 990–991; and, as a result, that it was unnecessary to consider whether Congress provided an adequate and effective substitute for habeas corpus in the DTA.

We granted certiorari. 551 U.S. ___ (2007).

II

As a threshold matter, we must decide whether MCA §7 denies the federal courts jurisdiction to hear habeas corpus actions pending at the time of its enactment. We hold the statute does deny that jurisdiction, so that, if the statute is valid, petitioners' cases must be dismissed.

As amended by the terms of the MCA, 28 U.S.C.A. §2241(e) (Supp. 2007) now provides:

"(1) No court, justice, or judge shall have jurisdiction to hear or consider an application for a writ of habeas corpus filed by or on behalf of an alien detained by the United States who has been determined by the United States to have been properly detained as an enemy combatant or is awaiting such determination.

"(2) Except as provided in [§§1005(e)(2) and (e)(3) of the DTA] no court, justice, or judge shall have jurisdiction to hear or consider any other action against the United States or its agents relating to any aspect of the detention, transfer, treatment, trial, or conditions of confinement of an alien who is or was detained by the United States and has been determined by the United States to have been properly detained as an enemy combatant or is awaiting such determination."

Section 7(b) of the MCA provides the effective date for the amendment of §2241(e). It states:

"The amendment made by [MCA §7(a)] shall take effect on the date of the enactment of this Act, and shall apply to all cases, without exception, pending on or after the date of the enactment of this Act which relate to any aspect of the detention, transfer, treatment, trial, or conditions of detention of an alien detained by the United States since September 11, 2001." 120 Stat. 2636.

There is little doubt that the effective date provision applies to habeas corpus actions. Those actions, by definition, are cases "which relate to . . . detention." See Black's Law Dictionary 728 (8th ed. 2004) (defining habeas corpus as "[a] writ employed to bring a person before a court, most frequently to ensure that the party's imprisonment or detention is not illegal"). Petitioners argue, nevertheless, that MCA §7(b) is not a sufficiently clear statement of congressional intent to strip the federal courts of jurisdiction in pending cases. See *Ex parte Yerger*, 8 Wall. 85, 102–103 (1869). We disagree. . . .

We acknowledge, moreover, the litigation history that prompted Congress to enact the MCA. In *Hamdan* the Court found it unnecessary to address the petitioner's Suspension Clause arguments but noted the relevance of the clear statement rule in deciding whether Congress intended to reach pending habeas corpus cases. See 548 U.S., at 575 (Congress should "not be presumed to have effected such denial [of habeas relief] absent an unmistakably clear statement to the contrary"). This interpretive rule facilitates a dialogue between Congress and the Court. Cf. *Hilton v. South Carolina Public Railways Comm'n*, 502 U.S. 197, 206 (1991); H. Hart & A. Sacks, *The Legal Process: Basic Problems in the Making and Application of Law*, 1209–1210 (W. Eskridge & P. Frickey eds. 1994). If the Court invokes a clear statement rule to advise that certain statutory interpretations are favored in order to avoid constitutional difficulties, Congress can make an informed legislative choice either to amend the statute or to retain its existing text. If Congress amends, its intent must be respected even if a difficult constitutional question is presented. The usual presumption is that Members of Congress, in accord with their oath of office, considered the constitutional issue and determined the amended statute to be a lawful one; and the Judiciary, in light of that determination, proceeds to its own independent judgment on the constitutional question when required to do so in a proper case.

If this ongoing dialogue between and among the branches of Government is to be respected, we cannot ignore that the MCA was a direct response to *Hamdan*'s holding that the DTA's jurisdiction-stripping provision had no application to pending cases. The Court of Appeals was correct to take note of the legislative history when construing the statute, see 476 F. 3d, at 986, n. 2 (citing relevant floor statements); and we agree with its conclusion that the MCA deprives the federal courts of jurisdiction to entertain the habeas corpus actions now before us.

III

In deciding the constitutional questions now presented we must determine whether petitioners are barred from seeking the writ or invoking the protections of the Suspension Clause either because of their status, *i.e.*, petitioners' designation by the Executive Branch as enemy combatants, or their physical location, *i.e.*, their presence at Guantanamo Bay. The Government contends that noncitizens designated as enemy combatants and detained in territory located outside our Nation's borders have no constitutional rights and no privilege of habeas corpus. Petitioners contend they do have cognizable constitutional rights and that Congress, in seeking to eliminate recourse to habeas corpus as a means to assert those rights, acted in violation of the Suspension Clause.

We begin with a brief account of the history and origins of the writ. Our account proceeds from two propositions. First, protection for the privilege of habeas corpus was one of the few safeguards of liberty specified in a Constitution that, at the outset, had no Bill of Rights. In the system conceived by the Framers the writ had a centrality that must inform proper interpretation of the Suspension Clause. Second, to the extent there were settled precedents or legal commentaries in 1789 regarding the extraterritorial scope of the writ or its application to enemy aliens, those authorities can be instructive for the present cases.

A

The Framers viewed freedom from unlawful restraint as a fundamental precept of liberty, and they understood the writ of habeas corpus as a vital instrument to secure that freedom. Experience taught, however, that the common-law writ all too often had been insufficient to guard against the abuse of monarchial power. That history counseled the necessity for specific language in the Constitution to secure the writ and ensure its place in our legal system.

Magna Carta decreed that no man would be imprisoned contrary to the law of the land. Art. 39, in *Sources of Our Liberties*, 17 (R. Perry & J. Cooper eds. 1959) ("No free man shall be taken or imprisoned or dispossessed, or outlawed, or banished, or in any way destroyed, nor will we go upon him, nor send upon him, except by the legal judgment of his peers or by the law of the land"). Important as the principle was, the Barons at Runnymede prescribed no specific legal process to enforce it. Holdsworth tells us, however, that gradually the writ of habeas corpus became the means by which the promise of Magna Carta was fulfilled. 9 W. Holdsworth, A *History of English Law*, 112 (1926) (hereinafter Holdsworth).

. . . The writ was known and used in some form at least as early as the reign of Edward I. *Id.*, at 108–125. Yet at the outset it was used to protect not the rights of citizens but those of the King and his courts. The early courts were considered agents of the Crown, designed to assist the King in the exercise of his power. . . . Over time it became clear that by issuing the writ of habeas corpus common-law courts sought to enforce the King's prerogative to inquire into the authority of a jailer to hold a prisoner. . . .

Even so, from an early date it was understood that the King, too, was subject to the law. As the writers said of Magna Carta, "it means this, that the king is and shall be below the law." 1 F. Pollock & F. Maitland, *History of English Law*, 173 (2d ed. 1909); see also 2 Bracton *On the Laws and Customs of England*, 33 (S. Thorne transl. 1968) ("The king must not be under man but under God and under the law, because law makes the king"). And, by the 1600s, the writ was deemed less an instrument of the King's power and more a restraint upon it [citation omitted].

Still, the writ proved to be an imperfect check. Even when the importance of the writ was well understood in England, habeas relief often was denied by the courts or suspended by Parliament. Denial or suspension occurred in times of political unrest, to the anguish of the imprisoned and the outrage of those in sympathy with them.

A notable example from this period was *Darnel's Case*, 3 How. St. Tr. 1 (K. B. 1627). The events giving rise to the case began when, in a display of the Stuart penchant for authoritarian excess, Charles I demanded that Darnel and at least four others lend him money. Upon their refusal, they were imprisoned. The prisoners sought a writ of habeas corpus; and the King filed a return in the form of a warrant signed by the Attorney General. *Ibid.* The court held this was a sufficient answer and justified the subjects' continued imprisonment. *Id.*, at 59.

There was an immediate outcry of protest. The House of Commons promptly passed the Petition of Right, 3 Car. 1, ch. 1 (1627), 5 Statutes of the Realm 23, 24 (reprint 1963), which condemned executive "imprison[ment] without any cause" shown, and declared that "no freeman in any such manner as is before mencioned [shall] be imprisoned or deteined." Yet a full legislative response was long delayed. The King soon began to abuse his authority again, and Parliament was dissolved. See W. Hall & R. Albion, *A History of England and the British Empire*, 328 (3d ed. 1953) (hereinafter Hall

& Albion). When Parliament reconvened in 1640, it sought to secure access to the writ by statute. The Act of 1640 . . . expressly authorized use of the writ to test the legality of commitment by command or warrant of the King or the Privy Council . . . and not until 1679 did Parliament try once more to secure the writ, this time through the Habeas Corpus Act of 1679. . . . The Act, which later would be described by Blackstone as the "stable bulwark of our liberties," . . . established procedures for issuing the writ; and it was the model upon which the habeas statutes of the 13 American Colonies were based, see Collings, *supra*, at 338–339.

This history was known to the Framers. It no doubt confirmed their view that pendular swings to and away from individual liberty were endemic to undivided, uncontrolled power. The Framers' inherent distrust of governmental power was the driving force behind the constitutional plan that allocated powers among three independent branches. This design serves not only to make Government accountable but also to secure individual liberty. . . . Because the Constitution's separation-of-powers structure, like the substantive guarantees of the Fifth and Fourteenth Amendments, see *Yick Wo* v. *Hopkins*, 118 U.S. 356, 374 (1886), protects persons as well as citizens, foreign nationals who have the privilege of litigating in our courts can seek to enforce separation-of-powers principles, see, *e.g.*, *INS* v. *Chadha*, 462 U.S. 919, 958–959 (1983).

That the Framers considered the writ a vital instrument for the protection of individual liberty is evident from the care taken to specify the limited grounds for its suspension: "The Privilege of the Writ of Habeas Corpus shall not be suspended, unless when in Cases of Rebellion or Invasion the public Safety may require it." Art. I, §9, cl. 2 . . . The word "privilege" was used, perhaps, to avoid mentioning some rights to the exclusion of others. (Indeed, the only mention of the term "right" in the Constitution, as ratified, is in its clause giving Congress the power to protect the rights of authors and inventors. See Art. I, §8, cl. 8.)

Surviving accounts of the ratification debates provide additional evidence that the Framers deemed the writ to be an essential mechanism in the separation-of-powers scheme. In a critical exchange with Patrick Henry at the Virginia ratifying convention Edmund Randolph referred to the Suspension Clause as an "exception" to the "power given to Congress to regulate courts." See 3 *Debates in the Several State Conventions on the Adoption of the Federal Constitution*, 460–464 (J. Elliot 2d ed. 1876) (hereinafter Elliot's Debates). A resolution passed by the New York ratifying convention made clear its understanding that the Clause not only protects against arbitrary suspensions of the writ but also guarantees an affirmative right to judicial inquiry into the causes of detention. See Resolution of the New York Ratifying Convention (July 26, 1788), in 1 Elliot's Debates 328 (noting the convention's understanding "[t]hat every person restrained of his liberty is entitled to an inquiry into the lawfulness of such restraint, and to a removal thereof if unlawful; and that such inquiry or removal ought not to be denied or delayed, except when, on account of public danger, the Congress shall suspend the privilege of the writ of *habeas corpus*"). Alexander Hamilton likewise explained that by providing the detainee a judicial forum to challenge detention, the writ preserves limited government. As he explained in Federalist No. 84:

> "[T]he practice of arbitrary imprisonments, have been, in all ages, the favorite and most formidable instruments of tyranny. The observations of the judicious Blackstone . . . are well worthy of recital: 'To bereave a man of life . . . or by violence to confiscate his estate, without accusation or trial, would be so gross and notorious an act of despotism as must at once convey the alarm of tyranny throughout the whole nation; but confinement of the person, by secretly hurrying him to jail, where his sufferings are unknown or forgotten, is a less public, a less striking, and therefore a *more dangerous engine* of arbitrary government.' And as a remedy for this fatal evil he is everywhere peculiarly emphatical in his encomiums on the *habeas corpus* act, which in one place he calls 'the bulwark of the British Constitution.'" C. Rossiter ed., p. 512 (1961) (quoting 1 Blackstone *136, 4 *id.*, at *438).

Post-1789 habeas developments in England, though not bearing upon the Framers' intent, do verify their foresight. Those later events would underscore the need for structural barriers against arbitrary suspensions of the writ. Just as the writ had been vulnerable to executive and parliamentary encroachment on both sides of the Atlantic before the American Revolution, despite the Habeas Corpus Act of 1679, the writ was suspended with frequency in England during times of political unrest after 1789. . . .

In our own system the Suspension Clause is designed to protect against these cyclical abuses. The Clause protects the rights of the detained by a means consistent with the essential design of the Constitution. It ensures that, except during periods of formal suspension, the Judiciary will have a time-tested device, the writ, to maintain the "delicate balance of governance" that is itself the surest safeguard of liberty. See *Hamdi*, 542 U.S., at 536 (plurality opinion). The Clause protects the rights of the detained by affirming the duty and authority of the Judiciary to call the jailer to account. See *Preiser* v. *Rodriguez*, 411 U.S. 475, 484 (1973) ("[T]he essence of habeas corpus is an attack by a person in custody upon the legality of that custody"); cf. *In re Jackson*, 15 Mich. 417, 439–440 (1867) (Cooley, J., concurring) ("The important fact to be observed in regard to the mode of procedure upon this [habeas] writ is, that it is directed to, and served upon, not the person confined, but his jailer"). The separation-of-powers doctrine, and the history that influenced its design, therefore must inform the reach and purpose of the Suspension Clause.

B

The broad historical narrative of the writ and its function is central to our analysis, but we seek guidance as well from founding-era authorities addressing the specific question before us: whether foreign nationals, apprehended and detained in distant countries during a time of serious threats to our Nation's security, may assert the privilege of the writ and seek its protection. The Court has been careful not to foreclose the possibility that the protections of the Suspension Clause have expanded along with post-1789 developments that define the present scope of the writ. See *INS* v. *St. Cyr*, 533 U.S. 289, 300–301 (2001). But the analysis may begin with precedents as of 1789, for the Court has said that "at the absolute minimum" the Clause protects the writ as it existed when the Constitution was drafted and ratified. *Id.*, at 301.

To support their arguments, the parties in these cases have examined historical sources to construct a view of the common-law writ as it existed in 1789—as have *amici* whose expertise in legal history the Court has relied upon in the past. See Brief for Legal Historians as *Amici Curiae*; see also *St. Cyr, supra*, at 302, n. 16. The Government argues the common-law writ ran only to those territories over which the Crown was sovereign. See Brief for Respondents 27. Petitioners argue that jurisdiction followed the King's officers. See Brief for Petitioner Boumediene et al. 11. Diligent search by all parties reveals no certain conclusions. In none of the cases cited do we find that a common-law court would or would not have granted, or refused to hear for lack of jurisdiction, a petition for a writ of habeas corpus brought by a prisoner deemed an enemy combatant, under a standard like the one the Department of Defense has used in these cases, and when held in a territory, like Guantanamo, over which the Government has total military and civil control.

We know that at common law a petitioner's status as an alien was not a categorical bar to habeas corpus relief. . . . We know as well that common-law courts entertained habeas petitions brought by enemy aliens detained in England—"entertained" at least in the sense that the courts held hearings to determine the threshold question of entitlement to the writ. . . .

We find the evidence as to the geographic scope of the writ at common law informative, but, again, not dispositive. Petitioners argue the site of their detention is analogous to two territories outside of England to which the writ did run: the so-called "exempt jurisdictions," like the Channel Islands; and (in former times) India. There are critical differences between these places and Guantanamo, however. . . .

Each side in the present matter argues that the very lack of a precedent on point supports its position. The Government points out there is no evidence that a court sitting in England granted habeas relief to an enemy alien detained abroad; petitioners respond there is no evidence that a court refused to do so for lack of jurisdiction.

Both arguments are premised, however, upon the assumption that the historical record is complete and that the common law, if properly understood, yields a definite answer to the questions before us. There are reasons to doubt both assumptions. Recent scholarship points to the inherent shortcomings in the historical record. . . . We decline, therefore, to infer too much, one way or the other, from the lack of historical evidence on point. . . .

IV

Drawing from its position that at common law the writ ran only to territories over which the Crown was sovereign, the Government says the Suspension Clause affords petitioners no rights because the United States does not claim sovereignty over the place of detention.

Guantanamo Bay is not formally part of the United States. See DTA §1005(g), 119 Stat. 2743. And under the terms of the lease between the United States and Cuba, Cuba retains "ultimate sovereignty" over the territory while the United States exercises "complete jurisdiction and control." See Lease of Lands for Coaling and Naval Stations, Feb. 23, 1903, U.S.-Cuba, Art. III, T. S. No. 418 (hereinafter 1903 Lease Agreement); *Rasul*, 542 U.S., at 471. Under the terms of the 1934 Treaty, however, Cuba effectively has no rights as a sovereign until the parties agree to modification of the 1903 Lease Agreement or the United States abandons the base. See Treaty Defining Relations with Cuba, May 29, 1934, U.S.-Cuba, Art. III, 48 Stat. 1683, T. S. No. 866.

The United States contends, nevertheless, that Guantanamo is not within its sovereign control. This was the Government's position well before the events of September 11, 2001. See, *e.g.*, Brief for Petitioners in *Sale* v. *Haitian Centers Council, Inc.*, O. T. 1992, No. 92–344, p. 31 (arguing that Guantanamo is territory "*outside* the United States"). And in other contexts the Court has held that questions of sovereignty are for the political branches to decide. See *Vermilya-Brown Co.* v. *Connell*, 335 U.S, 377, 380 (1948) ("[D]etermination of sovereignty over an area is for the legislative and executive departments"); see also *Jones* v. *United States*, 137 U.S. 202 (1890); *Williams* v. *Suffolk Ins. Co.*, 13 Pet. 415, 420 (1839). Even if this were a treaty interpretation case that did not involve a political question, the President's construction of the lease agreement would be entitled to great respect. See *Sumitomo Shoji America, Inc.* v. *Avagliano*, 457 U.S. 176, 184–185 (1982).

We therefore do not question the Government's position that Cuba, not the United States, maintains sovereignty, in the legal and technical sense of the term, over Guantanamo Bay. But this does not end the analysis. Our cases do not hold it is improper for us to inquire into the objective degree of control the Nation asserts over foreign territory. As commentators have noted, "'Sovereignty' is a term used in many senses and is much abused." See 1 Restatement (Third) of Foreign Relations Law of the United States, §206,

Comment *b*, p. 94 (1986). When we have stated that sovereignty is a political question, we have referred not to sovereignty in the general, colloquial sense, meaning the exercise of dominion or power . . . , but sovereignty in the narrow, legal sense of the term, meaning a claim of right. . . . Indeed, it is not altogether uncommon for a territory to be under the *de jure* sovereignty of one nation, while under the plenary control, or practical sovereignty, of another. . . . Accordingly, for purposes of our analysis, we accept the Government's position that Cuba, and not the United States, retains *de jure* sovereignty over Guantanamo Bay. As we did in *Rasul*, however, we take notice of the obvious and uncontested fact that the United States, by virtue of its complete jurisdiction and control over the base, maintains *de facto* sovereignty over this territory. See 542 U.S., at 480; *id.*, at 487 (Kennedy, J., concurring in judgment).

Were we to hold that the present cases turn on the political question doctrine, we would be required first to accept the Government's premise that *de jure* sovereignty is the touchstone of habeas corpus jurisdiction. This premise, however, is unfounded. For the reasons indicated above, the history of common-law habeas corpus provides scant support for this proposition; and, for the reasons indicated below, that position would be inconsistent with our precedents and contrary to fundamental separation-of-powers principles.

A

The Court has discussed the issue of the Constitution's extraterritorial application on many occasions. These decisions undermine the Government's argument that, at least as applied to noncitizens, the Constitution necessarily stops where *de jure* sovereignty ends.

The Framers foresaw that the United States would expand and acquire new territories. See *American Ins. Co.* v. *356 Bales of Cotton*, 1 Pet. 511, 542 (1828). Article IV, §3, cl. 1, grants Congress the power to admit new States. Clause 2 of the same section grants Congress the "Power to dispose of and make all needful Rules and Regulations respecting the Territory or other Property belonging to the United States." Save for a few notable (and notorious) exceptions, *e.g.*, *Dred Scott* v. *Sandford*, 19 How. 393 (1857), throughout most of our history there was little need to explore the outer boundaries of the Constitution's geographic reach. When Congress exercised its power to create new territories, it guaranteed constitutional protections to the inhabitants by statute. . . .

Fundamental questions regarding the Constitution's geographic scope first arose at the dawn of the 20th century when the Nation acquired noncontiguous Territories: Puerto Rico, Guam, and the Philippines—ceded to the United States by Spain at the conclusion of the Spanish-American War—and Hawaii—annexed by the United States in 1898. At this point Congress chose to discontinue its previous practice of extending constitutional rights to the territories by statute. . . .

In a series of opinions later known as the Insular Cases, the Court addressed whether the Constitution, by its own force, applies in any territory that is not a State. See *De Lima* v. *Bidwell*, 182 U.S. 1 (1901); *Dooley* v. *United States*, 182 U.S. 222 (1901); *Armstrong* v. *United States*, 182 U.S. 243 (1901); *Downes* v. *Bidwell*, 182 U.S. 244 (1901); *Hawaii* v. *Mankichi*, 190 U.S. 197 (1903); *Dorr* v. *United States*, 195 U.S. 138 (1904). The Court held that the Constitution has independent force in these territories, a force not contingent upon acts of legislative grace. Yet it took note of the difficulties inherent in that position. . . .

These considerations resulted in the doctrine of territorial incorporation, under which the Constitution applies in full in incorporated Territories surely destined for statehood but only in part in unincorporated Territories. . . . As the Court later made clear, "the real issue in the *Insular Cases* was not whether the Constitution extended to the Philippines or Porto Rico when we went there, but which of its provisions were applicable by way of limitation upon the exercise of executive and legislative power in dealing with new conditions and requirements." *Balzac* v. *Porto Rico*, 258 U.S. 298, 312 (1922). It may well be that over time the ties between the United States and any of its unincorporated Territories strengthen in ways that are of constitutional significance. Cf. *Torres* v. *Puerto Rico*, 442 U.S. 465, 475–476 (1979) (Brennan, J., concurring in judgment) ("Whatever the validity of the [Insular Cases] in the particular historical context in which they were decided, those cases are clearly not authority for questioning the application of the Fourth Amendment—or any other provision of the Bill of Rights—to the Commonwealth of Puerto Rico in the 1970s"). But, as early as *Balzac* in 1922, the Court took for granted that even in unincorporated Territories the Government of the United States was bound to provide to noncitizen inhabitants "guaranties of certain fundamental personal rights declared in the Constitution." 258 U.S., at 312; see also *Late Corp. of Church of Jesus Christ of Latter-day Saints* v. *United States*, 136 U.S. 1, 44 (1890) ("Doubtless Congress, in legislating for the Territories would be subject to those fundamental limitations in favor of personal rights which are formulated in the Constitution and its amendments"). Yet noting the inherent practical difficulties of enforcing all constitutional provisions "always and everywhere," *Balzac, supra*, at 312, the Court devised in the Insular Cases a doctrine that allowed it to use its power sparingly and where it would be most needed. This century-old doctrine informs our analysis in the present matter.

Practical considerations likewise influenced the Court's analysis a half-century later in *Reid*, 354 U.S. 1. The petitioners there, spouses of American servicemen, lived on American military bases in England and Japan. They were charged with crimes committed in those countries and tried before military courts, consistent with executive agreements the United States had entered into with the British and Japanese governments. *Id.*, at 15–16, and nn. 29–30 (plurality opinion). Because the petitioners were not themselves military personnel, they argued they were entitled to trial by jury. . . .

That the petitioners in *Reid* were American citizens was a key factor in the case and was central to the plurality's conclusion that the Fifth and Sixth Amendments apply to American civilians tried outside the United States. But practical considerations, related not to the petitioners' citizenship but to the place of their confinement and trial, were relevant to each Member of the *Reid* majority. And to Justices Harlan and Frankfurter (whose votes were necessary to the Court's disposition) these considerations were the decisive factors in the case. . . .

Practical considerations weighed heavily as well in *Johnson* v. *Eisentrager*, 339 U.S. 763 (1950), where the Court addressed whether habeas corpus jurisdiction extended to enemy aliens who had been convicted of violating the laws of war. The prisoners were detained at Landsberg Prison in Germany during the Allied Powers' postwar occupation. The Court stressed the difficulties of ordering the Government to produce the prisoners in a habeas corpus proceeding. It "would require allocation of shipping space, guarding personnel, billeting and rations" and would damage the prestige of military commanders at a sensitive time. *Id.*, at 779. In considering these factors the Court sought to balance the constraints of military occupation with constitutional necessities. *Id.*, at 769–779; see *Rasul*, 542 U.S., at 475–476 (discussing the factors relevant to *Eisentrager's* constitutional holding); 542 U.S., at 486 (Kennedy, J., concurring in judgment) (same).

True, the Court in *Eisentrager* denied access to the writ, and it noted the prisoners "at no relevant time were within any territory over which the United States is sovereign, and [that] the scenes of their offense, their capture, their trial and their punishment were all beyond the territorial jurisdiction of any court of the United States." 339 U.S., at 778. The Government seizes upon this language as proof positive that the *Eisentrager* Court adopted a formalistic, sovereignty-based test for determining the reach of the Suspension Clause. See Brief for Respondents, 18–20. We reject this reading for three reasons.

First, we do not accept the idea that the above-quoted passage from *Eisentrager* is the only authoritative language in the opinion and that all the rest is dicta. The Court's further determinations, based on practical considerations, were integral to Part II of its opinion and came before the decision announced its holding. See 339 U.S., at 781.

Second, because the United States lacked both *de jure* sovereignty and plenary control over Landsberg Prison, see *infra*, at 34–35, it is far from clear that the *Eisentrager* Court used the term sovereignty only in the narrow technical sense and not to connote the degree of control the military asserted over the facility. See *supra*, at 21. The Justices who decided *Eisentrager* would have understood sovereignty as a multifaceted concept. See Black's

Law Dictionary, 1568 (4th ed. 1951) (defining "sovereignty" as "[t]he supreme, absolute, and uncontrollable power by which any independent state is governed"; "the international independence of a state, combined with the right and power of regulating its internal affairs without foreign dictation"; and "[t]he power to do everything in a state without accountability"); Ballentine's Law Dictionary with Pronunciations, 1216 (2d ed. 1948) (defining "sovereignty" as "[t]hat public authority which commands in civil society, and orders and directs what each citizen is to perform to obtain the end of its institution"). In its principal brief in *Eisentrager*, the Government advocated a bright-line test for determining the scope of the writ, similar to the one it advocates in these cases. See Brief for Petitioners in *Johnson* v. *Eisentrager*, O. T. 1949, No. 306, pp. 74–75. Yet the Court mentioned the concept of territorial sovereignty only twice in its opinion. See *Eisentrager*, *supra*, at 778, 780. That the Court devoted a significant portion of Part II to a discussion of practical barriers to the running of the writ suggests that the Court was not concerned exclusively with the formal legal status of Landsberg Prison but also with the objective degree of control the United States asserted over it. Even if we assume the *Eisentrager* Court considered the United States' lack of formal legal sovereignty over Landsberg Prison as the decisive factor in that case, its holding is not inconsistent with a functional approach to questions of extraterritoriality. The formal legal status of a given territory affects, at least to some extent, the political branches' control over that territory. *De jure* sovereignty is a factor that bears upon which constitutional guarantees apply there.

Third, if the Government's reading of *Eisentrager* were correct, the opinion would have marked not only a change in, but a complete repudiation of, the Insular Cases' (and later *Reid*'s) functional approach to questions of extraterritoriality. We cannot accept the Government's view. Nothing in *Eisentrager* says that *de jure* sovereignty is or has ever been the only relevant consideration in determining the geographic reach of the Constitution or of habeas corpus. Were that the case, there would be considerable tension between *Eisentrager*, on the one hand, and the Insular Cases and *Reid*, on the other. Our cases need not be read to conflict in this manner. A constricted reading of *Eisentrager* overlooks what we see as a common thread uniting the Insular Cases, *Eisentrager*, and *Reid*: the idea that questions of extraterritoriality turn on objective factors and practical concerns, not formalism.

B

The Government's formal sovereignty-based test raises troubling separation-of-powers concerns as well. The political history of Guantanamo illustrates the deficiencies of this approach. The United States has maintained complete and uninterrupted control of the bay for over 100 years. At the close of the Spanish-American War, Spain ceded control over the entire island of Cuba to the United States and specifically "relinquishe[d] all claim[s] of sovereignty . . . and title." See Treaty of Paris, Dec. 10, 1898, U.S.-Spain, Art. I, 30 Stat. 1755, T. S. No. 343. From the date the treaty with Spain was signed until the Cuban Republic was established on May 20, 1902, the United States governed the territory "in trust" for the benefit of the Cuban people. *Neely* v. *Henkel*, 180 U.S. 109, 120 (1901); H. Thomas, *Cuba or the Pursuit of Freedom*, 436, 460 (1998). And although it recognized, by entering into the 1903 Lease Agreement, that Cuba retained "ultimate sovereignty" over Guantanamo, the United States continued to maintain the same plenary control it had enjoyed since 1898. Yet the Government's view is that the Constitution had no effect there, at least as to noncitizens, because the United States disclaimed sovereignty in the formal sense of the term. The necessary implication of the argument is that by surrendering formal sovereignty over any unincorporated territory to a third party, while at the same time entering into a lease that grants total control over the territory back to the United States, it would be possible for the political branches to govern without legal constraint.

Our basic charter cannot be contracted away like this. The Constitution grants Congress and the President the power to acquire, dispose of, and govern territory, not the power to decide when and where its terms apply. Even when the United States acts outside its borders, its powers are not "absolute and unlimited" but are subject "to such restrictions as are expressed in the Constitution." *Murphy* v. *Ramsey*, 114 U.S. 15, 44 (1885). Abstaining from questions involving formal sovereignty and territorial governance is one thing. To hold the political branches have the power to switch the Constitution on or off at will is quite another. The former position reflects this Court's recognition that certain matters requiring political judgments are best left to the political branches. The latter would permit a striking anomaly in our tripartite system of government, leading to a regime in which Congress and the President, not this Court, say "what the law is." *Marbury* v. *Madison*, 1 Cranch 137, 177 (1803).

These concerns have particular bearing upon the Suspension Clause question in the cases now before us, for the writ of habeas corpus is itself an indispensable mechanism for monitoring the separation of powers. The test for determining the scope of this provision must not be subject to manipulation by those whose power it is designed to restrain.

C

As we recognized in *Rasul*, 542 U.S., at 476; *id.*, at 487 (Kennedy, J., concurring in judgment), the outlines of a framework for determining the reach of the Suspension Clause are suggested by the factors the Court relied upon in *Eisentrager*. In addition to the practical concerns discussed above, the *Eisentrager* Court found relevant that each petitioner:

"(a) is an enemy alien; (b) has never been or resided in the United States; (c) was captured outside of our territory and there held in military custody as a prisoner of war; (d) was tried and convicted by a Military Commission sitting outside the United States; (e) for offenses against laws of war committed outside the United States; (f) and is at all times imprisoned outside the United States." 339 U.S., at 777.

Based on this language from *Eisentrager,* and the reasoning in our other extraterritoriality opinions, we conclude that at least three factors are relevant in determining the reach of the Suspension Clause: (1) the citizenship and status of the detainee and the adequacy of the process through which that status determination was made; (2) the nature of the sites where apprehension and then detention took place; and (3) the practical obstacles inherent in resolving the prisoner's entitlement to the writ.

Applying this framework, we note at the onset that the status of these detainees is a matter of dispute. The petitioners, like those in *Eisentrager,* are not American citizens. But the petitioners in *Eisentrager* did not contest, it seems, the Court's assertion that they were "enemy alien[s]." *Ibid.* In the instant cases, by contrast, the detainees deny they are enemy combatants. They have been afforded some process in CSRT proceedings to determine their status; but, unlike in *Eisentrager, supra,* at 766, there has been no trial by military commission for violations of the laws of war. The difference is not trivial. The records from the *Eisentrager* trials suggest that, well before the petitioners brought their case to this Court, there had been a rigorous adversarial process to test the legality of their detention. The *Eisentrager* petitioners were charged by a bill of particulars that made detailed factual allegations against them. See 14 United Nations War Crimes Commission, Law Reports of Trials of War Criminals, 8–10 (1949) (reprint 1997). To rebut the accusations, they were entitled to representation by counsel, allowed to introduce evidence on their own behalf, and permitted to cross-examine the prosecution's witnesses. See Memorandum by Command of Lt. Gen. Wedemeyer, Jan. 21, 1946 (establishing "Regulations Governing the Trial of War Criminals" in the China Theater), in Tr. of Record in *Johnson* v. *Eisentrager,* O. T. 1949, No. 306, pp. 34–40.

In comparison the procedural protections afforded to the detainees in the CSRT hearings are far more limited, and, we conclude, fall well short of the procedures and adversarial mechanisms that would eliminate the need for habeas corpus review. Although the detainee is assigned a "Personal Representative" to assist him during CSRT proceedings, the Secretary of the Navy's memorandum makes clear that person is not the detainee's lawyer or even his "advocate." See App. to Pet. for Cert. in No. 06–1196, at 155, 172. The Government's evidence is accorded a presumption of validity. *Id.,* at 159. The detainee is allowed to present "reasonably available" evidence, *id.*, at 155, but his ability to rebut the Government's evidence against him is limited by the circumstances of his confinement and his lack of counsel at this stage. And although the detainee can seek review of his status determination in the Court of Appeals, that review process cannot cure all defects in the earlier proceedings. See Part V, *infra.*

As to the second factor relevant to this analysis, the detainees here are similarly situated to the *Eisentrager* petitioners in that the sites of their apprehension and detention are technically outside the sovereign territory of the United States. As noted earlier, this is a factor that weighs against finding they have rights under the Suspension Clause. But there are critical differences between Landsberg Prison, circa 1950, and the United States Naval Station at Guantanamo Bay in 2008. Unlike its present control over the naval station, the United States' control over the prison in Germany was neither absolute nor indefinite. Like all parts of occupied Germany, the prison was under the jurisdiction of the combined Allied Forces. See Declaration Regarding the Defeat of Germany and the Assumption of Supreme Authority with Respect to Germany, June 5, 1945, U.S.-U.S.S.R.-U.K.-Fr., 60 Stat. 1649, T. I. A. S. No. 1520. The United States was therefore answerable to its Allies for all activities occurring there. Cf. *Hirota* v. *MacArthur*, 338 U.S. 197, 198 (1948) *(per curiam)* (military tribunal set up by Gen. Douglas MacArthur, acting as "the agent of the Allied Powers," was not a "tribunal of the United States"). The Allies had not planned a long-term occupation of Germany, nor did they intend to displace all German institutions even during the period of occupation. . . . The Court's holding in *Eisentrager* was thus consistent with the Insular Cases, where it had held there was no need to extend full constitutional protections to territories the United States did not intend to govern indefinitely. Guantanamo Bay, on the other hand, is no transient possession. In every practical sense Guantanamo is not abroad; it is within the constant jurisdiction of the United States. See *Rasul*, 542 U.S., at 480; *id.*, at 487 (Kennedy, J., concurring in judgment).

As to the third factor, we recognize, as the Court did in *Eisentrager*, that there are costs to holding the Suspension Clause applicable in a case of military detention abroad. Habeas corpus proceedings may require expenditure of funds by the Government and may divert the attention of military personnel from other pressing tasks. While we are sensitive to these concerns, we do not find them dispositive. Compliance with any judicial process requires some incremental expenditure of resources. Yet civilian courts and the Armed Forces have functioned alongside each other at various points in our history. See, *e.g.*, *Duncan* v. *Kahanamoku*, 327 U.S. 304 (1946); *Ex parte Milligan*, 4 Wall. 2 (1866). The Government presents no credible arguments that the military mission at Guantanamo would be compromised if habeas corpus courts had jurisdiction to hear the detainees' claims. And in light of the plenary control the United States asserts over the base, none are apparent to us.

The situation in *Eisentrager* was far different, given the historical context and nature of the military's mission in post-War Germany. When hostilities in the European Theater came to an end, the United States became responsible for an occupation zone encompassing over 57,000 square miles with a population of 18 million. See Letter from President Truman to Secretary of State Byrnes, (Nov. 28, 1945), in *8 Documents on American Foreign Relations*, 257 (R. Dennett & R. Turner eds. 1948); Pollock, "A Territorial Pattern for the Military Occupation of Germany," 38 *Am. Pol. Sci. Rev.*, 970, 975 (1944). In addition to supervising massive reconstruction and aid efforts the American forces stationed in Germany faced potential security threats from a defeated enemy. In retrospect the post-War occupation may seem uneventful. But at the time *Eisentrager* was decided, the Court was right to be concerned about judicial interference with the military's efforts to contain "enemy elements, guerilla fighters, and 'were-wolves.'" 339 U.S., at 784.

Similar threats are not apparent here; nor does the Government argue that they are. The United States Naval Station at Guantanamo Bay consists of 45 square miles of land and water. The base has been used, at various points, to house migrants and refugees temporarily. At present, however, other than the detainees themselves, the only long-term residents are American military personnel, their families, and a small number of workers. The detainees have been deemed enemies of the United States. At present, dangerous as they may be if released, they are contained in a secure prison facility located on an isolated and heavily fortified military base.

There is no indication, furthermore, that adjudicating a habeas corpus petition would cause friction with the host government. No Cuban court has jurisdiction over American military personnel at Guantanamo or the enemy combatants detained there. While obligated to abide by the terms of the lease, the United States is, for all practical purposes, answerable to no other sovereign for its acts on the base. Were that not the case, or if the detention facility were located in an active theater of war, arguments that issuing the writ would be "impracticable or anomalous" would have more weight. See *Reid*, 354 U.S., at 74 (Harlan, J., concurring in result). Under the facts presented here, however, there are few practical barriers to the running of the writ. To the extent barriers arise, habeas corpus procedures likely can be modified to address them. See Part VI–B, *infra*.

It is true that before today the Court has never held that noncitizens detained by our Government in territory over which another country maintains *de jure* sovereignty have any rights under our Constitution. But the cases before us lack any precise historical parallel. They involve individuals detained by executive order for the duration of a conflict that, if measured from September 11, 2001, to the present, is already among the longest wars in American history. See *Oxford Companion to American Military History*, 849 (1999). The detainees, moreover, are held in a territory that, while technically not part of the United States, is under the complete and total control of our Government. Under these circumstances the lack of a precedent on point is no barrier to our holding.

We hold that Art. I, §9, cl. 2, of the Constitution has full effect at Guantanamo Bay. If the privilege of habeas corpus is to be denied to the detainees now before us, Congress must act in accordance with the requirements of the Suspension Clause. Cf. *Hamdi*, 542 U.S., at 564 (Scalia, J., dissenting) ("[I]ndefinite imprisonment on reasonable suspicion is not an available option of treatment for those accused of aiding the enemy, absent a suspension of the writ"). This Court may not impose a *de facto* suspension by abstaining from these controversies. See *Hamdan*, 548 U.S., at 585, n. 16 ("[A]bstention is not appropriate in cases . . . in which the legal challenge 'turn[s] on the status of the persons as to whom the military asserted its power' " (quoting *Schlesinger* v. *Councilman*, 420 U.S. 738, 759 (1975))). The MCA does not purport to be a formal suspension of the writ; and the Government, in its submissions to us, has not argued that it is. Petitioners, therefore, are entitled to the privilege of habeas corpus to challenge the legality of their detention.

V

In light of this holding the question becomes whether the statute stripping jurisdiction to issue the writ avoids the Suspension Clause mandate because Congress has provided adequate substitute procedures for habeas corpus. The Government submits there has been compliance with the Suspension Clause because the DTA review process in the Court of Appeals, see DTA §1005(e), provides an adequate substitute. Congress has granted that court jurisdiction to consider whether the status determination of the [CSRT] . . . was "(i) consistent with the standards and procedures specified by the Secretary of Defense . . . and (ii) to the extent the Constitution and laws of the United States are applicable, whether the use of such standards and procedures to make the determination is consistent with the Constitution and laws of the United States." §1005(e)(2)(C), 119 Stat. 2742.

The Court of Appeals, having decided that the writ does not run to the detainees in any event, found it unnecessary to consider whether an adequate substitute has been provided. In the ordinary course we would remand to the Court of Appeals to consider this question in the first instance. See *Youakim* v. *Miller*, 425 U.S. 231, 234 (1976) *(per curiam)*. It is well settled, however, that the Court's practice of declining to address issues left unresolved in earlier proceedings is not an inflexible rule. *Ibid.* Departure from the rule is appropriate in "exceptional" circumstances. See *Cooper Industries, Inc.* v. *Aviall Services, Inc.*, 543 U.S. 157, 169 (2004); *Duignan* v. *United States*, 274 U.S. 195, 200 (1927).

The gravity of the separation-of-powers issues raised by these cases and the fact that these detainees have been denied meaningful access to a judicial forum for a period of years render these cases exceptional. The parties before us have addressed the adequacy issue. While we would have found it informative to consider the reasoning of the Court of Appeals on this point, we must weigh that against the harms petitioners may endure from additional delay. And, given there are few precedents addressing what features an adequate substitute for habeas corpus must contain, in all likelihood a remand simply would delay ultimate resolution of the issue by this Court. . . .

Under the circumstances we believe the costs of further delay substantially outweigh any benefits of remanding to the Court of Appeals to consider the issue it did not address in these cases.

A

Our case law does not contain extensive discussion of standards defining suspension of the writ or of circumstances under which suspension has occurred. This simply confirms the care Congress has taken throughout our Nation's history to preserve the writ and its function. Indeed, most of the major legislative enactments pertaining to habeas corpus have acted not to contract the writ's protection but to expand it or to hasten resolution of prisoners' claims. . . .

There are exceptions, of course. . . .

The two leading cases addressing habeas substitutes, *Swain* v. *Pressley*, 430 U.S. 372 (1977), and *United States* v. *Hayman*, 342 U.S. 205 (1952), likewise provide little guidance here. The statutes at issue were attempts to streamline habeas corpus relief, not to cut it back.

The statute discussed in *Hayman* was 28 U.S.C. §2255. It replaced traditional habeas corpus for federal prisoners (at least in the first instance) with a process that allowed the prisoner to file a motion with the sentencing court on the ground that his sentence was, *inter alia*, "'imposed in violation of the Constitution or laws of the United States.'" 342 U.S., at 207, n. 1. The purpose and effect of the statute was not to restrict access to the writ but to make postconviction proceedings more efficient. It directed claims not to the court that had territorial jurisdiction over the place of the petitioner's confinement but to the sentencing court, a court already familiar with the facts of the case. As the *Hayman* Court explained,

"Section 2255 . . . was passed at the instance of the Judicial Conference to meet practical difficulties that had arisen in administering the habeas corpus jurisdiction of the federal courts. Nowhere in the history of Section 2255 do we find any purpose to impinge upon prisoners' rights of collateral attack upon their convictions. On the contrary, the sole purpose was to minimize the difficulties encountered in habeas corpus hearings by affording the same rights in another and more convenient forum." *Id.*, at 219.

See also *Hill* v. *United States*, 368 U.S. 424, 427, 428, and n. 5 (1962) (noting that §2255 provides a remedy in the sentencing court that is "exactly commensurate" with the pre-existing federal habeas corpus remedy).

The statute in *Swain*, D. C. Code Ann., §23–110(g) (1973), applied to prisoners in custody under sentence of the Superior Court of the District of Columbia. Before enactment of the District of Columbia Court Reform and Criminal Procedure Act of 1970 (D. C. Court Reform Act), 84 Stat. 473, those prisoners could file habeas petitions in the United States District Court for the District of Columbia. The Act, which was patterned on §2255, substituted a new collateral process in the Superior Court for the pre-existing habeas corpus procedure in the District Court. See *Swain*, 430 U.S., at 374–378. But, again, the purpose and effect of the statute was to expedite consideration of the prisoner's claims, not to delay or frustrate it. See *id.*, at 375, n. 4 (noting that the purpose of the D.C. Court Reform Act was to "alleviate" administrative burdens on the District Court).

That the statutes in *Hayman* and *Swain* were designed to strengthen, rather than dilute, the writ's protections was evident, furthermore, from this significant fact: Neither statute eliminated traditional habeas corpus relief. In both cases the statute at issue had a saving clause, providing that a writ of habeas corpus would be available if the alternative process proved inadequate or ineffective. *Swain*, *supra*, at 381; *Hayman*, *supra*, at 223. The Court placed explicit reliance upon these provisions in upholding the statutes against constitutional challenges. See *Swain*, *supra*, at 381 (noting that the provision "avoid[ed] any serious question about the constitutionality of the statute"); *Hayman*, *supra*, at 223 (noting that, because habeas remained available as a last resort, it was unnecessary to "reach constitutional questions").

Unlike in *Hayman* and *Swain*, here we confront statutes, the DTA and the MCA, that were intended to circumscribe habeas review. Congress' purpose is evident not only from the unequivocal nature of MCA §7's jurisdiction-stripping language, 28 U.S.C.A. §2241(e)(1) (Supp. 2007) ("No court, justice, or judge shall have jurisdiction to hear or consider an application for a writ of habeas corpus . . ."), but also from a comparison of the DTA to the statutes at issue in *Hayman* and *Swain*. . . . When Congress has intended to replace traditional habeas corpus with habeas-like substitutes, as was the case in *Hayman* and *Swain*, it has granted to the courts broad remedial powers to secure the historic office of the writ. In the §2255 context, for example, Congress has granted to the reviewing court power to "determine the issues and make findings of fact and conclusions of law" with respect to whether "the judgment [of conviction] was rendered without jurisdiction, or . . . the sentence imposed was not authorized by law or otherwise open to collateral attack." 28 U.S.C.A. §2255(b) (Supp. 2008). The D.C. Court Reform Act, the statute upheld in *Swain*, contained a similar provision. §23–110(g), 84 Stat. 609.

In contrast the DTA's jurisdictional grant is quite limited. The Court of Appeals has jurisdiction not to inquire into the legality of the detention generally but only to assess whether the CSRT complied with the "standards and procedures specified by the Secretary of Defense" and whether those standards and procedures are lawful. DTA §1005(e)(2)(C), 119 Stat. 2742. If Congress had envisioned DTA review as coextensive with traditional habeas corpus, it would not have drafted the statute in this manner. Instead, it would have used language similar to what it used in the statutes at issue in *Hayman* and *Swain*. Cf. *Russello* v. *United States*, 464 U.S. 16, 23 (1983) ("'[W]here Congress includes particular language in one section of a statute but omits it in another section of the same Act, it is generally presumed that Congress acts intentionally and purposely in the disparate inclusion or exclusion'" (quoting *United States* v. *Wong Kim Bo*, 472 F. 2d 720, 722 (CA5 1972))). Unlike in *Hayman* and *Swain*, moreover, there has been no effort to preserve habeas corpus review as an avenue of last resort. No saving clause exists in either the MCA or the DTA. And MCA §7 eliminates habeas review for these petitioners.

The differences between the DTA and the habeas statute that would govern in MCA §7's absence, 28 U.S.C. §2241 (2000 ed. and Supp. V), are likewise telling. In §2241 (2000 ed.) Congress confirmed the authority of "any justice" or "circuit judge" to issue the writ. Cf. *Felker*, 518 U.S., at 660–661 (interpreting Title I of AEDPA to not strip from this Court the power to entertain original habeas corpus petitions). That statute accommodates the necessity for factfinding that will arise in some cases by allowing the appellate judge or Justice to transfer the case to a district court of competent jurisdiction, whose institutional capacity for factfinding is superior to his or her own. See 28 U.S.C. §2241(b). By granting the Court of Appeals "exclusive" jurisdiction over petitioners' cases, see DTA §1005(e)(2)(A), 119 Stat. 2742, Congress has foreclosed that option. This choice indicates Congress intended the Court of Appeals to have a more limited role in enemy combatant status determinations than a district court has in habeas corpus proceedings. The DTA should be interpreted to accord some latitude to the Court of Appeals to fashion procedures necessary to make its review function a meaningful one, but, if congressional intent is to be respected, the procedures adopted cannot be as extensive or as protective of the rights of the detainees as they would be in a §2241 proceeding. Otherwise there would have been no, or very little, purpose for enacting the DTA.

To the extent any doubt remains about Congress' intent, the legislative history confirms what the plain text strongly suggests: In passing the DTA Congress did not intend to create a process that differs from traditional habeas corpus process in name only. It intended to create a more limited procedure. See, *e.g.*, 151 Cong. Rec. S14263 (Dec. 21, 2005) (statement of Sen. Graham) (noting that the DTA "extinguish[es] these habeas and other actions in order to effect a transfer of jurisdiction over these cases to the DC Circuit Court" and agreeing that the bill "create[s] in their place a very limited judicial review of certain military administrative decisions"); *id.*, at S14268 (statement of Sen. Kyl) ("It is important to note that the limited judicial review authorized by paragraphs 2 and 3 of subsection (e) [of DTA §1005] are not habeas-corpus review. It is a limited judicial review of its own nature").

It is against this background that we must interpret the DTA and assess its adequacy as a substitute for habeas corpus. The present cases thus test the limits of the Suspension Clause in ways that *Hayman* and *Swain* did not.

B

We do not endeavor to offer a comprehensive summary of the requisites for an adequate substitute for habeas corpus. We do consider it uncontroversial, however, that the privilege of habeas corpus entitles the prisoner to a meaningful opportunity to demonstrate that he is being held pursuant to "the erroneous application or interpretation" of relevant law. *St. Cyr*, 533 U.S., at 302. And the habeas court must have the power to order the conditional release of an individual unlawfully detained—though release need not be the exclusive remedy and is not the appropriate one in every case in which the writ is granted. See *Ex parte Bollman*, 4 Cranch 75, 136 (1807) (where imprisonment is unlawful, the court "can only direct [the prisoner] to be discharged"); R. Hurd, *Treatise on the Right of Personal Liberty, and On the Writ of Habeas Corpus and the Practice Connected with It: With a View of the Law of Extradition of Fugitives*, 222 (2d ed., 1876) ("It cannot be denied where 'a probable ground is shown that the party is imprisoned without just cause, and therefore, hath a right to be delivered,' for the writ then becomes a 'writ of right, which may not be denied but ought to be granted to every man that is committed or detained in prison or otherwise restrained of his liberty'"). But see *Chessman* v. *Teets*, 354 U.S. 156, 165–166 (1957) (remanding in a habeas case for retrial within a "reasonable time"). These are the easily identified attributes of any constitutionally adequate habeas corpus proceeding. But, depending on the circumstances, more may be required.

Indeed, common-law habeas corpus was, above all, an adaptable remedy. Its precise application and scope changed depending upon the circumstances. . . . It appears the common-law habeas court's role was most extensive in cases of pretrial and noncriminal detention, where there had been little or no previous judicial review of the cause for detention. . . .

There is evidence from 19th-century American sources indicating that, even in States that accorded strong res judicata effect to prior adjudications, habeas courts in this country routinely allowed prisoners to introduce ex-culpatory evidence that was either unknown or previously unavailable to the prisoner. . . .

The idea that the necessary scope of habeas review in part depends upon the rigor of any earlier proceedings accords with our test for procedural adequacy in the due process context. See *Mathews* v. *Eldridge*, 424 U.S. 319, 335 (1976) (noting that the Due Process Clause requires an assessment of, *inter alia*, "the risk of an erroneous deprivation of [a liberty interest;] and the probable value, if any, of additional or substitute procedural safeguards"). This principle has an established foundation in habeas corpus jurisprudence as well, as Chief Justice Marshall's opinion in *Ex parte Watkins*, 3 Pet. 193 (1830), demonstrates. Like the petitioner in *Swain*, Watkins sought a writ of habeas corpus after being imprisoned pursuant to a judgment of a District of Columbia court. In holding that the judgment stood on "high ground," 3 Pet., at 209, the Chief Justice emphasized the character of the court that rendered the original judgment, noting it was a "court of record, having general jurisdiction over criminal cases." *Id.*, at 203. In contrast to "inferior" tribunals of limited jurisdiction, *ibid.*, courts of record had broad remedial powers, which gave the habeas court greater confidence in the judgment's validity. See generally Neuman, "Habeas Corpus, Executive Detention, and the Removal of Aliens," 98 *Colum. L. Rev.* 961, 982–983 (1998). . . .

. . . The present cases fall outside these categories, however; for here the detention is by executive order.

Where a person is detained by executive order, rather than, say, after being tried and convicted in a court, the need for collateral review is most pressing. A criminal conviction in the usual course occurs after a judicial hearing before a tribunal disinterested in the outcome and committed to procedures designed to ensure its own independence. These dynamics are not inherent in executive detention orders or executive review procedures. In this context the need for habeas corpus is more urgent. The intended duration of the detention and the reasons for it bear upon the precise scope of the inquiry. Habeas corpus proceedings need not resemble a criminal trial, even when the detention is by executive order. But the writ must be effective. The habeas court must have sufficient authority to conduct a meaningful review of both the cause for detention and the Executive's power to detain.

To determine the necessary scope of habeas corpus review, therefore, we must assess the CSRT process, the mechanism through which petitioners' designation as enemy combatants became final. Whether one characterizes the CSRT process as direct review of the Executive's battlefield determina-tion that the detainee is an enemy combatant—as the parties have and as we do—or as the first step in the collateral review of a battlefield determi-nation makes no difference in a proper analysis of whether the procedures

Congress put in place are an adequate substitute for habeas corpus. What matters is the sum total of procedural protections afforded to the detainee at all stages, direct and collateral.

Petitioners identify what they see as myriad deficiencies in the CSRTs. The most relevant for our purposes are the constraints upon the detainee's ability to rebut the factual basis for the Government's assertion that he is an enemy combatant. As already noted, see Part IV–C, *supra*, at the CSRT stage the detainee has limited means to find or present evidence to challenge the Government's case against him. He does not have the assistance of counsel and may not be aware of the most critical allegations that the Government relied upon to order his detention. The detainee can confront witnesses that testify during the CSRT proceedings. But given that there are in effect no limits on the admission of hearsay evidence—the only requirement is that the tribunal deem the evidence "relevant and helpful,"—the detainee's opportunity to question witnesses is likely to be more theoretical than real.

The Government defends the CSRT process, arguing that it was designed to conform to the procedures suggested by the plurality in *Hamdi*. Setting aside the fact that the relevant language in *Hamdi* did not garner a majority of the Court, it does not control the matter at hand. None of the parties in *Hamdi* argued there had been a suspension of the writ. Nor could they. The §2241 habeas corpus process remained in place. Accordingly, the plurality concentrated on whether the Executive had the authority to detain and, if so, what rights the detainee had under the Due Process Clause. True, there are places in the *Hamdi* plurality opinion where it is difficult to tell where its extrapolation of §2241 ends and its analysis of the petitioner's Due Process rights begins. But the Court had no occasion to define the necessary scope of habeas review, for Suspension Clause purposes, in the context of enemy combatant detentions. The closest the plurality came to doing so was in discussing whether, in light of separation-of-powers concerns, §2241 should be construed to forbid the District Court from inquiring beyond the affidavit Hamdi's custodian provided in answer to the detainee's habeas petition. The plurality answered this question with an emphatic "no." *Id.*, at 527 (labeling this argument as "extreme"); *id.*, at 535–536.

Even if we were to assume that the CSRTs satisfy due process standards, it would not end our inquiry. Habeas corpus is a collateral process that exists, in Justice Holmes' words, to "cu[t] through all forms and g[o] to the very tissue of the structure. It comes in from the outside, not in subordination to the proceedings, and although every form may have been preserved opens the inquiry whether they have been more than an empty shell." *Frank* v. *Mangum*, 237 U.S. 309, 346 (1915) (dissenting opinion). Even when the procedures authorizing detention are structurally sound, the Suspension Clause remains applicable and the writ relevant. See 2 Chambers, *Course of Lectures on English Law, 1767–1773*, at 6 ("Liberty may be violated either by arbitrary *imprisonment* without law or the appearance of law, or by a lawful magistrate for an unlawful reason"). This is so, as *Hayman* and *Swain* make clear, even where the prisoner is detained after a criminal trial conducted in full accordance with the protections of the Bill of Rights. Were this not the case, there would have been no reason for the Court to inquire into the adequacy of substitute habeas procedures in *Hayman* and *Swain*. That the prisoners were detained pursuant to the most rigorous proceedings imaginable, a full criminal trial, would have been enough to render any habeas substitute acceptable *per se*.

Although we make no judgment as to whether the CSRTs, as currently constituted, satisfy due process standards, we agree with petitioners that, even when all the parties involved in this process act with diligence and in good faith, there is considerable risk of error in the tribunal's findings of fact. This is a risk inherent in any process that, in the words of the former Chief Judge of the Court of Appeals, is "closed and accusatorial." See *Bismullah III*, 514 F. 3d, at 1296 (Ginsburg, C. J., concurring in denial of rehearing en banc). And given that the consequence of error may be detention of persons for the duration of hostilities that may last a generation or more, this is a risk too significant to ignore.

For the writ of habeas corpus, or its substitute, to function as an effective and proper remedy in this context, the court that conducts the habeas proceeding must have the means to correct errors that occurred during the CSRT proceedings. This includes some authority to assess the sufficiency of the Government's evidence against the detainee. It also must have the authority to admit and consider relevant exculpatory evidence that was not introduced during the earlier proceeding. Federal habeas petitioners long have had the means to supplement the record on review, even in the postconviction habeas setting. See *Townsend* v. *Sain*, 372 U.S. 293, 313 (1963), overruled in part by *Keeney* v. *Tamayo-Reyes*, 504 U.S. 1, 5 (1992). Here that opportunity is constitutionally required.

Consistent with the historic function and province of the writ, habeas corpus review may be more circumscribed if the underlying detention proceedings are more thorough than they were here. In two habeas cases involving enemy aliens tried for war crimes, *In re Yamashita*, 327 U.S. 1 (1946), and *Ex parte Quirin*, 317 U.S. 1 (1942), for example, this Court limited its review to determining whether the Executive had legal authority to try the petitioners by military commission. See *Yamashita, supra*, at 8 ("[O]n application for habeas corpus we are not concerned with the guilt or innocence of the petitioners. We consider here only the lawful power of the commission to try the petitioner for the offense charged"); *Quirin, supra*, at 25 ("We are not here concerned with any question of the guilt or innocence of petitioners"). . . . We need not revisit these cases, however. For on their own terms, the proceedings in *Yamashita* and *Quirin*, like those in *Eisen-*

trager, had an adversarial structure that is lacking here. See *Yamashita, supra*, at 5 (noting that General Yamashita was represented by six military lawyers and that "[t]hroughout the proceedings . . . defense counsel . . . demonstrated their professional skill and resourcefulness and their proper zeal for the defense with which they were charged"); *Quirin, supra*, at 23–24; Exec. Order No. 9185, 7 Fed. Reg. 5103 (1942) (appointing counsel to represent the German saboteurs).

The extent of the showing required of the Government in these cases is a matter to be determined. We need not explore it further at this stage. We do hold that when the judicial power to issue habeas corpus properly is invoked the judicial officer must have adequate authority to make a determination in light of the relevant law and facts and to formulate and issue appropriate orders for relief, including, if necessary, an order directing the prisoner's release.

C

We now consider whether the DTA allows the Court of Appeals to conduct a proceeding meeting these standards. . . .

The DTA does not explicitly empower the Court of Appeals to order the applicant in a DTA review proceeding released should the court find that the standards and procedures used at his CSRT hearing were insufficient to justify detention. This is troubling. Yet, for present purposes, we can assume congressional silence permits a constitutionally required remedy. In that case it would be possible to hold that a remedy of release is impliedly provided for. The DTA might be read, furthermore, to allow the petitioners to assert most, if not all, of the legal claims they seek to advance, including their most basic claim: that the President has no authority under the AUMF to detain them indefinitely. (Whether the President has such authority turns on whether the AUMF authorizes—and the Constitution permits—the indefinite detention of "enemy combatants" as the Department of Defense defines that term. Thus a challenge to the President's authority to detain is, in essence, a challenge to the Department's definition of enemy combatant, a "standard" used by the CSRTs in petitioners' cases.) At oral argument, the Solicitor General urged us to adopt both these constructions, if doing so would allow MCA §7 to remain intact.

The absence of a release remedy and specific language allowing AUMF challenges are not the only constitutional infirmities from which the statute potentially suffers, however. The more difficult question is whether the DTA permits the Court of Appeals to make requisite findings of fact. The DTA enables petitioners to request "review" of their CSRT determination in the Court of Appeals, DTA §1005(e)(2)(B)(i), 119 Stat. 2742; but the "Scope of Review" provision confines the Court of Appeals' role to reviewing whether the CSRT followed the "standards and procedures" issued by the Department of Defense and assessing whether those "standards and procedures" are lawful. §1005(e)(C), *ibid.* Among these standards is "the requirement that the conclusion of the Tribunal be supported by a preponderance of the evidence . . . allowing a rebuttable presumption in favor of the Government's evidence." §1005(e)(C)(i), *ibid.*

Assuming the DTA can be construed to allow the Court of Appeals to review or correct the CSRT's factual determinations, as opposed to merely certifying that the tribunal applied the correct standard of proof, we see no way to construe the statute to allow what is also constitutionally required in this context: an opportunity for the detainee to present relevant exculpatory evidence that was not made part of the record in the earlier proceedings.

On its face the statute allows the Court of Appeals to consider no evidence outside the CSRT record. In the parallel litigation, however, the Court of Appeals determined that the DTA allows it to order the production of all "'reasonably available information in the possession of the U.S. Government bearing on the issue of whether the detainee meets the criteria to be designated as an enemy combatant,'" regardless of whether this evidence was put before the CSRT. See *Bismullah I,* 501 F. 3d, at 180. . . . For present purposes, however, we can assume that the Court of Appeals was correct that the DTA allows introduction and consideration of relevant exculpatory evidence that was "reasonably available" to the Government at the time of the CSRT but not made part of the record. Even so, the DTA review proceeding falls short of being a constitutionally adequate substitute, for the detainee still would have no opportunity to present evidence discovered after the CSRT proceedings concluded.

Under the DTA the Court of Appeals has the power to review CSRT determinations by assessing the legality of standards and procedures. This implies the power to inquire into what happened at the CSRT hearing and, perhaps, to remedy certain deficiencies in that proceeding. But should the Court of Appeals determine that the CSRT followed appropriate and lawful standards and procedures, it will have reached the limits of its jurisdiction. There is no language in the DTA that can be construed to allow the Court of Appeals to admit and consider newly discovered evidence that could not have been made part of the CSRT record because it was unavailable to either the Government or the detainee when the CSRT made its findings. This evidence, however, may be critical to the detainee's argument that he is not an enemy combatant and there is no cause to detain him.

This is not a remote hypothetical. One of the petitioners, Mohamed Nechla, requested at his CSRT hearing that the Government contact his employer. The petitioner claimed the employer would corroborate Nechla's contention he had no affiliation with al Qaeda. Although the CSRT determined this testimony would be relevant, it also found the witness was not reasonably available to testify at the time of the hearing. Petitioner's counsel, however, now represents the witness is available to be heard. If a detainee can present reasonably available evidence demonstrating there is no basis for his continued detention, he must have the opportunity to present this evidence to a habeas corpus court. Even under the Court of Appeals' generous construction of the DTA, however, the evidence identified by Nechla would be inadmissible in a DTA review proceeding. The role of an Article III court in the exercise of its habeas corpus function cannot be circumscribed in this manner.

By foreclosing consideration of evidence not presented or reasonably available to the detainee at the CSRT proceedings, the DTA disadvantages the detainee by limiting the scope of collateral review to a record that may not be accurate or complete. In other contexts, *e.g.*, in post-trial habeas cases where the prisoner already has had a full and fair opportunity to develop the factual predicate of his claims, similar limitations on the scope of habeas review may be appropriate. . . . In this context, however, where the underlying detention proceedings lack the necessary adversarial character, the detainee cannot be held responsible for all deficiencies in the record.

The Government does not make the alternative argument that the DTA allows for the introduction of previously unavailable exculpatory evidence on appeal. It does point out, however, that if a detainee obtains such evidence, he can request that the Deputy Secretary of Defense convene a new CSRT. Whatever the merits of this procedure, it is an insufficient replacement for the factual review these detainees are entitled to receive through habeas corpus. The Deputy Secretary's determination whether to initiate new proceedings is wholly a discretionary one. . . . And we see no way to construe the DTA to allow a detainee to challenge the Deputy Secretary's decision not to open a new CSRT. . . . Congress directed the Secretary of Defense to devise procedures for considering new evidence, see DTA §1005(a)(3), but the detainee has no mechanism for ensuring that those procedures are followed. DTA §1005(e)(2)(C), 119 Stat. 2742, makes clear that the Court of Appeals' jurisdiction is "limited to consideration of . . . whether the status determination of the Combatant Status Review Tribunal with regard to such alien was consistent with the standards and procedures specified by the Secretary of Defense . . . and . . . whether the use of such standards and procedures to make the determination is consistent with the Constitution and laws of the United States." DTA §1005(e)(2)(A), *ibid.*, further narrows the Court of Appeals' jurisdiction to reviewing "any final decision of a Combatant Status Review Tribunal that an alien is properly detained as an enemy combatant." The Deputy Secretary's determination whether to convene a new CSRT is not a "status determination of the Combatant Status Review Tribunal," much less a "final decision" of that body.

We do not imply DTA review would be a constitutionally sufficient replacement for habeas corpus but for these limitations on the detainee's ability to present exculpatory evidence. For even if it were possible, as a textual matter, to read into the statute each of the necessary procedures we have identified, we could not overlook the cumulative effect of our doing so. To hold that the detainees at Guantanamo may, under the DTA, challenge the President's legal authority to detain them, contest the CSRT's findings of fact, supplement the record on review with exculpatory evidence, and request an order of release would come close to reinstating the §2241 habeas corpus process Congress sought to deny them. The language of the statute, read in light of Congress' reasons for enacting it, cannot bear this interpretation. Petitioners have met their burden of establishing that the DTA review process is, on its face, an inadequate substitute for habeas corpus.

Although we do not hold that an adequate substitute must duplicate §2241 in all respects, it suffices that the Government has not established that the detainees' access to the statutory review provisions at issue is an adequate substitute for the writ of habeas corpus. MCA §7 thus effects an unconstitutional suspension of the writ. In view of our holding we need not discuss the reach of the writ with respect to claims of unlawful conditions of treatment or confinement.

VI

A

In light of our conclusion that there is no jurisdictional bar to the District Court's entertaining petitioners' claims the question remains whether there are prudential barriers to habeas corpus review under these circumstances.

The Government argues petitioners must seek review of their CSRT determinations in the Court of Appeals before they can proceed with their habeas corpus actions in the District Court. . . .

In cases involving foreign citizens detained abroad by the Executive, it likely would be both an impractical and unprecedented extension of judicial power to assume that habeas corpus would be available at the moment the prisoner is taken into custody. If and when habeas corpus jurisdiction applies, as it does in these cases, then proper deference can be accorded to reasonable procedures for screening and initial detention under lawful and proper conditions of confinement and treatment for a reasonable period of time. . . . Here, as is true with detainees apprehended abroad, a relevant consideration in determining the courts' role is whether there are suitable alternative processes in place to protect against the arbitrary exercise of governmental power.

The cases before us, however, do not involve detainees who have been held for a short period of time while awaiting their CSRT determinations. Were that the case, or were it probable that the Court of Appeals could complete a prompt review of their applications, the case for requiring temporary abstention or exhaustion of alternative remedies would be much stronger. These qualifications no longer pertain here. In some of these cases six years have elapsed without the judicial oversight that habeas corpus or an adequate substitute demands. And there has been no showing that the Executive faces such onerous burdens that it cannot respond to habeas corpus actions. To require these detainees to complete DTA review before proceeding with their habeas corpus actions would be to require additional months, if not years, of delay. The first DTA review applications were filed over a year ago, but no decisions on the merits have been issued. While some delay in fashioning new procedures is unavoidable, the costs of delay can no longer be borne by those who are held in custody. The detainees in these cases are entitled to a prompt habeas corpus hearing.

Our decision today holds only that the petitioners before us are entitled to seek the writ; that the DTA review procedures are an inadequate substitute for habeas corpus; and that the petitioners in these cases need not exhaust the review procedures in the Court of Appeals before proceeding with their habeas actions in the District Court. The only law we identify as unconstitutional is MCA §7, 28 U.S. C. A. §2241(e) (Supp. 2007). Accordingly, both the DTA and the CSRT process remain intact. Our holding with regard to exhaustion should not be read to imply that a habeas court should intervene the moment an enemy combatant steps foot in a territory where the writ runs. The Executive is entitled to a reasonable period of time to determine a detainee's status before a court entertains that detainee's habeas corpus petition. The CSRT process is the mechanism Congress and the President set up to deal with these issues. Except in cases of undue delay, federal courts should refrain from entertaining an enemy combatant's habeas corpus petition at least until after the Department, acting via the CSRT, has had a chance to review his status. . . .

⟨✒⟩

In considering both the procedural and substantive standards used to impose detention to prevent acts of terrorism, proper deference must be accorded to the political branches. See *United States* v. *Curtiss-Wright Export Corp.*, 299 U.S. 304, 320 (1936). Unlike the President and some designated Members of Congress, neither the Members of this Court nor most federal judges begin the day with briefings that may describe new and serious threats to our Nation and its people. The law must accord the Executive substantial authority to apprehend and detain those who pose a real danger to our security.

Officials charged with daily operational responsibility for our security may consider a judicial discourse on the history of the Habeas Corpus Act of 1679 and like matters to be far removed from the Nation's present, urgent concerns. Established legal doctrine, however, must be consulted for its teaching. Remote in time it may be; irrelevant to the present it is not. Security depends upon a sophisticated intelligence apparatus and the ability of our Armed Forces to act and to interdict. There are further considerations, however. Security subsists, too, in fidelity to freedom's first principles. Chief among these are freedom from arbitrary and unlawful restraint and the personal liberty that is secured by adherence to the separation of powers. It is from these principles that the judicial authority to consider petitions for habeas corpus relief derives.

Our opinion does not undermine the Executive's powers as Commander in Chief. On the contrary, the exercise of those powers is vindicated, not eroded, when confirmed by the Judicial Branch. Within the Constitution's separation-of-powers structure, few exercises of judicial power are as legitimate or as necessary as the responsibility to hear challenges to the authority of the Executive to imprison a person. Some of these petitioners have been in custody for six years with no definitive judicial determination as to the legality of their detention. Their access to the writ is a necessity to determine the lawfulness of their status, even if, in the end, they do not obtain the relief they seek.

Because our Nation's past military conflicts have been of limited duration, it has been possible to leave the outer boundaries of war powers undefined. If, as some fear, terrorism continues to pose dangerous threats to us for years to come, the Court might not have this luxury. This result is not inevitable, however. The political branches, consistent with their independent obligations to interpret and uphold the Constitution, can engage in a genuine debate about how best to preserve constitutional values while protecting the Nation from terrorism. Cf. *Hamdan*, 548 U.S., at 636 (Breyer, J., concurring) ("[J]udicial insistence upon that consultation does not weaken our Nation's ability to deal with danger. To the contrary, that insistence strengthens the Nation's ability to determine—through democratic means—how best to do so").

It bears repeating that our opinion does not address the content of the law that governs petitioners' detention. That is a matter yet to be determined. We hold that petitioners may invoke the fundamental procedural protections of habeas corpus. The laws and Constitution are designed to survive, and remain in force, in extraordinary times. Liberty and security can be reconciled; and in our system they are reconciled within the framework of the law. The Framers decided that habeas corpus, a right of first importance, must be a part of that framework, a part of that law.

The determination by the Court of Appeals that the Suspension Clause and its protections are inapplicable to petitioners was in error. The judgment of the Court of Appeals is reversed. The cases are remanded to the Court of Appeals with instructions that it remand the cases to the District Court for proceedings consistent with this opinion.

It is so ordered.

Justice Souter, joined by Justices *Ginsburg* and *Breyer*.

I join the Court's opinion in its entirety and add this afterword only to emphasize two things one might overlook after reading the dissents.

Four years ago, this Court in *Rasul* v. *Bush*, 542 U.S. 466 (2004) held that statutory habeas jurisdiction extended to claims of foreign nationals imprisoned by the United States at Guantanamo Bay, "to determine the legality of the Executive's potentially indefinite detention" of them, *id.*, at 485. Subsequent legislation eliminated the statutory habeas jurisdiction over these claims, so that now there must be constitutionally based jurisdiction or none at all. Justice Scalia is thus correct that here, for the first time, this Court holds there is (he says "confers") constitutional habeas jurisdiction over aliens imprisoned by the military outside an area of *de jure* national sovereignty, (dissenting opinion). But no one who reads the Court's opinion in *Rasul* could seriously doubt that the jurisdictional question must be answered the same way in purely constitutional cases, given the Court's reliance on the historical background of habeas generally in answering the statutory question. See, *e.g.*, 542 U.S., at 473, 481–483, and nn. 11–14. Indeed, the Court in *Rasul* directly answered the very historical question that Justice Scalia says is dispositive; it wrote that "[a]pplication of the habeas statute to persons detained at [Guantanamo] is consistent with the historical reach of the writ of habeas corpus," 542 U.S., at 481. Justice Scalia dismisses the statement as dictum, but if dictum it was, it was dictum well considered, and it stated the view of five Members of this Court on the historical scope of the writ. Of course, it takes more than a quotation from *Rasul*, however much on point, to resolve the constitutional issue before us here, which the majority opinion has explored afresh in the detail it deserves. But whether one agrees or disagrees with today's decision, it is no bolt out of the blue.

A second fact insufficiently appreciated by the dissents is the length of the disputed imprisonments, some of the prisoners represented here today having been locked up for six years, (opinion of the Court). Hence the hollow ring when the dissenters suggest that the Court is somehow precipitating the judiciary into reviewing claims that the military (subject to appeal to the Court of Appeals for the District of Columbia Circuit) could handle within some reasonable period of time. See, (opinion of Roberts, C. J.) ("[T]he Court should have declined to intervene until the D.C. Circuit had assessed the nature and validity of the congressionally mandated proceedings in a given detainee's case"); ("[I]t is not necessary to consider the availability of the writ until the statutory remedies have been shown to be inadequate"); ("[The Court] rushes to decide the fundamental question of the reach of habeas corpus when the functioning of the DTA may make that decision entirely unnecessary"). These suggestions of judicial haste are all the more out of place given the Court's realistic acknowledgment that in periods of exigency the tempo of any habeas review must reflect the immediate peril facing the country.

It is in fact the very lapse of four years from the time *Rasul* put everyone on notice that habeas process was available to Guantanamo prisoners, and the lapse of six years since some of these prisoners were captured and incarcerated, that stand at odds with the repeated suggestions of the dissenters that these cases should be seen as a judicial victory in a contest for power between the Court and the political branches. See (Roberts, C. J., dissenting); (Scalia, J., dissenting). The several answers to the charge of triumphalism might start with a basic fact of Anglo-American constitutional history: that the power, first of the Crown and now of the Executive Branch of the United States, is necessarily limited by habeas corpus jurisdiction to enquire into the legality of executive detention. And one could explain that in this Court's exercise of responsibility to preserve habeas corpus something much more significant is involved than pulling and hauling between the judicial and political branches. Instead, though, it is enough to repeat that some of these petitioners have spent six years behind bars. After six years of sustained executive detentions in Guantanamo, subject to habeas jurisdiction but without any actual habeas scrutiny, today's decision is no judicial victory, but an act of perseverance in trying to make habeas review, and the obligation of the courts to provide it, mean something of value both to prisoners and to the Nation.

10

The Rule of Law and the Judiciary
in Times of Crisis[1]

Let us begin with a truism: The rule of law when applied has actual consequences to the ideology, goals, objectives, purposes, and desires of one group or another. The question is rarely whether the law applies to a given situation, but whether the law of expediency will prevail over the law in a given situation.

In chapter 1, we reviewed the first debate on the use of Presidential power. In this chapter we will begin with the two men most responsible for the structure of the American Constitutional republic, Madison and Hamilton. Although history found these two men on the opposite side of the debate on Presidential power to determine foreign policy, both men held similar views on how to protect the rule of law in the actual implementation of government. Much ink has been spilled over the question of "how" and to "what" extent the Judicial Department of the United States should exercise deference to the political branches in times of war and national security crisis, and the Supreme Court for more than a century has wrestled with both the defining and the maintaining of the Constitutional boundaries of powers allotted to the Congress and the President in such times. In the last of the four cases to address the assertions of Presidential power by the Bush Administration in the post-9/11 world, Justice Kennedy observed in *Boumediene* that "liberty and security can be reconciled; and in our system they are reconciled within the framework of the law." This chapter will continue on Justice Kennedy's theme by reviewing *why* the judiciary and the rule of law have a role in national security policy during times of crisis.

On June 14, 1788, Alexander Hamilton published his famous Federalist Papers #78 essay defending the independence of the Judicial Department in the proposed Constitution. In defending the Constitutional provisions appointing members of the Judicial Department to "hold their Offices during good Behavior" whose "compensation . . . shall not be diminished during their Continuance in Office,"[2] Hamilton wrote that the development of these protections, in order to guarantee an independent judiciary, was "one of the most valuable of the modern improvements in the practice of government."[3] His reason for why it was one of the most valuable improvements is significant to the question of why the actions of the Bush Administration regarding the capture and detention of Al Qaeda and other suspected terrorists in the "War on Terror" is any of the Court's business.

Hamilton asserted that judicial appointment "during good Behavior" and the prohibition of reduction in compensation of judicial officers were key aspects to protecting the Judicial Department from encroachments by the other two Departments as well as a way to protect liberty and the Constitution. The principle of judicial independence for judges in a monarchy, Hamilton wrote, "is an excellent barrier to the despotism of the prince; in a republic *it is a no less excellent barrier to the encroachments and oppressions of the representative body. And it is the best expedient which can be devised in any government, to secure a steady, upright, and impartial administration of the laws.*"[4] The ability of members of the Judicial Department, in the proposed Constitutional system of checks and balances, to be free from arbitrary removal or monetary threats to their livelihood ensures judicial "firmness and independence," which Hamilton wrote must "be justly regarded as an indispensable ingredient . . . , and, in a great measure, [establishes the Judicial Department as] the citadel of the public justice and the public security."[5] But why is an independent and permanent judiciary indispensable to public justice and public security? The answer goes directly to the power of judicial review, limited government, Constitutional supremacy, the protection of liberty and the rule of law.

⁓

Chief Justice Edward Coke in 1610 wrote that "It appears in our books that in many cases the common law will control acts of Parliament and sometimes adjudge them to be utterly void; for when an Act of Parliament is against common right and reason, or repugnant, or impossible to be performed, the common law will control it, and adjudge such an Act to be void."[6]

Hamilton, reflecting this principle of judicial independence and judicial review established by English common law, was an original proponent of judicial review for the national courts and the truism that it is the province of the Judicial Department to say what the law is. In Federalist Papers #78 Hamilton wrote,

The complete independence of the courts of justice is peculiarly essential in a limited Constitution. By a limited Constitution, I understand one which contains certain specified exceptions to the legislative authority; such, for instance, as that it shall pass no bills of attainder, no *ex post facto* laws, and the like. *Limitations of this kind can be preserved in practice no other way than through the medium of courts of justice, whose duty it must be to declare all acts contrary to the manifest tenor of the Constitution void. Without this, all the reservations of particular rights or privileges would amount to nothing.*

Some perplexity respecting the rights of the courts to pronounce legislative acts void, because contrary to the Constitution, has arisen from an imagination that the doctrine would imply a superiority of the judiciary to the legislative power. It is urged that the authority which can declare the acts of another void, must necessarily be superior to the one whose acts may be declared void. As this doctrine is of great importance in all the American constitutions, a brief discussion of the ground on which it rests cannot be unacceptable.

There is no position which depends on clearer principles, than that every act of a delegated authority, contrary to the tenor of the commission under which it is exercised, is void. *No legislative act, therefore, contrary to the Constitution, can be valid.* To deny this, would be to affirm, that the deputy is greater than his principal; that the servant is above his master; that the representatives of the people are superior to the people themselves; that men acting by virtue of powers, may do not only what their powers do not authorize, but what they forbid.

If it be said that the legislative body are themselves the constitutional judges of their own powers, and that the construction they put upon them is conclusive upon the other departments, it may be answered, that this cannot be the natural presumption, where it is not to be collected from any particular provisions in the Constitution. It is not otherwise to be supposed, that the Constitution could intend to enable the representatives of the people to substitute their *will* to that of their constituents. It is far more rational to suppose, that *the courts were designed to be an intermediate body between the people and the legislature, in order, among other things, to keep the latter within the limits assigned to their authority. The interpretation of the laws is the proper and peculiar province of the courts.* A constitution is, in fact, and must be regarded by the judges, as a fundamental law. It therefore belongs to them to ascertain its meaning, as well as the meaning of any particular act proceeding from the legislative body. If there should happen to be an irreconcilable variance between the two, that which has the superior obligation and validity ought, of course, to be preferred; or, in other words, the Constitution ought to be preferred to the statute, the intention of the people to the intention of their agents.

Nor does this conclusion by any means suppose a superiority of the judicial to the legislative power. It only supposes that the power of the people is superior to both; and that *where the will of the legislature, declared in its statutes, stands in opposition to that of the people, declared in the Constitution, the judges ought to be governed by the latter rather than the former.* They ought to regulate their decisions by the fundamental laws, rather than by those which are not fundamental.[7]

Hamilton asserted that the role of the Judicial Department is to be "inflexible and uniform [in the] adherence to the rights of the Constitution, and of individuals, which we perceive to be indispensable in the courts of justice" both in the area of enforcement of limited government as well as treating as void "injury of the private rights of particular classes of citizens, by unjust and partial laws." Judicial action, making such unjust partial laws void, "operates as a check upon the legislative body in passing them."

Hamilton explained that the "courts must declare the sense of the law." The role of the Judicial Department, Hamilton proposed, was that they act as "the bulwarks of a limited Constitution against legislative encroachments" and through judicial independence the Courts

> guard the Constitution and the rights of individuals from the effects of those
> ill humors, which . . . have a tendency . . . to occasion dangerous innovations
> in the government. . . , that the representatives of the people, whenever a mo-
> mentary inclination happens to lay hold of a majority of their constituents [be-
> come], incompatible with the provisions in the existing Constitution. . . .Until
> the people have, by some solemn and authoritative act, annulled or changed the
> [Constitution], it is binding upon themselves collectively, as well as individually;
> and no presumption, or even knowledge, of their sentiments, can warrant their
> representatives in a departure from it, prior to such an act. But it is easy to see,
> that it would require an uncommon portion of fortitude in the judges to do their
> duty as faithful guardians of the Constitution, where legislative invasions of it
> had been instigated by the major voice of the community.

James Madison in Federalist Papers #48–50 lamented that in designing a government and a Constitution to govern the powers of government, the "mere demarcation on parchment of the constitutional limits of the several departments, is not a sufficient guard against those encroachments which lead to a tyrannical concentration of all the powers of government in the same hands."[8] He concluded that appeal to the general public by one or two of the branches against the actions of the third for violations of Constitutional powers would not prevent tyranny because in such a contest "passion, not reason" will prevail.[9] Thus concluding, in his famous Federalist Papers #51, that "ambition must be made to counteract ambition" for "if men were angels, no government would be necessary [and if] angels were to govern men, neither external nor internal controls on government would be necessary." Madison explained that the answer to the problem that written law alone is not enough to govern the government, is to institutionally separate each Department with its own interests, purposes and constituency, as well as provide each with enough power to be distinct so as to control the usurpations of powers by the others. Madison's model divided governmental power between the states and the federal government (vertical federalism), between the three Departments of the national government (horizontal federalism), and divided the Legislative Department into two distinct chambers; one designed to provide inclusion of all classes and types of citizens (the House of Representatives) and one to represent the states (the Senate). Hamilton's model centralized the judicial power of the national government into one Department and divided the judicial power of the nation between the state courts and federal courts with the U.S. Constitution being the supreme law over both. Although the making of law and policy would be denied to the judicial power of the nation, the judicial power of the nation would be granted final authority to enforce the Constitutional boundaries established by the Supreme Law of the Land. In such a divided governmental system the political process would *in toto* provide protections of civil rights and liberties for all citizens.

THE MADISONIAN AND HAMILTONIAN MODELS: "WHY" THE COURTS HAVE A ROLE

While Madison in Federalist Papers #51 depended on the structure and dynamics of "politics" and human nature to protect individual liberty and freedom, Hamilton in Federalist Papers #78 focused on how the Judicial Department would function within this dynamic and how to use the rule of law and the supremacy of the Constitution, as the supreme law of the land, to maintain control of the predominant Department of the National Government—the Congress.

Congress, in the Madisonian model, was the Department most feared as a source of tyranny. To prevent the Congress from becoming tyrannical, Madison divided it into two branches with different political sources of power and membership. With the most powerful[10] of the three Departments divided, Congress was designed, nonetheless, to be able to check the activity of the other two Departments.[11] For example, during the debate over ratification the Anti-Federalists asserted that the Constitution allowed Congress to raise and support a standing army in times of peace, which in the late eighteenth century was considered a direct threat to liberty. Hamilton addressed this concern in Federalist Papers #26 by observing that

> the legislature of the United States will be obliged, by this provision, once at least in every two years, to deliberate upon the propriety of keeping a military force on foot; to come to a new resolution on the point; and to declare their sense of the matter, by a formal vote in the face of their constituents. They are

not at liberty to vest in the executive department permanent funds for the support of an army, if they were even incautious enough to be willing to repose in
it so improper a confidence.

Thus Congress was envisioned to review military policy, beginning with
the preliminary issue of deciding whether to maintain the military, every
two years. In fact, it was obligated to do so. Only after reviewing that policy
was Congress to determine continued funding. But Congress, due to "political" constraints rather than "constitutional" ones, has failed for decades, if
not centuries, to be the *primary* Department that *determines* military policy
and approves it before continuing to fund it. Because it is an unquestioned
"political" fact that the Congress will fund Presidential use of military force
once deployed into a hostile environment, Congress has lost one of the key
Constitutional controls on the Presidential power. As a "political" matter,
the President will always have supporters in Congress for his military actions as well as those who believe Congress does not have a plenary role in
national security or foreign policy matters in the first place. But aside from
this, it is also a "political" fact that those who oppose funding Presidential
military deployments without prior Congressional approval are accused of
failing to "support the troops" and threatening American national security.
Congress has failed to assert the Constitutional principle that Congressional
opposition to funding a military policy implemented prior to its approval
is required by the Constitution. Because Congress, as an institution, focuses
on the political aspects of Presidential action, rather than on its role as the
source of funding and approval of military offensive action, it has lost the
Constitutional plenary control over military deployment and war policy. In
1990 it was asserted by the Bush 41 Administration that Congress had no
Constitutional authority to require the Administration to seek its approval
to use force against Iraq. In a 1996 *Frontline* interview, then Former Secretary
of Defense Cheney explained that he opposed President George H. W. Bush
going to Congress to seek authorization to use military force to extract Iraq
from Kuwait. Vice President Cheney's comments in the 1996 interview and
his impact on the Constitutional assertions of executive power by the second
Bush Administration were examined in a *Frontline* 2007 documentary.

   NARRATOR: As secretary of defense, Cheney argued the president should
not seek congressional authorization for the Gulf war.
   Rep. MICKEY EDWARDS (R-OK), 1977–'92: The leadership in Congress
generally was telling the first President Bush, "You have to get permission from
Congress to go into the Gulf war." The president didn't think that was the case.
He resisted it.
   RICHARD CHENEY, Fmr. Defense Secretary: [*Frontline* 1996] I argued that
we did not need congressional authorization, and that legally and from a constitutional standpoint, we had all the authority we needed.

JACK GOLDSMITH: Secretary of Defense Cheney's advice was that it was unnecessary and imprudent—unnecessary because the Constitution did not require it, imprudent because Congress might say no.

RICHARD CHENEY: [*Frontline* 1996] If we'd lost the vote in the Congress, I would certainly have recommended to the president that we go forward anyway.

NARRATOR: In the end, Cheney's view did not prevail. The president agreed to a congressional vote.[12]

Another reason Congress only functions as a secondary force of political control and a check on executive power[13] is because it does not (assuming it ever did) function as the primary Constitutional institution for policy and governance, but rather it functions as an institution dominated by political party politics in support of or in opposition to the policies of the party holding the Presidency. Congress is a conglomerate of interests, some of which are always supportive of the President's primacy over Congress in times of war or national crisis. Since Congress functions within the dynamics of political party politics rather than as an institution designed to check the power of the President, and since the Executive Department is a unitary branch with one person governing at its apex, the President always has the political upper hand in policy design and implementation.

A third reason Congress does not exercise primacy in military affairs is that Congress, over two hundred years of history, has acquiesced to the assertion of sole Presidential power to use the military without advanced consent of Congress. Summarizing the history and the fact of Congressional acquiescence Deputy Assistant Attorney General John Yoo testified before the Senate Judiciary Committee, Subcommittee on the Constitution, Federalism and Property Rights:

> Congress also has the power to declare war. This power to declare a legal state of war and to notify other nations of that status once had an important effect under the law of nations, and continues to trigger significant domestic statutory powers as well, such as under the Alien Enemy Act of 1798 (50 U.S.C. § 21) and Federal surveillance laws (50 U.S.C. §§ 1811, 1829, 1844). But this power has seldom been used. Although U.S. Armed Forces have, by conservative estimates, been deployed well over a hundred times in our Nation's history, Congress has declared war just five times. *This long practice of U.S. engagement in military hostilities without a declaration of war demonstrates that previous Presidents and Congresses have interpreted the Constitution as we do today.*
>
> As the United States rose to global prominence in the post–World War II era, Congress has provided the President with a large and powerful peacetime military force. Presidents of both parties have long used that military force to protect the national interest, even though Congress has not declared war since World War II. President Truman introduced U.S. Armed Forces into Korea in 1950 without prior congressional approval. President Kennedy claimed con-

stitutional authority to act alone in response to the Cuban missile crisis by deploying a naval quarantine around Cuba. Presidents Kennedy and Johnson dramatically expanded the U.S. military commitment in Vietnam absent a declaration of war.

In response to President Nixon's expansion of the Vietnam War into Laos and Cambodia, Congress approved the War Powers Resolution, but that resolution expressly disclaimed any intrusion into the President's constitutional war power. Accordingly, Presidents Ford, Carter, Reagan, and the first President Bush have committed U.S. Armed Forces on a number of occasions. In these cases, the administration has generally consulted with, notified, and reported to Congress, consistent with the War Powers Resolution.

President Clinton deployed U.S. Armed forces in Somalia, Haiti, and Bosnia—all without prior congressional authorization. In 1999, the Clinton administration relied on the President's constitutional authority to use force in Kosovo. Assistant Secretary of State Barbara Larkin testified before Congress that April that "there is no need for a declaration of war. Every use of U.S. Armed Forces, since World War II, has been undertaken pursuant to the President's constitutional authority. . . . This administration, like previous administrations, takes the view that the President has broad authority as commander in chief and under his authority to conduct foreign relations, to authorize the use of force in the national interest."

In short, Presidents throughout U.S. history have exercised broad unilateral power to engage U.S. Armed Forces in hostilities. Congress has repeatedly recognized the existence of presidential constitutional war power, in the War Powers Resolution of 1973, and more recently in S.J. Res. 23.[14]

During the same Senate hearing, Louis Fisher, Senior Specialist in Separation of Power with the Congressional Research Service testified as to the "original intent" of the Founders to place the power to declare war with the Congress:

While the "original intent" of many constitutional provisions is debatable, there is no doubt about the framers' determination to vest in Congress the sole authority to take the country from a State of peace to a State of war. From 1789 to 1950, lawmakers, the courts, and the executive branch understood that only Congress could initiate offensive actions against other nations. . . .

Admittedly, some scholars—particularly John Yoo—argue that the framers designed a system to "encourage presidential initiative in war" and that the Constitution's provisions "did not break with the tradition of their English, state, and revolutionary predecessors, but instead followed in their footsteps.". . . Suffice it to say that had the framers adopted the English model, they wouldn't have written Articles I and II the way they did. Here it is unnecessary to debate the framers' intent. It is enough to look at the plain text of the Constitution. If the framers had indeed adopted "the traditional British approach to war powers," they would have written Article II to give the President the power to declare war, to issue letters of marque and reprisal, and to raise armies, along with other powers of external affairs that are reserved to Congress.

I won't repeat here the many statements of framers who believed that they had stripped the Executive of the power to take the country to war. At the Philadelphia convention, George Mason said he was "against giving the power of war to the Executive, because not to be trusted with it. . . . He was for clogging rather than facilitating war." At the Pennsylvania ratifying convention, James Wilson expressed the prevailing sentiment that the system of checks and balances "will not hurry us into war; it is calculated to guard against it. It will not be in the power of a single man, or a single body of men, to involve us in such distress; for the important power of declaring war is vested in the legislature at large." The power of initiating war was vested in Congress. To the President was left certain defensive powers "to repel sudden attacks."

The framers gave Congress the power to initiate war because they believed that Presidents, in their search for fame and personal glory, would have too great an appetite for war. John Jay, generally supportive of executive power, warned in Federalist No. 4 that "absolute monarchs will often make war when their nations are to get nothing by it, but for purposes and objects merely personal, such as a thirst for military glory, revenge for personal affronts, ambition, or private compacts to aggrandize or support their particular families or partisans. These and a variety of other motives, which affect only the mind of the sovereign, often lead him to engage in wars not sanctified by justice or the voice and interests of his people."

In studying history and politics, the framers came to fear the Executive's potential appetite for war. Has human nature changed in recent decades to permit us to trust independent presidential decisions in war? The historical record tells us that what Jay said in 1788 applies equally well to contemporary times.

John Yoo recognizes that Congress has the constitutional power to check Presidential wars: It can withhold appropriations. Congress "could express its opposition to executive war decisions only by exercising its powers over funding and impeachment." The spending power, he writes, "may be the only means for legislative control over war." Constitutionally, this kind of analysis puts Congress in the back seat. Yoo allows Presidents to initiate wars and continue them until Congress is able to cut off funds. The advantage to the President is striking. Executive wars may persist so long as the President has one-third plus one in a single chamber to prevent Congress from overriding his veto of a funding cutoff.[15]

During his oral testimony, Fisher asserted that for "over . . 160 years" in American history it was acknowledged by Congress and the President that "when the country goes from the state of peace to a state of war, the President comes to Congress for authority in advance" but admitted that "over those years, 160 years, there were examples where Presidents used military force without authority from Congress. But those are fairly small-scale actions, chasing bandits over the borders and doing various things, certainly not major military actions."[16] Although Fisher is correct that the Founders rejected the British model of exclusive executive power to declare (formally start / engage) and implement (conduct / respond to hostilities) war, Congress has acquiesced in maintaining the distinction between these two powers. Although it is well settled that the President has the power to respond or repel military actions against the United States, over the past two centuries the Congress has ceded to the President the power to declare (formally start) war or to use military power offensively prior to Congressional approval. It is no answer to assert that although various Presidents have used "military force without authority from Congress," they were only "small-scale" uses. The significance in Presidential use of the military prior to Congressional approval is that it occurred in the first place *without* Congressional resistance, thus establishing the legitimacy of the use of that power.[17] The result of Congressional acquiescence of its power to declare (formally start / engage) war prior to Presidential use of military power is that it is now convincingly asserted that the President was never subject to Congressional prior approval in the first place.[18]

> Some commentators . . . argue that the vesting of the power to declare war gives Congress the sole authority to decide whether to make war. This view misreads the constitutional text and misunderstands the nature of a declaration of war. Declaring war is not tantamount to making war—indeed, the Constitutional Convention specifically amended the working draft of the Constitution that had given Congress the power to make war. An earlier draft of the Constitution had given to Congress the power to "make" war. When it took up this clause on August 17, 1787, the Convention voted to change the clause from "make" to "declare." 2, *The Records of the Federal Convention of 1787*, at 318–19 (Max Farrand ed., rev. ed. 1966) (1911). A supporter of the change argued that it would "leav[e] to the Executive the power to repel sudden attacks." *Id.* at 318. Further, other elements of the Constitution describe "engaging" in war, which demonstrates that the Framers understood making and engaging in war to be broader than simply "declaring" war. *See* U.S. Const. art. I, § 10, cl. 3 ("No State shall, without the Consent of Congress . . . engage in War, unless actually invaded, or in such imminent Danger as will not admit of delay."). . . . If the Framers had wanted to require congressional consent before the initiation of military hostilities, they knew how to write such provisions.[19]

But the Bush Administration's assertion of plenary Presidential power over foreign policy is not novel in American political[20] and Constitutional thought.[21] The first great debate over Presidential power occurred within the Washington Administration over the President declaring the United States neutral during the war between Great Britain and France in 1793.[22] Jefferson and the Republicans were incensed that the President would declare neutrality in a war, an act which they believed favored Great Britain. Madison, on Constitutional theory grounds, opposed the President's decision, asserting in essence that Congress, not the President, has the final authority to determine the foreign policy of the nation, especially the decision of whether the nation should or should not become engaged in military hostilities. Hamilton defended the decision and authority of President Washington, arguing in essence that the President as Commander-in-Chief was the responsible agent to determine what the nature of foreign affairs was and to take action to safeguard the nation. Although Hamilton accepted that Congress had the power to declare war, that power did not limit the President from determining the foreign policy of the nation even if that determination impacted or conflicted with the prerogatives of Congress. Although Hamilton acceded to the fact that only Congress could change the legal status of the nation from peace to war, it was for the President to act in the formation and implementation of foreign affairs as the sole representative of the nation until Congress formally determined that war replaced peace. It is to Hamilton that the origin of the "unitary President" and "sole organ" theories of executive power are to be credited.[23]

It is not asserted that the title of Commander-in-Chief was an empty title in the first place, but that Congress has abdicated its supremacy over the decision to use military force offensively and that the assertions by the Bush Administration based on strong affirmations of the "unitary President" and "sole organ" theories of Presidential power in domestic and foreign policy are not without precedent. Hamilton and Madison assumed that such assertions would be made; the problem has been that Congress has not asserted its powers to counteract such assertions. The result is that the President is now the plenary "political" power in our Constitutional system.

Within a month of the attacks of 9/11 President Bush, under his powers as Commander-in-Chief, created a military commission system to try terrorists outside of the Uniform Code of Military Justice or the civilian courts. By executive proclamation he also determined that "it is not practicable to apply in military commissions under this order the principles of law and the rules of evidence generally recognized in the trial of criminal cases in the United States district courts."[24] The Bush Administration further asserted that Congressional action was not needed to create the commissions and the courts had no authority to review the decisions made by the President regarding his classification of individuals as enemy combatants. Within three years of such absolutist positions of executive power, the Bush Administration encountered significant judicial resistance[25] as well as political resistance both domestically and internationally. Although President Bush was correct to assert that, as Commander-in-Chief, he had the power to create military commissions,[26] and detain enemy combatants captured during the war on terror,[27] the Supreme Court rejected the Bush Administration's proposition that under his powers as Commander-in-Chief he could hold such enemy combatants indefinitely[28] without a formal hearing governed by laws and rules of evidence recognizable in civilian or military criminal proceedings.[29] The Supreme Court affirmed Presidential power to create commissions but rejected the assertion by President Bush that under his power as Commander-in-Chief alone, he had the authority to create a military commission system intentionally outside of the requirements of the Uniform Code of Military Justice and the Geneva Convention.[30] Although Congress and the President together have the authority to limit the jurisdiction of the Court, the Supreme Court determined that the statutory and Constitutional right to challenge unlawful detention through the Great Writ of Habeas Corpus is a principle that supersedes the political needs to detain suspected terrorists without any meaningful review.[31] The Supreme Court also rejected the proposition by the Bush Administration that the enemy combatant detention facility established at Guantanamo Bay, Cuba, was outside of the United States, the jurisdiction of the Judicial Department and U.S. Constitutional requirements.[32]

Even in times of war the rule of law must govern a society, otherwise in times of stress such a society lives under the rule of men and as such never lived under the former.[33]

THE RULE OF LAW AND WHY IT MATTERS

Nothing is more fitting for a sovereign than to live by and within the laws, nor is there any greater sovereignty than to govern according to the due process of law, and the sovereign ought properly to yield to the tradition and process of law that makes him king.[34]

In our Constitutional system, as it functions today, there are only three external factors that control the Executive Department. It was only the dictates of these three external controls on Presidential power, for example, that forced the Bush 41 and later the Bush 43 Administrations to go to Congress for authorization to use military force against Iraq (1991), Afghanistan (2001), and Iraq (2003), respectively.

The first factor involves the *dynamics of Presidential political power*. The dynamics of Presidential political power are comprised of three aspects: Constitutional limits, institutional power and political power. The Constitutional limits on the Presidency involve the restrictions on the power of the President imposed by the text of the Constitution itself and by Congressional action—that is, the Twenty-Second Amendment or Congressional statutes specifically prohibiting action. The institutional power of the Presidency includes the "inherent" or "executive" power to act. The theories of "executive privilege," "unitary President," "inherent powers," and "sole organ" all reflect the range of institutional power of the chief executive. Lastly, political power defines the ability of a specific President at any given time during his administration to achieve or prevent action. This power defines what the President wants to do and can do without and/or over "political" resistance.

The second external control on the Executive Department is the support of *the principles of separated and limited powers* by the American people. The popular support for these principles becomes evident through the "political" demands of individual members of Congress, the media, academics, and other interested groups. Both Bush Administrations asserted that the President had the authority to use force against Iraq and that the President was not required to seek and gain Congressional approval. Popular understanding of the principles of separation of powers led to demands for submission of the policy to Congress for a formal vote forcing both administrations to comply with the principles of separation of powers—that is, Congress, not the President, has the Constitutional power to declare war or otherwise authorize offensive military action. Without organized and consistent popular demands that the President submit to this popular view of the Constitution, neither Bush Administrations would have sought Congressional action on its plans to go to war against Iraq.

The third external control on the Executive Department is *the supremacy of the rule of law* (as defended by the Judicial Department) and the assent of the American people to the results of the application of the rule of law. Because the principle of the supremacy of law and its implementation through the rule of law has prevailed through American history as the governing value of the Constitution itself, the boundaries of Presidential power have been made "legally" and "politically" subservient to the voice of the rule of law, the judiciary.

Hamilton wrote in Federalist Papers #22, "The fabric of American empire ought to rest on the solid basis of the consent of the people. The streams of national power ought to flow immediately from that pure, original fountain of all legitimate authority." In Federalist Papers #81 Hamilton spoke of the power of the sovereign, the people and the rule of law in the Constitutional system. The principles of the rule of law should be more than cavalierly acknowledged, for "without the law there can be no freedom and without justice there can be no law."[35] More importantly, history has no example of a democracy, republic, or society long enduring without falling into tyranny when rule *by* law (law of expediency) is employed over the rule *of* law.

Reflecting on the history of Rome, the historian Cornelius Tacitus remarked that the rule of a single man is the only remedy for a country in turmoil. As history has proven, in a democracy, through the demands of *pro bono publico*, the people can elect a republic into dictatorship or tyranny if placed under sufficient social, political, military and/or economic stress. So it was in 47 BCE when the Roman Senate elected Julius Caesar dictator after he defeated Pompey in a civil war (49–48 BCE), which Caesar himself started when he entered Rome with his army in defiance of the Senate and Roman law. Under his dictatorship Caesar initiated various political and economic reforms including providing land and grain to the poor to ensure that there was no starvation in Rome. Upon his assassination, the benign dictator was declared a God by the people. In 31 BCE, after twelve years of civil war resulting from the assassination of Caesar, Octavian unified power into himself. With the assent of the Roman people the Roman Senate, in January 27 BCE, continued to effectively end the Roman Republic by bestowing on Octavian exclusive military and political powers, control over the major provinces of the Republic, and appointing him with the title Augustus (a religious title of near divinity) for life; the very titles and powers that Caesar was assassinated, on March 15, 44, BCE, for seeking. Centuries after the election of Octavian as a near divinity and primary ruler of Rome, the First French Republic fell in 1793. Under the instigation and applause of an armed mob, the French National Convention passed the September 1793 resolution ordering the arrest of its Girondist members and established the policy of terror as the chosen means to protect the ideals of the revolution from internal enemies.[36] The revolution to establish *Liberté, Egalité,* and *Fraternité* and the principles of the *Declaration of the Rights of Man* were abandoned for social order, the promise of safety, and victory over the enemy. The result being the rise of Robespierre and the Jacobins, the reign of terror, the establishment of the government of the guillotine, the death of more than ten thousand Parisians, and later, the rise of Emperor Napoleon. It was under the threat of internal economic and political disorder, more than a century later, that the Germans ended the Weimar Republic in March 1933 through the passage of the Enabling Act ("Law to Remedy the Distress of the People and the Nation"). The March 1933 act gave Hitler and his government lawmaking power independent of the legislative supremacy of the Reichstag. The Reichstag remained a rubber stamp for Hitler until the fall of the Third Reich in May 1945.

Those who believe that the process of democracy, by itself, guarantees "justice and the rule of law . . . forget that the popular will can rule with or without constitutional and legal limits. Without constitutional and legal limits, popular will can be as destructive as, or even more destructive than, the unfettered discretion of 'the few.'"[37] Madison made the same observation more than two centuries ago during the ratification debates on the Bill of Rights. In a letter to Jefferson on October 17, 1788, he wrote on the limits of depending on written law alone to keep the power of government in control. He observed,

> [T]he invasion of private rights is chiefly to be apprehended, not from acts of government contrary to the sense of its constituents but from acts in which the government is the mere instrument of the major number of the constituents. . . . Wherever there is an interest and power to do wrong, wrong will generally be done, and not less readily by a powerful and interested party than by a powerful and interested prince.[38]

One of the protections against electing away individual and structural freedoms is to establish that those freedoms are above the political process and above governmental power to disregard; to establish, value and defend the governing of government by the rule "of" law above rule "by" law.

> The difference between "rule by law" and "rule of law" is important. Under the rule "by" law, law is an instrument of the government, and the government is above the law. In contrast, under the rule "of" law, no one is above the law, not even the government. The core of "rule of law" is an autonomous legal order. Under rule of law, the authority of law does not depend so much on law's instrumental capabilities, but on its degree of autonomy, that is, the degree to which law is distinct and separate from other normative structures such as politics and religion. As an autonomous legal order, rule of law has at least three meanings. First, rule of law is a regulator of government power. Second, rule of law means equality before law. Third, rule of law means procedural and formal justice.[39]

In essence the rule of law, as a principle, establishes that raw political or military might is not the essence of governance. Rule of law, a Lockean concept,[40] is a moral principle that asserts that although the king is above men, the king is under law and the King is king because of the *Law*. Rule by law is based on a different premise. Rule by law, a Hobbesian concept,[41] is based on the observation that "[s]ince the ruler is the source of all law, and stands above the law, there are no limits or effective checks on the ruler's arbitrary power."[42] The Hobbesian observation of rule by law was not new in his time, for many a millennia before, long before the days of David, the prophet Samuel defined the absolute power of the sovereign over his kingdom, people, and the administration of the law and justice.[43]

In a society under the rule of law, the law governs the people and the government. Conversely, in a society under rule by law, the law governs the people and the government governs the law. The difference was exampled in November 2007 when Pakistani President Pervez Musharraf suspended his country's Constitution, fired the Chief Justice of the Supreme Court and declared martial law. His suspension of the Constitution was done partly due to fears of political and social disruption; in the wake of the assassination attempt on his significant political rival, former Prime Minister Benazir Bhutto; as well as due to concerns that the Pakistani Supreme Court would rule that his election to a third term as President was unconstitutional. Musharraf was elected President while holding the position of Chief of the Army during the election which was in violation of the Pakistani Constitution. Rather than risking the decision of the Court, President Musharraf suspended the Constitution and removed the Chief Justice and other members of the Court viewed as a threat to his reelection. The suspension of the Constitution was lifted, but only after a new and more friendly Court was constituted. Such is a government by the rule by law. Conversely, it was due to internal institutions and the Pakistani people supporting the principles of the rule of law, along with international pressure, that resulted in the lifting of the martial law, reinstatement of the Constitution and Musharraf surrendering the position of Chief of the Army in compliance with the Constitution. It was also the application of the rule of law and the Pakistani parliament threatening impeachment that led to the resignation of Musharraf in August 2008.

Put simply, rule by law puts the government above the law; thus not being subject to it, the government does not have to follow the law when doing so frustrates its desires. A government based on the rule of law has no such latitude. The rule of law frustrates the government for it protects the individual from governmental power and the "ill temper" of society through the requirements of procedural due process as well as equal protection under the law.

The answer to *why* the actions of a President are subject to judicial scrutiny draws from the English Common Law principles of the rule of law that Hamilton and Madison wrote into the Constitution. These principles that executive power is subject to the law and not superior to it were developed centuries before the Philadelphia Convention. In the early thirteenth century Lord Justice Henry Bracton in his treatise *On the Laws and Customs of England* wrote on the importance of the rule of law and its sovereignty over the executive power of the King or in our language the President.

> His power, therefore, is that of justice and not of injustice and since he himself is the author of justice, an occasion of injustice ought not arise from the source whence justice comes, and likewise he who has the right from his office to prohibit others, ought not commit this same injustice himself. . . . Indeed it is said that he is king from ruling well and not from reigning, because he is king while he rules well and he is a tyrant when he oppresses with violent domination the people under his charge. Let him temper his power through the law which is the bridle of power, that he might live according to the law because a human law has established it as inviolable that the laws bind the lawgiver (lator), and elsewhere in the same (lex humana) it is said that it is worthy of the majesty of one who reigns that the prince avow himself bound by the laws.[44]

Lord Justice Bracton explained *why* executive power should be under the law by invoking the basis of English Common Law.

> The King himself must be, not under Man, but under God and the Law, because the law makes the king. . . . For there is no king where arbitrary will dominates, and not the law. And that he should be under the law because he is God's vicar, becomes evident through the similitude with Jesus Christ in whose stead he governs on earth. For He, God's true Mercy, though having at His disposal many means to recuperate ineffably the human race, chose before

all other expedients the one which applied for the destruction of the devil's work; that is, not the strength of power, but the maxim of Justice, and therefore he wished to be under the Law in order to redeem those under the Law. For he did not wish to apply force, but reason and judgment.[45]

And so therefore, the king ought to [do likewise], lest his power remain unchecked (infrenata). Therefore there ought to be none greater than he in the administration of justice (in exhibitione juris), but he ought to be the least, or nearly so, in submitting to judgment if he seeks it.[46]

The king ought, therefore, to exercise the power of justice as the vicar and minister of God on earth because that power is from God alone; however, the power of injustice is from the devil and not from God, and the king will be the minister of him whose work he does. Therefore while he does justice he belongs to the Eternal King; when he turns toward injustice he is the minister of the devil.[47]

Under the Rule of Law, the *Law* makes the King, King; it is not the King that makes *law*, *Law*. It was under the principle that the sovereign must not act contrary to the law for the sovereign is under the Law and the sovereign is sovereign because of the Law, that Chief Justice Edward Coke in 1610 ruled that parliamentary laws that violate the higher Common Law were void.[48] In November 1607 Chief Justice Coke, while standing before King James, defending the independence of the Judiciary and the supremacy of law; echoed Lord Justice Bracton, and answered the King's protest of judicial supremacy over the administration of criminal justice, saying *"Rex non debet esse sub homine, sed sub Deo et lege, quia lex facit regem."*[49] Centuries before Hamilton and Madison drafted the Constitution it was an accepted principle of Western government that it was for the judiciary to hold the law sovereign over Kings and Presidents. The principle that the law is sovereign over executive power is as old as the Scriptures as reflected in the Old Testament *Book of Esther*: "Whatever is written in the King's name and sealed with the King's signet ring no one can revoke," not even the King himself.[50]

DEFENDING THE RULE OF LAW: THE ROLE OF HAMILTON'S LEAST DANGEROUS BRANCH IN TIMES OF WAR AND CRISIS

With all its defects, delays and inconveniences, men have discovered no technique for long preserving free government except that the Executive be under the law, and that the law be made by parliamentary deliberations. Such institutions may be destined to pass away. But it is the duty of the Court to be last, not first, to give them up.[51]

Is it enough to say that because Congress has abdicated its role as the primary check on Presidential power, it falls to the Judiciary to place practical checks on President Bush's assertions of broad and sole executive power in the "War on Terror"? Does Hamilton's view in Federalist Papers #78 that it is the duty of the Judicial Department to be the "faithful guardians of the Constitution, where legislative invasions of [the Constitution] had been instigated by the major voice of the community," equally apply in the face of Presidential action in time of war? Has history changed Hamilton's model to require the Judicial Department "to be an intermediate body between the people and the legislature [as well as the Executive], in order, among other things, to keep the latter within the limits assigned to their authority [?]" Does the Constitution itself demand judicial action and review of Presidential assertions of power?

Article VI, Clause 2 of the Constitution reads in part, "This Constitution, and the Laws of the United States which shall be made in Pursuance thereof . . . shall be the supreme Law of the land." Article III, Section 2 of the Constitution reads in part, "The Judicial Power shall extend to all Cases, in Law and Equity, arising under this Constitution [and] the Laws of the United States." Hamilton explained, in Federalist Papers #80, that "cases . . . arising under this Constitution" refers to cases involving prohibitions and limitations proscribed in the text of the Constitution itself. Thus the Constitution, which creates the three Departments, is supreme above all laws passed and all actions taken under its name and authority. The Judicial Department is empowered to hear all disputes "in Law" arising under the Constitution. As Hamilton reminds, "Laws are a dead letter without courts to expound and define their true meaning and operation. . . . [A]ll nations have found it necessary to establish one court paramount to the rest, possessing a general superintendence, and authorized to settle and declare in the last resort a uniform rule of civil justice."[52] Beginning with the assumption that the political branches cannot act outside of the Constitution and that the Constitution is not only "law" but the Supreme Law of the Land, the Judiciary has the power to hear disputes arising from Congressional and Presidential activity under the authority of the Constitution. The category of actions by the President either in domestic or in foreign affairs does not mitigate the fact that the Judiciary has the authority to hear assertions of violations of law by the President. Thus the question of *why* the judiciary has a role in addressing how President Bush uses executive power to meet the post–September 11 world is answered. The question of *how* and to *what extent* the Judicial Department advances or limits the use of executive power in times of war and national crisis, as well as *what limits* the Judicial Department places upon itself to assess specific Presidential actions in times of war or crisis under judicial review, is a separate question.[53]

CONCLUSION

The organizing principle of any society, Mr. Garrison, is for war. The authority of the state over its people resides in its war powers.[54]

Democracy, in and of itself, does not guarantee freedom nor does the rule of law, in and of itself, guarantee the supremacy of the law. Cultural, social, legal, and political institutions must support the rule of law and the supremacy of the law for both to successfully resist the overstepping of governmental power. Hamilton and Madison valued this truth and drafted a Constitution to both ensure that the American Constitutional system would be based on the rule of law as well as ensure that the government in practice could ensure the supremacy of law and avoid the concentration of political power, the very definition of tyranny. Madison presumed that power balanced against power would provide the practical mechanisms to allow the rule of law to prevail. Part of that balance is the institutional separation of legislative, executive, and judicial functions. Hamilton envisioned that the Judicial Department would protect the principle of limited government, declare laws in violation of the Constitution void and protect individuals from the "ill humor" of the majority, which could cause injury to "the private rights of particular classes of citizens."

It is the business of the Judicial Department to provide protection and "judgment" as to the boundaries of majority rule. Hamilton intended the judiciary to defend the provisions and limitations of the Constitution against the "ill tempers" of the people and the Departments of government that are subject to those passions. The President is just as subject to those "ill tempers" of the public as Congress. In fact, he is more so as demonstrated by the public reaction to the terror of September 11. It was to the President, not the Congress, that the people turned to for protection, and it was to the Presidency that demands for action were levied. As a result, the nation approved the assertions made by President Bush that as Commander-in-Chief it is his duty, and sole power, to protect the American people from terror. It was only as the "ill temper" of the people cooled and the President was perceived as extending his power beyond what the nation was prepared to tolerate in the long term that the courts, and later the Congress, acted to restrict his assertions of sole power.[55]

The same principles of Constitutional boundaries that limit the public and its representatives in Congress, which Hamilton wrote the judiciary was authorized to enforce, are the same boundaries that limit the powers of the President acting as Commander-in-Chief. Although the "how" of judicial review of Presidential action is open to discussion, the "why" of judicial review of such actions is settled by the Constitution itself. As Hamilton concluded, "the Constitution ought to be the standard of construction for the laws, and that wherever there is an evident opposition, the laws ought to give place to the Constitution. But this doctrine is not deducible from any circumstance peculiar to the plan of the convention, but from the general theory of a limited Constitution."[56] Under the U.S. Constitution, the rule of law, the muse of justice, finds her voice in Hamilton's least dangerous branch.

As the actions of Congress exercising its powers are subject to the mirror of the Constitution, so are the actions of the President subject to the same mirror. The actions placed before the mirror of the Constitution are the President's business. The holding of the Constitutional mirror and declaring what it beholds in the reflection is the Court's business.

NOTES

1. This chapter is a revised version of an article originally published in the *Journal of the Institute of Justice & International Studies* 8 (2008): 120 and the paper "Enemy Combatants, Detention and the War on Terror: Why This Is Any of the Court's Business" presented at the 2008 Terrorism and Justice: The Balance for Civil Liberties Conference, University of Central Missouri, Warrensburg, Missouri, February 2008.

2. U.S. Constitution, Article 3, Section 1.

3. Federalist Papers #78.

4. Ibid.

5. Ibid.

6. *Dr. Bonham's Case* 8, Cokes Report, part 8, 114, 118 (1610), 77 Eng. Rep. 638, 652 (C.P. 1610). See also William Blackstone and William Gardiner Hammond, *Commentaries on the Laws of England* (San Francisco: Bancroft-Whitney, 1890) and Sir John Baker, "Human Rights and the Rule of Law in Renaissance England," *Northwestern Journal of International Human Rights* 2, (Spring 2004): 3–23.

7. Federalist Papers # 78 (emphasis added in part).

8. Federalist Papers # 48.

9. Federalist Papers # 49–50.

10. "[T]he legislative department" Madison wrote in Federalist Papers # 48, "alone has access to the pockets of the people, and has in some constitutions full discretion, and in all a prevailing influence, over the pecuniary rewards of those who fill the other departments, a dependence is thus created in the latter, which gives still greater facility to encroachments of the former."

11. Madison in Federalist Papers # 48 described the Congress and its powers compared to the Executive and Judicial as follows:

> But in a representative republic, *where the executive magistracy is carefully limited*; both in the extent and the duration of its power; and *where the legislative power is exercised by an assembly*, which is inspired, by a supposed influence over the people, *with an intrepid confidence in its own strength*; which is sufficiently numerous to feel all the passions which actuate a multitude, yet not so numerous as to be incapable of pursuing the objects of its passions, by means which reason prescribes; *it is against the enterprising ambition of this*

department that the people ought to indulge all their jealousy and exhaust all their precautions. The legislative department derives a superiority in our government from other circumstances. *Its constitutional powers being at once more extensive,* and less susceptible of precise limits, it can, with the greater facility, mask, under complicated and indirect measures, the encroachments which it makes on the co-ordinate departments. It is not unfrequently a question of real nicety in legislative bodies, whether the operation of a particular measure will, or will not, extend beyond the legislative sphere.

On the other side, *the executive power being restrained within a narrower compass, and being more simple in its nature,* and the judiciary being described by landmarks still less uncertain, projects of usurpation by either of these departments would immediately betray and defeat themselves (emphasis added).

12. "Cheney's Law," *Frontline*, 2007, http://www.pbs.org/wgbh/pages/frontline/cheney/etc/script.html.

13. Congress has the power to impeach and remove the President for "other high Crimes and Misdemeanors" and leaving aside what the full meaning of Article II, Section 4 is, it has never been used or threatened upon Presidential use of military offensive force without prior Congressional authority.

Although the legal and Constitutional scope of the purpose of impeachment is open to debate, it is a fact that impeachment is viewed more through political lenses than constitutional ones. To the party holding the Presidency, impeachment is viewed as an act of "partisan politics" or "criminalizing policy disputes" while the party not holding the Presidency views impeachment as a legitimate tool of the legislative branch to oppose Presidential "abuse of power" and Congressional protection of Constitutional principles. If Article II, Section 4 provided Congress with an additional institutional power to check the power of the President to act without prior Congressional authorization, it has been lost both due to Congressional failure to use it as such as well as to the historical politicization of the process during the Andrew Johnson and William Clinton Administrations, the impeachment hearings during the Richard Nixon Administration being the notable exception.

14. Senate Judiciary Committee, Subcommittee on the Constitution, Federalism and Property Rights, *Applying the War Powers Resolution to the War on Terrorism*, April 17, 2002 S. HRG. 107–892 Serial no J-107-74 at 12 (emphasis added).

15. Ibid., 16–17 (internal citation omitted).

16. Ibid., 14.

17. In his September 2001 memo John Yoo explained the significance of historical Congressional acquiesce to Presidential use of military power without prior Congressional approval as follows:

The historical practice of all three branches confirms the lessons of the constitutional text and structure. The normative role of historical practice in constitutional law, and especially with regard to separation of powers, is well settled. Both the Supreme Court and the political branches have often recognized that governmental practice plays a highly significant role in establishing the contours of the constitutional separation of powers: "a systematic, unbroken, executive practice, long pursued to the knowledge of the Congress and never before questioned . . . may be treated as a gloss on 'executive Power' vested in the President by § 1 of Art. II." *Youngstown Sheet & Tube Co.,* 343 U.S. at 610–11 (Frankfurter, J., concurring). Indeed, as the Court has observed, the role of practice in fixing the meaning of the separation of powers is implicit in the Constitution itself: "'the Constitution . . . contemplates that practice will integrate the dispersed powers into a workable government.'" *Mistretta v. United States*, 488 U.S. 361, 381 (1989) (citation omitted). In addition, governmental practice enjoys significant weight in constitutional analysis for practical reasons, on "the basis of a wise and quieting rule that, in determining . . . the existence of a power, weight shall be given to the usage itself—even when the validity of the practice is the subject of investigation." *United States v. Midwest Oil Co.*, 236 U.S. 459, 473 (1915).

John C. Yoo, "The President's Constitutional Authority to Conduct Military Operations Against Terrorists and Nations Supporting Them" (memorandum opinion for Timothy Flanigan, Deputy Counsel to the President, September 25, 2001) in *The Torture Papers: The Road to Abu Ghraib*, ed. Karen J. Greenburg and Joshua L. Dratel (New York: Cambridge University Press, 2005), 14 (internal citation omitted).

18. Citing prior opinions by the Office of Legal Counsel, John Yoo asserted that

the Constitution confides in the President the authority, independent of any statute, to determine when a "national emergency" caused by an attack on the United States exists.

. . . the President's role under our Constitution as Commander in Chief and Chief Executive vests him with the constitutional authority to order United States troops abroad to further national interests such as protecting the lives of Americans overseas.

. . . constitutional practice over two centuries, supported by the nature of the functions exercised and by the few legal benchmarks that exist, evidences the existence of broad constitutional power.

. . . Thus, there is abundant precedent, much of it from recent Administrations, for the deployment of military force abroad, including the waging of war, on the basis of the President's sole constitutional authority.

Yoo, "The President's Constitutional Authority to Conduct Military Operations Against Terrorists and Nations Supporting Them," 23, 12, 13, and 17 respectively.

19. Ibid., 6–7.

20. Arthur H. Garrison, "National Security and Presidential Power: Judicial Deference and Establishing Constitutional Boundaries in World War Two and the Korean War," *Cumberland Law Review* 39, no. 3 (2008/2009): 609–84.

21. See chapter 1 and the Pacificus–Helvidius debates between Hamilton and Madison.

22. Arthur H. Garrison, "The Internal Security Acts of 1798: The Founding Generation and the Judiciary during America's First National Security Crisis," *Journal of Supreme Court History* 34, no. 1 (2009): 1–27.

23. See *United States v. Curtiss-Wright Export Corp*, 299 U.S. 304 (1936) for the seminal case of judicial recognition of the President as the "sole organ" of American foreign policy through his powers as Commander-in-Chief and the vesting of the executive power of the United States within the Office of the President. But see *Youngstown Sheet and Tube Co. v. Sawyer*, 343 U.S. 579, 634 (1952) for Justice Jackson's concurring opinion, which has since become the seminal governing opinion on determining the boundaries and limits of Presidential power. See *Hamdan v. Rumsfeld*, 548 US 557 (2006), *Medellin v. Texas*, 552 U.S. 491, 128 S. Ct. 1346, 170 L. Ed. 2d 190 (2008) and *Boumediene v. Bush* and *Al Odah v. United States* 553 U.S. 723 (2008).

24. President Bush Presidential Military Order of November 13, 2001: "Detention, Treatment and Trial of Certain Non Citizens in the War against Terrorism, in Greenburg and Dratel, *The Torture Papers*, 26.

25. *Rasul v. Bush*, 542 U.S. 466 (2004), *Hamdi v. Rumsfeld*, 542 U.S. 507 (2004), *Hamdan v. Rumsfeld*, 548 U.S. 557 (2006) and *Boumediene v. Bush* and *Al Odah v. United States* 553 U.S. 723 (2008).

26. See *Ex Parte Quirin*, 317 U.S. 1 (1942), *Duncan v. Kahanamoku*, 327 U.S. 304 (1945), *Johnson v. Eisentrager*, 339 U.S. 763 (1950) and *Madsen v. Kinsella*, 343 U.S. 341 (1952). For additional scholarship, Congressional Research Service papers, and information on military commissions, see U.S. Department of State web page, *U.S. Military Commissions and Tribunals*, http://fpc.state.gov/fpc/c12784.htm.

27. See *Ex parte Quirin*, 317 U.S. 1 (1942) and *Hamdi v. Rumsfeld*, 542 U.S. 507 (2004).

28. See *Boumediene v. Bush* and *Al Odah v. United States* 553 U.S. 723 (2008).

29. See *Hamdi v. Rumsfeld*, 542 U.S. 507 (2004).

30. See *Hamdan v. Rumsfeld*, 548 U.S. 557 (2006).

31. *Rasul v. Bush*, 542 U.S. 466 (2004) and *Boumediene v. Bush* and *Al Odah v. United States*, 553 U.S. 723 (2008).

32. *Rasul v. Bush*, 542 U.S. 466 (2004).

33. See similar conclusions by the judiciary in *Ex parte Merryman*, 17 F. Cas. 144 No. 9,487 (1861) and *Ex parte Milligan*, 71 U.S. 2 (1866).

34. Lord Justice Henry Bracton, *On the Laws and Customs of England*, vol. 2, 305–06, quoted in Martin Krygier, "The Rule of Law: Legality, Teleology, Sociology," *University of New South Wales Faculty of Law Research Series* 65 (2007): 7, http://law.bepress.com/cgi/viewcontent.cgi?article=1067&context=unswwps.

35. "Nullification," *Law and Order* (television program), 1997.

36. Arthur H. Garrison, "The Theory and Application of Terrorism: A Review of Historical Development," in *Terror: From Tyrannicide to Terrorism*, ed. Brett Bowden and Michael T. Davis (Brisbane: University of Queensland Press, 2008).

37. Bo Li, "What Is the Rule of Law? *Perspectives* 2, no. 4 (2001), http://www.oycf.org/oycfold/httpdocs/Perspectives2/10_022801/what_is_law.htm (originally cited as *Perspectives* 1, no. 5 (2000), http://www.oycf.org/Perspectives/5_043000/Contents.htm.)

38. Robert A. Rutland and Charles F. Hobson, eds., *The Papers of James Madison*, vol. 11 (Charlottesville: University Press of Virginia, 1977), 296–300.

39. Li, "What Is the Rule of Law?" Ibid. note 37.

40. John Lock, in his 1689 book *Two Treatises On Government* (published in the colonies in 1773), took a less pessimistic view of human nature than Hobbes and asserted that in the state of nature all men were equal with each other in "a state of perfect freedom of acting and disposing of their own possessions and persons as they think fit within the bounds of the law of nature." Lewis F. Abbott, *Two Treatises on Government: A Translation into Modern English* (Manchester, UK: Industrial Systems Research, 2009), 70. But man formed society and government because although all men were free, equal, and able to organize their affairs as they saw fit, "in the state of nature . . . the enjoyment of it is very uncertain . . . the enjoyment of the property he has in this state is very unsafe, very unsecure. This makes him willing to . . . join in society with others, who are already united, or have a mind to unite, for the mutual preservation of their lives, liberties and estates, which I call by the general name, property" (123). The rule of law is a Lockean theory in that it provides that security of life, liberty, and property while preserving most of the rights that man enjoyed in the state of nature.

41. Thomas Hobbes, in his book *Leviathan* (1651), provided the foundation of modern western social contract political theory with his proposition that man's natural nature is for war and conflict and government was established in order to protect the right to life, liberty, and property. Hobbes asserted that in the state of nature life was "solitary, poor, nasty, brutish, and short" and government was instituted to create order and institute safety. Thus the social contract required man to submit to the sovereign power of government in order to live in safety. Rule by law is a Hobbesian theory in that rule by law is how the sovereign creates order by force of its own will and determination. Under the rule by law, the individual is under the law but the sovereign is above it. The full citation of Hobbes's famous description of the nature of man is as follows:

> Whatsoever therefore is consequent to a time of war, where every man is enemy to every man, the same consequent to the time wherein men live without other security than what their own strength and their own invention shall furnish them withal. In such condition there is no place for industry, because the fruit thereof is uncertain: and consequently no culture of the earth; no navigation, nor use of the commodities that may be imported by sea; no commodious building; no instruments of moving and removing such things as require much force; no knowledge of the face of the earth; no account of time; no arts; no letters; no society; and which is worst of all, continual fear, and danger of violent death; and the life of man, solitary, poor, nasty, brutish, and short.

Thomas Hobbes, *Leviathan*, parts I and II, edited by A. P. Martinich (Peterborough, ON: Broadview Press, 2005), part I: chap. 13, 95–96.

42. Kenneth Winston, The Internal Morality of Chinese Legalism: Working Paper, SSRN, 2005, http://ssrn.com/abstract=757354 (accessed August 18, 2009).

43. "This will be the manner of the king that shall reign over you: He will take your sons, and appoint *them* for himself . . . to reap his harvest, and to make his instruments of war, and instruments of his chariots. And he will take your daughters . . . And he will take your fields, and your vineyards, and your oliveyards, *even* the best *of them*, and give *them* to his servants. And he will take the tenth of your seed, and of your vineyards, and give to his officers, and to his servants. And he will take your menservants, and your maidservants, and your goodliest young men, and your asses, and put *them* to his work. He will take the tenth of your sheep: and ye shall be his servants" (1 Samuel 8:1-17, KJV).

44. Lord Justice Henry Bracton, *On the Laws and Customs of England* quoted in S. J. T. Miller, "The Position of the King in Bracton and Beaumanoir," *Speculum* 31 no. 2 (1956): 263, 269.

45. Lord Justice Henry Bracton, *On the Laws and Customs of England*, quoted in Ernst Hartwig Kantorowicz, *The King's Two Bodies: A Study in Mediaeval Political Theology* (Princeton, NJ: Princeton University Press, 1997), 156.

46. Lord Justice Henry Bracton, *On the Laws and Customs of England*, quoted in Miller, "The Position of the King in Bracton and Beaumanoir," 263, 272.

47. Ibid., 269.

48. *Dr. Bonham's Case*, 8 Cokes Report, part 8, 114, 118 (1610), 77 Eng. Rep. 638, 652 (C.P. 1610).

49. Let the King not be under any man, but he is under God and the Law, because the law makes the King.

In 1607 King James asserted that he had the authority to sit as a judge on the King's Bench to hear a case involving a charge of treason on his own authority and that the judges of the Bench had no authority to hear the case upon his determination to sit as judge. Chief Judge Coke ruled that that the King had no such authority and guilt of crime was for the court to determine. In *Prohibitions Del Roy* (1607) EWHC KB J2312, Cokes Report, 64, 65; 77 Eng. Rep.1342, 1343, http://www.bailii. org/ew/cases/EWHC/KB/1607/J23.html. Chief Justice Coke wrote,

> The King in his own person cannot adjudge any case, either criminal or betwixt party and party; but it ought to be determined and adjudged in some Court of Justice, according to the law and custom of England.
> The King may sit in the King's Bench, but the Court gives the judgment. No King after the conquest assumed to himself to give any judgment in any cause whatsoever which concerned the administration of justice, within the realm; but these causes were solely determined in the Courts of Justice. . . .
> . . . then the King said, that he thought the law was founded upon reason, and that he and others had reason, as well as the Judges: to which it was answered by me, that true it was, that God had endowed His Majesty with excellent science, and great endowments of nature; but His Majesty was not learned in the laws of his realm of England, and causes which concern the life, or inheritance, or goods, or fortunes of his subjects, are not to be decided by natural reason but by the artificial reason and judgment of law, which law is an act which requires long study and experience, before that a man can attain to the cognizance of it: that the law was the golden met-wand and measure to try the causes of the subjects; and which protected His Majesty in safety and peace: with which the King was greatly offended, and said, that then he should be under the law, which was treason to affirm, as he said; to which I said, that Bracton saith, *quod Rex non debed esse sub homine, sed sub Deo et lege.*

50. *Esther* 8:8, New King James Version. Lord Bracton echoed the scriptural principle that the king is bound by the Law and by the laws he himself makes as follows:

> Let him, therefore, temper his power by law, which is the bridle of power, that he may live according to the laws, for *the law of mankind has decreed that his own laws bind the lawgiver*, and elsewhere in the same source, it is a saying worthy of the majesty of a ruler that *the prince acknowledges himself bound by the laws.*

Lord Justice Henry Bracton, *On the Laws and Customs of England*, vol. 2, quoted in Martin Krygier, "The Rule of Law: Legality, Teleology, Sociology," *University of New South Wales Faculty of Law Research Series* 65 (2007): 7. http://law.bepress.com/cgi/ viewcontent.cgi?article=1067&context=unswwps (emphasis added).

51. *Youngstown Sheet & Tube v. Sawyer*, 343 U.S. 579, 655 (1952) (Justice Jackson, concurring).

52. Federalist Papers # 22.

53. See William Brennan, "The Quest to Develop a Jurisprudence of Civil Liberties in Times of Security Crises," *Israel Yearbook on Human Rights* 18 (1988): 11–21; Arthur Garrison, "The Judiciary in Times of National Security Crisis and Terrorism: Ubi Inter Arma Enim Silent Leges, Quis Custodiet Ipso Custodies?" *American Journal of Trial Advocacy* 30, no. 1 (2006): 165–230.

54. *JFK*, DVD (Warner Home Video, 1991).

55. See Arthur Garrison, "The War on Terrorism on the Judicial Front, Part II: The Courts Strike Back," *American Journal of Trial Advocacy* 27, no. 3 (2004): 473–516; Arthur Garrison, "*Hamdan v. Rumsfeld*, Military Commissions, and Acts of Congress: A Summary," *American Journal of Trial Advocacy* 30, no. 2 (2006): 339.

56. Federalist Papers #81.

11

A Summary of Cases

PART I: NATIONAL SECURITY, THE RISE OF PRESIDENTIAL POWER, THE RULE OF LAW, AND THE DEVELOPMENT OF CONSTITUTIONAL BOUNDARIES ON POLITICAL NECESSITY AND THE WAR POWER

CHAPTER 2: THE SUPREME COURT AND PRESIDENTIAL AUTHORITY IN TIMES OF NATIONAL CRISIS

Little v. Berreme (1804)
- The implementation of a Presidential policy does not make it Constitutional based on the order itself. If the act violated statutory law, the Presidential order does not make it lawful.

U.S. v. Smith (1806) (Circuit)
- The Commander-in-Chief power does not allow the President to declare that a state of war exists.

Ex parte Bollman and Swartwout (1807)
- Only Congress can suspend the writ of habeas corpus.

Martin v. Mott (1827)
- The President, as Commander-in-Chief, has the power to call out the militia. The President is the sole agent to determine if the exigency arises to call out the militia. His determination is conclusive.

Luther v. Borden (1849)
- The President, as Commander-in-Chief, has the power to call out the militia to suppress a rebellion within a state upon request from the legitimate state government. The President has the authority to determine if the request is from the legitimate government.

Fleming v. Page (1850)
- The Commander-in-Chief's power is specific to the use of the military to secure military victory but his powers are governed by legislative action.

Durand v. Hollins (1860) (Circuit)
- "As executive head of the nation, the President is made the only legitimate organ of the General Government, to open and carry on correspondence or negotiations with foreign nations, in matters concerning the interests of the country or of its citizens."

Ex parte Merryman (1861) (Circuit)
- The President does not have the power to order an arrest and confinement of an American citizen in times of war when the federal courts are open and functioning under the authority of and loyal to the Constitution and the United States.

Prize Cases (1866)
- The President, as Commander-in-Chief, is authorized by the Constitution to meet the challenge of war regardless of Congressional recognition that formal war has been declared against the United States. The President is authorized to meet an armed rebellion as war with appropriate military action.

Ex parte Milligan (1866)
- The President, as commander in chief, cannot subject a civilian to military arrest and military justice when he is not a member of the military and has not engaged in disloyal service to the enemy of the United States in time of war. Martial law cannot be imposed where the federal courts are open and loyal to the United States.

Chinese Exclusion Case (1889)
- A request by England for the United States to commit military forces in concert with other world powers to secure certain guarantees from China could not be honored because the warmaking power of the United States belongs to Congress and the President has no authority to order aggressive use of the military without Congressional approval.

Cunningham v. Neagle (1890)
- The President, as chief executive, has the authority to act to ensure that the laws are faithfully executed through both direct authorization by a specific statute as well as reasonable inferences of power from specific statutes and the Constitution itself.

COMMUNISM, RED SCARES, NATIONAL SECURITY FREE SPEECH AND THE SUPREME COURT

CHAPTER 3: WORLD WARS, THE RED SCARE, AND FREE SPEECH I: WORLD WAR I, THE FIRST RED SCARE (1917–1920), AND FREE SPEECH

Bad Tendency Theory Cases (Lower Courts)

United States v. Motion Picture Film "The Spirit of 76" (1917)
- In times of national security threat, speech that was protected during peace can become liable and subject to sanction. The First Amendment does not protect speech that threatens national security.

Goldstein v. United States (1919)
- In a criminal trial of sedition under the Espionage Act of 1917 truth is not a defense to seditious speech if the speech, under the circumstances, will tend to create the danger that the government has a right to prevent.

Shaffer v. United States (1919)
- In a criminal trial of sedition under the Espionage Act of 1917 criminality is established if the speech, regardless of truth, has the natural tendency and effect calculated to produce the result made illegal.

Opposition to the Bad Tendency Theory (Lower Courts)

Masses Publishing Co. v. Patten (1917)
- Political speech, by definition, could not violate the Espionage Act of 1917. Only willfully false statements known to be false could establish liability under the Espionage Act.

United States v. Hall (1918)
- Speech by itself cannot sustain a charge of willful obstruction of recruiting of the military; actual obstruction and injury must be proven to establish violation of the Espionage Act. Mere speech, without more, cannot sustain a conviction.

Bad Tendency Theory and the Supreme Court

Schenck v. United States (1919)
- The judgment of whether speech, political or not—true or not, is judged by the time, place and circumstances of the utterance.
- "Whether the words used are in such circumstances and are of such a nature as to create a clear and present danger that they will bring about the substantive evils that Congress has a right to prevent."

Frohwerk v. U.S. (1919)
- The First Amendment is not an absolute protection. Not all speech is protected.

Debs v. United States (1919)
- Political speech intended to cause or encourage the evil Congress had sought to prevent; criminal liability was established under the Espionage Act.

Abrams v. U.S. (1919) (Holmes and Brandeis defect)
- The clear and present danger test requires that the evil that Congress sought to prevent must be an immediate danger, not a theoretical one, occurring due to the speech; and the speaker must have the specific intent to bring about that danger by the speech.
- The "ultimate good desired is better reached by the free trade in ideas . . . in the competition of the market" of ideas.

Congressional War Powers

Wilson v. New (1917)
- Congress has the power to act to prevent a national emergency and govern interstate commerce and labor disputes during a time of war.

Aver v. United States (1918)
- The draft is Constitutional.

Hamilton v. Kentucky Distilleries (1919)
- Congressional use of war powers is Constitutional so long as there is a rational relationship between its action and the evil sought to be prevented.

Ruppert v. Caffey (1920)
- Congressional use of its war powers is not confined to the specific grants of power listed in the Constitution. Congress has the inherent powers to act to meet the needs of the nation.

Bloch v. Hirsh (1921)
- So long as the action by Congress is not such that it is futile or has no reasonable relation to the desired goal, the Court will not second-guess the utility or propriety of the action.

The First Red Scare

Ex parte Jackson (1920)
- Habeas case resulting from the Palmer Raids. Court held that the raids were unlawful due to the lack of warrants and excessive force. Further, that the deportation hearings violated due process.

Colyer v. Skeffington (1920)
- Habeas cases resulting from the second round of Palmer Raids. Court issued a detailed report on the unlawful activities of the federal agents and flawed deportation hearings.
- Held that membership in Communist Party, without more, was not sufficient to authorize deportation (reversed by the Court of Appeals).

CHAPTER 4: WORLD WARS, THE RED SCARE, AND FREE SPEECH II: WORLD WAR II, THE SECOND RED SCARE (1947–1957), FREE SPEECH, AND THE LOYALTY OATH CASES

War Powers

United States v. Curtiss-Wright (1936)
- Presidential foreign policy powers differ from domestic powers in both source and scope.
- President is the sole organ of foreign policy.
- Congressional power in foreign policy is much more limited than its power over domestic policy.
- In foreign policy the President is plenary.

Ex parte Quirin (1942)
- The President has the power as Commander-in-Chief to create military commissions for the violations of the laws of war.
- Congress has the power to determine what the laws of war are and to authorize the President to implement and punish violations of the laws of war.
- Citizenship does not bar punishment for the violation of the laws of war.
- *Ex parte Milligan* held that the military may not place its hand on a civilian who has not acted in support of military forces which are at

war with the United States. Military jurisdiction is established through active membership in the U.S. Armed Forces or through belligerent activity against the United States in time of war.

Duncan v. Kahanamoku (1944)
• The President does not have the power to close federal courts and impose military law during a time of war in a state or part of state that is loyal to the United States in which the Courts are open and functioning.

Lichter v. United States (1948)
• Held the Enemy Alien Act (1798) was Constitutional.
• It is for the political branches to determine if the nation is at war and when hostilities have ended.
• Congressional determinations on what methods it chose to implement its war powers are not within the purview of the Court so long as the methods used were necessary and proper in the implementation of its war powers.

Chicago and Southern Air Lines v. Waterman S.S. Corp. (1948)
• Presidential power in foreign policy is inherent in his powers as Commander-in-Chief and as the sole organ of foreign policy.
• The Judiciary does not have the power to pass on the political judgments of the President in areas of foreign policy.
• Political judgments of the President are not judicially reviewable.

United States ex rel Knauff V. Shaughnessy (1950)
• The President by statute and through his inherent powers as Commander-in-Chief has the power to exclude aliens from entrance into the United States.

Toth v. Quarles (1955)
• Congress cannot authorize the seizure of an American citizen who has been discharged from the military by the military for trial under military law for crimes committed while such an individual was in the military.

Reid v. Covert (1957)
• Congress cannot authorize military trials of dependents of active military personnel.

Free Speech

Whitney v. California (1927)
• The Court upheld a California statute that criminalized belonging to an organization that advocated, taught, or aided in activities or speech

to overthrow the government or change in industrial ownership or effect political change.
- The Court held that the law did not violate the First Amendment because the Amendment does not prevent the government from outlawing speech that is inimical to the public welfare or endangers the foundations of organized government.
- Last Supreme Court case supporting the "bad tendency" doctrine. See *Brandenburg v. Ohio*, 395 US 444 (1969) for formal overturning of *Whitney*.

Hartzel v. United States (1944)
- The Court held that prosecutions under the Espionage Act of 1917 require a specific intent to cause impairment or interference with military recruitment and that the possibility of such impairment must be "clear and present danger."
- Mere advocacy of opposition to the war, alone, does not merit violation of the law.
- The tendency of speech to interfere with the government, by itself, was no longer sufficient—"bad tendency" doctrine was functionally disavowed.

Denaturalization and Freedom of Thought/Association

Schneiderman v. United States (1943)
- Can a naturalization determination be voided upon government assertion that the finding of adequacy of citizenship was made in error?
- The Court held that association with or membership in the Communist Party, per se, is not enough to denaturalize a citizen on theory that such membership is proof of lack of loyalty to the United States.
- Court held that the government must establish by "clear, unequivocal, and convincing" evidence that a certificate of naturalization was illegally procured.

Baumgartner v. United States (1944)
- The Court held that the government can not denaturalize a citizen for the views that he develops after being naturalized.
- The Court held that the rights of citizenship granted upon naturalization are to be protected with greater diligence than review of loyalty before citizenship is granted.

Bridges v. Wixon (1945)
- Membership in the Communist Party, per se, is not enough evidence to authorize deportation.

Knauer v. United States (1946)
- Citizenship gained through naturalization is equal to citizenship gained through birth.
- Affirmed *Schneiderman* and *Baumgartner*.

Girouard v. United States (1946)
- Religious prohibition against serving in the military does not establish a false taking of the oath of citizenship.

The Second Red Scare

American Communications Association v. Douds (1950)
- The Court held that the labor Management Relations Act of 1947 which required labor unions to certify that its directors were not members or supporters of the Communist Party was Constitutional.
- The Court held that it was not unreasonable (using the rational basis standard) for Congress to conclude that community control of unions would pose a threat of labor strikes and production disruption to facilitate its goals of overthrowing the government and/or the economic system of the United States.

Garner v. Board of Public Works (1951), *Gerende v. Election Board* (1951), and *Adler v. Board of Education* (1952)
- Held that state loyalty oath was Constitutional.
- State and local government can require an employee to take an oath or submit an affidavit of not currently or previously being a member of the Communist Party before being eligible to hold or run for local or state positions.

Dennis v. United States (1951)
- The Court, by plurality vote, affirmed the conviction of the twelve members of the national board of the Communist Party.
- Court affirmed the application of the "clear and present danger" test to criminal statutes that involved the use of speech to establish criminal conduct.

Tenny v. Brandhove (1951)
- Vindictiveness of Congressional investigative committees, per se, does not establish civil liability.

Joint Anti-Fascist Refuge Committee v. McGrath (1951)
- An organization has a due process right to address being placed on the Attorney General's subversive organization list.

Wiedman v. Updegraff (1952)
- The Court held that *Garner, Gerende,* and *Adler* require that an oath and/or affidavit of non membership in a subversive organization required that the individual had specific knowledge of and supported the subversive goals and objectives of the organization.
- Mere membership, without specific knowledge of subversive goals and objectives, was not sufficient to bar an individual from satisfying the requirements of an oath of loyalty.

Cole v. Young (1956)
- Dismissal based on an agency head determination that a federal employee is a threat to the interests of national security violates due process if the employee is not given fair notice of what activities and organizations will trigger a determination of disloyalty or a finding that a person is a threat to national security.

Schware v. Board of Bar Examiners (1957)
- The Court held that membership in the Communist Party in the 1930s cannot establish the lack of moral character regarding admission to the bar.

Konigsberg v. State Bar of California (1957)
- Affirmed that membership in the Communist Party, per se, is not evidence of a lack of moral character and could not form the basis for rejection for admission to the bar.
- The Court held that organizational membership, political views and writing that criticize the government cannot be used to establish bad moral character.

Jencks v. United States (1957)
- The Court held that the defendant, an accused member of the Communist Party, had a right to FBI records regarding prior reports by an informant when the informant testified at trial against Jencks.
- The Court ruled that if the government refused to produce the documents due to concerns of national security, then the government would have to dismiss the case against Jencks.

The Red Monday Cases and the End of the Second Red Scare

Yates v. United States (1957)
- The Court held that under the Smith Act prohibition to "organize" an association to "advocate" violence or the overthrow of the government applied to the creation of such an organization. This prosecution under the act against the organizers of the socialist party could

only be brought thirteen years (statute of limitations) from the date of organization. The prosecution in 1951 was past the date since the Communist Party was formed in 1945.

- The Court held that "advocacy" of the overthrow of the government without the intent to initiate or cause such a result is protected by the First Amendment.

Watkins v. United States (1957)

- The Supreme Court held that a witness can claim Constitutional protections during a Congressional investigation hearing.
- Congressional investigation committees must provide a witness with an explanation of why a question is pertinent to the purpose of the committee before requiring the witness to answer if such witness refuses initial questioning.

Sweezy v. New Hampshire (1957)

- The plurality held that the Fourteenth Amendment applied the principle of the First Amendment to state investigations of speech that was academic in nature.
- The Court held that the Fourteenth Amendment applied the principles of *Watkins* to state legislative investigative committees. The Court reasoned that the authority and scope of the Attorney General's investigative was too broad and undefined to provide a witness with the proper notice of purpose and responsibility to answer questions.

Service v. Dulles (1957)

- The Court reversed a finding by the Secretary of Defense that Dulles was disloyal because federal regulations required him to conduct a complete review of the case and not simply affirm a decision by the Loyalty Review Board of the Civil Service Commission.

PART II: SEPTEMBER 11, 2001, TERRORISM, AND THE VINDICATION OF THE RULE OF LAW

CHAPTER 8: ENEMY COMBATANTS: IS THE PRESIDENT'S DESIGNATION ENOUGH?

Hamdi v. Rumsfeld (2004)
- The Court held that the President has the authority to declare a person an enemy combatant but that determination is not beyond judicial review.

CHAPTER 9: CAPTURED TERRORISTS: GUANTANAMO BAY, MILITARY COMMISSIONS, AND HABEAS CORPUS

Rasul v. Bush (2004)
- The Court held that the detainees at Guantanamo had the right under the federal habeas corpus law to challenge their detention and classification as enemy combatants in federal court.

Hamdan v. Rumsfeld (2006)
- The Court held that although the AUMF had activated the war powers of the President, neither the AUMF nor the DTA authorized the creation of military commissions that were violative of the UCMJ. The Court held that the UCMJ—an Act of Congress—governed the procedures of Presidential created military commissions and the current procedures did not meet the UCMJ standards.

Boumediene v. Bush (2008)
- The Court held that the detainees at Guantanamo have a Constitutional right to seek habeas corpus review because the U.S. exercises de facto sovereignty over Guantanamo, Cuba.
- The Court held that MCA, which restricted judicial review of the procedures and determinations of military commissions, amounted to a suspension of the writ of habeas corpus. The Court held that the suspension of the writ can only be accomplished by direct invocation of that power by Congress and the judicial stripping section of the MCA was held unconstitutional.

Index

Abbott, Lewis F., 445n40
ABM treaty, 280
Abrams v. US (1919), 107, 161, 162, 452; majority opinion, 108; on speech constraints in times of war, 110
absolute power, 241–42
abstract doctrine, 196n239
ACLU. *See* American Civil Liberties Union
act(s): Adamson, of 1916, 111; Alien and Sedition, of 1798, 91; Alien Deportation, of 1918, 115, 152; Alien Registration, 156, 160; Civil Aeronautics, 134; Commander-in-Chief power, 45; Communist Control, 1954, 158; Defense Production, 240; Department of Defense Appropriation, of 1994, 277; Detainee Treatment, 320; Enabling, 436; Enemy Aliens, of 1798, 132, 133; Executive, 8; Foreign Intelligence Surveillance, 285; Habeas Corpus, of 1863, 50, 59–60, 69, 74, 82; Internal Security (The McCarran Act), 158; Judiciary, of 1789, 51; Labor Management Re-lations (1947), 169; Military Commission, 321, 349; National Labors Relations, 169; National Security, 276; New Hampshire Subversive Activities, 185; Non-Detention, 1950, 301; Organic, 139, 140; of Parliament, 424; Renegotiation, 131; Sedition, of 1798, 99, 110, 119; Sedition, of 1918, 92, 103, 143; Selective Service, of 1917, 111, 131; Smith, 160, 163, 175; Syndicalism, 189n75; Taft-Hartley, 181, 240
action: administrative, 214; Bush, George W., and, 282; Commander-in-Chief and, 4; governmental, 182; legislation and, 80; police, 238, 243; President, during times of war, 24; Presidential, 24, 244, 255; *Presidential Military Order of November 13, 2001: Detention, Treatment and Trial of Certain Non Citizens in the War Against Terrorism* (2001), 289–90; violence, 150. *See also* executive action
Act of Parliament, 424
Adams, John, 21

461

About the Author

Arthur H. Garrison is the senior criminal justice instructor at the Philadelphia Campus of Kaplan University (Thompson Institute). He has published in various academic journals including the *Juvenile and Family Court Journal*; *Criminal Justice Studies*; *Court Review*; *American Journal of Forensic Psychology*; *Police Studies*; *Journal of Police and Criminal Psychology*; *Professional Issues in Criminal Justice*; *Youth Violence and Juvenile Justice*; *Journal of Police and Criminal Psychology New England Journal on Criminal and Civil Confinement*; the *American Journal of Trial Advocacy*; *Issues in Child Abuse Accusation*; the *Journal of Supreme Court History*; the *Journal of the Institute of Justice and International Studies*; and the *Cumberland Law Review* on a wide variety of criminal justice topics including constitutional law and history. Mr. Garrison holds a BA in political science with a minor in history (1990) from Kutztown University of Pennsylvania, a MS in criminal justice (1995) from West Chester University of Pennsylvania, and a doctor of law and policy (Summer 2011) from Northeastern University.